POLITICAL
LEARNING
in
ADULTHOOD

POLITICAL
LEARNING
in
ADULTHOOD

A Sourcebook of Theory and Research

Edited by

Roberta S. Sigel

The University of Chicago Press
Chicago and London

Roberta S. Sigel, Distinguished Professor of Political Science at Rutgers University, is a pioneer in the study of adult political socialization. Her many publications include *The Political Involvement of Adolescents* (with Marilyn Hoskin) and the edited collections *Political Socialization: Its Role in the Political Process* and *Learning about Politics: Studies in Political Socialization.*

The University of Chicago Press, Chicago 60637
The University of Chicago Press, Ltd., London
© 1989 by The University of Chicago
All rights reserved. Published 1989
Printed in the United States of America

98 97 96 95 94 93 92 91 90 89   54321

Library of Congress Cataloging-in-Publication Data
Political learning in adulthood.
   Bibliography: p.
   Includes index.
   1. Political socialization.   I. Sigel, Roberta S.
JA76.P5928   1988   306'.2   88-20522
ISBN 0-226-75693-9
ISBN 0-226-75694-7 (pbk.)

Contents

Introduction:
Persistence and Change

ROBERTA S. SIGEL

The year 1959 saw the publication of Herbert Hyman's Political Socialization—a slim little volume which was to launch a whole subfield of political
science by that very name. The theme of the book was that political behavior
is *learned* behavior and that learning begins in childhood and, in many respects, is completed by adolescence. "The importance of such a formulation
to understanding the stability of political systems is self-evident—*humans
must learn their political behavior early and well and persist in it*" (Hyman
1969, p. 10; emphasis in original). Yet, as he lamented, one "seeks far and
wide for any extended treatment of political behavior as *learned* behavior,
despite the fact that this is patently the case" (p. 9). His book was meant to
exhort social scientists to study childhood learning and socialization, so that
adult politics can be better understood.

The exhortation was taken so seriously by political scientists that ten years
later, in a preface to the paperback edition, Hyman could write: "now—by
1969–the study of political socialization has become a large-scale enterprise"
(p. v). With virtually no exception, this large-scale enterprise focused almost
exclusively on childhood political socialization (although by the mid 1970s
studies of adolescents were included.)[1] Apparently students of the subject
accepted as "self-evident" and "patently" certain that such early learning
would remain relevant for and persist into adulthood. Scholars, therefore, saw
no need to test empirically whether indeed political learning has been largely
completed—as Hyman suggested–by the first years in high school.[2]

It is perhaps no coincidence that Hyman's advice was so readily accepted.
Political scientists, especially in the post–World War II period, were particularly concerned with questions of political stability and the survival of stable
democracies. David Easton's systems analysis (1953, 1965), with its emphasis on system support, is an outstanding example of this effort. In these works
Easton postulated that the stability of democratic regimes rested on the diffuse
support of their citizenry reflected in the rather positive sentiments citizens

harbored for the political system in general and its institutions specifically. These supportive attitudes were seen to function like a reservoir of good will on which the authorities could draw—within limits—during occasional periods of hard times. In a later work with Dennis (1969) Easton postulated that citizens acquire this diffuse support early in childhood when the young person feels trusting and affectionate toward political authority figures. As the young person matures into adulthood, he tends to maintain these positive attitudes although, of course, he will divest himself of some of his political naiveté. Political scientists studying political socialization resonated to the Eastonian paradigm for two reasons: (1) Studies of adults and of young people tended to confirm the presence of stable, positive feelings for the government and its authorities within the American public, and (2) the tendency to locate the roots for such positive sentiments in childhood experiences fitted well with the increasing popularity of psychoanalytic theories which trace adult dispositions and behavior patterns back to childhood experiences. It is not surprising, therefore, that the system-analytic perspective became the dominant one in political socialization research.

And so by the 1960s political socialization had become a "growth stock" and the fastest growing subfield in the political science literature (Greenstein 1970, p. 969) By political socialization most researches understood "the process by which people acquire relatively enduring orientations towards politics in general and towards their own particular systems" (Merelman 1987).[3] The great majority of studies concentrated on analyzing childhood cognitions and affect, although more recently adolescents were included as well (Jennings and Niemi 1974; Sigel and Hoskin 1981). Much of the analysis reflected a developmental perspective.[4] In addition, heavy emphasis was placed on the agents of socialization, especially the family and the school, which were seen as the transmitters of society's sociopolitical heritage, with the child being seen as the essentially passive, willing recipient of the agents' "lessons." As Wrong (1971) commented, the political socialization literature presented us with an "oversocialized" model of man.

Absent from the early socialization literature was attention to the particular historical or structural settings in which socialization takes place and inquiry into the persistence into adulthood of the "relatively enduring orientations." The implicit assumption, occasionally stated explicitly, was that little change should be anticipated during adulthood or, more precisely, that most observable change probably constituted nothing but elaborations of values internalized earlier. The process of individual development was assumed to have been completed with the onset of adulthood.

The authors represented in this volume clearly do not subscribe to the notion that learning and development are completed by adulthood; rather they see them as constituting a lifelong process. A second theme is that such learning is highly dependent on the social setting in which it takes place, and they attempt to specify the conditions for change and/or continuity. Finally, the third theme they stress is that socialization is essentially an interactive process by which persons are influenced by their environment and in turn influence the latter.

Before elaborating on these themes, we need to make clear that the stress on the probability of significant transformation occurring during adulthood, i.e., making a case for the so-called lifelong openness perspective, is, of course, not tantamount to an assertion that what was learned early in life has no bearing on later orientations. Clearly, much in the value system that was acquired and internalized during childhood, adolescence, and early adulthood structures how people perceive and react to new experiences (the so-called primacy or persistence-through-life principle). No doubt, as Glenn (1980, p. 605) speculates, "some values are likely to be more stable than others; some attitudes are likely to be more stable than other attitudes, and some beliefs are certainly more stable than other beliefs." Among the more stable beliefs and attitudes, we might presume, are those touching on very basic values, such as freedom, equality, and attachment to religious or ethnic groups. Some of them, we might assume, have by adulthood become part of a person's sociopolitical identity (although even here the evidence is far from conclusive just how impervious to outside forces one's identity is). What evidence we have from the work on adolescents shows that many dispositions observed in the adult public are already present in teenagers. Their view of the good citizen (a person who must take an interest in public affairs as well as obey the law) is one adolescents share with adults (Jennings and Niemi 1974; Sigel and Hoskin 1981). Loyalty, patriotism, and pride in the nation are other components of the image, although Sigel and Hoskin have characterized youngsters' pride as "relative pride" to indicate that affect is tempered by a good deal of criticism (just as it is in the adult population). Cognitively, Jennings and Niemi as well as Sigel and Hoskin found high school seniors to be as well or poorly informed (depending on one's standards) as the adult population. We can, therefore, say that much of the foundation for political life—affect, cognition, and participation—is in place as the young person reaches adulthood.

Not until the mid 1970s—perhaps in response to the protest movements of the late 1960s—did some students of political socialization begin to raise doubts concerning the evidence for this persistence-through-life model (Searing et al. 1973; Connell 1972; Tedin 1974). Echoing such doubts, David O. Sears in a 1975 review article wrote "it seems likely that the early rush of enthusiasm for preadolescents will gradually be replaced with attention to the entire life span." Two years later Sigel and Hoskin (1977, p. 259) voiced a similar complaint about "the relative neglect of adults" and called for a more developmental, life-span approach to the field.

Such an approach had become fairly prevalent in allied disciplines, notably psychology and sociology. For example, Inkeles and Smith (1974, p. 235) considered the behavioral changes they observed in six developing nations to constitute "evidence that major transformations are possible in fully matured adults" and no "man need be permanently limited to the attitudes, values, and modes of acting he develops in his early life" (p. 277). In a similar vein Knox (1977, p. 1) wrote that the "realization of adult potential has become the sign of our times"; and the earlier focus on child and adolescent development began to be complemented by "attention to the dynamics of the process by which adult life unfolds." In short, these disciplines began to adopt a developmental perspective when studying adults.

As stated before, this developmental perspective has not yet become an integral part of political science research. Attention to political socialization over the entire life span—especially attention to adult *development* broadly defined—is still the exception rather than the rule. While we do have much information on how adults at a given moment act or react—their vote, their policy preferences, and so on—we lack systematic knowledge of whether such behavior is a carryover from values learned during childhood or whether it has arisen in response to changed social or personal circumstances not anticipated in childhood, i.e., whether it was learned during a specific time in the adult's or the nation's history. Nor do we know whether these observed dispositions and behaviors are likely to remain stable or will undergo even further transformation.

In this volume we hope to demonstrate the utility of adopting a life-span, developmental approach for the study of adult political behavior. We begin with the assumption that childhood and adolescence build the foundation of one's worldview (or at least a good part of it). But a foundation cannot convey a clear picture of what the finished edifice will look like, and whether changes in the original blueprint or master plan have to take place before the building is complete. We have every reason to anticipate changes in the "building program" as the person matures. For one thing, experiences during adulthood play a crucial part in this building process precisely because adults are exposed in the course of their lives to many different and often unanticipated political experiences. Many of these new experiences demand striking a balance between values learned and internalized earlier in life and the need to adopt and welcome new behaviors which may conflict with the former. Moreover, adults have to assume a far greater number of diverse roles than they had to adopt during their youth, and not all of these roles will necessarily push the individual in the same political direction. Consequently, childhood will not have offered them adequate anticipatory preparation to "perform" without some additional learning occurring.

Similarly, the phenomenon of individual aging—with all the physical, cognitive, and emotional changes it involves—is another change process which childhood socialization cannot anticipate but with which the maturing adult has to learn to cope. Many of these individual changes at times affect and possibly modify the person's political outlook. For example, the staunch free enterpriser who during youth and middle age wanted the government off his back and out of his pocket, now, having reached the age of sixty-five, wants the same government to provide him with an old-age pension, low-cost housing, and so on.

Not only do we need to reflect on the ways in which individuals change or fail to change as they mature, we also need to acknowledge the social setting in which this occurs. After all, even individual change does not take place in a social vacuum. As C. Wright Mills (quoted by Morris, Hatchett, and Brown in chapter 7 this volume) commented: "Whatever else he may be, man is a social and historical actor who must be understood, if at all, in close and intricate interplay with social and historical structures." What individuals come to expect of the political system and how they visualize their obligations to it are highly dependent on the social and political setting in which people find themselves. For example, the definition of the good citizen varies from country to country but has been shown to vary also among classes within the same country and, even more specifically, to vary by age *and* class. Thus Sigel and Hoskin (1981) found working-class youth to emphasize obedience to law whereas upper-class adolescents stressed the participatory aspects of citizenship somewhat more. Or, to cite another example, while adolescents in the U.S. may hope that public education will prepare them adequately for adult living, adults in turn may expect that society will find uses for their labor and talents; and the aged may expect that society will be sufficiently caring to permit them to live out their days in dignity. As humans age and develop, so do their needs. These needs in turn may help restructure what individuals expect and demand of society and the political system, but their expectations in turn reflect the social structure in which they live.

So far we have stressed individual change over the life span. We next need to examine the impact societal change has on individuals. It is, of course, a truism that societies as well as individuals change, but it is equally clear that the two are inextricably interwoven. Humans' political outlooks often are challenged and even altered as the society's political agenda changes, but humans in turn also challenge and at times succeed in changing society. These are two themes that need to be included in the study of adult political socialization. To illustrate the first, let us return to the example of the sixty-five-year-old. Had he turned sixty-five in 1920, the expectation of a government pension would never have occurred to him! Society has changed sufficiently in the interim that in 1988 he feels entitled to a pension. Two chapters in this book (Laufer's and Horowitz's) document how major historical catastrophes profoundly alter, perhaps even de- and resocialize individuals. Not only extraordinary events, however, have this potential but so do the many ordinary tasks men and women encounter in the course of daily living.[5] The chapters on the civil rights movement and the women's movement are illustrations of the other theme, namely, humans' ability to influence society and thereby contribute to a resocialization of the mass public. Individuals—whether adults or children—are not just passive recipients who accept whatever society and its agents ordain; they are also actors.

To conclude, we conceive of individuals as both actors and acted-upon who have a lifelong capacity to learn and change, although differing from each other in their capacity and inclination for learning. Political socialization, therefore, is an ongoing, continuous process. Brim and Kagan (1980, p.1) in a volume on human development clearly state this perspective:

> humans have a capacity for change across the entire life span. It [their book] questions the traditional idea that experiences of the early years, which have a demonstrated contemporaneous effect, necessarily constrain the character of adolescence and adulthood. . . . Many individuals retain a great capacity for change, and the consequences of the events of early childhood are continually transformed by later experiences, making the course of human development more open than many have believed.

To explore the nature of humans' capacity for political change is the objective of this volume. In it we seek to provide a very broad overview of what is known up to now about adult political socialization, in order to find answers to a number of questions: What happens in the political development of adults as they go about the business of living? To what extent do the political stances and actions of men and women remain essentially unchanged as the person faces new personal and/or social contingencies, and to what extent do they change? Phrased this way, the questions clearly suggest that we assume both continuity and change in political outlook will characterize the adult political socialization process. The challenge is to discover when the one is more likely to be dominant than the other.

Given the sparse and fragmentary body of knowledge about adult political socialization, we have no illusion that this volume can constitute a definitive answer to the questions just raised. Rather we hope (in the words of Erikson, 1986, p. 1) "to engage in the kind of aerial reconnaissance most of us try to undertake before we move on foot into a new research terrain. That means that I cannot help but be more attentive to the broader contours of the terrain than to its finer grains and textures."

We begin the volume by looking first at the impact of age and aging. Delli Carpini examines the extent to which generational replacements in and of themselves account for social change, making a distinction between episodic and incremental change. Steckenrider and Cutler ask: "Are there stages in an aging individual's political life cycle that can be traced to maturation from youth to old age?" These two introductory chapters are meant to establish the book's theme, namely, that political continuity as well as political change are neither the exclusive product of individual maturation nor of sociopolitical circumstances but rather of the interaction of the two.

The next section focuses on the world of work as one type of status transition experienced by most young adults. Four chapters focus on four very different types of work environment: the world of manual and/or skilled labor (Lafferty); the helping or human-service industry (Dressel and Lipsky), the military (Lovell and Stiehm); and the world of political leadership (Renshon).

Nonanticipated, "normal" life transitions which are affected by major changes in the sociopolitical environment are examined in the third section. We have singled out the civil rights (Morris, Hatchett, and Brown) and the women's liberation movements (Carroll) as two social movements which are playing major roles in the post–World War II world. The accelerated pace of migration from rural to urban centers and across nation-states constitutes yet another important change of the period which–like the birth or rebirth of the other two social movements—makes major rather than minor social demands on individuals. Hoskin's chapter on migration addresses that problem.

The impact of events which constitute the most abrupt and potentially life-threatening situations brings the volume to an end. Laufer contributes a chapter on war and Horowitz one on terrorism and terror. Surely events of such magnitude constitute the most serious rifts with one's past and hence illuminate particularly vividly individuals' adaptation and/or resistance to forced resocialization.

The authors of each chapter will look for evidence of continuity and change—socialization and resocialization—in the social contexts, i.e. the social environment, on which they focus. Social environment is defined very broadly, so as to include social structures and movements as well as historical events. Our selections distinguish between those social environments and the life experiences related to them for which the individual had some, however imperfect, preparation (the world of work) and those for which he or she lacks such preparation (war or political imprisonment). We further differentiate these life experiences according to the degree to which the individual has control over them (the decision to migrate) and those over which he or she lacks such control (war or unemployment). Another distinction we make focuses on the life-threatening or life-enhancing character of the event. Underlying these distinctions, of course, lies the assumption that change-proneness, i.e. resocialization, will vary not only with the individual's chronological age and circumstances but with the discontinuity and severity of each such event.

Finally, we need to point out that we have adopted a very broad definition of the term "political." In contrast to most standard definitions which tend to restrict themselves to "what government and its agencies do, how citizens react to it, and what if anything, they do about it" (Sigel and Hoskin, 1981, p. 40), we include in the definition all those activities (partisan, communal, or group) and attitudes which have the potential and/or the objective to "affect the quality and character of our public lives" (p. 41), as well as "those opinions held by private persons which governments find it prudent to heed" (Key 1961, p. 14).

In the conclusion the editor, by synthesizing the preceding chapters, will present an overview of what can be said with some degree of definitiveness about political continuity and change over the adult life course.

Any edited volume by its very nature has to be selective. This applies particularly to the one at hand. Given the paucity of research on adult socialization, it proved impossible to focus on many important areas of life that could illustrate human capacities for political persistence and change. Availability of materials dictated the inclusion of some topics and the exclusion of others. For example, we included two chapters on social movements (the civil rights and the women's liberation movement) but had to exclude other contemporaneous social movements—for example the peace movement and the environmental one—because they had not been sufficiently covered from a political socialization perspective. Though both exclusions and inclusions are by necessity somewhat arbitrary, we hope nonetheless to have singled out at least a few of the major dimensions conducive to adult political socialization. If this highly selective volume will spur others to begin systematic research in adult political socialization, it will have served its purpose.

Notes

1. The "classic" early childhood socialization studies are: David Easton and Jack Dennis, *Children in the Political System* (New York: McGraw-Hill, 1969); Fred I. Greenstein, *Children and Politics* (New Haven: Yale University Press, 1965); and Robert D. Hess and Judith Torney, *The Development of Political Attitudes in Children* (Chicago: Aldine, 1967). The two studies of adolescents are M. Kent Jennings and Richard G. Niemi, *The Political Character of Adolescence: The Influence of Families and Schools* (Princeton: Princeton University Press, 1974), and Roberta S. Sigel and Marilyn B. Hoskin, *The Political Involvement of Adolescents* (New Brunswick: Rutgers University Press, 1981).

2. Hyman himself did not advocate stopping political socialization research at that stage. Speaking of his own book, he writes near the end (p. 98) that "The earlier discussion represents, so-to-speak, the child moving in a stable world. Now, by contrast, the child is stable but the world is moving." In the next paragraph, however, he

holds that although "the idea has plausibility," researching it would be "attended by great difficulty." Moreover, on the basis of the evidence presented by him, he concludes "the doctrine must be regarded in a *modest* light" (p. 98; emphasis added).

3. For the many different meanings attached to the term, see F. I. Greenstein, "A Note on the Ambiguity of 'Political Socialization': Definitions, Criticisms and Strategies of Inquiry," *Journal of Politics* 32 (1970): 969–77.

4. The most commonly used perspective is that of Jean Piaget.

5. These "normal" developments take on added significance when societies undergo very rapid sociopolitical change. Then anticipatory childhood socialization may well be irrelevant for adult behavior. The United States is said to be one country experiencing extraordinarily fast rates of change (Brim and Kagan 1980; Toffler 1970).

References

Brim, O. G., Jr., and J. Kagan, eds. 1980. *Constancy and Change in Human Development.* Cambridge, Mass: Harvard University Press.

Connell, R. W. 1972. "Political Socialization in the American Family: The Evidence Reexamined." *Public Opinion Quarterly* 36:323–33.

Easton, D. 1953. *The Political System.* New York: Alfred A. Knopf.

———. 1965. *A Systems Analysis of Political Life.* New York: John Wiley and Sons.

———, and J. Dennis. 1969. *Children in the Political System.* New York: McGraw-Hill.

Glenn, N. D. 1980. "Values, Attitudes, and Beliefs." In O. G. Brim, Jr. and J. Kagan, eds., *Constancy and Change in Human Development.* Cambridge: Harvard University Press, 596—640.

Erikson, K. 1986. "On Work and Alienation." *American Sociological Review* 51: pp. 1–8.

Greenstein, F. I. 1970. "A Note on the Ambiguity of 'Political Socialization': Definitions, Criticisms and Strategies of Inquiry." *Journal of Politics* 32: 969–77.

Hyman, H. H. 1969. *Political Socialization: A Study in the Psychology of Political Behavior.* New York: The Free Press.

Inkeles, A., and D. H. Smith. 1974. *Becoming Modern: Individual Changes in Six Developing Countries.* Cambridge, Mass: Harvard University Press.

Jennings, M. K., and R. G. Niemi. 1974. *The Political Character of Adolescence: The Influence of Families and Schools.* Princeton: Princeton University Press.

Key, V. O. 1961. *Public Opinion and American Democracy.* New York: Alfred A. Knopf.

Knox, A. B. 1977. *Adult Development and Learning.* San Francisco: Jossey Bass.

Merelman, R. M. 1987. "The Role of Conflict in Children's Political Learning." Mimeograph.

Searing, D. O., J. J. Schwarts and A. E. Lind. 1973. "The Structuring Principle: Political Socialization and Belief Systems." *American Political Science Review.* 67:415–42.

Sears, D. O. 1975. "Political Socialization," In F. I. Greenstein and N. W. Polsby, eds., *Handbook in Political Science.* Vol. 4. Reading, Mass.: Addison-Wesley.

Sigel, R. S., and M. B. Hoskin. 1981. *The Political Involvement of Adolescents*. New Brunswick, N.J.: Rutgers University Press.

————. 1977. "Perspectives on Adult Political Socialization—Areas of Research." In S. A. Renshon, ed., *Handbook of Political Socialization*. New York: The Free Press, pp. 259–93.

Tedin, K. L. 1974. "The Influence of Parents on the Political Attitudes of Adolescents." *American Political Science Review* 68:1579–92.

Toffler, A. 1970. *Future Shock*. New York: Random House.

Wrong, D. 1961. "The Oversocialized Concept of Man in Modern Society." *American Sociological Review* 26:183–93.

Part I

Introduction:
Age and Political Socialization

Chronological age and political thought are linked—at least in some aspects. For one thing, certain political behaviors, such as voting or running for office, are age-dependent. For another, the ability to reason logically, to think abstractly, and to apply such thought to concrete situations—all prerequisites for meaningful political thought—are age-dependent. The three-year-old is incapable of such things. Most adolescents and adults have reached a stage of cognitive development that should enable them to engage in such thought (provided they are motivated to think about politics). Not a great deal more in the line of basic cognitive development should be anticipated over the adult life-course. Which is not to say that increases in available information, interest, and life experiences cannot enrich the quality and sophistication of political thought as the person matures. It merely asserts that political cognition probably undergoes relatively few transformations as a person reaches middle age and then old age. Individuals who found it difficult at eighteen to think in terms of abstract political principles will, in all likelihood, experience similar difficulties at forty years of age—all other things being equal.

Political attitudes, issue preferences, interest and involvement in politics, on the other hand, do undergo changes over the adult life-span. These are less dependent on a person's cognitive maturity than on his or her life experiences—education, occupation, reference group, and the times in which the person lives. Here is where we can anticipate considerable change with chronological age and change in life circumstances. Evidence is increasing that as men and women assume new roles or are exposed to new experiences (such as parenthood, corporate office, combat in war) their political outlook often changes in tandem.

Chronological age, of course, is not a perfect indicator of these transitions (some people become full-time members of the labor force at sixteen while others, especially professionals, do not enter it until thirty years of age or even older). Nor can we assume that major historical events have the same impact on everyone who is of the same chronological age. The military draft during the Vietnam War affected eighteen-year-old male college students very differently than it did high-school students or dropouts. Consequently it is next to impossible, if not actually impossible, to attribute political attitudes and attitude changes exclusively to chronological age—as the two chapters which follow make abundantly clear.

Chronological age, nonetheless, is a sufficiently rough indicator of these transitional stages to be used widely by social scientists when commenting on the political-attitude changes they are observing. In discussing age and politics it is customary to distinguish three periods; young adulthood (usually eighteen to thirty); middle age, and old age (sixty or sixty-five and over). There are few far-reaching observations that can be made as yet concerning probable attitude changes over these three stages. The evidence, though, is quite strong that participation (as measured by voting and active participation in politics) follows a curvilinear path, with young adults the least involved and middle-aged the most, but some controversy exists (as will be discussed later) over just how uninvolved the aged (at least those under seventy) really are. Other areas for which data exist deal with political alienation, preferred ideology, issue orientation, and the growth of conservatism with age; but here too controversy prevails.

Two population groups have, over the past two decades, been singled out for particular attention: young adults and the aged. The unrest of the 1960s generation spawned interest in the politics of young adults. Questions were asked concerning their alleged idealism (Flacks 1971) their lack of commitment or their alienation (Keniston 1960 and 1968), their general attachment to the political system (Barnes and Kaase 1979), and their post-materialism (Inglehart 1985).

In "normal" times it is assumed that young adults are so preoccupied with the assumption of adult roles and the transition from the dependent status in the parental home to that of independent adult that they seem to have little interest or energy left for becoming actively engaged in politics. On the other hand, young people (adolescents and adults) are said to be less disenchanted with the government, to trust it more and generally to be more idealistic than their elders. They are alleged to be particularly critical of compromises made by adults, compromise being considered a form of hypocrisy. This state of mind is captured by the popular saying, "those who are not idealistic at sixteen have no heart; those who are still idealistic at sixty have no head."

On the surface it may well seem that the 1960s generation, with its demonstrations and protests, corroborates the notion of idealism and refutes that of young people's political uninvolvement. Certainly these widely publicized protests gave the appearance of deeply involved young people. Closer examination, however, reveals that such involvement characterized a relatively small segment of young adults (heavily concentrated on certain college campuses and in specific communities) but did not necessarily strike a responsive chord among young people in general and was actually opposed by some youths (Kasschau et al. 1974). Moreover, its intensity subsided with the conclusion of the Vietnam War. Protests, however, were not limited to objection to the war but ran the gamut of championing civil rights, greater student involvement in the governance of the educational establishment, and newer, nontraditional life styles—thereby offering some indication of idealistic predisposition during youth. But again, such predispositions and activities were not as widespread as the publicity would seem to indicate. Even during the sixties and certainly since—as shown by Delli Carpini among others—the evidence suggests that young adults, then as now, are relatively uninvolved, being more preoccupied with other developmental tasks.

What does, however, characterize young adults since the mid-1960s more than in earlier times is their political cynicism or lack of trust in their government. Jennings and Niemi's panel studies (1974, 1981) noted a startling drop in trust among them. "Whereas in 1965 they were extraordinarily more positive than were their parents, by 1973 they had become equally negative" (Jennings and Niemi 1981, p. 173). This spectacular drop cannot be attributed to maturation alone but rather is a vivid example of period effects as they interact with the aging process. "Under the impetus of events beginning in the middle 1960's, however, this generation was catapulted well beyond what probably characterized most preceding cohorts" (Jennings and Niemi 1981, p. 174). Conceivably, the impact of disillusioning governmental performance has a more devastating impact on *young* adults precisely because childhood political socialization had lead them to expect so much more of their government (Sigel and Hoskin 1981). Discontinuities such as these, one might assume, tend to alter the speed and direction of normal developmental processes.

With the growth of the elderly population in the U.S., it is the aged who have become the subject of many studies. Making definitive statements about the relationship of old age to politics is no easier than making statements about aging in general. Take for example the very question of old age. People (and people in different cultures) vary in how they feel about being old, and even whether they feel old upon reaching sixty or seventy years of age. For example, 38 percent of those sixty years and older identified themselves as old but 55 percent did not, and it is age-consciousness that made a difference in the two groups' political outlook. Cutler (1975) in an analysis of the 1972 National Election Study found that on economic issues the subjectively old took a more liberal position, especially with regard to government medical-aid programs; but on other so-called social issues (such as abortion and environmental policies) they were more traditional. "Age clearly has a different meaning to different individuals who share the same general position in the life cycle" (Cutler 1975, p. 390).

In addition, the very concept of old age is undergoing revision in keeping with societal changes. Thus in 1974 Bernice Neugarten introduced the concept of the young old (those under seventy-five years of age) and the old old. Currently attempts are being made to subdivide the old olds even further into the olds and the very olds (those over eighty-five) in order to reflect more accurately the different degrees of sociopolitical involvement characteristic of the three groups. The 1968 Glenn and Grimes article cited by Steckenrider and Cutler and a more recent review by Edinger (1985) have cast serious doubt on the notion, once widely subscribed to, that with old age comes political disengagement or growing conservatism on political issues. As for disengagement, Steckenrider and Cutler go even further and conclude "age *per se* is not a significant factor . . . and disengagement theory is considered to be disconfirmed." Edinger (1985) contrasted the political orientations and behaviors of the elderly with those of the young and middle-aged and found that in the United States the elderly did not vary greatly from younger cohorts in interest, turnout, sense of political efficacy and issue orientations. "In the United States, the divergence for the aged appears . . . more confined to old people of seventy and over" (Edinger 1985, p. 59). but even here the differences are not dramatic. In fact Edinger suggests that assigning all elderly people (those sixty-five and older) to one category—as is customarily done in survey research—conceals a good deal of diversity "in the political orientations and behavior of an age group that is coming to encompass two generations of retired people" (p. 64).

Another age-related question that is receiving increased attention concerns the likelihood that the elderly will develop a cohesive group consciousness stemming from age-related needs that could be met only by increased government services (Ragan and Dowd 1971; Riley 1968; 1969; 1973; Foner 1974). So far the evidence tends to suggest that the elderly constitute a sufficiently heterogeneous group to make the advent of group consciousness and political mobilization unlikely in the near future. Stating that the elderly do not seem—at least yet—to have the potential of forming a cohesive movement is not to deny that they do exert a good deal of political pressure, especially through the organizations with which they are affiliated. Among the most effective of these is the American Association of Retired People, with its 24 million members. But even in this highly active organization a good deal of controversy prevails concerning parts of its political agenda, reflecting the heterogeneous nature of its membership. Moreover, members often join less for political motives and more to take advantage of other benefits, such as insurance, travel discounts, and so on.

In comparison with what we know of the elderly, our knowledge of the link between politics and middle age is even less. Are there specific age-related experiences unique to the various phases of middle age that might also give rise to political restructuring? For example, does the phenomenon of burnout observed in middle-aged professionals, especially those working in large bureaucracies, lead to changes in political outlook? For the most part political scientists and sociologists have had little to say about political transformations during middle age. One exception to this generalization is presented by the feminist literature which has sought to reflect on the political implications of various stages in a woman's life (Klein 1984; Sapiro 1983). Klein points out that lower fertility and higher longevity rates make for a much prolonged empty-nest stage, beginning at an earlier point in middle age. The long empty-nest stage, she holds, offers a partial explanation for the growth of the women's liberation movement in the last two decades.

Another age-related question which calls for more systematic investigation is whether certain ages are more change-prone than others. Steckenrider and Cutler, as does Delli Carpini, suggest that young adulthood—because of the pileup of role transitions—may be such a period. As young adults become older, the possibility for change remains, although the likelihood decreases somewhat with each successive life-stage (Nunn, Crockett, and Williams 1978; Cutler and Kaufman 1975; Glenn 1974). But even here the data are far from conclusive. To be sure, the "published evidence seems to support the aging-stability thesis, on balance, but it deals with a very restricted range of attitudes" (Glenn 1980, p. 611). The attitudes examined are, for the most part, party identification, political interest, voting behavior, and ideological self-identification and will be discussed in the chapters that follow.

So far we have addressed mainly the question of chronological age, as though age per se can explain political outlook. That, of course, is patently not the case. Steckenrider and Cutler hold that more important than chronological age are the social roles individuals assume. These, as they show, have more relevance for the development of the political self than does chronological age. In their chapter they focus on role transitions, since in their opinion "perhaps the most promising and still uncharted keys to the mysteries connecting aging and political dispositions lie in the sequence of roles associated with adult maturation and aging." As they see it, "any new role can expose the individual to conditions and experiences that may lead to significant attitudinal and behavioral change."

The roles most likely to expose the individual to such change-productive experiences that they single out for discussion are college student, breadwinner, spouse, parent, and old person. Other life experiences that one might mention would be migration, military service, especially in wartime, and permanent unemployment (some of which will be discussed in this volume).

To decide to which to attribute observed change—to role transition or to chronological age—is difficult indeed. Did young Hal in Shakespeare's *King Henry V* give up childish pranks and self-indulgence because he suddenly had grown up, or did ascendance to the throne cause him to show more responsible behavior? Or is the disengagement some think they can detect in retirees in their withdrawal from social involvement (Cummings and Henry 1964), really a function of biological aging rather than of the loss of a meaningful role, especially in such youth-oriented societies as ours? After all, "movement into old age involves major *social losses* including central roles and their responsibility, authority and rewards. Finally, there is basic *role discontinuity,* with no preparation for such losses and no substitution of new norms, responsibilities, and rights. The conditions have profound implications for the prospective socialization to old age" (Rosow 1974, p. 27; emphasis in original).

Distinguishing between change due to aging and change attributable to role transition is but one of the difficulties that confront us when trying to generalize about the role aging plays in politics. We encounter even more formidable difficulties when we try to distinguish life cycle effects from period effects, cohort effects, and generational ones. Historical events of major proportions, say a war, affect people of all ages (period effects) but they may well affect one age cohort (young men of draft age) much more directly than another age cohort (those too old to be called up for military duty). Even members of the same age cohort may experience the same historical event in very different ways. The young combat soldier is much more likely to become shaped by his war experience (see Laufer in this volume) than another young man who works in a defense plant. Finally, some experiences simply cannot be shared by people who have not lived through them. Those who came of age during the Great Depression were shaped by it indelibly, so much so that we speak of a Depression generation. To disentangle these various effects from each other is, as Steckenrider and Cutler as well as Delli Carpini explain, an all but impossible task.

Generational replacement is yet another factor which complicates the already complex picture. As Delli Carpini points out, every thirty years "the reigns of government are handed to a completely new set of leaders, the unavoidable result of our mortality . . . generational replacement is all inclusive as well. That is, every aspect of society and every individual within that society is affected by it." For example, generational replacement, according to Delli Carpini, rather than partisan reorientations explains the decline in partisanship over the past decade. But this replacement, as he also points out, need not involve major change; much of it, on the contrary, tends to be incremental and evolutionary, thus providing for much continuity and minimal demands for individual attitude change.

Generational replacement not only affects the attitudes of the new entrants but has the potential to shape the attitudes of the old-timers as well. Inglehart (1985) showed that the increase in secular thinking and the rejection of restraints on individual self-expression, though most characteristic of the postwar generation, also affected the older ones, albeit not nearly to the same degree. Inasmuch as old and young live in the same world, the possibility that the older generation can change in response to ideas advanced by the younger one cannot be dismissed offhand, especially in countries exposed to the omnipresence of the mass media and their tendency to deaccentuate group-based differences.

Not only do we need to enhance our understanding of period, cohort, and life cycle effects, we also need to be sensitive to national variations and subgroup variations and how they may modify the relationship between chronological age and political outlook. For example, receptivity to attitude change with respect to political as well as life-style issues seems greater among young adults from middle-class backgrounds (especially if they attend college) than for those from working-class backgrounds, the latter being more prone to continue endorsing the conservative life-style ideas of the parental generation (Kasschau et al. 1974). Similarly, the pain of the transition to old age varies not only by social class but also by ethnic group. Among Italian-Americans, the transition to old age seems to progress with less sense of isolation and feelings of being devalued than among the Anglo-American aged. The difference, conceivably, could be attributed to the fact that the former put high value on interdependence and the latter on independence. Italian-Americans become socialized from early childhood to place family interests above individual ones. Dependence in old age can then be perceived as a natural progression rather than as a stigma.

In short, any attempt to theorize about the relationship between chronological age and political persistence or change is confronted with the formidable task of trying to decide whether an observation is attributable to age alone or whether it is attributable to such confounding factors as period effects or cohort effects; generational replacement; national or subnational differences, or any combination thereof. The two chapters by Steckenrider and Cutler and Delli Carpini squarely face that difficulty. Delli Carpini points to the need for developing a more solidly based generational theory. The major emphasis of his chapter deals with the role played by generations in effecting or resisting political change. Of particular interest is his discussion of subgenerational units—each of which experiences the main events of a period somewhat differently, depending on its chronological age at the time of first encounter with the new event. Encountering novelty for which one has been unprepared by socialization, he holds, has different effects than having seen variations of it—even if only as a spectator—prior to reaching adulthood. He concludes his chapter by drawing our attention to the importance of the identification problem which needs to be solved before one can build a definitive generational theory and outlines a methodology suited for such an undertaking.

To build generational theories not only calls for new methodological approaches, it also requires longitudinal investigations. With the exception of the pioneer work by Jennings and Niemi (1974, 1981)—which up to now extends over a fifteen-year period—no longitudinal studies exist in political science which follow young people over an extended time. And certainly none exist that follow them from youth to old age. Such studies, though costly and probably impractical, would help us to determine which—if any— basic values and orientations, internalized during childhood or adolescence, will be maintained throughout adulthood, albeit in a different form. One might, for example, ask whether adults who as children were taught the value of thrift and self-reliance are less sympathetic to social-welfare legislation than youth brought up to show empathy and concern for the less fortunate. The evidence supplied by Delli Carpini and others (Markus and Jennings 1985) suggests that at least as far as the Yuppie generation is concerned, its earlier life-style liberalism was not subsequently translated into economic liberalism. But inasmuch as few of the studies on the Yuppies are based on longitudinal data, we really don't know whether or not this economic conservatism is indicative of attitude change, or merely illustrates that social and economic liberalism do not necessarily occupy the same domain.

At this time we have to conclude that, notwithstanding all the significance attached to childhood political socialization, the jury is still out as to its importance. Nor do we yet have definitive evidence as to the significance of the aging process per se. Much of it, as we have seen, is inconclusive; some evidence lends weight to the stability thesis, some to the openness-to-change one. Moreover, even when we can present very nonambiguous findings, such as the greater stress on patriotism and a strong military posture among older people, we still cannot be sure that these phenomena really are due to aging rather than to different generational socialization experiences. Consequently, as Glenn (1980, p. 634) so aptly writes, "Few confident conclusions can now be made only because the needed work has not been done."

R.S.S.

References

Barnes, S., M. Kaase et al. 1979. *Political Action Mass Participation in Five Western Democracies*. Beverly Hills, Calif.: Sage Publications.
Cummings, E., and W. Henry. 1964. *Growing Old: The Process of Disengagement*. New York: Basic Books.

Cutler, S. J. and R. L. Kaufman. 1975. "Cohort Changes in Political Attitudes: Tolerance of Ideological Nonconformity." *Public Opinion Quarterly* 39: 63–81.

Easton, D., and J. Dennis. 1969. *Children in the Political System.* New York: McGraw-Hill.

Edinger, L. 1985. "Politics of the Aged: Orientations and Behavior in Major Liberal Democracies." *Zeitschrift für Gerontologie* 18: 57–64.

Flacks, R. 1971. *Youth and Social Change.* Chicago: Markham.

Foner, A. 1974. "Age Stratification and Age Conflict in Political Life." *American Sociological Review* 39: 187–96.

Glenn, N. D. 1974. "Aging and Conservatism." *The Annals* 415: 176–86.

———. 1980. "Values, Attitudes, and Beliefs." In O. G. Brim, Jr., and J. Kagan, eds., *Constancy and Change in Human Development.* Cambridge: Harvard University Press, 596–640.

Greenstein, F. 1965. *Children and Politics.* New Haven: Yale University Press.

Hyman, H. 1959. *Political Socialization.* Glencoe: The Free Press.

Inglehart, R. 1985. "Intergenerational Change in Politics and Culture: The Decline of Traditional Values." Paper delivered at the 1985 annual meeting of the American Political Science Association.

Jennings, M. K., and R. G. Niemi. 1974. *The Political Character of Adolescence: The Influence of Families and Schools.* Princeton: Princeton University Press.

———. 1981. *Generations and Politics: A Panel Study of Young Adults and Their Parents.* Princeton: Princeton University Press.

Kasschau, P. L., H. E. Ransford, and V. L. Bengtson. 1974. "Generational Consciousness and Youth Movement Participation: Contrast in Blue and White Collar Youth." *Journal of Social Issues* 30: 69–94.

Keniston, K. 1960. *The Uncommitted: Alienated Youth in American Society.* New York: Harcourt, Brace and World.

———. 1968. *Young Radicals: Notes on Committed Youth.* New York: Harcourt, Brace and World.

Klein, E. 1984. *Gender Politics.* Cambridge: Harvard University Press.

Markus, G. B., and M. K. Jennings. 1985. "Of Yuppies, Enddies and the Formation of Political Generations." Paper prepared for delivery at the 1985 annual meeting of the American Political Science Association.

Neugarten, B. L. 1974. "Age Groups in American Society and the Rise of the Young-Old." *The Annals* 415: 197–98.

Nunn, C. Z., H. H. Crockett, Jr., and J. A. Williams, Jr. 1978. *Tolerance for Nonconformity.* San Francisco: Jossey-Bass.

Ragan, P. K. and J. J. Dowd. 1971. "The Emerging Political Consciousness of the Aged: A Generational Interpretation." *Journal of Social Issues* 27: 137–58.

Riley, M. W. 1973. "Aging and Cohort Succession: Interpretations and Misinterpretations." *Public Opinion Quarterly* 37: 35–49.

Riley, M. W., et al. 1968. *Aging and Society.* Vol. 1, *An Inventory of Research Findings.* New York: Russell Sage Foundation.

Riley, M. W., A. Foner, B. Hess, and M. L. Toby. 1969. "Socialization for the Middle and Later Years." In David A. Goslin, ed., *Handbook of Socialization Theory and Research.* Chicago: Rand McNally.

Rosow, I. 1974. *Socialization to Old Age*. Berkeley: University of California Press.

Sapiro, V. 1983. *The Political Integration of Women. Roles, Socialization and Politics*. Urbana: University of Illinois Press.

Sigel, R. S., and M. Hoskin. 1981. *The Political Involvement of Adolescents*. New Brunswick, N.J.: Rutgers University Press.

Wasmund, K. 1982. *Jugendliche. Neue Bewusstseinsformen und politische Verhaltensweisen*. Stuttgart: Ernst Klett.

One

Age and History: Generations and Sociopolitical Change

MICHAEL X. DELLI CARPINI

All is flux, nothing stays still. . . . Nothing endures but change.
                                                    Heraclitus

Introduction

It is the possibility of change in the human condition that underlies both the practice and the study of politics. History is chronicled by deviations from the past. Political philosophies have come into existence, individuals have risen to power, governments have toppled, because of the promise of change or the fear of it. Even a preoccupation with stability, which characterizes many political ideologies, governments, and traditions of research, is driven by the specter of potential change.

Politics is the art/science of controlling changes in the human condition. Not surprisingly, therefore, institutions, processes, periods, and moments of real or potential change dominate its study. It is at points of discontinuity, such as the outbreak of war or the peaceful transfer of power among competing elites, that visions of Utopia and Armageddon flick momentarily into our collective mind's eye. Even periodic change that occurs under the constraints of carefully developed rituals, traditions, and institutions contains the possibility of major disjunctures from the past and so also evokes the hopes and fears associated with the unknown. Of course, such controlled change is usually much less traumatic for the political system. Indeed, one of the major functions of political institutions is to cope with the inevitability of change in a way that maximizes its predictability. In the United States, for example, the holding of periodic, staggered elections, the existence of a two-party system, the separation of powers, and so on, all work to channel political change along a predictable, moderate course (Burnham 1970; Ginsberg 1982).

It is in this context of continuity and change that the importance of generations to the study of politics is best understood. There is no more fundamental transfer of power, and therefore no more fundamental *potential* for change, than that which occurs between generations. This is so because, unlike any other type of change, it is *inevitable,* it is *all-inclusive,* and it is *untested.*

Generational change is inevitable. As noted by Ferrari (1874), approximately every thirty years the reigns of government are handed to a completely new set of leaders, the unavoidable result of our mortality (cited in Braungart and Braungart 1984; Marias 1970). Generational replacement is all-inclusive as well. That is, every aspect of society and every individual within that society is affected by it. The collected cultural, social, economic, and political systems of humanity are left to the care of each new generation. Even in the most affluent modern societies, the cycle of birth and death means that entire populations are replaced every century. Finally, in addition to being inevitable and inclusive, generational replacement involves the filling of societal roles by individuals who are, by definition, untested in those roles. If "all the world's a stage," every thirty years or so the actors are replaced not by seasoned veterans but by their understudies. In the light of personnel replacement of this magnitude, the transfer of power that occurs in elections, or through assassinations, or even in revolutions, pales. This generational process cuts across all eras and all types of political systems. From monarchies to democracies, no type of system is free from this inevitable changing of the guard.

Despite the magnitude of the physical reality of generational replacement, however, generationally inspired sociopolitical changes are more the exception than the rule. An analogy to this change in the individuals who make up a society is the changing physiology of the human body. Over time the cells that make up an individual die and are replaced by new ones. Over the course of an individual's life, almost all of the cells of the body are replaced several times. In terms of the *physical* makeup of the person, it is not inaccurate to say that the individual standing before you at age fifty is not the same person who stood before you at age thirty. And yet to argue that these are different persons in the same sense that you and I are different people is to miss something important. In spite of the (almost) total replacement of individual cells, much has not changed. Each new cell is not free to take on an entirely new function but instead takes on the responsibility of the particular cell it replaces. Groups of cells combine in ways that vary only imperceptibly from those they have replaced. Hands do not need to relearn how to tie a shoe, feet and legs do not relearn how to walk. One's personality survives the physical metamorphoses, memories and experiences intact.

A person maintains individuality in spite of such physical changes because one's personal genetic coding orchestrates these changes down to the most minute detail, and because the cells of the brain, in which reside the sum of what one has learned about oneself and about the world, are not periodically replaced. The result is a life span that, despite physical changes of growth and ultimately of decay, allows for the cumulation and the synthesis of experiences. Without this continuity each new moment would be as if the first.

The process of continuity and change in the human body is analagous to generational replacement in the body politic. With the passage of time, individuals die and are replaced by new ones. Eventually an entire generation of people is replaced. The new generation does not enter the system as it pleases but is molded into preestablished roles, classes, and the like. In addition, the experiences of prior generations are not completely lost but are transmitted to the new generation. Of course the body politic does not undergo this process of replacement without some changes, but the actual change relative to the potential change is usually quite small.

To carry the analogy a bit further, socialization is the societal equivalent of genetic coding, and political institutions are equivalent to the human brain. That is, members of a new generation do not develop their values, opinions, and behaviors independently of the generation they are replacing, but instead learn them from that generation. This learning of what values to hold, as well as how and when to express them, is at the heart of the political socialization literature and places the study of generations firmly within that school (Easton and Dennis 1969). Institutions such as the family, schools, the media, and the workplace are the agents of this socialization process (Dawson et al. 1977; Dennis 1973). In that they serve as both the repositories of the cumulative values of prior generations and the transmitters of those values to future generations, their role is analogous to that of the human brain.

There are, of course, limits to the analogy with the human body. Unlike genetic coding, socialization, even in the most controlled of societies, is a very imperfect process. The political socialization literature establishes quite clearly that while the transmission of values, opinions, and behaviors through socializing agents does occur, it is a complex, interactive process that seldom results in the exact replication of specific orientations from sender to receiver (Chaffee et al. 1970; Dawson et al. 1977; Elden 1981; Jennings and Niemi 1974, 1981; Klapper 1960; Langton and Jennings 1968). These agents only partially influence the orientations of new generations. In addition, because the social, economic, political, and cultural environment is extremely changeable, new generations are often socialized under unique circumstances that are not controlled by any single agent. Finally, the pluralistic nature of most modern societies means that different socializing agents often send different, competing messages. It is in this inability of society to control all the relevant aspects of the socializing environment, and in the resultant inability to guarantee its own replication, that the potential for generational change resides. In fact, the biggest distinction between the study of political socialization in general and the particular study of generations is that the former emphasizes *continuity* in attitudes, opinions, and behaviors between socializer and socialized while the latter focuses on *discontinuity*. Generations play a key role in the interpretation of certain historical periods (Europe in the first half of the nineteenth century and again in the early twentieth century; the 1930s in those countries hit by the Great Depression; and the 1960s on a global scale) precisely because they were times of conflict between generations (Braungart 1982, 1984; Braungart and Braungart 1984). In many ways, the study of political generations becomes important when the process of political socialization fails.

Generational Replacement and Rates of Political Change

To study generational politics is to study mass political change. The concept of mass political change, however, can refer to a variety of occurrences. In the history of the United States, one need only consider the revolt from England and the attempted revolt of the South from the North, the sudden changes in voting patterns that marked the 1890s or the 1930s, or the gradual decline in partisan support in the twentieth century to see the range this concept includes. While there are many dimensions along which mass political change can be distinguished, an important one for the study of generations is the rate at which it takes place. One of the first students of American politics to emphasize rates of political change was V. O. Key, Jr. In 1955 Key wrote his seminal piece on critical change in U.S. politics. In it he noted the tendency in the electorate for sudden, radical shifts in support for competing political elites. Four years later he published a second article emphasizing gradual demographic change and its incremental impact on mass opinions and behaviors. While Key was focusing on electoral politics in the United States exclusively, his basic distinction between episodic and incremental change is applicable to the general study of mass opinions and behaviors.

Perhaps the best example of research on dramatic alterations in the established opinions and behaviors of a population is the work on critical elections (Key 1955; Sundquist 1973; Burnham 1965, 1970). These studies concentrate on brief, intense periods during which fundamental shifts in mass support for particular elites and/or agendas take place. Such shifts are triggered by new issues that challenge established coalitions in both the mass population and among political elites. Often a particularly intense event (such as a war or a depression) serves as the catalyst for the emergence of new political coalitions, agendas, and opinions. Realignments are the exceptions that define the rule. That is, they are occasional adjustments to the political system that are distinct from more normal patterns and that ultimately define those patterns.

At the other end of the spectrum is the study of evolutionary change in opinions and behaviors. Such change is often more difficult to detect, especially over short periods of time. It results not from sudden reactions to brief periods of intense politics but from gradual economic, social, and political development. The work of Nie, Verba, and Petrocik (1979) or Inglehart (1977) exemplifies research of this genre, though much of Burnham's work could be placed here as well.

While distinguishing between episodic and evolutionary political change is a useful technique for studying mass politics, one must not lose sight of the links between the two kinds of change. In particular, these extreme types of political change are interconnected in two ways. First, incremental change is the condition that exists between periods of more dramatic, intense activity. That is, rather than conceptualizing the normal pattern within political periods as one of stasis, it is more accurate to characterize it as a period of gradual change, with the rate and nature of the shift determined by the social, economic, and political parameters set during the more dramatic periods of upheaval.

Second, and perhaps more important, the nature of critical change is determined in part by the evolutionary shifts in mass politics that preceded it. While issues and events no doubt trigger such change, the reaction to those issues and events (indeed sometimes their very occurrence) can only be understood in light of the more subtle movements that occurred since the last such "eruption." In short, the political orientations of a population over time are best understood by considering not only episodic change and incremental change but also the interaction between the two. This interaction is particularly important in the study of generations.

Both episodic and incremental change involve the impact of issues, events, and social and economic developments on the pattern of mass political attitudes and behaviors. These patterns necessarily develop over time, however, and over time the individuals who make up a population also change, due largely to the natural cycles of birth and death. If, in addition to documenting change, one is interested in explaining its sources, a distinction must be made between aggregate change resulting from net shifts within individuals who already are part of the population, and that resulting from the replacement of one set of individuals with another.

Consider the concept of incremental change discussed above. If one finds a gradual loss of support for the Democratic party over a twenty-year span, that loss could be the result of either former supporters becoming slowly disenchanted with the party or older citizens dying and being replaced by a new generation that is less enamored of the Democratic party right from the start (or some combination of both processes). Determining the actual reason for the loss of support is critical both for understanding the nature of the change and for speculating on its long-term consequences.

For example, generational replacement was a critical component in the decline in partisanship in the 1960s and in the more recent rise in Republican party adherence among new voters, though the exact role of generational change (relative to life cycle and period effects, which will be discussed later) is still being debated (Abramson 1979, 1983; Beck 1974; Claggett 1981; Converse 1976, 1979; Crittenden 1962; Cutler 1969–70; Delli Carpini 1986; Glenn 1972, 1977; Glenn and Hefner 1972; Knoke and Hout 1974; Nie et al. 1979; Shively 1979). The bulk of the evidence suggests that the choice of a particular party (or of independence) is determined primarily by generational forces and secondarily by period effects. There is also some evidence of slightly increased partisanship generally and Republican affiliation specifically with age. Finally, it appears that the strength of party attachments, once formed, also increases slightly with age.

While generational replacement may appear more relevant in discussions of evolutionary change, even dramatic shifts in opinions and behaviors can result from alterations in the makeup of the population. Andersen, for instance, finds that most of the rapid rise in support for the Democratic party in the 1930s can be attributed to first-time voters and not to disenchanted Republicans (1979a, 1979b). While many of these new voters were immigrants or long-time citizens who had forgone their franchise, a large percentage of them were members of a new generation that had slowly been changing the makeup of the eligible electorate.

The Biological, Psychological, and Historical Foundation of Generations

Distinguishing between change resulting from the succession of generations and change attributable to other sources is both methodologically and theoretically difficult. Methodological issues are considered later in this chapter. Here some theoretical issues are discussed. One of the most important and difficult issues in the study of generations is the distinction between an "age cohort" and a "generation." While there is general agreement in the literature concerning this distinction (Braungart and Braungart 1984; Delli Carpini 1986; Jansen 1975; Marias 1968; Ortega y Gasset 1962), the influence of early writings that did not distinguish between biological and sociological definitions of generation can still be found in the literature.

While concern with generational conflict can be traced back four thousand years (Braungart and Braungart 1984; Lauer 1977), current thinking about generations is strongly influenced by two schools of thought: the nineteenth-century French positivists and the largely German romantic-historical movement of the nineteenth and early twentieth centuries (Braungart and Braungart 1984; Jansen 1975). The positivists saw a strong link between the biological process of aging and the sociopolitical process of generational replacement. As a result, their study of generations (much like those of the ancient Greeks) emphasized stages of psychological and biological development through the individual life cycle. In addition, inasmuch as biological development was inevitable, so too was the regular occurrence of generational replacement. The influence of generations on the sociopolitical process was, therefore, viewed as occurring with clock-like regularity. Ferrari (1874), for example, believed that approximately every thirty years a new generation left its mark on the political landscape (cited in Braungart and Braungart 1984; Marias 1968). There were, of course, areas of disagreement within this school of thought. The impact of generations over time was seen by some (such as Ferrari) as cyclical and by others as unilinear (Jansen 1975). In addition, some generations, for a variety of reasons, are more likely to have an impact on society than are others. The two unifying themes among the positivists, however, were the importance of life-cycle stages to generational development and a somewhat mechanistic view of generational replacement.

The legacy of the French positivists can be seen in much of the current research on generations. Research that emphasizes the link between generational development and individual biological and psychological development has at least some of its roots in this tradition (Beck 1974; Delli Carpini 1986; Inglehart 1977; Jennings and Niemi, 1974, 1981). In addition, the conceptualization of generations as systematic, equal-sized age cohorts is still found in much of the empirical research (Abramson 1975, 1979, 1983; Abramson and Inglehart 1986; Converse 1976; Cutler 1969–70, 1977; Kritzer 1983; Glenn 1977). This approach is especially prevalent in the research on partisanship discussed above, though it exists as well in the study of other topics, such as post-materialism (Abramson and Inglehart 1986), alienation (Cutler and Bengston 1974), and political efficacy and trust (Abramson 1983).

A somewhat different view of generations developed out of the romantic-historical movement of mid-nineteenth-century Germany. Though early thinkers on the subject were often influenced by *both* positivism and romantic-historicism (Dilthey 1976), in the latter school the concept of a biological age cohort was more clearly distinguished from that of a generation as a sociopolitical force. Not every age cohort necessarily develops into what Dilthey (1875) called a "social generation" (cited in Braungart and Braungart 1984; Esler 1982; Jansen 1975; Marias 1968; Schorske 1978). An age cohort is simply a group of individuals who all fall into the same age group at a particular time: all individuals who are between the ages of eighteen and twenty-eight in 1984 for example. Nothing is implied concerning the individuals who make up this cohort beyond the similarity in ages. A generation, in contrast, implies some shared experiences, some common bond that is "imprinted" on a particular age cohort within a population (Mannheim 1972).

The distinction between an age cohort and a generation is laden with implications. Most importantly and despite the etymology of the word (genos), it suggests that "generations are made, not born" (Braungart and Braungart 1984, p. 350). That is, an age cohort is a "potential generation" that may or may not develop the common bond that transforms it into an "actual generation" (Mannheim 1972).

How is it possible that the inevitable process of biological lineage does not always translate into distinct sociological generations? The answer, for the romantic-historicists, lay in the deemphasis of psychological and biological stages of development and greater emphasis on sociological and historical forces. While the relative openness of youth to new ways of thinking was still considered important to generational development, it was the interaction of this tendency with intellectual (Ortega y Gasset 1974), social and historical (Dilthey 1976; Mannheim 1972), and political (Heberle 1951) forces that was the key (Braungart and Braungart 1984). The possibility of a new generation existed with the coming of age of each new cohort, but the actuality of a new generation, as well as the specific attitudes that developed and the specific ways in which those attitudes were expressed, depended on the external environment.

Contemporary research on generations and politics in part reflects a synthesis of the positivist and historical schools of thought, and in part reflects a continued debate on the relative merits of each approach. Generational personae develop out of the combination of social forces and personal life-cycle stages. This "imprinting" results from a process that lies somewhere between the socialization of an individual and the development of an entire political culture. On the one hand, unique personality development results from the interaction of the self, the socializing experiences of family, peers, school, the mass media, and other social agents, and the idiosyncratic experiences derived from one's daily routine. A national culture, on the other hand, is the summation of those personal traits, socializing experiences, and historical occurrences that are common to most individuals within a society. Generations result from a similar process, but one that acts on a particular age cohort within the population. That is, generations result from a "socialization" process that is less general than that for an entire culture, but more general than the unique experiences of particular individuals.

The logic behind the notion of generational development lies in the assumption that there is an interaction between age and experiences. This interaction occurs in two ways. First, there is a tendency for people within the same age cohort to be exposed to similar historical, social, cultural, and political experiences. The rise of mass education, the Vietnam War, the development of the home computer--these all affected the entire society of the United States in many ways, but they also provided unique experiences to different age cohorts. Certain age cohorts were the first to enjoy the opportunity to be gained from extensive public education; certain age cohorts were required to fight in Vietnam; certain age cohorts are growing up with computers as part of their daily routine. The sum of these common experiences, opportunities, and situations creates a "Zeitgeist" or historical spirit that bonds the individuals who are a part of it (Mannheim 1972; Lambert 1972). Beck (1974), for example, makes a convincing argument that it was experiencing the Depression (and the parties' responses to it) as young voters that seared a Democratic partisanship on a generation of Americans in the 1930s. Later generations could not hold the same intensity of opinions precisely because they had not experienced the same events.

The second assumption underpinning the age-experience link is that different age groups perceive and react to the same experience in different ways because of the particular stage of personal and social development they have reached when the event occurs. That is, not only is each generation likely to have a unique set of experiences, but each is also likely to react to the same experiences in different ways. In this vein, Inglehart (1977, 1981, 1984) demonstrates that the economic and political security of the 1950s and 1960s had a unique and lasting impact on the youth of Western Europe and the United States. Those raised during that period are significantly more likely to demonstrate "post-materialist" tendencies: liberal political and social values and opinions, an internationalist rather than nationalist worldview, a rejection of traditional institutions and cultural norms, and a greater acceptance of system-challenging forms of political participation. This distinctiveness occurred despite the fact that older cohorts also experienced the changed economic and political climate of this era.

Generational "Imprinting" and Stages of Personal Development

While there is a general consensus on the role of both life cycle and sociohistorical forces in the process of generational development, there are still several theoretical and conceptual gray areas. One of these areas is the age at which a generational profile is most likely to form. The rebelliousness and the relatively unformed identity that characterize adolescence make it an important stage. This assumption has its roots in both psychological theory (Freud 1964; Erikson 1968; Piaget 1967; Kohlberg 1968) and in sociological theory (Mannheim 1972; Heberle 1951; Eisenstadt 1956, 1963). Psychological theory provides explanations for the openness of youth to attitudes, opinions, and behaviors that differ from those of their elders (Feuer 1969). Stages of cognitive (Piaget), psychological (Freud; Erikson), and moral (Kohlberg) development make the *very* young unlikely to have acquired the basic stuff from which to develop a distinct identity, and make older individuals more resistant to such new developments. Sociological theory provides explanations for how this very individual process can, in certain circumstances, result in the development of social and political orientations that cut across an entire cohort.

Despite the conceptual emphasis on adolescence, there is some disagreement on the specific years involved in generational development. Often the years from the late teens to midtwenties, a period that straddles late adolescence and young adulthood, are assumed to be critical. For Mannheim (1972) and Rinalta (1968, 1979) the years from seventeen to twenty-five are crucial, for Lambert (1972) the years from eighteen to twenty-six, for Ortega (1961, 1962) fifteen to thirty, and for Heberle (1951) twenty to thirty. The logic behind these assumptions is clear enough. It is the age at which individuals first step out into the world as independent adults that is central to the formation of each generation's unique personality. However, while there is much that is attractive about this notion, for several reasons one should be cautious in accepting it as a general rule.

First, since the idea of a generational personality is based on the idea of individual personalities that share a common worldview, it seems overly simplistic to select one stage of early development as necessarily dominant in the process. Developmental theorists such as Erikson (1968), Maslow (1962), and, to an extent, even Freud (1964) would agree that early adulthood is an important stage, but certainly it is not the only, not the first, and not the last stage at which personality development takes place. To the extent that generational development is based upon the commonalities found in the development of individual personalities, then it too must be forming at various (and varying) stages. Certain writers on generational politics (Ortega, for example) are sensitive to this issue and discuss stages of generational development that extend beyond adolescence and young adulthood.

One might argue that while it is analogous to individual development, generational development is a distinct process that follows distinct patterns. In particular, since generational development involves the impact of larger social and historical forces, it stands to reason that the age at which one first steps out into the world as a somewhat independent adult is critical to that process. Even if, however, one did accept that the processes of individual and generational development are largely unrelated (something that runs counter to the literature on generations itself), it still does not follow that early adulthood must be the critical stage. One certainly would not want to argue that historical, cultural, economic, and social forces do not affect the development of individuals prior to their emergence from the family, or that such forces do not act in similar ways on similar age groups. In addition, the particular age at which one begins to outgrow childhood ties is culture- and time-bound. The point at which one first feels the grasp of the outside world was arguably well before the age of seventeen or eighteen in the England of the mid-1800s, in the United States of the 1930s, and, for very different reasons, the contemporary era in the United States.

A final objection to the often exclusive emphasis placed on adolescence and young adulthood is the implication that, beyond this age, change that has a unique impact on an entire generation and which becomes part of that generation's personality is unlikely. Again, it is not the case that socialization at the individual level ends with young adulthood (Sigel and Hoskin 1977), nor that historical forces, among others, stop affecting a generation as a group. Why, then, should we assume that a generation's personality will not form its most distinctive characteristics later in life? In sum, while the prominence of adolescence and young adulthood in the study of generations is probably warranted, more attention needs to be paid to generational development that occurs before and after these stages of the life cycle (Delli Carpini 1984, 1986).

No matter what age (or ages) one considers critical, the definition of generations as the interaction of history and particular age cohorts can be difficult to apply. This definition is based on static notions of aging and history, although both are continuous processes. Consider that you have defined "The Depression generation" as individuals who were between seventeen and twenty-six during the Depression, and the "World War II generation" as individuals who were of that age during that war. Aside from the problem of establishing cutoff dates for periods such as a depression, you have the added problem that a good portion of one generation falls into the age group of the other. In other words, the idea of labeling particular generations and distinguishing them from others is really an artificial characterization of a dynamic process as a categorical one in order to gain a deeper understanding of the consequences of such processes. This problem is exacerbated by the notion put forth above that generations develop their personalities at various ages.

Does all this mean that generational analysis cannot or should not be done, that it is too fluid a process to allow characterizations beyond the most qualitative discussions? Probably not, though the issues raised above do affect the way such research is done. The key lies in returning to the underlying premise of a generation: the juncture of historical events and of age cohorts through time. Proper analysis should therefore start with the question: a generation in regard to what? If one is interested in studying the ramifications of the Depression, then one can talk about the Depression generation. One cannot necessarily distinguish it entirely from other generations that might, under other circumstances, be equally worthy of study. It is, in a sense, only a useful fiction.

Beyond this, however, the points raised above suggest that not only must a researcher choose from among alternative historical boundaries, he or she must consider the age cohort (or cohorts) most likely to be affected by the events selected. Tolley (1973), examining the effects of the Vietnam War (and the more general threat of nuclear war) on a new generation of Americans, focuses on children from seven to fourteen years old. Dalton (1977), in testing Inglehart's thesis of a post-materialist generation, emphasizes the years from eight to twelve. Whalen and Flacks (1984), interested in the generational effects of "the sixties," interviewed individuals who were in their late teens or early twenties during the 1967–71 period. And an examination of the generational impact of the Depression might very legitimately focus on cohorts that were long-time members of the work force—people between the ages of thirty and sixty for instance.

Generations, Consciousness, and Self-Consciousness

While there is agreement that generational development implies the existence of a common worldview among its members, it is unclear how conscious of this commonality such members need be. Again, an examination of the writings on generations reveals a core of agreement surrounded by differences in specific applications. Much of the more historical literature suggests that self-awareness of generational distinctions is a critical part of the process of generational development (Braungart and Braungart 1984; Jansen 1975; Mannheim 1972; Marias 1968; Ortega y Gasset 1962). The importance of self-consciousness is in the link between it and generational-based action: "An age group is transformed into a generation when its members are aware of their uniqueness, feel a sense of solidarity, and join together to become an active force for social and political change" (Braungart and Braungart 1984, p. 350). The more quantitative and behavioral analyses of generations place less emphasis on the importance of self-awareness, instead using attitudinal and behavioral differences between generations as evidence of the process at work (Abramson 1975, 1979, 1983; Claggett 1981; Converse 1976; Delli Carpini 1986; Jennings and Niemi 1974; 1981; Markus 1983).

The study of self-awareness in the generational process can be informed by the literature on class, race, and sex consciousness (Alford 1963; Klein 1984; Poole and Zeigler 1984; Shingles 1981; Verba and Nie 1972). In that literature, the development of a group self-consciousness often changes the nature of the attitudinal and behavioral divisions between, for example, blacks and whites, but seldom is seen as the sine qua non for differences of any kind to exist. For example, distinctions in the social and political attitudes, opinions, and behaviors of different classes exist in the United States (Erikson et al. 1980) despite the remarkably low level of class consciousness. While the nature of the distinctions and the degree of conflict that results from them changes as class consciousness increases, one would be misguided to assume that without class consciousness there are no manifestations of class differences. In fact, the development of consciousness often decreases rather than increases differences between the groups involved. For example, differences in political participation between blacks and whites are reduced as black consciousness increases (Verba and Nie 1972; Shingles 1981).

Rather than seeing self-consciousness as a necessary element in generational formation, it is perhaps better to see it as an ingredient that affects the particular way in which a generation (or some portion of a generation) expresses its distinctiveness. Generations, paralleling workers, blacks, and women, might be more likely to become politically active or even disruptive when they develop a certain level of consciousness. Jennings (1987) and Jennings and Niemi (1981), for example, found that members of the sixties generation who were active in protests during that period (and so probably more conscious of their generational identity) were by far the most distinct on a host of political opinions and behaviors. They were also the most likely to maintain that distinctiveness over time.

Alternately, a generational consciousness might never develop, yet generational differences might be crucial to the emergence of race, class, or sex consciousness. Sigel and Reynolds (1979–80), for example, found significant differences between generations in their acceptance of feminism, with women in college during 1975–76 generally more supportive of feminist issue positions than their parents (who were college graduates of the same institution). In sum, generational self-awareness, like that based on other important divisions in society, does not cause the development of group divisions, but develops because such divisions already exist.

The Role of Social, Cultural, Historical, Economic, and Political Forces

As with the relationship between generations and consciousness, the relationship between generations and social, cultural, historical, economic, and political forces is well established but not always fully established. For example, while most theorists acknowledge that an interaction of historical and personal forces is at work, there is a good deal of disagreement concerning whether the mainspring of generations is social processes (Mannheim 1972; Dilthey 1875; Inglehart 1977, intellectual thought (Mentre, 1920; Ortega y Gasset, 1961, 1962), cultural developments (Dickstein 1977), political events (Heberle 1951; Eisenstadt 1956, 1963; Rinalta 1979), or psychological processes (Feuer, 1969). Rather than seeing it as an either-or situation, it is better to consider the generational process as dependent on all of these forces. The "personality" of any particular generation depends on the unique combination of forces that exists as the members of that generation mature. At different times and for different generations, the dominant force and therefore the dominant impact might come from very different parts of the complex environment in which we live. The difficulty in generalizing about this process is made clearest by noting the numerous discontinuities in it: While every thirty years or so the potential for a new generation arises, generations as social and political forces do not always materialize.

More important than attempting to rank-order various elements of human existence according to their impact on generational development is understanding the specific dynamics of how this process occurs. Critical in understanding these dynamics is distinguishing between the roles of social, cultural, political, historical, and economic environments as triggering mechanisms that *develop* a distinct generation, and the role of these environments in channeling the specific way in which generational distinctiveness is *expressed*.

Consider the role of these environments in the development of a generation. As the quote from Heraclitus, used to introduce this chapter, suggests, change is a given in the human condition. Change occurs at different rates, however, both across time and across the different environments within which humans interact. The rate of change and the locus of change are the keys to understanding generational development (Braungart 1980, 1982, 1984). It is in periods of rapid change and social discontinuity that generational development is most likely to occur (Delli Carpini 1986; Gurr 1970; Smelser 1963, 1968). This rapid change can be largely political, as with the rise of youth movements in Europe in the 1800s (Braungart and Braungart 1984) and in the years following World War I (Hamilton and Wright 1975; Heberle 1951; Loewenberg 1974). Economic change can also serve as the catalyst, as with the Depression generation of the 1930s (Draper 1967; Simon 1967) and, in a very different way, with the baby-boom generation of the 1960s (Delli Carpini 1986; Jones 1980). Even technological changes can be instrumental in generational development. Nowhere is this clearer than with the impact of technologies such as nuclear power and arms, and the electronic media on the development of the 1960s generation (Braungart and Braungart 1980; Delli Carpini 1986; Gitlin 1980).

Of course while one aspect of the environment might stand out as critical to the development of a new generation, most periods of great generational conflict have involved discontinuity that cuts across the social, political, economic, and cultural environments. It is for this reason that generational change is more common and extreme in modern societies, where change is rapid and all-inclusive (Bettelheim 1963; Braungart and Braungart 1984; Eisenstadt 1963; Mannheim 1972).

The social, political, economic, and other environments are also instrumental in determining the way in which generational distinctiveness is expressed. For example, while a political event (World War I) led to the development of a distinct generation in Europe, a sizable portion of that generation expressed its views by rejecting politics (Rinalta 1979). Similarly, while much of the distinctiveness of the 1960s generation was triggered by political events, one of the most enduring characteristics of that generation is its alienation and disengagement from politics (Gilmour and Lamb 1975; Delli Carpini 1986). Alternately, while the 1930s generation was formed out of the ashes of an economic collapse, the particular way in which its members expressed their views was very much shaped by the outbreak of World War II (away from domestic economic grievances and towards support for the war effort). In short, the social, economic, and political environments both *create* and *channel* new generations, and these are two distinct processes. It is in the latter process (channeling) that the role of culture and intellectual thought plays its most significant role, in that it is in this sphere that blueprints for change are most clearly presented (Mentre 1920; Ortega y Gasset 1961, 1962).

The Concept of Generational Units

The complexity of the socioeconomic, political, cultural, and intellectual environments not only complicates the way in which particular generations differ one from another, but also complicates the internal development of generations. That is, since generations result from the interaction of bio-psychological development and historical circumstances, and since these forces come together in different ways for different segments of society, each generation is likely to comprise distinct generational units (Mannheim 1972) or subgenerations (Delli Carpini 1986). This is even more likely in modern societies where change is more rapid and populations more heterogeneous.

Subgenerational differences result from real distinctions in each unit's "identity" and from differences in the ability and/or opportunity to express that identity. For example, while the Depression of the 1920s and 1930s was felt by almost everyone who lived in North America and Europe, the specific nature of that impact varied from class to class and from country to country. Socioeconomic forces exerted distinct pressures on different groups (certain classes and certain countries were harder hit than others). In addition, classes and nationalities internalized similar pressures in different ways. In the United States individualism and the strong Protestant work ethic made self-blame a much more likely response than system-blame, especially among the working class. Since national and class cleavages cut across generations as well, this combination of disparate pressures and disparate reactions to similar pressures leads to differences in the profiles of specific generational units.

The way in which newly formed attitudes are *expressed* also varies across social cleavages such as class and region. This is so in part because the dynamics discussed above lead to the formation of different attitudes, but also because the same attitudes lead to different opinions and behaviors, depending upon the opportunities presented by the sociopolitical, economic, and intellectual environments (Bennett 1980). To continue with the Depression example, workers in the United States vented their dissatisfaction by turning to the relatively moderate Democratic party, while in Europe the development of radical worker, socialist, and communist parties was more common. This was so in part because of differences in the political and economic institutions of the United States and Europe, which channeled behaviors in significantly different ways (Burnham 1970; Lipset and Rokkan 1967; Piven and Cloward 1977).

To take a more recent example, much of the debate concerning the rise of a "new class" in advanced industrial societies (Brint 1984; Bruce-Briggs 1979) implicitly and explicitly centers on the development of a generational unit out of the interaction of class (white-collar professionals), age (under forty), and history (the economic and social environment of the 1960s and 1970s). Whether this new class is liberal or conservative depends in part on what attitudes were originally internalized, but also depends on how those attitudes are tapped in particular circumstances. Hence, the same "new class" can be seen as liberal or conservative, depending on the issue involved or the nature of the times (Bruce-Briggs 1979).

Generational units often develop out of more traditional cleavages in a society, such as sex, race, and class. For example, studies of the generation raised in the United States in the 1960s suggest that young women are more feminist and more liberal than older women (Sigel and Reynolds 1979–80). There is also some evidence to suggest that differences in political involvement, information, and participation between men and women is much less pronounced in the more recent generation, though the extent of these changes is debatable (Jennings and Niemi 1981). Differences between blacks and whites in levels of political involvement, efficacy, information, and participation also seem much less pronounced in "the sixties generation" than in preceding ones (Jennings and Niemi 1981), though racial differences do still exist. In addition, differences between blacks and whites on policy stands and partisan preference remain strong, and in some cases are even stronger within the new generation, with blacks generally more liberal and more Democratic (Jennings and Niemi 1981). Abramson (1975, 1983), however, does not attribute the recent increases in Democratic leanings among blacks to generational replacement, seeing it instead as a more general period effect.

Perhaps the greatest evidence for a generational unit is found among the college-educated within the sixties generation. The college-educated members of this generation stand out, both from older individuals of similar education and from their less-educated peers, as more politically and socially liberal, politically involved, and participatory (Brint 1984; Kasschau et al. 1974; Ladd 1984; Lipset and Ladd 1972; Roberts and Lang 1985). These differences persist over time as well. The extent to which this distinctiveness is specifically the result of the college experience; is the result of a person having been a student during a unique political period; or is some more subtle self-selection process that is detectable before a person enters college is un-clear (Jennings and Niemi 1981), though undoubtedly all of these processes are involved. Additionally, the differences may be as attributable to class as to educational differences (Brint 1984; Delli Carpini 1986; Kasschau et al. 1974; Simon et al. 1969).

Even more specific generational units can be identified, often by combining the larger categories of sex, race, education, and class. College-educated women (Sigel and Reynolds 1979–80), or "working women" (Andersen and Cook 1985; Blydenburgh and Sigel 1983), both much more prevalent in re-cent generations, are quite distinctive in their political involvement, their lib-eralism, and their opinions on "women's issues." Young urban professionals (yuppies) also display distinctive political opinions and behaviors (Markus and Jennings 1985), though whether this distinctiveness can be characterized as more liberal or more conservative, or whether it is even all that unique is a matter of some debate (Delli Carpini and Sigelman 1986). Recent exami-nations of "the new class" of professionals often include generational com-ponents, though again the extent to which this new class is more liberal, more conservative, or a little of both is very unclear (Brint 1984; Bruce-Briggs 1979).

Some generational units are based upon nontraditional cleavages that are unique to the historical circumstances involved in a particular generational process. Inglehart's new breed of liberal—the post-materialist—is essentially a generational unit whose common bond is having reached the Maslovian stage of "self-actualization." Evidence that activists or protestors of the 1960s are still politically distinct from others in their generation and from members of prior generations can also be interpreted as the discovery of an important generational unit (Jennings 1987; Jennings and Niemi 1981; Roberts and Lang 1985). Even the "new class" and "yuppie" theses described above might be characterized in these nontraditional terms.

Slight differences in age can also lead to important subgenerational distinc-tions. Again, this results from the importance of age and history in the pro-cess of generational development, and from the dynamic quality of both. More specifically, there are at least two types of socialization experiences that need to be distinguished: direct and indirect. Direct socialization refers to the learning and imprinting that occurs by being in the age cohort centrally in-volved in the events under consideration (being of working age during the Depression, or of high school or college age during the sixties, for example). This is not to say that only those who actually experience particular events (lose a job, go to war, participate in a sit-in), can be part of a generation. Rather it is to distinguish cohorts, many of whose members had such direct experiences, from those that, due to their collective age at a certain historical point, were less likely to have such "opportunities." Indirect socialization refers to a more passive process of learning (being a child during the Depression or during the 1960s). This process is much closer to the traditional view of socialization found in the political science literature, but is often ignored in generational studies. Both types of socialization have important ramifications for the development of each generation's profile, but the dynamics of that impact are different (Delli Carpini 1986; Rinalta 1979). Again, these differences can result from either the *formation* or the *expression* of generational distinctiveness.

The 1960s, for example, clearly affected individuals who were in their teens and individuals who were in their preteens. The differences in age undoubtedly led to the development of somewhat different attitudes and opinions, inasmuch as the cognitive, psychological, and moral development of teens and preteens is quite different. To the extent that similar worldviews did develop out of the experience of the sixties, however, the opportunity to express those views in particular ways was quite different for the cohort reaching young adulthood in 1968–73 and that reaching adulthood in 1976–81 (Delli Carpini 1986). Jennings and Niemi (1981) find significant differences in political involvement, trust, efficacy, policy stands, and participation between age cohorts who directly experienced the sixties (high school seniors in 1965) and those who were indirectly socialized by it (high school seniors in 1973). The latter cohort was less efficacious and trusting of the system, less politically engaged, and more conservative than the former. In my own research I also found differences between those who were between thirteen and twenty-four in the sixties and those who were slightly older or younger. My finding, paralleling those of Jennings and Niemi, was that the youngest cohorts were the least supportive of the political system, and the least politically involved, while the "experienced" cohorts were the most likely to have liberal political leanings and an alternative political agenda. Unlike Jennings and Niemi, however, I found even the experienced cohorts to be relatively disengaged from the political system, when compared to prior generations.

The acknowledgment of distinct subgenerations does not come at the expense of a more holistic view of generational development. Rather, subgenerations are often the particular manifestations of forces that are affecting the entire generation. The particular way in which different segments of the generation internalize those forces, or the particular way in which they externalize them often differ. Such intra-age variability (Braungart and Braungart 1984) indicates an interaction between generation and social status, but does not preclude the existence of an independent main effect as well. All four of the acknowledged periods of heightened generational activity demonstrate intragenerational divisions. The Young Europe generation of the early to mid-1800s pitted the progressive "Germania Burschenschaften" against the conservative "Arminia Burschenschaften" (Braungart 1984; Braungart and

Braungart 1984). The intragenerational conflicts of the early 1900s set communists and socialists against more traditional and even reactionary forces in Europe and the Soviet Union. Similar splits, this time among a new generation of communists, socialists, and fascists, were common in Europe and the United States during and after the Great Depression. Religious and nationalist generational units were common at this time as well. And in the 1960s, youth-dominated movements on the left and right, fueled by ideology, issues of national liberation, and religious conviction, were a worldwide occurrence (Braungart 1984; Braungart and Braungart 1984).

Despite these subgenerational divisions, however, all four periods still demonstrate strong intergenerational splits that allow for characterizations to be made about the successor generation. These commonalities seem to be at the level of deep-seated attitudes or values (Braungart, 1982 Braungart and Braungart 1984; Delli Carpini, 1986; Inglehart 1977; Knutson 1972; Mannheim 1972; Renshon 1974). Just as one can talk about cultures without denying the existence and importance of subcultures, one can also talk about both generations and subgenerations as legitimate social phenomena. My own research on the sixties generation (1986) demonstrates that, despite the existence of important subgenerational differences, there is a clear and consistent profile that distinguishes that generation from preceding ones: more liberal, more likely to have an alternative political agenda, less supportive of the political system, less likely to be involved in mainstream politics, more Democratic in its vote, but less Democratic in its long-term party allegiance. Similarly, Yankelovich (1974, 1984), while noting subgenerational differences, can speak of a generation raised in the 1960s and early 1970s that is identifiable in its liberalism on social issues and its rejection of many traditional norms, values, and institutions.

The Asymmetrical Nature of Generations

Throughout this chapter a fine line has been walked between biological and historical forces. Generations are clearly children of both. While at the level of general theory the *periodic* interaction of age and history resulting in generations seems reasonable, the *dynamic* nature of both processes as they operate in reality complicates matters. At the individual level, daughters and sons do come of age and "replace" their parents in thirty-or forty-year cycles. At the aggregate level, however, this replacement is spread out, with births and deaths, hirings and retirements, and so on, constantly occurring. Similarly, as discussed earlier, many of the economic, political, and technological developments that are relevant to generational change occur gradually and without much reflection. This fact helps to explain why generational distinctiveness at the level of, for example, the 1960s generation, is not a regular occurrence. It also suggests that the process of generational change, like social and political change of any kind, has an evolutionary side to it as well (Delli Carpini 1986). When birthrates either increase for a short period of time or rise and fall with a certain regularity, the potential for generational distinctiveness is increased. Similarly, when historical events or changes occur rapidly, marking distinct shifts in the sociopolitical environment, the potential for generational distinctiveness is increased. When both these elements are present, the possibility of dramatic generational differences is greatest. The 1960s and 1970s were years of tremendous generational conflict precisely because they brought together an unusually large cohort that was born in a rather short period of time and a historical period that was filled with unprecedented political, social, cultural, and economic change (Jones 1980; Delli Carpini 1986).

When historical and life-cycle forces are not packed into relatively small units of time, the process of generational replacement becomes less visible. While change associated with such replacement is undoubtedly less dramatic and more difficult to detect, it would be wrong to assume that it is either nonexistent or irrelevant. The research of Inglehart (1971, 1977, 1981, 1984) and of Nie et al. (1979) clearly demonstrates that generational change has important political and social implications even when it occurs in evolutionary fashion.

What does all this suggest for the empirical study of generations? Fundamentally, it suggests that one cannot look at a population at a particular point in time, neatly divide it into equal age groups, and call each a generation. Generational analysis requires either starting with a particular age group and considering the key forces that act as direct and indirect socializing agents in the development of its unique personality, or starting with a particular set of events or a period (what Ortega calls a "zone of dates") and examining the way in which it directly or indirectly affects the personality of different generations. In addition, it suggests that the problem of overlap makes a definitive analysis of multiple generations in a single study extremely difficult in the best of circumstances and impossible in many situations. One can do such analysis with biological age cohorts but not with generations.

Life-Cycle, Period, and Interaction Effects

As if the specific components of generational change were not complicated enough, one must also contend with individual change beyond that attributable to a generation. In particular, one must consider the effects of age that are not due to its interaction with historical and societal forces but that are more directly associated with the aging process and change related to the passage of time. Many changes take place within an individual as he or she grows older. Many of these changes are not likely to affect how one views the social and political world, but some will. In particular, processes such as cognitive development, the routinization of attitudes and behaviors through repetition, and the continuous refinement of those attitudes and behaviors through personal life-experiences and contact with the social and political world, can clearly lead to changes over time (Abramson 1983; Campbell et al. 1960; Hudson and Binstock 1976; Hudson and Strate 1985; Jennings and Niemi 1981; Milbrath and Goel 1977; Wolfinger and Rosenstone 1980; Nie et al. 1974). One's attitude about the effectiveness of elections for choosing political leaders, for example, is determined in part by the capacity of an individual to grasp the theory underlying the electoral process, in part by the gathering of specific information about the actual mechanics of the process, and in part by one's repeated experience with the process over time. All of these elements are related to the life cycle.

The specific way in which the life cycle affects the development of attitudes, opinions, and behaviors depends on the particular attitudes, opinions, and behaviors involved. Even so, several general observations can be made about how this process is conceptualized. The greatest area of disagreement centers on the rate at which the life cycle affects learning and socialization. Logically, almost any pattern can be defended, from a straight linear model (Delli Carpini 1986; Wolfinger and Rosenstone 1980), to step-function models that emphasize critical stages of development (Erikson 1968; Kohlberg 1968; Piaget 1967), to curvilinear models that suggest changing rates of learning. Such curvilinear models usually suggest that the rate of learning slows with advancing age, though the point at which this slowing begins ranges from childhood (Davies 1977; Knutson 1974; Renshon 1975) to old age (Campbell et al. 1960; Verba and Nie 1972), depending on the substantive issue and the theoretical perspective involved. Some curvilinear models even allow for the possibility of "forgetting" or "unlearning," as in the case of the rise and fall in political participation with age (Campbell et al. 1960; Verba and Nie 1972).

Inasmuch as all of the above models (as well as more complex hybrids) can be defended on logical and theoretical grounds, it would seem that the decision as to which is the more appropriate should be settled empirically. Unfortunately this is not possible, since the same empirical finding can be interpreted in a number of different ways. Consider, for example, that one finds that the probability of voting is relatively low between the ages of eighteen and twenty-five, increases between the ages of twenty-six and forty-four, remains about the same from forty-five to fifty-five, and begins to decline thereafter. Even if one can establish that these findings are not the result of generational differences (no easy task in and of itself, as shall be discussed below), it is still possible that the changing rates of "learning" are not due to the life cycle. It is possible, for example, that the youth culture of the period in question disdains voting as evidence of "selling out," and so young people are less likely to vote. Alternately, it is possible that the issues of the day do not address the concerns of the elderly, and so they do not vote. It is even possible that the accelerated participation in middle age reflects the coincidental fact that young adults and middle-aged people benefit most from the political institutions of advanced industrial societies. In short, deciding upon the structure of life-cycle effects is primarily a conceptual task. It depends upon what one is willing to include as part of the life-cycle process. Much of what one might consider "natural" life-cycle stages of development are, upon reflection, class-, culture-, and time-bound (consider recent evidence that voting is less likely to decrease after the age of fifty-five than was once the case). Jennings and Niemi (1981) distinguish such class-, cultural-, and time-bound effects from generational and life-cycle ones, calling the former "contextual effects." Many life-cycle and generational theorists are not so sensitive to such issues, however. Even the psychological, cognitive, and moral stages of theorists such as Freud, Piaget, and Kohlberg are highly susceptible to criticisms of cultural and class ethnocentrism.

This suggests that a truly parsimonious and "pure" definition of the life cycle would be divorced (as much as possible) from cultural and other kinds of idiosyncracies. The effects of culture, class, generations, historical circumstances, and the like could then be examined as separate forces or as forces that *interact* with the life cycle at different points and in different ways. Looked at from this perspective, let me offer the following general characteristics of the life cycle.

First, there does not appear to be any theoretical or empirical reason to assume that one ever stops the iterative process of learning and reevaluating (Gergen and Ullman 1977; Searing et al. 1976). Second, when the entire life cycle from birth to death is considered, the rate of learning and changing appears to slow (Dennis 1973; Dawson et al. 1977). However, when only adulthood is considered, the rate of change directly attributable to the effects of the life cycle are *essentially* linear. That is, once the rapid psychological, moral, cognitive, and educational developments associated with childhood and adolescence have occurred, there are no solid biological or experiential arguments to suggest that there is less change and development in one's forties than in one's thirties, or in one's sixties than in one's fifties, and so on (short of the physical and mental infirmities that can be associated with very old age). Third, the pattern of change associated with the life cycle should be relatively constant from one generation to another, when other factors are controlled for. The concept of the life cycle assumes a process that is similar for all groups and for all age cohorts over time. While members of one generation may hold attitudes different from those of members of another one, the independent effects of aging on those attitudes should be the same.

In addition to the effects of the life cycle, there is one other independent effect on the development of attitudes, opinions, and behaviors to consider: period effects. By period effects is meant social, political, cultural, and economic events that affect all generations and all age cohorts in a similar manner. Watergate had some important generational and life-cycle effects that impressed children in one way, new participants in the electoral process in a different way, and long-time participants in yet a third way; but it also had a more general effect that operated in a constant manner across all generations and all age groups. This would be considered a period effect. The effect of mass-media campaigns on the loosening of partisan ties for all cohorts in a society, or the increased participation across the board that results from a particularly important or interesting election are also examples of period effects. Such effects can be short-lived (as with the increased participation due to the dynamics of a particular election) or long-lasting (as with the loosening of partisan attachments), but the defining characteristic is its uniform impact on all members of the polity.

A final type of effect to consider is that resulting from the *interaction* of generation, life-cycle, and period effects. While each of the three former concepts are theoretically and methodologically distinct, it is possible for additional effects on political attitudes, opinions, and behaviors to result from the interaction of two (or more) of them. For example, a man who is twenty-five years old in 1984 holds certain attitudes towards civil rights that are in part determined by his age, in part determined by his generation, and in part determined by the political atmosphere of the period. His attitudes will also be determined, however, by the unique interaction of his age and generation, or his age and the period. Such interactions are important to a more complete understanding of the effects of generation, the life cycle, and distinct periods on political orientations. For example, my research (1986) suggests that the *interaction* of life cycle with generation (that is, being a member of the sixties generation) has the effect of "pulling" one back into the political mainstream over time. This effect is *in addition* to the separate "main effects" of aging and of generational differences. Beck and Jennings (1979) demonstrate that the belief that conservatives participate at greater rates than liberals is the result of the interaction of ideology and political periods, and not something inherent in a particular ideology per se. And Wolfinger and Rosenstone (1980) show that the decline in voting among the elderly is not a life-cycle effect but results instead from the interaction of age and generational differences in education and income.

Generalizability, Levels of Analysis, and the Selection of Data

Translating the theoretical and conceptual issues discussed above into models that allow for empirical testing is not an easy task. In addition to deciding which of the numerous variations on the generational theme is most appropriate, the researcher must also specify the model in a way that does justice to the theory, while allowing for a decomposition of intra- and intergenerational forces, as well as period, life-cycle, and interaction effects. And all this must be done in a way that is sensitive to the strengths and weaknesses of the data that are available.

The information used to test or illuminate generational theory runs the gamut from qualitative impressions to highly quantified data, and from system-level to individual-level evidence of change. As with all research, the selection of data involves tradeoffs. In generational research, the major tradeoffs center around the issues of generalizability and the level of analysis.

The issue of generalizability is a thorny one. While there is not a logical distinction between the level of generalization and the amount and quality of detail, there is often a practical one. In-depth interviews with a limited number of political activists from the 1960s can provide incredibly rich detail concerning generational development, period effects, and changes that occur with age, but the question remains as to the applicability of these findings to other activists from the same generation, to activists from other generations, or to the 1960s generation as a whole (Bellah et al. 1985; Boyte 1980; Broder 1981; Gilmour and Lamb 1975; Peck 1985; Whalen and Flacks 1984). Alternately, studies that emphasize generalizability to an entire population (Delli Carpini 1986) can suffer from a lack of detail concerning things such as intragenerational distinctions, the specific impact of particular elements of the sociopolitical environment, the richness of the generational profile, and so on. Research that is generalizable at one level usually fails at another. Even when comparisons are made to the generation being replaced, studies of a single generation (Braungart and Braungart 1980; Delli Carpini 1986; Draper 1967; Jennings and Niemi 1981; Loewenberg 1974; Wohl 1979) can only be impressionistically related to the generational process as a whole. They are essentially case studies, no matter what the ability to generalize to members of the cohort in question. Studies of student movements (Altbach 1967; Altbach and Laufer 1972; Altbach and Peterson 1972; Lipset and Altbach 1969; Lipset and Ladd 1972; Meyer and Rubinson 1972; Weinberg and Walker 1969) often cut across several generations, but the data are usually limited to a few periods (most often the 1930s and the 1960s) and of course the findings can be applied only to the generational unit of students and not to the 1930s and 1960s generations per se. Studies that focus on one aspect of change can not generalize to others. My own study of the 1960s generation (1986) is limited to political orientations, while Yankelovich's work focuses on social values (1972, 1974, 1984).

All this is not to criticize these studies or to suggest that completely generalizable studies are even possible. Rather it is to suggest that the complexity of the concept of generation, its interaction with historical, socioeconomic, and biological processes, and the limitations of available data make definitive studies of generational theory next to impossible. One must therefore select data that allow for the most acceptable mix of generalizability and qualitative depth on the theoretical dimensions of generational theory that are most central to one's research. One should also be explicitly aware of what these trade-offs are and how they affect the interpretations of findings. What level of generalization is reasonable? To what population? Under what historical circumstances? Can the effects of generation, periods, and/or the life cycle be distinguished with any confidence?

A related issue in the selection of data is the level of analysis. While most studies, by the very nature of generational development, consider both systemic and individual change, inevitably a choice between the two must be made. Is one centrally interested in the generational process as it manifests itself at the level of parent-child transmission (Bengston and Black 1973; Cutler 1977; Flacks 1967; Jennings and Niemi 1974, 1981; Stacey 1977; Tedin 1974)? Such "lineage effects" (Bengston and Cutler 1976; Braungart and Braungart 1984) are best studied using individual-level data that generally include parent-child interviews and preferably also include some aspect of a panel design (Jennings and Niemi 1981; Newcomb et al. 1967). If one is interested in aggregate levels of generational change (but still concerned with attitudinal change), then cross-sectional surveys repeated over time are appropriate (Abramson, 1975, 1979, 1983; Abramson and Inglehart 1986; Claggett 1981; Converse 1976; Cutler 1969–70; Delli Carpini 1986; Glenn 1972, 1977; Glenn and Hefner 1972; Inglehart 1977), though panel studies can be utilized at this level as well (Jennings and Niemi 1981). Sigel and Brookes' study of how events can change children's support for the political system (1974) uses both cross-sectional and panel surveys in its research design.

Theories or interests that apply to specific subgenerations (such as students, activists, the middle class, women) need panels or cross-sectional surveys that provide enough interviews with the desired category of people to allow for meaningful generalizations. Often such subgroups are too small to be drawn from more general surveys and so require specially designed samples. Such surveys are quite rare, especially ones that have been conducted over time. The classic example of such a survey is the Bennington College study (Newcomb 1943; Newcomb et al. 1967). Sigel and Reynolds' study of two generations of college-educated women (1979–80), and Roberts and Lang's analysis of Princeton graduate students (1985) are also examples of the utilization of specialized data sets.

Occasionally studies of individual people are used to illuminate the larger process of generational change (Crosby 1984; Kearney 1984; Post 1984; Rinalta 1984). Most often these are biographical studies of prominent or exceptional individuals and serve as case studies of particular generational units (such as political elites) rather than of entire generations. Rinalta's examination of Vera Brittain's *Testament* (1984) is probably an exception to this, however, with Brittain's personal experiences providing insights into her generation as a whole.

Generational change can go beyond questions of individual and aggregated opinions, attitudes, and behaviors. More systemic levels of analysis include changes in the economic, political, cultural, social, and intellectual environments that both cause and result from generational change. Such analyses are the most difficult to conduct systematically, and yet in many ways understanding change at this level is the goal of all generational research. The most common approach for this kind of research is historical and institutional (Mannheim 1972; Draper 1967; Eisenstadt 1956; Esler 1974; Heberle 1951; Tilly et al. 1975). Naturally, as emphasis on historical processes increases, the level of specificity concerning attitudinal and behavioral change decreases. This results from limits in the ability to deal with all the diverse aspects of generational change in a single study and from the lack of detailed, systematic attitudinal data prior to the late 1930s. Often demographic and behavioral data (census figures on occupation and income, statistics on migration patterns, aggregate voting, and so on) serve as the link between sociohistorical and individual/cohort processes of generational change (Jones 1980; Klein 1984).

Since most contemporary behavioral studies of political generations depend on some form of survey research (usually multiple cross-sectional surveys), let me spend a little more time dealing with some of the issues that are of particular relevance to this kind of data. In my own study of the 1960s generation, I relied upon the series of National Election Studies (NES) designed and carried out by the Inter-University Consortium for Political and Social Research at the University of Michigan from 1952 to 1980. The choice of the NES was relatively easy, once the criteria for this study were established. First, it was necessary to find a set of surveys that provide national samples. Second, it was necessary that these surveys include a wide array of both political and social variables, as well as demographic characteristics. Third, the questions asked at various times had to be comparable. Fourth, the surveys had to span a period that began prior to the sixties, and to the entry of individuals who were part of the sixties generation into the electorate, and that continued beyond the years designated as the sixties. Only the NES surveys met all these requirements.

The choice of these surveys was not without drawbacks, however. In many cases the survey questions available do not address the attitudes or actions that most distinguish the sixties generation and the 1960s from what preceded them. This is especially true in the area of antisystem or untraditional behavior. While this always poses a difficulty for the secondary analysis of data, it is a particular problem when the goal of the research is to uncover change. Surveys, especially surveys repeated over time, are designed within the context of a particular system and a particular period. In addition, they are designed by individuals who are themselves part of that environment. As a result, the surveys themselves are bounded by that dominant perspective; for it to be any different would require a prescience that is unlikely. This means, however, that while one can hint at the outer bounds of opinions and behaviors of the new generation, one must be content to show how this generation differed from preceding ones relative to the political structure that already existed. For example, while I could show that the new generation was less likely to vote than prior generations, I could only speculate whether this represented a movement away from participation in politics, or a shifting of political modes from voting to, for instance, involvement in grass-roots organizations. Where possible, one can supplement the central analysis with additional data, but the nature of the conclusions drawn from such less systematic analyses must necessarily be more tentative. As a result, research on generations often focuses more on deviations from past norms and less on the specific development of new norms.

Methodological Issues

Political change arising from generational replacement, the life cycle, and/or period effects has been studied empirically in many different ways. Again, the biggest distinction in methodology is between studies that emphasize individual and cohort change and those that emphasize the larger historical process. Concerning the former, methods of analysis have ranged from straightforward comparisons of attitudes and behaviors across time and groups (Cutler and Bengston 1974; Cutler 1977; Glenn and Hefner 1972; Glenn 1977; Jennings and Niemi 1981) to more complex multivariate designs based upon linear regression (Abramson 1979; Claggett 1981; Converse 1976; Delli Carpini 1986), categorical regression (Kritzer 1983), and dynamic modelling (Markus 1983). In the choice of a method of analysis each researcher attempts both to document time- and age-related change and to reduce it to its causal components, doing so in a way that introduces the greatest fit between the assumptions underlying the methodological and substantive theories involved.

Central to this notion of fit is the "identification problem." This problem is encountered when one has more unknowns to explain than can be independently estimated from the data. In the particular case of change believed to be caused by some combination of life-cycle, period, and generational effects, this means that knowing an individual's (or group's) location on two of these characteristics fully determines his or her location on the third, making an independent estimate of the latter's impact impossible. For example, if we know that an individual is thirty years old, and that the data were collected in 1972, then we know with certainty of which generation that individual is a member. Similarly, if we know the generation and year, we must know the age group, or if we know the generation and age, we must know what year the data were collected in. This problem is made more complicated when interaction effects are included, since the number of unknowns is increased without increasing the ability of the data to provide information.

While the identification problem is most often referred to and dealt with in the use of statistical models, in fact it is a conceptual problem that has relevance to any study of generations, no matter what the mode of inquiry. Distinguishing among the "contributions" of age, generation, historical circumstances, and their interactions is as important in a biographical examination of Gladstone as it is in a historical examination of student protestors in the 1960s or in a statistical analysis of the opinions of the youth of the 1980s. The specific language used in these various approaches may differ. Some of the "terms" may be implicit rather than explicit in research that is more qualitative. The consequences of ignoring certain effects may be more obvious in statistical research. And yet the importance of distinguishing these forces to the best of one's ability remains across all methods of inquiry. Since statistical analysis lays out the different variables and their interrelationships in relatively precise ways, in the following discussion I will discuss the identification problem and its various solutions in statistical terms. The relevance of the issues raised to research on generations that does not employ statistics should be kept in mind, however.

In statistical research the solution to the identification problem, assuming one is working with cross-sectional data gathered over a number of years, depends upon the nature of the substantive issue under consideration and the theoretical assumptions one is willing to make in order to provide information that otherwise cannot be obtained directly. The most common approach to avoiding the identification problem is to provide additional information (side information) that allows the researcher to assume that one or more of the hypothesized effects (life-cycle, period, generational, or the interaction effects) to be either zero or of some independently estimable magnitude. If one assumes an effect to be zero, then that term can be eliminated from the model, making the remaining terms identifiable. Suppose, for example, that we are interested in the changing racial composition of the United States. Such a change could be due to generational differences (different birth rates could lead to one generation having a larger or smaller percentage of blacks for instance), or to period differences (blacks might immigrate to the United

States during a particular period at unusual rates because of changing immigration laws or because of conditions abroad). It is a safe assumption, however, that changes are not due to the life cycle. One does not change race with age. Thus, one can use cross-sectional data over time to estimate the effects of generational replacement and period differences without encountering the identification problem.

Research on generations (including nonstatistical research) that ignores the effects of aging, historical periods, or interactions is implicitly "solving" the identification problem by setting these terms to zero. Problems arise, however, when these unstated assumptions prove overly simplistic. For example, ignoring the effects of specific periods led most political observers to first underestimate the importance of issues in the vote choice of the American public, and then to overestimate their importance (Campbell et al. 1960; Nie et al. 1976, 1979; Pomper 1975).

If it is unrealistic to assume away one of the effects, it is still possible to avoid the identification problem by using side information. With this approach, one attempts to estimate one or more of the effects independently, and then uses this estimate in a more complicated model, utilizing other data. Claggett (1981), for example, estimated generational effects on partisanship for the period from 1952 to 1964, and then used this estimate in a more complicated model for the 1964 to 1976 period. In short, this approach involves changing one of the unknowns to a known, and then estimating the model with this information included.

Kritzer (1983) suggests a way of estimating multiple effects that is not based upon assumptions concerning the *impact* of some of those effects but upon assumptions concerning the *structure* of such impacts. He argues that the identification problem arises only when the independent variables involved are linear combinations of each other. If only one of the variables is assumed to be linear, while the others are assumed to be categorical (or dummy variables), the model is identified. In his example concerning partisanship, Kritzer argues that the life-cycle effect is largely linear, while generational and period effects are categorical, leading to an identified model.

Consider the example involving age, generation, and period used above to introduce the identification problem, and the solutions offered to get around such a problem. What Kritzer's approach suggests is that the use of dummy variables in the model combines the simplifying notions underlying (1) setting certain effects to zero and (2) providing independent estimates of those effects. That is, either an effect is zero (someone is not a member of a particular generation, or the year is not 1972), or the effect is constant for all members of the category. Put another way, data set up in this fashion do not determine with certainty in which generation or period all individuals or responses should be placed. Instead the data determine only those in which they should not be placed. One knows, for example, that an individual is not part of a particular generation if his score is zero, but this information cannot be combined with the age variable to determine the time period. Nor can it be combined with the period variable to determine the respondent's age. This element of independence, when considered in the data as a whole, results in an identified model.

The research described above concerning solutions to the identification problem equates generations with equal-sized age cohorts. The earlier discussion of the theoretical and conceptual dimensions of generations suggests that this may be an unrealistic approach. A more theoretically developed conceptualization of generational change allows one to borrow from these methodological approaches but also suggests the need to modify or adapt them. Consider that you are interested in studying the political impact of the sixties generation (and its subgenerations) on the distribution of political attitudes, opinions, and behaviors in a political system. Suppose also that you are trying to remain consistent with some of the subtleties of the process discussed earlier in this chapter. In some ways you are at an advantage, in that, unlike the attempts to examine generational change discussed above, your concern is only with the impact of a single generation, and a particular period. This allows you not only to simplify parts of the model but also to use information about the population prior to the 1960s as side information. However, a more theoretically rigorous definition of generations and an expectation of not only all three main effects but also interaction effects make your particular methodological needs unique.

For example, it was suggested above that the way in which the world imprints different generations is unique and that, as a result, any examination that attempts to uncover generational differences must be sensitive to such idiosyncratic configurations. Does this mean that in order to understand the 1960s and the generation that grew up in that decade one must first document the distinct impact of all prior generations and all prior periods? While such documentation may in fact be desirable, it would be a task of overwhelming proportions. The usual solution is to assume away much of the uniqueness of what one might call "generational crystallization" and to use equally proportioned age cohorts as surrogates for the more complex notion of generation. While in many cases this may be acceptable, given the arguments presented above, such a solution would be inappropriate for this analysis. How then does one simplify the reality of political change in a way that is consistent with this notion of generational change?

One possible solution (Delli Carpini 1986) is based loosely on Kritzer's observation concerning linear and nonlinear change. Consistent with earlier discussion, political change brought about by the life cycle is assumed to be essentially linear. That is, the process of aging, and the incremental experi-

encing and learning about the world that is a part of the process, is conceptualized as affecting one's political orientations at a relatively constant rate.
This does not imply that the life cycle must affect all political orientations,
nor that it must be the same for different types of attitudes and actions. It only
says that such an effect, when it does exist and when separated from other
sociological, cultural, historical, and biological effects, is essentially linear.

The effects of the generation one is born into and the period one reacts to
are, on the other hand, nonlinear. Knowing the attitudes, opinions, and behaviors of one generation need not tell us much about the attitudes, opinions,
and behaviors of earlier or subsequent generations, once the effects of the life
cycle have been accounted for. This is due to the fact that each generation
develops its identity from a unique combination of historical, cultural, social,
economic, political, and even biological circumstances. Similarly, periodic
events and the reaction to those events by different generations are discrete
and nonlinear (Ryder 1965).

How does distinguishing linear from nonlinear effects help to overcome the
problem of developing a context for the introduction of a new generation?
The answer lies in the essentially random nature of period and generational
effects when considered on a wide array of people and events. While the
characteristics of each generation, each event or period, and the reaction of
generations to events are clearly not random, there is no reason to expect a
consistent, linear pattern of characteristics, events, or reactions to be developed across a number of generations (Ryder 1965). For example, while there
are clear reasons to expect those socialized in the Depression to develop a
unique political character that is attributable (in part) to that experience, nothing about the development of that generation allows one to say much about
the character of preceding or following generations. This is especially true
when one considers not two or three generations but many.

Similarly, while one can offer explanations for the reaction of individuals
and groups to specific periods, the events of a particular period provide little
to predict the details of the next. It is difficult to argue a linear progression in
the Roosevelt, Truman, Eisenhower, Kennedy, Johnson, Nixon, Ford, Carter,
and Reagan years, and even more difficult to argue for such a progression in
the specific events that constitute the substance of those periods. What is the
linear link between the Depression of the 1930s and JFK's assassination?
Between World War II and Watergate?

If one accepts that the effects of generation and period are nonlinear, especially across individuals who represent several different generations and
who have experienced the events of many different periods, then it can be
assumed that the linear relationship that does exist between age and political
orientations in the population that grew up before the 1960s is due primarily
to the life cycle. While this assumption is of little use if one is interested in

determining the political effects of generations and periods prior to the 1960s, it is invaluable for studying the effects of a new generation and particular periods.

The strength of the measure is that it distinguishes life-cycle effects from those of generation and period without introducing unacceptably artificial definitions of the latter two concepts. In addition, it allows one to estimate a more realistic model of the effects of a particular period and a particular generation by allowing one to include a greater number of hypothesized effects without encountering the identification problem. In any event, the point of this discussion is less to demonstrate the utility of this particular operationalization of the life-cycle effect than again to point out that generational research, like generational theory, is a matter of making reasoned tradeoffs that allow for a more detailed examination of one aspect of generational change at the expense of a detailed examination of some other aspect. One is always forced to simplify assumptions, ignore possible sources of change, limit the scope of analysis, and so on. The key then becomes doing so in a way that involves the fewest costs for the aspects of generational change that are most central to one's theory and research. A diversity of methodological approaches should not be viewed as evidence of incoherence in the study of generations, but as evidence of the complexity of the endeavor.

A Summary and Synthesis

I would like to end this chapter by synthesizing some of the issues raised in the previous pages. While this synthesis falls short of a theory of generations, it contains the elements upon which such a theory might be based. I shall begin with a brief summary of the key concepts discussed in this chapter. An "age cohort" is a collection of all individuals born within an indeterminate but continuous set of years. This set of years is usually narrow (between one and ten years), but the limits are determined by the purpose of the research and by the nature of the historical environment. A "period" is a finite set of years that can be distinguished from the years immediately preceding and following it along one or more dimensions of human existence. These dimensions include the social, political, economic, cultural, intellectual, technological, and natural environments of particular systems but are not logically limited to them. "History" is a summary term for the combination of the social, political, economic, cultural, intellectual, technological, and natural environments of particular systems over time. A "generation" is an age cohort whose values, attitudes, opinions, and/or behaviors have been shaped in relatively stable and unique ways by history. Generations react to specific historical circumstances in unique ways because different age cohorts tend to experience different aspects of that history, and because different age cohorts, due to their relative location in the life cycle, tend to interpret the same historical experiences in different ways.

While part of the definition of a generation focuses on its unique reaction to specific historical periods, this is not the same as saying that the attitudes of a generation need to differ from those of preceding or succeeding generations. Imagine that a particular age cohort reacts to a political scandal by becoming engaged in politics at a much greater rate than it would have otherwise. Imagine as well that the preceding generation was unaffected by the scandal but was already unusually engaged in politics as a result of the particular historical circumstances of its past. Alternately, imagine that this older generation was affected by the scandal by becoming less engaged in politics, but that this merely lowered their level of political engagement to that of the new generation. In both of these scenarios it is possible that the old generation and the young one would be indistinguishable in terms of their level of political involvement. And yet it would be inaccurate to suggest that the process of generational development had not occurred. In short, distinct worldviews are a possible outcome of the process of generational replacement, but not a necessary outcome. Viewed in this way, the issue becomes one of identifying the elements that make generational distinctiveness more likely.

One of these elements is the *rate* of population replacement. When members of an older generation die and/or when members of a new generation are born at unusually rapid rates, the potential for distinct generations increases. This is due in part to the presence of a "critical mass," which increases the likelihood that an age-based subculture will develop. Related to this issue of the rate of population replacement is the *variability* of population replacement. Short periods of very distinct birth rates are more likely to lead to generational distinctiveness than less clearly defined or more extended ones. This is so because it *concentrates* the biological and life-cycle elements of the generational process.

The rate and variability of historical developments are also critical to generational distinctiveness. During periods of rapid change the likelihood that an age cohort will have experiences that are different from those of prior generations (as well as different from those that prior generations had when they were at the same point in the life cycle as the new cohort) increases. During times of variable rates of change, when critical events are concentrated in relatively short, distinct periods, this likelihood is increased further.

Since history is a summary of several more specific dimensions of human experience, one can talk about historical concentration not only across time but also across dimensions. The probability of generational distinctiveness increases when change is occurring in the social, political, economic, and other environments simultaneously.

Members of a generation can be conscious of their unique situation in the same way that other important groups and classes are, but this is not a necessary element of generational development. It is likely, however, that the circumstances described above, which increase the probability of generational distinctiveness, also increase the probability of generational self-consciousness. Such self-consciousness, in turn, changes the substance of generational distinctiveness.

The development of a generational profile and the specific opportunity to express it are two related but fundamentally distinct processes. Historical change is still central to the latter process, though in a slightly different way than in the former. In periods of rapid, concentrated historical change, the environment that is critical for the shaping of a generation's common worldview may be very different from the environment that exists when members of the generation become significant actors in the social, economic, political, and other systems. Also, the dimension of the historical environment that is most influential in shaping the worldview of a generation need not be the same dimension that is central in expressing this new worldview. In fact, since a rejection of some aspect of a previous generation's worldview is often an important part of generational development, it is likely that the successor generation will select a new avenue in which to pursue its goals. A new generation might develop a distinct profile as a result of the political and technological environments (the threat of nuclear annihilation, perhaps) but express that uniqueness not politically or technologically but through a cultural statement (the "Punk" movement). The specifics of this process are unclear but should be conceptualized as the opportunities for the focusing of generational energies provided by a system at a particular historical point. These circumstantial and structural "stress points" result from the interaction of the nature of the generational profile, the nature of the particular system, and the generation's sociopolitical location in that system (which is in part determined by biological age). Generational self-conciousness probably increases the likelihood of a generation expressing itself in some unique way. The specific details of a generation's self-image undoubtedly affect the particular way in which it expresses itself.

Just as the process of generational development can be incremental or radical, the expression of it can result in either evolutionary or revolutionary changes in the system within which it takes place. This again depends upon both the nature of the generational profile and on the specific opportunities presented to express that distinctiveness. The legacy of generational replacement might be a gradual decrease in participation or a dramatic political revolt. Whether such change is dramatic or incremental depends in part on whether the generation, due to earlier birth rates, enters the adult population relatively quickly or more slowly over time. It also depends upon the opportunities that are available for political participation. A generation that, from its early development, appears sure to have a dramatic impact as adults, might never actually materialize as a sociopolitical force, while a generation that is less remarkable in its youth may, under the right circumstances, be the catalyst for more dramatic change later in life. Again, the point is that processes of development and of expression are separate.

The above discussion applies to generations as a whole. Just as history affects different age groups in different ways, however, it can also affect *segments* of new age cohorts in different ways. Women, poor people, blacks experience the world in a very different way than do men, rich people, whites. This is as true for the young as it is for the old, though the specific differences may change. In short, all of the processes applicable to whole generations are also occurring for different generational units, or subgenerations. A subgeneration can even be based upon finer age distinctions within larger cohorts. The same forces that increase the likelihood of generational distinctiveness and self-conciousness and that shape the way in which this distinctiveness is expressed also operate on subgenerations. Because each subgeneration brings together different mixes of biological and historical forces, and different opportunities for expression, each has the potential for developing subgenerational profiles that differ not only from other members of their age cohort, but also from older members of their particular subgroup. These distinct profiles can occur in addition to a more inclusive generational one, or, because of unique historical and biological circumstances, might occur in lieu of the more general one. The stronger the forces that lead to an overall generational profile, the less likely it is that dramatically distinct subgenerations will form. Again, a distinction must be made between the formation and the expression of, in this case, subgenerational worldviews. A generation might, for example, form a single dominant set of attitudes, but different subgenerations may express those attitudes in very different ways. Which subgenerations are important at any particular time depends upon the nature of class, race, sex, age, and other divisions that exist in the system in question. If social, political, economic, and other differences between men and women do not exist, then the juncture of age and history that results in a generational profile should not result in subgenerational profiles based upon sex.

Both aging and history are continuous processes that not only affect the development of a generation but also exert independent influence on the development and expression of attitudes, opinions, and behaviors. As a result, both need to be included in any attempt to isolate the unique impact of generations on historical change. In addition, the interactions among generations, age, and history need to be considered. For example, declining turnout among the elderly might be considered part of the life-cycle effect if interactions are ignored. If they are included, this drop-off becomes better understood as the result of the interaction between age and a historical period, during which the structure of political institutions (limited access to polling places, the lack of easily available transportations, and the like), the nature of the political agenda, and the limits of medical science interact with being elderly in such a way as to decrease both the incentive and the ability to vote. Additionally, the decline might result from the interaction of age and generation. That is, a particular generation might have certain characteristics (low education, poor civic training, unusual physical ailments) that do not affect turnout during the prime of life but that, coupled with the additional burdens of old age, work to depress turnout. It is important to see that the inclusion of interaction effects is as much a conceptual as a methodological consideration, in that it defines what kinds of effects one wishes to attribute to particular sociological, political, and physiological forces. Aging is both a physiological and a cultural experience. To the extent that it is cultural, its impact on attitudes, opinions, and behaviors will vary from period to period and from generation to generation. It is this situation-based aspect of aging that is best conceptualized as an interaction effect.

The Nature and Possibilities of Generational-Based Change

One cannot talk about generational development without talking about socialization. Socialization is the process by which people learn the norms, values, and beliefs of a particular system (or subsystem), as well as how and when these norms, values, and beliefs should be expressed. The agents of socialization are the institutions of society: family, school, work, the media, and so on. These institutions are the repository of the collected history of a system, as well as the transmitters of that history. Were the environments in which the institutions of a society exist never to change, those institutions would never change, and so socialization would result in the constant replication of society and its members. It is the changing, often unpredictable environment, which both results from and leads to changes in institutions, that prevents socialization from working as a mechanical process of replication. Generational distinctiveness develops out of these cracks in the die of socialization.

Acknowledging that generations can differ does not mean that these differences are lasting or that they are fundamental. If institutions are the repository and the transmitters of a society's norms, values, and beliefs, then for generations to be critical agents of change themselves, they should have some effect on a society's institutions. Without such institutional change it is unlikely that a generation can maintain its behavioral differences, and without behavioral differences, attitudinal differences either fade away, or are repressed, surfacing in idiosyncratic psychological and sociological ways. Put another way, "deauthorization" (Braungart and Braungart, 1984), or the rejection of the norms and values of older generations, may result from the cracks in the socialization process, but "authorization" of a new set of norms and values requires a restructuring of institutions. The nature of the generational process makes deauthorization of the old a much more likely development than authorization of some new set of arrangements. This is so because the rejection of old norms is most likely to happen when a generation is young and first coming to grips with a society's institutions. The development and maintenance of new norms requires some degree of institutional power and organization. But this is most likely to occur much later in the life cycle. And by this time, the socializing effects of old institutional structures are likely to have pulled the generation back to the societal norms (Delli Carpini 1986). This temporal separation of rebelliousness and power is probably the greatest obstacle to lasting generation-based change.

This is not to say that generational change is not important to the development of a society over time. Rather it is to suggest that there are at least three types of such change that need to be considered (beyond cosmetic changes in life-style). The first might be called "destructive" change, and refers to the tendency towards deauthorization described above. Such change presents the possibilities of more constructive, permanent change but can also be solely destabilizing. In and of itself it is unlikely to have a lasting impact on a system, but should be thought of as the raw material for other kinds of change.

The second kind of change is "restructuring." Restructuring change involves the institutional development and support that is required for the maintenance and transmission of alternate norms, values, and behaviors. Such change is more difficult and therefore much less likely to occur. It can occur by a new generation actually providing both the leadership and the "foot soldiers," but it more likely involves members of a new generation throwing their support behind nonmainstream movements or ideas that already exist in the environment (support among the German youth for Nazism and the Hitler Youth, for example).

The third kind of change, "adaptive" change, is one that is much less considered in the literature on generations. Since generations develop out of cracks in the wall of socialization, the real discontinuities that exist are actually between the environment and the *older* generations. That is, older generations that were socialized under a certain set of conditions find themselves in a rapidly changing environment in which old rules no longer apply. New generations develop in this changed environment, and so do not feel a discontinuity with it, but do feel one with the older generations and their no longer applicable norms. Viewed in this way, generational change is simply a way for the institutions of society to adjust themselves to a changing environment and for the development of a population that is prepared to follow these new rules. In fact, it is the older generations that may be potentially the most revolutionary (or, more accurately, reactionary), since it is their norms that are most at odds with the realities of the society in which they live. However, the process of aging again acts as a safety valve for society, this time with the cold finality of death.

Consider the changing attitudes towards women in the workplace. Generational differences in both attitudes and behaviors suggest that a new generation has at least begun the process of deauthorizing traditional views on this topic. There is even evidence of limited structural change in institutions such as the workplace and the family. Is this restructuring originating from the new generation, or did economic decline in the United States create a condition in which families needed two incomes to maintain a standard of living that one could once provide? In the latter case, generational change is adaptive, leading to an acceptance among the young of conditions that already exist. In the former case it is restructuring. The difference for understanding the dynamics of generational change is profound. If generations are more often adaptive than restructuring, then the real value of generational research may lie in what it tells us about the de facto norms, opinions, behaviors, and institutions of the generation being replaced. When society looks at a new generation in many ways what it sees is a reflection of itself, not as it would like to be but as it really is.

References

Abramson, Paul R. 1975. *Generational Change in American Politics.* Lexington, Mass.: Heath.

———. 1979. "Developing Party Identification: A Further Examination of Life Cycle, Generational, and Period Effects." *American Journal of Political Science* 23 (February): 78–96.

———. 1983. *Political Attitudes in America.* San Francisco: W. H. Freeman.

Abramson, Paul R., and Ronald Inglehart. 1986. "Generational Replacement and Value Change in Six Western European Societies." *American Journal of Political Science* 30: 1–25.

Alford, Robert. 1963. *Party and Society.* Chicago: Rand McNally.

Altbach, Philip G. 1967. "Students and Politics." In Seymour Martin Lipset, ed., *Student Politics.* New York: Basic Books.

Altbach, Philip G., and Robert S. Laufer, eds. 1972. *The New Pilgrims: Youth Protest in Transition.* New York: David McKay.

Altbach, Philip G., and Patti McGill Peterson. 1972. "Before Berkeley: Historical Perspectives on American Student Activism." In Philip G. Altbach and Robert S.

Laufer, eds., *The New Pilgrims: Youth Protest in Transition*. New York: David McKay, pp. 13–31.

Andersen, Kristi. 1979a. "Generation, Partisan Shift, and Realignment: A Glance Back at the New Deal." In Nie et al., *The Changing American Voter*. Cambridge: Harvard University Press, pp. 74–95.

———. 1979b. *The Creation of a Democratic Majority*. Chicago: University of Chicago Press.

Andersen, Kristi, and Elizabeth A. Cook. 1985. "Women, Work, and Political Attitudes." *American Journal of Political Science"* 29: 606–25.

Beck, Paul A. 1974. "A Socialization Theory of Partisan Realignment." In Richard Niemi, ed., *The Politics of Future Citizens*. San Francisco: Jossey-Bass, pp. 199–219.

Beck, Paul A., and M. Kent Jennings. 1979. "Political Periods and Political Participation." *American Political Science Review* 73: 737–50.

Bellah, Robert, Richard Madsen, William Sullivan, Ann Swidler, and Steven Tipton. 1985. *Habits of the Heart*. Berkeley: University of California Press.

Bengston, V. L., and K. D. Black. 1973. "Intergenerational Relations and Continuities in Socialization." In P. B. Baltes and K. W. Schaie, eds., *Life-Span Development Psychology: Personality and Socialization*. New York: Academic Press.

Bengston, Vern L., and Neil E. Cutler. 1976. "Generations and Intergenerational Relations: Perspectives on Age Groups and Social Change." In Robert H. Binstock and Ethel Shanas, eds., *Handbook of Aging and the Social Sciences*. New York: Van Nostrand.

Bennett, W. Lance. 1980. *Public Opinion in American Politics*. New York: Harcourt, Brace, Jovanovich.

Bettelheim, Bruno. 1963. "The Problem of Generations." In Erik Erikson, ed., *Youth: Change and Challenge*. New York: Basic Books.

Blydenburgh, John C., and Roberta S. Sigel. 1983. "Key Factors in the 1982 Elections as Seen by Men and Women Voters: An Exploration into the Vulnerability Thesis." Paper presented at the American Political Science Association meeting, Chicago.

Boyte, Harry C. 1980. *The Backyard Revolution*. Philadelphia: Temple University Press.

Braungart, Richard G. 1980. "Youth Movements." In J. Adelson, ed., *Handbook of Adolescent Psychology*. New York: John Wiley.

———. 1982. "Historical Generations and Youth Movements: A Theoretical Perspective." Paper presented at the World Congress of Sociology meeting, Mexico City.

———. 1984. "Historical Generations and Generational Units: A Global Pattern of Youth Movements." *Journal of Political and Military Sociology* 12: 113–35.

Braungart, Richard G., and Margaret M. Braungart. 1980. "Political Career Patterns of Radical Activists in the 1960s and 1970s: Some Historical Comparisons." *Sociological Focus* 13: 237–54.

———. 1984. "Generational Politics." *Micropolitics* 3: 349–415.

Brint, Steven. 1984. "New Class and Cumulative Trend Explanations of the Liberal Political Attitudes of Professionals." *American Journal of Sociology* 90: 30–71.

Broder, David. 1981. *The Changing of the Guard*. New York: Penguin Books.

Bruce-Briggs, B., ed. 1979. *The New Class?* New Brunswick, N.J. Transaction Books.

Burnham, Walter Dean. 1965. "The Changing Shape of the American Political Universe." *American Political Science Review* 59: 7–28.

———. 1970. *Critical Elections and the Mainspring of American Politics*. New York: Norton.

Campbell, Angus, Philip E. Converse, Warren E. Miller, and Donald E. Stokes. 1960. *The American Voter*. New York: John Wiley.

Chaffee, Steven H., L. Scott Ward, and Leonard B. Tipton. 1970. "Mass Communication and Political Socialization." *Journalism Quarterly* 47: 647–59; 666.

Claggett, William. 1981. "Partisan Acquisition v. Partisan Intensity: Life-Cycle, Generation, and Period Effects."*American Journal of Political Science* 25: 193–214.

Converse, Philip E. 1976. *The Dynamics of Party Support: Cohort-Analyzing Party Identification*. Beverly Hills: Sage Publications.

———. 1979. "Rejoinder to Abramson." *American Journal of Political Science* 23: 97–100.

Crittenden, John. 1962. "Aging and Party Affiliation." *Public Opinion Quarterly* 26: 648–57.

Crosby, Travis L. 1984. "Gladstone's Decade of Crisis: Biography and the Life Course Approach." *Journal of Political and Military Sociology* 12: 9–22.

Cutler, Neil. 1969–70. "Generation, Maturation, and Party Affiliation: A Cohort Analysis." *Public Opinion Quarterly* 33: 583–88.

———. 1977. "Political Socialization Research as Generational Analysis: Cohort Approach versus the Lineage Approach." In *The Handbook of Political Socialization*, ed. Stanley A. Renshon. New York: The Free Press, pp. 294–326.

Cutler, Neil and Vern L. Bengston. 1974. "Age and Political Alienation." *Annals of the American Academy of Political and Social Science* 415: 160–75.

Dalton, Russell. 1977. "Was There a Revolution? A Note on Generational versus Life Cycle Explanations of Value Differences." *Comparative Political Studies* 9: 459–74.

Davies, James C. 1977. "Political Socialization: From Womb to Childhood." In *Handbook of Political Socialization*, ed. Stanley A. Renshon. New York: The Free Press.

Dawson, Richard E., Kenneth Prewitt, and Karen S. Dawson. 1977. *Political Socialization*. Boston: Little, Brown.

Delli Carpini, Michael X. 1984. "Politics and the 1960s: Generational, Period, and Life Cycle Effects." Paper presented at the Southern Political Science Association meeting, Savannah.

———. 1985. "Generations and Politics: The Political Involvement of the Sixties Generation." Paper presented at the Midwest Political Science Association meeting, Chicago.

———. 1986. *Stability and Change in American Politics: The Coming of Age of the Generation of the 1960s*. New York: New York University Press.

Delli Carpini, Michael X., and Lee Sigelman. 1986. "Do Yuppies Matter? A Test of Competing Explanations of the Political Distinctiveness of Young Urban Professionals." *Public Opinion Quarterly* 50: 502–18.

Dennis, Jack, ed. 1973. *Socialization To Politics*. New York: John Wiley.

Dickstein, Morris. 1977. *Gates of Eden*. New York: Basic Books.

Dilthey, W. 1976. *Selected Writings,* trans. H. P. Rickman. Cambridge: Cambridge University Press, 1976.

Draper, H. 1967. "The Student Movement of the Thirties: A Political History." In R. Simon, ed., *As We Saw The Thirties*. Urbana: University of Illinois Press.

Easton, David, and Jack Dennis. 1969. *Children in the Political System: Origins of Political Legitimacy*. New York: McGraw-Hill.

Eisenstadt, Shmuel N. 1956. *From Generation to Generation: Age Groups and Social Structures*. London: The Free Press.

———. 1963. "Archetypal Patterns of Youth." In Erik Erikson, ed., *Youth: Change and Challenge*. New York: Basic Books.

Elden, J. Maxwell. 1981. "Political Efficacy at Work: The Connection Between More Autonomous Forms of Workplace Organization and a More Participatory Politics." *American Political Science Review* 75: 43–58.

Erikson, Erik H. 1968. *Identity, Youth and Crisis*. New York: Norton.

Erikson, Robert S., Norman Luttbeg, and Kent L. Tedin. 1980. *American Public Opinion*. New York: John Wiley.

Esler, A. 1974. *The Youth Revolution*. Lexington, Mass.: D.C. Heath.

———. 1982. *Generations in History: An Introduction to the Concept*. Williamsburg, Va.: William and Mary College Press.

Ferrari, Giuseppe. 1874. *Teoria dei Periodi Politici*. Milan: Hoepli.

Feuer, Lewis S. 1969. *The Conflict of Generations*. New York: Basic Books.

Flacks, Richard. 1967. "The Liberated Generation: An Exploration of the Roots of Student Protest." *Journal of Social Issues* 23: 52–75.

Freud, Sigmund. 1964. *New Introductory Lectures on Psychoanalysis,* trans. James Strachey. New York: Norton.

Gergen, Kenneth J., and Matthew Ullman. 1977. "Socialization and the Characterological Basis of Political Activism." In *Handbook of Political Socialization,* ed. Stanley A. Renshon. New York: The Free Press.

Gilmour, Richard, and Richard Lamb. 1975. *Political Alienation in Contemporary America*. New York: St. Martin's Press.

Ginsburg, Benjamin. 1982. *The Consequences of Consent: Elections, Citizen Control, and Popular Acquiescence*. Reading, Mass., Addison-Wesley.

Gitlin, Todd. 1980. *The Whole World Is Watching*. Berkeley: University of California Press.

Glenn, Norval D. 1972. "Sources of the Shift to Political Independence: Some Evidence from a Cohort Analysis." *Social Science Quarterly* 53: 494–519.

———. 1977. *Cohort Analysis*. Beverly Hills: Sage Publications.

Glenn, Norval D. , and Ted Hefner. 1972. "Further Evidence on Aging and Party Identification." *Public Opinion Quarterly* 36: 31–47.

Gurr, Ted R. 1970. *Why Men Rebel*. Princeton: Princeton University Press.

Hamilton, R. F., and J. Wright. 1975. *New Directions in Political Sociology*. Indianapolis: Bobbs-Merrill.

Heberle, R. 1951. *Social Movements*. New York: Appleton-Century, Crofts.

Hudson, Robert B., and Robert H. Binstock. 1976. "Political Systems and Aging."

In Robert H. Binstock and Ethel Shanas, eds., *Handbook of Aging and the Social Sciences*. New York: Van Nostrand, pp. 369–400.

Hudson, Robert B., and John Strate. 1985. "Aging and Political Systems." In Robert H. Binstock and Ethel Shanas, eds., *Handbook of Aging and the Social Sciences*. 2d ed. New York: Van Nostrand Reinhold, pp. 554–85.

Inglehart, Ronald. 1971. "The Silent Revolution in Europe: Intergenerational Change in Post-industrial Societies." *American Political Science Review* 65: 991–1017.

———. 1977. *The Silent Revolution*. Princeton: Princeton University Press.

———. 1981. "Post-materialism in an Environment of Insecurity." *American Political Science Review* 75: 880–900.

———. 1984. "Generational Politics and Cultural Change." Paper presented at Conference on Changing Political Culture of Youth in Western Democracies, Lake Como, Italy.

Jansen, N. 1975. *Generational Theory*. Johannesburg: McGraw-Hill.

Jennings, M. Kent. 1987. "Residues of a Movement: The Aging of the American Protest Generation." *American Political Science Review* 81: 367–82.

Jennings, M. Kent, and Richard G. Niemi. 1974. *The Political Character of Adolescence*. Princeton: Princeton University Press.

———. 1981. *Generations and Politics*. Princeton: Princeton University Press.

Jones, Landon Y. 1980. *Great Expectations*. New York: Ballantine Books.

Kasschau, Patricia L., H. Edward Ransford, and Vern L. Bengston. 1974. "Generational Consciousness and Youth Movement Participation: Contrasts in Blue Collar and White Collar Youth." *Journal of Social Issues* 30: 69–94.

Kearney, Robert N. 1984. "The Mentor in the Commencement of a Political Career: The Case of Subhas Chandra Bose and C. R. Das." *Journal of Political and Military Sociology* 12: 37–47.

Key, V. O., Jr. 1955. "A Theory of Critical Elections." *Journal of Politics* 17: 3–18.

———. 1959."Secular Realignment and the Party System." *Journal of Politics* 21: 198–210.

Klapper, Joseph T. 1960. *The Effects of Mass Communication*. New York: The Free Press.

Klein, Ethel. 1984. *Gender Politics*. Cambridge, Mass: Harvard University Press.

Knoke, David, and Michael Hout. 1974."Social and Demographic Factors in American Political Party Affiliation, 1952–72." *American Sociological Review* 39: 700–713.

Knutson, Jeanne. 1972. *The Human Basis of Polity*. New York: Aldine Atherton.

———. 1974. "Prepolitical Ideologies: The Basis of Political Learning." In Richard Niemi and Associates, *The Politics of Future Citizens*. San Francisco: Jossey-Bass.

Kohlberg, Lawrence. 1968. "Moral Development." In *The International Encyclopedia of the Social Sciences*. New York: Macmillan.

Kritzer, Herbert M. 1983. "The Identification Problem in Cohort Analysis." *Political Methodology* 9: 35–50.

Ladd, C. Everett. "Opinion Roundup: Values." 1984. *Public Opinion* 6: 21–40.

Lambert, T. Allen. 1972. "Generations and Change: Towards a Theory of Generations as a Force in Historical Processes." *Youth and Society* 4 (September): 21–46.

Langton, Kenneth P., and M. Kent Jennings. 1968. "Political Socialization and the High School Civics Curriculum in the United States." *American Political Science Review* 62: 852–67.

Lauer, R. H. 1977. *Perspectives on Social Change.* Boston: Allyn and Bacon.

Lipset, Seymour Martin, and Philip G. Altbach, eds. 1969. *Students in Revolt.* Boston: Houghton Mifflin.

Lipset, Seymour Martin, and Everett Carl Ladd. 1972. "The Political Future of Activist Generations." In Philip G. Altbach and Robert S. Laufer, eds., *The New Pilgrims: Youth Protest in Transition.* New York: David McKay, pp. 63–84.

Lipset, Seymour Martin, and Stein Rokkan, eds. 1967. *Party Systems and Voter Alignments: Cross National Perspectives.* New York: The Free Press.

Loewenberg, P. 1974. "A Psychohistorical Approach: The Nazi Generation." In A. Esler, ed., *The Conflict of Generations in Modern History.* Lexington, Mass.: D.C. Heath.

Mannheim, Karl. 1972. "The Problem of Generations." In Philip G. Altbach and Robert S. Laufer eds., *The New Pilgrims.* New York: David McKay (originally published in 1928).

Marias, J. 1968. "Generations: The Concept." 1968. In D. Sills, ed., *Encyclopedia of the Social Sciences.* New York: Macmillan.

———. 1970. *Generations: A Historical Method.* University, Ala.: University of Alabama Press.

Markus, Gregory B. 1983. "Dynamic Modelling of Cohort Change: The Case of Political Partisanship." *American Journal of Political Science* 27 (November): 717–39.

Markus, Gregory B., and M. Kent Jennings. 1985. "Of Yuppies, Enddies, and the Formation of Political Generations." Paper presented at the American Political Science Association Meeting, New Orleans.

Maslow, Abraham. 1962. *Towards a Psychology of Being.* Englewood Cliffs: D. Van Nostrand.

Mentre, François. 1920. "Les Générations Sociales." Paris: dissertation.

Meyer, J. M., and R. Rubinson. 1972. "Structural Determinants of Student Political Activity: A Comparative Interpretation." *Sociology of Education* 45: 23–46.

Milbrath, Lester W., and M. L. Goel. 1977. *Political Participation.* Chicago: Rand McNally.

Newcomb, Theodore. 1943. *Personality and Social Change.* New York: Dryden.

Newcomb, Theodore, Kathryn E. Koenig, Richard Flacks, and Donald Warwick. 1967. *Persistence and Change: Bennington College and Its Students After 25 Years.* New York: John Wiley.

Nie, Norman H., Sidney Verba, and Jae-On Kim. 1974. "Political Participation and the Life Cycle." *Comparative Politics* 6: 319–40.

Nie, Norman H., Sidney Verba, and John R. Petrocik. 1976. *The Changing American Voter.* Cambridge, Mass.: Harvard University Press.

———. 1979. *The Changing American Voter.* Enlarged Edition. Cambridge, Mass.: Harvard University Press.

Ortega y Gasset, J. 1961. *The Modern Theme.* New York: Harper and Row.

————. 1962. *Man and Crises*. New York: W. W. Norton.

————. 1974. "The Importance of Generationhood." In A. Esler, ed., *The Youth Revolution*. Lexington, Mass.: D.C. Heath.

Peck, Abe. 1985. *Uncovering the Sixties*. New York: Pantheon.

Piaget, Jean. 1967. *Six Psychological Studies*. New York: Random House.

Piven, Frances Fox, and Richard A. Cloward. 1977. *Poor People's Movements*. New York: Pantheon.

Pomper, Gerald M. 1975. *Voters' Choice: Varieties of American Electoral Behavior.* New York: Dodd, Mead.

Poole, Keith, and Harmon L. Zeigler. 1984. *Women, Public Opinion, and Politics*. New York: Longman.

Post, Jerrold M. 1984. "Dreams of Glory and the Life Cycle: Reflections on the Life Cycle Course of Narcissistic Leaders." *Journal of Political and Military Sociology* 12: 49–60.

Renshon, Stanley. 1974. *Psychological Needs and Political Behavior.* New York: The Free Press.

————. 1975. "The Role of Personality Development in Political Socialization." In David Schwartz and Sandra Kenyon Schwartz, eds., *New Directions in Political Socialization*. New York: The Free Press.

Rinalta, Marvin. 1968. "Generations in Politics." In D. Sills, ed., *Encyclopedia of the Social Sciences*. New York: Macmillan.

————. 1979. *The Constitution of Silence: Essays on Generational Themes*. Westport, Conn.: Greenwood Press.

————. 1984. "Chronicler of a Generation: Vera Brittain's Testament." *Journal of Political and Military Sociology* 12: 23–35.

Roberts, Carl W., and Kurt Lang. 1985. "Generations and Ideological Change: Some Observations." *Public Opinion Quarterly* 49 (Winter): 460–73.

Ryder, N. B. 1965. "The Cohort as a Concept in the Study of Social Change." *American Sociological Review* 30: 843–61.

Schorske, C. E. 1978. "Generational Tension and Cultural Change: Reflections on the Case of Vienna." *Daedalus* 107: 111–22.

Searing, Donald, Gerald Wright, and George Rabinowitz. 1976. "The Primacy Principle: Attitude Change and Political Socialization." *British Journal of Political Science* 6: 83–113.

Shingles, Richard. 1981. "Black Consciousness and Political Participation." *American Political Science Review* 75 (March): 76–91.

Shively, W. Phillips. 1979. "The Development of Party Identification among Adults: Exploration of a Functional Model." *American Political Science Review* 73: 1039–54.

Sigel, Roberta S., and Marilyn Brookes. 1974. "Becoming Critical about Politics." In Richard G. Niemi, ed., *The Politics of Future Citizens*. San Francisco: Jossey-Bass.

Sigel, Roberta S., and Marilyn Brookes Hoskin. 1977. "Perspectives on Adult Political Socialization—Areas of Research." In S. A. Renshon, ed. *Handbook of Political Socialization*. New York: The Free Press, pp. 259–93.

Sigel, Roberta S., and John Reynolds. 1979–80. "Generational Differences and the Women's Movement." *Political Science Quarterly* 94: 635–48.

Simon, R. J. 1967. *As We Saw The Thirties*. Urbana: University of Illinois Press.

Simon, William, John H. Gagnon, and Donald Carns. 1969. "Working Class Youth: Alienation without an Image." *New Generation* 51: 15–21.

Smelser, N. J. 1963. *Theory of Collective Behavior.* New York: The Free Press.

———. 1968. *Essays in Sociological Explanation.* Englewood Cliffs, N.J.: Prentice-Hall.

Stacey, B. 1977. *Political Socialization in Western Society: An Analysis from a Life-Span Perspective.* New York: St. Martin's Press.

Sundquist, James L. 1973. *The Dynamics of the Party System.* Washington D.C.: Brookings Institution.

Tedin, Kent L. 1974. "The Influence of Parents on the Political Attitudes of Adolescents." *American Political Science Review* 68: 1579–92.

Tilly, C. L., and R. Tilly. 1975. *The Rebellious Century, 1830–1930.* Cambridge, Mass.: Harvard University Press.

Tolley, Howard, Jr. 1973. *Children and War.* New York: Teachers College Press.

Verba, Sidney, and Norman Nie. 1972. *Participation in America.* New York: Harper and Row.

Weinberg, I., and N. Walker. 1969. "Student Politics and Political Systems: Toward a Typology." *American Journal of Sociology* 75: 77–96.

Whalen, Jack, and Richard Flacks. 1984. "Echoes of Rebellion: The Liberated Generation Grows Up." *Journal of Political and Military Sociology* 12: 61–78.

Wohl, R. 1979. *The Generation of 1914.* Cambridge: Cambridge University Press.

Wolfinger, Raymond E. and Steven J. Rosenstone. 1980. *Who Votes.* New Haven: Yale University Press.

Yankelovich, Daniel. 1972. *The Changing Values on Campus.* New York: Washington Square Press.

———. 1974. *The New Morality: A Profile of American Youth in the 70s.* New York: McGraw-Hill.

———. *New Rules.* 1984. New York: Random House.

Two

Aging and Adult Political Socialization: The Importance of Roles and Transitions

JANIE S. STECKENRIDER AND NEAL E. CUTLER

One of the most intriguing questions for analysts of political behavior focuses on the relationship between the *aging process* and political dispositions. Are there stages in an aging individual's "political life cycle" that can be traced to maturation from youth to old age? The maturing and aging individual undergoes an interaction of physiological, psychological, sociological, and role changes. Typically paralleling these numerous changes is life-course political continuity; but almost as often there can be modifications, adjustments, or even dramatic alterations in an individual's political attitudes and political behavior.

If we approach political socialization from a multidisciplinary perspective (Cutler 1977a), clues can be gleaned about both political change and continuity. Perhaps the most promising and still uncharted paths to the mysteries connecting aging and political dispositions lie in the sequence of roles associated with adult maturation and aging, e.g., student, spouse, wage-earner, parent, retiree, and—increasingly in today's age-conscious society—"old person."

Adult Political Change: Levels of Analysis

In contrast to the systems- or macro-perspective toward political socialization (e.g., Almond 1960; Easton 1965; Easton and Dennis 1969), the individual- or micro-level perspective of the present paper examines how, when, and why individuals acquire particular political attitudes, beliefs, and behaviors. Thus, political socialization has been defined as the "process through which an individual acquires his particular political orientations—his knowledge, feelings and evaluations about his political world" (Dawson et al. 1977, p. 33). This broad definition encompasses all phases and studies of individual opinion formation, such as the early voting behavior studies (Berelson et al. 1954; Lane 1959; Campbell et al. 1960; Lipset 1960); children's benevolent feelings toward political authorities, particularly the president (Greenstein 1960), the role of the family, school and peers as agents of political socialization (Langton 1969; Jennings and Niemi 1974), the influence of health and body image on political attitudes (Schwartz et al. 1975), and the potential impact of "subjective age identification" among the elderly (Cutler 1983).

It is the micro-perspective that is concerned with the gradual, incremental, and lifelong process of developing an individual's "political self" (Mead 1934)—a complex synthesis of feelings about nationalism and patriotism, identification with a particular political party and with political and social groups, ideological positions, attitudes and evaluations of specific political issues, personalities and political events, knowledge and experience with political structures and procedures, and one's self-image of rights, responsibilities, and positions in the political world (Dawson et al. 1977, p. 40).

Adults vs. Children

Despite the fact that nearly all the political socialization literature focuses on children and adolescents, an individual's political self does not magically crystallize upon reaching the legal age of political adulthood—which itself includes such variations as eighteen for voting, twenty-five for membership in the House of Representatives, thirty for the Senate, and thirty-five for the presidency. Instead, the political self has a dynamic and constantly changing complexion throughout the life cycle. The basic and early political learning does, of course, provide a foundation for adult political orientations, but childhood is a time of "incomplete socialization" (Rose 1960) because it cannot sufficiently prepare an individual for the volume and variety of political and social experiences that the adult will encounter (Sigel 1970, p. 427).

Analyses of adult political socialization identify three clusters of explanations as to why political socialization is continuous throughout the life cycle—why adults are susceptible to political change: (1) societal-level phenomena, (2) time-lag or temporal aspects, and (3) changes in the individual's life situation. These three explanations need not, of course, be mutually exclusive.

Societal phenomena include events such as wars, depressions, and international and domestic realignments. Similarly, rapid and widespread development and diffusion of transportation and communication technology have clearly produced social, economic, and political changes that have in turn produced alterations in political expectations and perceptions. The Depression, for example, caused changes in expectations about the fundamental role of government's responsibility to society. And while perhaps atypical, wartime and post—World War II events clearly affected the political orientations of German and Japanese adults (Kuroda 1965). Granted, the usual tendency is for basic political orientations to persist throughout the adult years; but they are influenced by the world of significant, real political events and can be dislodged or changed by those events.

The *time-lag* dimension of adult political change is also influenced by societal changes and reflects the time lag between childhood political learning and the later acquisition of explicitly political roles. The changed social or political world renders the political orientations acquired earlier less relevant or incomplete for the current circumstances. Brim (1968) notes that the modern industrial world provides novel situations for which childhood socialization could not prepare the individual, including variations over time in basic political-cultural values, general policy choices, and the political contexts in which political choices must be made.

A parallel temporal consideration is the time lag between youthful political learning and the assumption of "real" political roles as citizens. Childhood can provide only partial anticipatory socialization for the roles of voter, taxpayer, campaign contributor, and party activist. Running for the vice presidency of the sixth-grade soccer club may (in Eastonian terms) engender the input of support for democratic institutions, but clearly many of the norms and values surrounding adult political roles can be learned only "on the job" and may radically differ from those learned in childhood.

The *acquisition of new roles and life experiences* characterizes the third explanation as to why individuals undergo political change throughout the life cycle. Life-cycle events after high school are significant and numerous—college, entry into the labor force, marriage, parenthood, home ownership and neighborhood involvements, memberships in new and different kinds of organizations, retirement, widowhood. Each new set of life-course transitions has the potential of creating new role relationships, thereby producing new experiences, social environments, and political responsibilities and opportunities any of which can lead to changed political outlooks. It is this third set of factors, new roles in adulthood, on which this chapter focuses in examining political changes that occur over the adult life-course. We suggest that the new roles can lead to socialization or resocialization and can result in new or changed political values and attitudes. In this context we concur with Rowe and Kahn's recent analysis which, although focused on physical and mental declines associated with aging, applies also to the issue of age-related socialization:

> We believe that the role of aging per se in these losses has often been overstated and that a major component of many age-associated declines can be explained in terms of life style, habit, diet, and an array of psychosocial factors extrinsic to the aging process. (Rowe and Kahn 1987, p. 143)

While the focus here is on the *capacity* for adult role change to produce adult political change, this is certainly not to argue against those conceptual and empirical writings which point to the volume and importance of childhood political socialization. Many, if not most, of an individual's basic political orientations are relatively stable throughout the life cycle. In commenting on the early acquisition and relative consistency of party identification, for example, Dawson et al. (1977, pp. 80–81) suggest that the core of the political self is indeed acquired in childhood and remains quite stable, becoming the filter or perceptual screen to evaluate later political stimuli.

By contrast, adult political socialization is generally conceived as being more relevant to specific events, programs, and personalities, which are more susceptible to change than basic social and political identifications and general beliefs about political institutions (Searing, Wright, and Rabinowitz 1976). Yet, even the "very basic political outlooks can be changed during the adult years" (Dawson et al. 1977, p. 81). And in this way we are brought full circle: what is the relationship between the aging process and political dispositions?

Role Transitions, Aging, and Socialization

The utility of role transitions in understanding adult political socialization is in part based on the connections among the concepts of *role, socialization, and the aging process*. Consequently, as a prelude to the more detailed overview of age, role, role transitions, and political dispositions, we first consider several definitions of socialization, the expectations and sanctions associated with roles, an example of how various roles and expectations become intertwined, and the transition of roles over the life cycle.

While socialization and role transition are not synonymous, the former typically being considered as a broader and more basic set of experiences than the latter, nonetheless a number of definitions of socialization do either explicitly focus upon or include elements of the learning and internalizing of the skills, expectations, and obligations of new roles. Furthermore, the potential overlap of the concepts of socialization and role transition is especially germane in the context of aging and adult socialization precisely because adult development and aging may be seen as a serial process of role change and role transition, with each role demanding at least some additional knowledge and skills (Bengtson and Haber 1983).

What Is "Socialization"?

In much of the literature socialization is defined as the process by which one learns to perform various roles adequately. Brim (1966) views socialization among adolescents and adults as largely a matter of role learning. Clausen (1968, p. 21) includes role learning with childhood training, education, enculturation, and development of social character as aspects of socialization. For George Herbert Mead (1934) the socialization process is discovering what society expects of us in various roles. But perhaps the most clearly identified connection between aging, socialization, and role transition is given by social gerontologist Matilda White Riley. Riley (1976) sees socialization as *teaching individuals at each life stage how to perform new roles,* to negotiate allocated procedures, to adjust to changed roles, and to relinquish old roles.

Effective socialization means internalizing the beliefs, conforming to the shared expectations, and taking on the basic standards of society or a group related to a particular role. Every role brings with it socially defined norms or rules of behavior which are determined by cultural ideas of appropriateness. For example, in current Western societies the role of parent has associated norms or expectations of providing one's children with adequate food, shelter, clothing, and protection from physical abuse, among other responsibilities. With any role there is an acceptable range of variation in behavior, style, quality, and degree of commitment to the role expectations. Even the parent role allows the individual latitude in the interpretation of what is deemed "adequate," but this role, like all others, has limits to acceptable variations.

Role Expectations and Sanctions

Following from the above, the key element in socialization is the role expectations from others, or oneself, that may involve change in one's beliefs, attitudes, motives, or values. The expectations may be from a self-initiated motivation to change to be *more acceptable to oneself,* e.g., to relabel oneself as a fiscal conservative so as to correlate economic attitudes with an occupational promotion, or to appear *more acceptable to others,* e.g., adopt a more popular style of teaching so as to meet the expectations of a new dean. The expectations associated with some roles require only simple additions or expansions of existing skills and create little conflict. For example, the grandparent role is in many ways similar to the parent role and, furthermore, the grandparent has already been a parent (Kornhaber 1985, p. 164). Other role expectations may demand major changes in an individual's orientations or create discontinuity with what was learned earlier, i.e., prisoner of war (Brim 1966, p. 196). Whether self-initiated or originating from others, and regardless of the degree of discontinuity created, "the awareness of a new constellation of expectations and behavior occurs with each new role or status, producing a distinctive reconstruction, or transformation, of one's identity" (Bengtson and Haber 1983, p. 77).

The character and degree of the demands made by the role expectations depend upon the existence and degree of associated *sanctions*. Sanctions can be rewards or punishments, and can range from formal and severe (imprisonment) to the informal raising of an eyebrow. The degree to which the role expectations will be binding on an individual is determined by the extent to which the significant others or society is willing to impose sanctions and on the desire of the role occupant to conform to role expectations (Jaros and Grant 1974, p. 275). In *Men at the Top,* Presthus (1964) illustrates that some individuals simply cannot and do not want to internalize the expectations and values incumbent on a new role.

A Congressional Example. A classic example of roles, and their accompanying expectations and sanctions, is provided by Fenno's hypothetical member of the Appropriations Committee of the House of Representatives (Fenno 1966, pp. 160–67). The committee member occupies several roles simultaneously—legislator, public leader, party member, spouse—each with its complex of expectations. For example, the representative's colleagues on the Appropriations Committee expect her to work hard, develop a policy specialization, restrain partisan party rhetoric inside the committee, accept the judgment of other specialists, and compromise on issues. Committee colleagues have both positive and negative sanctions to encourage her reciprocity and compromise and to ensure committee unity. Positive sanctions include a prized subcommittee chairmanship, additional staff assistance, and special help from senior committee members. Just as powerful are negative sanctions of assignment to an undesirable subcommittee, social isolation, or removal from the committee.

Operating simultaneously are expectations from the Congress as a whole, the political party, constituents, spouse, and the individual's self-expectations. The party wants its position represented and aggressively pursued by its representatives on the committee. Access to financial contributions and to the party's leadership imply both positive and negative sanctions. The presence of multiple roles, and their possibility of conflict, is well illustrated by the fact that all representatives have multiple committee assignments, each directed by different personalities, styles, and political strategies. Similarly, every legislator is simultaneously called upon to be both "delegate" from her own constituency and "trustee" acting on behalf of the good of the commonwealth, a conflict experienced by members of a state as well as the national legislature (e.g., Wahlke et al. 1962).

By contrast, constituents, who hold the ultimate rewards and sanctions via the vote, seldom perceive their representatives' obligations to internal committee and congressional roles, and naturally focus instead on policy benefits. Legislators retain nonpolitical roles with still other expectations and sanctions, such as those of spouse and parent. The committee expectation of hard work may conflict with these roles if there is no time left to spend with the family or if the individual's health is jeopardized. And for many politicians, perhaps the strongest expectations and sanctions are intrapersonal—resolving all of these various expectations with his or her self-image.

In some cases the conflicting expectations of multiple roles, as in the congressional example, lead to pronounced role strain, at times prompting the role occupant to exit. Sigel and Pindur (1969), for example, report that some members of local school boards and city councils found these multiple expectations so stressful that they advised their offspring against entering politics, and confessed that their respect for and trust in the political process was steadily becoming eroded. In sum, it is clear that for citizen and political elite alike, multiple roles, with multiple and overlapping patterns of expectations and sanctions, represent the canvas on which the picture of adult political socialization is sketched.

Roles over the Life Course

The life course has traditionally been perceived as a progression of "orderly" changes from infancy to old age with biological and sociocultural timetables "governing" the sequence of role transitions (Cain 1964; Ryder 1965; Clausen 1972). These ordered stages generally include child, student, employee, spouse, parent, grandparent, retiree, and widow. To use the metaphor of statistical vocabulary, however, these stages are *ordinal* rather than *interval* in nature, as there are both historical and cross-sectional variations surrounding the chronological time at which identifiable life stages may occur. In recent decades, for example, marriage has come later in life, and retirement earlier. And as Bengtson and Haber note, within modern society "socioeconomic status can influence the age at which major events can occur," e.g., working-class males leave school and enter the workforce earlier, and are retired earlier than middle-class males (1983, p.75).

However, even this ordinal progression of role transitions is being increasingly challenged by a variety of nontraditional or "asynchronous" life-stage role acquisitions, e.g., as females choose the role of parent prior to or with no intent of making the transition to spouse by marriage; as large numbers of older persons enter or return to the role of student by enrolling in college courses; and as remarried men and women renew the role of spouse and parent at, sometimes, older than usually expected chronological ages.

Each new role carries with it recognizable expectations of acceptable patterns of activity, responsibility, and privilege that differ from other stages. During the progression through the life course the individual learns to adapt to new roles and relinquish old ones, and to accumulate knowledge and attitudes and social experiences (Neugarten and Hagestad 1976, p. 36).

Roles can be acquired through rather different kinds of developmental sequences. For example, one role can be serially dependent on another—e.g., the widow role requires having been a spouse. Or, one role can be entered by achievement but its successor role entered by ascription, as when a corporate vice president is faced with age-based mandatory retirement. And roles can, of course, be either voluntary (club member) or largely involuntary (family member). While the political consequences of the nature of a role's origin represents a class of analytic questions that has yet to be addressed (e.g., the political consequences of voluntary versus mandatory retirement), the key point here is that, in addition to its origin, any new role can expose the individual to conditions and experiences that may lead to significant attitudinal and behavioral change.

The life cycle can be divided into fundamental stages with numerous variations in detail and subdivision, from infancy through adulthood, to stages within adulthood, and even stages within old age. Where Shakespeare identified seven ages of man—from a "muling and puking" infant to old age described as "second childishness and mere oblivion"—Erikson's (1950) commonly used conception of the life course includes eight stages of psychological development based on personality and individual experiences (for details, see Renshon, chap. 6, in this volume). Neugarten and Peterson (1957) identified four periods in adulthood, each with its own characteristic behavior—young adulthood, maturity, middle age, and old age.

Rosow's *Socialization to Old Age* (1974) provides a more comprehensive demarcation of the adult life course—young adulthood (complete education and start work), marriage, parenthood, middle age (raise family), grandparenthood, and old age (widowhood, retirement, illness). Although the timing may differ by social class, ethnicity, or gender, most adults may expect to go through this progression of roles. Neugarten (1974) identified two distinct sociodemographic groups of older men and women—the "young old" and the "old old"—who differ not only in their chronological age (65–74 versus 75 +) but in terms of a broad range of health, wealth, and social characteristics, and ultimately in their public-policy needs and demands.

Age and Role Transition

The connection between age and role transition over the life course is not as obvious as it may sometimes seem. Age is only a rough indicator of the number and types of roles that are open (and closed) to individuals. And the relationship of age to role, imperfect as it is, changes over history and even within an individual's (or a cohort's) own lifetime. Entering and exiting some roles is closely age-linked (voting at eighteen; retirement at sixty-five—both which have changed within the last twenty years), but others are only indirectly age related, such as motherhood or occupational advancement (Riley 1976, pp.196–98).

In addition, age can serve to link complexes of otherwise differentiated roles. Old age, for example, can simultaneously bring the role of retiree, member of a national politically-involved organization, grandparent, widow, and community elder. At the same time, the relationship between age and these major life stages is not invariant across society. As mentioned earlier, for example, the developmental relationship between age and role can be influenced by socioeconomic status: the lower the socioeconomic level, the sooner in the life course a particular role transition occurs. Individuals of lower socioeconomic status were found to be far more likely to complete their education and enter the labor force at an earlier age. Females of lower socio-economic status, moreover, were found to take on new roles at an earlier age than comparable males (Neugarten et al. 1965).

Different patterns in the timing of role transitions reflect social norms as to the age when a particular event should occur. Furthermore, the age-appro-priate norms for a particular role transition can vary throughout history, as illustrated by the "empty nest" phenomenon (period after children leave home). Females born in 1920 averaged age fifty-two at the marriage of their last child compared to a female born in 1880 who was fifty-six at this major event. Another important historical change is that 80 percent of the 1920 cohort shared this final launching with their husbands whereas only 50 per-cent of the 1880 cohort did (Glick and Parke 1965). Aside from recent de-mographic patterns, these "empty nest" patterns serve to illustrate that (a) chronological age, behavior, and role are only imperfectly linked over the life cycle, and (b) even when age-specific or "age appropriate" values and norms can be identified, they are susceptible to redefinition in even relatively short historical periods. The corollary proposition, of course, is that the political socialization associated with significant role transition similarly cannot be precisely linked to specific chronological ages. In sum, the interplay of role, age, socialization, and politics is no less heterogeneous or variable than the society these concepts seek to elucidate.

Age, Role, and Political Dispositions

The concept of roles and role transitions is, thus, an important explanatory key in answering our original question concerning the socialization relation-ship between the aging process and political dispositions. These important landmarks in adult life can effect socialization or resocialization to new polit-ical orientations. Adult (re)socialization occurs not necessarily because an individual rejects the values and behavioral patterns learned in childhood but because they may be inadequate or irrelevant for the new or modified roles taken on as an adult. The adult either wants or is forced to learn new, different, or additional ways of thinking, feeling, and behaving politically to cope with the new demands accompanying the new role (Sigel and Hoskin 1977). Many of these demands are no doubt caused by new roles which lead the individual to experience new people, new expectations, new environments, new needs. Brim addresses the force of demands and expectations for change:

> Even though some of the expectations of the society are relatively stable through the life cycle, many others change from one age to the next. We know that society demands that the individual meet these changed expectations, and demands that he alters his personality and behavior to make room in his life for newly significant persons such as the family members, his teachers, his employer and his colleagues at work. (Brim 1970, pp. 18–20)

Political Participation

The use of role transitions might help explain the so-called "linear relationship" often said to exist between age and political participation. Milbrath and Goel (1971) reported that voting turnout was lowest among young voters, increased and peaked for individuals in their forties and fifties and dropped among individuals over sixty. Later analyses have convincingly shown that statistical controls diminish or eliminate the decrease in participation at the end of the life course (Verba and Nie 1972, chap. 9). Glenn and Grimes (1968) and Cutler (1983) found a similar monotonic relationship between age and political interest. These patterns of political behavior and age may be further understood through a role-transition perspective.

While young adults (late teens and early twenties) are the least concerned with politics and have the lowest voter turnout rate of any age group, this life-stage does show an increase over the pre-teen period in the individual's involvement and interest in the events of the political world and in greater crystallization of the political self (Dawson and Prewitt 1969, pp. 50–51). The low participation rate during young adulthood reflects the individual's preoccupation with *multiple role transitions*—completion of education, labor-force entry, marriage and family formation—activities that take precedence over civic duties and public concerns (Glenn and Grimes 1968; Verba and Nie 1972). Indeed, Glaser and Strauss (1971) observe that the greatest synchronization of roles occurs around the period of early adulthood, where a "pile-up" of role transitions occurs.

With time, individuals increasingly are socialized into their new roles and are exposed to different conditions that influence political behavior. Milbrath and Goel (1971), for example, report that *integration into the community* (clearly a broad collection of new personal, familial, fiscal, and social roles) intervenes between age and political participation. Political participation and political interest peak in middle age, which marks the stage in one's life when an individual is almost completely socialized into the multiple roles assumed in early adulthood. The major role transitions of the middle and later life stages, (retirement, empty nest, widowhood, eligibility for public entitlement programs) are more likely to affect the political self in terms of attitudes toward public policy benefits than in modes of political action in pursuit of those policies. Indeed, where aging was once thought to almost automatically bring about a "disengagement" from participatory roles, continuity of social participation and behavioral style across life stages is now recognized as the modal pattern of normal adult development and aging (Reedy 1983).

On the other hand, there is increasing evidence that in the United States both the society and the citizenry are becoming increasingly "age conscious" (Cutler, Pierce, and Steckenrider 1984; Gurin, Miller and Gurin 1980). This suggests that for some people, the arrival at a new complex set of roles (retirement, leisure, public benefits, income and health concerns, etc.) may stimulate an interest in political activity where little political interest beyond voting had before been present (e.g., Trela 1971; Cutler 1981b). Thus, just as early adulthood may be characterized by a density of role transitions, so we would hypothesize that the beginning of the young-old stage of the life cycle reflects a relatively high density of role transitions, the consequence of which is a life stage characterized by new political socialization.

Political Attitudes

It is possibly in the area of political attitudes that role transitions may have their greatest impact on adult political socialization. Since the publication of the classic *The American Voter* in 1960, political scientists have recognized that a large portion of voters adopt a *group-benefits* orientation on political issues, i.e., citizens interpret their political world in terms of policies toward their significant social groups. In turn, the assessed significance of different social groups flows from the individual's roles and life situation. Thus, change in roles can alter both the structure of an individual's group associations and their relative salience. The likely result, then, is a process not simply of attitude or opinion change but new socialization experiences in which attitude change is one of several components.

As one example of this role or group-benefits model connecting adult socialization and political attitudes, we can consider a reinterpretation of a series of studies showing age changes in attitudes toward federal government sponsorship of national health insurance. A number of studies have shown that attitudinal support of federal programs aimed at providing health care insurance increases with chronological age—or, in this reinterpretation, as a function of reaching a life stage corresponding to the new role of entitlement program beneficiary.

Campbell (1962, 1971) concluded that older voters more than younger were supportive of such insurance proposals not from an ideological perspective but from a group-benefits perspective. A more extensive analysis reconfirmed the cross-sectional age pattern across a sequence of national surveys, i.e., that support for government-financed health insurance increased as one entered the life stage that would most benefit from such a program (Schreiber and Marsden 1972). A formal cohort analysis applied to these data verified the conclusion that it was indeed aging and not generational cohort or historical period effects that produce the increased support for this policy benefit among the older respondents (Cutler and Schmidhauser 1975). While this is not necessarily evidence of resocialization, as contrasted with attitude change, the age-related pattern of change is consistent with an older adult role-socialization model.

This explanation is further supported by a different kind of analysis of these same data. Using the concept of *subjective age identification* (individuals who identify themselves with old age in a positive sense), a cross-sectional study found a strong association between subjective feelings of old age and support for federal medical insurance (Cutler 1983). That is, among all respondents age sixty and older, those with a higher subjective identification with old age were more likely to support the federal health-insurance policy proposal. The study was not focused on the concepts of role or adult political socialization. However, from this role perspective, it may be hypothesized that subjective age identification represents an operational indicator of an individual's having made the role transition into old age.

Major Role Transitions

We now explore some of the major role transitions during the life course, focusing on the political attitudes and behavior that have been found to be associated with these transitions. The intent is to illustrate the usefulness of the concept of role transitions as an explanatory tool in the analysis of political socialization. It should be emphasized, however, that not all of these role transitions have been comprehensively researched from a political perspective; consequently, this discussion is as much the rough outline of a research agenda as it is a review of the extant literature.

College

Most surveys have found that college education is correlated with more liberal opinions, especially on noneconomic issues such as race, tolerance of dissent, and internationalism. Granted, not all college students or graduates are highly tolerant, unprejudiced, or generally liberal, but individuals tend to become more so with college. The classic Bennington study done in the 1930s found that students were more politically liberal than their parents, and that their level of liberalism increased with the school years. The freshmen women were found to hold relatively middle-class conservative political views reflecting their middle-class background, but were found to have been considerably transformed, in large part through the influence of their network of reference group affiliations, by their senior year, and supported liberal "New Deal" policies (Newcomb 1943). In similar studies replicated at other institutions and in later years, the same results have emerged.

Changes in political orientations during the college years are not invariably or directly caused by the faculty or specific courses. Even introductory political science courses were found not to be able to increase political participation or interest (Somit et al. 1958; Schick and Somit 1963). On the other hand, education at teachers' colleges was found to have trained students to have greater respect for the political authority and the established regime than did liberal arts colleges. Although teachers were different in many ways, there were substantial similarities, especially related to the inappropriateness of political expression in the classroom. Jennings and Ziegler (1970) concluded that these similarities were due to the ethics of the profession and the socialization of the preparation.

No definitive consensus has yet been reached concerning whether political differences among different college majors are the consequence of different curricula as socializing agents, different types of schools, or are due largely to the impact of self-selection, i.e., that persons with different personal as well as political ideologies tend to select different college majors and careers, e.g., engineering versus social work. In isolated cases, the faculty may be important in transmitting liberal political orientations, but the influence of the faculty seems to be filtered through the more persuasive college environment, particularly the peer group and subculture (Newcomb 1943; Lane 1968; Feldman and Newcomb 1971).

A more persuasive explanation of the socializing influence of the college experience is found in the concept of role and role transition. The transition to the college community brings a new environment with sustained exposure to peers. The accompanying socialization process leads to the internalizing of the social norms of the college peer group. The classic view, of course, is that the college reference group facilitates liberal political attitudes.

The Bennington study demonstrated the instrumental importance of the norms of the peer group in the socialization process at this life stage. The study found, for example, that the most popular women also had the most liberal political attitudes; that some women consciously became liberal for social acceptance; and that women who depended on the college for their social life adopted more liberal political outlooks than women who participated largely in off-campus social interaction or who spent most weekends at home. Jacobs (1957) later supported the Bennington findings but concluded that the socializing effect of college was to soften prior political views and persuade individuals to reconsider previous values.

In what is clearly recognized as the most comprehensive political study on this topic—a seventeen-year national longitudinal study of the high school graduating class of 1965—Jennings and Markus (1986) support the basic findings of the classic studies. "Yuppie Baby Boomers" (defined as those with a college degree, in a professional or managerial job, and having a household income of $30,000 or more) were found to have significant political differences from their non-Yuppie classmates. These Yuppies and non-Yuppies share a fairly conservative outlook on economic policy; the Yuppies, however, are overwhelmingly liberal on social issues where the non-Yuppies are conservative (see Delli Carpini, chap. 1, in this volume). Another political difference was evidence in the 1968 and 1972 presidential votes of these two groups of 1965 high school seniors: where the Yuppies evenly split their votes between the two major party candidates, the non-Yuppies gave a greater percentage of their vote to Nixon in both elections.

The significance of the college experience in this trend is suggested by the fact that in 1965 the "future Yuppies" and their non-Yuppie classmates were fairly conservative and virtually indistinguishable on a number of issues such as trust in government and school integration. However, those who went on to college became more liberal on social and economic issues during their Vietnam-era college years. After college, the Yuppies retained their liberal position on social issues but became more conservative on economic issues.

These latter findings, plus the historical context of the Bennington study, suggest that the socializing influences of college role transitions are not always politically liberalizing. To be sure, the "broadening" of the world of ideas and experience that new peers, facts, and concepts bring about suggests an opening or "liberalizing" process. At the same time many conservatives have been to college and many to graduate school. If reference-group influences helped to socialize politically liberal perspectives in the 1930s, the same dynamic may well help to explain the politically conservative atmosphere on college campuses in the 1980s. The more general proposition, then, is that role transition, here from adolescent to college student, serves to introduce contemporary broader societal and historical themes to the student, i.e., what cohort analysts (e.g., Glenn 1977) refer to as *period effects:* liberalizing in a liberal period, conservatizing in a conservative period. In sum, then, research should focus on the *process* of role transition as socialization agent, and not just on the presumed intellectual content of the college experience.

Work Roles

In modern society work work has become the primary focus of life for most men and, increasingly, women. Consequently, roles and role transitions associated with work are among the most significant sources of adult socialization, quite often with both indirect and direct political consequences. Among work-related role transitions are those associated with initial entry to the labor force, and then role transitions associated with changes in one's occupation or workplace and, later, with one's exit from the labor force. The socialization that surrounds the role of wage earner is so central that it can shape the individual's political beliefs and ideology, habits and lifestyle, status in society, and even self-image.

The role transition to wage earner includes several clusters of changes: new interpersonal relations, new latitude in decision-making, new job commitment, new environment, and new norms and expectations. Although entry into the labor force is not typically a political act, there is no other role transition that has the same potential political impact (Sigel and Hoskin 1977, p. 272).

The workplace itself can provide an initial and comprehensive introduction to politics and lead to certain political attitudes and behaviors (see Lafferty, chap. 3, in this volume). Industrial work has been identified as a source of political and psychological alienation, especially among young workers (Hampden-Turner 1970; Rothschild 1972). The skill level of the worker's task was also found to have attitudinal consequences. Among automobile workers in the same plant, those with higher skilled and individualized jobs were most satisfied with the workplace and less cynical about work, authority, trade unionism, and the system in general (Lipsetz 1963).

Other studies have related the type of work to general contentment with (perceived) authority, and found individuals with the most routine work to be the most alienated (Dahl 1970). Sigel, Snyder and Delli Carpini (1982) found self-employed individuals, regardless of income level, to constitute the most satisfied group and also found a connection between type of work, work satisfaction, and political alienation. And while the connection of job (dis)satisfaction to political beliefs and actions is more often indirect, the concepts of class identification and class consciousness provide a framework for the more direct, albeit conditional, relationship of work to politics (Riley, 1976).

The occupation can be a direct agent of socialization in terms of skills that are transferable to the political environment. Pateman (1970) argues that participation in the workplace affects politicalization in several ways, among them training for and incentive to participate in politics, a decrease in political alienation, and an increase in self-esteem. Lafferty (chap. 3 in this volume) though generally supportive of workplace participation, is less sanguine about its impact on political participation. In their classic cross-national study of the participatory *Civic Culture*, Almond and Verba (1963) found that individuals who were consulted about decisions on the job and who felt free to protest job decisions had a higher political efficacy. As a more specific example, in one set of studies programs to professionalize local police forces included training to increase self-respect and assertiveness. These skills later had political consequences in police demands for unionization, competitive compensation, and strikes (Reiss 1971; Halpern 1974).

Another common transference to the political arena is from success on the job to increased investment in community affairs. For many, the sense of being successful in work transmits to a feeling of obligation for community involvement and widens the number of memberships in work-related and community-oriented organizations. Conversely, lack of occupational success or fulfillment can lead to low levels of community involvement—the pattern being to do a good job but to leave job concerns at work and "retire into the heart-warming circle of kin and friends" (Wilenksy 1961, p. 235).

A major part of the link between work-related role transitions and political socialization focuses on interpersonal relations and work associates. In their early voting study Berelson et al. (1954) found a strong relationship between the partisanship of friends and co-workers and the individual's voting intention. In cross-pressure situations among work associates, the individual is likely to seek reinforcement of his own views among like-minded colleagues (Finifter, 1974).

The shared political outlooks of work colleagues document the pervasive socialization that occurs in the work role. Businessmen, for example, tend to share politically relevant attitudes toward religion, taxation, work incentives, welfare, government limits on profits, and other areas of concern (Whyte 1956; Lewis and Stewart 1961; Ewing 1964). On the other hand, much variation on specific issues exists among businessmen due to the specific context of their work—individual entrepreneur, employee, large or small business, corporate-employed (Sigel and Hoskin 1977). Bernstein (1953), for example, found that small businessmen tend to adopt laissez-faire political views while corporate executives are less inclined toward laissez-faire and unrestricted competition. An emphasis on the importance of being responsive to public opinion to maintain a good public image is more characteristic of large than small businessmen (Reagan 1963).

Other occupations also have been shown to have widely shared beliefs. The medical profession (Stevens 1971; Roback 1974), lawyers (Carlin 1966), civil servants and foreign bureaucrats (Eulau and Quinley 1970; Dressel and Lipsky, chap. 4, in this volume), and even the nonpolitical military (Janowitz 1964; Huntington 1967; Lovell and Stiehm, chap. 5, in this volume) were found to have widely shared political beliefs and attitudes. The political and social perspective associated with an occupation or profession virtually has an existence of its own since it is continually reinforced and maintained over time through the network of work associates.

Thus, the utility of the concept of roles and role transitions is most vividly detected through changes in the work role. An individual entering the role of boss for the first time, for example, is confronted with new problems and develops new perspectives toward such things as production schedules, company policies, worker efficiency, labor unions, and authority (Bengston and Haber 1983). A promotion or a job change brings a new circle of work associates and job conditions, causing the individual to adapt his interests, beliefs, motives, and habits to the expectations of the new colleagues.

Studs Terkel's interviews with employed men and women (1974) abound in examples of resocialization in the course of changes in employment status. For example, assembly-line workers told Terkel they could observe vast changes in behavior and attitudes toward work and workers among former colleagues who had been promoted to the role of foreman. Even in the same job, a new boss, colleague, or subordinate can cause alterations in one's political self. These new associates and new role expectations bring new social experiences, reference groups, and attitudes to the individual that may have political consequences.

Marriage

Often coinciding with transition to the wage-earner role is the major life event of marriage, which also brings new demands and expectations for the individual. For most men and women marriage means a new definition of self and major changes in life patterns. The spouse role entails new patterns of communication, economic demands, social and community interaction, all with significant potential for change in basic political perspectives and on contemporary political issues. Overall, becoming a spouse leads to major alterations, as shown by the greater personality change found among young marrieds in an empirical comparison with a control of unmarrieds (Vincent 1964).

The 95 percent political party agreement among couples found in the early voting studies implied that personal and social change brought about by marriage extended to political views (Lazarsfeld et al. 1944; Campbell et al. 1954). Not explored in the early works was the possibility of selection of a mate on political grounds—which is rare in the United States. (Selection on social grounds of course, also not explored in these early studies, can produce the result of similar partisanship.) Nevertheless, Newcomb's twenty-five-year Bennington follow-up study found some pattern of selective mating on political criteria. Although most of the women did marry men of high social status, those women with the most liberal attitudes had been careful to marry men who shared their liberal views and thus were atypical of their social group (Newcomb et al. 1967). Beck and Jennings (1975), however, later concluded that *conversion* of the husband or wife better accounted for the similarity of partisanship than selective mating. Clearly the temporal or period-effects aspects of this conversion-versus-selection dimension of adult political socialization need to be more systematically explored.

The early studies assumed that if the married couple did not initially agree, it was the wife who realigned her views (Key 1961; Bone and Ranney 1976). Beck and Jennings later concluded that this was generally the direction of the conversion, but their evidence also confirmed that the political changes with marriage were not exclusively one-sided, and that some husbands changed, too (Beck and Jennings 1975). Using the wife's report of her husband's politics, Newcomb et al. (1967) also found that the political change in a marriage was not inevitably in the direction of wife-to-husband but could be mutual. Marriage influences couples to strive toward consensus of partisanship. Still, it must be acknowledged that, despite who might change and whatever the direction, social and economic similarity account partially for partisan similarity in marriage. And while most of the empirical studies of the political consequences of marriage deal with party identification, and while it may be assumed that the dynamics of selection, conversion, and balance that follow the transition to marital roles is similar for other political attitudes, further research is clearly necessary.

Parenthood

The second fundamental new role acquired in adulthood, after marriage, is parenthood, a role transition identified by some as a traumatic developmental event in the life course (Holmes and Rahe 1967). This "crisis" is caused not just by the role expectations envisioned by the parent, but also because of the direct demands of the child. LeMasters (1957) points out that "new parents are unprepared for the realities of actually living with a baby and have romanticized the role of parenthood so that there is an observable impact of the first-born child upon the adult personality as his highly immediate and imperative needs demand the attention of the parent." This crisis perception was found by Dyer (1963) among new parents and was not due to an unplanned or undesired pregnancy. Feeling that "crisis" is too strong a label, Hobbs (1968, p. 417) suggested that "it would seem more accurate to view the addition of the first child to the marriage as a period of transition which is somewhat stressful than to conceptualize beginning parenthood as a crisis." Regardless of whether termed a crisis or just "somewhat stressful," parenthood is a major role transition with new demands and expectations that can lead to personality change.

The changes that come about with parenthood are numerous. The parents' freedoms are curtailed and, even in the context of contemporary feminism, the mother in particular often finds herself cut off from recreation and community participation and increasingly dependent upon the marriage for economic and emotional support. Children bring increased economic demands and the need for more living space. As the children age, a sharper division of household labor develops with the female typically becoming responsible for most of the household tasks; at the same time the amount of husband-and-wife interaction decreases (Clausen 1972).

Research on female life satisfaction demonstrates the potential for change in social and political attitudes during this life stage. Clausen (1972) found that women had the lowest satisfaction with their living standards when the children were in the preadolescent years. It is feasible that such life dissatisfaction transfers to dissatisfaction with community affairs and politics, thereby contributing to (along with the demands of parenting itself) reduced participation and interest in political affairs. Lynn and Flora (1973) as well as Sapiro (1983) offer alternate explanations for reduced levels of political interest and participation. Lynn and Flora attribute it to the severely restricted communication networks available to women with young children. Sapiro, in a related vein, argues that restricted resources (time and energy in addition to material resources) as well as role definitions (motherhood and family life being defined as essentially private roles) block women's full participation in the political life of the nation.

A major politically relevant dimension of adult socialization linked to parenthood is increased involvement in a variety of community organizations. For example, parents become more interested in the community partly because of the children's need to play outside—leading to increased importance attached to neighborhood recreational facilities (Clausen 1972). Since parks and schoolyards are public facilities, city and county politics take on new importance. Members of appointed and elected local zoning, planning, and schools boards no doubt begin these "political careers" in nonpolitical family-related organizations.

More directly, educational programs and facilities and local taxes become areas of increased involvement and concern for the parent (Sigel and Hoskin 1977). Having children in school often translates into new categories of social participation—PTA, Scouts, teacher's aide, baby-sitting co-ops, Little League coach. These additional memberships in even nonpolitical social groups often lead to increased political discussions and ultimately to increased political participation (Kirkpatrick 1974; McCourt 1977). Cutler (1981b) found that the strength of the relationship among age, political participation, and voluntary-association membership is directly dependent on the type of association to which the individual belongs (e.g., school-related organizations for parents, recreational groups for retirees), a finding consistent with the role transition model of adult socialization. Parenthood also can lead directly to increased political activity, encompassing both the content and direction of attitudes and behavior, e.g., parents who actively promote or fight school busing for integration, or who write their congressman to support or oppose federal aid to parochial schools.

The role socialization that occurs in parenthood is not a unidirectional process from parents to children, but a dyadic process of mutual influence. Although research typically focuses on parents as agents of socialization for children, in fact parents continue to be developing and changing individuals, who continually have the experiences and strains of socialization and resocialization (Brim 1966). More specifically, Bengtson and Kuypers (1971) describe socialization as a negotiation process between parents and children, persons at different stages in their respective life cycles. They point out that both generations have a *developmental stake* in the relationship. The young want to establish their own existence, style, and attitudes whereas the parent generation wants to continue its sense of social order and instill its value in its "social heirs." Therefore, each brings different perceptions to the intergenerational relationship and behaves in response to its own stake in the developmental process.

Sigel and Reynolds' study of mothers and their college-attending daughters (1979) offered one such instance of the negotiation process and also offered evidence of the dyadic process of mutual influence, with mothers crediting daughters with having contributed to maternal resocialization with respect to gender roles. What is important for a discussion on the socialization of parents is that this relationship is constantly undergoing change and renegotiation which can lead to changes in attitudes and behavior of the parents.

Old(er) Age

There are a number of major role transitions that occur as individuals enter the later years of the life cycle. Given the weakening of the relationship between chronological age and "traditional" age norms—as people live longer and, for example, retire earlier—it may be more appropriate in this context to talk about *older age* than *old age*. For example, Neugarten's seminal analysis a decade ago classified the older population in functional and social as well as chronological terms as *the young-old* and *the old-old*—with the argument that the social and political and policy expectations of these two groups would also be distinguishable (Neugarten 1974). The young-old include men and women age fifty-five to seventy-four, most of whom are retired and healthy—the "wellderly." By contrast, many of the public stereotypes of "old age" do not fit these younger persons, and more accurately depict the old-old stage, seventy-five and older, where many but certainly not all individuals are less healthy, less wealthy, less mobile, and less independent—the "illderly." In terms of public policy distinctions, a generally accurate but obviously oversimplified view would be that the major concern of the young-old is with income security, while the preeminent policy concern of the old-old is with the health and the health-care delivery system.

These two identifiable stages of old age encompass a number of role transitions pertaining to the family and marriage, the work role, to one's relationship to government services and benefits, and often (especially among the old-old) to health and medical institutions. At this life stage, role transition takes place at a relatively accelerated pace: within a relatively short span of years, the individual may see the youngest child leave home, retire from a life-long occupation, experience the death of his or her spouse, become eligible for pensions, Social Security, and Medicare benefits, and develop chronic illness. These changes, separately and collectively, affect the individual's self-image (Cutler 1982a), and are thus likely to affect political dispositions as well.

This discussion is not to imply that all changes in the later life-stages are negative or simply losses. For the young-old, especially, aging may bring a freedom from day-to-day parenting and occupational responsibilities, the new acquisition of leisure and free time, the capacity to pursue new (or old) interests, including politics. The positive identification of older people with their age has certainly increased in the past two decades (Cutler, Pierce, and Steckenrider 1984). Nonetheless, from the perspective of changes in politically relevant dispositions that are rooted in role transition, the relevant focus is change from (i.e., out of) those roles that occupied the individual's life in the most central way for the largest amount of time—including the roles of parent, worker, and spouse, changes for which we should expect adjustment and resocialization.

An especially significant and widespread change during the later stages of the life cycle is retirement; by age sixty-five, only 20 percent of males and 8 percent of females are still in the labor force (Foner and Schwab 1981, p. 3 [1976 data]). The adjustment to retirement can take many forms and depends largely on financial, social, and emotional factors. Many individuals experience a lowered standard of living, loss of social contacts and work associates, a loss of prestige and power, and an end to the central purpose in life. If an individual had not achieved his or her occupational goals, retirement also means the loss of a last chance. Adjustment to retirement is especially difficult for successful individuals highly involved in their job, more so than for those who earlier turned to family and leisure for satisfaction (Clausen 1972). Retirement, like the empty-nest transition, can have negative or positive consequences for the individual. For example, in reviewing eight studies of "retirement satisfaction" published across the period from 1965 to 1978, Foner and Schwab (1981, pp. 57–58) found that typically only 60–65 percent of retirees expressed satisfaction with retirement.

Comparable to the changes brought on by retirement, many females find the launching of the children to bring vast changes and adjustments in self-image. For some, especially those whose life centered around children, the empty-nest role can be traumatic or even a crisis filled with loneliness and emptiness. In fact, the maternal role loss was a common characteristic of middle-aged females hospitalized for depression and emotional illness (Saprina et al. 1970).

More positive consequences result for other women who view the empty-nest stage as a relief from economic responsibilities, household chores, and supervision of children. In fact, in a national survey Schwartz (1970) found that empty-nest females averaged higher morale than their counterparts with children still at home. Women in this stage of life increased activities with their husbands outside the home, felt increased freedom and independence, and had more time to spend with their husbands and friends. Traumatic or not, the launching of one's children does indicate changes in the female, both positive and negative, which can include political changes as well.

A role that has yet to receive much scholarly attention is the politically relevant one acquired by most people in old age for the first time—direct recipient of government services and financial benefits. Virtually all individuals age sixty-five and older receive Social Security benefits and Medicare coverage. Smaller but significant numbers of older people participate in government programs such as the social and nutrition programs under the Older Americans Act, Supplementary Security Income, state and federal housing for senior citizens, and property-tax relief programs for senior citizens. These programs increase individuals' contact with the bureaucracy and increase their interest in political issues concerning programs of which they are beneficiaries.

For example, because an individual is a recipient of Social Security or Medicare, he or she is more inclined to pay attention to political messages and actions concerning these areas—which may result in increased participation, i.e., an illustration of the "group benefits" orientation in *The American Voter.* This situation is well illustrated by the intense politics surrounding the Social Security reforms of 1982 (Light 1985). In addition, the politics surrounding the social and nutritional services of the Older Americans Act, while focused on programs whose budgets are in the millions rather than Social Security's billions of dollars, have been seen to be especially intense and salient to older persons because of the direct manner in which such programs can affect their daily lives (Cutler 1984).

Becoming active in the context of Social Security benefits or local social services programs in old age may, for some persons, be little different from going out on strike while employed, and therefore is an example of the *stability of socialization* which maintains itself into old age. On the other hand, if becoming a recipient of Social Security influences an older individual to change his behavior by increasing political participation or becoming a political activist on the issue (or related issues), this behavioral change may be one way to identify the (re) socialization of older men and women.

A significant direction for future research remains whether this is resocialization or merely the reorienting of a predisposition. The importance of this research direction, furthermore, is signalled by the well-documented erosion of partisanship in the United States over the past two decades (e.g., Abramson 1976; Asher 1984). Additionally, the results of Abramson's (1976) cohort analyses and Jennings and Niemi's (1981) longitudinal parent-child analyses clearly conclude that this decline in partisanship is generational in nature, and is concentrated in the large baby-boom cohorts. Combining these demographic, partisan, and gerontological trends, Cutler (1981a) concludes that aging-oriented issues of public policy may at least in part take on the electoral functions which for prior cohorts were performed by party identification. Consequently, the degree to which the politicization precipitated by Social Security (at the national level) or social services (at the local level) reflects continuity or change, socialization or resocialization—and especially when the size of the aging baby boom is taken into account—looms as an especially significant issue for political socialization research.

Furthermore, many nongovernmental benefits emphasize the role-transition nature of aging, as found in an expanding range of "senior citizen" discounts. In 1983, for example, one telephone company began a nationwide program of "Silver Pages" specialized directories. And since such private as well as public age-directed benefits are consistent with the "group benefits" orientation toward politics, it should not be surprising that studies clearly show that self-reported political interest increases with age for both men and women of both higher and lower education levels (Glenn and Grimes 1968; Cutler 1983).

Illness often accompanies the old-old life stage and with it comes changed demands and expectations for the individual that can have political consequences. Although data on older people are lacking, the studies of children concerning health and body image concluded that health experiences and body images bear regular, significant, and causal association with basic social and political attitudes, behavior, and processes. The individual's degree of well-being, especially the lack of chronic illness, was significantly and positively associated with personality, satisfaction with family dynamics, level of general social participation, and relations with peers (Birch et al. 1970; Pless and Douglas 1970; Mechanic 1959).

One consequence of a health condition or disability is the limits on the individual's sociopolitical participation resulting either from the physical limitations or the inward focus on oneself rather than on society and politics (Saprina et al. 1970). Schwartz (1970) reported that college students who perceived themselves as low in personal energy tended to adopt relatively withdrawn or passive political behavior orientations; and also that health problems decreased social and political participation and the amount of political information and satisfaction with the political system (Schwartz et al. 1975). Such studies argue that health difficulties lead to low or diminished sociopolitical interest and participation, and it is the later years of life that are most consistently associated with increased disability and chronic illness. Clearly, there needs to be more investigation into the political consequences of illness and physical disabilities that disproportionately occur at the later stage of the life cycle.

It was once thought that voter participation and political interest of older individuals showed a drop-off from middle age. Originally, such "disengagement" was believed to be an inherent dimension of "normal aging," prompting individuals to withdraw from a broad variety of social contacts and political activity (Cumming and Henry 1961). Later analyses challenged disengagement theory, finding little evidence that political participation substantially decreased with age. When participation measured by voter turnout was statistically corrected for such relevant factors as education, length of residency and gender, such old-age drop-off almost disappeared: voters over sixty-five were found to differ little from other age groups (Verba and Nie 1972).

Furthermore, among cohorts socialized in the early decades of this century (today's older population), women were found to vote consistently less than their male "cohort mates," and since today's older population is disproportionately female, the fall-off in participation among the old is largely accounted for by gender rather than by age (Glenn and Grimes 1968). And because contemporary older individuals have less formal education than the young—another cohort effect rather than aging effect—controlling for education also decreases the drop-off among today's older voters (Glenn and Grimes 1968; Verba and Nie 1972). Consequently, with appropriate statistical controls, age per se is not a significant factor in political behavior, and disengagement theory is considered to be disconfirmed. In fact, the opposite may be more likely as a comparison of turnout in presidential election years with off-year congressional elections shows that older individuals actually have higher turnout rates than younger people in off-year, primary, and local "low stimulus" elections (Cutler 1976).

As noted earlier, political interest generally follows the same pattern in regard to age as political participation. Early mass media studies, for example, found that age was related to increased reading of public-affairs news and editorials and decreased reading of sports and comic sections (Schramm and White 1954). Controlling for gender and education places the highest political interest at age 60+ and, as with political participation, the differences between educational levels and the sexes are greater than exist between age groups (Cutler 1977b). An analysis of a large number of surveys concluded that the old take great interest in current public affairs and that, when controlling for education, there are no significant differences between age groups (Glenn 1969). As with political participation, there is no evidence of disengagement among older individuals in terms of political interest.

Overall, many of the roles assumed in old age suggest increased political interest and participation. Retirement and the empty-nest stages provide freedom from responsibilities and more time to devote to politics. Men and women who were never "on welfare" and who do not consider personal or business "tax breaks" as direct government benefits to them, may find themselves in the role of "recipients"—which can lead to increased political attention, information, and ultimately participation.

An important and clearly related pattern among older people today is the propensity to become members of mass organizations (Cutler 1981b, 1982b) such as the 24-million-member American Association of Retired Persons, and the 3-million-member National Council of Senior Citizens. Many of these organizations have a clear political agenda (Pratt 1976), but even their nonpolitical functions can increase the older person's political interest and involvement (Nie and Verba 1972; Trela 1971, 1972; Cutler and Mimms 1977).

Concluding Comments

The concepts of roles and role transitions contribute an important dimension to understanding the ontogeny of political attitudes and behavior over the life span. Student, spouse, parent, wage earner, and retiree are major stages in the life cycle and the movement into them involves new social contexts, new colleagues, new activities, all of which can lead to adaptation, alterations, or reversals in political attitudes or behavior. In concluding, however, we note three caveats concerning the utility of the concepts of role and role transitions.

The first concerns the continuity of personal identity. Under some circumstances adulthood can be a period of (re)socialization, but *continuity* is the rule, not the exception (Bengtson 1973). Much of what is learned in childhood is or can be made to be consistent with adult social roles, and does not need to be dramatically rejected or converted (see Renshon, chap. 6, in this volume). Personality, relations with significant others, ethnic memberships, values, styles, and even many roles themselves are marked more by continuity than by discontinuity.

Second, any discussion of age also involves generations and cohorts (see Delli Carpini, chap. 1, in this volume). Even age-connected roles and their associated expectations and demands differ markedly from cohort to cohort. Successive cohorts will be influenced by different conditions and events of the environment and the cohort's characteristics (Bengtson, Cutler, Mangen, and Marshall 1985). For example, today's highly educated young (i.e., tomorrow's elderly) will bring new perspectives, attitudes, and styles of behavior to the roles exited by the relatively less educated contemporary elderly. The transition to the parent or the grandparent role is certainly different in the mid-1980s than for those who arrived at these roles twenty or thirty years ago (Bengtson 1985).

Similarly, the societal age consciousness that has helped to expand the ranks of the politically active 24-million member American Association of Retired Persons suggests that the political resources and issue agenda of older persons are dramatically different than they were thirty or even fifteen years ago (Pratt 1976). While observed change may simply be attitude change, it is also clear that the roles in which chronologically older persons find themselves are different from the roles of young and middle adulthood. Since old age today is in many ways itself different from old age yesterday, then the political socialization involved encompasses more than the simple extension of either personally prior or socially prior continuity.

Finally, just as older individuals do not uniformly agree on all different political attitudes and strategies, neither is role incumbency likely to define politically homogeneous groups of people; becoming a grandparent or retiree, like becoming old itself, does not instantly eradicate all the other personal and social attachments which contribute to the political self. Factors such as gender, education, and social status remain central in the formation and expression of political dispositions, even as role transitions affect those dispositions.

Role and role transitions have been largely ignored in the systematic investigation of political attitudes and behavior over the life span. There is but little research on how roles are involved in political changes and which role transitions have more extensive political consequences. Future research needs to look at the expectations and demands surrounding the major life roles, how these expectations are internalized and transmitted, and the connection of the roles to the political self. The focus needs to be on the changing roles across the life span, and longitudinal studies need to follow individuals through adulthood with respect to their roles. Political variations *within* holders of similar roles, of course, need to be explored as well. Above all, we need to systematically assess the interplay of the continuity we assume is established in childhood and adolescent socialization, and the inevitable changes we know are experienced by living human beings undergoing major life transitions. Only then can we more fully respond to the question of the relationship of the aging process to political dispositions.

References

Abramson, P. R. 1976. "Generational Change and the Decline of Party Identification in America, 1951–1974." *The American Political Science Review* 70: 469–78.

Almond, G. A. 1960. "Introduction: A Functional Approach to Comparative Politics." In G. A. Almond and J. S. Coleman, eds., *Politics of the Developing Areas.* Princeton: Princeton University Press.

Almond, G. A., and S. Verba. 1963. *The Civic Culture.* Princeton: Princeton University Press.

Asher, H. B. 1984. *Presidential Elections and American Politics.* 3d ed. Homewood, Illinois: The Dorsey Press.

Bart, P. 1971. "Depression in Middle Aged Women." In V. Gornick and B. K. Moran, eds., *Women in Sexist Society.* New York: New American Library.

Beck, P. A., and M. K. Jennings. 1975. "Parents as 'Middle-Persons' in Political Socialization." *Journal of Politics* 37: 83–108.

Bengtson, V. L. 1973. *The Social Psychology of Aging.* Indianapolis: Bobbs-Merrill.

———. 1985. "Diversity and Symbolism in Grandparent Roles." In V. L. Bengtson and J. R. Robertson, eds., *Grandparenting.* Beverly Hills: Sage, pp. 11–25.

Bengtson, V. L., and D. Haber. 1983. "Sociological Perspectives on Aging." In D. S. Woodruff and J. E. Birren, eds., *Aging: Scientific Perspectives and Social Issues,* 2d ed. Monterey, Calif.: Brooks/Cole Publishing, pp. 72–93.

Bengtson, V. L. and J. Kuypers. 1971. "Generational Differences and the Developmental Stake." *Aging and Human Development* 2: 249–60.

Bengtson, V. L., N. E. Cutler, D. J. Mangen, and V. R. Marshall. 1985. "Generations and Social Change." In R. Binstock and E. Shanas, eds., *Handbook of Aging and the Social Sciences,* 2d ed. New York: Van Nostrand.

Berelson, B., P. Lazarfeld, and W. N. McPhee. 1954. *Voting.* Chicago: University of Chicago Press.

Bernstein, M. H. 1953. "The Political Ideas of Selected American Business Journals." *Public Opinion Quarterly* 17: 258–67.

Birch, H., J. D. Gussow, and J. Dye. 1970. *Disadvantaged Children, Nutrition and School Failure.* New York: Harcourt Brace and World.

Bone, H. A., and A. Ranney. 1976. *Politics and Voters,* 4th ed., New York: McGraw-Hill.

Brim, O. G. 1966. "Socialization through the Life Cycle." In O. G. Brim and S. Wheeler, eds., *Socialization after Childhood*. New York: Wiley.

———. 1968. "Adult Socialization." In J. Clausen, ed., *Socialization and Society*. Boston: Little, Brown.

———. 1970. "Socialization after Childhood." In R. Sigel, ed., *Learning about Politics*. New York: Random House.

Cain, L. D. 1964. "Life Course and Social Structure." In R. B. L. Faris, ed., *Handbook of Modern Sociology*. Chicago: Rand McNally.

Campbell, A. 1962. "Social and Psychological Determinants of Voting Behavior." In W. Donahue and C. Tibbitts, eds., *Politics of Age*. Ann Arbor: University of Michigan Press.

———. 1971. "Politics through the Life Cycle." *Gerontologist* 11: 112–17.

Campbell, A., G. Gurin, and W. E. Miller. 1954. *The Voter Decides*. New York: Harper and Row.

Campbell, A., P. E. Converse, W. E. Miller, and D. E. Stokes. 1960. *The American Voter*. New York: Wiley.

Carlin, J. 1966. *Lawyers' Ethics: A Survey of the New York City Bar*. New York: Russell Sage Foundation.

Clausen, J. A. 1968. "A Historical and Comparative View of Socialization Theory and Research." In J. A. Clausen, ed., *Socialization and Society*. Boston: Little, Brown.

———. 1972. "The Life Course of Individuals." In M. W. Riley, M. Johnson, and A. Foner, eds., *Aging and Society*. Vol. 3, *A Sociology of Age Stratification*. New York: Russell Sage Foundation.

Cumming, E., and W. Henry. 1961. *Growing Old: The Process of Disengagement*. New York: Basic Books.

Cutler, N. E. 1976. "Resources for Senior Advocacy: Political Behavior and Partisan Flexibility." In P. A. Kerschner, ed., *Advocacy and Age: Issues, Experiences, and Strategies*. Los Angeles: University of Southern California Press, pp. 23–40.

———. 1977a. "Political Socialization Research as Generational Analysis: The Cohort vs. the Lineage Approach." In S. A. Renshon, ed., *Handbook of Political Socialization*. New York: The Free Press, 1977, p. 297.

———. 1977b. "Demographic, Social-Psychological, and Political Factors in the Politics of Aging: A Foundation for Research in Political Gerontology." *American Political Science Review* 71: 1011–25.

———. 1981a. "Political Characteristics of Elderly Cohorts in the Twenty-first Century." In S. Kiesler, J. N. Morgan, and V. Oppenheimer, eds., *Aging: Social Issues*. New York: Academic Press, pp. 127–57.

———. 1981b. "Toward an Age-Appropriate Typology for the Study of Participation of Older Persons in Voluntary Associations." *Journal of Voluntary Action Research* 9: 9–19.

———. 1982a. "Subjective Age Identification." In D. J. Mangen and W. A. Peterson, eds., *Research Instruments in Social Gerontology*. Minneapolis: University of Minnesota Press, pp. 731–87.

———. 1982b. "Voluntary Association Participation and Life Satisfaction: Replication, Revision, and Extension." *International Journal of Aging and Human Development*. 14: 127–37.

―――. 1983. "Age and Political Behavior." In D. S. Woodruff and J. E. Birren, eds., *Aging: Scientific Perspectives and Social Issues*. 2d ed. Monterey: Brooks/ Cole, pp. 409–42.

―――. 1984. "Federal and State Responsibilities and the Targeting or Resources within the Older Americans Act: The Politics of Multiple Agenda-Setting." *Policy Studies Journal* 13: 185–96.

Cutler, N. E., and G. E. Mimms. 1977. "Political Resources of the Elderly: The Impact of Membership in Nonpolitical Voluntary Associations upon Political Activity." Paper presented at the Annual Meeting of the American Political Science Association, Washington, D.C.

Cutler, N. E., and J. R. Schmidhauser. 1975. "Age and Political Behavior." In D. S. Woodruff and J. E. Birren, eds. *Aging: Scientific Perspectives and Social Issues*. New York: Van Nostrand.

Cutler, N. E., R. C. Pierce, and J. S. Steckenrider. 1984. "Age and Politics: How Golden is the Future?" *Generations* 9: 38–43.

Dahl, R. 1970. *After the Revolution*. New Haven: Yale University Press.

Dawson, R. R., and K. Prewitt. 1969. *Political Socialization*. Boston: Little, Brown.

Dawson, R., K. Prewitt, and K. Dawson. 1977. *Political Socialization*. 2d ed. Boston: Little, Brown.

Deming, M. B., and N. E. Cutler. 1983. "Demography of the Aged." In D. S. Woodruff and J. E. Birren, eds., *Aging: Scientific Perspectives and Social Issues*. 2d ed. Monterey: Brooks/Cole, pp. 18–51.

De Sola Pool, I., S. Keller, and R. A. Bauer. 1956. "The Influence of Foreign Travel on Political Attitudes of American Businessmen." *Public Opinion Quarterly* 20: 161–75.

Dyer, E. D. 1963. "Parenthood as Crisis: A Re-Study." *Journal of Marriage and the Family* 25: 196–201.

Easton, D. 1965. *A Systems Analysis of Political Life*. New York: Wiley.

Easton, D., and J. Dennis. 1969. *Children in the Political System*. New York: McGraw-Hill.

Erikson, E. 1950. *Childhood and Society*. New York: Norton.

Eulau, H., and H. Quinley. 1970. *State Officials and Higher Education*. New York: McGraw-Hill.

Ewing, D. 1964. *The Managerial Mind*. Glencoe: The Free Press.

Feldman, K., and T. M. Newcomb. 1971. *The Impact of College on Students: An Analysis of Four Decades of Research*. San Francisco: Jossey-Bass.

Fenno, R. 1966. *The Power of the Purse: Appropriations Politics in Congress*. Boston: Little, Brown.

Finifter, A. W. 1974. "The Friendship Group as a Protective Environment for Political Deviants." *American Political Science Review* 68: 607–25.

Foner, A., and K. Schwab. 1981. *Aging and Retirement*. Monterey: Brooks/Cole.

George, L. K. 1980. *Role Transitions in Later Life*. Monterey: Brooks/Cole.

Glaser, B., and A. Strauss. 1971. *Theory of Status Passage*. Chicago: Aldine.

Glenn, N. D. 1969. "Aging, Disengagement, and Opinionation." *Public Opinion Quarterly* 33: 17–33.

———. 1975. "Psychological Well-Being in the Post-Parental Stage: Some Evidence from National Surveys." *Journal of Marriage and Family* 37: 105–10.

———. 1977. *Cohort Analysis.* Beverly Hills: Sage Publications.

Glenn, N. D., and M. Grimes. 1968. "Aging, Voting, and Political Interest." *American Sociological Review* 33: 563–75.

Glick, P. C., and R. Parke, Jr. 1965. "New Approaches in Studying the Cycle of the Family." *Demography* 2: 187–202.

Greenstein, F. I. 1960. "The Benevolent Leader: Children's Image of Political Authority," *American Political Science Review* 54: 934–45.

Gurin, P., A. H. Miller, and G. Gurin. 1980. "Stratum Identification and Consciousness." *Psychological Quarterly* 43: 30–47.

Halpern, S. 1974. *Police Association and Department Leaders.* Lexington: Lexington Books.

Hampden-Turner, C. 1970. *Radical Man: The Process of Psycho-Social Development.* Cambridge: Schenkman.

Hobbs, D. F. 1965. "Parenthood as Crisis: A Third Study." *Journal of Marriage and Family* 27: 367–72.

———. 1968. "Transition to Parenthood: A Replication and Extension." *Journal of Marriage and Family* 30: 413–17.

Holmes, J. H., and R. H. Rahe. 1967. "The Social Readjustment Rating Scale." *Journal of Psychosomatic Medicine* 11: 219–25.

Huntington, S. P. 1967. *The Soldier and the State.* Cambridge: Harvard University Press.

Jacobs, P. E. 1957. *Changed Values in College: An Exploratory Study on the Impact of College Teaching.* New York: Harper and Row.

Janowitz, M. 1964. *The Military in the Political Development of New States.* Chicago: University of Chicago Press.

Jaros, D., and L. Grant. 1974. *Political Behavior.* New York: St. Martin's Press.

Jennings, M. K., and G. Markus. 1986. "Yuppie Politics." *ISR Newsletter,* August 1986. Ann Arbor: Institute of Social Research, University of Michigan.

Jennings, M. K., and R. G. Niemi. 1981. *Generations and Politics: A Panel Study of Young Adults and Their Parents.* Princeton: Princeton University Press.

Jennings, M. K., and R. G. Niemi. 1974. *The Political Character of Adolescence: The Influence of Family and Schools.* Princeton, N.J.: Princeton University Press.

Jennings, M. K., and H. Zeigler. 1970. "Political Expression Among High School Teachers: The Intersection of Community and Occupational Values." In R. S. Sigel, ed., *Learning about Politics.* New York: Random House.

Jones, L. Y, 1981. *Great Expectations.* New York: Ballantine.

Key, V. O. 1961. *Public Opinion and American Democracy.* New York: Knopf.

Kornhaber, A. 1985. "Grandparenthood and the 'New Social Contract.'" In V. L. Bengtson and J. F. Robertson, eds., *Grandparenthood.* Beverly Hills: Sage Publications.

Kirkpatrick, S. A. 1974. *Quantitative Analysis of Political Data.* Columbus, Ohio: Merrill.

Kuroda, Y. 1965. "Agencies of Political Socialization and Political Change: Political Orientations of Japanese Law Students." *Human Organization* 24: 328–31.

Lane, R. E. 1959. *Political Life*. Glencoe, Ill.: The Free Press.

———. 1968. "Political Education in the Midst of Life's Struggles." *Harvard Education Review* 38: 468–94.

Lane, R. E, and D. Sears. 1964. *Public Opinion*. Englewood-Cliffs: Prentice-Hall.

Langton, K. P. 1969. *Political Socialization*. London: Oxford University Press.

Lazarsfeld, P., B. Berelson, and H. Gaudet. 1944. *The People's Choice*. New York: Duell, Sloan, and Pearce.

LeMasters, E. E. 1957. "Parenthood as Crisis." *Journal of Marriage and Family* 19: 352–55.

Lewis, R., and R. Stewart, 1961. *The Managers*. New York: Mentor Books.

Light, P. 1985. *Artful Work: The Politics of Social Security Reform*. New York: Random House.

Lipset, S. M. 1960. *Political Man*. Garden City, N.J.: Doubleday.

Lipsetz, L. 1963. "Work Life and Political Attitudes: A Study of Manual Workers." *American Political Science Review* 28: 69–75.

Lynn, N., and C. Flora. 1973. "Motherhood and Political Participation: The Changing Sense of Self." *Journal of Political and Military Sociology* 1973: 91–103.

McCourt, K. 1977. *Working-Class Women and Grass Roots Politics*. Bloomington: Indiana University Press.

Mead, G. H. 1934. *Mind, Self, and Society*. Chicago: University of Chicago Press.

Mechanic, D. 1959. *Medical Sociology*. New York: The Free Press.

Milbrath, L. W., and M. L. Goel. 1971. *Political Participation*. 2d ed. Chicago: Rand McNally.

Monroe, A. 1975. *Public Opinion in America*. New York: Harper and Row.

Neugarten, B. L. 1974. "Age Groups in American Society and the Rise of the Young-Old." *Annals of the American Academy of Political and Social Sciences* 415: 187–98.

Neugarten, B. L, J. Moore, and J. Lowe. 1965. "Age Norms, Age Constraints and Adult Socialization." *American Journal of Sociology* 70: 710–17.

Neugarten, B. L., and W. A. Peterson. 1957. "A Study of the American Age Graded System." *Proceedings of the Fourth Congress of the International Association of Gerontology*, vol. 3.

Neugarten, B. L., and G. O. Hagestad. 1976. "Age and the Life Course." In R. Binstock and E. Shanas, eds., *Aging and the Social Sciences*. New York: Van Nostrand Reinhold.

Newcomb, T. M. 1943. *Personality and Social Change: Attitude Formation in a Student Community*. New York: Dryden Press.

Newcomb, T. M., K. Keonig, R. Flacks, and D. Warwick. 1967. *Persistence and Change: Bennington College and Its Students after Twenty-Five Years*. New York: Wiley.

Pateman, C. 1970. *Participation and Democratic Theory*. New York: Cambridge University Press.

Pless, I., and J. Douglas, 1970. *Chronic Illness in Childhood*. University of Rochester School of Medicine and Dentistry.

Pless, I., and K. J. Roghmann. 1970. "Chronic Illness and Its Consequences." Paper presented to the 1970 Annual Meeting of the American Public Health Service.

Pratt, H. 1976. *The Gray Lobby.* Chicago: University of Chicago Press.

Presthus, R. 1964. *Men at the Top.* New York: Oxford University Press.

Reagan, M. D. 1963. *The Managed Economy.* New York: Oxford University Press.

Reedy, M. N. 1983. "Personality and Aging." In D. S. Woodruff and J. E. Birren, eds., *Aging: Scientific Perspectives and Social Issues.* 2d ed. Monterey, Calif.: Brooks/Cole, pp. 112–36.

Reiss, A. 1971. *The Police and the Public.* New Haven: Yale University Press.

Riley, M. W. 1976. "Age Stratification in Society." In R. Binstock and E. Shanas, eds., *Aging and the Social Sciences.* New York: Van Nostrand Reinhold.

Roback, T. 1974. "Occupational and Political Attitudes: The Case of Professional Groups." In A. Wilcox, ed., *Public Opinion and Political Attitudes.* New York: Wiley.

Rose, A. 1960. "Incomplete Socialization." *Sociology and Social Research* 44: 244–50.

Rosow, I. 1974. *Socialization to Old Age.* Los Angeles: University of California Press.

Rothschild, E. G. H. 1972. "In More Trouble." *New York Review of Books,* March.

Rowe, J. W., and R. L. Kahn. 1987."Human Aging: Usual and Successful." *Science,* July 10, 1987: 143–49.

Ryder, N. B. 1965. "The Cohort as a Concept in the Study of Social Change." *American Sociological Review* 30: 843–61.

Sapiro, V. 1983. *The Political Integration of Women: Rules, Socialization, and Politics.* Urbana: University of Illinois Press.

Saprina, J., et al. 1970. "Differences in Perception between Hypertensive and Normatensive Populations." *Psychosomatic Medicine* 33: 239–55.

Schick, M., and A. Somit. 1963. "The Failure to Teach Political Activity." *American Behavioral Scientist* 6: 5–8.

Schramm, W., and D. White. 1954. "Education and Economic Status as Factors in Newspaper Readings: Conclusions." In W. Schramm, ed., *The Process and Effects of Mass Communication.* Urbana: University of Illinois Press.

Schreiber, E. M., and L. R. Marsden. 1972. "Age and Opinions on a Government Program of Medical Aid." *Journal of Gerontology* 27: 95–101.

Schwartz, D. C. 1970. "Perceptions of Personal Energy and the Adoption of Basic Behavioral Orientations to Politics." Paper presented to the International Political Science Association. Munich, 1970.

Schwartz, D. C., J. Garrison, and J. Alouf. 1975. "Health, Body Images and Political Socialization." In D. Schwartz and S. K. Schwartz, eds., *New Directions in Political Socialization.* New York: The Free Press.

Searing, D., G. Wright, and G. Rabinowitz. 1976. "The Primacy Principle: Attitude Change and Political Socialization." *British Journal of Political Science* 83–113.

Sigel, R. S. 1970. "Socialization in Adulthood: The Importance of Role." In R. Sigel, ed., *Learning about Politics.* New York: Random House.

Sigel, R. S., and M. Hoskin. 1977. "Perspectives on Adult Political Socialization—

Areas of Research." In S. A. Renshon, ed., *Handbook of Political Socialization.* New York: The Free Press.

Sigel, R. S., and W. Pindur. 1969. "Self-Image as a Guide to Representational Behavior." Paper presented at the Annual Meeting of the American Political Science Association, New York City.

Sigel, R. S., and J. Reynolds. 1979–80. "Generational Differences in the Women's Movement." *Political Science Quarterly* 94: 635–48.

Sigel, R. S., R. Snyder, and M. X. Delli Carpini. 1982. "Does It Make a Difference How You Feel about Your Job? Work Satisfaction and Political Orientations." Paper presented at the Annual Meeting of the American Political Science Association, Denver.

Somit, A., J. Tannenhaus, W. Wilke, and R. Cooley. 1958. "The Effects of the Introductory Political Science Course on Student Activities toward Personal Political Participation." *American Political Science Review* 52: 1129–32.

Stevens, R. 1971. *American Medicine and the Public Interest.* New Haven: Yale University Press.

Sussman, M. 1976. "The Family Life of Older People." In R. Binstock and E. Shanas, eds., *Handbook of Aging and the Social Sciences.* New York: Van Nostrand Reinhold.

Terkel, S. 1974. *Working.* New York: Pantheon Books.

Trela, J. E. 1971. "Some Political Consequences of Senior Centers and Other Age Group Memberships." *Gerontologist,* 11: 118–23.

———— 1972. "Age Structure of Voluntary Associations and Political Self-Interest among the Aged." *Sociological Quarterly* 13: 244–52.

Verba, S., and N. Nie. 1972. *Participation in America.* New York: Harper and Row.

Vincent, C. E. 1964. "Socialization Data in Research on Young Marrieds." *Acta Sociologica.*

Wahlke, J. C. et al. 1962. *The Legislative System.* New York: Wiley.

Whyte, W. 1956. *The Organization Man.* Garden City: Doubleday.

Wilensky, H. 1961. "Life Cycle, Work Situation and Participation in Formal Associations." In Robert Kleemeier, ed., *Aging and Leisure.* New York: Oxford University Press.

Part II

Introduction:
The World of Work

"Narrowly speaking, the way a man or a woman makes a living is not a political act (unless they choose to make politics their profession) and might therefore seem to fall outside the topic of political socialization. In actuality, however, there is probably no other phase in a person's life of the same political impact—or potential impact—as his work situation" (Sigel and Hoskin 1977, p. 272). Working for a living is a fact of life for almost all adult males and increasingly for most adult females. Employed men and women spend more of their waking hours at their occupational tasks than they do at any other single activity. Moore (1969, p. 861) has gone so far as to assert that "in temporal terms, occupation is challenged only by the family as the major determinant and locus of behavior." Moreover, in the United States "work tends to be seen not only as a means to an end but as a value in and of itself. To work is tantamount to being socially responsible and individually worthy. Not to work—from choice or inability—is a human failing bordering on immorality" (Sigel et al. 1982, p. 1).

Preparatory Socialization

Childhood and adolescence can offer some preparatory socialization to the world of work. Parental training, for example, can affect it. Miller and Swanson (1958) noted that the type of business setting in which a father works (entrepreneurial versus bureaucratic) affected his child-rearing style. These differences in turn conditioned offsprings to differential responses to authority relationships likely to be encountered in the work world. Blue collar families here and abroad (Kohn 1969) value discipline and conformity in their offsprings over creativity and independence—traits which probably are very functional for their offsprings' adult tasks provided they too will enter blue-collar jobs. Schools, with their emphasis on punctuality, neatness, scheduling, and rule-consciousness (not to mention their intellectual training), also must be considered a potential source of preparatory work socialization.

Gainful employment after school hours and during vacations—a frequent practice in the United States—has been considered another potential socializer. Opinion is divided as to its social and potentially political value. It had been rather commonly accepted "wisdom" that such work was beneficial in that it built character, taught young people responsibility and respect for property and money—all qualities congenial to life in a capitalist society. Some dissident voices have been raised recently (Greenberger and Steinberg 1986), arguing that the type of work most teenagers perform might have the very opposite effect, encouraging "indiscretionary spending" rather than frugality and facilitating the growth of work habits counterproductive to a solid work ethic, thereby actually encouraging bad attitudes toward work. Too little is known about this aspect of preparatory socialization for one to say just what part teenage employment plays.

Nor do we know what role the mass media, especially TV and the movies, play. Might their generally glamorized pictures of adult work settings be dysfunctional as a socializer? For one thing, the majority of work settings are middle-and upper-status ones; there are far more lawyers, doctors, and executives portrayed in leading roles on the screen than there are coal miners, truck drivers, waitresses, and saleswomen. Could this suggest to the young person, first of all, that it is crucial to aspire to high-status positions and, secondly, does it perhaps unduly glamorize the nature even of these allegedly more glamorous or exciting occupations? What, if any, are the political consequences when these high expectations are not fulfilled in the adult's work life? There are no definite answers to any of these questions but it is fairly clear that childhood socialization to the world of work can, at best, only be partially preparatory to the realities that await youth in the adult world.

Adult Work Settings

Lafferty, in chapter 3 here, holds that as "a setting for political learning, the industrial workplace is the least studied of the political socialization phenomena." Nor have many other work settings been studied from a socialization perspective (for a brief review, see Sigel and Hoskin 1977). Yet it is clear that in the adult world work does function as a political socializer. It does so in a variety of ways, both direct and indirect. Let us turn first to some direct ones. All occupations make some work-related demands on those who engage in them, but some actually demand or give rise to specific sociopolitical values, and the holding of such values is essential to functioning efficiently in the occupation. Several of the human-service industries illustrate this point. In an earlier review article (Sigel and Hoskin 1977, p. 275) we argued that social work is an occupation which virtually demands one sociopolitical outlook which precludes others; social workers are not apt to view poverty as an indicator of having fallen from divine grace, nor are they likely to look upon it as just retribution for laziness and/or lack of intelligence. . . . the occupation as a whole is unthinkable without the philosophical assumption of society's responsibility for its poor and disabled.

In chapter 4 Dressel and Lipsky, who consider the desire to help unfortunate people to be "the centerpiece of professional education," nonetheless show that even this centerpiece can and has been modified or reinterpreted by new entrants in the profession who may have a different interpretation as to what it means to help clients. Nor is the profession's beliefs unaffected by the social climate of the time, the nature of the community where it is practiced, and the demands society makes on it, to name but a few factors.

It suffices to cite just two more examples of political socialization in the professions. Journalism schools in their function as socializing agents aim to socialize their students into specific attitudes toward government/press relations and into vigilant protection of the profession's first-amendment rights. The military is another profession that assumes a socializing role. Dedication to the nation, ahead of family and even self, is demanded of the professional soldier, according to Lovell and Stiehm, in chapter 5. And although the "United States armed forces traditionally have looked askance at political indoctrination," as they assert, their chapter as well as the work of other students of the military indicates that military training does tend to shape members' political views, especially as it pertains to the officer corps. Their chapter also makes interesting observations concerning the ways in which elite status in an organization contributes to uniformity of outlook. Steckenrider and Cutler, in chapter 2, referred to other professions that act as agents of political socialization, but so far not too many professions have been studied in depth, at least not from a political socialization perspective. Yet it is fairly plausible to assume that many professions require or at least induce a certain view of the political world and that such views may differ from profession to profession (even though they may be of similar social status), depending on the profession's mission. Training and common interests see to that. To summarize, "occupations are important socializers and teachers of values, especially those like the professions that come to constitute 'communities' with shared normative standards for conduct, even outside of work" (Kanter 1976, p. 42).

While it is not too difficult to discover that specific professions and occupations subscribe to a certain generalized outlook on the world and perhaps even on the role of government, it has been far more difficult to establish a link between specific issue-preferences and specific occupations. We lack detailed information about the ways in which certain professions socialize their members to specific political preferences. "Indeed, it is striking just how little attention has been paid to work in studies of adult socialization. While there has been research on how people are socialized *into* jobs, there has been virtually none on the socialization effects of jobs for other life settings" (Kanter 1976, p. 46). This lack of information is in some part attributable to the fact that most of our data are derived from large-scale national sample surveys. Such instruments do not permit us to decompose the various occupations into finely graded segments, tuned to capturing the nature and mission of each occupation. Longitudinal studies reaching back to childhood and adolescent socialization would be particularly useful here in that they might shed light on the extent to which job choices—and with them consonant social philosophy—are a function of early socialization or, conceivably, constitute a deliberate break with it, perhaps an act of youthful rebellion. Equally useful would be panel studies which could document the nature of the socialization process in a given work setting.

Socialization to nonprofessional occupations may be less overt but still is apt to be influential. Modern industrial, capitalist societies make certain personal demands on the worker, such as time-consciousness, punctuality, respect for private property, ability to follow written instructions, and so on. Moreover, "strict hierarchies of authority responsive to the imperatives of machine production, and the separation of product and producer, all are part of this milieu, and require particular personal properties of those who are to master its requirements" (Inkeles and Smith 1974, p. 4). But industrial tasks very often are monotonous, repetitive, and demand little intellectual involvement on the part of the practitioner (Form 1973). More importantly, the very simplicity of the task is said to have effects beyond the task itself. Kohn and his associates found substantive complexity of work tasks to be conducive to intellectual flexibility and adult development regardless of the occupational status or financial rewards involved. "It also bears on many facets of off-the-job psychological functioning, ranging from valuation of self-direction to self-esteem to authoritarian conservatism to intellectual flexibility" (Kohn 1980, p. 198). He argues that such flexibility maintains itself and even grows over the life span but is dependent on "the meaningful challenges the work itself poses (or fails to pose)" (p. 206).

One could infer from Kohn's findings that lower levels of self-esteem, greater intellectual rigidity, and even political conservatism could be the consequence of nondemanding, monotonous work routines. In this vein Sheppard and Herrick's 1972 study of young assembly-line workers attributed their low sense of political efficacy and high political alienation to the deadening, nonchallenging nature of their job routine. Having obtained higher levels of formal education than earlier generations of assembly-line workers, they found the lack of control of their work routine and the simplicity of it jarring and unacceptable.

The discontent of these younger workers stands in marked contrast to older workers' greater acceptance of the work routine described so vividly in the work of Studs Terkel (1972, 1981). While we lack much solid empirical work to explain the difference in reactions, a plausible explanation might be that childhood socialization did not prepare the younger worker for his frustration with certain types of industrial work. Being urged (by the schools and the media) to think for himself and being led to believe that hard work—in the land of unlimited opportunity—would eventually lead to a more challenging work-related existence, he now may feel that he has been misled. As Korn-hauser (1965) observed, it is sad indeed that modern industrial work-routines ask so little of men and women who have so much more to give. Many of their fathers and grandfathers, by contrast, arrived in the plants, mills, and factories either from subsistence rural settings or were immigrants who came here from mean, impoverished circumstances and entered the American econ-omy on its lowest rungs which, though low in every respect, probably still constituted an improvement over the conditions they had left behind. In short, their level of expectation was considerably lower than that of their sons and grandsons, and because their expectations were modest, it is conceivable that they also were less dissatisfied, in spite of the fact that their working condi-tions might have been worse than are those of the sons and grandsons. Thus it is not only the work routine itself but the expectations one brings to it that have the potential to alter one's political outlook.

Karl Marx was not the only one who conjectured that deadening and often poorly rewarded work routines would lead to political alienation from the system and eventually to revolt against it. "An almost classic preoccupation among analysts of American society has been the failure of the society to generate a radical working class in pursuit of socialist goals" (Rosenblum 1973, p. 1). The unwillingness of the industrial work force to challenge the system, however, does not mean that workers, especially unionized industrial ones, have not sought to use economic and political means to improve their economic situation. Workers are among the staunchest and best-organized advocates for improvement in working conditions, better pay, shorter work weeks, and several other social welfare measures likely to result in a some-what altered balance in the status quo. These economic demands, however, cannot be equated with a strong desire to redistribute the wealth and even less with any objections to the capitalist system (Nie et al. 1976; Schlozman and Verba, 1979; Hochschild, 1981). Nor are blue-collar workers particularly lib-eral when it comes to other political issues (foreign affairs, civil liberties, alternate life styles, protection of the environment.) If anything, they tend toward conservatism. Most favor a strong defense posture, are more support-ive than the rest of the population of certain military postures of the U.S., and are generally less opposed to the use of force.[1] They are also among the most anti-Communist elements in the population. In fact, most of manual labor is a strong defender of the American version of democracy as taught in the schools and propagated by the media. No data exist to establish that this conservatism is a result of schooling and most likely should instead be attributed to familial and religious and/or ethnic ties (Sigel and Hoskin 1977). When the system fails to provide what is anticipated, American workers have been shown to be more inclined to blame the specific company—or even to blame themselves—than to blame the system (Chinoy 1955). Lafferty's study of Norwegian workers showed that the propensity toward radicalism—where it existed at all—probably had more to do with parental predispositions than with the work-setting itself—one more intimation that people bring a good deal of intellectual and affective "baggage" to any new setting.

What about less ideological aspects? How does the political involvement of workers compare with that of other groups? What evidence we have suggests that blue-collar participation in community affairs, voluntary associations, and political causes is relatively low (Verba and Nie 1972; Campbell et al. 1960; Kornhauser 1965; Shepard 1971), although voting turnout (at least in unionized plants) is on a par with the rest of the population (Kornhauser et al. 1956; Delli Carpini 1986). Whether or not such relatively low political involvement should be attributed to the work routine and seen as symptomatic of political alienation rather than being related to educational and other resources is an unanswered question.

It also would be highly misleading were we to focus exclusively on blue-collar work routines in our search for signs of political alienation. As more and more white-collar people work in large institutions—whether public or private—they too confront conditions conducive to alienation, such as monotonous work routines, close supervision, and hierarchical structures. In fact, one topic which deserves far closer attention than it has received up to now concerns the effect on white-collar employees of automation and computerization. As work routines in offices and stores become more and more mechanized and are broken down into smaller and smaller segments, "workers play an increasingly reduced role. . . . they apply but a fraction of their skill and knowledge to the task at hand, and often lose their sense of the larger logic of the productive process in the bargain" (Erikson 1986, p. 2). Sarason (1977) noted that it is the very size and bureaucratization of some health-delivery systems that lead to "burnout" and alienation among employees long before they have reached retirement age, frequently causing them to leave the profession. Dressel and Lipsky make similar comments concerning the social welfare bureaucracy. In many instances, such employees—much like industrial labor before them—are resorting to unionization in order to regain control over their work environments. Again, as in the case of the workers on whom Lafferty reports, dissatisfaction does not take the form of hostility to the political system or attempts to alter it in fundamental ways. It is fairly clear that, at least in the United States, unfavorable work environments have not socialized workers and employees into radical ideological commitment, let alone radical activity. A question which cannot be answered as yet is whether discontent with lack of control over one's working life is the reason why political participation—as measured by voting turnout, organizational involvement, and so on—is so low and seems to be decreasing steadily.[2]

Giving workers more control over their work routines has frequently been advocated as a remedy for this situation. Participation in the workplace has been endorsed by political scientists not so much from a desire to make workers more satisfied or productive but out of the belief that such participation would socialize them to active involvement in the political process of the outside world. As Verba and Nie (1972, p. 3) asserted, "effective [political] participation depends on opportunities to participate in other spheres—family, school, voluntary associations, the workplace." Almond and Verba's five-nation study (1963, p. 363) demonstrated to them that the participatory workplace played a particularly crucial role in socializing for democratic citizenship. Lafferty's chapter here (chap.3) is devoted to testing that proposition by focusing almost exclusively on the effects of participation in industrial workplaces. He reaches the conclusion that participation does have an effect but only on some people and under some conditions. Consequently it remains a moot question whether participation in the workplace has the socializing function attributed to it by Pateman (1970) and others.

The central role that work occupies in political socialization can be further illustrated by the impact unemployment has on political interest and activity. In a classic early study of unemployment, Jahoda et al. (1933) vividly documented the catastrophic effect of the prospect of prolonged unemployment on political involvement. Previously active and engaged Austrian textile workers became apathetic, cut their ties with social organizations in which they had been active, and generally withdrew from political involvement. And this in spite of the fact that most of them had been members of a socialist party! It is, therefore, not surprising to find that in the United States—which lacks a similar labor-oriented party—steelworkers in Ohio (Buss and Hofstetter, 1981) who either faced the prospect of unemployment or already found themselves unemployed also withdrew from involvement. Seemingly then, acute external crises, such as prolonged unemployment, have the potential to attenuate, if not actually imperil, patterns of behavior to which one had been previously socialized.

Another, perhaps more indirect, way in which work functions as a political socializer has to do with the status enjoyed by one's occupation. Occupation designates not only what one does to earn a living, it also indicates to the world at large as well as to oneself a status in society which brings with it certain resources, skills, knowledge, prestige. It is highly probable that self-esteem is not totally independent of status. "We define ourselves, and are defined by others by what we do: our work" (Sarason 1977, p. 1). Blauner (1964) compared high-status blue-collar workers—the so-called aristocrats of labor (in this case, a study of printers)—with economically depressed, lower-status ones and found the former but not the latter to score high in self-esteem. In their case, as prevails generally, self-esteem and community involvement also were related. The effectiveness of a group's community involvement, however, is not independent of its social standing. Dressel and Lipsky, for example, in chapter 4, question how much "public creditibility and political clout" the social-work profession can exercise, given its "own possible marginality." This is a crucial question that should be raised with respect to other similar professions whose membership may be highly trained but lacking in prestige. The attempts of several of them to unionize (for example, public-school teachers) no doubt is an attempt to attain through organizational strength the power denied them by lack of social status.

In general, the very attributes which bestow high status on an occupation, such as education and income, also involve work routines that call for skills in speaking and writing, aptitude for interpersonal relations or leadership, and some autonomy in decision-making. Work routines such as these, mastered successfully, not only tend to be related to a sense of personal efficacy but are also of crucial importance for political involvement, since these skills after all constitute the essence of the political process. Consequently, it is not surprising that active political involvement and occupational status are related (Campbell et al. 1960; Key 1961). Possession of such characteristics seems to be especially crucial for the attainment of positions of political leadership—as Renshon demonstrates (in chap. 6)—and is a partial explanation why few major political leaders in the United States have risen from the ranks of blue-collar labor.

The section which follows puts the spotlight on four very different occupations. They were chosen not only because they varied from each other in work routines but because they also varied in the intensity and extensiveness of the socialization experience to which the employees are exposed. Of the four occupations selected, three have in common that work takes place in large, highly structured, and hierarchical organizations. They consequently reflect the reality of work settings as they prevail for a majority of today's employed people in the United States. By contrast, the fourth focuses on an elite and rather individualistic occupation—that of political leader. Of the first three, one deals with manual or unskilled labor. The other two are service professions and probably enjoy somewhat higher social status. These are the military and the social welfare sector. Whereas all three seek to socialize new recruits into the nature of the work routines they are to perform, socialization into the military and into social welfare work goes well beyond that, because their practitioners are expected to internalize the work ethos consonant with the institution's mission. Of the two the military—often characterized as a total institution—calls for the most complete socialization and/or resocialization. It seeks to fuse the professional and the personal so completely that the individual soldier takes on a new identity after basic training.

Lafferty, in chapter 3, on worker participation, alerts us to the moderating roles played by intervening institutions, such as labor unions, which can effect the socialization process in significant ways. Of particular interest here is the differential impact union membership has on women and on men. What he has to say about the importance of employee participation in the decision-making process is a topic whose significance reaches well beyond its effect on blue-collar labor and deserves more attention than it has received so far.

Dressel and Lipsky, who focus on social welfare work in chapter 4, consider it to be a component of what Lipsky (1980) has labeled the street-level bureaucracy. He defines street-level bureaucrats as "public service workers who interact directly with citizens in the course of their jobs, and who have substantial discretion in the execution of their work" (p. 3). He includes in this category, in addition to social welfare workers, teachers, police officers, other law enforcement officials, health workers "and many other public employees who grant access to government programs and provide services with them" (p. 3). Although most of these professions are normally regarded as relatively low-level occupations, they are of critical importance precisely because the employee's discretionary power can bestow or deny the public certain benefits of the social system. The social welfare bureaucracy—because it delivers most of these services to usually needy sectors of the public— symbolizes a specific political philosophy concerning government's obligation to help the needy. One would assume, therefore, that people who did not subscribe to this philosophy would probably not choose the profession of social worker.[3] What happens, though, to this philosophy of social empathy once the social worker encounters (a) his client and (b) the large bureaucracy with its case-overload, its myriad of rules, and its impersonality? What are the dilemmas he or she encounters in the course of this work, and what changes in philosophy or practice do workers experience as they seek to cope? Under these conditions idealism and altruism can on occasion turn into cynicism and conservatism.

Lovell and Stiehm's study of the military in chapter 5 offers an example of socialization in "an intense, total environment" which aims to control just about every aspect of a person's life, thoughts, and values. Military socialization, if successful, thus goes beyond training for work-related competence (that it shares with all forms of work training); it even goes beyond instilling certain professional beliefs and values in recruits (that it shares with other professions). Rather, its aim is to restructure the recruit's sense of self and his or her place in the organization and in society. The very nature of the rites of passage to which the recruit is exposed is designed to accomplish that end. Lovell and Stiehm write that if "the intended messages are received then, a recruit should finish basic believing in the military's near-total effectiveness." But, they ask, is the message received in full, do the lessons learned closely approximate what the military intended? This is an important question one must ask of all socialization agents. Each of the first three chapters in this part of the volume raises it in one way or another.

The last chapter, dealing with the socialization of political leaders, adopts a different perspective. Renshon seeks to explore what light developmental psychological theories can shed on the political socialization of leaders. He consequently pays a great deal of attention to the emotional transformations a leader experiences as he moves from childhood to youth to maturity. Although he stresses more than did the preceding three chapters the crucial role played by individual personality, he shares with them the conviction that the constraints of the work setting and the nature of the political times and system affect the socialization even of political leaders. Those who seek to resist these constraints or are unable to shape them constructively, he shows, tend to experience much failure and eventual defeat in their leadership role. Beyond that his chapter differs in yet another way from the other three. Given the nature of the material available on leaders, Renshon has considerably more opportunity to forge a link between childhood socialization and adult behavior. Very few such longitudinal observations can be made for most other types of work. One striking exception—pointing to the persistence of childhood socialization—comes from a study of automobile workers during the 1952 presidential election. All worked in the same plant and belonged to the same labor union (UAW), which carried out a strong mobilization drive on behalf of the Democratic ticket. Still, of those whose fathers were or had been Republicans a majority (51 percent) voted for the Republican candidate whereas those with Democratic fathers all but unanimously voted Democratic (Kornhauser et al. 1956, p. 43). While it would no doubt be very important to know more about the childhood background of all types of currently employed men and women, the evidence furnished by the chapters in this section points to the crucial importance of the work experience itself in socializing individuals.

To conclude, we have today a large body of literature on work and its organization but relatively little on the way work socializes men and women once they are engaged in it. And when it comes to reaching conclusions as to the *political* socialization function of work, we can at best speculate or draw tentative inferences from sociological and psychological studies on the topic. All of these point in the direction "that the relationship between everyday work experiences and the development and expression of political views is a real and complex one worthy of . . . further inquiry" (Delli Carpini 1986, p. 24).

R.S.S.

Notes

1. Women and black workers, however, are seen as less conservative with respect to these issues. Carroll (chap. 8 in this volume) and others have pointed to the important ways in which paid employment shapes women's outlook.

2. The literature on job satisfaction is voluminous, but here too results are far from conclusive. See C. Frederick Herzberg, *Work and the Nature of Man* (London: Staples Press, 1968); Robert Blauner, "Work Satisfaction and Industrial Trends in Modern Society," in Reinhard Bendix and Seymour Martin Lipset, eds., *Class, Status, and Power*, 2d. ed. (New York: The Free Press, 1966, pp. 474–87); Roberta S. Sigel, Robin Synder, and Michael X. Delli Carpini, "Does it Make a Difference How You Feel about Your Job? Work Satisfaction and Political Orientations." Paper presented at the 1982 Annual Meeting of the American Political Science Association.

3. The extent to which self-selection into occupations plays a role in accounting for similarities in views among people in the same occupation is another topic in adult socialization which has not yet received adequate scholarly attention.

References

Almond, G. A., and S. Verba. 1963. *The Civic Culture: Political Attitudes and Democracy: Political Attitudes and Democracy in Five Nations*. Princeton: Princeton University Press.

Blauner, R. 1964. *Alienation and Freedom*. Chicago: University of Chicago Press.

Buss, T. F. and R. Hofstetter. 1981. "Communication, Information and Participation During an Emerging Crisis." *The Social Science Journal* 18: 81–91.

Campbell, A., P. Converse, W. Miller, and D. Stokes. 1960. *The American Voter*. New York: John Wiley.

Chinoy, E. 1955. *Automobile Workers and the American Dream*. Garden City, N.Y.: Doubleday.

Delli Carpini, M. X. 1986. "Work and Politics: A Decomposition of the Concept of Work and an Investigation of Its Impact on Political Attitudes and Actions." *Political Psychology* 7: 117–40.

Erikson, K. 1986. "On Work and Alienation." *American Sociological Review* 51: 1–8.

Finifter, A. W., ed. 1972. *Alienation and the Social System*. New York: John Wiley and Sons.

Form, W. 1973. "Auto Workers and Their Machines: A Study of Work, Factory, and Job Satisfaction in Four Countries." *Social Forces* 52: 1–15.

Greenberger, E., and L. Steinberg. 1986. *When Teenagers Work. The Psychological and Social Costs of Adolescent Employment.* New York: Basic Books.

Hochschild, J. L. 1981. *What's Fair? American Beliefs about Distributive Justice.* Cambridge: Harvard University Press.

Inkeles, A., and D. H. Smith. 1974. *Becoming Modern: Individual Change in Six Developing Countries.* Cambridge: Harvard University Press.

Jahoda, M., P. F. Lazarsfeld, and H. Zeisel. 1933. *Die Arbeitslosen von Marienthal.* Leipzig: Hirzel.

Kanter, R. M. 1976. *Work and Family in the United States.* New York: Russell Sage.

Key, V. O. 1961. *Public Opinion and American Democracy.* New York: Alfred A. Knopf.

Kohn, M. L. 1969. *Class and Conformity: A Study in Values.* Homewood, Ill.: Dorsey.

———. 1980. "Job Complexity and Adult Personality." In Neil J. Smelser and Erik Erikson, eds., *Themes of Work and Love in Adulthood.* Cambridge: Harvard University Press, pp. 193–212.

Kornhauser, A. W. 1956 *When Labor Votes.* New York: University Books.

———. 1965. *The Mental Health of the Industrial Worker.* New York: John Wiley and Sons.

Lipsky, M. 1980. *Street-Level Bureaucracy Dilemmas of the Individual in Public Services.* New York: Russell Sage.

Miller, D. R., and G. E. Swanson. 1958. *The Changing American Parent.* New York: John Wiley.

Moore, W. E. 1969. "Occupational Socialization." In D. A. Goslin, ed., *Handbook of Socialization Theory and Research.* Chicago: Rand McNally, pp. 861–884.

Nie, N. H., S. Verba, and J. R. Petrocik. 1976. *The Changing American Voter.* Cambridge: Harvard University Press.

Pateman, C. 1970. *Participation and Democratic Theory.* New York: Cambridge University Press.

Rosenblum, G. 1973. *Immigrant Workers: Their Impact on American Labor Radicalism.* New York: Basic Books.

Schlozman, K. L. and S. Verba. 1979. *Injury to Insult.* Cambridge: Harvard University Press.

Sarason, S. 1977. *Work, Aging, and Social Change: Professionals and the One Life–One Career Imperative.* New York: The Free Press.

Seeman, M. 1959. "On the Meaning of Alienation." *American Sociological Review* 24: 783–91.

Shepard, J. M. 1971. *Automation and Alienation: A Study of Office and Factory Workers.* Cambridge: MIT Press.

Sheppard, H. L., and N. Q. Herrick. 1972. *Where Have All the Robots Gone?* New York: The Free Press.

Sigel, R. S., R. Snyder, and M. X. Delli Carpini. 1982. "Does it Make a Difference How You Feel about Your Job?" Paper presented at the Annual Meeting of the American Political Science Association.

Sigel, R. S., and M. B. Hoskin. 1977. "Perspectives on Adult Political Socialization." In S. A. Renshon, ed., *Handbook of Political Socialization*. New York: The Free Press, pp. 259–93.

Terkel, S. 1972. *Working*. New York: Ballantine Books.

———. 1981. *American Dreams: Lost and Found*. New York: Ballantine Books.

Verba, S., and N. H. Nie. 1972. *Participation in America*. New York: Harper and Row.

Three

Work as a Source of Political Learning Among Wage-Laborers and Lower-Level Employees

WILLIAM M. LAFFERTY

As a setting for political learning, the industrial workplace is easily the least studied of all political-socialization phenomena.[1] Studies of socioeconomic status and politics are legion; studies of class and politics ample; studies of occupation and politics sparse; and studies of industrial labor and politics *very* sparse. In the area of political participation, for example, which Milbrath and Goel (1977) have made into one of the best-documented bibliographical areas of the discipline, we find not a single study devoted to intraindustrial variance. We do know, of course, that there is a general tendency for "blue-collar" or "manual-labor" occupations to be less involved in conventional political behavior, but we also know: (1) that the tendency can be strongly reversed by organizational factors (Rokkan and Campbell 1960; Verba, Nie, and Kim 1978; Lafferty 1981) and (2) that the tendency is strongly related to *other* socioeconomic factors—childhood class position, level of education, occupational opportunity—which are seldom controlled for.

What we must aim for, therefore, is an understanding of blue-collar labor which allows us to pinpoint, both theoretically and empirically, the specific effects of different industrial settings. What is it about industrial workplaces which might either change or reinforce basic patterns of political socialization acquired prior to entry into the workforce?

Though the question appears simple enough, it leads, as we shall see, to a labyrinth of causal explication. For reasons both representative and synthetic, I propose that we traverse the maze along two broad theoretical paths: Marxism and social liberalism. The first guides us according to a general notion of sociotechnical determinism, informing as to what manual labor seems to lead to in the way of ideology and action; while the second points in the direction of learning and authority, providing an understanding of the possible effects which changes in work organization imply. The overall purpose of the analysis is a clarification of the relationship between specific types of industrial workplaces and the orientations and competencies which lead to either involvement in or rejection of electoral-based politics. In addition to the major studies in the area, reference will be made to a recent national survey on "Democracy in Norway" where the issues under discussion were given major attention.[2]

The Marxist Perspective

In the classical Marxist view, the relationship between industrial labor and political consciousness and action was, in theory at any rate, a broadly determined one. The nature of industrial wage-labor itself, as an integral part of the capitalist mode of production, would eventually condition the proletariat to an understanding of its exploited position, which would in turn lead to a proletarian revolution. The key dynamic of the model is the theory of alienation, i.e. the belief that the separation of the worker from his or her product creates an internal tension in the species-specific need for an integration of socialized human sensibility with nature (see, e.g., Ollman 1971; Mészáros 1970). It is the psychological stress of alienation (though none of the classical Marxists ever described it *as* a psychological phenomenon) which leads the class of wage-laborers to a joint recognition of their plight, thereby objectifying their position *as* a class vis-à-vis the owning class, so as, ultimately, to see the need for political action.

Michael Mann (1973, p. 13) has effectively captured the essence of the post-alienation process in terms of four main elements of the class:

identity: "the definition of oneself as working-class, as playing a distinctive role in common with other workers in the production process."

opposition: "the perception that the capitalist and his agents constitute an enduring opponent to oneself."

totality: "the acceptance of the two previous elements as the defining characteristics of (a) one's total social situation and (b) the whole society in which one lives."

an alternative: "a goal toward which one moves through the struggle with the opponent."

Though Marx himself *mostly* assumed that this process would automatically work itself out in history, later analysts, including Mann, have placed greater emphasis on the dialectical nature of the process. The elements of the process are viewed not as a linear and uniform development within a relatively predictable duration but as (in light of a growing body of evidence) being open to specific cultural and organizational influences. Workers are never workers without historical and cultural traditions; industrialization is never a monotypical experience, either in national context, sequence, or timing; and the response of labor is neither necessarily solidaristic or univocal (Lafferty 1971, 1974; Gusfield 1970; Lipset 1983). Nearly every documented relationship in this area has been shown to have its exception, and the rapid changes in both the division of labor and sociotechnical organization continue to compound the evidence.

Though not always acknowledged by the more committed proponents of neomarxist analysis, Marxist-inspired empiricists have contributed greatly to the relativization of the materialist learning model. In summarizing the major contributions in this area, we can work with the general concept of *political radicalism*. The goal is not a detailed summary of the literature, however, but an overview of the major insights and problems encountered in the area. What we must try to determine is the degree to which occupational characteristics per se contribute to the phenomena in question. Assuming from the outset that sociotechnical effects are always relativized by the cultural, historical, institutional, and systemic configurations of each national setting, we nonetheless search for those indicators and perspectives which point toward occupational invariance in learning.[3]

Industrial Labor and Political Radicalism

The notion that the industrial working class in general would constitute the leading edge of political revolution has been proven so definitively wrong as to warrant little further speculation. There is virtually not a single country which has experienced a revolution from within where industrial labor has provided crucial leadership. Revolutions have traditionally been led by disenchanted upper-class and middle-class intellectuals, and usually fought out by peasant and/or military renegades.

If we wish to explore the logic of the Marxist model further, therefore, we must, in the first instance, revert to the level of political ideology. If the industrial proletariat has not "exploded" en masse in revolution against the political system, where and under what circumstances has it at least given its support to socialism as a political program?

At the broadest level of analysis, Seymour Martin Lipset has recently summarized his life-long interest in "the sources of working-class politics" in the form of two general propositions:

> . . . the more rigid the status demarcation lines in a country, the more likely the emergence of working-class-based parties. Where industrial capitalism emerged from a feudal society, with its emphasis on strong status lines and barriers, the growing working class was viewed as a *Stand,* a recognizable social entity. . . . Contrastingly, in nations that were "born modern," which lacked a feudal and aristocratic past, class position was less likely to confer a sense of shared corporate identity.

. . . the ways in which the dominant strata reacted to the nascent working-class movements conditioned their orientations. Where the working class was denied full political and economic citizenship, strong revolutionary movements developed. Conversely, the more readily working-class organizations were accepted into the economic and political order, the less radical their initial and subsequent ideologies. (Lipset 1983, p. 2)

Lipset's detailed case-by-case analysis of the literature on national labor movements provides both a clear perspective on the historical specificity of varying ideological responses as well as a general framework for understanding the institutional features and ideological proclivities conditioning blue-collar labor today. Though the situation is clearly not free from exceptions, there emerges a relatively concise picture of cross-national variance. Countries within the Anglo-Saxon tradition, with either relatively weak feudal "Stände" backgrounds or none at all, and with an early history of democratic rights are characterized by labor movements which are both more moderate and more "open" in terms of labor-party relations.

At the other extreme, in those countries where feudal traditions were relatively strong, and where the extension of rights to the working class was opposed prior to World War I (most typically, France, Germany, Italy, Spain), the working class has tended toward radical subcultures and organizations which have been relatively poorly integrated into the national decision-making process. In between, are some of the smaller countries of Europe (most typically Scandinavia and the Netherlands), which had relatively nonrigid preindustrial status systems and an early history of rights extension and organizational inclusion. These movements are characterized by reformism coupled with a high degree of worker-party association and highly developed corporate-pluralist systems.

The clear relevance of Lipset's overview for the present problem is the understanding that blue-collar occupations present the worker with different settings for ideological learning in different national contexts. The choice of ideological alternatives is thus both structured as to availability (vis-à-vis electoral politics) and "colored" in relation to specific national histories. There will be variation in blue-collar workplaces as to possible ideological profiles and identities, but it will be a contextually determined variation.

Of particular interest in electoral research at present, however, is the question of the degree to which the class-based differences across national units are in fact diminishing. From a number of different research directions, and with clear intellectual roots in the earlier "end-of-ideology" debate, there is growing evidence that class-related factors are playing an increasingly minor role in predicting party identification and political ideology. The so-called "new politics" sees electoral ideological preferences as gradually being disassociated from factors such as occupation in lieu of an increased predictability on the basis of values and life-style. As Western democracies become increasingly "postindustrial" or "postmaterialist," the effects of economic and occupational factors diminish.[4]

The relevance of these perspectives for the problem at hand is the prospect that manual or blue-collar labor may lose its predictive power in relation to socialist ideology in those European contexts where it has remained strong. Whether or not this takes place, however, is not unrelated to what is actually happening in the systems under study. The fact that Western societies are changing the profile of their occupational structures in the direction of fewer manual (industrial) and more service-sector workers is enough in itself to account for the decline in "class-polarization" effects (i.e., the Alford index, Alford 1963). Not all studies manage to control for the specific occupation-ideology relationship, however, so that there are open questions in many cases as to just what the decline in class-related factors is due to. In Scandinavia, for example, it has been pointed out that "class development" is attributable to three different types of processes in Norway, Sweden, and Denmark (Worre 1980). Although the long-term trend seems to be moving in the direction of declining support for worker-oriented ideologies within the blue-collar workforce, *considerable* cross-national differences persist. While the pressures to vote for a socialist or social-democratic alternative are still very strong on the industrial shop floors of Scandinavia, they are, for example, virtually nonexistent in the United States.

As a general phenomenon, therefore, the political learning experience of manual labor is structured in terms of national-industrial "schools." The development toward postindustrialism means declining proportions of traditional blue-collar workers, which in turn means a declining relevance of industrially oriented socialist ideologies. The technologizing of production and increasing predominance of service occupations does not mean, however, a decline in lower-level, routinized wage-labor. To the contrary, there is strong evidence of a growing "deskilling" of labor even as the classic blue-collar jobs are phased out (Braverman 1974; Wood 1982; Littler 1982).

In the most highly developed Western societies, therefore, we are confronted with a period of transition away from the pattern of politics and the division of labor that has served as a basic paradigm for analysis and prediction since the coincident development of democratization and industrialization (often referred to as "the Lipset-Rokkan paradigm," from Lipset and Rokkan 1967). Insofar as industrial labor *does* exert a systematic socializing effect, it will, in the future, be most clearly manifest and of most decisive importance in the industrializing sector of the Third World. Considering the enormous differences between this phase of industrialization and the Western experience, we should hardly expect any great similarity in labor response across the two processes.

Should there be any similarity, it would have to be related to what appears to be the only intraindustrial dimension that shows a *relatively* clear pattern of cross-national consistency in radical-vs.-moderate labor response. Even though the first control for blue-collar political socialization must be at the level of national experience, there does seem to be a structural characteristic of industrial workplaces themselves which tends toward cross-national invariance.

I refer, in a very general way, to the internal organizational form attaching to different types of industrial activity. If one inspects the literature and reviews of the literature on the relationship between occupation and political radicalism, there emerges a picture of certain labor conditions which seem to be related to radical ideology (at least in an electoral context) and possibly more radical forms of direct action. The occupational types which stand out in this regard are: forestry workers, miners, dockworkers, large-scale construction workers, shipbuilders, and steel and metal workers (Lipset et al. 1954; Allardt 1964, 1976; Allardt and Pesonen 1967; Soares and Hamblin 1967; Petras and Zeitlin 1967; Lafferty 1974).

In trying to grasp an underlying dimension which might account for radical invariance across these diverse productive activities, it is again worthwhile to turn to Seymour Martin Lipset. As early as 1954 Lipset et al. identified six factors which seemed to be most typically related to the combination of mining and forestry on the one hand and electoral leftism on the other. These factors were divided into three "types of deprivation"—*insecurity of income, unsatisfying work,* and *low prestige status*—and three "facilitating conditions"—*good intraclass communications, low expectation of mobility,* and *lack of traditionalism* (Lipset et al. 1954, p. 1143). As Lipset does not explicitly state how mining and forestry are generally characterized by a "lack of traditionalism," and as there is no necessary connection between the two, we can neglect this particular feature.

The other five features indicate a work situation which is understandable as a setting that would condition workers in a radical rather than a moderate, more reformist direction.[5] The work is physically hard, routinized as to task, and unpredictable as to duration, and with very low social status. It is labor in one of its most negative forms: heavy, noncontractual work to survive. It is also work which, because of its sociotechnical nature and (usually) regional isolation in nonindustrial settings, provides little prospect of upward mobility, either on or off the job. The lack of a differentiated and open organizational structure is, however, also the source of a unimodal occupational identity and a high level of intraworkforce communication.

It is exactly this type of situation which the Scandinavian labor sociologist Sverre Lysgaard (1961) has identified as the basis for generating a strong, more-or-less spontaneous "worker collective." In Lysgaard's perspective, conditions of proximity, similarity of task, and a common "problem situation" both on and off the job lead to a greater degree of group interaction, identification, and problem interpretation. By implication, the more structurally rigid the sociotechnical process accompanying the type of productive activity in question (mining and labor-intensive forestry), the stronger the sense of worker collectivity and the clearer the needs for a class-based alternative ideology. Without other organizational structures in the immediate situation, the clearest and most practical problem solution is simply to reverse the values in power and prestige by transferring ownership and control to the workers.

The generality of the Lipset-Lysgaard perspective is strengthened when we bring in the other industrial types which have shown radical tendencies: large-scale construction projects, shipbuilding, dockworkers, commercial farming and fishing, and open-hearth steel and metal production. All of these activities have the same general features of work organization in relation to the same general type of "product." They involve large numbers of workers in similar tasks with low prestige and heavy, mostly exposed work loads under a numerically small but sharply differentiated and asymmetrical management. As the product is either a large-scale impersonal "project" (dams, ships, roads) or partially processed raw materials (ore, lumber, fish, alloys), there is little ability to see individual effort reflected back from the labor process, and greater reason to experience the collective nature of the enterprise. The result seems to be a generalized socialization effect in the direction of collectivist radical ideology.

By implication, one should also expect a tendency towards moderate labor ideology in those work settings which are characterized by lighter work loads, higher occupational status, secure employment, upward mobility on the job (i.e., greater intragroup competition) and a weaker worker-collective. Other than to point out that this expectation is borne out by the demonstrated strength of reformist electoral alternatives in the more advanced industrial countries in general, one can refer to little more in the way of data. As with most other phenomena, it is the atypical which attracts most interest, and communism has traditionally been atypical in the countries most studied by Western empiricists. To my knowledge, there are only two large-scale studies which test for *both* radical and moderate support on the basis of the same models for the same data (Allardt and Pesonen 1967; Lafferty 1974). The point is a crucial one for nearly all generalizations in this area, since the vast majority of studies are ecological, i.e. based on aggregate data for geographic subunits. Without adequate controls for *other* electoral ideologies within the same analysis, there is always the possibility that proven predictors of radicalism are also associated with both moderate and rightist ideologies.[6]

Be that as it may, in those studies which have controlled for the relative strengths of other ideologies, there is a clear tendency for moderate socialism (social democracy) to be relatively more popular in the more developed and differentiated industrial regions (differentiated as to both the internal division of labor and competitive wage-labor opportunities [Lafferty 1974, chaps. 8 and 9; Allardt and Pesonen 1967, pp. 354–55]). The more craft-oriented the industrial branch and the more diversified the general industrial setting, the greater the possibility for an *exclusively* moderate preference.

In sum, therefore, there is limited evidence that certain types of occupational structures do condition manual laborers in the direction of particular ideological responses. Allowing for all demonstrated and possible exceptions, and allowing too for the historic specificity of many of the findings, there seems to be a general radical-moderate dimension which is reflective of the work quality, labor status, product type, market position, mobility potential, and—perhaps most important—degree of diversified integration in, or categoric isolation from, the structure of authority and responsibility accompanying the sociotechnical productive process itself.

The implications for the Marxist learning model are, however, dubious. While the structural perspective may be both interesting and challenging for Third World countries that, to a certain degree, may still be experiencing similar conditions of production in the areas in question, the same conditions have long since been the subject of both technological and organizational innovation in the West. The modes of production in question are either being phased out altogether; transferred to less demanding and sophisticated labor markets; or being radically changed by technology. Both the labor-intensive occupations themselves and the radical traditions they have fostered are fading into the Western history books. Other so-called hi-tech occupations are replacing them—and many of these may be equally low in status, physically demanding, hierarchical, and task-homogeneous (clerical work and the assembly of technological components)—but the contextual factors affecting these workplaces are so different from those affecting the earlier settings as to render predictions uncertain.

Occupational Structure and Labor Ideology in Norway

So as to illustrate the problem in a contemporary setting, and at the same time bring in a greater degree of variable control, I shall illustrate the above by looking briefly at data from a recent Norwegian national survey. Norway is, of course, one of the most highly developed economic systems in the West, as well as an exceptionally strong case for organized labor. What, we can ask, is the relationship between the conditions of labor at the lowest level of the occupational hierarchy and political ideology in a "social democratic state"? Further, are the relationships revealed the result of occupational factors per se, or are there other *prework* factors which must be taken into consideration?

Though Norway is in many ways atypical, the presentation should none-theless provide a clear understanding of the more specific difficulties involved in isolating workplace effects on political learning. As implied earlier, at this stage of development the field of adult political socialization requires clarity of approach and analysis rather than synopses of findings. The Norwegian case is thus offered as an analytical example.

The data to be presented derive from a national survey undertaken in 1981 on "Democracy in Norway: Participation and Basic Values." One of the major purposes of the survey was to develop a broad-based understanding of the relationship between work and politics. Respondents were questioned in de-tail as to the characteristics of their work situation, their social and political engagement, and a large number of ideologically relevant issues. Interviews were completed for 1,170 respondents, which means that occupational sub-categories are rather small; nonetheless they are indicative for Norway as a whole.

For present purposes, I must limit the discussion to the occupational cate-gories at the lowest level of the division of labor. These include manual work-ers, wage-labor members of the crafts and trades, and lower-level employees in commerce and the services. The latter are included because they constitute the "vanguard" of poorly paid, routinized, white-collar labor. Most of them (76 percent) are women. As a problem for adult political socialization, they represent a challenge which is both growing in importance and different in nature. If the workplace *does* have "politicizing" effects, and if these effects are important for both ideological persuasion and political practice, lower-level women employees must overcome the effects of *both* class and patriar-chy. Contrary to the situation in Marx's England, where women and children constituted a major segment of the industrial proletariat *without citizenship*, we are now confronted by a working class which is both technologically and sexually bifurcated under conditions of full political entitlement.

In trying to unravel the possible occupational-ideological dependencies of this situation, we began by contrasting several indexes of ideologically rele-vant phenomenon. These included measures of political radicalism, socialist values, political alienation, and direct-action values. These measures were then checked against a broad number of work-related indicators, including income; the nature of the industrial branch or sector; size of workplace; level of job demands (routine and tempo); level of "job discretion" (autonomy in relation to both job tasks and organizational hierarchy); and degree of poten-tial job mobility (opportunities for training and advancement).

The results were consistently negative for all bivariate relationships. Though several tendencies were revealed in the direction expected, none reached even a minimum level of significance. Despite the fact that the job measures employed generate considerable variance in other analytic contexts, they showed no consistent effect on political ideology.

There was, however, a single relatively minor exception. In relation to an index of "political radicalism," the division between blue-collar workers and low-level employees proved to be just barely significant, with the former slightly more radical than the latter.[7] Knowing the gender-specific nature of the subdivision, we took this relationship as a point of departure for an analysis of the effect of occupational socialization in relation to both preoccupational and other status-related factors. The results of the analysis proved highly instructive as to both the nature of the problem and the need for a comprehensive multivariate approach.

To start with, we found, not unexpectedly, that there was a relatively strong interaction effect in the relationship between type of job and gender. The direction of the effect was quite unexpected, however. Although women employees were clearly the most conservative subgroup (followed by male employees), it was women manual workers who were clearly the most radical subgroup. Though the overall effect was small, women workers were, in terms of average scores, five times more radical than male workers; seven times more radical than male employees; and ten times more radical than women employees.

With these results as a baseline occupational effect (the only one of significance), we then searched for other variables with plausible effects on political radicalism. Three bivariate relationships emerged as significant: the degree of union activity, particularly maternal party preference, age, and parental party preference during childhood (Jennings and Niemi in their 1974 study of adolescents made similar observations concerning maternal influence). Together with the gender/work variable, these three variables enabled us to probe deeper into the question of continuity and change. How much was the gender/work relationship a result of occupational characteristics, and how much was it a reflection of preoccupational or extraoccupational characteristics?

The answers can be very briefly reported. Under conditions of mutual control, the direct effect of gender/work on political radicalism reduces to insignificance. This is due to three coincident effects.

First, for reasons which are probably peculiar to the Norwegian setting, there is a clear tendency for radicalism to increase with age. Since most new jobs are in the service sector, and since most of these are taken by younger women, the general trend toward youthful conservatism (in 1980–81) is reflected in the gender/work variable.

Second, there is an equally strong tendency for union activists to prefer radical leftist options. Since unionization is stronger in the blue-collar occupations, workers, and—unexpectedly—particularly women workers, score higher on the radicalism scale.

Finally, there is the effect of preoccupational socialization. Not unexpectedly, there is in Norway—as in many democracies—a very strong tendency for adult ideological preference to reflect parental party preference during childhood. Though most of this effect works directly on radical-conservative preferences, some of it also seems to influence and work through job selection and job type. There is a combined tendency, in other words, for children of socialist-leaning parents to choose blue-collar occupations and children of bourgeois-leaning parents to choose service occupations.[8]

Taken as a whole, the results of the Norwegian project indicate that job characteristics themselves exert very little effect on adult ideological preference. In terms of relative explanatory power, a ranking of the four variables discussed above shows that parental party preference alone accounts for nearly 60 percent of the variance in political radicalism. Age contributes an additional 24 percent; union activism another 15 percent; and the combined effects of gender and work less than 2 percent.

Ideological orientation is thus primarily attributable to family socialization and secondarily to a nonspecific effect related to aging. As it is difficult to understand the latter effect as a result of the aging process itself, it seems reasonable to attribute it to a generational effect deriving from either radicalizing work conditions (of the type outlined above) or a general radical political climate during the early work-life of the older cohorts (see Delli Carpini, chap. 1, in this volume). Norwegian workers and lower-level employees between the ages of fifty and sixty-five had entered the workforce (assuming minimum education) in the 1932–47 period. This was a period of strong radical attraction to the left and equally strong rejection of the right, beginning with the Great Depression and concluding with the struggle against fascist occupation. The learning effects of this period *could* account for the greater radical proclivity of those over fifty; just as Norway's recent conservative resurgence is to a large degree attributable to a "new-right" attraction among today's youth (Lafferty and Knutson 1981).

Either way, we are confronted with factors which are both external to the production process itself (as a learning setting) and seemingly of a more permanent ideological nature. If so, we are left with a single work-related factor which may function as an element of change in adult socialization: union organization and activity. What emerges as most interesting here, however, is the fact that this variable is as weak as it is. Causal analysis shows that union activity *is* strongly related to the nature of the work sector—i.e. mining and manufacturing, commercial activity, personal services, etc.—and that the relationship remains strong when controlled for gender, parental party preference, age, and manual-vs.-permanent employment. This means that there is a clear work-sector effect on union organization and activity but that the effect is not "carried through" with equal strength to political radicalism.

What this indicates in turn is that there are clearly differentiated socializing effects attaching to the work sector in regard to the level of union activity, but that these differences are only slightly reflected in ideological orientation. The work sectors which are positively related to union activity are mining, petro-chemicals, raw metals, shipbuilding, and the production of heavy machinery. In other words, those same types of occupation which were shown above to have been previously related to radicalism (in Norway), tend now to be re-lated only to unionism. Those branches showing a most negative relationship to unionism are wholesale and retail trade, restaurants and hotels, and other "personal services." Other branches show, in general, no relationship at all with the variable.

If we relate these results to the general Marxist learning model, it appears that, in a highly developed society such as Norway, the nature of the work process itself tells us practically nothing about the radical or moderate pro-clivities of workers. When it comes to radicalism, it is the factors which are external to work itself which mainly account for ideological variance. Union-ism in general is also related to ideological preference, but it is an effect which does not mediate the nature of work itself. The latter effect does make clear, however, that the general ideological profile of a country will stand in direct relation to the degree of labor organization.

It could be objected, of course, that it is not differences *within* the lower categories of the division of labor which should be decisive but rather the differences between these categories and all *other* categories of work. In re-lation to the problem at hand, however, the foregoing analysis renders the question moot. Even if workers and lower-level employees are more prone to radical socialist orientation than other occupational categories, we now know that it is not an effect attributable to the conditions of work. As it turns out, the bivariate relationship between political radicalism and the different cate-gories of the occupational spectrum is relatively weak at the outset and re-duces to minimal significance when controlled for the same measures which proved important for workers and lower-level employees (parental party pref-erence, age, and occupational-group activity, including employer organiza-tions). To the degree that the Marxist learning model is dependent on work characteristics as a vital element of predicted class-ideology conjunctions, it is clearly irrelevant for Norwegian political culture.

In addition to the substantive findings for Norway, the above analysis illus-trates the clear need for both numerous relevant indicators and thorough sta-tistical control in this problem area. The overwhelming majority of empirical studies have, however, been highly particular case studies within specific na-tional settings at specific points in political history (e.g., Lipsitz 1964; Mur-phy and Morris 1961; Goldthorpe et al. 1968; Seeman 1972, 1975; Glantz 1958; Manis and Meltzer 1954). Very few of these studies operate with either comprehensive measures of political ideology or thorough controls for either cross-sectional or extraneous occupational effects. I hope that the analysis reported above can serve as an indication of what is minimally necessary for broad-based generalizations in this area.

Social Liberalism

A second major perspective on the adult learning potential of routinized low-status labor is the tradition of social liberalism. The roots of this tradition are usually traced to the work of John Stuart Mill, who is seen as a major bridge between the laissez-faire values of "classical liberalism" (or "utilitarianism") and the values of socialism. Mill's concern was for the dehumanizing effects that large-scale capitalist industrialism had on the lower classes. As the conditions of the modern proletariat—men, women, and children—became obnoxiously visible, Mill and his immediate English followers took upon themselves the task of finding solutions within the general sphere of liberalist values. The core idea of the approach was the notion of lower-class education: education for the purpose of executing the function of democratic (*liberal* democratic) citizenship (cf. Thompson 1970, 1976; Macpherson 1977). This "education" was clearly understood by Mill to involve both formal schooling in state-supported schools and the informal education one could receive through an expanded participation in decision-making processes in general.

In the terms of Thompson's recent exposition, the guiding principle of Mill's approach was an overriding democratic need for both competent leadership and personal development (1976). If democracy is to survive and prosper, it must find a way to coincidentally procure an effective and stable mode of governance along with a developing and increasingly competent citizenry. Decrying (and fearing) the socio-organizational determinism of Marxism, on the one hand, and deploring the neglectful determinism of unfettered market capitalism, on the other, Mill sought to improve the one without embracing the other.

It is from and within this general tradition—as later pursued in differing ideological shades by G. D. H. Cole, Sidney and Beatrice Webb, Ernest Barker, R. H. Tawney, and John Dewey—that a broad subfield of "democracy and learning" has gradually emerged in the social sciences. This subfield can truly be said to be one of the very few areas in social research which is specifically devoted to the question of adult socialization.[9]

The orientation itself arises from a conviction that class conditions are biased in socialization consequences and that such consequences not only can but should be remedied by changing central areas of adult experience. Contrary to the Marxist model, which originally hoped and expected that the negative learning experiences of the proletariat would produce the class opposition necessary for revolutionary conflict, the social-liberalist position hopes and trusts that the relations of production can be at least harmonized (and at most democratized) so as to condition citizens to the demands and advantages of political democracy.

The one views adult learning as leading to revolution and a new system of equality of condition; the other sees it as the means to an improved system of equality of capacity. The faith that Marxism places in changing property relations, social liberalism places in changing personal relations.

The beliefs and values of social liberalism have been reflected in several subfields of the social sciences, most importantly industrial sociology, administrative science, human relations, group dynamics, and studies of "the quality of working life (QWL)." All of these areas have been concerned with different facets of the relationship between the technical, organizational, and interpersonal characteristics of work, on the one hand, and the personalities, capacities, values, attitudes, and performance of workers, on the other. The vast majority of these studies (and the literature *is* vast) have been concerned with what Ambrecht (1975) refers to as the "internal" dynamics and consequences of work variation. How do changes in work variables affect personal and interpersonal characteristics as these work back on and affect the productive process itself? It is safe to say that most of these studies have been concerned with "humanizing" the work situation of large-scale, routinized industrial labor: an attempt, so to say, to apply the social-liberal perspective within the capitalist sphere of production itself.[10]

Mill's original vision had to do, however, with the relationship *between* work and democratic citizenship. As a specific problematic, this question was not brought to the forefront of contempory democratic research prior to Carole Pateman's massively influential *Participation and Democratic Theory* (1970). With explicit reference to Mill's work (viewed, however, as a source secondary to Rousseau), Pateman made a case for what she termed the "educational effect" of workplace participation, a case that has dominated the discussion since. The strength of Pateman's argument was twofold: she effected a clear boundary-setting within the so-called "classical theory" of democracy between its representative and participatory traditions, and she moved the entire discussion of participation from normative polemics to normative empiricism. It was the right book at the right time: both a correction and a stimulus in an area of growing practical and theoretical interest.

Had not "participation" become a central issue in labor-management relations at about the same time as Pateman's book appeared, there most probably would have been little more to report on in the present context. As it is, the problem which she presented and defended has become an outstanding example of the promise and frustration attaching to normative-empirical research. It is also as clear an example of the difficulties encountered in the area of adult political socialization as one is likely to find. Pateman's "two hypotheses" on the relevance and validity of participatory theory—the central role of work in shaping political orientations and the particular learning effects deriving from participatory authority structures—place the question of adult political learning squarely on the normative-empirical line. Numerous researchers, with numerous interests, have taken up her challenge, and, though the issue is far from resolved, it is greatly clarified. In the following, I will argue that, more than fifteen years later, we still do not know if Pateman's hopeful expectations are *generally* valid. But we do know what those expectations reasonably imply, and we know further what must be present, empirically, to decide if they are in fact fulfilled.[11]

The clarification of Pateman's problematic has progressed along both theoretical and empirical lines. The need for theoretical clarification derives largely from the fact that the original formulation was strongly colored by the democratic debates of the 1960s. A major purpose was to clarify and reorient the normative discussion so as to make the participatory position acceptable on different grounds than had theretofore been the case. Much of the presentation was thus of an oppositional, critical nature. The substance of the participatory learning theory was sketched out and strongly defended, but details were lacking. It has, therefore, been up to succeeding "participationists" and their critics to fill out the approach by specifying more clearly just what type of political learning is involved, so as to be able to move on to problems of operationalization and testing.

It is still most worthwhile, however, to begin with one of Pateman's own statements on the nature of the proposition:

> The theory of participatory democracy is built round the central assertion that individuals and their institutions cannot be considered in isolation from one another. The existence of representative institutions at national level is not sufficient for democracy; for maximum participation by all the people at that level socialization, or "social training," for democracy must take place in other spheres in order that the necessary individual attitudes and psychological qualities can be developed. This development takes place through the process of participation itself. The major function of participation in the theory of participatory democracy is therefore an educative one, educative in the very widest sense, including both the psychological aspect and the gaining of practice in democratic skills and procedures. (1970, p. 42)

We find in this statement all the essentials of a reformulation of the social-liberalist position:

First, there is no reference to either class relationships or property relationships as essential elements of the proposition. The posited causality between participation, learning, and democratic citizenship is generalized within the existing order. Neither Pateman, nor any of the other researchers who build strongly on her work, introduce the problem of ownership as a necessary preliminary to the discussion. It is not that they don't see the issue as relevant; just that it is not considered to be conceptually essential to the learning thesis in question.[12]

Second, we see the "central assertion" as to the interdependency between individuals and their institutions. It is this premise more than any other which casts the Pateman persuasion as a theory of adult socialization. Personalities and personal capabilities are viewed—almost exclusively, one might say— as products of institutional socialization. The underlying conviction is Rousseau's notion of "man as a social product": a *tabula rasa* filled in by the guiding strictures of contingent authority structures. Individuals are neither biologically nor socially determined, but merely institutionally conditioned. Not only can that conditioning be modified by revising institutional settings and procedures, but that is the *only* way it can and should be modified.

Third, we see an all-important contextual aspect of the position: its specific formulation in relation to the weaknesses of existing "representative institutions at the national level." Pateman's concern, and the concern of social liberalism in general, is primarily in the problem of eliminating inequalities in the usage of national democratic opportunities. Participation at the national level is "not sufficient." It must be supplemented so that it can be maximized. Pateman was not, therefore—as so many of her critics, both friendly and otherwise, would have her—an advocate of communitarianism. She was not primarily concerned with creating new personalities of a self-effacing, other-oriented, altruistic bent, but rather with developing and improving the capacities necessary to function as responsible and effective democratic citizens. Her position can thus be seen as primarily a thesis on political learning for greater political justice, not a thesis on expressivist, self-esteem politics (Elster 1983a, 1983b) or on communitarianism (Kelso 1978).

What has perhaps caused confusion on this point is a final aspect of her position: the posited results of the learning in question. While the "gaining of practice in democratic skills and procedures" is straightforward, and directly in line with a number of John Stuart Mill's own formulations, the "psychological aspect" is clearly much more vague. A close reading of Pateman reveals, however, that what she is primarily referring to here is a sense of political efficacy: a view of oneself as an entitled and capable citizen. She also refers to a great deal of research which indicates that greater discretion on the job leads to other feelings of well-being, satisfaction, and self-esteem, but she is careful not to give these results equal status with the notion of political competence and efficacy.

Taken together, the four aspects of Pateman's approach constitute what appears to be a very specific proposition within the area of adult socialization. If industrial workers, who are otherwise relatively inactive in traditional electoral politics, are given greater opportunity to participate in the decisions affecting their daily work situations, they will gradually learn the rules and techniques of democratic decision-making, and they will gradually develop a personal sense of political competence and efficacy which should in turn motivate them toward more active political citizenship. Once workplace democracy is fully instituted—which means conditions of what Pateman calls "full participation," rather than "pseudo" or "partial" participation (1970, pp. 68–71)—the relationship between socioeconomic status and political participation should be dissolved. Beyond this major goal of equality in the conditions of instrumental democratic citizenship, Pateman also mentions that participation may increase both citizen responsibility toward and integration in the democratic collectivity, but these are only briefly referred to as "subsidiary hypotheses" (p. 43).

Democratization and Political "Spillover": The Development of the Proposition

Within the general area of industrial or occupational sociology, the type of proposition put forth by Pateman is known as "the spillover effect" (Gardell 1976; Staines 1980). As opposed to the notion that work has little intrinsic importance for most blue-collar workers—that work primarily fulfills an instrumentalist, "compensatory" function through its economic rewards—the spillover approach sees work as a major source of extraoccupational values and behavior patterns. Pateman's proposition thus goes to the heart of an empirical controversy in the sociology of labor which is at least as old as Dubin's work from the 1950s (1958), and which was given most prominent attention in a political context by the work of Goldthorpe et al. (1968) in Great Britain.[13]

The first line of defense for Pateman's proposition as descriptive theory is, therefore, against those who would question its basic socialization premise from the outset. Even so central a figure in the spillover tradition as Bertil Gardell, who has contributed enormously to the understanding of job conditioning, has warned against a lack of balance between the compensatory and socializing aspects of work (1976).

Such warnings obviously have little appeal for the proponents of workplace democracy. They are spillover theorists of the first—or rather second—order. Not only do they predict work-derived changes in personality, interpersonal relations, and social perceptions (the traditional dependent variables of spillover sociologists), but they anticipate that these changes carry through to the level of political action. In Ambrecht's (1975) elucidation of the idea, for example, the implied causality is seen as spanning both the "intraorganizational" and "extraorganizational" effects of "changes in organizational struc-

ture," with the extraorganizational effects stipulated as both "increased political efficacy" and "increased political activity." Likewise, Elden's (1981)
influential "three-step-model" covers the "design of work organization,"
"quality-of-working-life consequences," and "political consequences."

The importance of these model stipulations by empirically oriented researchers lies in their clear investment in the *total* range of the postulated
learning effects. This is necessary to make the problem interesting for adult
political socialization, since the question of nonpolitical spillover effects is
relatively clearly established. Staines's (1980) review of the spillover-
compensation controversy is resolved in favor of spillover, with the apparent
exception of heavy physical labor, where spillover is, understandably, at a
minimum. The "cutting edge" of Pateman's proposition—and therein the reason for her dominant role in the present work—is thus at the point of conversion between social-psychological and political effects.

Even within this clearly formulated and relatively narrow dependent-
variable range the problem is far from simple. The fact is that most spillover
studies acknowledge the clear possibility that spillover works both ways, i.e.
that off-the-job activities and change can also reflect back on individual job
behavior. The same problem has, of course, been central to the discussion of
the relationship between feelings of political efficacy and political participation: Which comes first? The question is far from academic in the present
context since Pateman herself makes no serious mention of the problem, accepting instead the implied unidirectional causality from workplace involvement to sense of efficacy to political action. We can thus identify an initial
point of critical control for extraneous effects in the logic of the proposition
itself; i.e. the need to demonstrate that any variation in both feelings of political efficacy and political involvement are primarily the result of altered working conditions and not the reflection of other extraoccupational influences.

A second vital point of control arises in connection with the variable to be
manipulated: workplace democratization. The key question here is, how
much democratization is necessary, where, for how long, to provide the predicted results?

Though somewhat unclear on this point, Pateman indicates that, while a
sense of political efficacy can probably be developed that is proportionate to
the quality of participation ("pseudo," "partial," or "full") at a "lower level"
of decision-making ("control of day-to-day shop floor activity"), the other
major aspect of the proposition—skill and understanding in the ways, means,
and consequences of democratic decision-making—will have to be developed
at the "higher level" ("decisions that relate to the running of the whole enterprise"). For reasons of empirical necessity (i.e. a general lack of higher-level
democratization), the follow-up studies have generally focused only on the
prospect and consequences of lower-level participation. Interestingly enough,

however, the majority of analyses have not stipulated criteria of workplace democratization at this level, but have instead concentrated on criteria of job autonomy or job routinization. Whether or not these latter, task-oriented descriptions are part of an overall change in authority structures is a question that is usually neglected. To my knowledge, there are only two studies in the entire literature (Elden 1976, 1981, and Greenberg 1975, 1981a, 1981b, 1983) which include both specific schemes of democratization and specifically political dependent variables. A high degree of autonomy on the job is clearly not necessarily the same as participation in decision-making.

Finally, there is the question of theoretical precision and control in relation to the "predemocratic" situation, both as to the nature of the authority structure and the question of worker selection. The essence of the participatory proposition lies, once again, in its expectations for change. If one begins with a work setting which, for any number of possible contextual or historical reasons, is already politically activized without being internally democratized, or if one fails to control for exceptional factors in worker recruitment, the hypothesis may already be saved from the outset. Perhaps the greatest weakness in the entire persuasion in this regard is a near total neglect of the theoretical and empirical consequences of labor organization. (A problem to be illustrated below.) The theory builds on the prospect that blue-collar workers are disproportionately politically passive because they are made, or at least maintained, passive at work. Whether they actually are passive, and why they are or are not, must be demonstrated and not presumed.

In sum, the theory of adult socialization which supports and informs the Pateman variant of workplace democracy is a theory of political learning based on occupational role change in democratized authority structures. As such, it poses strong and clear demands for the control of antecedent, processual, and consequential factors. As the following brief overview of the field makes clear, these demands have proved difficult to accommodate.

Democratization and Political Activization: The Findings

There is a broad consensus among researchers in this area that there are very few empirical studies which manage to cover the entire causal range of the participatory proposition (Ambrecht 1975; Elden 1976, 1981; Greenberg 1975, 1981; Cooper 1984). With only one exception (Almond and Verba 1965), none of the studies referred to by Pateman demonstrate the postulated political consequences. Cooper (1984), in the most comprehensive review of the literature to date, cites several works which *seem* to show that greater work autonomy contributes to greater community and political activity, but the overall impression is immediately qualified:

While all of these studies are clearly suggestive of potentially politicizing effects of increased autonomy, they do not address the question of "democratization" directly. The structural characteristics of
work that have been found to be related to political potency, efficacy,
and involvement in outside social and political organizations are, at
best, only partial indicators of the democratized work structure.
Furthermore, in all cases "autonomy" has been conceived as an individual measure—i.e. the extent of decision making, flexibility,
and discretion involved in one's own job, not in interaction with a
well-defined, governing group of co-workers. More importantly,
none of these studies have involved a change to a democratized ar-
rangement from a traditional work set-up. (Cooper 1984, p. 77)

Among the major contributions, there have in fact emerged only two studies which consistently are given high scores for having conceived, operationalized, and demonstrated the proposition: Elden's (1976, 1981) study of "self-
managing" work groups in a California paper-product factory, and Karasek's
(1978) study of Swedish panel data from national surveys in 1968 and 1974.
In addition to these two projects, it is important to look at the first and only
comparative effort by Almond and Verba (1965), as well as the important
analysis of worker-owned plywood cooperatives in the American northwest
by Greenberg (1975, 1981a, 1981b, 1983). These studies not only provide
us with the best data available in the area, they clearly illustrate the difficulties
encountered in producing empirical confirmation of the normative thesis.
Discussion of them will be followed up by further reference to the Norwegian
project introduced above.

The Almond and Verba Study. In what remains as the only comparative analysis of adult political socialization, Almond and Verba show that, for four of
the five nations studied, workers who reported that they were "consulted on
the job" had considerably higher scores on "feelings of subjective political
competence" than did workers who were not consulted (1963, table 11.6).
The differences were, moreover, stronger for "unskilled" than for "skilled"
labor, and they were also apparently "cumulative" when viewed against reports of decision-making participation in both the family and school. The
latter analysis indicated that subjective political competence was highest for
those reporting all three types of decision-making experience, but it also
showed (for three of the five cases) that job participation was seemingly
enough to positively outweigh nonparticipation in either family or school
(Tables 11.7 and 11.8).

The strength of Almond and Verba's data lies in the confirmation of the
expected pattern across very diverse national settings, as well as in the controls for previous "nonpolitical" participatory experience. The major weak-

ness is the quality of the participation indicator, which is derived solely from personal reports on consultation without adequate controls for education. The clear differences among unskilled laborers (where education should not be a decisive factor) represent, however, findings of exceptional consistency and importance in this area. Of equal, but less encouraging, interest, is the fact that Almond and Verba's innovative comparative analysis has never (to my knowledge) been followed up within political science.

The Elden Study. Max Elden's study of autonomous work groups in a modern paper-product factory in Califonia is acknowledged to be one of the first and best studies specifically to employ the Pateman proposition. This is because Elden also devoted considerable attention to the logic of the proposition, integrating a broad spectrum of alternative theoretical approaches as well as a thorough update of the literature (1981).

Though Elden's study is meticulously thought-out and executed (with participant observation, in-depth interviews, and multiple-item, multiple-scale questionnaires), there are a number of operational-methodological weaknesses.

First, for reasons beyond his control, he was not allowed (by the firm leadership) to inquire as to off-the-job political activity. His dependent variables thus contain only a single measure with political content: a four-item index of political efficacy. Aside from the fact that interpretation of this particular index is extremely difficult, there is the further problem that the strongest relationship reported—that between political efficacy and an index for "satisfaction with work"—is barely significant (Elden 1981, p. 50).[14]

Even the meaning of this slight relationship is, however, open to question. First of all, there is the rather interesting problem that the relationship itself is for *internal* variation in what is assumed to be a relatively democratized workplace. Here we have the question of why some of the workers are "more satisfied" and possessed of greater feelings of political efficacy, while others (the clear majority) are not. Lacking controls for other, nondemocratized, work processes, we would like to know why the democratization scheme is selective in its posited consequences.

Of even greater importance, however, is the fact (pointed out by Elden) that none of the analyses carried out are *causal*. The method employed is a very special form of dimensional analysis (the so-called "McQuitty method" (1957) of correlational "clusters"). This technique tells us nothing about whether the presumed independent variables are in fact meaningfully related to the measure of political efficacy, nor do we have any controls for the final relationship itself. Because of the large variation in the size of the bivariate "path" correlations, there is a strong possibility that the efficacy measure is not significantly affected by the crucial democratization variables.

Finally, there is the problem of external controls for nonjob characteristics, particularly education. Elden admits that the workforce in general at his plant was "relatively young, well-educated, affluent, and mobile" (1976, p. 173). This means that we should expect, from the outset, higher general scores on the political efficacy scale, as efficacy has been demonstrated in countless other studies ("overwhelmingly" so, according to Milbrath and Goel [1977, p. 60]) to be related to higher social status. It is also clearly related to political activity itself, a variable which, as we have seen, is not covered by Elden's study. The possibility is thus present that Elden's workers are subjectively efficacious for reasons not adequately controlled for. Elden does report that education was later introduced into the dimensional analysis. But as a method of control, the McQuitty technique leaves a number of questions unanswered; the relationship between education and political efficacy is, for example, not reported.

For all of these reasons, Elden's highly important study must be seen— insofar as the Pateman proposition is concerned—as a relatively weak case of confirmation.

The Karasek Study. The fact that Robert Karasek's (1978) study of male Swedish workers is so often presented as the strongest available evidence for the thesis in question is due to both the size and nature of the sample. Karasek's is the only analysis which: (a) presumes to have all the elements of the problem; (b) has a data sample which is both large (N = 1,451) and nationally representative; and (c) is also "longitudinal" (i.e. contains data on change over time). In general, the study is thorough, imaginative—and relatively difficult to grasp. Space allows for only the briefest of comments.

The strength of the analysis is generally portrayed as lying in the fact that it contains two separate measures of political activity, and that it clearly shows that conditions of "job discretion" and "job demands" are positively related to these measures, both synchronically and over time. Here again, there are reasons for accepting the findings with some caution.

To begin with, Karasek's analysis is based on the *entire* nonrural male labor-force in Sweden. The sample thus ranges across the entire hierarchy of occupational stratification, thereby posing particular problems for the control of nonwork status effects. This is particularly crucial since the independent measures of "job discretion" and "job demands" are not related to any specific democratization schemes but are derived solely from personal job reports (cross-checked against expert rankings). The variable, "job discretion," for example, is really a measure of "skill discretion" which is constructed from personal reports on both the level of education required for the job and the degree of perceived repetition of job task. Not only are there no indicators of specific decision-making procedures, but the most problematic control variable—education—is built into the analysis at the start.

Second, the two measures of political activity are also very special. "Elite political participation" refers to "speaking at meetings, writing articles, attempts to influence, filing complaints on one's behalf"; and "mass political participation" refers to "political or labor union activity (more than passive membership), and demonstrations" (Karasek 1978, p. 12). Both measures appear to be at the opposite margins of traditional "political" activity—a fact which is clearly confirmed by the results of the synchronic analysis. Whereas "elite" activity shows the strongest single relationship with discretion and demands (in comparison with six nonpolitical forms of leisure activity), "mass" activity actually shows *directly opposite* tendencies. Here it is the workers with "the most demanding and restrictive jobs" (the "oppressed workers" as Karasek calls them) who are *most* active in "labor and political organizations" (p. 15). Karasek's comment on this latter finding that "We cannot say . . . that the 'socialization' process which can account for the majority of our other activity patterns applies universally" is a clear understatement of one of the study's most significant negative findings.

As for the longitudinal analysis, Karasek here relies on panel data between 1968 and 1974. On the basis of changes in self-reports on job discretion and job demands, it is reported that "workers who have become more 'passive' have reduced their participation in political activity" over the six-year period. It is also reported in the study's conclusions that "political participation declines as jobs become 'passive'" (p. 25). If I understand Karasek's presentation here correctly, however, this conclusion is not supported by the data (table 3). What the data indicate is that *all* categories of reported job change show increases in total political activity between the two time-points, but that those who report more "active" job characteristics at the second time-point also report somewhat greater levels of political activity.[15] Furthermore, there is no mention of the possibility that changes in job description can be attributed to job mobility, or that such mobility could itself be attributable to other social-developmental variables.

For this and other reasons, Karasek's study does not represent, in my opinion, as clear a case of confirmation as is usually maintained. To the contrary, the findings on "mass political action" constitute a direct contradiction of the thesis. What is at issue here is the entire understanding of worker socialization as a result of either collective organization or job characteristics. As mentioned above, the former is almost totally neglected in the workplace socialization literature, despite clear evidence of the mobilizing effects which labor organizations have on working-class citizens (Verba, Nie, and Kim 1978; Lafferty 1981, 1984; Damgaard 1980).

The Greenberg Study. Though hardly a favorite among worker-participation enthusiasts, Edward Greenberg's study of worker-owned plywood factories is by far the most thorough and decisive in the area. The ambivalence with which Greenberg's findings have been received is attributable to the negative image they cast over the socializing hopes (as to both learning theory and ideologicization) of participation advocates. The latter are generally invested in the social-liberalist belief that participatory involvement will, in and of itself, lead to more active and public-oriented citizens, but Greenberg shows that, while increased activity *may* result, it is neither due solely to the participatory experience itself nor is it very public-oriented. The clear implication of Greenberg's project is that workplace democracy never functions in an ideological vacuum and will therefore never render context-free results. Despite the fact that the plywood co-ops fulfilled all the criteria for a fully democratized workplace, and that they had been in operation for more than twenty years at the time of the study, the results did not resemble Pateman's expectations. Or did they?

The question is necessary because in many ways Greenberg's study raises more doubts than it resolves. It is for this reason, of course, that the study warrants a central place in the field. Having attended to all three of the critical control points outlined above, Greenberg's findings emerge as lucid, valid— and provocative.

The study can be summarized in terms of two major conclusions: (1) Worker-owners were clearly more active in local political affairs than were workers in similar production enterprises which were not democratized. The effect also held within the co-ops themselves: the more active participants at work were also clearly more politically active in the community (Greenberg 1981b). (2) Worker-owners were *not*, however, more "public-spirited," "altruistic," or "egalitarian" in their socioeconomic values and beliefs. To the contrary, they showed greater preference for "classic-liberal," "market-oriented" values than did the workers at the traditional, hierarchic plywood plants (1981a).

As a major qualifying factor in relation to both of these conclusions, Greenberg also presents data on the motivational basis for joining the co-op to begin with. He here shows that the chief reason for choosing this organizational option was "pecuniary": i.e. "it would be a good financial investment;" "the wages were good;" or "I wanted a guaranteed job in case times got bad." Furthermore, political activity in the community was correlated with these reasons (primarily the first two), but not with other reasons of a more cooperative organizational nature.

The major implication of Greenberg's study—which he has himself generalized into a comprehensive contextual approach to the problem (Greenberg

1983)—is that the Pateman proposition, in either its primary "political-activization" sense or its secondary "public-spirited" sense, cannot be tested without information about the ideological and motivational makeup of the "predemocratic" workforce. Stated another way, Greenberg's study indicates that, whereas workplace democracy *may* heighten interest-protecting political activity off the job (we don't know how active the "pecuniary" worker-owners were prior to entering the cooperative), the ideological nature of that activity is unpredictable.

Work and Political Involvement in Norway

It was with the specific intent of clarifying the more questionable aspects of the major studies in the area that the Norwegian democracy project aimed at a thorough coverage of workplace characteristics in its national survey. As one of the two or three leading Western countries in the area of democratized (not democratic) decision-making processes at work, Norway provides the minimum conditions for a national-survey approach.[16] Before comprehensive and standardized probes can be used constructively on a national basis, there must be something to survey. In Norway, there are three major types of generalized democratization reforms, covering three different levels of decision-making within a broad spectrum of industrial, business, and service enterprises (Lafferty 1984; Gustavsen and Hunnius 1981; Elden 1979). First, there is the legal prescription for at least one-third worker representation on the governing bodies of all joint stock companies with more than fifty employees (with numerous other private and public concerns following suit). Second, there is the provision through negotiated agreements for fifty-fifty worker-management representation on numerous types of production, personnel, and safety councils at the middle level of management. And, finally, there is the comprehensive provision for rights to information, consultation, control over work tasks, and training at the level of individual work-procedures included in the Work Environment Act of 1977.

Using a variety of measures to tap activity in all three areas, the project conducted analyses of both the institutional and personal aspects of workplace democratization. Measures of efficacy (similar to those used by Almond/Verba and Elden) and measures of actual political involvement (in "conventional" local and national electoral politics) were checked against the existence of democratic reforms at work as well as the actual level of involvement in these reforms. Thorough controls were made for both the nature of the occupational setting (size, branch, type of production, etc.) and for the socioeconomic characteristics of the subpopulation. The following references are again only for blue-collar workers and lower-level employees.

The most significant results in the present context can be succinctly stated as constituting a clear case of confirmation for a "strong" variant of the Pate-man thesis. The findings indicate a marked tendency for political involvement off the job to increase with both the degree of institutional democratization and the level of personal involvement in decision-making processes (Lafferty 1985). The more democratized the workplace and the greater the autonomy and decision-making involvement of the individual worker, the greater the degree of involvement in conventional political activities. The bivariate cor-relations are stronger for individual involvement than for the degree of insti-tutional reform, and the levels of association are only slightly reduced under controls for union membership, education, and gender.

Furthermore—and perhaps of greatest importance for the question of con-tinuity vs. change—the effect of workplace involvement was also indepen-dent of political socialization in the family. Based on a measure of the amount of political discussion which respondents had engaged in with their parents, family socialization proved to be an equally strong and *separate* predictor of conventional political involvement. The relationship between the two types of socialization was again controlled for union involvement, education, and gender, with no meaningful reduction in the strength of the two correlations.[17]

These findings constitute the strongest single case of empirical support for the Pateman proposition yet provided. They are based on a large-scale na-tional sample; with a necessary minimum of democratization reforms in ef-fect; with the necessary variables for adequate operationalization and control; and with—as documented by the above overview of the earlier studies—a fair share of pretest skepticism on the part of the principal investigator. The overall implication of the results is clear. *Widespread democratization of rou-tinized labor processes on the basis of uniform legal reforms contributes an independent positive effect to democratic citizenship.*

As with all studies of such diverse and interdependent social phenomena, there are certain "footnotes" of direct relevance for further analysis. First, the Norwegian study does not contain data on the effects of change itself. Tech-nically, we cannot say definitively that it is democratization as a process over time which has produced the spillover effects. Because the study controls, however, for those variables which normally account for high levels of polit-ical involvement, there is no obvious reason to believe that current activity patterns reflect "predemocratic" proclivities. The burden of falsification has at a minimum been shifted into new areas of understanding.

Second, it is important to report that the results of the Norwegian project do *not* confirm a "weak" version of the Pateman proposition: the expectation that workplace involvement should also increase feelings of political efficacy. There was, in fact, no relationship between the two types of phenomena. Numerous subanalyses indicated that the reason for this was that political efficacy is largely an upper-status phenomenon, *and* that it is more a result of feedback from actual political participation than a reflection of other background determinants. The Pateman learning-effect appears, in other words, to work directly on political involvement among low-status occupations without having to be first developed through convictions of political efficacy. The learning models enunciated by Ambrecht and Elden (as well as the dominant learning model in the study of political participation in general) require substantial revision.

Had the report from the Norwegian project stopped here, we would, at a minimum, have established a clear benchmark for further research and discussion. The project has, however, pushed the problematization somewhat further in relation to a variable of increasing importance in the area: gender. Space allows for only two brief references, both deriving from the analysis of statistical interaction. As opposed to the normal practice (particularly in the area under investigation) of limiting analyses to "zero-order" relationships and additive effects, interaction analysis recognizes the possibility of multiplicative effects deriving from combinations of variable categories and levels. While the results from such analyses seldom invalidate robust additive explanations, they can provide important insights into critical deviant subareas.

This was the case for the Norwegian data in relation to the combination of gender and union organization. As stated above, both of these variables were introduced as separate control variables in relation to the socialization effects of both family and workplace without having any serious effect on the model. When they were combined, however, into separate categories of organized and unorganized men and women, two findings of interest emerged.

First, while the relationship between workplace involvement and conventional political involvement remains equally strong for organized men and women and for unorganized men, it is totally nonexistent for unorganized women (nearly all of whom are lower-level employees). We thus have an important nuance on the basic results stressed above. Unionization is apparently a contributory factor for women, but not for men, when it comes to the spillover effect between work and politics. Unorganized men manage to convert the learning experiences of job autonomy to political action without the supporting context of collective organization, while unorganized women apparently do not. The results can thus be said to offer a challenge to the position's original gender-neutral formulation: a challenge which Carole Pateman not only explicitly accepts but strongly endorses (see her article in Crouch and Heller 1983, pp. 3–34).

Second, there is a similar insight with direct relevance for Greenberg's perspective on the dependency between ideology and context. Norway is, in Greenberg's terminology, a "market-mediated society" (Greenberg 1983). By this he means that the power position of the labor movement is such as to be able to intervene in, and "mediate," market relationships, both directly through collective bargaining and indirectly through the political power of the state. Having found that workplace democracy in a "nonmediated" society like the United States does not live up to the ideological expectations of the more socialist-oriented formulations of the theory ("public-spiritedness" and a greater attraction to collectivist equality), he speculates that the effect might nonetheless obtain in a society like Norway.

Having at hand a broad spectrum of survey data on attitudes, values, and beliefs, the Norwegian project was able to investigate Greenberg's hypothesis in considerable detail. If we concentrate only on the gender/unionization interaction, the results show that there is no relationship at all between measures of "public-spiritedness vs. market capitalism" and workplace involvement for men (whether organized or not), but that there is a slight positive relationship for unorganized women and a very strong positive relationship for organized women. The interaction between gender and collective organization thus appears to have an even more decisive influence on political ideology than it does on political involvement. Women who are autonomous and active in workplace decision-making are consistently more "public-spirited," "collectivist," or "egalitarian" than either uninvolved women or men in general.

These latter results raise questions of a type which the line of research here reported has thus far neglected: questions as to the differential effects of gender integration in both work and organized labor. Being less affected and less benefited by the ideologies and stratagems of *both* business and organized labor, women are seemingly more open than men for exactly that type of learning effect posited by the "public-spirited" hypothesis. Lower-status women who become activated through workplace events objectify the barriers and limitations attaching to the male-dominated spheres of business and labor, and thereby see their own interests as best served by more general collectivist solutions. If so, the differences between a "mediated" and "nonmediated" market society may lie in directions considerably different from those anticipated by Greenberg. A transcendence of capitalist interests in the direction of public-spirited socialism may also require a transcendence of institutionalized male dominance on both sides of the corporatist bargaining table. Or is it perhaps even the case that the struggle against patriarchy is the only remaining way to public-spirited socialism?

Conclusions

The present chapter has concentrated on the problem of adult political learning as a reflection of job characteristics at the lower end of the occupational hierarchy. By treating the problem in terms of the Marxist and social-liberalist orientations, I have tried to cover in analytic depth the elements of the most prevalent approaches in the area. The goal has been to explicate the nature of the problem *as* a research problem, rather than to resummarize a broad spectrum of existing findings, problematizations, and overviews. By concentrating only on those contributions which have specifically introduced the political aspect of the problem (here interpreted as "conventional politics"), I have given priority to problem-specificity rather than breadth-of-findings.[18]

From the point of view of the question of continuity vs. change in adult socialization patterns, we can derive two very different sets of generalizations from the two problem-areas investigated.

Insofar as the relationship between routinized labor and political ideology is concerned, there is a clear tendency toward a weakening of this dependency in advanced industrial settings. Whereas certain occupational situations have, under conditions of intense industrialization and ideological polarization, been associated with relatively "radical" worker responses, these dependencies become attenuated in the course of "postindustrial" development. Not only does the scope of "blue-collar labor" shrink—with a gender-specific shift in lower-status labor from industry to commerce and the services—but there also develops an increasingly "abstract" relationship between work and politics. What is left of the industrial sector consists of progressively better-organized, better-trained, and better-paid *men*. Their strategic position in relation to both state and economy is strong, integrated, and generally supportive. Depending on the institutional links between labor organizations and political parties (which vary considerably from country to country), ideological tendencies will be, at the most, weakly determined by organizational pressures, and, at the least, free-floating in the electoral or ad-hoc-movement market.

Either way, the overriding general tendency is for basic values to be more determinative of ideological preference than occupational situs. In sum, insofar as the conditions of industrial labor exert an independent effect on adult ideology, they do so through the mediation of labor organizations with diverse ideologies. The weaker the ties of these organizations to political parties, the weaker the mediation of ideology, and the greater the play of extraoccupational learning (conditioning) factors. Whereas blue-collar labor was once of an integrated piece with the socializing conditions of working-class life and culture, it is now of a piece with corporatist postindustrial consumerism.[19]

The situation is very different within the lower echelons of commercial and service labor. Less organized, less educated, less well paid, and mostly female, these multicolored "collars" have not yet developed a distinct organizational-ideological profile. We have, in fact, very little to go on in the way of empirical studies of the ideological consequences of woman-dominated routinized labor in these areas, but we have good reason to assume that, even if the type of structural conditions outlined by Lipset should also prove "radicalizing" here, the result will in all probability be a new variant of feminist socialism. If large numbers of women are concentrated in highly routinized jobs with poor pay, poor mobility, and authority structures which are asymmetric as to *both* status and gender, the question of continuity vs. change in political ideology will, eventually, be put to a critical test. More than any other area, perhaps, it is here that future research on adult political learning offers its greatest promise (see Carroll, chap. 8, in this volume).

Finally, a brief comment on the second major problem area covered: workplace democratization. Operating on the conviction that this is an area with a particular relevance for the question of adult political learning, the treatment here has gone into critical-analytical depth in relation to both normative theory and empirical research. As a central feature of the social- liberalist tradition, workplace democratization goes to the heart of the continuity-vs.-change problem. As normative theory, the goal of the persuasion has been to argue for the transformative potential of democratized authority structures at work, and as an empirical subfield, the task has been to substantiate that norm. In trying to clarify both the theory and the findings, I have portrayed the normative aspect as being characterized by a general positive bias in both the generation and interpretation of results. With only a single major exception (Greenberg), the search for confirmation has been presented as successful, though, as I have tried to show, there is fair room for critical dissent.

It was thus as a skeptical adherent that the author approached his own analysis of the proposition—and I was that much more surprised when the results turned out as positive as they did. Having stipulated the type of critical controls that a decisive analysis of the proposition should attend to, and having applied these controls as well as possible in relation to a representative national data base, I was pleased to see the results emerge as clearly supportive of the normative predictions. The institutionalization of democratic reforms in Norwegian workplaces has had a clear positive effect on conventional political involvement.

So as not to conclude on *too* positive a note, however, let me round off with a final word of caution. As already indicated, the entire participatory orientation is strongly optimistic as to the political learning potential of workplace democracy. This is as it should be in normative-empirical research where a major goal of the enterprise is to change things for the better. In addition to the problem of interpretation which such enthusiasm can lead to, there is also a danger of benign neglect. Altering the authority structures of our daily work-settings may lead to an improved quality of overall citizen involvement; but it will also surely lead to greater citizen burdens. The making of decisions is clearly one of the more stressful tasks with which the human animal is confronted. To increase the range and depth of decision-making involvement is to diffuse the costs of democracy, as well as the potential benefits. Discontinuities in adult political socialization will not be achieved without the conflict and pain that any self-change process involves.

The point is, of course, obvious—which is why it is such a major problem for the participationist persuasion, where it has been widely and systematically neglected. Adult political learning—if it is to have any consequential significance—is more like a form of psychotherapy than gymnastics. Changes for the better will not be won at the cost of a few stiff muscles but only at the labored cost of a more mature and responsible body politic.

Taken together, the analyses of the Marxist and social-liberalist perspectives point toward a more general set of conclusions for the broader question of occupation and political learning. On the one hand, both analyses indicate the need for a high degree of contextual relativization in the area. The determinative nature of low-status work settings was already weak under the relatively standard conditions of early industrialization and has only become more so with the move towards postindustrialism. Under current conditions of workplace organization, with shorter work weeks, more flexible and less burdensome technologies, wide variations in the pattern and degree of unionization, and highly trained, ideologically conscious personnel staffs, prediction is tricky indeed. In an age where professional "motivators" are playing an increasingly more active role in structuring large-scale workplaces, the interdependence between technology and ideology becomes highly tenuous. When it comes to the relative strength of the factors affecting political learning on the job, the cultural factor seems to be clearly ascendant.

This leads, however, to a complementary perspective of equal importance. Regardless of how manipulable modern work settings may be, there is a "bottom line" for socialization analysis in the fact of manipulability itself. No matter which combination of technology, organization, and industrial subculture is employed, the resulting totality will rest upon and function through a specific *authority system*. If there is a common denominator for the Marxist and social-liberalist perspectives, it rests in a presumed impulse toward personal autonomy: an impulse which, if frustrated, fosters a combination of underdeveloped personal competence (and performance) with an antisystem orientation.

An emphasis on authority systems as the essential factor in occupational socialization thus provides a focal point which is both ontologically valid and normatively explicit. As such, it provides a necessary touchstone for a more context-free and cumulative development of the subfield.[20]

Notes

1. With the sole exception of Sigel and Hoskin (1977), I have not found any reference to the workplace as a setting for political socialization in any of the standard

overviews of the subfield. Allardt's (1976) important contribution on "work and political behavior" covers many of the central problem areas but not with explicit reference to the socialization theme. The normal practice is to pursue the institutional aspect of socialization through the family and the school, and then jump to the effects of the mass media (Dennis 1973; Niemi 1973; Niemi and Sobieszek 1977). Even the specific treatment of "adult socialization" in the International Encyclopedia of the Social Sciences (Brim 1972) makes no mention of work as a socializing agent.

2. The data reported in the present chapter derive from the project "Democracy in Norway: Participation and Basic Values." The project has been led by the author and financed by the Norwegian Research Council for Science and the Humanities, the Ministry of Local Government and Labor, and the Institute of Political Science, University of Oslo. The sample survey was carried out by the Central Bureau of Statistics in January and February 1981 on the basis of random selection from the national population register. The total sample consists of 1,170 respondents. Unless other citations are mentioned, the specific findings reported here can be found in an internal project report available from the author.

3. Summary perspectives of the literature in this area are available in Lafferty (1974), Allardt (1976), and Lipset (1981, 1983). See also the brief but insightful treatment by Sigel and Hoskin (1977, pp. 277–279). Also of interest, but with less of a "conventional" political orientation, is the macrohistorical perspective provided by Sabel (1982).

4. The combined effects of the postindustrial process itself and the current research persuasion which is monitoring it (the "new politics") leads attention away from the specific relationship between different types of occupation and political ideology. As referred to below, the literature in the area of ideological change, party loyalties, radicalism vs. conservatism, etc., is primarily concerned with problems of "dealignment" or "realignment" in what have been relatively stable class-politics relationships. The analysis of these processes is mainly undertaken in relation to models that contrast the effects of ideational (values, attitudes, beliefs) as opposed to structural (class, status, age, gender) factors. The ability to derive meaningful generalizations as to the changing relationship between *occupation* and political ideology from these works is slight indeed.

For a good cross-section of the "new-politics" literature, with numerous cross-national references, see Lipset 1981, 1983, 1985; Dalton et al. 1984; Baker et al. 1981; Barnes and Kasse 1979; Ladd and Hadley 1978; Inglehart 1977; and Budge et al. 1976.

5. It must be remembered that I am referring here to "radicalism" as a question of choice among proferred electoral, ideological alternatives. We must assume that if workers are not *made aware of* radical alternatives, they will not question authority structures beyond spontaneous outbursts in reaction to acute suppression. Electoral ideology in the form of party programs can thus be said to accommodate all four elements of Mann's (1973) worker-consciousness scheme (see text). The first question to be addressed to the ideological aspect of political learning at work is thus one of ideological availability (Lafferty 1974, chap. 4).

6. Most studies of radicalism, either to the right or left, concentrate only on the specific ideology of interest, i.e. they focus on either communism or fascism as a

manifestation of something *different*. The normal procedure is to search for explanatory factors in relation to the relative strength of the radical manifestation, which in most cases is measured by electoral support or party membership. What is usually neglected, however, is the possibility that the same areas which show strong communist or fascist strength may also show relatively strong support for other, even directly opposite, ideologies. The highly controversial discussion in political psychology as to the distinctness of rightist and leftist extremist tendencies has not made its mark on the subfield of political ecology.

7. For the sake of relative comparison in the present context, all findings from the Norwegian project will be made in terms of the eta and beta coefficients of the well-known multivariate classification analysis technique (MCA: see, e.g., Nie et al. 1975). The correlation between "political radicalism" and occupational type (worker/low-level employee) was eta = .16, with the workers showing a radical edge. Unless otherwise stated, all findings are for the combined subgroup of workers (N = 237) and lower-level employees (N = 135) only.

The index of "political radicalism" is an additive index computed from three separate measures: (1) *Party identification* along a spectrum of ten major parties, from the neoliberalist Progressive party on the right to both Soviet- and Chinese-oriented communist parties on the left. (2) *Ideological self-placement* on a right-left scale from 1 to 10. (3) *Attitude toward social change,* varying from "the entire social system should be radically changed" to "several of the reforms carried out recently should be reversed." The resulting index is normatively distributed across the subgroup and strongly reflects the type of "radicalism" covered by the literature under review.

8. The measure of "parental party preference" is based on two questions as to which political party the respondent's parents "were supporters of" during childhood. Interestingly enough, it was the maternal preference which was the best predictor of political ideology. The overall multivariate results are the same, however, regardless of which parental measure is included in the model.

The relevant coefficients for the full MCA-model are as follows: maternal party preference (eta = .33, beta = .29); age (eta = .24, beta = .19); union involvement (eta = .23, beta = .16); and gender/work (i.e. combination of gender and worker vs. lower-level employee) (eta = .17, beta = .06). Eta indicates bivariate association without controls; beta the relative effect with all other predictors controlled for.

9. For three recent contributions within this orientation with particular relevance for the issues emphasized here, see Barber (1984), Garforth (1979), and Kieffer (1981).

10. For some of the more relevant surveys in relation to the current problem, see Blumberg (1973), Bolweg (1976), Crouch and Heller (1983), Elden (1981), Emery and Phillips (1976), Greenberg (1975), Kaplan (1975), O'Toole (1973), Sheppard and Herrick (1972), Strauss and Rosenstein (1970), Wall and Lischeron (1977), and Wilpert and Sorge (1984). See also the continuing stream of reports in the journals *Human Relations, Industrial Relations, Administrative Science Quarterly,* and *Economic and Industrial Democracy.* Perhaps the most relevant and innovative line of research in this general area (relevant for the problem of political socialization without discussing

the political aspect specifically) is the work of Melvin Kohn (Kohn 1969, 1985; Kohn and Schooler 1983; Mortimer 1985).

11. The normative aspect of Pateman's work has been commented upon so extensively as to defy simple reference. For a sampling of positive and negative perspectives, see Kelso (1978, chap. 8), Lafferty (1975), Schonfeld (1975), and Weinstein (1974). For an important follow-up and expanded formulation of the entire participatory persuasion (with an introduction by Pateman herself) see Mason (1982), and for Carole Pateman's own "reflections" on her earlier position, see her article in Crouch and Heller (1983, pp. 107–20).

12. The non-Marxist understanding of ownership in this connection is that it consists more of a "bundle of rights" than of a determinant asymmetric relationship. Thus one may have a high degree of workplace democratization with or without worker ownership, and worker ownership without the democratization of decision-making. See, e.g., Bernstein (1980) and Dahl (1970, 1982, 1985). For the clearest empirical illustration of the relevance of this perspective, see the work of Greenberg referred to in the text.

13. Dubin's (1958) argument was that work is not a "central life interest" for the majority of industrial workers. Rather than being "work oriented," most workers are "community oriented." In this view, work is a necessary "extrinsic" activity which provides the means to compensate for its own burdens and burdening status. Goldthorpe et al. endorsed Dubin's position in their study of English workers in Luton, but they preferred the expressions "work-centered," "family-centered," "leisure-centered," etc. as a nuance on the Dubin dichotomy. Their persuasion as to the importance of work from a "spillover" perspective, is clearly expressed as follows: "workers' lives are sharply dichotomised between work and non-work. Work experiences and relationships are not likely to be carried over into 'out-plant' life, and workers are unlikely to participate in 'social' activities associated with work—e.g. in works clubs and societies or in other than what are seen as economically urgent or essential trade union activities" (Goldthorpe et al. 1968, p. 39). A comprehensive theoretical discussion of the differences between the "compensatory" and "spillover" approaches, with special relevance for workplace democratization, is available in Elden (1976, pp. 68–89).

14. There are numerous variants of the so-called "Michigan" attitude battery employed by Elden. In its basic form, the instrument consists of a given number of statements reflecting personal attitudes to the political system in general or to the individual's role as citizen in that system. When used positively, the battery is thought to reflect "political efficacy," and when used negatively to measure "political alienation." Two major problems with the probe are the bias associated with "response-set" (primarily the tendency to agree with negatively formulated statements), and the question of whether the statements actually measure personal characteristics, or whether they are, in fact, not perceived as descriptive statements of political phenomena which do not necessarily imply either alienation or efficacy.

In an earlier community study in Norway, Lafferty (1981) tested for both of these methodological difficulties by alternating the positive and negative formulations of the statements, and by applying the same battery to both a representative sample of the population *and* local political leaders. The results showed, not surprisingly, clear evidence of response-set. Factor analysis revealed a dominant principal component composed of the alternate negative and positive formulations, with no substantive meaning in terms of attitudes. Even more dismaying, however, was the revelation that for several of the probes, the elected local politicians were on the average more "alienated" than the population as a whole! The implication is clear: interpretation of the standard "political-efficacy" and "political-alienation" measures must be made with great circumspection.

15. According to Karasek's table 3, those who report a more "passive" job content at the end of the panel period (1968 to 1974) also report an average increase in the frequency of reported political acts of + .456. Those who report no change in job situation, report average changes in political activity of + .536, and those who report "active" job changes (greater job discretion and higher job demands) report average changes of + .811. The figures are for a national sample of all employed Swedish males between the ages of eighteen and sixty (N = 1,638: Karasek 1978, table 3). The report has, unfortunately, never been published.

16. Overviews of industrial democracy in Europe are available in Jenkins (1974), Levinson (1974), Gustavsen (1981), IDE (1981), Carby-Hall (1977), with updates on new reforms in the journal on *Economic and Industrial Democracy*. For the United States, see Hunnius et al. (1973), Deutsch and Albrecht (1983), Zwerdling (1978), and Rothschild-Whitt (1984).

17. The eta coefficient for the relationship between the measure of workplace involvement (which measures individual activity in relation to the three levels of democratization reported in the text) and the measure of political involvement (which measures individual activity in relation to a hierarchy of electoral politics) was .29 (p. = .001). When included in a multivariate (MCA) model with union involvement, education, gender, and "parental political interaction" (frequency of political discussion with both parents during childhood), the relationship is reduced to beta = .26, which is still significant at p = .001. Most important is the fact that the relationship between the two types of involvement (work and politics) is completely linear. The average level of political activity is greater for every incremental category of workplace involvement, both before and after the multivariate control. The coefficients for parental political interaction, which was the only other significant predictor in the model, were eta = .29 and beta = .29.

18. The approach chosen does not imply, of course, that many of the other phenomena which have been studied in relation to occupational characteristics—such as feelings of personal alienation and the tendency to strike—do not have political relevance. It is simply the author's conviction (based on the type of findings reported in the first section of the present chapter) that these aspects of ideology and behavior have proved very unsystematic in their relation to political action in a broad conventional sense. It is also the case, however, that in neither of these areas has there been much attention to specific problems or models of adult political learning.

19. On an individual level, the relationship between class background and current ideology can be illustrated by a series of cross-classifications of structural and ideological determinants. The Norwegian data show, for example, that ideological predictability is in general very weak if you only consider the occupational position of the respondent's father in connection with the occupational position of the respondent.

Manual laborers who had manual laborers for fathers, for example, are nearly equally divided on both sides of the conservative-radical index. *Within* the subgroup, however, there is a strong relationship between the ideological preferences of parents and the ideological preferences of children. Whereas 64 percent of workers with parents who voted for "socialist" parties are "radical," the corresponding figure for those whose parents voted "bourgeois" is only 30 percent. The effect is even stronger for blue-collar workers from middle-class homes. Here, the effect of father's occupation alone is exactly nil: the sample is divided evenly on both sides of the radical/conservative median. When we control for parental electoral preference, however, the ideological effect is strong and linear. Of workers from middle-class, socialist-leaning homes 75 percent are "radical," as opposed to only 28 percent for those with middle-class, bourgeois-leaning backgrounds.

Together with the results discussed in the text on the effects of one's own occupation (which were shown to be extremely slight), these findings indicate that sociostructural factors are insignificant when it comes to the ideological preferences of blue-collar laborers. The question of consistency vs. change for this occupational grouping is strongly biased in the direction of ideological conditioning within the family. In the context of adult learning and workplace socialization, this indicates that changes in family-based ideologies will only come about in work settings which have a strong affective component for the individual worker. Insofar as the workplace is character- ized by a strong "worker collective" (Lysgaard 1961), the potential for "converting" "conservative" workers should be strong. If, on the other hand, the workplace is per- meated by management values with a strong company identity, the socialization ad- vantage should lie on the side of deradicalization. In this light, the general tendency toward a more "human" corporate ideology can be seen as an important "cultural" determinant of the current conservative resurgence, particularly in a social-democratic state like Norway.

20. To be more concrete, one can imagine a program which attempts to integrate the basic normative persuasion of Pateman (1970) with the macrocontextual approach of Greenberg (1983); the working-class consciousness perspective of Mann (1973); *and* the highly developed (and sadly neglected) conceptual approach to authority sys- tems worked out by Eckstein and Gurr (1975). Schonfeld's (1975) early critique of Pateman represents a partial attempt in this direction.

References

Alford, R. 1963. *Party and Society.* Chicago: Rand McNally.

Allardt, E. 1964. "Social Sources of Finnish Communism: Traditional and Emerging Radicalism." *International Journal of Comparative Sociology* 5: 49–72.

———. 1976. "Work and Political Behavior." In *Handbook of Work Organization and Society,* ed. R. Dubin, pp. 807–33. Chicago: Rand McNally.

Allardt, E., and P. Pesonen. 1967. "Cleavages in Finnish Politics." In *Party Systems and Voter Alignments: Cross-National Perspectives,* ed. S. M. Lipset and S. Rok- kan, pp. 325–66. New York: The Free Press.

Almond, G., and S. Verba. 1965. *The Civic Culture.* Boston: Little, Brown.

Ambrecht, B. C. 1975. "Work Organization and Adult Political Socialization." Paper for the annual meeting of the Western Political Science Association, Seattle.

Baker, Kendall L., R. J. Dalton, and K. Hildebrandt. 1981. *Germany Transformed: Political Culture and the New Politics.* Cambridge: Harvard University Press.

Barber, B. 1984. *Strong Democracy: Participatory Democracy for a New Age.* Berkeley: University of California Press.

Barnes, S., and M. Kaase. 1979. *Political Action: Mass Participation in Five Western Democracies.* Beverly Hills: Sage Publications.

Bernstein, P. 1980. *Workplace Democratization: Its Internal Dynamics.* New Brunswick, N.J.: Transaction Books.

Blumberg, P. 1973. *Industrial Democracy: The Sociology of Participation.* New York: Schocken Books.

Bolweg, J. F. 1976. *Job Design and Industrial Democracy.* Leiden: Nijhoff.

Braverman, H. 1974. *Labor and Monopoly Capital.* New York: Monthly Review Press.

Brim, O. G., Jr. 1972. "Adult Socialization." *International Encycolpedia of the Social Sciences* 12: 555–62.

Budge, I., I. Crewe, and D. Farlie. 1976. *Party Identification and Beyond.* London: John Wiley.

Carby-Hall, J. R. 1977. *Worker Participation in Europe.* London: Croom Helm.

Cooper, T. 1984. "The Socialization Effects of Workplace Participation." M.A. thesis, University of Oregon.

Crouch, C., and F. A. Heller, eds. 1983. *Organizational Democracy and Political Processes.* Vol. 1 of *International Yearbook of Organizational Democracy for the Study of Participation, Cooperation, and Power.* Chichester: John Wiley.

Dahl, R. A. 1970. *After the Revolution?* New Haven: Yale University Press.

———. 1982. *Dilemmas of Pluralist Democracy: Autonomy vs. Control.* New Haven: Yale University Press.

———. 1985. *Preface to Economic Democracy.* Berkeley: University of California Press.

Dalton, R., S. C. Flanagan, P. A. Beck, et al. 1984. *Electoral Change in Advanced Industrial Democracies: Realignment or Dealignment?* Princeton: Princeton University Press.

Damgaard, Erik. 1980. *Folkets Veje i Dansk Politik.* Copenhagen: Schultz Forlag.

Dennis, J. 1973. *Socialization to Politics: A Reader.* New York: John Wiley.

Deutsch, S., and S. Albrecht. 1983. "Worker Participation in the United States: Efforts to Democratise Industry and the Economy." *Labour and Society* 8: 243–69.

Dubin, R. 1958. *The World of Work: Industrial Society and Human Relations.* Englewood Cliffs: Prentice-Hall.

Eckstein, H., and T. R. Gurr. 1975. *Patterns of Authority: A Structural Basis for Political Inquiry.* New York: John Wiley.

Elden, M. 1976. "Democracy at Work for a More Participatory Politics: Worker Self-management Increases Political Efficacy and Participation." Ph.D. dissertation, University of California, Los Angeles.

———. 1979. "Three Generations of Work Democracy Experiments in Norway." In

The Quality of Working Life: The European Experiment, ed. C. Cooper and E. Mumford. London: Associated Business Press.

———. 1981. "Political Efficacy at Work: The Connection between More Autonomous Forms of Workplace Organization and a More Participatory Politics." *American Political Science Review* 75: 43–58.

Elster, J. 1983a. "Offentlighet og deltagelse." In *Deltaker-demokratiet,* ed. T. Bergh, pp. 13–29, Oslo: Universitetsforlaget.

———. 1983b. *Sour Grapes: Studies in the Subversion of Rationality.* Cambridge: Cambridge University Press.

Emery, F., and C. Phillips. 1976. *Living at Work.* Canberra: Australian Government Publishing Service.

Gardell, B. 1976. "Reactions at Work and Their Influence on Nonwork Activities." *Human Relations* 9: 885–904.

Garforth, F. W. 1979. *John Stuart Mill's Theory of Education.* London: Martin Robertson.

Glantz, O. 1958. "Class Consciousness and Political Solidarity." *American Sociological Review* 23: 375–83.

Goldthorpe, J. H., D. Lockwood, F. Bechhofer, and J. Platt. 1968. *The Affluent Worker: Political Attitudes and Behaviour.* Cambridge: Cambridge University Press.

Greenberg, E. S. 1975. "The Consequences of Worker Participation and Control: A Clarification of the Theoretical Literature." *Social Science Quarterly* 56: 191–209.

———. 1981a. "Industrial Democracy and the Democratic Citizen." *Journal of Politics* 43: 964–81.

———. 1981b. "Industrial Self-management and Political Attitudes." *American Political Science Review* 75: 29–42.

———. 1983. "Context and Cooperation: Systematic Variation in the Political Effects of Workplace Democracy." *Economic and Industrial Democracy* 4: 191–223.

Gusfield, J. R., ed. 1970. *Protest, Reform, and Revolt.* New York: John Wiley.

Gustavsen, B. 1981. "Industrial Democracy." In *Nordic Democracy,* ed. Erik Allardt et al., pp. 324–58. Copenhagen: Det Danske Selskab.

Gustavsen, B., and G. Hunnius. 1981. *New Patterns of Work Reform: The Case of Norway.* Oslo: Universitetsforlaget.

Hunnius, Gerry, G. David Garson, and John Case, eds. 1973. *Workers' Control: A Reader on Labor and Social Change.* New York: Random House.

IDE. 1981. *Industrial Democracy in Europe.* Oxford: Clarendon Press.

Inglehart, R. 1977. *The Silent Revolution: Changing Values and Political Styles among Western Publics.* Princeton: Princeton University Press.

Jennings, M. Kent, and Richard Niemi. 1974. *The Political Character of Adolescence—The Influence of Families and Schools.* Princeton: Princeton University Press.

Kaplan, L. 1975. "The Literature of Participation to Realism." *College and Research Libraries* 36: 473–79.

Karasek, R. A. 1978. "Job Socialization: A Longitudinal Study of Work, Political and Leisure Activity." Revised working paper no. 59. Stockholm: Swedish Institute for Social Research.

Kelso, W. A. 1978. *American Democratic Theory: Pluralism and Its Critics*. Westport, Conn.: Greenwood Press.

Kieffer, C. H. 1981. "The Emergence of Empowerment: The Development of Participatory Competence among Individuals in Citizen Organizations." Ph.D. dissertation, University of Michigan.

Knutsen, O., and W. M. Lafferty. 1981. "Høyrebølgen i et generasjonsperspektiv." In *Høyrebølgen: Epokeskifte i Norsk Politikk?*, ed. Tor Bjørklund and Bernt Hagtvet, Oslo: H. Aschegoug, pp. 235–62.

Kohn, M. L. 1969. *Class and Conformity: A Study in Values*. Homewood, Ill.: Dorsey Press.

———. 1985 "Unresolved Issues in the Relationship between Work and Personality." Thematic address at the annual meeting of the American Sociological Association, Washington, D.C. Mimeographed.

Kohn, M. L., and C. Schooler. 1983. *Work and Personality: An Inquiry into the Impact of Social Stratification*. Norwood, N.J.: Ablex.

Ladd, E. C., and C. D. Hadley. 1978. *Transformations of the American Party System*. New York: W. W. Norton.

Lafferty, W. M. 1971. *Economic Development and the Response of Labor in Scandinavia*. Oslo: Universitetsforlaget.

———. 1974. *Industrialization, Community Structure, and Socialism*. Oslo: Universitetsforlaget.

———. 1975. "Participation and Democratic Theory: Reworking the Premises for a Participatory Society." *Scandinavian Political Studies* (Old series) 10: 53–70.

———. 1981. *Participation and Democracy in Norway: The "Distant Democracy" Revisited*. Oslo: Universitetsforlaget.

———. 1983. "Political Participation in the Social Democratic State: A Normative-Empirical Framework for the Analysis of Decision-making Involvement in Norway." *Scandinavian Political Studies* (New series) 6: 281–308.

———. 1984. "Workplace Democratization in Norway: Current Status and Future Prospects, with Special Emphasis on the Role of the Public Sector." *Acta Sociologica* 27: 123–38.

———. 1985. "Decision-making Involvement and Socioeconomic Resources in Norway: A Normative-Empirical Analysis." *Scandinavian Political Studies* (New series) 8: 1–32.

Lafferty, W. M., and O. Knutsen. 1984. "Leftist and Rightist Ideology in a Social Democratic State: A Survey-based Analysis of Norway in the Midst of the Conservative Resurgence." *British Journal of Political Science* 14: 345–67.

Levinson, C., ed. 1974. *Industry's Democratic Revolution*. London: George Allen & Unwin.

Lipset, S. M. 1981. *Political Man: The Social Bases of Politics*. Expanded and updated edition. Baltimore: The Johns Hopkins University Press.

———. 1983. "Radicalism or Reformism: The Sources of Working-class Politics." *American Political Science Review* 77: 1–18.

————. 1985. *Consensus and Conflict: Essays in Political Sociology.* New Brunswick, N.J.: Transaction Books.

Lipset, S. M., P. F. Lazarsfeld, A. H.Barton, and J. Linz. 1954. "The Psychology of Voting: An Analysis of Political Behavior." In *Handbook of Social Psychology,* Vol. 2, ed. G. Lindzey. Cambridge, Mass.: Addison-Wesley.

Lipset, S. M., and S. Rokkan. 1967. *Party Systems and Voter Alignments: Cross-National Perspectives.* New York: The Free Press.

Lipsitz, L. 1964. "Work Life and Political Attitudes: A Study of Manual Workers." *American Political Science Review* 58: 951–62.

Littler, C. R. 1982. *The Development of the Labor Process in Britain, Japan and USA.* London: Heinemann.

Lysgaard, S. 1961. *Arbeiderkollektivet: En Studie i de Underordnedes Sosiologi.* Oslo: Universitetsforlaget.

Macpherson, C. B. 1977. *The Life and Times of Liberal Democracy.* Oxford: Oxford University Press.

McQuitty, L. L. 1957. "Elementary Linkage Analysis for Isolating Orthogonal and Oblique Types and Typal Relevancies." *Educational and Psychological Measurement* 17: 207–29.

Manis, J. G. and B. N. Meltzer. 1954. "Attitudes of Textile Workers to Class Structure." *American Journal of Sociology* 60: 30–35.

Mann, M. 1973. *Consciousness and Action among the Western Working Class.* London: Macmillan.

Mason, R. 1982. *Participatory and Workplace Democracy: A Theoretical Development in Critique of Liberalism.* Carbondale: Southern Illinois University Press.

Mészáros, I. 1970. *Marx's Theory of Alienation.* London: Merlin Press.

Milbrath, L., and M. L. Goel. 1977. *Political Participation: How and Why Do People Get Involved in Politics?* 2d. ed. Chicago: Rand McNally.

Mortimer, J. T. 1985. "Discussion of Melvin Kohn's 'Unresolved Issues in the Relationship between Work and Personality'." Paper presented at the Thematic Session on Work and Personality, annual meeting of the American Sociological Association, Washington, D.C.

Murphy, R. J., and R. T. Morris. 1961. "Occupation Situs, Subjective Class Identification, and Political Affiliation." *American Sociological Review* 26: 383–92.

Nie, N., C. H. Hull, J. G. Jenkins, K. Steinbrenner, and D. H. Bent. 1975. *SPSS: Statistical Package for the Social Sciences.* 2d. ed. New York: McGraw-Hill.

Niemi, R. G. 1973. "Political Socialization." In *Handbook of Political Psychology,* ed. J. N. Knutson. San Francisco: Jossey–Bass, pp.117–38.

Niemi, R. G., and B. I. Sobieszek. 1977. "Political Socialization." *Annual Review of Sociology* 3: 209–33.

Ollman, B. 1971. *Alienation: Conception of Man in Capitalist Society.* London: Cambridge University Press.

O'Toole, J., ed. 1973. *Work in America: Report of a Special Task Force to the Secretary of Health, Education, and Welfare.* Cambridge, Mass.: MIT Press.

Pateman, C. 1970. *Participation and Democratic Theory.* Cambridge: Cambridge University Press.

Petras, J., and M. Zeitlin. 1967. "Miners and Agrarian Radicalism." *American Sociological Review* 32: 578–85.

Rokkan, S., and A. Campbell. 1960. "Norway and the United States of America." *International Social Science Journal* 12: 69–99.

Rothschild-Whitt, Joyce. 1984. "Worker Ownership: Collective Response to an Elite-Generated Crisis." *Research in Social Movements, Conflict and Change*, vol. 6: 167–94.

Sabel, C. F. 1982. *Work and Politics: The Division of Labor in Industry.* Cambridge: Cambridge University Press.

Schonfeld, W. R. 1975. "The Meaning of Democratic Participation." *World Politics* 28: 134–58.

Seeman, M. 1972. "Alienation and Engagement." In *The Human Meaning of Social Change,* ed. A. Campbell and P. E. Converse. New York: Russell Sage Foundation, pp.467–527.

———. 1975. "Alienation Studies." *Annual Review of Sociology* 1: 91–123.

Sheppard, H., and N. Herrick. 1972. *Where Have All the Robots Gone?* New York: The Free Press.

Sigel, R. S., and M. B. Hoskin. 1977. "Perspectives on Adult Political Socialization—Areas of Research." In *Handbook of Political Socialization: Theory and Research,* ed. S. A. Renshon. New York: The Free Press.

Soares, G. S. D., and R. L. Hamblin. 1967. "Socio-economic Variables and Voting for the Radical Left: Chile, 1952." *American Political Science Review* 61: 1053–65.

Staines, G. L. 1980. "Spillover versus Compensation: A Review of the Literature on the Relationship between Work and Nonwork." *Human Relations* 33: 111–29.

Strauss, G., and E. Rosenstein. 1970. "Workers' participation: A Critical View." *Industrial Relations* 9: 197–214.

Thompson, D. F. 1970. *The Democratic Citizen.* Cambridge: Cambridge University Press.

———. 1976. *John Stuart Mill and Representative Government.* Princeton: Princeton University Press.

Verba, S., N. H. Nie, and J. Kim. 1978. *Participation and Political Equality: A Seven-Nation Comparison.* Cambridge: Cambridge University Press.

Wall, T. D., and J. A. Lischeron. 1977. *Worker Participation: A Critique of the Literature and Some Fresh Evidence.* London: McGraw-Hill.

Weinstein, M. A. 1974. "Utopian Pluralism: Review Essay on Recent Contributions." *Journal of Voluntary Action Research* 3: 27–35.

Wilpert, B., and A. Sorge, eds. 1984. *International Perspectives on Organizational Democracy.* Vol. 2 of *International Yearbook of Organizational Democracy for the Study of Participation, Cooperation, and Power.* Chicester: John Wiley.

Wood, S. 1982. *The Degradation of Work.* London: Hutchinson.

Worre, T. 1980. "Class Parties and Class Voting in the Scandinavian Countries." *Scandinavian Political Studies* (New series) 3: 299–320.

Zwerdling, D. 1978. *Workplace Democracy.* New York: Harper.

Four

Political Socialization in Social Welfare Work

PAULA DRESSEL AND MICHAEL LIPSKY

In social welfare as in other public services the accuracy, effectiveness, and affect of the interaction between social welfare workers and their clients constitute a large part of what citizens get from welfare agencies. It follows that what workers bring to the encounter represents an important constituent of welfare policy. This review of political socialization in social welfare work is therefore not simply an exercise in exploring changing attitudes as workers go through an occupational life cycle. It is also an assessment of how an important component of a critical public service is fashioned.

If the study of politics is concerned with the exercise of power and influence in the distribution of values in a society, it is clear that there are at least two political dimensions to social welfare work. The most obvious is the nature of the work itself. Welfare workers are agents of the state, whether they are employed in public or private agencies. As such, they mediate relations between the general public, policy-makers, and agency administrators on the one hand and the beneficiaries of goods and services on the other. Equally political but less obvious is the status and treatment of welfare workers as employees of social agencies. These two dimensions are intricately intertwined. They determine to a large extent the credibility and resources that welfare workers bring to interactions with clients and to interest-group politics in formal political channels.

In the following discussion our remarks are confined to social welfare workers in government-supported public and private nonprofit social welfare agencies who deliver assistance benefits and personal services to designated recipient groups through direct contact with the target population. The work of these "street-level bureaucrats" (Lipsky 1980) encompasses programs as varied as protective services, community mental health, AFDC, child and adult day care, meals provision, and transportation assistance, all of which fall under the broad umbrella of human services or social welfare.

At this point a few introductory distinctions are in order. First, we use the

Lundberg 1958). They have found that, although within specializations in social work there is no significant difference among recruits on measures of dogmatism (Koepp 1963), students do differ on assertiveness by social work specialization, with majors in planning, community organization, and group work scoring higher than clinical and casework students (Hess and Williams 1974; Cournoyer 1983). Merdinger's (1982) undergraduate social work majors scored higher than economics and management majors but were similar to psychology majors on measures of student evaluations of human nature (trustworthiness, altruism, will and rationality) (see Cryns 1977).

Students have also been assessed on attitudes and values directly relevant to social work. Varley (1963) found no significant differences in her cross-sectional research between beginning and graduating social work students on orientations toward equal rights, service, psychodynamic-mindedness, and universalism. She speculated quite appropriately that the findings may be a result of student cohort differences rather than a statement about the impact of professional education. Of particular interest are her findings that older students with previous welfare work experience showed a decline in adherence to the values studied while lower-class, low-income students showed the greatest favorable value changes upon exposure to formal social work education. Here again, however, "decline" and "change" are at best tenuous interpretations when utilizing cross-sectional data.

Several studies addressed students' attitudes about poverty and public dependency. While Grimm and Orten (1973) reported no gender difference in attitudes toward the poor, Cryns (1977) noted that male students have a greater tendency to attribute individual rather than structural explanations to both poverty and economic success. On the other hand, both studies found that having prior welfare work experience and having family responsibilities are related to less favorable attitudes about the poor. Furthermore, Grimm and Orten discovered significant associations between positive orientation and undergraduate major (sociology or social work) (also Merdinger 1982), undergraduate institution (public, non-Southern), high socioeconomic status, and area of professional specialization (especially community organization).

Finally, with regard to work-relevant attitudes, Carlton and Jung (1972) and Rubin and Johnson (1984) documented students' preferences for individual casework and private practice, respectively, as their overriding occupational interests. The studies' consistent results are particularly interesting since they were conducted over a decade apart in very different sociopolitical climates regarding welfare issues. Carlton and Jung's findings are also intriguing in light of strong emphasis within social work education and its professional literature in the late 1960s and early 1970s on community action and social change. The authors themselves question the apparent inconsistencies among emphases in the professional literature, the content in graduate education, and students' career goals. Yet we are aware of no studies that terms "social welfare worker," "human service worker," "service provider," and "social worker" interchangeably; they are intended to refer to a broad category of personnel linked by common structural positions within and across service agencies.

Second, while welfare employees have certain working conditions in common with other street-level bureaucrats such as teachers and police officers (Lipsky 1980), for some purposes, as in this essay, the work of the latter may be usefully analyzed separately, as it embraces different, if implicit, political credos and is carried out in sociopolitical environments that are distinctly different than those of other street-level occupations. In a discussion of political socialization it is therefore critical to distinguish among various arenas in which street-level bureaucrats operate.

Third, we concentrate exclusively on paid staff working within social welfare agencies rather than on volunteers or individual fee-for-service entrepreneurs. This focus simplifies later discussions of workers' pre-occupational orientations and motivations and the impact of work experiences on political views and behaviors. Our selection of subjects, however, does not deny the importance of investigating individuals engaged in social welfare either as volunteers or on a private entrepreneurial basis. Nor does it diminish the need for examining street-level bureaucrats working in nonwelfare settings. Rather, it is intended to establish conceptual boundaries for a literature that is abundant, even within the parameters of specific occupational roles.

Throughout the chapter the term "political" is utilized in a broad sense. We are interested in individual and collective values and activities regarding and affecting the allocation of goods and benefits through both formal and informal channels and mechanisms. The willingness (or refusal) of a service provider to receive a call from a client late at night is no less a political act by our definition than is the consent by a social agency to permit workers to engage in client voter registration. Furthermore, we view political socialization as both a latent and a manifest process (see Almond and Verba 1963). Alteration in or reinforcement of one's political values and behaviors derives from a variety of work experiences, not only those in which political instruction is overt. From our perspective service workers undergo political socialization by observing ways in which their coworkers informally accommodate conflicting agency demands in the same sense that they undergo political socialization from attending workshops outlining changes in the policies their agencies implement.

Our final preliminary remarks further explicate the approach we take in the subsequent analysis. First, we agree with critics who contend that the field of political socialization should give more attention to the sociopolitical context in which socialization occurs (Sigel and Hoskin 1977; Sigel 1983; Delli Carpini, chap. 1, in this volume). We therefore offer summary comments on the shifting historical and political climates within which social welfare work is undertaken, the changing organization of the work over time, demographic variations in the composition of the welfare workforce longitudinally, and the implications of the foregoing for political socialization.

Second, we concur with the call to study political socialization as a process as well as a set of outcomes (Schwartz and Schwartz 1975; Sigel and Hoskin 1977). Consequently, we devote considerable attention to the microdynamics of the welfare workplace, focusing on how political socialization occurs as well as what its consequences are.

Third, we endorse the view that individuals are interactive agents in the socialization process rather than passive recipients of political information (Dennis 1973; Schwartz and Schwartz 1975; Rosenberg 1985).[1] Thus, we address both the political orientations that welfare workers bring to the job and the diverse ways in which they respond cognitively and behaviorally to the demands and opportunities of their work roles. Throughout our discussion we touch at least briefly on research being done on particular topics, and offer critiques of that research as well as suggestions for further investigation. Much of the material cited has not been undertaken as "political socialization" research per se; nevertheless, it provides information relevant to the specialization and its advancement.

The Sociopolitical Context of Welfare Work

A thorough understanding of political socialization in social welfare work must take account of the prevailing sociopolitical climate in which the work is undertaken, the structural contours of the workplace, and the social status of personnel inhabiting the work roles. These factors affect the attitudes workers bring to the socialization experience, the specific content of political learning, and the ability of workers to translate political interests into political action, to name a few issues. They also alert us to the possibility of period and cohort effects on the politics of social welfare workers.

Sociopolitical Climate

The sociopolitical climate within which social welfare activities takes place has fluctuated considerably over time. Public support, policy preferences, and service ideologies vary, often markedly, from one period to another, betraying an underlying cultural ambivalence about social welfare and its clientele. Under changing historical circumstances there have been varying political influences on and responses by welfare workers. For example, the Great Depression of the 1930s and the War on Poverty of the 1960s prompted action for social change by welfare workers and recipients; in contrast, these groups have tended to be relatively quiescent in the 1980s, a period characterized by social welfare contraction. Political socialization of the 1930s and 1960s revolved around community organization and systemic problem analysis in an expanding welfare state, while the political mood during the scientific philanthropy movement of the late 1800s and the fiscal crisis of this decade emphasizes individual initiative, agency accountability, and worker efficiency in the face of limited resources and retrenchment. Some students of social welfare document the political values and behaviors of social welfare students and workers in specific historical periods. For example, Bremner (1956) describes the tenets of scientific philanthropy from 1873 to 1893; Spano (1982) details the activism of the rank-and-file movement of the 1930s; and Rubin and Johnson (1984) note the private practice/psychotherapeutic orientation of contemporary graduate students. Other authors provide detailed accounts of the microprocesses by which politics unfolds in contemporary social welfare agencies. Street, Martin, and Gordon (1979) describe the homogenization of client treatment; Lipsky (1980) documents how welfare policy is made at the agency level; and Dressel (1984) shows how both clients and welfare come to be scapegoated when welfare policies fail. These writings acknowledge the importance of the sociopolitical context for understanding welfare workers' politics. For the most part, however, empirical studies in social work education and social service delivery give only passing mention to larger social forces that impact on the issues being addressed. Often such reference is provided as an ex post facto explanation of the findings rather than as a guiding consideration in the overall development of the research project.

Workplace Organization

The changing organization of social welfare work is a second contextual factor that influences the nature of political socialization. At least three significant trends in workplace arrangements and accompanying demands on employees for particular kinds of job preparation have occurred within this century: professionalization, deprofessionalization, and proletarianization.

Since the early 1900s efforts have been undertaken with varying levels of commitment and varying degrees of success to create and consolidate the profession of social work and to limit job access in social welfare organizations to the professionally trained. Graduate programs in universities have been established, journals have been founded, and occupational specialization has proceeded apace. Likewise, social welfare professionals have regularly lobbied, often successfully, to impose licensing and degree requirements on state governments and within state and local personnel classifications. One underlying rationale for professionalization of social welfare work was to promote social workers' political credibility. It was thought that enhanced occupational status would offer welfare workers greater leverage in the political process, thereby enabling them to achieve policies beneficial to their clienteles. In other words, workers' improved credibility would eventually trickle down to welfare clients, whose needs would in turn be legitimized. We are aware of no research, however, that has tested this hypothesis. For example, it would be interesting to test legislators' or workers' attitudes toward clients in states where licensure is mandated and those where it is not (introducing needed controls, of course). One might also compare legislators' attitudes toward social welfare professionals in these states.

Efforts toward professionalization have contributed to changes in the internal composition of the occupation. Specifically, the requirements and prerequisites of professionalization have opened avenues of upward mobility for men in an otherwise female-intensive workforce (Dressel, forthcoming). Men are found disproportionately in faculty and dean positions in professional schools (DiNitto, Martin, and Harrison 1984) and in administrative slots in social agencies (Szakacs 1977; U.S. Equal Opportunity Commission 1977; NASW 1984). Their superordinate locations in the hierarchy of the social welfare industry suggest that men are thus more likely to be powerful socialization agents for a direct service workforce that is made up disproportionately of women. Consequently, any analysis of agency politics should not overlook the possibility of gender politics at work as well. Qualitative "backstage" research on female service workers' informal conversations with one another could provide rich data on this dimension of the workplace.

The countertrend of deprofessionalization has challenged professionalization efforts at particular historical junctures. Deprofessionalization refers to the reduction of education or training requirements for employment in social welfare work. This dynamic was most evident in the 1930s and 1960s. In these decades expansive social welfare legislation generated thousands of jobs that could not be filled by the limited number of available professional workers. Further, in the 1960s it was deemed desirable to open up opportunities to black workers who lacked professional credentials. Legislative mandates of the 1960s for maximum feasible client participation in service agencies led to the creation of paraprofessional positions in a host of welfare activities (Brager 1965; Gartner 1971).

In the current decade deprofessionalization occurred as a response to fiscal difficulties and to specific judicial decisions. Many states, in order to reduce payrolls or comply with affirmative action directives, undertook civil service reclassification to lower educational requirements for social welfare workers (Karger 1981; Pecora and Austin 1983). One clear political effect of deprofessionalization is ensuing conflict between professional and nonprofessional agency workers. The former have sought to guard their positions and prerogatives through professional associations, while the latter have joined unions in an attempt to protect their interests (Shaffer 1979; Tambor 1983; NASW

News 1985). Regrettably, the politics of occupational self-interest in welfare work is seldom addressed as an empirical concern or as a professional controversy. Here again qualitative "backstage" research on informal conversations among professional and nonprofessional line staff and during associational and union meetings is a useful starting point for determining the phenomenological parameters of this issue.

Proletarianization has frequently accompanied deprofessionalization. To an extent, social welfare work has experienced rationalization, or the separation of work tasks into components performed by different individuals who collectively achieve greater efficiency than a single individual performing the whole task. A typical outcome of rationalization is proletarianization, or a deskilling of work, loss of control over the complete work product, and loss of autonomy in the work process. In welfare work proletarianization takes such forms as the separation of client screening and intake from casework functions (Vondracek, Urban, and Parsonage 1974; Finch 1976b; Piliavin and Gross 1977; Funiciello and Sanzillo 1983) and the utilization of computers and computer technicians to perform tasks previously performed by skilled caseworkers (Vondracek, Urban, and Parsonage 1974; Boyd, Hylton, and Price 1978; Schoech and Arangio 1979). Social policies of the 1960s that mandated utilization of welfare clients in social agencies and fiscal pressures of the 1970s and 1980s for greater agency efficiency and lower employee costs have undergirded trends toward proletarianization of the welfare workplace (Patry 1978). This trend, along with deprofessionalization, has engendered tensions between professional and nonprofessional workers over issues of hiring and layoffs and between agency workers and administrators over issues of job autonomy and the quality of the client experience.

The fluid structural contours of the welfare workplace affect political socialization contexts in significant ways, at least in terms of who become significant socialization agents, the level of control welfare workers have over their tasks, the degree of conflict within the ranks of social agency personnel, and the quality of services received by welfare clientele. Insofar as workplace satisfactions or discontents influence workers' broader political stances and motivations (see Sigel and Hoskin 1977; Delli Carpini et al. 1983; and Lafferty, chap. 3, in this volume), these trends affect larger concerns of citizenship as well. The speed of, and the manner in which, the dynamics of professionalization, deprofessionalization, and proletarianization unfold, and the political climate within which they unfold, will influence the process and products of political socialization in social welfare work.

Worker Social Status

Still another contextual factor relevant to political issues for welfare workers is the broader social status of those employed in human service work. Historically the occupation has been among a limited number of arenas offering at least semiprofessional employment to groups rendered marginal to the private sector economy: women of all racial and ethnic groups and oppressed racial and ethnic men[2] (Collins 1983; Vetter, Babco, and Jensen-Fisher 1983). The proletarianization of certain aspects of the work and the creation of paraprofessional positions opened avenues of employment for lower-income individuals as well. The demographic composition of the social welfare workforce raises significant questions regarding political socialization, only a few of which have been addressed by social scientists.

For example, does the predominance of women in line staff positions diminish the likelihood of political activism by front-line welfare workers? Sapiro (1983) noted that women are less likely than men to convert their political interests into activism. She also concluded from her data analyses (1982, 1983) that women's political activities are altered by their parental status, especially if they are single parents. It would be useful to have comparative data by gender, marital and parental status, and level of job-specific political activism to assess how these factors interplay for front-line staff in social welfare agencies. A more fundamental gender-relevant issue is researchers' disproportionate emphasis on formal political participation rather than informal, or street-level, politics. The former is undertaken more by social policymakers and agency administrators, who are disproportionately men, while the latter represent important political behaviors engaged in at levels where women predominate. To a degree implementation studies (see Hargrove 1975; Lipsky 1978) and feminist reconceptualizations of politics (Boals 1975; Sapiro 1983) are addressing this bias and thereby bring women centrally into research on politics. The arbitrary boundary between public and private behaviors is being challenged, and heretofore private issues are now coming to be understood as having political content as well.

Another intriguing question concerns welfare workers whose employment represents upward mobility. How do they accommodate conflicting demands from former and new reference groups? Limited evidence from research on graduate social-work students reveals that students with lower socioeconomic backgrounds are less sympathetic toward the poor (Grimm and Orten 1973). This finding fundamentally challenges the hopes of some optimists that integration of the public work force would, among other things, result in greater rapport between workers and clients. This research does not address how these attitudes may be mediated by professional training or formal work experience, however. Gilkes' (1983) description of black women community workers "going up for the oppressed" is an excellent model for further investigation along this line. Her research described the dialectics of utilizing positions of authority for the betterment of one's own people.

A related question surrounds the likelihood of worker-client coalitions, as former clients themselves become welfare agents. What factors contribute to or undermine the potential for joint political action? Berman and Haug (1973) and Feild, Holley, and Holley (1980) documented paraprofessionals' strong interest in upward mobility within the service agency, providing an empirical basis for the claim that paraprofessionals are likely to align themselves with the agency rather than with the target population (Grosser 1966; Adams and Freeman 1979). Furthermore, is client interaction with welfare agencies facilitated by the presence of indigenous paraprofessionals, as anticipated by the framers of client participation legislation? Limited evidence suggests paraprofessional success in voter registration and family casework (Gartner 1971). It appears, however, that success is often measured in terms of inputs (what tasks paraprofessionals perform) rather than outputs (such as quality of client-worker interaction).

Another important issue is the degree to which the competing dynamics of professionalization and deprofessionalization generate or exacerbate gender, race, and class tensions among social welfare employees. Insofar as these trends reflect or promote cleavages along demographic lines of social stratification, it seems likely that occupational controversies will become intermixed with charges of elitism or discrimination. If so, we need to ask to what extent political attitudes developed in the workplace effect employees' general political orientations regarding economic issues and civil rights. For example, will white workers' previous support for civil rights erode when their own jobs are threatened? Will all workers be willing to settle for wage freezes in the face of job scarcity? Ongoing retrenchment of the work force in virtually all public services currently affords a critical time for such research to be conducted, especially since many employment debates have posited the values of affirmative action and seniority in direct opposition to each other.

A final illustration of questions that can be raised by the social status of welfare employees is how their gender, racial, or economic marginality affects public opinion or policy decisions about social welfare benefits and services. How much public credibility and political clout can they foster, despite the low status of their clients and their own possible marginality? In short, the social status of the welfare work force may be a crucial factor in issues ranging from the interpersonal dynamics of worker-client relationships to the legislative successes or failures of social welfare policies.

Workplace Dynamics

Research focusing on the welfare workplace as an arena for political socialization may be said to treat three key issues: inputs, processes, and outcomes. *Inputs* refer to the "raw materials" that workers bring to their employment in social welfare agencies: general and specific political attitudes, particular motivations for undertaking welfare work, and their level and kind of work-related training or education, to name a few. *Processes* refer to how political socialization unfolds in day-to-day, face-to-face interactions among welfare workers, and with clients and a host of significant others. This focus examines the content and sources of political messages available to workers and how they cognitively process them. Outcomes are the cognitive and behavioral consequences of political learning for workers themselves, their clients, and the political systems in which they are embedded.

We shall examine each of these issues in some detail. Prior to a review, however, it is essential to note that the bulk of available research, especially on inputs and outcomes, has serious methodological shortcomings. First, although cross-sectional research designs are frequently employed, researchers are nonetheless inclined to draw conclusions about aging effects (see Steckenrider and Cutler, chapter 2, and Delli Carpini, chapter 1, in this volume regarding distinctions among aging, cohort, and period influences in political socialization). Second, most studies fail to treat how the sociopolitical climate of the time during which the research was conducted may have influenced the findings. Consequently, it is hazardous to compare similar studies undertaken years apart or even within different political administrations. Finally, the populations from which most samples are obtained are severely limited, often to a single graduate school or agency. Generalization to an entire occupation with diverse practitioners and work settings on the basis of these studies is thus hazardous.

Inputs

Literature about inputs relevant to issues of political socialization covers at least three major themes: (1) generalized political attitudes and personality attributes of persons entering social work education or practice; (2) specific political attitudes central to welfare work performance; and (3) the impact of formal social work education on students' attitudes and beliefs. Most research has utilized social work student samples because of their ready availability. However, because a rather high proportion of social welfare practitioners does not have formal social work training (see Gartner 1971), one must be cautious about generalizing the findings to all practitioners. Caution is especially in order in light of our earlier discussion of the impact of deprofessionalization on the composition of the work force.

A variety of general political attitudes and personality characteristics of social work students has been investigated. Researchers have found that people recruited to social work education are generally more liberal than their peers. For example, studies have reported that graduate social work students are less authoritarian than graduate students in other majors (Kidneigh and

directly investigate how these competing influences are mediated by individuals training to be practitioners.

The final major dimension of inputs into the politics of welfare work is socialization within professional schools. Because many states do not require licensure of social workers and many social welfare positions do not require formal social work training, a large proportion of social welfare workers do not undergo this socialization experience. For those who do, there are conflicting claims regarding its impact. Despite the profession's long-standing commitment to specialized social work education as requisite preparation for employment in social agencies, some writers (Hayes and Varley 1965) maintain that professional training has little empirically demonstrated effect on trainees. Alternatively, others (Hepworth and Shumway 1976) document statistically significant changes in selected areas of development. These studies are based on various assumptions about the kinds of attributes, skills, and knowledge graduating students should possess. Yet the assumptions themselves are problematic, given the persistent debate historically and disagreement at any one time about the appropriate mission of the social work curriculum (Levy 1968; Dinerman 1982).

While the foregoing research is concerned with schools' influence on students, it is also relevant to question students' reciprocal impact on their educational experience. In short, do students themselves affect the educational process? One especially interesting, if limited, report focuses on minority social work students engaged in internships in an agency setting (Olmstead 1983). The case study described how students' criticisms prompted changes in agency staffing, client outreach, and diagnosis and treatment strategies. All of the changes were instituted to enable the agency to be more responsive to its minority clientele. In particular, students became aware of the potential for client mistrust of service systems, the need for outreach for both clients and minority staff members, and the utility of a diagnostic shift from individual pathology to an ecological model and treatment plan. The agency responded to students' criticisms by developing a new case-recording format consistent with an ecological model, conducting a course for agency personnel on an ecological approach to casework, holding workshops for staff to raise their awareness of minority issues, and taking steps in hiring that realized designated affirmative action goals. In short, because field internships are a central component of both undergraduate and graduate education, and because students enter professional training with varying career goals, it would be fruitful to investigate ways in which they may alter both agency and university operations.

Processes

The processes of political socialization through on-the-job experiences have been the subject of considerable research and conceptualization, most recently in a flurry of studies on burnout. A common theme running through much of the work in this area is the inherent dilemmas encountered by people who perform social welfare functions. In particular, workers face two central and related problems that require political resocialization: role conflict from incompatible client and agency needs and normative conflict between organizational and professional expectations.

Welfare workers are supposed to help people. That expectation is the centerpiece of professional education and the expressed reason many providers choose the occupation (Pins 1963). Most workers expect to accomplish this mission through employment in a welfare bureaucracy. But in doing so, welfare workers, in effect, become mediators between the needs of clients and the resources of their employing agency. This structural position is fraught with tension because clients and employers evaluate providers' performances on the basis of very different, and often contradictory, criteria. The priority need of clients is to obtain a benefit or service; agencies offer benefits or services, of course, but within budgetary constraints. At the same time agencies are expected to serve the interests of the larger community by protecting taxpayers' or contributors' investments (Scott 1969; Howe 1980) and to maintain their own organizational stability and growth.

Abstractions such as these frequently become operationalized as role conflict for social welfare workers. For example, an agency administrator may urge providers to divert clients from one program to another more visible one, regardless of the advisability of change for the client, in order to engender community support for the agency. Or a supervisor preparing a grant proposal may impose a short paperwork deadline on a caseworker despite the latter's already full calendar of home visits. Or a client may contact a provider with a self-proclaimed emergency at the time a worker is also due at an important staff meeting. The latter two illustrations reflect the inevitable time conflicts that workers experience.

Another source of role conflict is the scarcity of financial resources for accommodating the needs of all eligible clients (see Scott 1969; Maslach and Pines 1977; Maslach and Jackson 1978; Pines and Maslach 1978; Lipsky 1980; Helmer 1982; Dressel 1984, on lack of time and funds). The persistent lack of funds and time adequate to address needs makes rationing of services and benefits necessary. With the minimal assistance of typically broad guidelines for targeting aid and attention, workers routinely must decide who gets the available limited resources and who does not. None of these dilemmas has an immediately clear or consistently appropriate resolution. Although welfare workers may have been trained to tend to clients' needs and believe in their primacy, they are less likely to be prepared for the dilemmas surrounding that mission. Consequently the role conflicts characteristic of social welfare work mandate resocialization.

Theoretically, normative or ideological systems offer guidance for the resolution of role conflicts. In the case of social welfare, however, there are also normative conflicts between professional and bureaucratic belief systems (Billingsley 1964; Lubove 1969; Finch 1976a; Robin and Wagenfeld 1977; Rein and Rabinovitz 1978; Reamer 1983). The norms of the social work profession view the client as the provider's primary allegiance; bureaucratic norms expect workers' commitment to be to the employing agency and its policies. The competing normative systems often create additional concrete dilemmas for welfare workers. For example, how can the worker assist a client's quest for independence if the agency's funding is premised on ongoing client dependence? How can the worker be both efficient and effective in processing cases if the agency caseload quota allows workers only fifteen minutes with each client? As with role conflicts, there are no easy solutions to the normative conflicts experienced by welfare workers.

Both types of dilemmas, role conflict and normative conflict, must be resolved daily by welfare workers,[3] despite their lack of formal preparation for handling the contradictions. The decisions they make every day from one agency to the next in order to manage competing demands collectively sum into social policy generated from the bottom up. This is the sense in which street-level bureaucrats make welfare policy, regardless of whether they do so inadvertently or systematically. Furthermore, how they manage or resolve the inherent work dilemmas can entail political resocialization in the face of unexpected circumstances.

The research on welfare workers' responses to on-the-job experiences describes a rich repertoire of attitudinal and behavioral coping skills. Studies are less clear about the conditions under which workers favor one strategy over another for the resolution of conflict; nor are they clear about the agents, channels, or mechanisms through which workers learn adaptive responses. At least three cognitive and three behavioral adaptations are reported in the literature.

Some workers manage the conflicts of their jobs through cognitive reorganization of the stressful situation. Often stress reduction is achieved through role-bargaining, comparisons, or philosophical orientations. Role-bargaining refers to the intrapersonal negotiation of an appropriate performance level for one's role (Goode 1960). Through such negotiation workers variously reduce their own expectations for what they can accomplish (Lipsky 1980; Dressel 1984), keep professional distance between themselves and their clients (Levy 1970; Pines and Maslach 1978), engage in ritualistic decision-making (Levy 1970; Handler and Hollingsworth 1971; Street, Martin, and Gordon 1979), and "goof off" (Levy 1970).

Another strategy in the face of conflict is the utilization of comparisons (Thibaut and Kelley 1959). Regardless of the built-in frustrations, when workers compare their jobs favorably to their occupational alternatives or to the jobs or work settings of others, they are less troubled by the aforementioned conflicts. Similarly, workers who approach service provision with a philosophical or religious orientation tend not to be bothered by work dilemmas (Dressel 1984). As we discuss later, the diminution of stress through employment of the latter two cognitive devices has political consequences just as surely as does the more active strategy of role-bargaining.

Welfare workers also confront job conflicts by changing their behaviors, most notably through role manipulation (Levy 1970; Wasserman 1971; Maslach and Pines 1977; Brager and Holloway 1978; Maslach and Jackson 1978; Pines and Maslach 1978; Dressel 1984), norm violation (Levy 1970; Brager and Holloway 1978; Dressel 1984), and social action (Gilkes 1983; Dressel 1984).

Role manipulation refers to control over the activation or deactivation of role relationships (Goode 1960; Sarbin and Allen 1968). The various forms it takes in response to work conflicts include compartmentalization of work and nonwork time and activities (or, "not taking the job home"), temporary curtailment of work responsibilities through absenteeism and time off, elimination of the entire work role through resigning one's position or part of the work role through the delegation of selected responsibilities, and expansion of certain work responsibilities in order to avoid others (see Sieber 1974).

Norm violation is behavior that challenges the formal and informal expectations of the job. It ranges from client abuse to rule-breaking on behalf of the client and is usually accompanied by attempts to explain deviant conduct in culturally appropriate terms (see Scott and Lyman 1968; Stokes and Hewitt 1976). For example, workers who voice negative feelings about clients may deny that these feelings affect their ability to accord clients fair treatment; alternatively, workers who violate policy guidelines in order to obtain service for a particular client may justify their action as consistent with the ultimate purpose of the social agency. Such explanations reduce workers' cognitive dissonance; as we argue later, they are also likely to produce alterations in work ethics over the long term.

A final response to job dilemmas is social action on the part of service workers to restructure the arrangements of their tasks or work situations and thereby eliminate the sources of conflict. Social actions include behaviors such as lobbying for passage of particular legislation or administrative regulations, registering clients to vote, and joining colleagues or clients in political coalitions. Unlike the aforementioned responses, social action challenges the organization of the work itself, the relationships of the workplace, and/or the sociopolitical conditions that foster service dilemmas. Even if social action is unsuccessful, it can reduce workers' frustrations over role conflicts by allowing them to believe that they seek long-term solutions to the inherent contradictions of their jobs. It is intended to effect permanent solutions, whereas other coping mechanisms are designed largely to provide short-term relief to frustrated employees. Social action as a response to work conflicts is clearly political in nature; role manipulation and norm violation also have significant political consequences, albeit more subtle ones.

Outcomes

Because providers' responses to work dilemmas are varied, the consequences of their responses are varied as well. More likely than not, however, the cognitive and behavioral changes they undergo serve to perpetuate the dilemmas and inadequacies of the social welfare system rather than to challenge or transform it. What are transformed instead are the altruistic orientations that many workers bring to the job. The political consequences of workers' resocialization are felt by workers themselves, their clients, and the larger welfare enterprise.

Workers' adaptive measures offer at least short-term relief from job stresses. Indeed, providers employing favorable comparisons or positive philosophies may even be oblivious to the troubles of their work. Individuals who utilize role bargaining and role manipulation as ways of coping often subvert the service ideals which brought them to social work in the first place. They do so in the name of being realistic about limitations of the welfare workplace rather than seeing those limitations as problematic. Over time they are likely to come to believe in the adjustments as optimal practice, thereby crystallizing their accommodation to work problems (see Zajonc 1968, and Stokes and Hewitt 1976). This is true of workers who employ comparisons and philosophical orientations as well as those involved in role bargaining and role manipulation.

On the other hand, workers for whom coping strategies are unsuccessful are likely to engage in high absenteeism as a preliminary step to leaving welfare work altogether. Consequently, the workplace achieves equilibrium by the resocialization of those workers who remain and the eventual expulsion of those who are unable or unwilling to change. Accordingly, Gilkes (1983) found that community workers oriented to social change did not give priority to job tenure. Rather, they realized that the confrontations they initiated would inevitably result in their having to leave one work setting for another.

What impact does resocialization have on clients? Role manipulation virtually guarantees that clients will have to deal with multiple service providers over time, the result of which is likely to be a fragmented service experience. Role bargaining contributes to worker detachment in interaction with clients and the possibility that lowered expectations will become self-fulfilling prophecies. It also functions to undermine universalism as a service ideal. That is, workers may decide to salvage their original service ideals for at least some of their clients. However, such rationing of energy is based on workers' personal biases and preferences, often favoring less needy and more bureaucratically astute clients at the expense of less articulate and needier ones (Street, Martin, and Gordon 1979; Lipsky, 1980). The former types of clients conceivably are also likely to be the recipients of worker norm violations in the form of rule-bending. The latter types, on the other hand, may become scapegoats for worker frustrations and perhaps be subject to hostility and verbal or even physical abuse.

The larger welfare enterprise is left unchallenged by workers' accommodations to its shortcomings and contradictions. Organizations are deprived of the feedback they normally require if they are to become self-correcting (Hirschman 1970; Landau 1973). Indeed, blame for workplace frustrations becomes displaced on "difficult," "demanding" clients or on workers themselves who "can't cope." Insofar as these misplaced shorthand analyses of "what's wrong with the welfare system" fit into the broader cultural climate of public opinion and the political climate of particular interest-group pressures, good will may erode toward both welfare workers and their clients. Under such circumstances, agendas for welfare retrenchment are easier to realize.

In short, the typical scenario of political socialization in social welfare work emphasizes provider accommodations to workplace problems. The erosion of pre-occupational service ideals is rationalized as functional for workers' mental health, efficient job performance, and agency staffing stability. Underlying problems go unchallenged. The consequences of resocialization include the subversion of basic social work principles, the scapegoating of clients and providers, and ideological justifications for cutbacks in welfare commitments.

An alternative scenario exists wherein providers challenge welfare decisions and workplace arrangements and seek social change on behalf of themselves or their clients. While it is not so commonplace as the scenario of accommodation, political activism is by no means incompatible with welfare work ideologies or mandates. Indeed, the professional and practitioner literature offers ongoing debate on the appropriate parameters for and anticipated outcomes of welfare workers' political activities (Galper 1975; Horejsi, Walz, and Connolly 1977; Adams and Freeman 1979; Tambor 1979; Alexander 1980; Wolk 1981; Matthews 1982; Funiciello and Sanzillo 1983; Lightman 1983; Salcido 1984). Attention has been directed toward (a) coalition-building with and on behalf of clients, (b) occupational self-interest politics, and (c) participation in formalized political channels.

Before summarizing the debates and findings in each area, we must note several shortcomings of the literature. First, writings on these issues tend to be prescriptive rather than empirical. Debates regarding the appropriate political roles of welfare workers are themselves symbolic socialization agents for practitioners; however, the limited research lends only minimal empirical insight into the abundant rhetorical claims. Second, empirical articles typically focus on case studies or limited survey samples, severely restricting broader generalization. Third, the research all too often fails explicitly to address the sociopolitical climate of the time during which data are collected. An underlying, if unintended, assumption of such oversight is that welfare workers' politics are treated as issues embedded solely in the nature of their work tasks and structural locations in social agencies. Yet the most cursory examination of social welfare history teaches that human service workers are most likely to be politically mobilized when major social movements are engaging the broader society. Finally, the literature for the most part leaves unexamined the factors that converge to generate worker politicization for the purpose of change rather than accommodation.

With these limitations in mind, we turn first to politics expressed in conjunction with client interests and client-interest groups. Professional ethics of social work dictate practitioner advocacy on the client's behalf. As we noted earlier, at the microlevel advocacy is manifest in such day-to-day actions as rule-bending or refusal to activate dehumanizing regulations. At the macrolevel rather widespread coalitions of workers and clients have emerged from time to time, most recently in the 1960s around welfare rights and in the 1980s around worker registration of clients to vote. These activities seem to be promoted by broader sociopolitical events: expansive federal social legislation and civil rights movements in the former case, and assaults on the federal social welfare agenda by elected officials in the latter case. The absence of similar large-scale efforts by welfare workers and clients within relatively quiet sociopolitical periods suggests that service workers and recipients take their political cues from social forces apart from the worker-client dyad or localized agency concerns. It further suggests that their political activities in the absence of broader supports are unlikely to be successful (Adams and Freeman 1979). Utilizing theoretical and conceptual tools from the literature on social movements and the dissemination of social action, researchers might fruitfully focus on the mechanisms whereby broad social movements infiltrate and inform localized politics, how welfare workers and clients come to identify their concerns as intertwined with larger social forces, and the dynamic ways in which local and national political actions enhance, impede, or otherwise influence one another.

What impact worker-client political coalitions have on day-to-day welfare practice is clearer than their impact on larger political dynamics. There is case-study documentation, for example, of coalitions changing the representation on specific committees, altering their goals and forging improved worker-client understanding (Marquardt and Camp 1977). However, any wider impact of worker-client political coalitions is difficult if not impossible to document. Although interest groups frequently lay claim to responsibility for the passage of specific legislation or the implementation or blockage of administrative regulations, the causal chain is never unambiguous.

Because the mandate of welfare workers is to help others, considerable controversy surrounds the extent to which providers should seek their own occupational interests. As noted earlier, self-interest politics is expressed through two primary channels, the professional association and the union. Membership in these bodies tends to be delineated by level of education and job function, both of which are correlated with race and social class. Consequently, MSW professionals, who are likely to be middle-class and disproportionately white, express their concerns through the professional associations; BSW and nondegree paraprofessionals, who are more likely than their MSW counterparts to be working class and nonwhite, gravitate toward unions. The differences between associations and unions go beyond membership characteristics to philosophies, goals, and tactics (Alexander 1980). Unions emphasize adversarial relationships with management and stress economic issues, while professional associations incorporate management in a quest for a larger good and professional autonomy. Union tactics frequently involve power struggles, whereas professional struggles often are resolved by reliance on codes of ethics or the findings of investigatory studies. The ideology of professionalism in social welfare work encourages putting client welfare above that of the worker. Workers' class interests become subordinated as a result (Tambor 1979). In contrast, unions highlight class issues. Some observers (Alexander 1980) see the two types of employee organizations as oppositional; others (Lightman 1982) argue for a division of labor between them in the interest of all workers. Still others (Oppenheimer 1975) maintain that the changing treatment of professional workers due to growing proletarianization of the workplace will propel them toward unionization. Empirical studies are limited in their focus to issues such as workers' attitudes toward one or the other vehicle of political expression (Shaffer 1979; Lightman 1982), and attitudes toward work stoppages or strikes (Lightman 1983). As in the case of claims about worker-client coalitions, it is possible to document distributive instances of change brought about by pressures from professional associations and unions, but aggregate claims are less readily substantiated. Substantiation of broad claims of influence requires either detailed historical or political economic analyses that are large in scope, or in-depth "behind-the-scenes" case studies of the intricate maneuverings and complex variables that produce certain outcomes. These kinds of research are regrettably scarce in the literature of social welfare work.

Finally, a few studies have addressed social workers' activism through formal political channels such as campaign activities and political contributions. On the basis of limited evidence, it can tentatively be argued that service workers seem to be more politically active than the general population. Within the profession, however, workers in direct services were significantly less likely than their colleagues in community organization or social workers in administration or teaching to be politically active (Wolk 1981). Furthermore, political activity and influence are not necessarily correlated. Matthews (1982) found that social workers as a group were not viewed as especially influential in the legislative process, thereby reinforcing the claim that their success may be contingent on alignment with larger, more powerful organizations or social movements.

In summary, the quest for social change within and beyond social agencies is a persistent, if secondary, dynamic of the welfare workplace. Some service workers challenge workplace problems and contradictions as an integral orientation to their everyday work. From time to time large numbers of workers are moved to political action through interest group coalitions and formal electoral channels. We know very little, however, about what influences some workers to become change agents at work while their counterparts, instead, work in ways that reinforce the arrangements of the welfare enterprise.

Beyond the Workplace

In the preceding overview of the literature on political socialization in social welfare work we have shown that both continuity and change are recurring themes of the workplace and those who study it. The themes are manifested on the one hand in the resocialization of many workers to accommodate the work's limitations; workers' actions consequently reproduce and elaborate the existing welfare system. In effect, individual change enables institutional stability. On the other hand, some workers (few most of the time and larger numbers at specific historical junctures) retain their original ideals even in the face of workplace pressures; their actions are oriented to change within social welfare institutions that will facilitate the realization of their original ideals. In this case the persistence and tenacity of individual beliefs promote institutional change. Both dynamics highlight interactions between the micro- and macro-levels of the workplace and demonstrate the mutuality of influence between workers and the work setting as agents of reorganization and resocialization, respectively.

To be sure, the literature in this area has serious shortcomings that make generalized conclusions tenuous. We have already noted the asociological, ahistorical, and atheoretical character of much research, its historically biased emphasis on formal political channels, the lack of longitudinal studies, the misleading conclusions drawn from cross-sectional data, limited student and practitioner samples, a lack of research on students' impact on university and internship settings, and the need for specification of conditions under which accommodation or change is likely to occur. In short, both theory and data in this area are far narrower than they should be and than a rich treatment of the subject matter demands.

Even with its shortcomings, however, the examination of welfare work as a locus for political socialization is potentially rich in what it can offer the broader study of adult political socialization. We suggest three theoretical perspectives offered by research on welfare workers that deserve attention beyond this particular work setting. They are (a) role stresses as a source of stability or change, (b) the interplay of individual political conduct and the larger political culture, and (c) the function of marginality as a research focus.

Role Stresses

Role stresses take a variety of forms and derive from various social situations (see Sarbin and Allen 1968; Gross 1970). Of particular interest to political socialization theorists are the concepts of role conflict, role frustration, and role inadequacy. Any of these experiences calls for some combination of alteration in individual role performance and environmental demand. Role conflict refers to the experience of incompatible expectations either from within oneself, from others, or from both sources. We have already illustrated certain role conflicts encountered by welfare workers as they try to satisfy needs of both employers and clients. Some time ago Ziegenhagen (1970) acknowledged the utility of this concept in political socialization. Role frustration and role inadequacy are counterpart concepts (see Bates and Harvey 1975). The former refers to the lack of situational resources and the latter refers to the lack of appropriate personal resources for adequate role performance. By way of illustration, welfare workers who do not have enough funds to address the needs of all clients are likely to experience role frustration, while those without specialized counseling skills may encounter role inadequacy in trying to function as a caseworker. All three role concepts highlight the lack of a person-situation "fit." The quest for the reduction of person-situation tensions is the stage on which political socialization gets played out. These concepts are applicable beyond work settings to wherever role stresses occur. For example, one could just as well examine shifting gender politics and resocialization in a two-career family with a newborn baby by utilizing these conceptual tools as we have done in applying them to the welfare workplace.

A related social psychological research tradition offers additional tools for political socialization theorists. The abundant writings on cognitive dissonance (see Zajonc 1968) attend to ways in which role stresses are managed and suggest how some management strategies produce accommodation while others generate change. For example, we have already noted that welfare workers readily assimilate the stresses of their work if they compare their jobs favorably to previously held positions or occupational alternatives. Cognitive dissonance theory also addresses the issue of commitment to one's choices once they are made. Here it could be helpful for understanding party allegiances and candidate preferences over time, even in the face of political adversity. As a final illustration, cognitive dissonance theory could be applied to understanding a people's eventual accommodation to or rebellion against outside domination. In the case of accommodation, cognitive distress is alleviated when public behavioral conformity influences private attitudinal change. Alternatively, rebellion represents the challenge of private ideology to the public conformity demanded by colonizers of the colonized.

Conduct and Culture

Another issue our discussion of welfare workers has raised concerns how individual political conduct shapes and is shaped by the larger political culture. We have noted that many people enter welfare work with strong altruistic motives and are confronted with environmental demands and situational dilemmas that frequently alter their behaviors. When workers' performances fall short of their ideals, they rationalize them with a variety of cognitive tools called aligning actions (Stokes and Hewitt 1976; Hunter 1984). Our discussion above of workers' coping strategies of role-bargaining and the use of comparisons and philosophical orientations illustrates the concept of aligning actions. The use of aligning actions acknowledges that service ideals are intact even if they are not presently operative; in other words, welfare workers attempt to preserve the larger cultural value of altruism in the face of pressures against it. However, aligning-action theorists argue that, over the long run, culture adjusts to conduct. That is, service ideals are likely to erode over time to bring them in line with what it is possible for welfare workers to accomplish. The literature on aligning actions has potential in political socialization research for exploring arenas in addition to the workplace. For example, one could study ways in which parents who verbally endorse equality but behave in discriminatory ways represent this contradiction to their children. Attention could also be given to what specific messages these children acquire from their parental socialization agents. Or one could study the voting record and campaign rhetoric of a staunch abortion foe whose district changes over time into a younger, increasingly urbanized, non-Catholic constituency. A focus on aligning actions provides conceptual linkage between everyday individual conduct and the larger cultural context which it either reinforces or challenges.

Marginality

Finally, we propose that researchers in adult political socialization stand to gain perhaps their greatest insights by focusing on marginal individuals in the social systems of their concern. By marginal individuals we mean persons whose social locations or status place them at junctures between competing social systems or forces. With regard to social welfare workers, indigenous paraprofessionals represent marginal people. Their work responsibilities derive from their similarity to clients, yet the work role posits a certain psychological and social distance from clients. Because of their marginality these individuals may be able to make the taken-for-granted premises of their social setting more obvious, if not transform them (Willie 1975), and in so doing expose the dominant political culture for study. In addition, because these persons clearly must negotiate dialectical pressures, they may render the process of negotiation more visible to the researcher. To illustrate the function of marginality further, if one wishes to gain greater understanding of gender, electoral, racial, or national politics, one could focus on single custodial fathers, female presidential and vice-Presidential candidates, black Republicans, and Soviet Jews, respectively. The suggestion to study marginal people is the structural counterpart to the recommendation of focusing on crises and transitions to better understand processual dynamics (see Erikson 1976).

To date, political socialization theorists have relied heavily on developmental and learning theories to ground and guide their work. We recommend adding the aforementioned interactionist and interpretive social psychological perspectives to the repertoire of theoretical tools. The interactionist and interpretive traditions have the potential for understanding the individual as a dynamic learner, negotiator, and shaper of political ideas and the political environment.

A Final Word

Social welfare work is changing. Increasingly, services are provided through private, nonprofit agencies under contract to government, and through private, profit-oriented agencies using third-party payments and individual fee-for-service relationships. More and more, computers are keeping track of client eligibility and entitlements. The welfare state, broadly defined, now includes alcoholism counseling provided by the employer, counseling through nonprofit corporations under contract to the courts, and outpatient psychotherapy paid for by health maintenance organizations.

Privatization and the changing organizational contexts in which it is practiced should have profound effects on social welfare work. These trends simultaneously promote the transformations in professionalization and deprofessionalization about which we wrote above. They also prefigure changes in the accountability structures of service, with implications for the nature of welfare workers' constituencies. We may perhaps pull some of the issues of socialization in social welfare together by reviewing the general importance of the following considerations for the nature of service to clients.

Recruitment to social welfare occupations is strongly affected by prevailing wages and benefits, and the relative status accorded to helping professions at any given time. It will be affected as well by the centrality of and support for social welfare institutions in the society. These have varied considerably over time and place in the recent past. Who enters social welfare work will also be affected by the structure of alternatives confronting new recruits. It would be wise to entertain the view that recruits to social welfare work vary in ability, background, and attitudes over time not only because such jobs are variably attractive but also because talented people will be able to go into different lines of work as racial and sex barriers fall or shift in society.

Social welfare workers may vary considerably in the backgrounds and predispositions they bring to the work, but these backgrounds by themselves clearly do not determine how workers practice. Rather, "backgrounds" may be said to be disciplined by the work structure in which people find themselves. Biases in the practice of social welfare may find expression to a greater degree than in other jobs because of the high discretion which characterizes these occupational roles. But this discretion in itself does not predict how or whether personal dispositions will be expressed. In other words, the existence of discretion does not itself lead to biased behavior on the part of workers.

Bureaucratic systems characterized by discretion among lower-level workers will also incorporate values and norms which at times will predispose workers to act according to personal preferences inappropriate to the job but normally will encompass discretionary impulses consistent with the preferences of their agencies. This is why it is possible to maintain *both* that frontline workers have great discretion *and* that agencies can hold workers accountable and retain control over policy.

If, indeed, the socialization of social welfare workers affects policy outcomes as well as service morale, analysts concerned with social welfare policy would be well advised to attend to the way workers are recruited, trained and initiated into the world of practice. These should be concerns not only of schools of social work and public managers but also of the broad constituency that continues to protect social welfare agencies against persistent attacks on their mission and claims to effectiveness.

Notes

1. Rosenberg's (1985) main argument, however, is not one with which we concur. His claims regarding the inadequacies of sociologically based political-socialization

research are based on a limited understanding of only normative theory in sociology; he completely overlooks the discipline's interpretive and interactionist traditions.

2. See Meyers (1984) for discussion of preference for the phrase "oppressed group" rather than "minority group."

3. Findings from national survey data on MSWs with membership in the National Association of Social Workers show that the particular stresses vary in degree and kind according to the area of practitioner specialization. For example, child welfare workers report significantly greater role and value conflicts than do family service and community mental health specialists (Jayaratne and Chess 1984).

References

Adams, Paul, and Gary Freeman. 1979. "On the Political Character of Social Service Work." *Social Service Review* 53: 560–72.

Alexander, Leslie B. 1980. "Professionalization and Unionization: Compatible after All?" *Social Work* 25: 476–82.

Almond, Gabriel A., and Sidney Verba. 1963. *The Civic Culture*. Princeton: Princeton University Press.

Bates, Frederick, and Clyde Harvey. 1975. *The Structure of Social Systems*. New York: Gardner.

Berman, Gerald S., and Marie R. Haug. 1973. "New Careers: Bridges or Ladders?" *Social Work* 18: 48–58.

Billingsley, Andrew. 1964. "Bureaucratic and Professional Orientation Patterns in Social Casework." *Social Service Review* 38: 400–7.

Boals, Kay. 1975. "Political Science." *Signs* 1: 161–74.

Boyd, Lawrence H., Jr., John H. Hylton, and Steven V. Price. 1978. "Computers in Social Work Practice: A Review." *Social Work* 23: 368–71.

Brager, George. 1965. "The Indigenous Worker." *Social Work* 10: 33–40.

Brager, George, and Stephen Holloway. 1978. *Changing Human Service Organizations*. New York: The Free Press.

Bremner, Robert H. 1956. "'Scientific philanthrophy', 1873–93." *Social Service Review* 30: 168–73.

Carlton, Thomas Owen, and Marshall Jung. 1972. "Adjustment or Change: Attitudes among Social Workers." *Social Work* 17: 64–71.

Collins, Sharon. 1983. "The Making of the Black Middle Class." *Social Problems* 30: 369–82.

Cournoyer, Barry R. 1983. "Assertiveness among MSW Students." *Journal of Education for Social Work* 19: 24–30.

Cryns, Arthur G. 1977. "Social Work Education and Student Ideology: A Multivariate Study of Professional Socialization." *Journal of Education for Social Work* 13: 44–51.

Delli Carpini, Michael X., Roberta S. Sigel, and Robin Snyder. 1983. "Does It Make Any Difference How You Feel About Your Work? An Explanatory Study of the Impact of Job Satisfaction on Political Orientations." *Micropolitics* 3: 227–51.

Dennis, Jack. 1973. "Major Problems of Political Socialization Research." In Charles G. Bell, ed., *Growth and Change: A Reader in Political Socialization,* pp.7–31. Encino, Calif.: Dickenson.

Dinerman, Miriam. 1982. "A Study of Baccalaureate and Master's Curricula in Social Work." *Journal of Education for Social Work* 18: 84–92.

DiNitto, Diana M., Patricia Yancey Martin, and Dianne F. Harrison. 1984. "Sexual Inequality among Social Work Faculty: An International Comparison." *International Social Work* 27: 27–36.

Dressel, Paula. 1984. *The Service Trap: From Altruism to Dirty Work.* Springfield, Ill.: Charles C. Thomas.

———. 1987. "Patriarchy and Social Welfare Work." *Social Problems* 34: 294–309.

Erikson, Kai T. 1976. *Everything in Its Path.* New York: Simon and Schuster.

Feild, Hubert S., William H. Holley, and Betty B. Holley. 1980. "Paraprofessional-client Similarity: Its effect on the Relation between Job Attributes and Performance." *Social Work Research and Abstracts* 16: 13–18.

Finch, Wilbur. 1976a. "Social Workers versus Bureaucracy." *Social Work* 21: 370–75.

———. 1976b. "Paraprofessionals in Public Welfare: A Utilization Study." *Public Welfare* 34: 52–57.

Fisher, Jacob. 1980. *"Social Work Today,* 1934–42, and the Dissenting Left for Which It Spoke." *Catalyst* 5: 3–23.

Funiciello, Theresa, and Tom Sanzillo. 1983. "The Voter Registration Strategy: A Critique." *Social Policy* 14: 54–58.

Galper, Jeffry H. 1975. *The Politics of Social Services.* Englewood Cliffs, N.J.: Prentice-Hall.

Gartner, Alan. 1969. "The Use of the Paraprofessional and New Directions for the Social Service Agency." *Public Welfare* 27: 117–25.

———. 1971. *Paraprofessionals and Their Performance.* New York: Praeger.

Gilkes, Cheryl Townsend. 1983. "Going Up for the Oppressed: The Career Mobility of Black Women Community Workers." *Journal of Social Issues* 39: 115–39.

Goode, William J. 1960. "A Theory of Role Strain." *American Sociological Review* 25: 483–96.

Grimm, James W., and James D. Orten. 1973. "Student Attitudes toward the Poor." *Social Work* 18: 94–100.

Gross, Edward. 1970. "Work Organization and Stress." In Sol Levine and Norman A. Scotch, eds., *Social Stress.* Chicago: Aldine.

Grosser, Charles F. 1966. "Local Residents as Mediators between Middle-class Professional Workers and Lower-class Clients." *Social Service Review* 40: 56–63.

Handler, Joel F., and Ellen Jane Hollingsworth. 1971. *The "Deserving Poor": A Study of Welfare Administration.* Chicago: Markham.

Hargrove, E. C. 1975. *The Missing Link: The Study of the Implementation of Social Policy.* Washington, D.C.: Urban Institute.

Hayes, Dorothy D., and Barbara K. Varley. 1965. "Impact of Social Work Education on Students' Values." *Social Work* 10: 40–46.

Helmer, D'Arcy J. 1982. "Iatrogenic Intraorganizational Processes as One Mediator of Burnout." In Robert F. Morgan, ed., *The Iatrogenics Handbook: A Critical Look at Research and Practice in the Helping Professions.* Toronto: IPI.

Hepworth, Dean H., and E. Gene Shumway. 1976. "Changes in Openmindedness as a Result of Social Work Education." *Journal of Education for Social Work* 12: 56–62.

Hess, Dolph, and Martha Williams. 1974. "Personality Characteristics and Value Stances of Students in Two Areas of Graduate Study." *Journal of Education for Social Work* 10.

Hirschman, Albert O. 1970. *Exit, Voice and Loyalty.* Cambridge: Harvard University Press.

Horejsi, John E., Thomas Walz, and Patrick R. Connolly. 1977. *Working in Welfare: Survival through Positive Action.* Iowa City: University of Iowa School of Social Work.

Howe, Elizabeth. 1980. "Public Professions and the Private Model of Professionalism." *Social Work* 25: 179–91.

Hunter, Christopher. 1984. "Aligning Actions: Types and Social Distribution." *Symbolic Interaction* 7: 155–74.

Jayaratne, Srinika, and Wayne A. Chess. 1984. "Job Satisfaction, Burnout, and Turnover: A National Study." *Social Work* 29: 448–53.

Karger, Howard J. 1981. "Burnout as Alienation." *Social Service Review* 55: 270–83.

Kidneigh, John C., and Horace W. Lundberg. 1958. "Are Social Work Students Different?" *Social Work* 3: 57–61.

Koepp, Edwin F. 1963. "Authoritarianism and Social Workers: A Psychological Study." *Social Work* 8: 37–43.

Landau, Martin. 1973. "On the Concept of Self-correcting Organization." *Public Administration Review* 33: 533–42.

Levy, Charles S. 1968. *Social Work Education and Practice, 1898–1955.* New York: Wurzweiler School of Social Work, Yeshiva University.

Levy, Gerald. 1970. "'Acute' Workers in a Welfare Bureaucracy." In Deborah I. Offenbacher and Constance H. Poster, eds., *Social Problems and Social Policy.* New York: Appleton-Century-Crofts.

Lipsky, Michael. 1978. "Standing the Study of Public Policy Implementation on Its Head." 1978. In W. Dean Burnham and Marth Wagner Weinberg, eds., *American Politics and Public Policy.* Cambridge, Mass.: MIT Press.

———. 1980. *Street-Level Bureaucracy.* New York: Russell Sage.

Lightman, Ernie S. 1983. "Social Workers, Strikes, and Service to Clients." *Social Work* 28: 142–47.

———. 1982. "Professionalization, Bureaucratization, and Unionization in Social Work." *Social Service Review* 56: 130–43.

Lubove, Roy. 1969. *The Professional Altruist.* New York: Atheneum.

Marquardt, Michael, and Ethel Camp. 1977. "The Worker-client Alliance: One Existing Model."In John E. Horejsi, Thomas Walz, and Patrick R. Connolly, *Working in Welfare: Survival through Positive Action.* Iowa City: University of Iowa School of Social Work.

Maslach, C., and S. E. Jackson. 1978. "Lawyer Burn-out." *Barrister* 8: 52–54.

Maslach, Christina, and Ayala Pines. 1977. "The Burn-out Syndrome in the Day Care Setting." *Child Care Quarterly* 6: 100–13.

Matthews, Gary. 1982. "Social Workers and Political Influence." *Social Service Review* 56: 616–28.

Merdinger, Joan M. 1982. "Socialization into a Profession: The Case of Undergraduate Social Work Students." *Journal of Education for Social Work* 18: 12–19.

Meyers, Barton. 1984. "Minority Group: An Ideological Formulation." *Social Problems* 32: 1–15.

NASW. 1984. "NASW Members—Selected Characteristics." Computer printout, table 13. October.

NASW News. 1985. "NASW Fights Erosion of Job Standards." 30: 6.

Olmstead, Kathleen A. 1983. "The Influence of Minority Social Work Students on an Agency's Service Methods." *Social Work* 28: 308–12.

Oppenheimer, Martin. 1975. "The Unionization of the Professional." *Social Policy* 5: 34–40.

Patry, Bill. 1978. "Taylorism Comes to the Social Services." *Monthly Review* 30: 30–37.

Pecora, Peter J., and Michael J. Austin. 1983. "Declassification of Social Service Jobs: Issues and Strategies." *Social Work* 28: 421–26.

Pines, Ayala, and Christina Maslach. 1978. "Characteristics of Staff Burnout in Mental Health Settings." *Hospital and Community Psychiatry* 29: 233–37.

Pins, Arnulf 1963. *Who Chooses Social Work? When and Why?* New York: New York Council on Social Work Education.

Piliavin, Irving, and Alan E. Gross. 1977. "The Effects of Separation of Services and Income Maintenance on AFDC Recipients." *Social Service Review* 51: 389–406.

Reamer, Frederic G. 1983. "Ethical Dilemmas in Social Work Practice." *Social Work* 28, no.1: 31–35.

Rein, Martin, and Francine F. Rabinovitz. 1978. "Implementation: A Theoretical Perspective." In Walter Dean Burnham and Marth Wagner Weinberg, eds., *American Politics and Public Policy.* Cambridge, Mass.: MIT Press.

Robin, Stanley S., and Morton O. Wagenfeld. 1977. "The Community Mental Health Worker: Organizational and Personal Sources of Role Discrepancy." *Journal of Health and Social Behavior* 18: 16–27.

Rosenberg, Shawn W. 1985. "Sociology, Psychology, and the Study of Political Behavior: The case of Research on Political Socialization." *Journal of Politics* 47: 715–31.

Rubin, Allen, and Peter J. Johnson. 1984. "Direct Practice Interests of Entering MSW Students." *Journal of Education for Social Work* 20: 5–16.

Salcido, Ramon M. 1984. "Social Work Practice in Political Campaigns." *Social Work* 29: 189–91.

Sapiro, Virginia. 1982. "Private Costs of Public Commitments or Public Costs of Private Commitments? Family Roles versus Political Ambition." *American Journal of Political Science* 26: 265–79.

———. 1983. *The Political Integration of Women: Roles, Socialization, and Politics.* Urbana: University of Illinois Press.

Sarbin, Theodore R., and Vernon L. Allen. 1968. "Role Theory." In Gardner Lindzey and Elliot Aronson, eds., *The Handbook of Social Psychology,* 2d ed. Reading: Addison-Wesley, 1968.

Schoech, Dick, and Tony Arangio. 1979. "Computers in the Human Services." *Social Work* 24: 96–102.

Schwartz, Sandra Kenyon, and David C. Schwartz. 1975. "New Directions in the Study of Political Socialization." In David C. Schwartz and Sandra Kenyon Schwartz, eds., *New Directions in Political Socialization.* New York: The Free Press.

Scott, Marvin, and Sanford Lyman 1968. "Accounts." *American Sociological Review* 33: 46–62.

Scott, W. Richard. 1969. "Professional Employees in a Bureaucratic Structure: Social Work." In Amitai Etzioni, ed., *The Semi-Professions and Their Organization.* New York: The Free Press.

Shaffer, Gary L. 1979. "Labor Relations and the Unionization of Professional Social Workers: A Neglected Area in Social Work Education." *Journal of Education for Social Work* 15: 80–86.

Sieber, Sam. 1974. "Toward a Theory of Role Accumulation." *American Sociological Review* 33: 576–78.

Sigel, Roberta S. 1983. "The Mass Media and the Political Environment." Paper presented at the annual meeting of the International Society for Political Psychology. Oxford, England.

Sigel, Roberta S., and Marilyn Brookes Hoskin. 1977. "Perspectives on Adult Political Socialization—Areas of Research." In Stanley Allen Renshon, ed., *Handbook of Political Socialization.* New York: The Free Press, 1977.

Spano, Rick. 1982. *The Rank and File Movement in Social Work.* Washington, D.C.: University Press of America.

Stokes, Randall, and John P. Hewitt. 1976. "Aligning Actions." *American Sociological Review* 41: 838–49.

Street, David, George T. Martin, Jr., and Laura Kramer Gordon. 1979. *The Welfare Industry: Functionaries and Recipients in Public Aid.* Beverly Hills: Sage Publications.

Szakacs, Juliana. 1977. "Survey Indicates Social Work Women Losing Ground in Leadership Ranks." *NASW News* 22: 12.

Tambor, Milton. 1983. "Declassification and Divisiveness in Human Services." *Administration in Social Work* 7: 61–68.

———. 1979. "The Social Worker as a Worker: A Union Perspective." *Administration in Social Work* 3: 289–300.

Thibaut, J. W., and H. H. Kelley. 1959. *The Social Psychology of Groups.* New York: John Wiley.

Transue, Judith. 1980. "Collective Bargaining on Whose Terms?" *Catalyst* 5: 25–37.

U.S. Equal Employment Opportunity Commission. 1977. *Minorities and Women in State and Local Government, 1975.* Vol. 1, *U.S. Statistical Summary.* Washington, D.C.: Government Printing Office.

Varley, Barbara K. 1963. "Socialization in Social Work Education." *Social Work* 8: 102–9.

Vetter, Betty M., Eleanor L. Babco, and Susan Jensen-Fisher. 1983. *Professional Women and Minorities: A Manpower Data Resource Service.* 4th ed. Washington, D.C.: Scientific Manpower Commission.

Vondracek, Fred W., Hugh B. Urban, and William S. Parsonage. 1974. "Feasibility of an Automated Intake Procedure for Human Services Workers." *Social Service Review* 48: 271–78.

Wasserman, Harry. 1971. "The Professional Social Worker in a Bureaucracy." *Social Work* 16: 89–96.

Willie, Charles V. 1975. "Marginality and Social Changes." *Society* 12: 10–13.

Wolk, James L. 1981. "Are Social Workers Politically Active?" *Social Work* 26: 283–88.

Zajonc, R. B. 1968. "Cognitive Theories in Social Psychology." In Gardner Lindzey and Elliot Aronson, eds., *The Handbook of Social Psychology.* 2d ed., vol. 1, pp. 320–441. Reading: Addison-Wesley.

Ziegenhagen, Edward A. 1970. "Political Socialization and Role Conflict: Some Theoretical Implications." In Roberta S. Sigel, ed., *Learning about Politics: A Reader in Political Socialization.* New York: Random House.

Five

Military Service and Political Socialization
JOHN P. LOVELL AND JUDITH HICKS STIEHM

Introduction

The political socialization that is an intended or unintended consequence of military service must be understood, first, in relation to the role that the military plays within and for society and, second, in relation to the authority that the military exercises over its members.

The justification military elites have given for seizing political power in dozens of coups d'état in recent decades (principally in Third World states) has reflected a carefully cultivated organizational self-image of praetorian responsibility. The military socialization process in such instances can be understood to have contributed to military intrusion into politics. In other political systems, however, civilian and military elites have been trying to use the socialization process to depoliticize the armed forces. Spain, Portugal, Brazil, Argentina, and the Philippines are examples (albeit with mixed results).

Military socialization in the two world superpowers involves considerations beyond politicization-depoliticization. These considerations stem from the massive resource commitments that are made to military goals, and from the global reach of the military influence of each of the powers. Both the U.S. and the USSR rely upon their armed forces to maintain and protect far-flung interests, and to check each other's influence and dominance. Each has a large military establishment with a formidable arsenal of nuclear and nonnuclear weaponry; each also has an even more sizeable military-industrial-scientific complex committed to ongoing military programs.

Neither the United States nor the Soviet Union has been faced in modern times with the threat of a military seizure of power. However, each has been faced with complicated problems involving the maintenance of political-governmental control of military policies and programs. The instrument of control in the Soviet Union is the Communist party. In the United States, the mechanism of control is somewhat more intricate. Rooted in a set of constitutional checks and balances, control ultimately is dependent upon (1) the internalization by American military professionals of attitudes and beliefs consonant with democracy and (2) the subordination of the military to elected civilian governmental leaders.

Although the role of the military varies from one political system to another, common to all is the symbolic importance of the military as *the* institution charged with the legitimate use of state violence. In fulfilling that charge, the military is entitled to ask its members both to kill on behalf of the state and to risk their lives on behalf of the state.

It is the authority to demand such sacrifices from its members that makes inquiry into the political socialization of the military so compelling. How is it, one must ask, that military institutions are able to elicit compliance with such formidable demands? Does the process of military socialization effect a radical if not total transformation of the preexisting attitudes, beliefs, and behavior of the members of these institutions? Are changes that occur effected as a result of coercion, appeals to patriotism, indoctrination, peer pressure, or other factors?

The focus in this essay will be on the political socialization of the United States armed forces, which more than virtually any other military organization have been the object of extensive systematic research by social scientists and by some military historians (Karsten 1984). It is not certain that the findings discussed below hold across national and cultural boundaries. Indeed, the long-range challenge is precisely one of identifying cross-cultural similarities and differences in military socialization.

Systematic research is more readily accomplished in some societies than in others, of course. Even in relatively open societies, however, the challenge is to go beyond statistically significant findings to politically significant ones. To do so requires supplementing survey and other data with more subtle and less quantifiable measures. It also requires attention to the political context of military socialization, and a willingness to make inferential interpretations of data.

Attention to the political context helps develop the questions about military socialization that require answers. The next section of the essay poses a variety of questions in order to set the stage for subsequent discussion. In the following section, the intentions of military and civilian elites who direct the process of military socialization are assessed. The actual results of socialization appear to differ somewhat from intentions. Those results are susceptible to empirical investigation, and are presented in the third section of the essay, along with an interpretation of the political significance of these results. In the final section, on "lessons learned," the previous interpretation is expanded and a set of conclusions is offered concerning the significance of the political socialization of the military for democratic politics.

Political Socialization of the Military: Some Current Questions

The political values and attitudes of the American armed forces have been a concern to those committed to the democratic process since the founding of the Republic. Such values and attitudes, and the socialization process that cultivates and maintains them, acquired added significance in the years since World War II. This is because the military we have known is not the military we have had since the emergence of the Cold War confrontation with the USSR. For the first time, we have something many of the Founders of the Republic warned against—a large standing army in peacetime. Today more than two million Americans wear military uniforms. Another million are directly employed by the military, and thousands of others are linked to it indirectly through work for defense contractors.

In addition, our military establishment has become an imperial one in the days since World War II. It now has bases and maneuver areas all around the globe. More than a quarter of American military personnel are stationed abroad. They are not flown in to protect immediate American interests; rather, they are stationed abroad to influence the outcome of disputes within or between other countries, to maintain the status quo, or to alter a regional balance in a direction considered favorable to U.S. interests. In short, the role is now freighted with politics; it is routinely used as an instrument of international policy/politics. Karl von Clausewitz would be comfortable with such a notion; but we Americans are entitled to concern about the political goals that are served, and about the attitudes and values that are cultivated in the armed forces in order to support particular political goals.

The modern military also differs from the pre–World War II military in being asked to serve as an instrument of deterrence. In such capacity, it is not asked to seek success in battle but rather (by its readiness) to prevent war from occurring. Further, when American troops are committed to battle, as they were in Korea and in Vietnam, the military has been asked to support limited objectives. The concepts of deterrence and limited war are both at variance with the "no substitute for victory" approach that has been traditional in the training of the American armed forces. Thus, it becomes important to ask whether or not the new concepts have fully taken root in the socialization process.

Moreover, in the years since American forces were extricated from Vietnam and military conscription was ended (1973), an all-volunteer armed force has been developed. The incentives used to attract recruits to it have been principally mercenary ones. We need to know the consequences of this new incentive system for the political socialization process.

A final dimension of change that distinguishes the modern U.S. military from that of earlier eras is the technological one. Preparation for the possibility of future war includes design and operation of ballistic missiles, nuclear explosives, laser and particle-beam weapons, satellite communication and anti-satellite weapons, and a host of other high-tech devices. Thus, military professionalization includes a heavy dose of specialized training. As military professionals acquire an expertise that sets them apart from civilians (including many in Congress who are charged with oversight of the military), do they also acquire attitudes and values at odds with the democratic values of the society? Or, conversely, has the modern military establishment become "civilianized" in values and self-image as well as in skill requirements, perhaps to a point that detracts from its ability to conduct war effectively? Some argue that trends such as scientism in military training, the blurring of the distinction between military and civilian expertise, the emphasis upon management in officer education, and the focus on making barracks life agreeable to enlisted personnel have all had a corrosive effect on military attitudes and preparedness.

Political Socialization of the Military: Lessons Intended

The United States armed forces traditionally have looked askance at political indoctrination (Wesbrook 1979). To be sure, "troop information" programs are a regular feature of training; and in wartime a special effort is made to justify the goals of war and combat objectives. But few military officials have enthusiasm for the idea that their training mission has a political dimension. When officers have displayed enthusiasm for such an approach to training, as army general William Walker did in the early 1960s with his "Pro-Blue" campaign of anti-Communist indoctrination that relied heavily on materials developed by the John Birch Society, their efforts sometimes have been deleterious to their careers (as Walker's most assuredly were—he was relieved of his command).

To argue that American military officials eschew involvement in political indoctrination is not to contend that they avoid seeking to instill values, attitudes, and beliefs that are highly salient to political life. On the contrary, there is an important political dimension to military socialization that is intended.

The military socialization process involves the training of thousands of men and women, enlisted and officers, every year. The armed forces publish instructions for trainees, and lesson plans and manuals for trainers—drill sergeants, or platoon leaders and company commanders. Basic training or "boot camp" is the common denominator for enlisted personnel; the academies' "plebe year" and ROTC's summer camp are the precommissioning experiences for prospective officers. It is during entry-level training that the most essential messages are transmitted. The primary activity is one of transforming "citizens into soldiers" (or sailors, marines, or airmen). The symbolism of patriotic identification with the state is ubiquitous; this is reinforced by rituals such as parades, flag-raising, and retreat ceremonies.

Otherwise there is little political content to the initial indoctrination the young man or young woman receives upon entering military service, beyond an occasional reference to defending "democracy and the free world," meeting "the Communist threat," and honoring "God and country". There is no American counterpart to the zambolit or political commissar whose role in the Soviet military remains central to the socialization process (Jones 1985).

Still, even beyond the explicit symbols of statehood and patriotism, there are a number of clear messages presented to American military recruits. One is that the military is competent, it is in control, it is in charge. Basic training (which is used as a shorthand here for the initial military training experience for officers-to-be as well as for enlisted personnel) takes place in an intense, total environment. Recruits are isolated from outsiders but have no privacy in relation to their peers (Faris 1975). The civilian world is left wholly behind. Even one's relationship to the time of day becomes altered, with a twenty-four-hour clock. Before new recruits arrive, the trainer is so carefully prepared that his checklist includes diluting the floor wax, obtaining sanitary napkins for the first-aid kit, and testing the mop wringers. Every requirement of the trainee is anticipated and met, including clothing, food, bedding, and time scheduling (U.S. Army Training Center 1983). The intent and effect of this total environment are to make the trainee experience the military as both omniscient and omnipotent, as a bandwagon worth joining.

But "joining" is more than signing up. The recruit must prove his or her worth to become part of "the team." Basic is a rite of passage; and only as a succession of tests of one's worthiness are met is admission to the group to be granted.

The daily schedule is demanding. Every element of life is defined. There is a correct way to arrange the content of each dresser drawer, and a correct way to place a hanger on a rack. Any other way is the wrong way. Physical demands also are severe. The precision, detail, and effort demanded are impossible of immediate achievement; but they are ultimately possible for most recruits. Because meeting the standards is difficult, success is valued; but success is also something most recruits are able to realize. Thus, the training is designed to have it both ways. It humbles and even humiliates the new recruit by demonstrating his or her initial incompetence or inferiority in relation to the demanding standards of the military. But trainers are expected to graduate most of their trainees, and do so. Ultimately, therefore, the training instills the pride of accomplishment and group identification.

Recruits are expected to set priorities in the following order: "my nation, my service, my unit, my fellows, my family, and (then) myself." Loyalty, then, is said to be owed to a collectivety, or to a number of them; the individualism of American political ideology is much muted. Group identity is established by the wearing of a uniform, by conformity to regulations such as those concerning haircuts, by rituals and gestures such as saluting, and even by use of a "lingo" that differentiates the group from outsiders. Colored berets, medals, and patches establish further distinctions. Thus, everyone is simultaneously part of the whole and part of something special. The message is group pride (which officers tend to identify through the erect posture, well-pressed uniforms, and crisp saluting) and group loyalty.

Conformity and compliance are fundamental values to be instilled, even among cadets and midshipmen who may aspire to rise through the officer ranks to become generals or admirals. One must learn to obey before one can learn to lead, the novice is told. Moreover, the leader in the American armed forces leads by example. This requires a departure from aristocratic notions of leadership that are prevalent in some other military establishments which preclude getting directly involved in the mundane and dirty chores. The "good leader" in the American military, by contrast, is one who will demonstrate how to clean a toilet bowl by plunging his or her own hand into the bowl and scrubbing it vigorously.

Each step of the training also is designed to foster a sense of responsibility among recruits: responsibility for themselves and their equipment, and responsibility for their buddies. "Wars are won or lost through teamwork"; that is the message. And "your life may depend on how well the guy in the next foxhole has learned that lesson, as his life may depend upon how well you have learned it!"

War is the ultimate test which members of the military must be prepared to meet. Consequently, they are taught to overcome the fear and inhibition that most individuals have about facing death and inflicting death, and that many have even about handling and using weapons. Because the recruits are primarily postadolescent males, this facet of basic training represents part of the test of manhood—and the Freudian symbolism of military weaponry serves to underscore this.

Of course, beyond the rite-of-passage element of weapons training and exercises simulating combat, it is thought that all service personnel, including men who may be destined for desk jobs and including women (who are excluded from combat positions by law and policy), should become aware of the essence of the institution of which they are a part. From such awareness, it is believed, will come an increased appreciation of the responsibilities of those who engage in that essential activity—fighting.

If the intended messages are received, then, a recruit should finish basic training believing in the military's near total effectiveness. The recruit should be proud to be a part of the military, loyal to it and its traditions, prepared to conform but also to accept responsibility, and, finally, prepared to fight to defend the country and its interests.

Lessons Learned: The Evidence

Erving Goffman has described barracks life in the military as an example of the functioning of a "total institution," that is, one that creates a controlled environment for its members, within which they work, play, and sleep (Goffman 1961). Precisely because of the totality of the control over the individual during basic training, one might suppose that the "lessons learned" by recruits would closely approximate those intended by the military. Even in instances in which the preexisting attitudes and values of recruits were at great variance with those desired by organizational officials, one might suppose the degree of control exercised would enable the military to effect dramatic attitudinal and behavioral changes.

Surprisingly, however, available research suggests that although important *behavioral* changes are effected during the first months of military training, enduring changes in attitudes and values are less substantial than one might expect. The relative absence of lasting change is particularly evident when one focuses on political socialization, which of course is but one dimension of the broader experience of military socialization, and one only marginally related to the training objectives of military officials.

In a review of the literature that supports a finding of only modest change, a number of distinctions need to be made. First, the distinction between socialization into the enlisted ranks and socialization into the officer corps is drawn with sufficient emphasis in the military that one must examine each separately. In the course of that examination, commentary will be provided also on some differences between socialization in the current all-volunteer armed force and socialization in the previous structure that included conscripts, draft-induced volunteers, and "true" volunteers. Second, although emphasis thus far has been on the initial rite of passage, during which training is designed to transform civilians into military personnel, attention will be paid to subsequent career experience as well. Third, because the armed forces are divided into specialized arms and branches of service, each of which tends to cultivate its own distinctive culture, variations among and within services will be explored. Finally, the nature and meaning of socialization varies to some extent according to the individual's sex, race, and ethnic and regional heritage. Moreover, the salience of such individual background characteristics has varied somewhat over time. Accordingly, we shall note some research findings related to background variables.

The Class Structure of the Military: Enlisted Ranks and Officer Corps

The officer-enlisted dichotomy that is maintained in the armed forces establishes a class system unlike any found elsewhere in American culture. Neither
civilian police nor firemen use the same kind of double career-ladder. The
extensive surveys that were conducted during World War II of the attitudes of
American GIs found that resentment of the privileged officer "caste" was
pronounced (Stouffer et al. 1949). An evident outcome of becoming socialized to the enlisted culture that obviously was unintended by military officials
was learning to gripe about "the brass."

On the other hand, an interesting change in enlisted attitudes by the time
of the escalating involvement of the United States in Vietnam in the late
1960s was reported by Charles Moskos (1970). A rift between those who
were in the service only on a short-term basis, whether in the enlisted or
officer ranks, and those who were making the military a career overrode the
resentments associated with the distinction between enlisted and officer.

Such a rift was part of a broader pattern of a breakdown in unit cohesion
(Henderson 1985). From the perspective of reform-minded officers and noncommissioned officers, the turbulence and dissent in the ranks in the late
1960s and early 1970s reflected a deplorable failure of leadership, especially
at the top of the military hierarchy. Ironically, however, from the perspective
of many dissident GI-organizers, the stifling of dissent by military authorities
was evidence of social control techniques that too often were successful. Indeed, changes initiated by the Army in response to internal dissent, such as
"rap sessions" in race relations, greater attention to procedural due process in
courts martial, and abolition of some menial chores such as KP detail, were
interpreted by some critics as an insidious effort by military officials to impose still greater control (see Radine 1977).

A more accurate interpretation of events in that turbulent period might be
that they represented a pattern of desperate and not always successful measures by military officials groping to maintain organizational legitimacy in
the eyes of their subordinates. The socialization process that under other circumstances had forged bonds of organizational cohesion had become dominated in many instances by leaders of dissident countercultures. What was
unusual about the functioning of the armed forces during this period was not
the discrepancy that emerged between formal authority and informal leadership but only the magnitude of the rift.

Even in the best of times, the socialization process serves in part to breed
challenges to military authority (and sometimes to civilian authority as well),
despite the pious hopes of officials that it will foster uniformly enthusiastic
compliance. A key lesson that every savvy soldier, sailor, and airman learns
is how to "beat the system" when necessary. Such lessons typically have their

origins not in hostility toward particular representatives of the hierarchy but in a predisposition to value personal autonomy and in an acquired recognition that in a large, impersonal, bureaucratic organization, things go wrong. Time is frittered away and snafus are commonplace. Adhering completely to "the regs" (regulations) gets no rewards, and may lead to missed opportunities to survive and even thrive.

Those who become particularly adept at seizing opportunities or even at dramatically flouting the system can become organizational folk-heroes, e.g. the trainee who finds a girl in town and stays out all night with her when he is supposed to be in bed in the barracks; the cadet who rides a motorcycle into the mess hall; the sailor who wins big in an unauthorized poker game with the petty officers. Even if caught and punished, the individual who has defied the system with style and daring can win approbation and a place in local history.

However, recognition of a "high-jinks" dimension of the socialization process ought not to obscure a more serious dimension associated with the inculcation of professional values and beliefs. This dimension of the process is most clearly apparent among those who have chosen to make the military a career. When social scientists have focused upon socialization at the officer level, they have tended to equate socialization with professionalization, following the studies of Samuel Huntington (1957) and Morris Janowitz (1960). Huntington identified the professional ethos of the officer corps as being one of "conservative realism," an ethos he found appropriate to the assigned function of the military as "managers of violence." This portion of Huntington's argument derived largely from the deduction of core values and beliefs from the nature of the military "mission," but Janowitz found a more varied pattern, based upon his review of documentary and interview data as well as an examination of secondary sources focusing on the military in the first half of the twentieth century.

One of Janowitz's working hypotheses that subsequent researchers have found particularly compelling is that over time the military profession (like many others) has become viewed by its practitioners as less of a "calling" and more of an "occupation." One result is increased appreciation of career benefits associated with the profession. Several empirical studies over the past decade provide further support for and refinement of this hypothesis (Moskos 1977; Janowitz 1977; Stahl, McNichols, and Manley 1980; Segal and Segal 1983; Segal and Yoon 1984).

An additional Janowitz hypothesis that is important to the issue of political socialization, and that has received subsequent study, is that the trend among American military officers has been to view their task as managerial (and to a lesser extent, technical), with a reduced emphasis on the "heroic-leader" self-image. Janowitz did not argue that "heroic-leader" and "managerial" self-images were mutually exclusive. On the contrary, most officers in the modern era would see their role in terms of both. However, it is the perceived trend toward managerial emphasis to the neglect of personal, "heroic" leadership (for example, by the infantry platoon leader) that came to concern many internal critics of the military. This problem reached crisis proportions during the later stages of the war in Vietnam and has continued to be a source of concern in the all-volunteer military (see, for example, Gabriel and Savage 1978; Hauser 1973; Sorley 1980; Vought 1982; U.S. Industrial College of the Armed Forces 1984).

The argument that officer socialization in the American armed forces has been teaching men and women how to manage but not how to lead is analogous to the provocative contention of Norman Dixon that the military socialization process breeds incompetence (Dixon 1976). Dixon's argument, like Huntington's, is derived deductively rather than inductively, although each author offers numerous examples in support of his argument. Thus, the Dixon thesis that military socialization fosters rigidity and, therefore, incompetence in battle is far from unchallengeable. Indeed, it seems equally likely that the military socialization process teaches flexibility. It is true that the military emphasizes hierarchy, obedience, meticulous attention to appearance, and detailed regulations; such emphasis lends the appearance of rigidity to military life. The counterpoint, though, is that individuals in the armed forces move regularly across and between continents; they go on hardship tours, often leaving families behind with whom they must reestablish relations upon their return. Further, they change bosses even more quickly than locations, and subordinates just as quickly. Moreover, they are expected to take on new assignments promptly and without complaint, even when those assignments are unrelated to the job they have been trained to do, or the job they have been doing. In short, the eternal watchword of the military could easily be, "stay flexible."

Perhaps more important to Dixon's argument than the proposition that rigidity is learned in the military, however, is his contention that the military career attracts individuals with anal-compulsive personalities. This interpretation tends to downplay the impact of professional socialization, and to emphasize social selection.

Numerous studies of socialization during the precommissioning stages at the service academies, in ROTC programs, and in officer candidate schools (OCS) have found that the changes effected are more modest than either critics or proponents of such programs imagine. Such, in general, was the finding of John Lovell's study of the socialization of West Point cadets (1962, 1964) and of several subsequent studies, including Edwin Lebby's analysis of the socialization of plebes at Annapolis (1970), William Lucas's study of ROTC cadets and midshipmen (1971), Peter Karsten's comparison of the views of

Annapolis midshipmen, ROTC cadets, and a civilian-student control group (1971), and James Dorman's ROTC study (1976).

Without attempting to provide a full account of pertinent research findings, we can describe the pattern as one in which the socialization process within the military reinforces preexisting values and beliefs rather than drastically altering them. As with entry into other professions, self-selection works to attract new members who already hold many of the values and beliefs which they are expected to acquire as products of professional socialization. They are, in effect, "presocialized."

Yet, it can be argued with some justification that such empirical findings do not fully address the issue of *political* socialization. Such a focus requires attention not only to changes of attitude that occur during training but also to military recruitment and retention patterns, and to the subtle reinforcement of particular modes of thought and action that the organizational culture provides.

Although scholars typically have considered it inappropriate to ask military respondents questions about political-party affiliation, some have gathered more general data on conservative or liberal leanings of military respondents. Not surprisingly, such studies affirm that members of the armed forces (particularly professionals or aspiring professionals such as cadets or midshipmen) tend to be more conservative than their civilian counterparts. However, the explanation seems to lie not so much with socialization as with the self-selection of conservatively oriented young people (Cochran and Luis 1974; Karsten 1971).

On the other hand, relatively few longitudinal studies have traced political attitudes over time during military socialization. One that did, a study of West Point cadets over four years, found senior respondents to be more conservative than they had been as plebes (Priest, Fullerton, and Bridges 1982). However, the finding may be an aberration explicable in terms of the beleaguered posture of the military in American society in the years covered by the survey (1971–75), resulting in a felt need of those who had elected to go to West Point in this period to justify their decision in terms consonant with hard-line policies. The significant increase that the authors found in cadet sensitivity to criticism and in general defensiveness seem supportive of such an interpretation (see also Just 1970; Ellis and Moore 1974.)

Furthermore, studies of first-term soldiers in the West German Bundeswehr and of U.S. Air Force cadets have found that authoritarian attitudes decreased rather than increased over a twelve-to-eighteen-month training period (Roghmann and Sodeur 1972; Campbell and McCormack 1957). Such a finding is consistent with research on postadolescent development generally, which associates emotional maturation and growth with a reduction in authoritarianism (Sanford 1962).

Another study of draftees in the Bundeswehr found that, after a year of service, soldiers were less politically alienated and showed more "democratic awareness" than had been characteristic at the outset of military service (Lippert, Schneider, and Zoll 1978). On the other hand, the authors found little evidence of planned socialization. Some of the apparent attitude changes, such as negative reactions to the Bundeswehr itself, were clearly contrary to the goals of indoctrination.

In a more recent study of U.S. Army enlisted men that sampled soldiers at various points throughout the career span, E. M. Schreiber has found that authoritarianism tends to increase with length of service following an initial period of decline (1979). He attributes the finding not to socialization per se (which his cross-sectional design could not identify confidently), but to the propensity of the more authoritarian soldiers to reenlist.

Comparable data on officers in the U.S. armed forces are relatively sketchy. However, historical experience is relevant. Peter Karsten has provided a vivid description of the emergence of a politically conservative U.S. naval "aristocracy" among Alfred Thayer Mahan and his fellow officers. The evidence is not so much that attitudes and beliefs were altered by the experience of serving in the Navy in that era but that membership in the "club"—the "naval aristocracy"—reinforced the conservative biases and perspectives of the select group (Karsten 1972).

Irving Janis has noted that when the sense of identification with a group is regarded as "special," feelings of solidarity are most likely to lead to "groupthink," which reduces the capacity of individual members to exercise judgment independent of group norms (1982). The modal attitudes and beliefs in the Navy of Mahan's times posed no threat to American democracy; the point is, however, that the student of the role of the military in politics needs to be attentive to the effects of military culture in reinforcing value biases and exerting pressures toward conformity, as well as to the intended changes in behavior and attitude which are effected.

Socialization beyond the Initial Rite of Passage

Although the initial rite of passage is the focal point for the military's intensive efforts to socialize its members, the socialization process should be viewed as ongoing. Empirical data are relatively scarce about the impact of subsequent career experiences. However, it is a reasonable surmise that because some of these experiences are particularly challenging, emotionally intense, and/or incongruous with civilian situations and problems, they are of particular importance in terms of military socialization (Elder 1986).

Combat clearly is one of these. Because political socialization in combat is the subject of another chapter in this volume (Laufer), it is necessary here only to underscore its importance by emphasizing the centrality of warfare to the raison d'être of the military.

In addition to the combat experience, some forms of training are accorded a special status within the military on the grounds that those who succeed in meeting the training's arduous demands have demonstrated that they have "the right stuff." Tom Wolfe found this to be true of the ordeal of test pilots and astronauts (Wolfe 1979). But the same could be said of the status accorded to the nuclear submarine program in the Navy (which for years included grueling interviews of candidates by Admiral Hyman Rickover); it is true of flight training in all of the services; of airborne training ("jump school"); Ranger training; and training for the special forces.

There can be no doubt that those who become entitled to wear pilot wings, jump wings, the Ranger tab, or a similar symbol of successful completion of an elite training program perceive themselves as different from—in important respects, superior to—peers who have not achieved these qualifications. However, the evidence suggests that any distinctiveness of attitudes held by members of a select unit reflects the reinforcement that success provides to preexisting values and beliefs. For example, in a study of airborne training, based upon participant-observation supplemented by structured interviewing, Cockerham (1973) found that those graduating from jump school prided themselves on having been action-oriented individuals even before they began airborne training. The dangers associated with the training, then, only provided an opportunity to test and affirm self-images and values.

Of course, some socialization effects are sufficiently subtle that they become evident only long after a particular socialization experience. In a survey of the attitudes of Army paratroopers toward participating in the quelling of civil disturbances (a mission that seemed likely in 1976 when the survey was conducted), Cockerham and Cohen (1979) found generally favorable attitudes displayed toward such an assignment. Willingness to accept an assignment that few American military leaders historically have regarded as desirable would seem to reflect an unusual commitment to the organization, perhaps stemming from the pride of association that elite units cultivate. Such an interpretation would seem compatible with Cockerham's finding that those most favorably disposed toward such assignments were those most contented with being in the army, and those with the strongest sense of being combat-ready.

Conversely, a soldier who becomes estranged from the military not only is likely to display a poor attitude toward assigned tasks but also to perform below standard and to be likely to incur disciplinary infractions. A study of estrangement in the Army found it to be higher among regulars than among trainees, suggesting that the long-term military socialization process may actually be counterproductive in this respect (Wesbrook 1980). On the other hand, a sense of alienation from the society (an outlook slightly more characteristic of trainees than of regulars) was even more pervasive than estrangement from the Army. In short, the modern all-volunteer Army appears to be recruiting a high percentage of individuals (roughly half, by Wesbrook's measures) who bring with them a profound distrust of their fellow citizens and a cynical view of what is required to get a fair break in American society. On the other hand, improved standards of recruitment in the 1980s were accompanied by a positive change in enlisted attitudes (Moskos 1986a).

Among officers, typically, there has been less cynicism and alienation than in the enlisted ranks. Also, those who are successful in moving up the promotion ladder are often rewarded for having positive attitudes (among other qualities). Because selection for advanced schooling in the military is one measure of career success, and to some extent a prerequisite for future promotion, the military schools provide a convenient locus for studying long-range effects of socialization among career military officers. In a comparison of the attitudes of military officers enrolled at the five war colleges (Army, Navy, Air, National, and Industrial College of the Armed Forces) with a survey of more than 1,000 business executives, Bruce Russett (1974) found significant differences that at first glance might seem to confirm that a military career results in a "military mind." Officers were more "hawkish" than were business executives, for example. On domestic issues, however, differences between military and civilian respondents were negligible. Moreover, Russett found, as had Janowitz (1960), that there was a diversity of opinion among military officers. In Janowitz's terms, many officers in the post–World War II military had become pragmatic in outlook, acknowledging Clausewitz's maxim that military means must serve political ends, and recognizing that armed force is but one of several instruments of foreign policy. Other military officers were more doctrinaire. The "absolutists," in Janowitz's terms, viewing war as an inescapable element of human existence, were uncomfortable with notions of "limited war" or of graduated applications of force in conflict situations. Instead, absolutists adhered to General Douglas MacArthur's oft-quoted view that "in war there is no substitute for victory."

The design of Russett's study did not permit him to attribute his findings to socialization. A different study, though, provides some evidence that advanced education on policy issues, such as that provided in the one-year program at the war colleges, does lead officers to become somewhat less absolutist and more pragmatic in their views (Brewer 1975). In any event, to the extent that attitude change had occurred during an eighteen-to twenty-year period of military socialization (the average military service of students at the war colleges), that change has clearly not been in the direction of a uniform political mind-set.

The Armed Services Subcultures

More plausible than the hypothesis that a military career produces a common set of values and beliefs (a "military mind") is the hypothesis that there are distinctive clusters, associated with the different socialization experiences of the various armed services. It is certainly true that the Army, Navy, Air Force, Marine Corps, and Coast Guard (a component of the military in time of war) nourish their own customs, traditions, lore, and training practices (Lovell 1979; Wamsley 1972; Patrow and Patrow 1986; Wells et al. 1976).

Indeed, even within these organizations, there tend to be distinctive organizational cultures associated with specialized subunits. For instance, the Navy has at least three distinct cultures; these are associated with the surface navy, naval aviation, and the submarine fleet. There are political implications of such differences, which are reflected in the policy priorities emphasized in each, as well as in the jockeying for top positions of influence within the Navy (Davis 1962).

Similar examples of rival cultures could be given within the Army and Air Force and, to a lesser extent (because they are smaller and more cohesive organizations) the Marine Corps and the Coast Guard. Yet the evidence supports a recurrent theme in this essay, that military socialization (whether viewed in the aggregate or in a distinctive organizational milieu) fosters distinctive group and individual behavior—carefully nurtured traditions, customs, practices—but does not appear to produce pronounced enduring changes in values, attitudes, and beliefs.

For example, in his study of Air Force officers, Margiotta (1976) noted some familiar patterns of rivalry between, say, bomber pilots affiliated with the Strategic Air Command (SAC) and fighter pilots of the Tactical Air Command (TAC). Regardless of organizational affiliation, though, most officers in his survey were moderately conservative in political outlook, with a variety of opinions among them regarding particular issues. Moreover, few believed that their views had changed much as a result of their military educational experience.

Another study of Air Force officers, this one focused on junior officers only a few years into their careers, suggests that even the changes of attitude that occurred in the past may be reduced in the future. Finding that modern junior officers in the Air Force accord less prestige to flying than did their predecessors, and are more inclined to identify with reference groups in the civilian sector, Wood (1980) concludes that the "civilianization" of the American military that Janowitz (1960) had observed (but had seen as limited in some important respects) is continuing in the Air Force.

Socialization Experience and Differences by Nationality,
Ethnic Heritage, Race, and Gender

"Civilianization" is an ambiguous concept. Wood uses it to highlight the identity crisis that he finds among Air Force junior officers, finding that they lack a clear image of themselves as military professionals distinct from civilian managers. Yet because "civil" is linked to "civic" etymologically, one could view "civilianization" as a process of *acquiring* an identity as citizen—as a fully integrated member of the civic order.

The role that military service has played in the inculcation of civic (citizen) consciousness among individuals previously denied full status as citizens is a fascinating and recurring theme in the American historical experience. It is a theme that accords much importance to the military in the area of citizen socialization. Its importance, though, varies considerably from one individual to another. Critical intervening variables are individual background characteristics, particularly those relating to nationality and ethnic origin, to race, and to gender.

The military socialization of aliens, for example, has been different in important respects from that experienced by those who have been born and raised in the United States. With the exception of a brief period early in the nineteenth century, male aliens intent on becoming U.S. citizens have been able to attain nationalization through military service. Hundreds of thousands of aliens became citizens in this way in the past; and in recent years, more than 30,000 aliens have been taking steps towards citizenship by serving in the all-volunteer armed forces of the United States (Jacobs and Hayes 1981). For such individuals, the military becomes the principal institutional mechanism through which one is first asked to internalize American values and beliefs. At times, it also has been the institution with the responsibility for teaching immigrants the English language (sometimes to the considerable frustration of both cadre and immigrant; see White 1971).

For second-generation immigrants—from Irish and Italians in an earlier era to Hispanics in the present one—military service has been an avenue of upward social mobility, and sometimes thereby of acquiring political influence. Blacks, too, have found military service to be a source of relatively secure employment and social mobility. Moreover, their military socialization experiences since World War II, together with those of whites with whom they have served in uniform, have had demonstrable effects on those being socialized, and in turn on public policy.

Racial segregation and prejudice were as commonplace in the armed forces as they were elsewhere in American society until World War II (Patton 1981). Especially in the last half of the war years, however, blacks were brought into closer contact with whites than previously, sometimes in units that were at least partially integrated racially. Landmark surveys of the attitudes of soldiers, conducted during World War II by a team of social scientists,showed that the more contact white soldiers had with black soldiers, the greater the receptivity was to racial integration of military units (Stouffer et al. 1949). Such evidence helped to persuade policy officials of the feasibility as well as of the desirability of racial integration in the services, which was implemented by the Truman administration.

In turn, subsequent experience has had the important political and social consequence of habituating white and black military personnel to work together as equals—and to work in situations in which whites are subordinate to blacks, as well as vice versa. Situations in which blacks have been in command in the military have been far more common in the enlisted (that is, noncommissioned officers) ranks than in the officer ranks; but the recent trend has been one of blacks attaining more promotions in the officer ranks as well. Although still not represented in the top officer grades (general and admiral) in proportion to their numbers in the services, it is significant that "blacks occupy more management positions in the military than they do in business, education, journalism, government, or any other significant sector of American society" (Moskos 1986b, p. 64).

Although racial integration has had a generally positive impact on the attitudes of military personnel, one cannot ignore evidence of the opposite effect. There have been episodes in which racial animosities were intensified rather than lessened by interracial contact in the armed forces, and others in which attitudes or behavior displayed by whites in racially integrated units were indistinguishable from those displayed in an earlier era of blatant discrimination.* Racism certainly has not been eliminated (Butler and Holmes 1981; Ingraham 1984). Moreover, gains that blacks have made in securing official compliance with affirmative action programs sometimes have been offset by white backlash.

Women, too, have experienced discrimination and, like blacks and other minorities that have been targeted for affirmative action, women in the military have been perceived as recipients of favoritism. The case of women is different, though, because *all* U.S. military women have been volunteers and because they have not been assigned to combat roles. This difference makes generalizations about women based on all-male data inappropriate. Yet few studies on the socialization of military women exist, and those that do are based on small samples over short periods of time.

The influx of women into the armed forces in unprecedented numbers during World War II was absorbed with only a marginal breakdown of traditional sex roles. However, the intrusion into a previously all-male domain was suf-

---

*A case in a point of return to seemingly proscribed practices of an earlier era was provided at the Citadel in the fall of 1986. Five white cadets dressed in hoods awakened a startled black freshman cadet and his Filipino roommate, and then left, leaving behind a charred paper cross. Convinced that this was evidence of the kind of racial harassment he would continue to experience, the black cadet resigned. *New York Times,* November 23, 1986, sec. 1, p. 26.

ficiently threatening to provoke a slander campaign that hampered recruitment into the WAAC/WAC, WAVES, Spars, and women Marines (Treadwell 1954, chap. 11). With the end of the war, all of the armed services drastically curtailed the numbers of women in their ranks.

Thus, from 1945 to 1972, women's roles in the military were limited. There were nurses and a small number of other women officers, many of whom commanded the roughly 1 percent of the enlisted force that was composed of women (mostly in clerical and medical assignments). During the decade 1972–82, women's numbers increased to roughly 10 percent of the total force; the women's corps were abolished, and women were assigned to a broad range of noncombat specialties. The changes in numbers, organization, and jobs were accomplished only in the face of considerable resistance. Senior officers understood the need for "manpower" in a time of recruitment difficulties, but work units and NCOs often found it hard to accept a handful of women into historically all-male housing and work environments.

In many respects, the discrimination and harassment experienced by women resembled that which had been experienced by men from racial and ethnic minorities. One typical response to the erosion of a unit's all-male environment was for its male members and leaders to assign more weight than ever to masculine values and capacities, particularly those associated with physical strength (Thomas 1986; Kanter 1975). Another was to oppose the principle of "women in the military" while treating one's "own" women quite decently.

One author (Campbell 1984) has argued that male prejudice against women increases as women intrude into domains of activity that men perceive as distinctly "masculine." It is also important to note, though, that much of men's resentment has focused on what they see as favoritism accorded women.

In one sense, men are quite right. Women are favored, in the important sense of sharing the benefits of military service while remaining exempt, by law and/or policy, from the military's most onerous task—killing—and also from its most final demand—dying (Goldman 1982; Stiehm 1980, 1981).

Given the differences, then, between (a) formal teaching and policies of the equality of the sexes, and (b) men's reactions and certain actual practices, women's military socialization has necessarily involved contradictory messages. Women have had to prove both their "mettle" and their "femininity" while being forbidden the core military activity. Nevertheless, many women emerge from service with a sense of pride at having met a worthwhile challenge. Often they have met this challenge while resisting or ignoring pejorative stereotypes assigned to them as well as verbal assaults from male peers. Moreover, in spite of their frustrations, military women tend to see themselves as treated better than women civilian workers (DeFleur and Warner

1984; Marsden 1986; Segal 1986), and it is clear that the military offers women relatively high pay and high levels of responsibility.

Official concern about women's capacities continues. In recent years, attention has shifted from doubts about women's "physical strength" and "time lost" to doubts about women's military "preparedness." The military's own evidence has shown that many women *can* do "men's" jobs (Schreiber and Woelfel 1979; Hoiberg 1978; Kalish and Scobey 1983). The "preparedness" argument, however, rests on the assumption that pregnancy and single-motherhood make an unacceptably high percentage of women unavailable for immediate, worldwide deployment and that, therefore, policies that permit the retention of pregnant women and single parents must be altered. (Women respond that if "preparedness" were examined in context, as "lost time" has been analyzed, it might be found that the differences between women's and men's preparedness are smaller than supposed.)

Many military women do accept the limitations placed on their service and would even agree that pregnancy should result in discharge. One interesting study showed that if the limitations on utilization of women in the military were reduced or eliminated, the number of women volunteering for service would not necessarily increase. Instead, there would be a different cross-section of women recruited, that is, differently presocialized women (Borack 1978). Thus, by limiting the number of women admitted to their ranks (all of them volunteers), the armed forces select those who accept the military as it is. Its role as a socializing agent is thereby minimized. In contrast, the military is under pressure to make adjustments in its own procedures or to engage in extensive resocialization of its male recruits, because large numbers of them are needed, and they come from diverse backgrounds with widely varying values.

The most important barrier to increasing the number of women in the military may be the prohibition against their use in combat, but there is also deep resistance quite apart from this prohibition. This can be seen most clearly in the case of the Air Force, in which few personnel see combat and in which there are few formal restrictions on the use of women. Despite including a higher percentage of women than the other services, the Air Force was directed by Congress recently to increase its use of women. This unusual mandate reflected the conviction of the legislature that the Air Force was not active enough in its effort to recruit women for positions for which they were qualified. Fewer women were recruited to the Air Force than the Army in the early 1980s, and they composed only 10 to 15 percent of the Air Force even though restrictions on their assignment were few. Moreover, Air Force recruiters were told not to expect to do better in large part because of women's low "propensity" (lack of presocialization) for enlistment (Ginovsky 1984, and Garamone, 1985).

At least two interesting and important policy issues regarding women in the military can be identified for the future. First, if Congress reinstates military conscription for men, will an effort be made to maintain or to increase the percentage of women in the military? Or will the ranks be filled with male draftees, and the number of military women reduced possibly to the former 1 or 2 percent of the total? Secondly, will the current taboo against assigning women to "combat roles" yield to a concern for equity of risk and obligation among the sexes? At present, congressional and military leaders express the belief that the American public would not tolerate women in combat. Yet at least one poll, using a nationwide sample, showed more than a third of the population supporting the use of women even in hand-to-hand combat! (Davis, Lauby, and Sheatsley 1983).

Military service has long been associated with citizenship (Janowitz 1983). This has been particularly true for immigrants, minorities, and those from nonprivileged sectors of American society; for them, the completion of a term of service has been proof of a fulfilled civic obligation. Thus, one must ask how women's citizenship is affected by failure to fulfill this particular obligation. More to the point, one must ask whether abolition of limits on women's participation in the armed services and combat would have as its most radical result women's "final, long-delayed acceptance as full citizens" (Stiehm 1981, p. 297).

The Research Agenda

Future studies, then, might focus not only on military socialization and its distinctive characteristics but also on the socialization of civilians concerning the military, its composition, and uses. Without claiming to provide a definitive research agenda, we can suggest several additional topics, each highly relevant to the political socialization of the military, about which further data and analysis are badly needed. One that has become of particular interest in the era of increasing military reliance on "high-tech" weapons systems and equipment is that of the effects of technology on socialization. As Arlinghaus notes (1981), the military's development and utilization of precision-guided munitions (PGMs, or "smart" weapons) and similarly sophisticated arms and equipment has been accompanied by numerous problems and has necessitated a restructuring of units and some major changes in training practices. As the shift to technology-intensive forces continues, the effects not merely on performance but also on the attitudes and beliefs of military personnel merits research attention.

The experience of different ethnic groups in military service continues to provide a needed focus for research. It seems probable that Hispanics, for example, will play an increasing role in American politics in coming years;

the political attitudes of the of the sizeable contingent of Hispanics in the military developed during such service are worthy of systematic study. Generalizations about military socialization need to be refined also through comparisons of the distinctive experiences of successive generations of service personnel (for example, with wars in Korea, in Vietnam, and against drugs). Finally, inquiry continues to be needed into the effects on the socialization process of the distinctive demands that the military makes upon its members. What are the difficulties of socializing for killing and dying, when the socialized do not wish to do either, and when the socializing agent only wants them to be prepared to do both?

Conclusions

For some individuals—for example, citizens who became naturalized as a result of service in the U.S. armed forces—military service has been an important source of political socialization. For most men and women who serve in the military, however, military service does not seem to produce major enduring changes of values and beliefs (although experiences such as combat may have far-reaching effects).

Thousands of young men and women in the United States enter the armed forces each year. Contrary to the anxieties of those who believe that they will become automatons, and contrary to the supposition of enthusiasts who imagine military service will effect a virtuous remolding of character, most veterans of military service emerge with preexisting values and beliefs largely intact.

Part of the explanation for the relative absence of change is that most of those who perform military service do so for a short period of time. In recent years, roughly a third of those entering the all-volunteer force did not even complete their first enlistment. Many others have lasted their initial commitment, but then failed to reenlist. In fact, fewer than 50 percent of all personnel in the all-volunteer force have had as many as four years of service. Turnover has been especially great in the ground-combat arms, an organizational setting especially distinct from civilian milieux and therefore a setting in which one might expect the socialization experience to be especially important (but see Bachman and Blair 1975).

There is, of course, special concern about the political attitudes of those who remain in the armed forces for a career—the military professionals. Their beliefs and values typically *are* distinct from the modal values and beliefs of the society as a whole. However, even their outlook must be seen largely as the product of initial self-selection, and of the subsequent winnowing and self-selection-out that occurs in the assignment and promotion processes. Also, attitudes are reinforced and refined by friendship patterns and by organizational customs, traditions, and practices.

Huntington's original formulation of the professional ethos of the military as one of "conservative realism" remains a reasonable shorthand. However, as noted above, the ethos varies from one organizational culture to another within the armed forces; it varies along generational lines, and it also varies according to an individual's most salient reference groups (for example, racial, ethnic, and gender groups).

Moreover, there are nuances and complexities. It is true that American military professionals tend to be more nationalistic than their liberal, civilian contemporaries; but often the former are more international than the latter in their outlook, experience, and knowledge. Military professionals do tend to value order and discipline in the political life of the society as well as in their professional domain; but of necessity they also place a premium on flexibility. Military professionals are generally comfortable with broad descriptions of their "mission," including defending American territory, democracy, and the capitalist free-enterprise system. Yet the quasi-socialist structure of the military system of post exchanges, medical care, and retirement benefits is viewed as an entitlement of service (although complaints are made about the inefficient functioning of the system).

Duty, honor, and loyalty to country remain core values in military indoctrination and socialization. But they are often internalized at such a high level of abstraction that their application to specific situations and circumstances may result in inconsistencies that are troublesome to the most thoughtful military professionals.

For example, the cultivation of a deep sense of personal honor has made American military professionals resistant to bribes, kickbacks, and similar forms of avaricious corruption to a degree that is remarkable both in absolute standards and in cross-national comparisons. Thus, to the extent that political socialization in the military has instilled a sense of personal integrity, the American polity has been well served.

On the other hand, the corrupting effect of prolonged military involvement in Vietnam included serious breaches of personal integrity among American military personnel. The falsification of reports in response to demands for quantifiable measures of success such as body counts became so commonplace that numerous dedicated professionals resigned their military commissions rather than condone corruption, hypocrisy, and cynicism.

The corruption of the American military during the Vietnam era was tacitly if not overtly encouraged by civilian officials intent on putting a respectable face on ill-conceived policies and commitments. Thus, corruption resulted not from the pursuit by military leaders of objectives and practices out of step with the directives of civilian leadership, but rather from the military's undue readiness to manipulate their institution in support of myopic goals.

In reflecting on the soldier and the state some twenty years after his classic work on the subject was published, Huntington observed (1978, p. 33) "the dilemma of military institutions in a liberal society can only be resolved by a military establishment that is *different from but not distant from* the society that it serves" (emphasis in the original).

Perhaps. But the *ways* in which the military differs are crucial. The demands generated internally or imposed upon the military to conform or to differ may be benign or may be insidious—the nature of these demands is critical.

Huntington concluded his 1957 account of *The Soldier and the State* by invidiously comparing the handsome and kempt grounds of West Point with the slightly tacky nearby town. To the extent that such invidious comparisons encapsulate not just a romanticized view of the military held by a civilian scholar but also a disdainful view of American society accepted by military professionals, there is cause for concern. One would hope that a lesson which would be part of the political socialization process of the American armed forces (and of civilians) is that it is the disorganized, nonhierarchical, inefficient, personalized, hurly-burly nature of democracy that permits it to work—that permits it to allow political testing, change, and adjustment. In that case, the value conferred in Huntington's tidy-academy/unkempt-town comparison should be reversed, for it is exactly the nonmilitary values that make the domestic use of the military unnecessary. This is accomplished by providing for many small, nonviolent trials by ordeal in a variety of arenas.

This is not to argue that West Point should emulate Highland Falls (the town outside the gate); military values are, or can be, a plus rather than a minus. The "conservative realism" of the modern military professional includes acceptance of the subordination of the military to civilian control. It also appears to have perpetuated a tradition of abstinence from active participation in politics through normal civilian channels such as voting and letters to members of Congress (Frantzich, 1982). But conservative realism does not guarantee that the military will not become politicized, nor does it guarantee that civilians will refrain from trying to use the military for partisan political ends.

Indeed, that process may have already begun. At one time, military personnel were not allowed to vote. Now the Pentagon has a Federal Voting Assistance Program. In 1984, military personnel and their dependents and associated employees voted at a higher rate than the national average (Young, 1986). Moreover, the Department of Defense had provided the Reagan-Bush Campaign Committee names and addresses of 14 million armed services members just before the November 1984 election (Burnham, 1986). As military weapons systems and military pay and benefits become campaign issues, one must anticipate that military personnel will become more politically active. Thus far, then, it is civilian elected officials who appear to be mobilizing the military. In the future, though, electoral politics could include military efforts to affect, even decide, political elections.

At present, let us assume that the military profession remains different from but not distant from the society. Contact is encouraged by shared formal education, which receives more emphasis in the modern era (for both officer and enlisted) than it did in an earlier era. In the military academies or in ROTC programs, for example, students take courses about American government as well as about foreign governments, and typically have more exposure to U.S. history than do their civilian peers. Moreover, postgraduate educational opportunities for military personnel in civilian universities are relatively abundant.

Certain assignments bring the military professional into contact with civilians on a routine basis. The career officer who rises to senior field-grade rank (lieutenant colonel or colonel in the Army, Marine Corps, or Air Force; commander or captain in the Navy) will have had an assignment or two in the Pentagon, rubbing shoulders with civilian staff and often with personnel in other Washington-area agencies. An assignment in a major metropolitan area, or on a college campus, or on a military installation with frequent contacts with a host community, is also likely.

But the results of this aspect of the career socialization process are not risk-free from the perspective of maintaining a healthy democracy. Relatively few (less than a third) of senior field-grade officers are selected for flag-rank (generals or admirals). Because those not selected are required by law to retire after thirty years of commissioned service, the incentive is high for officers to begin to reconnoiter possibilities for a follow-on civilian career years before retirement. This includes establishing contacts with defense contractors and other firms where the services of skilled military retirees would be particularly valuable. The situation is fraught with possibilities not merely of economic conflicts of interest but also of policy conflicts of interest. An officer's "after-service" interests can too easily be different from the military's interests.

At the level of flag-rank officers, similar potential risks are present; there are additional hazards as well. Without disparaging the accomplishments of the relatively small number of officers who move up the ladder to flag-rank, it is fair to say that the nature of the job at that level requires substantial political ability as well as professional skill (Mylander 1974). Military advisors at top levels may develop an affinity for the policy perspectives of their civilian bosses. In such instances, as Betts (1977) has observed, military values and beliefs may become so fused with the dominant civilian values and beliefs that the military no longer provides an independent, professional judgment. An additional danger is that zealous military supporters of particular policy positions may become willing agents of political machinations.*

On the other hand, alienation from the policies of civilian decision-makers can trigger politization among the military. The risk is that military personnel thereby politicized might be tempted to exert influence in collaboration with dissident elements in Congress or elsewhere in the political system.

In sum, should the politization of the U.S. military occur, its origin is not likely to derive from an intended process of attitudinal and behavioral change rooted in the experience of military service. Rather, its roots are likely to lie in the processes of self-selection and recruitment (whether through the present all-volunteer system or an alternative such as conscription or national service; see Sherraden and Eberly, 1982). These processes determine who enters the armed forces (and therefore what ideas and values are fed into the military from the society), and how closely military service is linked to prevailing conceptions of citizenship. If civilians place a high value on democratic governance, on civilian control of the military, and on citizen participation in the military, military professionals are likely to hold similar values.

Further, the politization of the military (or the avoiding of it) is tied to the processes of promotion and retention, processes which reward some members, encouraging them to stay and to assume positions of leadership, and which discourage others. The norms and values that define an organization's culture are largely controlled by the promotion process, and this in turn affects the socialization experience for subsequent generations of new recruits. Thus, the criteria that are applied in the selection to flag-rank of military officers are key determinants of the value system that the military establishment is able to sustain—thoroughly professional values or politicized ones. Crucial to the value outcome will be the degree to which the demands made upon military leaders by their civilian superiors are for professional as opposed to partisan loyalty.

Equally crucial will be the degree to which the military is widely regarded by its members as an opportunity. A military which is an avenue for upward mobility for a substantial number of citizens (as the U.S. military is now for many ethnic minorities) is quite different from a military consisting of large numbers of individuals who believe they could "do better" as civilians.

It is not easy to offer a formula for maintaining a civilian-military relation-

---

* The instances that began to come to light in late 1986 and early 1987 of clandestine activities by the National Security Council staff generally, and by individuals such as Marine Corps Lieutenant Colonel Oliver North in particular, provide vivid recent illustrations of the point. North and others evidently acted as secret emissaries in facilitating arms shipments to Iran and aid to the Nicaraguan Contras even at the risk of violating national (and perhaps international) law and congressional resolutions.

ship that accords with the tenets of democracy. What does seem clear is that a proper equilibrium between democratic and professional norms in a civil-military relationship cannot be forged by focusing solely on the military. However distinctive its values and traditions, the military establishment in a democracy has its roots in the society which it is organized to serve. Ultimately the political socialization that is critical is that of the citizenry and, in turn, that of its elected officials.

References

Arlinghaus, Bruce E. 1981. "'Dumb' Soldiers and 'Smart' Bombs: Precision-Guided Munitions and the All-Volunteer Force." In *Defense Manpower Planning: Issues for the 1980s*, ed. William J. Taylor, Jr., Eric T. Olson, and Richard A. Schrader. New York: Pergamon.

Bachman, Jerald G., and John D. Blair. 1975. "'Citizen Force' or 'Career Force'? Implications for Ideology in the All-Volunteer Army." *Armed Forces and Society* 2: 81–96.

Betts, Richard K. 1977. *Soldiers, Statesmen, and Cold War Crises*. Cambridge: Harvard University Press.

Binkin, Martin. 1984. *America's Volunteer Military: Progress and Prospects*. Washington, D.C.: Brookings Institution.

Borack, Jules I. 1978. *Intentions of Women (18–25 Years Old) to Join the Military*. Technical Report 78–84. San Diego: Navy Personnel Research and Development Center.

Brewer, Thomas L. 1975. "The Impact of Advanced Education on American Military Officers." *Armed Forces and Society* 2: 63–80.

Burnham, David. 1986. "Pentagon Faulted as Aiding G.O.P. Campaigns in 1984." *New York Times*, March 23, p.18.

Burrelli, David F., and David R. Segal 1982. "Research Note: Definitions of Mission Among Novice Marine Corps Officers." *Journal of Political and Military Sociology* 10: 299–306.

Butler, John Sibley, and Malcom D. Holmes. 1981. "Perceived Discrimination and the Military Experience." *Journal of Political and Military Sociology* 9: 17–30.

Campbell, D'Ann. 1984. *Women at War with America: Private Lives in a Patriotic Era*. Cambridge: Harvard University Press.

Campbell, Donald T., and Thelma H. McCormack. 1957. "Military Experience and Attitudes toward Authority." *American Journal of Sociology* 62: 482–90.

Cochran, Charles L., and Luis R. Luis. 1974. "Midshipmen Political Characterization and Academy Socialization." In *Civil-Military Relations*, ed. Charles L. Cochran. New York: Macmillan.

Cockerham, William C. 1973. "Selective Socialization: Airborne Training as a Status Passage." *Journal of Political and Military Sociology* 1: 215–29.

Cockerham, William C., and Lawrence E. Cohen, 1979. "Attitudes of U.S. Army

Paratroopers Toward Participation in the Quelling of Civil Disturbances." *Journal of Political and Military Sociology* 7: 257–69.

Davis, James A., Jennifer Lauby, and Paul B. Sheatsley. 1983. "Americans View the Military, Public Opinion in 1982." Technical report no. 131, April. Chicago: National Opinion Research Center.

Davis, Vincent. 1962. *Postwar Defense Policy and the U.S. Navy, 1943–1946*. Chapel Hill: University of North Carolina Press.

DeFleur, Lois B., and Rebecca L. Warner. 1984. "The Impact of Military Service on Women's Status: A Neglected Area of Inquiry." In *Women in the United States Armed Forces*, ed. N. Loring. Chicago: Inter-University Seminar on Armed Forces and Society, pp.1–17.

Dixon, Norman F. 1976. *On the Psychology of Military Incompetence*. New York: Basic Books.

Dorman, James E. 1976: "ROTC Cadet Attitudes: A Product of Socialization or Self-Selection?" *Journal of Political and Military Sociology* 4: 203–16.

Dornbusch, Sanford M. 1955. "The Military Academy as an Assimilating Institution." *Social Forces* 33 (May): 316–21.

Elder, Glen H., Jr. 1986. "Military Times and Turning Points in Men's Lives." *Developmental Psychology* 22: 233–45.

Ellis, Joseph, and Robert Moore. (1974). *School for Soldiers: West Point and the Profession of Arms*. New York: Oxford University Press.

Faris, John H. 1975. "The Impact of Basic Combat Training: The Role of the Drill Sergeant in the All-Volunteer Army." *Armed Forces and Society* 2: 115–27.

Frantzich, Stephen E. 1982. "Citizens in Uniform: Political Participation Among Military and Civilian Samples." *Journal of Political and Military Sociology* 10: 15–28.

Gabriel, Richard A., and Paul L. Savage. 1978. *Crisis in Command: Mismanagement in the Army*. New York: Hill and Wang.

Garamone, Jim. 1985. "Quotas on Recruiting Women to Continue." *The Air Force Times,* June 3, p.11.

Ginovsky, John. 1984. "Aspin, McCoy Square Off Over AF's Use of Women." *The Air Force Times,* March 19, p.28.

Goffman, Erving. 1961. *Asylums: Essays on the Social Situations of Mental Patients and Other Inmates*. Garden City: Doubleday, Anchor Books.

Goldman, Nancy Loring. 1982. *Female Soldiers—Combatants or Noncombatants?* Westport: Greenwood Press.

Hagan, Kenneth J., and William R. Roberts, 1986. *Against All Enemies: Interpretations of American Military History from Colonial Times to the Present*. Westport: Greenwood.

Hauser, William L. 1973. *America's Army in Crisis: A Study in Civil-Military Relations*. Baltimore: Johns Hopkins University Press.

Henderson, William Darryl. 1985. *Cohesion: The Human Element in Combat*. Washington, D.C.: National Defense University Press.

Hoiberg, Anne, ed. 1978. "Women as New 'Manpower'." Special issue of *Armed Forces and Society,* 4: 555–716.

Hunter, Edna J. Donald den Dulk, and John W. Williams. 1980. *The Literature on*

Military Families, 1980: An Annotated Bibliography. United States Air Force Academy.

Huntington, Samuel P. 1957. *The Soldier and the State: The Theory and Politics of Civil-Military Relations.* Cambridge: Belknap Press of Harvard University Press.

————. 1978. "The Soldier and the State in the 1970s." In *The Changing World of the American Military,* ed. Franklin D. Margiotta. Boulder, Colo: Westview.

Ingraham, Larry H. 1984. *The Boys in the Barracks: Observations on American Military Life.* Philadelphia: Institute for the Study of Human Issues.

Jacobs, James B., and Leslie Anne Hayes. 1981. "Aliens in the U.S. Armed Forces: A Historico-Legal Analysis." *Armed Forces and Society* 7: 187–208.

Janis, Irving L. 1982. *Groupthink* 2d ed. Boston: Houghton Mifflin.

————. 1977. "From Institutional to Occupational: The Need for Conceptual Clarity." *Armed Forces and Society* 4: 51–54.

————. 1976. "Military Institutions and Citizenship in Western Societies." *Armed Forces and Society* 2: 185–204.

Janowitz, Morris. 1960. *The Professional Soldier: A Social and Political Portrait.* New York: The Free Press.

————. 1976. "Military Institutions and Citizenship in Western Societies." *Armed Forces and Society* 2: 185–204.

————. 1977. "From Institutional to Occupational: The Need for Conceptual Clarity." *Armed Forces and Society* 4: 51–54.

————. 1983. *The Reconstruction of Patriotism: Education for Civic Consciousness.* Chicago: University of Chicago Press.

Jennings, M. Kent, and Gregory B. Markus. 1976. "Political Participation and Vietnam War Veterans: A Longitudinal Study." In *The Social Psychology of Military Service,* ed. Nancy L. Goldman and David R. Segal. Beverly Hills: Sage.

Jones, Ellen. 1985. *Red Army and Society: A Sociology of the Soviet Military.* Boston: Allen and Unwin.

Just, Ward. 1970. *Military Men.* New York: Knopf.

Kalish, Philip A., and Margaret Scobey, 1983. "Female Nurses in American Wars: Helplessness Suspended for the Duration." *Armed Forces and Society* 9: 215–44.

Kanter, Rosabeth M. 1975. "Some Effects of Proportions on Group Life: Skewed Sex Ratios and Responses to Token Women." *American Journal of Sociology* 82: 965–90.

Karsten, Peter. 1971. "'Professional' and 'Citizen' Officers: A Comparison of Academy and ROTC Officer Candidates." In *Public Opinion and the Military Establishment,* ed. Charles C. Moskos, Jr. Beverly Hills: Sage.

————. ed. 1986. *The Military in America: From the Colonial Era to the Present.* Rev. ed. New York: The Free Press.

————. 1972. *The Naval Aristocracy: The Golden Age of Annapolis and the Emergence of Modern American Navalism.* New York: The Free Press.

————. 1984. "The 'New' American Military History: A Map of the Territory, Explored and Unexplored." *American Quarterly* 36: 389–418.

Kirkpatrick, Samuel, and James L. Regens. 1978. "Military Experience and Foreign Policy Belief Systems." *Journal of Political and Military Sociology* 6: 29–47.

Lebby, David E. 1970. "The Professional Socialization of the Naval Officer: The Effect of Plebe Year at the U.S. Naval Academy." Ph.D. diss., University of Pennsylvania.

Lippert, Ekkehard, Paul Schneider, and Ralf Zoll. 1978. "The Influence of Military Service on Political and Social Attitudes: A Study of Socialization in the German Bundeswehr." *Armed Forces and Society* 4: 265–82.

Lovell, John P. 1962. "The Cadet Phase of the Socialization of the West Pointer." Ph.D. diss., University of Wisconsin.

————. 1979. *Neither Athens Nor Sparta? The American Service Academies in Transition*. Bloomington: Indiana University Press.

————. 1964. "The Professional Socialization of the West Point Cadet." In *The New Military*, ed. Morris Janowitz. New York: Russell Sage.

Lucas, William A. 1971. "Anticipatory Socialization and the ROTC." In Charles C. Moskos, Jr., ed., *Public Opinion and the Military Establishment*, pp. 99–134. Beverly Hills: Sage.

Margiotta, Franklin D. (1976). "A Military Elite in Transition: Air Force Leaders in the 1980s." *Armed Forces and Society* 2: 155–84.

Marsden, Martha A. 1986. "The Continuing Debate: Women Soldiers in the U.S. Army." In *Life in the Rank and File*, ed. David R. Segal and H. Wallace Sinaiko. Washington, D.C.: Pergamon-Brasseys.

Moskos, Charles C., Jr. 1970. *The American Enlisted Man*. New York: Russell Sage.

————. 1986a. "The American Enlisted Man in the All-Volunteer Army." In *Life in the Rank and File*, ed. David R. Segal and H. Wallace Sinaiko. Washington, D.C.: Pergamon-Brasseys.

————. 1977. "From Institution to Occupation: Trends in Military Organization." *Armed Forces and Society* 4: 41–50.

————. 1976. "The Military." *Annual Review of Sociology* 2: 55–77.

————. 1986b. "Success Story: Blacks in the Army." *The Atlantic* 257: 64–72.

Mylander, Maureen. 1974. *The Generals: Making It, Military-Style*. New York: Dial.

Patrow, Michael L., and Renée Patrow. 1986. "The Leathernecks: A Few Good Men. . . . And Women." In *Life in the Rank and File*, ed. David R. Segal and H. Wallace Sinaiko. Washington, D.C.: Pergamon-Brasseys.

Patton, Gerald W. 1981. *War and Race: The Black Officer in the American Military, 1915–1941*. Westport: Greenwood.

Priest, Robert, Terrence Fullerton, and Claude Bridges, 1982. "Personality and Value Changes in West Point Cadets." *Armed Forces and Society* 8: 629–42.

Radine, Lawrence B. 1977. *The Taming of the Troops: Social Control in the United States Army*. Westport: Greenwood.

Roghmann, Klaus, and Wolfgang Sodeur. 1972. "The Impact of Military Service on Authoritarian Attitudes." *American Journal of Sociology* 78: 418–33.

Russett, Bruce M. 1974. "Political Perspectives of U.S. Military and Business Elites." *Armed Forces and Society* 1: 79–108.

Sanford, Nevitt. 1962. "Developmental Status of the Entering Freshman." In *The American College*, ed. Nevitt Sanford. New York: John Wiley and Sons.

Schreiber, E. M. 1979. "Authoritarian Attitudes in the United States Army." *Armed Forces and Society*, 6: 122–31.

Schreiber, E. M., and John C. Woelfel, 1979. "Effects of Women on Group Performance in a Traditionally Male Occupation: The Case of the U.S. Army." *Journal of
Political and Military Sociology* 7: 121–34.

Segal, David R. 1986. "Personnel." In *American Defense Annual, 1986–1987*, ed.
Joseph Kruzel, chap.7 Lexington: Lexington Books for the Mershon Center, Ohio
State University.

Segal, David R., and Mady Wechsler Segal, 1976. "The Impact of Military Service
on Trust in Government, International Attitudes, and Social Status." In *The Social
Psychology of Military Service*, ed. Nancy L. Goldman and David R. Segal. Beverly Hills: Sage.

———. 1983. "Change in Military Organization." *Annual Review of Sociology* 9:
151–70.

Segal, David R., and Young Hee Yoon. 1984. "Institutional and Occupational Models
of the Army in the Career Force." *Journal of Political and Military Sociology* 12:
243–56.

Sherraden, Michael W., and Donald J., Eberly, eds. 1982. *National Service: Social,
Economic and Military Impacts*. New York: Pergamon.

Smith, A. Wade. 1983. "Public Consciousness of Blacks in the Military." *Journal of
Political and Military Sociology* 11: 281–300.

Sorley, Lewis. 1980. "Prevailing Criteria [of Combat Effectiveness]: A Critique." In
Combat Effectiveness: Cohesion, Stress, and the Volunteer Military, ed. Sam C.
Sarkesian. Beverly Hills: Sage.

Stahl, Michael J., Charles W. McNichols and T. Roger Manley 1980. "An Empirical
Examination of the Moskos Institution-Occupation Model." *Armed Forces and Society* 6: 257–69.

Stiehm, Judith Hicks. 1980. "Women and the Combat Exemption." *Parameters, Journal of the U.S. Army War College* 10: 51–59.

———. 1981. *Bring Me Men And Women: Mandated Change at the U.S. Air Force
Academy*. Berkeley: University of California Press.

Stouffer, Samuel A., et al. 1949. *The American Soldier: Adjustment During Army Life*
vol. 1. *The American Soldier: Combat and Its Aftermath*, vol. 2. Princeton: Princeton University Press.

Thomas, Patricia J. 1986. "From Yeomanettes to WAVES to Women in the U.S.
Navy." In *Life in the Rank and File*, ed. David R. Segal and H. Wallace Sinaiko.
Washington, D.C.: Pergamon-Brasseys.

Treadwell, Mattie E. 1954. *The Women's Army Corps*. United States Army in World
War II, Special Studies. Washington, D.C.: Office of the Chief of Military History,
Department of the Army.

U.S. Army Training Center. 1983. *The Ultimate Weapon, Drill Sergeant Handbook*.
Fort Dix Pam. 350–7, 15 December. Fort Dix, N.J.: USA Training Center.

U.S. Industrial College of the Armed Forces, Defense Management Study Group on
Military Cohesion. 1984. *Cohesion in the U.S. Military*. Washington, D.C.: National Defense University Press.

Vought, Donald. 1982. "American Culture and American Arms: The Case of Vietnam." In *Lessons from an Unconventional War*, ed. Richard A. Hunt and Richard
H. Shultz. New York: Pergamon.

Wamsley, Gary L. 1972. "Contrasting Institutions of Air Force Socialization." *American Journal of Sociology* 78: 399–417.

Wells, Ronald A., Robert L. Demichiell, Malcolm J. Williams, and Lawrence J. Korb. (1976). "The United States Coast Guard Academy: A Case Study of Institutional Impact." In *The System for Educating Military Officers in the U.S.*, ed. Lawrence J. Korb. Pittsburgh: International Studies Assn., Occasional Paper no 9.

Wesbrook, Stephen D. 1979. *Political Training in the United States Army: A Reconsideration.* Position papers in the Policy Sciences, no. 3. Columbus: Mershon Center, Ohio State University.

———. 1980. "Sociopolitical Alienation and Military Efficiency." *Armed Forces and Society* 6: 170–89.

White, Bruce. 1971. "The American Military and the Melting Pot in World War I." In *War and Society in North America*, ed. J. L. Granastein and R. D. Cuff. Toronto: Thomas Nelson.

Wolfe, Tom. 1979. *The Right Stuff.* New York: Farrar, Straus, and Giroux.

Wood, Frank R. 1980. "Air Force Junior Officers: Changing Prestige and Civilianization." *Armed Forces and Society* 6: 483–506.

Young, Sharon B. 1986. "Both Political Parties Used Overseas Voters." *Air Force Times,* January 20, p.8.

Six

Psychological Perspectives on Theories of Adult Development and the Political Socialization of Leaders

STANLEY RENSHON

The purpose of this chapter is to explore the contributions that theories of adult development, especially those with roots in the psychoanalytic tradition,[1] can make to the study of the adult political socialization of leaders. In doing so, one brings together a developing body of theory, concepts, and findings in an emerging area (the study of adult development) with a field, political socialization, whose raison d'être at its founding was understanding adult political behavior, but which (somewhat paradoxically) rarely directly studied adults. The number of studies which purposely link the two areas is relatively small. My task therefore is not only to review the literature that currently exists but to bring together under a unifying conceptual rubric some major themes of the adult development literature and suggest how they help to illuminate the process of adult political socialization for leaders.

The perspective of this essay is leader-centered. While fully recognizing that socialization is a reciprocal process between the individual and the environment, I examine the process of adult political socialization by focusing on the individual political leader. Such a focus does not negate the importance of the external environment in favor of "psychic reality," but it does view the latter from a somewhat different perspective than the traditional "oversocialized" view of the process (Wrong 1961). It should also be noted here that the use of the individual level of analysis, with its emphasis on the leader's motives, beliefs, skills, and experiences is not meant as a replacement for other levels of analysis but rather as a useful and necessary component for the development of theories of adult political socialization.

The concerns of the psychoanalytic tradition in adult development theories and the field of adult political socialization come together with a certain symmetry at their intersection with the study of political leaders. One reason for this is that the analytic tradition has been keenly concerned with issues of psychological development and the capacity for, and dynamics of, continuity, learning, and change. Spurred by the work of Erikson, Lifton, Levinson,

Kohut, and others, psychoanalytic theory has had to consider how character, self, and personality dynamics unfold not only during childhood but after it.

So, too, theories of adult political socialization, especially those dealing with political leaders, must of necessity consider how those persons orient themselves to the complex role and reality-demands of exercising political power. Clearly, important aspects of behavior in these roles will be anchored in adult experience. To give but one brief example, the adherence to the norms which at one time governed the maiden speeches of freshman United States senators (Matthews 1960) could hardly be easily ascribed to any other developmental period but adulthood. But even if we grant that some degree of learning political role-specifics must take place during adulthood, this does not necessarily resolve many other questions involving the adult development and political socialization of leaders.

The concept of development in adulthood implies that certain kinds of changes can and do take place. Similarly, the concept of socialization is almost synonymous with learning. Does this mean that all adult political learning implies development? In this essay, I distinguish between learning and development, and reserve the latter term for major changes in the way in which leaders approach their political responsibilities. Development, therefore, implies the integration of information or understandings which significantly alter the way leaders think and act. I distinguish two such types of development, reversal and elaboration. The former takes place when previous understandings and behaviors lead to a change in nature and direction of a characteristic, for example, when a leader who started out as a liberal Democrat becomes a conservative Republican. The second, elaboration, also involves an important change in understanding and perspective, but this change results more in a deepening and specification of that perspective than a reversal of it. The distinction between development as elaboration or as reversal is a matter of direction, not depth. I distinguish both of these types of development from the more role-specific kind of learning, such as when it is appropriate for a freshman senator to make a maiden speech. It should be kept in mind however, that when dealing with political leaders, even role-specific learning can have substantial consequences.

These are general conceptualizations of the adult political socialization process, but students of this process will want to ask a number of more specific questions. For example, if development or learning does take place in adulthood for political leaders, at what level of functioning does it occur? Is it only at the level of political or policy facts, or do more basic orientations like political beliefs and philosophy also change? And what of a leader's more basic psychological makeup, the character structure and sense of self? Do these too change in and through adulthood or do any changes necessitated by the performance of adult roles simply get overlaid on more static psychological foundations?

Finally, along these lines, we would want to know more about the nature of adulthood itself for political leaders. It is important to remember that most people, including political leaders, spend most of their lives as adults. What, then, are the relationships between the concerns of different periods of adulthood and the nature of political work and careers? Can theories of adult development help us to understand the functioning and decisional thrusts of political leaders at different stages of their lives and careers? Can they help to throw any light on the motivations which underlie a leader's concerns and performance?

A study of adult development theory in relation to political leaders would seem to offer a number of attractive perspectives for theories of adult political socialization. It would examine a group of adult persons whose political behavior is frequent, public, and consequential. It would, moreover, be examining persons for whom political roles shape their adult professional and to a substantial degree personal identities.

Utilizing theories of adult development as a lens for examining the socialization of leaders also raises the possibility of establishing a more direct temporal and situational link between psychological and political processes, especially as they are engaged through the medium of the leader's role. Early political socialization theory suffered from a gap between the purpose of its studies (understanding and predicting adult political behavior) and the age of many of its research subjects, who were generally not adults. Inferences therefore had to travel across wide spans of time, thus becoming vulnerable to Markov processes in the causal chain.

A similar problem occurred in attempting to link psychological process to political context. Early political socialization theory was interested in making predictions to general classes of political behavior, frequently giving less attention to specifying the nature of the context in which the behavior took place. An interest in "internal dispositions" is still widely believed to preclude such concerns.

Yet it is difficult to imagine a theory of adult political socialization, especially of political leaders, which does not pay substantial attention to context and the forces that are operative therein. The acts or omissions of political leaders are highly consequential, and to a large degree leaders must be responsive to real circumstances. This raises an important conceptual and theoretical question. How can a focus on processes which are essentially internal to the person (learning, development) be reconciled theoretically and conceptually with an adult position of responsibility which must of necessity take full account of the external world?

Finally, the use of theories of adult development to study the political socialization of leaders focuses us on a somewhat distinctive and important set of questions regarding the actual nature of political work and the skills and capacities necessary to accomplish it in a democracy. It is of course important to answer the question of whether leaders can learn and develop, and, if the answer is affirmative, to find out what, how, and when. But the reasons for asking these questions are not necessarily confined to building or refining our theories.

The skillful, ethical, and democratic exercise of political power in a structurally complex and heterogeneous society is no small accomplishment. If the skills associated with successfully accomplishing this can and do develop during adulthood, then we are certainly justified in asking how, if at all, such development can be facilitated. Learning about the exercise of political power would seem to be too important to be left solely to on-the-job training.

The focus of this essay then, will be on the adult sources of adult political behavior. Specifically, I will be interested in issues of continuity and change for those who exercise political power as well as in the process of exercising power itself. Before proceeding to a more detailed consideration of these themes in the context of adult development theory, however, I must first say a few words about the subject of my analysis, political leaders.

From Political Elites to Political Leadership

Theory and research on those who hold positions of power have undergone a marked shift in the past two decades. The major thrust of the initial phase can be summarized by the question, Who governs? In this phase, primary emphasis was given to identifying those who exercised power, and to the implications of such findings for questions concerning the degree of democratic decision-making in this society. More recently, there has been a shift from questions of identifying those who have political power to a more detailed examination of what such persons actually do. The first phase can be characterized as the study of political elites, while the second can be distinguished by its emphasis on political leadership.

The exact nature of the specialized roles connected with making authoritative decisions in any society, and of the persons who exercise those roles, is a central concern in political theory and analysis. Questions raised in the study of political elites and leadership go directly to the heart of the rationale for studying the political socialization of leaders. It is therefore worthwhile to examine briefly the two lines of research as a background to a discussion of theories of adult development.

Any attempt to identify political elites or leaders must rest on some initial understanding or definition. In the case of political elites, this has not been easy. Putnam (1973, p. 5) observes in his work that there is little consensus among social scientists about the definition of elites and proposes that political elites be defined simply as those who have more power than others. Lasswell (1965, p. 3), a pioneer in the empirical study of elites, argued that "any single definition of such a key term as 'elite' is inadequate." And David Boyd

(1973, p. 16), surveying the literature in preparation for his own study, noted that "even in a purely technical context, there is much confusion about the term." Defining who elites are is an important task, since one cannot otherwise study their life histories or their impact.

There are several possible ways to approach these difficulties. The identification of political elites might well follow from one's view of the political process. If, for example, politics is the study of who gets what (Lasswell 1936), then elites are simply those who get more of what there is to have. In this view elites and formal leadership roles are not synonymous, although they clearly overlap.

Another approach arises out of the view that politics concerns the authoritative allocation of scarce values in a society (Easton 1965), from which it would follow that political elites are those charged with making those allocations. This view has the advantage of clearly distinguishing political from nonpolitical elites. The former would be those charged with making society-wide decisions about scarce resources. The latter group, however influential in fact, would be distinguished by not being formally charged or accepted as having such authority.

Beyond questions of identifying political elites, this line of research also raised important questions about their functioning in a democratic society. Mill's power-elite theory (1956) envisioned a relatively small group of power-holders who decided important questions, most notably those in the area of national defense, while public debate and influence were channeled into other somewhat less important areas. Implicit in the power-elite argument is the belief that the interests and views of the elites are similar, if not essentially uniform.

Mills derived his theory from examining the career patterns of top-level business, government, and military personnel, but he had relatively little to say about the origins of the uniformity of outlook that he posited. With the advent of inventories of background information, it became possible to collect and analyze data that might bear upon this process. Early studies of the political socialization of elites attempted to do just that. Edinger and Searing pointed out the rationale for such studies: in an important early paper:

> Social circles, to use Simmel's concept, whose members have had similar experiences, are presumed to hold similar attitudes. The analysis of social background variables in this sense represents an attempt to classify the contexts of the aggregate socialization experiences in which elite attitudes are formed in order to explain the collective orientations of members of influential social circles. (1967, p. 430)

I will review this important line of research in more detail shortly, but here I primarily wish to undercore its focus and rationale. Its focus is on first identifying the members of the elite group and then asking what common background characteristics distinguish them. These commonalities are then assumed to account for similarities of political attitudes. This approach, and the research which it generated, is best described as social-background analysis.

It is clear that this line of research incorporates the most basic element of what might be called the socialization hypothesis, which is to say the view that what happens to a person earlier in life helps account for what attitudes that person later holds. Social-background analysis is much more concerned with establishing and accounting for uniformities of outlook than with examining what political elites actually do. It is exactly this change in focus, from a search for similarities of outlook and their origins to a focus on the actual nature of political work, which represents a real shift towards the concerns of a theory of adult political socialization.

Political Leadership and the Nature of Political Work

One advantage that adult development theories have as a framework for the study of adult political socialization is that they focus attention directly on the work of political leaders. The importance of work in the lives of adults is a recurring theme in that literature, and for good reason. Work is both a reflection of and a vehicle for a person's aspirations, skills, and accomplishments. It is also the context in which a person's character and sense of self are directly engaged.

A focus on the nature of political work therefore, provides a point at which personal characteristics directly intersect with political contexts and outcomes. But it is important to keep in mind that the connections are not necessarily linear. A political leader's approach to his work is partially a reflection of intentions (both conscious and otherwise) and skills, but these too reflect the imprint of environmental structure and process. To put it another way, the leader both makes and is made by the political role.

There is presently no typology of "political contexts." Nor is there substantial agreement about the actual tasks involved in various political roles. But a focus on political leadership represents one major way, but not necessarily the only one, in which the work of political leaders may be understood.

The study of political leadership owes much to the comprehensive framework formulated by Paige (1977), as well as to work by Burns (1978), Tucker (1981), Kellerman (1984, 1986), and Hermann (1986). Leadership is a relational concept and involves at least two entities, the leader and his constituencies and/or followers. Hermann (1986, p. 180) makes the point that "Leaders are leaders because they have followers—people who have granted them authority and to whom they are accountable." Leadership itself is something that leaders are expected to provide, and it is certainly one of the tasks of the political role, but it is also, as Burns (1978, p. 2) points out, more observed than understood.

The question of what constitutes political leadership has received varied answers. Kellerman (1984, p. 70) has noted at least ten general views of political leadership. These include political leadership (1) as a focus of group process, (2) as personality and its effects, (3) as the ability to induce compliance, (4) as the exercise of influence, (5) as behavior, (6) as a form of persuasion, (7) as a power relationship, (8) as an instrument of goal achievement, (9) as a differentiated role, and (10) as the initiation of structure. Hermann (1986, p. 168), in reviewing the literature on views of political leadership suggested her own fourfold image, including the leader as pied piper, as salesman, as puppet, and as firefighter.

Another approach has been to analyze the nature of political leadership by examining different types of leaders and their styles. Typologies of political leaders attempt to classify them on the basis of their location among one or more continua. For example, Burns (1978, p. 4) distinguishes between transactional and transforming leaders. The former pursue politics as usual. This means in essence, an exchange relationship, in which a leader's constituency exchanges authority for specific promises and results. The transforming leader, however, perceives a need on the part of his followers and acts on it, transforming both them and himself in the process.

Other typologies of political leaders and leadership style have also been suggested. Early on, Lasswell (1930, 1948) distinguished two groups, political and democratic personalities. Those in the first group were oriented towards the personal accumulation of power while those in the second were oriented to the sharing of political power. Among the former group, Lasswell also distinguished between agitators, administrators, and theorists, and among them various approaches to the role. In this typology, motivation is closely linked to role performance.

In a similar vein, Barber (1965), studying state legislators, distinguished four general types by motivation and performance: the advertiser, the spectator, the reluctant, and the lawmaker. The first was oriented to self-promotion and advancement, the second was motivated by a need for approval, the third by a sense of obligation, and the fourth by the policy challenge of the position. Somewhat later, in classifying presidents, Barber (1985) used two continua—the amount of energy invested in the role and the actor's feelings of satisfaction with it.

These attempts to develop typologies for particular political types are helpful in studying the work of political leaders for several reasons. First, they emphasize the basic connection of motivation, skills, and performance. Second, they do so within the context of a set of structured role expectations, requirements, and possibilities. Kotter and Lawrence's (1974) typology of mayoral behaviors, for example (which includes caretaker, ceremonial, executive, program entrepreneur, and personality/ individualist roles), allows us to know not only what kind of role a person chooses but also suggests what leadership roles are available or possible.

Every political role can be approached from three basic perspectives: formal statutory responsibilities (e.g., the president shall be the commander-in-chief); institutional opportunities connected with work responsibilities (e.g., in connection with their lawmaking function, congressmen may hold hearings); or new definitions of function which "invent" new role elements. In discussing the concept of presidential style, Barber (1985, p. 5) notes three tasks that every president must perform to some degree—homework, rhetoric, and interpersonal relations. None of these will be found, except in the most indirect way, in statutory empowerment. The president is required to inform Congress of the "state of the union," but the concept of rhetoric goes well beyond that. Nor can the necessity of homework be easily accommodated within the framework of specific or implied presidential powers.

Barber's suggestions about presidential style begin to establish what might be characterized as a functional approach to the nature of political work. He tries to discern aspects of the role that tap what must be done, but which go beyond formal requirements. These three "musts" of the presidential role are valuable and suggestive, but it seems likely that other requirements will need to be added. Other candidates for possible inclusion as important aspects of political roles include making decisions, handling stress,[2] and developing the capacity to learn.

This last factor, the capacity to learn, deserves some emphasis here, given its general importance and the concerns of this essay. The need for a capacity to learn is built into leadership roles. It is the leader, after all, who is charged by society to deal with contingency. Moreover, political circumstances do change, and even (perhaps especially) when they do not, a leader may have to create circumstances that will advance his goals. This implies some capacity to diagnose circumstances and act accordingly.

At another level, the political leader must translate philosophy into policy. This may take the form either of general formulations or specific initiatives. And beyond this lies the process of implementation, which itself requires a number of further decisions on the leader's part. Because the policy-making process takes place in a political context, shifting interests and alignments must be continually reassessed. Political success therefore implies the capacity to learn.

Whichever way we characterize the nature of political work, it will be necessary to take into account how that work fits with the leader's character structure and more general attributes of personality. Characteristics such as a leader's sense of personal control, self-esteem, degree of ambition, and career and political goals influence not only which of the formal requirements are stressed and which associated opportunities are selected but also the ways in which they are carried out. Analyses of leadership style and political work, therefore, must focus on questions of how as well as what.

One must ask then, how is the work of political leaders and of political leadership to be understood from both a dynamic and a developmental perspective? Some time ago, Lasswell succinctly phrased the need for such understanding:

> We want to discover what developmental experiences are significant for the political traits and interests of the mature. This means we want to see what lies behind agitators, administrators, theorists and other types who play on the public stage. Can we conceive of the development of the human personality as a functioning whole, and discern the turning points in the growth of various patterns of public life? (1930, p. 8)

To this, I would now add the question, how can theories of adult development help us to accomplish this?

The Political Socialization of Leaders: Early Studies

Early studies of the political socialization of elites attempted to explain uniformities in political orientations. Beginning with the Hoover Institute's RADIR studies (Lasswell and Lerner 1965), a number of studies approached this problem by examining the social characteristics and backgrounds of political elites. Although Lasswell and Lerner attempted to place their data in a developmental paradigm, other researchers were not so attentive to this dimension.

An early critique of this line of research by Edinger and Searing (1967) pointed out that most research of this kind simply tabulated background characteristics without attempting to say which background variables, if any, were associated with which attitudes. In their important paper, using data from a survey of German and French leaders, they were able to demonstrate that some background variables were more predictive than others for elite attitudes, and that even these associations varied by culture. In other words, the standard background variables that were at the heart of much of the elite political socialization research could not be empirically demonstrated to be consistently and strongly associated with elite attitudes (no link between attitudes and behaviors were assessed in this or similar studies).

Two years later, Searing (1969) sought to make an important point about the fallacy of linking background variables with current political attitudes. He used data from five nations in an attempt to study variations in the effect of background variables on the attitudes of political elites and to replicate the earlier findings noted above. The empirical results obtained the second time around confirmed the earlier findings and led to the important conclusion that "many standard background categories are plainly gross structural indices with little chance of classifying similar socialization experiences relevant to attitude formation and change" (1969, p. 491). Searing went on to note (p. 491) that "The occupational category, 'intellectual,' or 'level of education' category, probably circumscribes extremely different socialization experiences in different cultures and systems."

We can summarize and build upon Searing's critique of this line of research as follows. First, it draws an implicit (but not theoretical) link between "background variables" and political attitudes. In the typical study characteristics such as age, level of education, university specialization, marital status, size of town of birth, to name but five of thirty-eight background variables in the Searing study, are analyzed in empirical relation to a wide range of political attitudes (fifty-five in the Searing paper). Searing's research made two important points about the utility of forecasting elite attitudes from background variables. First, that in the absence of a theoretical rationale for collecting specific kinds of data, the correlations themselves would not be a useful path to theory development. Second, Searing's work raised questions about the usefulness of focusing on political attitudes in the context of elite socialization studies.

In the two studies just mentioned and the larger data bases on which they drew, it is unclear whether the questions asked tapped attitudes or more concrete policy opinions (see Edinger and Searing (1967), p. 437, for some illustrations of the kinds of questions asked, and pp. 438 and 440 for their discussion of the difference between manifest and latent attitudes; see also Searing 1969, p. 492). Searing equated a specific attitude with well-defined opinion towards particular objects, situations, or policies (a view I would not share), and not surprisingly found that it was among the most specific attitudes (opinions) that background variables fared most poorly. This led him to conclude that more general underlying orientations that are subjective, diffuse, and not easily expressed in likert formats of most survey research instruments might be a more useful approach to establishing a linkage.

But there are also problems in this line of research with the mismatch between the experiences that are part of the socialization process and the measures that serve as indicators of these experiences. Searing comes close to putting his finger on the difficulty when he says that in trying to forecast what he refers to as underlying orientations, "it will be necessary to refine background categories by way of generating data closer to relevant socialization experiences" (1969, p. 495). One might rephrase this insight by suggesting that it is the very subjective experience underlying placement in categories which gives them their meaning for elite socialization, and the match between the experiences and the categories cannot simply be assumed, as much of this line of research has tended to do.

These early studies also tended to mix together persons in different political roles as long as they were elites. This strategy probably increases the variation within the samples but not the capacity of the independent variables to account for the variance. To put the point more basically, presidents and congressmen are both part of the political elite, but there is little theoretical or empirical reason to believe that they should be grouped together for purposes of analyzing their role performance.

In order to make meaningful statements about political leaders, it would seem to be necessary and desirable to know more about the nature of particular kinds of political work. We would then be in a better position to say exactly what drives, orientations (whether general beliefs and values or specific attitudes or opinions), skills, and cognitive processes are relevant. Political socialization and leadership studies might then be in a better position to study the ways in which specific developmental experiences are related to specific features of political role performance.

While it is important to have a greater understanding of the actual work of political leaders, it would also be helpful to have available models of individual development which would help guide the study of adult political socialization. The social background studies were based on the view that early developmental experience was both formative and determinant. A theory of adult political performance that does not wish to assume that leaders are children in men's clothes will have to look for other models of development to supplement childhood-centered theories of political socialization. Before examining these new models however, let us turn briefly to examine the legacy of these early studies on the issue of development.

The Freudian Legacy and the Question of Adult Development

Attempts to analyze the social backgrounds of political elites in order to uncover patterns of socialization represent one line of theoretical approach. Another, best represented by the work of Harold Lasswell (1930, 1948), looked more directly at individual life histories. These early studies of the psychological sources of a leader's behavior examined aspects of the leader's past, especially childhood, for clues to understanding later political behavior.

The psychoanalytic framework that guided these studies entailed two related assumptions. The first was that unconscious and therefore unresolved conflicts originating in childhood would persist into adulthood and be instrumental in shaping political behavior. This is the assumption which lies behind Lasswell's well-known formula for political man, namely, that he displaces private motives (e.g., unresolved psychological conflicts) onto public objects and rationalizes the process in terms of public interest. Using the same framework, Wolfenstein's early psychoanalytic study of Lenin, Trotsky, and Ghandi found a basic similarity in all three revolutionary leaders:

> Each had an unusually ambivalent relationship with his father . . . .
> When the nature of the youth's relation to paternal authority is very
> much at issue, it is very likely that the individual will be responsive
> to occupations, of which revolutionary activity is one, which allow
> him to work through his conflicts. . . . The revolutionary is one who
> escapes from the burdens of Oedipal guilt and ambivalence by car-
> rying his conflict with authority into the political realm. (1967,
> p. 305)

The second assumption embedded within the early psychoanalytic framework concerns the process of repetition. The early psychoanalytic model posited that unresolved childhood conflicts would not only influence the leader's adult political behavior but would do so repeatedly. To paraphrase Santayana, those who do not resolve their conflicts are doomed to repeat them. Perhaps the most familiar example of this model for political scientists is the Georges' argument (1964, pp. 320-21) regarding Woodrow Wilson's very similar difficulties as president of Princeton University, governor of New Jersey, and president of the United States. In each case a similar confluence of external circumstances and internal dispositions combined to reproduce unfortunate political results. For Wilson, the external circumstances included a challenge in an area in which he held himself to be expert. A person or persons in opposition then came to personify the challenge and call into question Wilson's competence or final authority in the matter. Among the inner dispositions that were relevant to this process were Wilson's intense ambition, sense of rectitude, and desire for quick compliance from others once he had staked out an issue as "his authority domain."[3]

   Given that these two assumptions (childhood primacy and character repetition) dominated early work in the psychoanalytic study of the political socialization of leaders, it is important to assess their status in a psychologically grounded theory of adult development and political socialization. My analysis will focus on the concept of character, which stands at the center of a leader's personality system. It is at the level of character, the most basic and deepest level of a leader's psychological functioning, that questions of continuity and significant change may be seen in sharpest relief. Is the traditional psychoanalytic view of character-consistency and repetition to be modified in view of the findings of adult development theory? And what exactly are the implications of any such modifications for our understanding of how political leaders develop through their adult years?

The early psychoanalytic view on these questions is quite clear. Character patterns develop early in childhood and persist intact through adulthood. The early psychoanalytic studies of political leaders emphasized the repetitious defense against unconscious drives, a view which essentially equated character with defense. In this view, character persisted unchanged into *and through* adulthood and decisively influenced the actions of political leaders. Interestingly, even more recent psychological studies of political leaders, which adapt a neoanalytic perspective, arrive at roughly the same conclusions about the continuity of character through adulthood. Barber, for example, in considering the question of continuity and change in presidential character concludes that the weight of evidence favors the former over the latter, and notes that "Every character elaborates itself through life, but after thirty or forty years, character is rarely transformed" (1985, p. 526).

I will present evidence in this essay that casts doubt on Barber's position. These data will suggest that developmental transformations (in the sense of both reversals and deepenings discussed at the beginning of the essay) can and do take place during adulthood. Furthermore, given the institutional amplification of leaders' decisions and behaviors, a real question can be raised as to whether imposing the requirement of transformation as a criterion for change is not too stringent. Character "elaboration" might well have substantial impact on a leader's performance, even in the absence of character transformation. Finally, exactly what kind of development or elaboration (to use Barber's term) is possible, what are its sources, and how does it unfold during adulthood?

Freud himself discussed character somewhat in passing (1908B, 1961D). His early followers furthered this work by delineating certain character types (Abraham 1927, chap. 5, 14, 20; Fenichel 1945, pp. 463-540), but they did not develop a real theory of character.[4] Even Reich, whose work *Character Analysis* (1949) is the most sustained effort to examine the concept, views character as a form of defensive shield (cf. his discussion of character armor) around the basic levels of the personality system.

The early analytic theorists, like Fenichel, relying on the metapsychology of drive theory, saw character as "the habitual mode of bringing into harmony the tasks presented by internal demands and by the external world" (1945, p. 467). By using the word "habitual," Fenichel was underscoring the point that character represents an acquired, deeply anchored pattern of experience and response to inner strivings and external situations. Other formulations underscored another aspect of character, namely, that it represents a pattern of orientation and response to a wide range of experience. Characterological patterns, then, are not only to be found in specialized circumstances (e.g., relations to authority), or for only specialized "types" (e.g., obsessive characters). Rather character is best seen as the foundation for every person's personality structure. It is these aspects of character that lend credence to Barber's terse but apt description of character, which he sees as the basis of presidential performance, "as a person's stance as he confronts experience" (1985, p. 5).

The impact of early experiences and character on the adult political behavior of leaders, however, is more complex than commonly assumed in political psychology research. For example, while some of the origins of character may be viewed as "primitive," because of their early appearance in the person's life history, their "deep" location in the psychological structure, and so on, the behaviors that are influenced by them are not necessarily the same. By the time a leader has reached adulthood, motives, however deep their origin, will have been subjected to layers of subsequent experience and fused with conscious calculation. Moreover, there will be, in almost all cases, a developed set of skills available to the adult that help translate these motives into accomplishment and that were not available to the child. These represent one source of change and development in character during adulthood, but there are others.

Early analytic theory focused on impulse and defense as the basis of character, but character contains a substantial and important cognitive component (Shapiro 1965).[5] Even if we grant that the origin of character is to be found in impulse, these impulses in turn must take some more concrete form. One does not ordinarily, for example, experience a need for love in the abstract but in connection with a particular person or persons. It is the history of a particular need and its reception in the real world by emotionally important others that give rise to the cognitive components of character, belief, and expectation. Basic character beliefs about the nature of the world, whether it is responsive or not, whether people can be trusted or not, and the expectations that are generated in connection with these character beliefs, are a central but heretofore largely unrecognized element of character.

What implications do the existence of the cognitive elements in character have for issues of continuity and change in adult political development? One is to suggest an important source of possible change in character, namely, experience. If the real-world reception of needs gives rise to these character-level beliefs and expectations, then in theory they can be modified by the same process. To put the thought another way, if beliefs and expectations surrounding need arise from experience, they must be responsive to it.[6]

Extrapolating these processes to the political arena, I will suggest that significant mismatches between character-generated beliefs and expectations with formative political experience can result in significant modifications of leadership cognitive frameworks, with resulting implications for political decisions and behavior. I will discuss this process at greater length in connection with the political careers of Ronald Reagan and Richard M. Nixon somewhat later in this essay.

One major source of character continuity in the view of early psychoanalytic theorists was the fact that impulses and unresolved conflicts, the basic building blocks of character, were unconscious. This meant that, without specialized techniques for uncovering these conflicts (e.g., psychoanalysis), they continued, their strength undiminished, to play a strong role in adult repetitions. While unexamined conflicts do continue to affect an individual's behavior, it is not quite accurate to say that no change can take place except through treatment.

One major consequence of unresolved conflict is repeated patterns of behavior in specific types of situations. These patterns may not be obvious to a person in their teens, twenties, or perhaps ever. But some time ago Smith, Bruner, and White (1956) noted that some individuals can become aware over time of some of their behavioral patterns. Political leaders, in repeatedly confronting situations which arouse echoes of past unsuccessful experiences, may realize that certain situations are problematic for them (even if they do not fully appreciate why) and search for new solutions. George and George, for example, in discussing Woodrow Wilson's flawed political performance in certain situations, note (1964, p. 321):

> There is some evidence that Wilson sensed the dangers implicit in his compulsive ambition. To House, Wilson spoke of his nightmares in which he relived his struggles at Princeton, and that the pattern of success-defeat might repeat itself in the Presidency. . . . There is also some evidence that Wilson was casting around for ways of avoiding a repetition of his highly distressing experience as a reformer at Princeton. Thus, for a while, he cultivated the notion that with the passage of his major legislative program of 1913–14 the task of reforming American economic life along progressive principles had been completed. . . . The implication that he had already made his major political contribution suggests a rudimentary effort to find a means of protecting himself through resignation or, more likely, refusal of a second term against the compulsive ambition which was causing anxiety.

Similarly, Mazlish (1972, p. 125) suggests that former President Nixon, himself no stranger to repetitive patterns, had nonetheless managed to develop some methods of by-passing or otherwise dealing with problematic areas:

> No man reaches his position without a good deal of ability, and Nixon starts with strong cognitive powers: he is quick, shrewd, and possessed of a good memory. Moreover, he has turned his problems and weaknesses into strengths. Racked by indecision, he has learned how to plan and contrive ahead of time. Faced with the constant need to test himself, he has shown real courage on a number of occa-

sions. . . . Since 1962 he has matured, coming to grips with his fear of failure.

Perhaps, then, it is fair to say that all but the most rigid political leaders can develop in adulthood even at the level of character. However, we should not expect that changes at this level of leadership functioning are typically dramatic, although even small increments of change can have important political consequences the higher in the power hierarchy a leader rises. At other, less fundamental levels of leadership functioning, like political beliefs, values, and strategies, we would expect more capacity to learn and develop. It may well be the case that in democracies, with their institutional mechanisms for accountability, persons require some degree of development and learning in order to obtain and maintain political office.

Political careers, like other careers, generate within them certain recurring circumstances (e.g., disputes over policy, formal and informal methods of obtaining power, mechanisms for exercising it, etc.). It is certainly plausible to argue that certain of these may recurringly evoke responses in the leader that in some respect or to some degree are related to unresolved conflicts. On the other hand, all of the psychological accounts discussed above suggest that most leaders advance in their careers more in spite of than because of their unresolved areas of intrapsychic and interpersonal conflicts.

Theories of Adult Development as a Framework for Adult Political Socialization Theory

Erik Erikson's studies of Gandhi (1969) and Luther (1958)[7] make clear that development with the attendant possibilities of growth or decline are evident throughout adulthood. His work underscores the limits of the traditional psychoanalytic view. The adult identity crises of a Luther and of a middle-aged Gandhi are neither foretold nor required by their childhoods. The models that emerge from these studies are developmental elaboration and reversal, not repetition. But in spite of the importance of Erikson's work, there is somewhat of a dilemma in using it as *the* basis for theories of the adult political socialization of leaders. One problem is that both Gandhi and Luther were "great men." The question therefore arises as to whether their talents, skills, and developmental experiences are relevant for the larger number of political leaders who are not "great" and do not initiate vast social or political transformations.

Erikson's theory is very helpful in charting the relationship between the great man's personal strivings and the as yet unarticulated stirrings of collective need. Leadership, in these cases, as Erikson (1969, p. 408) makes clear, consists not only in articulating but in addressing the felt imbalances accumulated over time in such societies. It is less immediately clear, however, what Erikson's work suggests for the less transformational leaders, to use Burns' (1978, p. 4) term, who constitute the great majority of political leaders. What is needed are a set of models to fill in the terrain of adult development for more typical political leaders. A useful model to consider in this regard may be found in the work of Levinson and his colleagues (1978). It should be noted at the outset that Levinson's research is based on a sample of forty males (1978, p. 9), so that the theory drawn from it may be limited to male political leaders. On the other hand, Levinson has recently completed (forthcoming) a similar in-depth study of women, and while there are differences, the general contours of the model appear to hold for both men and women.

Levinson conceives of adult development in terms of three major periods, or eras. The ages at which each period begins and ends are somewhat individually variable. The first begins in early adulthood around the age of seventeen and extends through the age of forty. The second period is middle adulthood, which extends from approximately forty to sixty. The third period late adulthood, begins around the age of sixty. Within each major period there are a series of stable and transitional phases, each related to the major developmental tasks of the phase. While each phase has its own set of tasks, it is central to Levinson's theory that the major task of all stable phases, whatever the period, is the development of a stable life-structure.

The concept of life structure is deceptively simple. It is the "underlying pattern or design of a person's life at a given time" (Levinson 1978, p. 41). The life structure reflects a person's choices (both conscious and otherwise) given a particular configuration of the person's sociocultural world (race, class, family, political system, etc.), developing sense of self (some aspects of which are lived out, others inhibited), and participation in the world (his involvement in the roles of citizen, husband, friend, etc.). Adult development in Levinson's view *is* "the evolution of the life structure" (p. 42), viewed as "a patterning of self and world" (p. 47).

Levinson's model, like Erikson's, is psychosocial. Both posit a two-way relationship between psychosocial development and the external environment, but there are important differences between the two. For Erikson's "great men," the strength of their drives, coupled with some extraordinary skills (for example, the capacity to mobilize publics), played out in an institutionally hostile but psychologically receptive environment, enabled them to transform that environment. Levinson's subjects, on the other hand, are more typical than transformational. The story of their lives is not to be found in the profound transformations of society that great men's inner drives made possible, but rather in the building of a life structure within the confines of their sociocultural world.

Central to Levinson's argument is the finding that no life structure, how-

ever satisfactory in some respects, can fully allow expression of the contradictory or incompatible strivings that characterize individuals. The inability
to find expression of some of what we wish to be provides a basic mechanism
of change throughout adulthood. Levinson's model implies that individual
development and learning have roots not only in the need to do politically
successful work but also in carving out a place for expression of important
aspects of the leader's self as he builds a successful life structure centered
around a political career.

Levinson's model suggests that political careers, like others, will both facilitate and suppress aspects of the individual's self. We know very little at
this stage about the nature of the political career as a vechicle for the expression of the self and about what aspects of the self are favored or inhibited in
the process of building a political career. As stated earlier, there has been
discussion in the literature (Lasswell and Rogow, 1963; Greenstein, 1969,
pp. 44, 54–55) about the ways in which high-level political roles enable the
expression of ego-defensive feelings or actions, but less attention has been
paid to the ways in which political roles facilitate or inhibit the expression of
aspects of the self. During recent presidential campaigns, candidates have
come under intense personal scrutiny, and the trend appears to be accelerating. It seems plausible that one result of close scrutiny is inhibition; on the
other hand, political careers must certainly provide for expression of some
aspects of self or there would be few seeking office, and fewer yet wishing to
remain once there.

Before examining some further implications of Levinson's model for a
theory of the adult political socialization of leaders, I would like to explicate
briefly Levinson's ideas regarding the tasks of each adult period. If the general task of each developmental period and the particular stages within it is
to build a stable and satisfying life structure, it is also the case that each
period in adulthood has its own particular developmental tasks. Figure 6.1
sets out the major developmental stages.

For Levinson, the period from seventeen to twenty-two marks the transition
from pre- to early adulthood. The twin tasks of this period are to begin moving out of the pre-adult world and to explore the possibilities of creating the
first adult life structure. From about twenty-two to twenty-eight the task is to
establish a provisional structure between a valued self and a self valued by
society. The provisional life structure begins to give way to the age-thirty
transition, extending approximately from twenty-eight to thirty-three, which
provides an opportunity to correct the flaws of the first life structure. Levinson found that for most men in his sample the primary thrust was reform, not
revolution; nonetheless, for a large number of his subjects, the period was
fairly stressful, and this led Levinson to speak of an age thirty crisis.

The second adult life structure begins to take shape at the end of the age

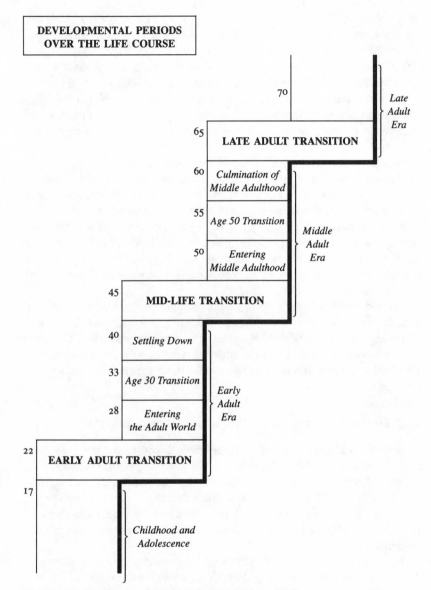

Figure 6.1.   The Seasons of a Man's Life (from Levinson 1978)

thirty transition and persists to about forty. Here Levinson talks about two primary tasks. First, the person strives to establish a *niche* in society, and, second, he works to "make it." It is during this period, from about thirty-six to forty that an important transition is frequently completed. A person starts out in this period at the bottom of the occupational ladder, but by the end of the period, if things go well, he is approaching a position of seniority. This latter period Levinson describes as "*becoming one's own man*" (1978, p. 60; emphasis in original). It is during this period that one speaks more strongly and confidently in one's own voice.

The late thirties mark both the end of early adulthood and the beginning of the mid-life transition. It is at this point that assessment of what one has and has not done takes on a new, more urgent tone. The passage of time increasingly weighs on these assessments, and if elements of the self which have not been given adequate expression are to be given it, new or modified life structures must be constructed.Levinson found that for many of his subjects this mid-life transition was a time of deep and significant self-reflection and turmoil. Some of his subjects abandoned the life structures they had created; others significantly modified them.

Levinson posits a further set of stages through later adulthood. These include an *age-fifty transition,* and a period from approximately fifty-five to sixty which he sees as devoted to building a second, middle-adult life structure. For about age sixty, Levinson posits yet another stage, a *late-adult transition* that terminates middle adulthood and creates the basis for starting late adulthood.

Adult Development and the Political Socialization of Leaders

We are now in a better position to explore more directly some implications of these theories of adult development for the study of political leaders, their careers and work. The discussion that follows has two interrelated themes. The first concerns the contribution of these theories to issues of continuity and change in political leaders, and the second concerns the applicability of these theories to specific aspects of leadership learning, performance, and development.

I begin with a discussion of the concept of the self and its role in theories of adult development and the political socialization of leaders. I will then examine the expression of the self through political life structures and the role that aspirations for the self play in political ambitions and the development of political careers. Finally, I will examine the very important set of interpersonal relationships (a leader's mentor, protégés, friends, and spouse) that help to define and shape adulthood, and the political life structure that the leader builds within his political career.

The Role of the Self and Self-esteem

Central to Erikson's theory of adulthood is the problem of identity, that core sense of the self that anchors beliefs, values, attitudes, skills, and so on. Like other concepts, that of the self has developed multiple meanings. One psychiatrist (Giovacchini 1975, p. 3) who has written extensively on the clinical understanding of the term notes, "This 'view of oneself' has alternately been referred to as 'the identity sense,' 'self-image,' and 'the self concept' . . . . [despite] the ubiquity of this concept there appears to be no uniform theoretical formulation regarding this particular ego function or its relationship to other ego systems." This statement notwithstanding, any student of the psychology of political leaders can still benefit from Erikson's discussion of the term.

Erikson notes that Freud's structural theory viewed the superego as containing two distinct sets of contents. The first includes all those internalizations and incorporations that represent primitive views of authority and necessity, while the second involves aspirations in the form of the ego-ideal. Erikson notes (1968, p. 210) that, "in contrast to 'blind morality,' [the] ego ideal . . . [is] more flexibly and consciously bound to the ideals of a particular historical era . . . [it] is closer to the ego function of reality testing: ideals can change." Erikson goes on to suggest that the ego ideal represents, "a set of to-be-striven for but forever not-quite-obtainable ideal goals for the Self, [while] ego identity could be said to be characterized by the actually obtained but forever to be revised sense of the reality of the Self within social reality" (1968, pp. 210–11). Erikson then proposes the term "self-identity" as the successful integration of multiple selves, "in an ensemble of roles which also secure social recognition." Identity, then, is a by-product of the ego's synthetic functions, namely, its capacity to integrate an individual's selves (both actual and aspired-to) within the context of available (or potentially available) roles.

In classic psychoanalytic theory, traumatic episodes were associated with the breakthrough of repressed impulses. For self-theory the major threats come from narcissistic vulnerabilities and threats to the cohesion and integrity of the self. In this paradigm, self-esteem becomes an essential psychological factor in maintaining an integrated and well-functioning self. What libido was to classic theory, self-esteem, or what Kohut (1971, p. 9) called "healthy narcissism,"[8] is for self-theory.

One implication of this change in perspective for theories of adult development in political leaders is that it leads away from compensation and repetition as central forms of adult functioning and learning. Where character and self are essentially viewed as compensatory, there is little room for adult political learning or development, and therefore little reason to study it. The emphasis in adult development theories on self- esteem and the development of the self also suggests a central dimension of leadership functioning and performance. If compensation is the key to leadership performance, then adult political socialization, especially as it deals with political leaders, would need to devote its energies to uncovering and tracing the experiences which make such measures necessary. On the other hand, if compensation is only one aspect, and perhaps in most leaders not the major aspect, of psychological functioning, then clearly a different developmental focus is in order.

Self-esteem is clearly related to the capacity for and the degree of political learning. In Sniderman's (1975) excellent treatment of the problem, he found that among a large and representative sample of political elites, self-esteem was not only empirically correlated with learning per se but also with what was learned. He found for example that "low self-esteem not only impairs cognitive efficiency in general but social learning in particular" (1975, p. 156). More particularly, elites in Sniderman's sample who suffered from low self-esteem were less likely to expose themselves to new political information, and when they did less likely to comprehend it. Finally, Sniderman found that "high self-esteem promotes commitment to democratic values; conversely low self-esteem increases the susceptibility to extreme political views" (1975, p. 199).

Sniderman's findings, based on a comprehensive and sophisticated use of survey research, help buttress similar findings in Barber's comparative studies of presidential character (1985). Barber notes that one of the characteristics of presidents with high self-esteem is the capacity to learn, both from experience and context. He gives by way of example the Bay of Pigs fiasco early in President Kennedy's first term. An important element in the failure of the decision process in that situation was Kennedy's reliance on others' evaluations which he did not subject to rigorous scrutiny, possibly because, at this stage, high self-esteem may have led him to a degree of overconfidence in his own decision-making. But after that failure Kennedy initiated a review of decision-making procedures and, more important, rethought his own role and the roles of his advisors. One result was that, by the time he was faced with the Cuban missile crisis, which many experts view as a success for him (see Janis 1982; Etheredge 1985), the decision process had been extensively revamped and Kennedy himself played a much more skeptical, probing role.[9] This example suggests that a strong sense of self-esteem may not keep leaders from making errors but is associated with learning from mistakes.

The Expression of the Self in the Political Life-structure

There is ample reason to look closely at the leader's political role as an important agency of adult political socialization. Unlike family, school, and other agencies of childhood political socialization, through which individuals must pass, the role of political leader is deliberately chosen. Given the importance of work for adults, including political work for those who choose it, we can expect the role to be important in shaping and developing the leader's adult sense of self.

This fit between intrapsychic development, developmental experience, and political role performance is complex, and no single theory or model can or should be expected to explain it all. Nor does the use of one theoretical lens necessarily preclude the helpful use of another. As an example of the "multiple lens" approach to understanding political leaders, consider the well-received psychobiography of Woodrow Wilson by Alexander L. and Juliette L. George (1964; originally published in 1956).

The Georges build their analysis on Lasswell's early formulation about power-seekers, namely, that they seek power to overcome low estimates of the self. As one examines this carefully drawn analysis, one can discern, along with the Georges' more specific psychoanalytic formulations, some themes of adult development theory. Here, for example, is young Woodrow Wilson, then thirty-three years old, writing to his wife about his feelings after the publication of his first book, in words that echo strongly Levinson's analysis of "becoming one's own man." "Have I told you," Wilson wrote to his wife, "that lately—since I have been here [Wilson had left the small-college environment of Bryn Mawr for a position at Wesleyan] a distinct *feeling* of maturity—or rather of maturing has come over me? The *boyish* feeling that I have so long had and cherished is giving place, consciously to another feeling—the feeling that I am no longer young . . . and that I no longer need hesitate (as I have so long and sensitively done) to assert myself and my opinions in the presence of and against the selves and opinions of old men, 'my elders'" (in George and George 1964, p. 27, emphasis in original). Here is a graphic description of finding one's personal and political voice and the sense of confidence that accompanies it. This accomplishment seems all the more important given the Georges' analysis of young Woodrow's difficulties with his extremely demanding and in some regards punitive father.[10]

Or consider Levinson's discussion of the different, often conflicting aspects of the self that are sometimes incapable of expression within one's life structure. Wilson had from very early in his childhood wanted to be a great statesman, and after graduating from Princeton enrolled at the University of Virginia to study law. He was now twenty-three years old, beginning to construct his first adult life structure. As he wrote to his future wife some years later, "The profession I chose was politics; the profession I entered was the law. I entered the one because I thought it would lead to the other" (in George and George 1964, p. 14). Wilson's legal career did not work out, and he spent more time listening to political oratory than engaging in it. Somewhat disheartened, he decided to study politics at Johns Hopkins University. He completed his degree and went off to his first teaching appointment, at Bryn Mawr College. Wilson's rise in the academic world was steady. By 1890, at the age of thirty-four, he had become a professor of politics at Princeton University and in a few years had achieved enormous success and prestige. Was Wilson happy or satisfied with the new life structure he had created? Absolutely not. Wilson is quoted as exclaiming to his brother-in-law, "I am so tired of a merely talking profession! I want to *do* something!" (in George and George 1964, p. 29). One can almost hear the echoes of Luther's famous fit in the choir, when he raved and shouted either "Ich bin's nit! Ich bin's nit!" or "Non sum! Non sum! "which Erikson translates (1958, p. 23) from the German as "It isn't me!" and from the Latin as "I am *not*!

Wilson's exasperation reflects the classic dilemma of a person who has created a life structure which to outsiders may appear enviable but which the person experiences as frustrating and intolerable. The choice here, as Levinson points out, is to either modify the life structure in a way which allows "voice" to those aspects of the self inhibited by the current life structure, or else break out of it and create a new one. Wilson's decision to resign as president of Princeton University and seek the governorship of New Jersey represents exactly such an attempt. The reason for it is not to be found in a stage-related imperative but rather in the ill fit between Wilson's deepest desire and the successful but unsatisfying life structure he had created.

Aspirations for the Self in Political Life: The Dream in Adult Development

Somewhere between fantasy and calculation lies the dream. It is, says Levinson,

> a vague sense of the self-in-adult world. It has the quality of a vision,
> an imagined possibility that generates excitement and vitality. . . .
> Whatever the nature of his Dream, a young man has the developmental task of giving it greater definition and finding ways to live it
> out. (1978, p. 91)

Levinson notes that the dream may take many forms. It may be concrete (winning the Nobel Prize), dramatic (being a great statesman), or mundane but fulfilling (being an excellent craftsman), but the one thing it cannot be without serious developmental consequences is absent. Levinson notes that "If the Dream remains unconnected to life, it may simply die and with it [a] sense of purpose" (1978, p. 92). And although it may have its origins in childhood and adolescence, "The Dream is a distinctively adult phenomenon" (1978, p. 93).

There can be little doubt of Woodrow Wilson's inner dream; it was to be a great statesman (George and George 1956, pp. xviii, 14, 23), and a giver of laws. In the latter he succeeded in sublimated form even as a college undergraduate; in the former he did not even as president of the United States. How might we account for this? The Georges argue that Wilson's failures revolved around an inability to compromise when he was exercising power, especially in those areas in which he personally involved himself. They carefully document a pattern of such difficulties, first at Princeton, then as governor of New Jersey, and finally as president. This pattern in turn, they relate to Wilson's childhood treatment by his father and his (Wilson's) resultant insecurely established sense of self and self-esteem. They contrast Wilson's flexibility in gaining power with his rigidity in exercising it in certain kinds of circumstances.

Let us take a brief look at this pattern from the standpoint of adult development theory, and more particularly at what Levinson notes about the changing nature of the dream during the mid-life transition. He observes that the dream derives in part from normal omnipotent fantasies in childhood and that some degree of grandiosity may be necessary for the young adult as he tries to construct an adequate structure for himself. Gradually however, this work requires an increasing amount of reality-testing and application if the life-structure is to be successful.

It is at the time of the mid-life transition that important modifications of the dream take place,[11] most importantly in those areas which are less directly reality-based. In this period, illusions (but not aspirations) must be given up if the remainder of the life cycle is not to be foolishly spent. Among the illusions that Levinson notes is "the illusion of omnipotence: as long as the hero is true to the Dream he is invincible; he may suffer momentary defeats and at times all may appear to be lost, but if he perseveres he will triumph" (1978, p. 247). One is reminded of Wilson's tortured path at the Paris Peace Conference and thereafter. It would seem that Wilson was so identified with his dream, and the grandiose and omnipotent elements were so unmodified by life experience, that compromise was tantamount to killing the dream and with it Wilson's idealized view of his self in the world.

One might ask, why this strong identification in the first place, and why the failure to modify the dream? One speculation about the identification is that it represents a powerful condensation of a number of elements. It represents a desire to be powerful and knowledgeable, and Wilson apparently experienced himself to be neither, in spite of his prodigious accomplishments. It also represents a certain kind of narcissistic generosity (he was, after all, giving humanity a legacy of peace), and virtue (rectitude was a central element in Wilson's value structure). Why wasn't Wilson able to modify his dream? One answer lies in the suggestion that persons with narcissistic vulnerabilities, such as a poorly established sense of self-esteem, are unable fully to integrate experience that calls into question their idealized sense of self.

Levinson's concept of the dream, and this discussion of Wilson's behavior regarding the League of Nations treaty, raises another aspect of adult development, the legacy. According to Levinson, the legacy defines to some degree the ultimate value of a person's life (for himself), and his claims on posterity. It includes all that he will pass on:

> For many men at mid-life, work is the most significant component of the life structure, and the major source of the legacy. . . . A man who develops and manages institutions—a political leader . . . would like his institution to be his monument, an edifice that he helped to create and will be part of his legacy. (1978, p. 219)

In Erikson's terms (1958, p. 242), the legacy is part of the crisis of generativity, in which a person looks at what he has generated and finds it either wanting or adequate. It is this evaluation and the subsequent attempt to modify or rectify one's legacy that Erikson puts at the center of the last developmental stage, that of old age, in which the central crisis is between integrity and despair.

There has been much speculation about the role of the leader's place "in history" as a source of political behavior. Presidents for example, are routinely thought to look towards their place in history at the end of their second terms, since they may not serve another. Theories of adult development suggest that the reasons for building a legacy have a firm psychological and developmental anchor and probably operate according to a somewhat different time schedule than simply the last few years of a leader's term of office. Concern for one's legacy is not simply a narcissistic indulgence, which would suggest it is mostly concerned with self-image. Rather for many (but not all) persons, the legacy represents one's link to the future and an extension of the self through time. It also represents a way in which the leader can try to insure that his values, beliefs, and hopes will continue to have influence when he is no longer present. Self-image may be the least part of such a concern. Such issues do not necessarily appear only at the time of the leader's last term in office but may well be present and a part of the mid-life transition(s) and the assessment of one's lifework (to date) at that juncture.

We can see here perhaps another reason why Wilson may have fought so hard for *his* League of Nations; it was to be his lasting political legacy. This may help to account for his stubbornness regarding the details of the treaty. There is no reason to assume that a leader who was inflexible in wielding power in areas closely tied to his own sense of self would be any more flexible when it came to defining his self (politically) for posterity.

The Wilson example suggests several points about the adult development of leaders in a democracy. It does seem fair to say, following Levinson, that the sense of self and its elaboration during adulthood is a major source of leadership motivation during adulthood. The task of political leaders at each stage of adulthood is to construct a life structure that allows the expression of many of the most important aspects of the self, while at the same time gaining recognition and confirmation from others of those choices and their results. The Wilson example suggests that this may be no easy matter. The process of democratic politics may impose particular constraints on leaders in this regard. The need to compromise policy or goals may place a special burden on those leaders whose dreams are to some degree compensatory (because of insufficiently established self-esteem) rather than functioning as guides for political action.

Political Socialization and Political Careers

The political career, like other forms of adult work, should provide satisfaction for individual needs and an opportunity for the expression of skills in the process. This does not mean however, that political careers are always the leader's first choice. For some, like Woodrow Wilson, the call of political life apparently began rather early. For others, equally oriented towards power once they became involved in politics, political careers had diverse origins. Glad (1980, p. 501) notes that for Jimmy Carter "The roots of [his] ambition . . . suggest he was propelled by a desire for recognition in *some* field, rather than a strong, burning interest in political goals." In other cases, a political career is a result of a first career-choice that didn't quite work. Richard Nixon tried, but failed, to obtain a job in a major New York law firm; he then returned to Whittier, California, and eventually took up a political career (but see Brodie, 1981, p. 154 for a different view regarding Nixon's political aspirations in Whittier).

Theories of adult development do not tell us why persons go into politics, but they can help us to understand what happens to them after their entry. Consider the question of learning about political roles. Obviously, specific information about these roles is generally a product of adult experience, except when political leadership is a family profession. Yet beyond concrete learning, we are also interested in whether and how early adult political experiences shape the developing political leader.

It seems clear that political careers, like others, progress in stages, and one crucial stage in any career is its beginning. Barber takes particular note of the political leader's first independent success. It is a time, according to Barber, when the novice leader combines and solidifies his worldview and character in a political context, and it leads to the development of a political style:

> In most biographical accounts this period stands out in stark clarity—the time of emergence, the time the young man found himself. . . . The *way* he did that is profoundly important to him. . . . Much later, coming into the Presidency, something in him remem-

bers this earlier victory and re-emphasizes the style that made it happen. (1985, p. 10, emphasis in original)

Barber offers other example of this phenomonon. Herbert Hoover's style of diligence, and the use of small groups to accomplish his goals, brought with it much success during his college years at Stanford and was a style that was repeated in the White House (Barber 1985, p. 128). Another example of the early adult development of a "political style" is Lyndon Johnson's wheeling and dealing while a college student at Southwest Texas State Teacher's College. This style combined raw energy with an ability to manipulate and manage interpersonal relations (Barber 1985, p. 135). This kind of early career experience should be separated from the "lessons of history" (Neustadt and May 1985) that a leader may gain from early experience in a policy area. Both are likely to be important, but different, sources of conduct for the leader. The former reflects a leader's relationship to the political process, while the other is more germane to understanding concrete policy choices.

It is worth noting here that there are other important early career experiences beyond the first success. Richard Nixon, for example, was considered a progressive in college and a "liberal" at Duke Law School, according to his classmates (Brodie 1981, p. 129; Mazlish 1972, p. 57). Yet after law school, Nixon went to Washington and briefly worked for the Office of Price Administration (OPA). Nixon recalls that experience in the following words:

I came out of college more liberal than I am today. . . . I became more conservative . . . after my experience at OPA. I also became greatly disillusioned about the bureaucracy and about what the government could do because I saw the terrible paperwork that people had to go through. For the first time when I was in OPA, I also saw that there were people in government who were not satisfied merely with interpreting the regulations, enforcing the law that Congress passed, but who actually had a passion to get into business and used their government jobs to that end. . . . They set me to think a lot. (in Mazlish 1972, p. 58)

This is, of course, Nixon's view of what prompted him to change. Yet whatever the objective accuracy regarding the conditions that Nixon describes, it seems clear that his experience at OPA did have some impact. Indeed if his recollection is accurate he actually experienced something of a political conversion. It is of interest, given our concerns, that this early adult conversion took place at the level of basic political beliefs. These beliefs are generally thought to be more deeply anchored in the personality system and more stable over time than political attitudes or opinions.

While Nixon's account of his political conversion early in his adulthood is somewhat open to debate, there are other instances of significant reversals of political development in response to early adult political experiences. Ronald Reagan, like Nixon, started out his political life as a liberal (in both cases it must be recalled that the terms "liberal," "Democrat," etc. had somewhat different meanings then). He was, like his father, a New Deal Democrat and as late as 1947 was a founding member of the Calfornia branch of the Americans for Democratic Action (ADA).

During this period Reagan became involved in the Screen Actor's Guild and in 1947 was elected its president. At this time, the union was the target of a take-over attempt by Communist sympathizers. Reagan became heavily involved in resisting this attempted take-over, and the experience had a very profound effect on his views about Communism. Other reasons have been advanced to explain Reagan's "conversion," most notably the impact of his wife, Nancy. But whatever other factors were responsible for facilitating or reinforcing that change, the evidence seems convincing that the union presidency itself and the fight against the take-over were important in the evolution of Reagan's political self.

The Nixon and Reagan examples are important for several reasons. First, they suggest that politically significant development can and does take place in adulthood. Beyond this obvious implication, they also point to the importance of acute disconfirmation in helping to bring about this change. In both instances, more liberal political beliefs changed in direct response to experiences which challenged and ultimately disconfirmed original philosophical and political assumptions.

The Mentor in the Adult Development of Political Leaders

A crucial dimension of adult life concerns interpersonal relationships, which along with work are a major component of adult life-structures. These include relations with friends, colleagues, marriage partners, and others who hold personal and professional significance. The ability to establish these kinds of relationships in adulthood is important, as is their quality. Vaillant (1977, p. 215), in his longitudinal study of a sample of men from college through their sixties, found that "to fail in intimacy was to forfeit mastery in the next stage of the adult life-cycle."

In a sense, much of political life involves interpersonal relationships, for example, the leader's relationships with followers, peers, other leaders, and so on. Neustadt (1960) has argued that presidential leadership consists of the ability to persuade, which of course involves the leader in interpersonal relationships. The kinds and nature of such relationships reveal a great deal about the leader's political style. Lyndon Johnson's famous ability to manipulate and cajole others represents one form of interpersonal persuasion, Franklin Roosevelt's use of cross-purpose staff assignments to insure diversity of advice, is another.

These professional relationships are a cornerstone of adult development, especially given the significance of work in adulthood. Yet, while professional relationships are an important part of the political work of leaders, they do not exhaust the range of important relationships. In this section and the two which follow, I will examine three areas of interpersonal relationships that are important for leaders aside from those that are strictly professional. I will begin with the role of the mentor in the leader's adult political development and then consider the role of the marriage partner and of friendships.

Beyond the first independent political success or other important primary adult political experience, adult development theories point to other important sources of the leader's adult political socialization. Among the most important adult experiences connected with role learning and advancement within a chosen profession is the development of a special, personal relationship with a somewhat senior person in that profession, the mentor. The mentor acts as a guide, sponsor, advisor, and friend. He introduces the novice into the profession, teaches him the ropes, acts as a resource and advisor in times of stress, and otherwise helps to nurture the novice's dream and create a life structure in which it can be realized.

These are important functions. Levinson argues that "Poor mentoring in early adulthood is the equivalent of poor parenting in childhood; without adequate mentoring a young man's entry into the adult world is greatly hampered" (1978, p. 338). One need not fully subscribe to the first part of his argument to appreciate the importance of the second. A number of recent studies (Kellerman 1978; Nelson 1978; Kearney 1984; Wilkins 1986), of political mentors have confirmed their importance in political careers.

The mentor relationship serves important functions for both parties. For the older political leaders, the young protégé may be part of a legacy, a chance for one's programs and values to transcend death. For the younger partner, such a relationship may be crucial when social mobility (which characterizes many leaders) cuts the novice leader off from the experiences of his parents.

Nelson's empirical study of mentor relationships in the House of Representatives helps to clarify some of these points. Nelson characterizes upwardly mobile young leaders as "mentor seeking," and suggests that they will become connected with older members of Congress, who he suggests may be "protégé-seeking " (1978, p. 68). It is clear enough why mentoring is important to the novice, but Nelson's research contains some interesting suggestions on the functions it might serve for the mentor. In examining the lives of speakers of the House, Nelson (1978, p. 73) found "a fascinating pattern, which I believe has enormous ramifications for the House itself. From 1936 to 1971 no speaker of the House had a son. Sam Rayburn had no children. John McCormack . . . had no children. Joe Martin never married." Nelson's analysis suggests that, for the mentor, the apprentice political leader may be seen as a "family" as well as a political heir.

Like other important interpersonal relationships, the mentor relationship is complex and sometimes difficult. The apprentice, for example, may welcome help in building a life-structure to contain his political dreams, but at the same he aspires to be "his own person" and not someone else's. For the mentor too, the relationship is complex and ambivalent. The mentor may view his protégé as part of the legacy of *his* dream, raising the possibility that the novice might not be as effective, good, or faithful to the dream as the mentor may want. Even if the novice is all these things, and the mentor is successful, the "student" will soon be lost to the "teacher." Success in developing an heir as part of one's legacy only serves to underscore one of the heir's primary functions, survival of the leader's work in some form, given the inevitability of death.

A final point is that we should not assume that if the mentoring process goes well psychologically for both parties the results will necessarily be beneficial for the political system. The mentor does, after all, transmit his or her insights about the workings of the system. In New York City recently, for example, a powerful city councilman was forced to resign from office amidst allegations of corruption. These charges were identical to those which had forced this man's mentor to resign from the same post some years before.

Marriage and the Adult Development of Political Leaders

We have noted that intimate relationships are, along with work, at the core of adult experience. The marriage partner of the political leader can play varied roles (Kellerman 1983). Eleanor Roosevelt played a role as moral alter-ego to her husband. Edith Wilson was a source of emotional support for her husband and played a crucial political role when he became incapacitated while president. Glad (1980, p. 500) has noted that Rosalynn Carter is a close confidant of her husband and also functions as a political "gate-keeper." These and other roles that marriage partners can play are politically relevant, but in this section I would like briefly to consider the role that marriage can play in shaping, even while reaffirming, the leader's developing political life-structure.

As an illustration, I turn to the political career of Ronald Reagan. As noted, Reagan was, by his own account, a political liberal at the time of his first career in acting. His first wife, Jane Wyman, was herself an actress, reflecting the commitment that both had made to this life-structure. That marriage broke up in 1947, about the same time that Reagan was fighting communist sympathizers in the Screen Actors Guild of which he had become president. Several years later, Reagan met, dated, and married Nancy Davis, the daughter of a prominent and politically conservative neurosurgeon. By most accounts, Nancy has had an enormous effect on Ronald Reagan. Barber (1985, p. 475) suggests that "no other person would rival her influence." Lou Cannon, a Reagan biographer (quoted in Barber 1985, p. 476), writes that "passive and pleasant, Ronald Reagan was married to a woman who was neither."

Barber credits Reagan's emerging political conservatism to his new social circle of rich, conservative friends and to the influence of his wife. He argues (1985, p. 476) that while Reagan's New Deal identifications are "easily explainable by family history . . . his [new] family had a markedly different equation and Reagan began to shift accordingly." This explanation has much to recommend it, but it tends to underestimate the extent to which the ideological shift was itself part of a larger, more complex process. This period in Reagan's life included the simultaneous deterioration of the twin pillars of his first adult life-structure (his marriage and career), his first executive leadership position (in the Screen Actors Guild) and the very emotionally charged experience of fighting communist influence in that union. The sequence would appear then to be as follows: first, a breakdown of the first life-structure; second, a highly charged transitional "political" role as head of a union under siege; and third, his meeting and subsequent marriage to Nancy Reagan.

The union role appears to have been crucial in reorienting Reagan. It was first of all a new role which provided some escape from a stalled acting career. Second, it proved to be a transitional role to a similar (executive) position in a different, more directly political context. Third, it provided an "apprentice" experience to the novice leader. Last, it seems to have been a very emotionally charged experience, one that apparently challenged Reagan's basic convictions about "how things worked."

It is within this developmental context that Nancy Reagan fits. What Barber suggests about her influence is not without foundation; at the level of character, it fits to some degree. Certainly an active, directed partner can have an enormous effect on a more passive one, especially if they share general values and feelings. Certainly too, Nancy has been an active and highly effective promoter of Reagan's second, political career. But it seems somewhat more accurate to see Nancy as ratifying, even while helping to shape, Reagan's second, political life-structure.

The Reagan life-history provides a good illustration of the ways in which changes in the aspects of a leader's life-structure contain within them the seeds of further adult development. These can include changes in career, ideology, and friendship circles, as well as marriage partners. In some areas of Reagan's later adult life we find developmental reversals, (e.g., at the level of political ideology). In others we find a transfer and deepening of skills that already had a strong developmental history, (e.g., communication skills applied to politics instead of acting). Lastly, in other areas of personality functioning, e.g., character, we find a certain continuity. The picture of adult development that emerges, in this case at least, is much more varied and complex than one of simple change or lack of it.

Friendships and the Adult Political Socialization of Leaders

Friendships are among the most important relationships of adulthood. They represent the mutually chosen association of persons on the basis of rough equality, shared views or interests, and feelings of liking and respect. The nature of (and capacity for) a person's friendships reflect important aspects of the person's interpersonal relations. As I have indicated before, a leader's interpersonal relationships are of interest to us because the exercise of political leadership and power in a democracy is itself an interpersonal process.

There are in our political system some barriers to the development of political friendships. The single-member, winner-take-all representational structure increases the competitiveness of the political process. This means that even among like-minded colleagues (a potential source of friendships) those with similar ambitions may well be competitors. Another potential source of difficulty may be found in the tendency of leaders to develop highly articulated policy views, which in a context of competition among leaders with similar perspectives can lead to an accentuation of differences and an increase in political and personal conflict. Last, the democratic political process entails a certain degree of strategic bargaining even among like-minded colleagues, but strategic cooperation is not the best building block for deep or enduring political friendships.

Yet the barriers to enduring friendships in politics are by no means the complete story. Recent political history contains a number of examples of such friendships. Among them are Woodrow Wilson and Colonel House, William McKinley and Mark Hanna, Franklin Roosevelt and Harry Hopkins, Richard Nixon and Charles (Bebe) Rebozo, and Ronald Reagan and Paul Laxalt. Political friendships may also occur between leaders of different countries. Ronald Reagan, for example, appears to have developed a genuine friendship with British Prime Minister Margaret Thatcher that has resulted in increased policy collaboration and trust between the two leaders.

The capacity for friendship reflects aspects of both internal psychological development and interpersonal relationships that are important for the exercise of political power. However, the importance of friendships for political leaders goes beyond the fact that leadership may be viewed as an interpersonal process. Friendships can also be instrumental in the leader's political learning. Every leader can benefit from honest advice, but there are barriers to receiving it. A leader's staff is often the most available potential source of "straightforward" advice, but for several reasons this potential is rarely fully realized. There is first of all the problem of selecting advisors who mirror the leader's views. It is assumed, frequently, that this is desirable. The National Governors' Association, in advising new governors about their staff, suggests (NGA 1978, p. 100; emphasis added) that the staff "must know the Governor—his hopes, his ideals, his standards and the directions he wishes to go . . . [and] *must be willing to accept these as their own.*" This approach insures administrative consistency but may do so at the expense of divergent policy views.

There is a further complication that arises in leader-staff relationships, and that is the latter's fusion of interests in the leader's advancement. The governors' association notes that (NGA 1978, p. 100) the staff's "energies and loyalties must be devoted unflinchingly to the achievement of the Governor's success." One wonders whether any concern on this point is necessary. The leader's staff enjoys power and prestige precisely because they work with a leader in power, not out of it. The problem comes in defining success and in the temptation to place political expediency before sound long-term, but politically unpopular, policy.

Finally, the leader may become increasingly invested in his own policy views over time and increasingly unwilling to entertain critical or contrary views. In this and other cases, a real political friendship can be an important mechanism for opening up the decision process. Senator Paul Laxalt, a senior United States senator and long-time friend of Ronald Reagan, has performed this function for the president a number of times. The lack of such friendships can be politically damaging. In Richard Nixon's disastrous campaign for the governorship of Calfornia in 1962, Brodie notes (1981, p. 459), "we have ample evidence that there was no one in the campaign who could or would stand up to Nixon when he insisted on overscheduling himself or continually avoided talking about state issues, which he found boring."

Friends can also be called upon to play other roles, for example, a supportive, nurturing role rather than an independent, advising one. Colonel House seems to have played such a role for his friend Woodrow Wilson. House wrote in his diary (quoted in George and George 1964, p. 125) that, when the president asked for his advice on the drafts of speeches, "I nearly always praise at first in order to strengthen the President's confidence in himself, which, strangely enough, is often lacking."

Close political friendships, like other central, psychologically important relationships, are complex. The Wilson-House friendship is a good illustration of this. House served as an advisor, diplomatic and domestic political trouble-shooter, and sympathetic supporter to Wilson. He was keenly aware of Wilson's need for emotional support and "was careful to nurture the impression that he was satisfied to work through Wilson, that he did not covet independent power" (George and George 1956, p. 126). Did House try to manipulate Wilson, making use of his knowledge of Wilson's vulnerabilities? The Georges suggest that he did, but go on to say (1956, p. 127),

> This is not to say that his motives were dishonorable or that he abused the confidence of his illustrious friend. His manipulative skills notwithstanding, House was not opportunistic in the matter of political ideals. He was . . . a conservative reformer, and he aspired to political achievement of the highest order. His political ideals happily coincided with Wilson's. Their collaboration otherwise would not have been possible, for however flexible his tactics, House was devoted to his convictions.

The close friendship of House and Wilson illustrates another (possible) aspect of a political leader's relationship with close political protégés. Kohut (1971, pp. 115,122–25) has discussed the phenomenon of twinship in close interpersonal relationships. In this kind of relationship the other person serves as an alter ego. In Kohut's view (1971, p. 122), "the alter-ego transference (twinship) in which not a primary identity but a likeness (similarity) with the object is established, corresponds to a more mature developmental phase." In this early work, Kohut noted (p. 115) that one characteristic of such intense relationships was that the person, "assumes that the analyist [or other] is either like him or similar to him, or that the analyst's [or other's] psychological makeup is like, or is similar." Keeping this close psychological bond in mind, consider how the Georges describe one aspect of the Wilson-House relationship (1964, p. 128; emphasis added):

> Wilson liked to believe there was some sort of mystical bond between himself and House. On numerous occasions when he placed House in charge of complex negotiations, he told the Colonel that the need for giving him instructions was obviated by the fact that *their thoughts and purposes were as one.*

Kohut, later in his career (1986), made some further observations about the functions of the twinship relationship that are relevant for our concern with political leaders. He noted that the concept of the alter ego is not only important in the development of identifications but also as a process in which ego capacities can be exchanged. In examining the phenomenon of major creative efforts in adulthood, Kohut noted that creativity is a psychologically exhausting and isolating process. The creative person may indeed stand alone in his understandings and thoughts, and furthermore may be, at least temporarily, emotionally drained by the creative process. In these cases, Kohut suggests, the creative person is not only emotionally bolstered by a twinship relationship with a confident, well-functioning other, but draws in some degree on that person's strength and conviction to bolster those qualities in himself. This raises the possibility that, for politically creative leaders engaged in the work of constructing new institutions, programs, and other political infrastructures and processes, these special kinds of friendships may serve as important facilitators of creativity.

I close this section with an illustration of one other kind of political friendship, which appears not to have directly served advice or esteem-bolstering functions. Former president Richard Nixon and Charles (Bebe) Rebozo first met in 1950 and became increasingly friendly. Brodie (1981, p. 472) reports that Rebozo was with Nixon during most his most important personal and political decisions from 1954 through his resignation. Nixon is a leader who did not develop close friendships during his political career. Indeed, the Watergate tapes reveal him saying, just after he had won a landslide reelection victory, "Nobody is a friend of ours. . . . Let's face it" (*New York Times*, 1974, p. 5). The continuity of this friendship is therefore striking, but so is its nature. Senator George Smathers is quoted (in Brodie 1981, p. 473) as saying, "I've seen him [Nixon] and Bebe sit in a room for long hours and never say a word." Another close observer of the friendship, Pat Hillings, pointed out (quoted in Brodie 1981, p. 472) that Nixon didn't have many friends, "only Bebe Rebozo, because no one else will do what Bebe does . . . [he] will sit all alone with him [Nixon] in a room for hours, saying nothing while Nixon writes away on that long yellow legal pad he's always got."

The Nixon-Rebozo friendship indicates a particular introspective style of interpersonal relationships which also finds expression in Nixon's other interpersonal/political relationships. The Watergate burglary and its aftermath reflect, among other elements, a set of assumptions about managing interpersonal relationships in politics. These events and the examples noted above suggest the ways in which a leader's style of interpersonal relationships frequently holds great significance for his or her behavior in the exercise of political power.

The Political Environment as a Source of Learning and Development for Leaders

Early research in political socialization of pre-adults examined a number of "agencies" of political learning including the family, school, peer group, and so on. The question therefore arises as to what agencies, if any, influence adult political learning and development. In this section I examine the two most important of these, the political environment and the leadership role itself.

Yet in an essay that examines the contributions of psychological theories of adult development, especially those with a psychoanalytic perspective, for theories of adult political socialization of leaders, questions arise. Psychodynamic theory gives great (some would say exclusive) weight to intra-psychic processes in the etiology of behavior. A question naturally arises as to the status of this issue in the theories I am considering in connection with the adult socialization of political leaders. Does the use of a psychoanalytic perspective require an emphasis on the intrapsychic aspects of leadership functioning? And if not, what exactly is the role of external constraints and political reality for the political development and learning of leaders? It is to these questions that I now turn.

The question of whether the internal dispositions of the political actor or the environment are determining factors in explaining political behavior is considered by Greenstein (1969, pp. 46–61) under the heading of "actor dispensability." Here one question is whether the situation is so compelling as to virtually require the same kind of behavior from political actors what-ever their internal dispositions. One question which follows from this is whether this kind of situation is typical.

With respect to the first question, that is whether political situations in general require actor compliance or allow discretion, Greenstein notes a num-ber of conditions that may favor internal sources of political action over en-vironmental ones. Included are ambiguous situations (whether because of novelty, complexity, or contradictory cues), the lack of socially standardized mental sets that might allow perception to structure ambiguity, intense per-sonal preferences, lack of sanctions attached to following one's personal views, greater affective involvement, and the greater effort demanded by the political act. To these Greenstein adds that even when all of the above factors run counter to the expression of internal dispositions relative to environmen-tal constraints, it will still be the case that certain spontaneous expressions of self will be evident. Even when there is very little room for personal varia-bility, according to Greenstein, there are likely to be variations in expressive, stylistic aspects of the behavior. These are not necessarily unimportant.

Greenstein's discussion is not directed specifically at understanding politi-cal leaders. He is interested in analyzing the general conditions under which internal dispositions and environmental factors will operate to produce polit-ical behavior. However, it could hardly be more obvious that many of the conditions that Greenstein lists as accentuating the importance of internal dispositions relative to environmental factors describe fairly persuasively the context of political leadership. Many acts of leadership take place in domestic and international situations that are novel, complex, and have contradictory indicators associated with them (Jervis 1976), or all three at once!

There are good reasons to believe that leaders are affectively engaged to some degree in their roles, although the degree does vary. Most leaders have expended considerable effort to reach their positions. Once there, their work takes on significance for them in numerous ways I have already discussed in considering the general importance of work in adult development. For these reasons, many political "acts" will tend to reflect strong personal preferences, another of Greenstein's criteria for a stronger role for internal dispositions. There would appear, then, to be ample room in the political leader's situational milieu for the operation and expression of the kind of "internal dispositions" I have been examining in adult development theory.

But what of the situations that do not admit so readily to the influence of these factors? What of situations that compel a particular response regardless of the person responding? As an illustration of a situation where there would be small variations in response, Greenstein gives the example of an American president faced with warning of an impending missile attack. He does not though, discuss what these variations might be. Among those we might consider are perceptions of whether the launch is an attack or an accident, whether it is massive or limited, how the president handles the stress of this experience, and whether, when everything is considered, he can really order a response that may result in the possibility of a nuclear winter. As Greenstein notes, in circumstances such as these "even small variations acquire profound interest."

These considerations of the ways in which environments differ as to the behaviors they either inhibit or encourage leads to a more general point. Social scientists have tended to treat uniformities of behavior as if they obviated the need to account for them, beyond pointing to the power of the environment. Conformity to contextual norms, for example, could be argued to reflect the power, not the absence, of internal dispositions. A variety of motives underlies responsiveness to external norms, including needs to be liked and belong, a decision (or need) to be polite, and so on . Responsiveness to the environment is frequently a decision, not an involuntary act.

There are other reasons to reconsider the supposed incompatibility of internal dispositions with a focus on the environment. Consider the motivational sources that result in leaders' paying close attention to the environment. Most, as I noted, have spent considerable time and effort to obtain their positions and to advance within them. Given this confluence of ambition and investment, would it make sense to assume that such goal-directed persons would be disinterested in the workings of the world around them, except when circumstances compelled them? Probably not. One of the very important aspects of adult political learning for leaders is that it is a highly motivated activity. Advancement and effectiveness within a political career are dependent, to a large degree, on such learning.

How do these considerations fit in with the use of psychological models in adult development theory, especially those with psychoanalytic roots? I noted before that psychoanalytic theory had emphasized "psychic reality" and downplayed actual experience. But, my discussion of both Erikson and Levinson suggests a very strong emphasis on the requirement to express these internal dispositions (the self), out there, in the external world. This is most fully articulated by Levinson's model, in which the building of the life-structure is a major "reality oriented" enterprise. But it is no less true of Erikson's discussion of both Gandhi and Luther. According to Erikson, each had an accurate understanding of the actual operation of the authority system he wished to change, including a keen sense of the effective levers of transformation that were available and their effects. Such knowledge and acuity were most certainly a substantial part, along with their (the leaders') personal distress, of their success in mobilizing others and transforming the system each found so inhospitable to the development of their selves.

Even a psychologically oriented approach to leadership socialization must begin by acknowledging the importance of the external political world and the leader's attempts to deal with it. On the other hand, no theory of the adult political socialization of leaders will get very far without giving attention to the ways in which the complex environments of leadership roles (about which we still know very little), coupled with the zones of discretion that are part of every leader's mandate, allow, even encourage, the expression of a wide range of internal dispositions.

What, then, appear to be important environmental sources of leadership development, learning, and performance? The first and among the most important of these are public issues themselves. Issues arise in many ways. Some are there before the leader arrives in office, for example, East-West relations which no president, whatever his inclination, can afford to ignore. Some issues develop while the leader is exercising power, for example, a governor confronting changes in state-federal fiscal relationships. Others develop because of the leader's interest or perspective. In all of these cases, some learning must go on. Leaders vary in the ways in which they learn best (some by experience, others by education, others by advice). But all must master, to some degree, highly complex issues. No leader can long afford displays of ignorance or incompetence, and even leaders with great public support cannot rest on their philosophical assumptions when complex issues of alternative policy in critical areas (for example, arms control) are at stake.

This, of course, is the material of *adult* political learning. Even relatively small increments of information can have important consequences for belief systems if the leader is powerful enough. Arms control may provide a useful illustration. There are many complex combinations of missile size, types, mode of basing and the like that can be assembled within the framework of a particular set of beliefs about the Soviet Union. From one perspective these "details" may seem to operate at the margins of big political question like war or peace, but these so-called marginal issues can in fact be central in defining a political process. The point here is that, contained within the myriad details that must be decided in any political role, there exists ample opportunity, indeed necessity, to learn.

Key political events are another aspect of the environment that has relevance for the leader's adult political socialization. Each historical period generates a number of watershed events. The meeting at Munich between Chamberlain and Hitler, the Vietnam War, the seizing of U.S. hostages in Iran, all are events which generate strong feelings for those involved. They also are events which afterwards seem to require or stimulate reflection and assessment in an effort to understand their meaning. These "lessons of the past" (Neustadt and May 1986), are a part of every leader's political cosmology. Does Munich reflect the basic folly of attempting to appease a power-oriented dictator? Does our experience in Vietnam reflect the futility of a "no-win" policy in war, or does it suggest the limits of U.S. power to maintain a government unable to foster and build legitimacy? The answers to these kinds of questions by those who lived through the events exert a powerful methaphorical force on the thinking of political leaders. Even if the events are "historical," their existence as part of the conventional wisdom or debate insures that the leader will take some position with respect to them.

While political events, either lived through or in their more symbolic lesson-form, are important aspects of the political environment as a socialization agency, they are not the only ones. A second important dimension of the political environment as a shaper of the leader's socialization and political learning is public expectation. This is especially the case in democracies, where accountability is a structural reality as well as a public expectation. Accountability takes different forms for different leadership roles. Whatever the role, however, it requires that leaders be able to make careful assessments of the boundaries within which they must operate.

A third dimension of the political context that acts as an agency of leadership socialization are the "rules of the game." These may be specific norms of the role, such as the expectation that junior senators will wait for some time before they make their first address to their colleagues. Expectations may come in other forms, too. Senior public officials in New York City, like their counterparts before congressional budget committees, frequently overstate the fiscal needs of their agencies in order to get more money from the mayor's budget, or at least not to lose any. Both sides know this strategy and compensate accordingly, but it is part of a long-standing norm and is thus not easy to break without suffering the consequences of being truthful but not believed.

There is one other aspect of the environment that deserves attention, and that is the actual work environment of the leader. Even good leaders need supportive, responsive environments in order to function adequately. Yet this aspect of leadership has rarely been mentioned (but see Dror 1978 for some preliminary formulations). The working environment includes both psychological and structural factors. Among the psychological factors is the degree of satisfaction that the leader obtains from different activities, especially as they relate to the capacity to express important aspects of his self. Another psychological aspect of the leader's work environment concerns the levels of political stress, their sources, and possible structural or other stress inhibitors. Political stress accompanies leadership roles (Hermann 1986: pp. 176-77). There is some research on the effects of political stress on leaders, but not much understanding of which kinds of events cause high stress. Some are quite obvious of course—a domestic or international crisis, for example—but these do not exhaust the sources of stress in leadership roles.

On the more structural side of the leader's work environment, there are such aspects as managing the leader's schedule and insuring the proper mix of time for different political and nonpolitical activities. Among the most important structural aspects of the work environment, however, is the management of decision-relevant information. Staff arrangements are important here not only because of issues of loyalty and knowledge of the leader's goals and values, but also because the structure and operation of the staff plays an important role in the policy process. The primary policy tasks of a leader's staff are policy option development and evaluation and education of the leader to these alternatives.

In all of these ways the political environments of leaders operate as an agency of adult political socialization. They do so in an indirect way by shaping the contexts in which political leaders must operate and also learn, and more directly by providing immediate challenges to the responsibilities of political leaders which require their attention. Within these boundaries, the work of building the leader's life-structure and political career takes place. We know very little about political careers from these perspectives, but adult development theories suggest that it would be useful to examine them.

Continuity and Change in Leaders, Beliefs, Values, and Decision-Making Styles in Adulthood

We have examined character and the self, two basic components of the leader's personality system, and found some evidence that change and development are possible and even likely in adulthood. But what of the other aspects of psychological functioning relevant to leadership roles? Are the leader's political beliefs, values, and decision-making routines also open to change during adulthood, and if so, what are the sources of change? I select these aspects of leadership functioning because they are crucial to the performance of leadership roles.

Let us begin with the leader's political beliefs. A belief is an assumption

(Rokeach 1960; Bem 1970); it is not independent of contextual "facts," but neither is it fully determined by them. The origin of belief is experience, its cognitive modes are extrapolation and generalization. One of its chief functions is to orient persons through understanding to action in the real world. If we carry over this view to politics, then a political belief is an assumption about the nature and operation of the political world that structures the leader's approach to political thinking and action.

Early research into elite political socialization indicated that it was beliefs, not attitudes, that might be the most useful, relevant level of analysis. Searing, for example, whose work on social background analysis I reviewed earlier, concluded that "it would seem that underlying orientations [beliefs] are the most promising dependent variables for a scientific social background approach to elite analysis (1969, p. 493). Since then, there have been several lines of development in research on the political beliefs of political leaders.

Putnam (1973) examined the political beliefs of leaders in Britain and Italy, specifically as they related to the harmonious or conflictual nature of society. He found that social class of origin was the single strongest predictor of the leader's images of social harmony or discord. The lower the political leader's original social class, the more likely he was to have a conflictual image of society (1973, p. 129). This suggests in general that there is some long-term stability in this kind of basic political belief that is related to social-class experience (which, however, was not specifically defined).

Another line of development in the analysis of the political leader's beliefs grows out of Leites's early work (1951) on "operational codes" and George's subsequent elaboration and modification of that work (1969, 1979; see also Holsti 1977, 1982; Hoaglan and Walker 1979). The operational code is a set of basic political beliefs about the nature and operation of the political world. George divides them into two basic groups, one philosophical, the other instrumental. Included in the first (1969 pp. 201–5) are the answers to such questions as, what is the "essential" nature of political life, what are the prospects for eventual realization of one's fundamental political values and aspirations, and how much mastery and control can one have over political events? Included in the instrumental set (1969 pp. 205–16) are the answers to such questions as, what is the best approach to selecting goals or objectives for political action, how are goals to be pursued most effectively, how is political risk to be calculated and controlled, what is the best timing of action, and what is the utility of different means of advancing one's interests?

In looking at the content of these two sets of basic beliefs it seems clear that the instrumental beliefs develop much later than the philosophical beliefs. While the instrumental beliefs may rest on deeper assumptions, they are not easily answered in the abstract. Rather they would appear to grow out of concrete political experiences. While I could find no empirical evidence bearing directly on this question, a plausible hypothesis would be that these kinds of beliefs, which are extremely important for a leader's decision-making in general as well as in particular cases, are the product of early adult political experience.

The philosophical beliefs however, represent a somewhat different situation. Answers to questions concerning mastery and control, the basic nature of political life, and the ability to realize one's political aspirations address fundamental and deeply anchored elements of a leader's belief system. They appear similar to the cognitive components of character (e.g., beliefs and expectations arising from experiences connected with the expression of needs and their reception), and I would hypothesize that they represent more stable belief elements.

There is some evidence that a leader's basic beliefs about the nature of the political world do remain stable over time. At the same time there is also some evidence to suggest that aspects of these belief systems can evolve over the course of adulthood. Johnson (1977) examined the operational code of former senator Frank Church at the time of his emergence in politics in 1956 and again at mid-career in 1972. He found substantial stability in these political beliefs in the period stretching from early adulthood through Church's mid-life transition. More specifically, in examining the two time periods, Johnson (1977, 113) asks,

> Could one have predicted much about the 1972 Church code back in 1956? The refinements and deepening convictions growing out of the Vietnam conflict of course, could not have been anticipated, nor could the very important change of attitudes about our allies and opponents as a result of the thaw in the Cold War. Nevertheless, the [political] beliefs that most characterize the man . . . stood out in bold relief in his 1956 campaign and have been sustained ever since . . . . the Church example suggests that the most fundamental dimensions of operational code develop early in the career and endure with few (albeit sometimes important) exceptions. The exceptions . . . were, in most instances, the result of crucial events in the international realm..

Johnson's research and conclusions are important in several respects. First, they indicate that at the level of basic political beliefs, we do find consistency over the course of a leader's adult political career. A second important point, however, is that there are changes in aspects of these beliefs systems, and they are not inconsequential. Furthermore, Johnson's research helps us to pinpoint the origins of these changes, namely, the leader's coming to grips with important changes in the specific area of political life that he is responsible for (in Church's case this was foreign affairs).

Beliefs serve several functions for political leaders. By helping to define the external world, they help organize perceptions of it. These perceptions, in turn, provide a foundation for political actions. If, to use the Leites-George operational code formulation, the essential nature of the political world is viewed as aggressive rather than potentially harmonious (or even merely competitive), a certain stance towards political events is in order on the part of the prudent leader. Beliefs also have a normative function, because the perceived "facts of political life" not only shape action but justify it. Thus if your political enemies will stop at nothing to defeat you, and survival is a major value, then strong steps are not only necessary but legitimate.

Political beliefs are not the only personal source of a leader's behavior. At the heart of decision is choice, and at the heart of choice lie values. There are several ways to approach the understanding of personal values. A value according to Rokeach, is "an enduring belief that a specific mode of conduct or end-state of existence is personally and socially preferable to alternative modes" (Rokeach 1972, p. 168). It is also possible that values will reflect individual psychological needs as well as more abstract preferences. Our interest here is in the word "enduring," and since, at least by Rokeach's definition, a value is itself a special form of belief, there would be an expectation that the leader's values and their relationship to each other would be somewhat stable. One example of long-term value stability is the case of Gandhi's nonviolence (what Rokeach would term an instrumental value), which Gandhi developed in the Ahmedebad strike of 1918 and continued until his death three decades later. Another example is to be found in the concept of a "presidential administration," whether Democratic or Republican, which implies a certain consistency of political and personal values over time on the part of the leader.

There are, however, reasons to suggest that the persistence of a leader's political values will not have quite the same degree of continuity as his basic political beliefs. From the standpoint of adult development theories, personal values are to some degree tied to the stage of a leader's life. The young, ambitious Woodrow Wilson is quite intent on "making it" in the early stages of his political career, but by the end of it he clearly has some concerns about what he will leave behind, his legacy. The political leader who has achieved political power will, in his forties and fifties, be concerned with creating something, the issue being in Erikson's term "generativity." This is a view of personal values which is more closely tied to developmental concerns.

Career and role mobility may also play a role in the development of values over adulthood. There are a number of career trajectories possible in political life. A person may enter politics laterally, or may start out in one position and advance to another, or may obtain and remain in a single political role. In most such cases, there is a degree of change in value perspective involved. The state legislator who wins a seat in Congress must make some adjustment in perspective to be successful; the same is true of a general who becomes president, or a congressman who becomes a senator. A congressman whose value structure coincides in large part with the constituencies that elected him, may when running for a state-wide office encompass other values also. Even within a single role, advancement to positions of leadership may well require the integration of new values, as in the case of a congressman who rises to the position of majority leader.

These adjustments do not mean that previous values must be or are abandoned. Rather, they reflect the need in political life to incorporate new and sometimes wider perspectives.

There are other aspects of the leader's politically relevant values that complicate the question of continuity and change over adulthood. The number of possible values is large; Lasswell and Kaplan (1950) list eight values (see also Lasswell 1971, pp. 42–43), Rokeach (1972) lists twenty-four (twelve "instrumental" and twelve "terminal") values, and so on. It is, of course, possible for a political leader to have a deep commitment to one or several values over adulthood, as nonviolence was for Gandhi or anti-Communism is for Ronald Reagan (Glad 1987). However, the multiplicity of possible political and personal values would seem to be a lever for change rather than for continuity.

There are several reasons to suspect this may be the case. Values like "freedom" or "equality," to take two from Rokeach's list have many potential meanings, in the abstract. But political leaders operate in a world that requires concrete manifestations of their values, e.g., policy. The problem with policy as a pure expression and instrument of values is at least fourfold. First, policies almost always incorporate more than one value. A leader must frequently choose among competing values, some of which he may find personally attractive, others not. In this case, a leader may only be able to accomplish what he wants if he includes what others want too. Second, the situation may be one of "tragic choice" (Calabresi and Bobbitt 1979). In this situation, there is "a necessity to choose between the 'unchoosable' and to allocate orders of priority and relative weights to values and goals all of which are absolute in themselves . . . [or] where indivisible costs must be imposed on particular and specified groups" (Dror 1986, p. 190). Third, development in the form of greater elaboration and sophistication may also take place in situations where there are two or more beneficial values that can not be realized in a particular policy, and a choice must be made. In examining this kind of value conflict in the British House of Commons (by a content analysis of Putnam's interviews there), Tetlock (1983, 1984) found that such value conflicts promote more integrated and complex ideological reasoning. Fourth, even if a preferred value is able to prevail in a leader's policy, the questions of how much and in what way(s) must still be answered.

These considerations suggest that while values in the abstract may be a product of pre-adult experience, there is opportunity, even necessity, for these values to develop during the course of political careers. This occurs because of external demands that determine which values must be considered (to take an obvious example, an impending nuclear attack requires consideration of different values than making policy regarding a national uniform speed-limit). In the course of political careers new political problems also arise that require new applications or understanding of a particular value. In this case, the application of "old" values to new problems provides a context in which values may be refined, extended, or otherwise modified. Beliefs and values are important for understanding the leader's approach to political roles and performance in them, and I have suggested that there is some degree of flexibility and potential development in each.

I now turn to another important aspect of most political roles, decision-making. Political decision-making begins with the process of organizing information to solve problems. In approaching political problem-solving, individuals employ their beliefs and values to process and evaluate information and alternatives. A critical part of this process is the way in which a leader perceives and processes information. I refer to these as standard political decision routines.

Standard political decision routines are at once both organizational and dynamic; they refer to the preferred ways of viewing and constructing the political world, as well as the logic by which decision proceeds. Putnam's (1973, pp. 43–44) factor analysis of the ideological style of his sample of political leaders found two distinct patterns of cognitive processing. One was a generalizer-particularizer continuum while the other was an inductive-deductive thinking continuum. More recently, as already noted, Tetlock found a relationship between cognitive style and political ideology.

The concept of cognitive style refers to the way a person organizes ("sees") the perceptual world, and then goes on to understand it. There is little research on when cognitive styles begin to develop, but one hypothesis is that they begin in childhood. What is clear is that cognitive style is not simply a matter of perceptual preference but becomes deeply anchored in character structure (Shapiro 1965).

A leader's cognitive style is an important part of political decision-making (Glad 1983). Anderson (1986) has argued that cognitive style is related to interpreting and assessing the state of the world and world events, argumentation and advocacy regarding policy options, and articulation of preferences and making a choice. To this, Orbovich (1986 p. 14) adds that it also influences the ways in which the leader sets up and functions with a policy advisory system.

Orbovich's assessment of the cognitive styles of Eisenhower and Truman captures some of the intrapsychic processes involved. In discussing Eisenhower, she notes that he relied on a combination of objective and subjective data, did not base his decisions on emotional and personal factors, and seemed at ease with multiple interpretations of the same data. Truman, on the other hand, at least at the outbreak of the Korean War, was not very intuitive in gathering and using information; he preferred facts and relied more heavily on his advisors' consensus.

Can cognitive style develop or even change over adulthood? I could find no evidence in the political psychology or adult development literatures directly bearing on this question. However, there is a body of clinical literature that deals with this question indirectly. Psychoanalytic psychotherapy is a specialized technique whose function is to bring about change in how people think, feel, and act. In their extensive review of the goals of such therapy, McGlashan and Miller, (1982) note at least eight areas of potential change that are by-products of a successful therapeutic experience. Among the categories relevant to our discussion are those of *reality acceptance* and *integrative capacity*. The first consists of five factors, among them improved reality testing(pp. 382–83). This includes the capacity to recognize reality, a willingness to test one's perceptions against those of others, and the capacity to distinguish past from present (e.g., a lessening of need-based perceptual distortion). Integrative capacity (pp. 384–85) includes the ability to tolerate ambivalence, a cluster of factors dealing with cognitive economy which includes a capacity for delay, reflection, remembering rather than acting, recalling of past errors to learn from them, and a certain degree of cognitive flexibility. These findings are not presented as suggestions for "psychiatry in high places," but rather to indicate that aspects of cognitive style can develop. On the other hand, the well-known difficulties associated with achieving such results suggest that, outside the consulting room, real development of these kinds of cognitive factors is more the exception than the rule. Perhaps not surprisingly, it may be easier to change *what* leaders think, rather than *how* they think.

Theory, Research, Method and Application in the Study of Adult Development and Political Leadership

In this essay I have examined some areas of importance in understanding and explaining the process of adult development and the political socialization of leaders. It should be clear however, that much remains to be done. In this section, I would like to raise some questions of theory, method, and research with the hope that they will stimulate the development of our knowledge in this area.

Let us turn first to theory. The study of the adult political socialization of leaders begins with a double theoretical task. It must not only find or build a useful theory of adulthood, it must also link that theory with theories from a wholly different area, that of political leadership. Theories in both areas are not at the point where they can simply be borrowed or easily blended. Adult development theories have suffered in part from being too broad-gauged, characterizing whole decades by single issues. These large periods of time, be they Erikson's eight stages (three in adulthood), Levinson's life-structures during the twenties, thirties, and so on, or others, need to be deaggregated. To do this we will need to have more detailed accounts of particular periods, which identify a fuller range of age- (or stage-) related concerns. Students of adult development and political leadership will, of course, have to take the next step, which is to identify how those concerns are relevant to leadership careers. If adult development theories suggest anything, it is that these points in the leader's unfolding life history will be reflected in different sets of personal/political concerns and should be manifest in their approach to the tasks of leadership.

In order to fill in these gaps in our knowledge, however, we will need specific studies of beginning leaders, emerging leaders, leaders who have settled into political careers, those who are at the peak of their political powers, and those who are at the conclusion of their political careers. Is the period of the emergence of political leaders their most creative, or is creativity in governing and policy-making a product of the more mature political leader? Presumably political leaders in their forties and fifties would be at the peak of their capacities, blending experience and commitment, but we know little about this very important stage in political careers. So, too, many political leaders rise to the highest positions of power in their sixties and even seventies, yet here too we know very little. Does political learning and/or development slow down or stop at this stage of leadership? Or, consider Erikson's view that later adulthood is the stage at which the leader may achieve wisdom. Is political wisdom the culmination of adult political socialization for political leaders, the ideal towards which all previous adult development was aimed?

What of activity, ambition, and commitment? Is there a decrease in a leader's active involvement in the daily routines of leadership as he or she approaches later adulthood? Does this constitute a form of leader desocialization? Or, on the other hand, is later adulthood a time when the leader is finally freed from the constraints of pressures of "making it," and can be fearless enough to do unprecedented political things? In the arts, the phenomonon of late-age creativity and boldness occurs often. The last works of Shakespeare, Rembrandt, Beethoven, Verdi, and more recently Ibsen and Yeats, all suggest that the last stages of the life cycle may bring release from conventional concerns and free the creative artist (leader?) to make major creative statements that represent both a continuation and culmination of his or her vision.

We also need to pay attention to the importance of common occurences during adulthood for political leaders. They can have profound effects. As the leader ages, children are born, parents get older and die, and all of these events serve as markers to the leader's advancing years. Some theorists of adult development have stressed the themes of approaching mortality and the experience of loss in the mid-adult years (Jaques 1965; Lifton 1983; but see Vaillant 1978, p. 221, for a different view), and there is evidence that personal loss can have profound political effects on leaders. Gilbert (1988) has argued that the death of Calvin Coolidge's son while Coolidge was president, destroyed his presidency. Gilbert notes that, as governor of Massachusetts, Coolidge established a very active and progressive administration and did the same thing in his first year as president, at which time his son died from an infection incurred while playing tennis at the White House. According to Gilbert, his son's death triggered an acute personal crisis for Coolidge, from which he and his presidency never recovered. In a similar vein, Jimmy Carter told two biographers (Mazlish and Diamond 1979, p. 158) that he began a thoroughgoing reassessment of his life, including his political career, when his father died in 1953. Thirteen years later, after being defeated in his first try for the Georgia governorship, Carter was plunged into an acute depression and personal crisis, from which he reemerged a "born-again" Christian, and incidently with renewed political ambition.

A third theoretical problem that must be squarely faced is that adult development theories suffer from being too male-centered. Most of the major theories of adult development (e.g., Erikson, Vaillant, Gould, and Levinson) have studied men. One result is that it is unclear as to the extent to which the models that have been developed so far apply equally to women. This problem carries over to the study of political leadership in a direct way, because one of the major theorists of adult development and political leadership, Erikson, has developed his work around two major male figures, Luther and Gandhi. Given that larger numbers of women are increasingly becoming part of the leadership structure in the United States and elsewhere, this major theoretical deficit will need to be addressed.

Turning from a focus on adult development theory, we can see that political leadership itself will have to be refined as a theoretical framework. At this point, we have far more categories of leadership types than clear understandings of what leaders actually do. In this chapter I have suggested that decision-making and interpersonal relations are key variables in the exercise of political power, but other important elements can doubtlessly be added. We can begin with the simple question of how the leader spends his or her time. One assistant to a state governor (Michaelson 1972, p. 7) estimated that his boss spent 27 percent of his time on public relations, 19 percent managing the state government, and 11 percent on "political leadership." Another more broadly based study of how governors used their time (Ransone, 1982, p. 96) noted that they spend 27 percent of their time managing state government, 18 percent working with the legislature, and 13 percent on ceremonial functions. Ransone (1982, p. 97), commenting on these data, notes that "apparently no time was devoted to policy making as such," but goes on to say that "it seems probable that a good deal of the activity under such headings as 'working with federal government' (7%), 'working with local government', and certainly at least part of 'political activity' (6%) had something to do with policy formation." One would guess that Ransone is probably correct, but the point is that we do not actually know. When we lack even the basic facts about what governors actually do, flights of conceptual theorizing about the nature of political leadership may seem somewhat premature.

When we do begin to look more closely at the actual exercise of power and/or leadership, it will be helpful to include "ordinary" leaders. The focus on the "great man" as leader is exciting and important but brings with it the danger of badly skewing the universe from which we draw our understandings. Once we gain a better understanding of the elements of exercising political power and/or leadership we can then begin to ask even more specific questions about political careers.

Are there particular, reoccurring dilemmas in the exercise of political power? The value trade-off dilemma in decision-making is one that comes readily to mind, but surely there are others. How does the leader handle these reoccurring aspects of leadership over time? What happens, for example, to some of the reoccurring feelings associated with the exercise of power? How is anger, disappointment, or grandiosity handled and what are the cumulative effects, if any, of such feelings over time? Political decisions, as I noted, often involve "tragic choices," which will result sometimes in substantial suffering. How does the leader reconcile the necessity for action and its consequences? Finally, we may ask about political idealism. Many leaders enter politics in part to shape the public order (this does not exclude other motivations). What happens to the sense of wanting to change or shape that order over a political career? Do persons who come to political life with a sense of social concern lose that over the years, in parallel with the loss of idealism that has been noted as one by-product of medical education?

Another reoccurring but poorly understood set of dilemmas revolve around ethical issues in the exercise of power. The ethics of political-power exercise would seem to be another area of leadership-learning that takes place within political roles rather than before them. However, the ethics of leadership discretion in the exercise of power have not been well explored. The political culture of democracies stresses norms of "legitimacy" and the "consent of the governed," with implicit agreements about the ways in which power will be exercised. I have already noted that the exercise of power reflects a set of interpersonal relationships (among leaders, between leaders and the public). But the leader's understanding of the obligations and responsibilities associated with these relationships is important in his or her actual behavior with regard to power. When, if at all, is it permissible for the leader to withhold information from the public? Is it ever permissible to mislead the public? When, if at all, is it permissible to harm an enemy, or mislead a friend?

The purpose of such questions is to find out more about the function of leaders in political roles. Consider in this regard the question of efficacy among political leaders. That variable has been used with great effectiveness in explaining political behavior among segments of the mass public, but how do such attitudes and the psychological foundations (sense of personal control) which underlie them work in the cases of political leaders? Should it be assumed that because leaders are in power they have high levels of political efficacy or personal control? Probably not. Does a leader's sense of personal control and political efficacy develop or evolve over the course of a political career, and if so in response to what factors? One hypothesis is that such orientations change in response to career advancement. Obtaining higher office may lead to greater feelings of personal control and political efficacy, but not necessarily. One former governor who become a United States senator told Matthews that in his former role everything seemed to revolve around him, but when he became senator "there was just a seat at the end of the table" (quoted in Paige 1977, p. 110).

All of these areas will increase *what* we know about adult development and political leadership, but the question remains of *how* we will find out. By now, the virtues and difficulties of the behavioral revolution have been extensively debated (Ascher 1986). Among the former, one would include a commitment to theoretical specificity, an attempt to disentangle personal preferences and beliefs from actual processes, a concern with developing accurate indicators of the concepts we wish to assess, and an interdisciplinary approach to the study of political life. Among the difficulties, I would include a focus on general laws to the exclusion of middle-range multivariate theories, an emphasis on technical measurement at the expense of theory, a neglect of the role of values in political research, and an insufficient concern with history, context, and application.

The most obvious research need in this new area is for more data, and all the usual methods can and should play a role. However, I would like to suggest that, in addition to the usual array of tools (surveys, interviews, historical records), we add to our list direct observation, coupled with intensive interviews. Most observations of political leaders take place at a distance. Consequently there is very little research in which the researcher both observes and asks questions. Some exceptions to this are Wolfinger's observation of New Haven mayor Richard C. Lee (1974), Matthews's observations of U.S. senators (1960), Richard Fenno's of congressmen (1978), and Muir's observations of California state legislators (1975).

What is needed is illustrated in part by the work of veteran writer John Hersey. Hersey (1951) was invited to spend time with Harry S. Truman at work in the White House. He later spent a week with Gerald Ford, while the latter was president, and also wrote an article about it (Hersey 1975). These accounts are a rich source of insight about leadership, but what is missing is a more sophisticated inquiry into the meaning of the events that Hersey observed. To get more of a sense of what further use could be made of such an opportunity, imagine Harold D. Lasswell spending a week with a president, attending meetings and discussing each day's events with him.

In the search for lawful relationships, behavioral research developed indices and applied them to samples from which it then extracted relationships. The assumption was that item meaning was invariant across persons. The point of observing and asking about leadership behavior is that it does not assume that a leader's understanding and our understanding of what is being done are necessarily the same. The relationship between the two would at least seem worth checking.

There are of course serious questions of access raised in studying political leaders and of their sophistication in dealing with questions we would like to ask (Clarke and Donovan 1980, p. 540). But a number of studies (Barber, 1965; Putnam, 1973; Clarke and Donovan, 1980) suggest that it can be done. One suggestion is to make better use of state and local-level officials, who are in general more accessible.

A study of the political socialization of leaders, especially from the perspectives I have been discussing, will involve asking different kinds of questions. The data will include dreams and aspirations, building a life-structure for the self in politics, the dilemmas of the role, and so on. They will not be easily captured by likert items, at least at first. However, if Erikson, Valliant, and Levinson are any guide, the effort is likely to prove worth the trouble.

There is a last issue in this section and the field of adult political socialization that deserves consideration, and that is the issue of application. Political socialization had at its outset an area where the results of its studies of political learning in children could have practical application. That area was the school, more specifically the social studies/political education curriculum. Patrick (1977) reviewed the affinity of educators interested in improving children's knowledge of their governmental institutions and processes and those whose research focused on specifying and understanding this knowledge. At the time, there were many joint projects (reviewed and assessed by Patrick 1977, pp. 212–16), including one by the American Political Science Association, to improve children's knowledge of their country's complex political system.

What of adult political socialization research? Is there, similarly, an area where theory and research might prove helpful in a policy-relevant way? I believe there is, and that the area is leadership development. Focusing on political leadership as an area of policy relevance may seem strange in a country which approaches leadership recruitment and performance from a free-market perspective. In this political culture, running for office and leadership evaluation is a matter of individual citizen choice. What, then, can theory and research in adult political socialization of leaders contribute?

The potential contributions may be seen in at least two areas (for others, see Paige 1977, pp. 221–23). First, such research can contribute to understanding and design of leadership environments. Some work along these lines is already taking place. As part of the report of the Commission on the Organization of the Government for the Conduct of Foreign Policy, Alexander George and his colleagues (1975) have analyzed and made recommendations regarding the organization of information for more effective leadership decision-making. These have been primarily in the ways that the leader can structure the flow of information to insure comprehensive exposure and evaluation of relevant data.

A second area is leadership preparation and development. It is somewhat ironic that in a political culture so concerned with political leadership, evaluation has received far more attention than preparation. This area, too, is beginning to develop. There are a number of programs that seek to orient persons who have just won elective office (mayors, congressmen), but the focus of these programs does not go far beyond orientation. So too, there are a number of mid-career programs for federal, state, and local officials geared towards substantive policy areas, and some which attempt to develop "operational" skills (management techniques, the use of computers). This researcher had been associated with one such program for a number of years, and has presented elsewhere (Renshon 1989, in press) some suggestions for furthering the process of preparing leaders for the exercise of political power.

Development in Adulthood among Political Leaders: A Final Note

In this essay I have reviewed some evidence for the existence of adult development in political leaders and suggested some factors which help account for it. In doing so, I have examined development and continuity in the leader's basic character structure, sense of self, basic political beliefs, values, and cognitive style. Is there a general conclusion that I can put forward here about learning and development in adulthood? Is adult political socialization best characterized by a "life-long persistence model" or a "life-long openness model" (Sears 1975)?

Looking over the theory and available data, I can suggest that both of these models are too linear to portray accurately what happens to political leaders in adulthood. Is there persistence in aspects of the political leader's character, self, beliefs, and so on? Of course there is; the personality system is a filter, not a sieve. Is there development in these same characteristics as the leader goes through adulthood? The evidence would suggest there is.

What, then, should our models of adult political socialization look like? A useful model would seem to be that of a mosaic, in which the various elements of the leader's personality system are hierarchically integrated but are themselves at different developmental levels. Each cluster of elements (character, self, etc.) would have its own developmental lines, which would suggest that they generally do not develop in step with each other.

There are a number of reasons to suspect this is the case. One reason is that the different elements of the personality system do not begin their progression along developmental paths from the same starting point. Second, development, when it does occur, is not always smooth. Developmental arrests, slowdowns, and even temporary reversals are possible. Third, each element of the personality system, even if development is possible and smooth, unfolds at a different pace. Character for example, may develop more slowly than political beliefs, even if there are not any developmental delays, etc. Fourth, different aspects of the leader's personality system are more available to the effect of environmental events. We would not expect a leader's basic sense of self, for example, to change dramatically in response to a policy setback, but we might expect a change in strategic approach (e.g., the instrumental belief-set of the operational code).

The theories and data I have discussed suggest that it is very important to be clear about the exact meaning of continuity and change. The concept of development does not necessarily exclude some degree of continuity; not, for that matter, does the concept of change. If we understand the concept of development to include only subtantial, "step-level" changes in psychological structures or functioning, or else dramatic reversals of what has existed before, we will be underestimating the degree of development that can and does occur. Development implies some degree of change, but it further implies that psychological structures and processes become more *elaborated, differentiated,* and *integrated.* These would appear to be useful distinctions to keep in mind in building theories of adult political socialization of leaders.

Notes

A number of individuals and several foundations were instrumental in the development of this paper and I would like to express my appreciation to them. This research was supported by a grant from the City University Faculty Award Program and by a grant to the author from the Earhart Foundation.

I am very appreciative of the careful reading given this manuscript by Professors James David Barber, Lloyd Etheredge, Alexander L. and Juliette L. George, and Barbara Kellerman. Dr. John Fiscalini of the William Alanson White Institute provided a close and very helpful reading of the manuscript. Professor Roberta Sigel was a most patient editor, and provided extremely valuable comments on successive drafts of the manuscript. I wish to also express my appreciation to the anonymous reviewer for the University of Chicago Press, whose suggestions were helpful.

The word "he" is generally used throughout this paper in referring to political leaders, and the usage is not accidental. It reflects the current state of adult development theories, which are largely based on studies of males. At this point therefore, their more general applicability to women leaders remains open. In addition, many studies of political leaders, done at a time when there were not large numbers of women in high office, also tend to lead to the use of the masculine article. I explore the implications of these points within the essay.

1. A useful set of essays which address some aspects of psychoanalytic theory and adult development may be found in Greenspan and Pollock (1980). An earlier consideration of adulthood, life history, and political leadership may be found in Renshon (1980). Briefer general treatments of adult development theory and political behavior can be found in Kellerman (1979), Baldino (1980), and Post (1980).

2. I will not deal here with the short-term effects of stress on political learning. Evidence indicates that it can be considerable (see for example (George 1974b: Janis and Mann 1977; Hermann 1979), and that it effects political learning in leaders. As a general rule, according to Hermann (1986, p. 176), "As stress increases, leaders tend to become more rigid; to reach conclusions more quickly; to focus less on the consequences of action; to see the present in terms of the past; to rely only on close associates, whose opinions and support can be counted on; and to take direct control of the decision making process." In short, substantial increases in stress tend to decrease political learning.

3. There is debate as to whether Woodrow Wilson's political rigidity stemmed from a medical problem (e.g., stroke) or a psychological problem. The latter position is put forward in Weinstein, et al. (1978/79). Detailed analysis and commentary on this controversy can be found in the June 1983 issue (vol.4, no.2) of *Political Psychology*.

Barber's more ego-psychological (1985, pp. 335–41, 380–85) analysis of Richard Nixon's classic decision-crises sequence provides another illustration of the ways in which character-based patterns of response reappear over the leader's political career. and one which isn't complicated by medical illness.

4. This is one reason why the criticism of Barber's conceptualization of character (see George et al. 1975, pp. 246–49), while accurate, somewhat underestimates the difficulties of drawing on such a theory from the clinical tradition. Barber has attempted, in the latest edition of his book (1985, pp. 529–41), to establish more firmly his character types within the framework of psychological theory. However, his effort serves to underscore the real nature of the problem. It is not that Barber's character types do not appear in the psychological theory, albeit under different names. Rather,

the more basic problem remains that there is no systematic theory of character from which to borrow in the psychological literature. Paradoxically, the concept of character is becoming increasingly important in clinical psychoanalytic theory and practice (Giovacchini 1975, 134–56).

5. Shapiro's work makes an important point that is often missed in studies of cognitive political psychology, namely, that both the structure and process of cognitive systems are embedded in characterological and developmental processes. Consider for example, the impulsive style of action and cognition (Shapiro 1965, pp. 134–56). He notes that impulsive action is characterized by a short period between thought and action. For nonimpulsive persons, the whim is the beginning of a complex process which involves the whim's relationship to long-standing needs, goals, and values. This process of elaboration and integration (of the whim) is short-circuited in the impulsive style. Shapiro then goes on:

> I have referred to the conspicuous lack of long-range planning by impulsive people. It might be imagined that this deficiency is a special and isolated one that simply follows from an inclination to quick action. Actually, lack of planning is only one feature of a style of cognition and thinking in which active concentration, capacity for abstraction and generalization and reflectiveness are all impaired. The fact is that the cognition of impulsive people is characterized by an insufficiency of active integrative processes that is comparable to the insufficiency of the integrative processes on the affective side. (1965, p. 147)

6. The importance of the power of the mismatch between expectation and experience is one fundamental tool available in the analytic situation to produce important changes at the level of character and interpersonal style, and therefore should not be ignored by students of the adult political socialization of political leaders. In brief, the process operates as follows. The patient comes to treatment with many assumptions and expectations rooted in prior experience. Gradually the nature and content of these become clear, first to the analyst, and then, through the therapeutic work, to the patient. The analyst, by not always meeting expectations, and by raising the issue of these mismatches in the course of the treatment, helps to provide "a corrective emotional experience" (Alexander 1948, pp. 286–87).

7. The theory on which these works basically build is Erikson's (1980, p. 129) eight-stage model of human development (infancy, early childhood, play age, school age, adolescence, young adulthood, adulthood, and mature age). It should be noted here that the model specifies five stages for the first seventeen years of life, and three for all of adulthood.

Erikson is not the first psychologist to write on adulthood (see, for example, the early papers of Rubinow [1933] and Buhler [1935]), but he is the first to formulate a psychoanalytic theory of the period.

8. There is a question—one that can not be fully treated in this context—of the relationship of narcissism to political leadership. There is an implicit (sometimes quite explicit) assumption in the use of the term that it denotes a form of pathology. McIntyre (1983, p. 484 n.4) suggests, "there are some grounds for believing that political leaders frequently belong to the narcissistic personality type." In that paper, he sug-

gests that Sir Oswald Mosley's shift from the Labor party to fascism can be explained in part by the failings of a narcissistic personality as it approaches mid-life. Along similar lines, Rhoads and Stern (1981 p. 280) note that "narcissistic problems might be rather common among the highest group of political office holders. . . . the accolades and privileges and powers of office might. . . . sustain exaggerated perceptions of grandiosity . . . and . . . conceal the shallowness of object relations."

To keep the question of leadership and narcissism in perspective, it should be noted that analytic theory distinguishes two very different kinds of narcissism. The first sees narcissism as a normal and healthy line of development. Writing about the principle narcissistic configurations, Kohut notes (1971, pp. 27–28), "Under optimal developmental conditions, the exhibitionism and grandiosity of the archaic [that is, pre-Oedipal) self are gradually tamed, and the whole structure gradually becomes integrated into the adult personality and supplies the instinctual fuel of our ego-syntonic ambitions and purposes . . . and for important aspects of our self-esteem. . . . If the child suffers severe narcissitic traumas, then the grandiose self does not merge into . . . the ego but is retained in its unaltered form and strives for the fulfillment of its archaic aims."

Kernberg (1975, pp. 315–42) also distinguishes between healthy and pathological narcissism, and notes several levels of the latter. These range from the "narcissistic problems of neurotic patients to the more severely disturbed patients who project onto others aspects of their grandiose self, and then identify with the person on that basis. In this later, more pathological case, both the internal object world is extremely primitive and undifferentiated, and the interpersonal relations are based primarily on very primitive fantasies. It obviously makes some difference where the political leader lies along this continuum.

9. Recent evidence suggest that President Kennedy's decision-making was not as comprehensive as originally thought. A good overview of the new evidence regarding the decision-making process during the Cuban missile crisis may be found in Bright, Nye, and Welch (1987).

10. Weinstein (1981) has disputed the Georges' contention regarding Woodrow Wilson's relationship with his father. More recent works, however, by Bongiorno (1985) and Stern (1987) tend to support the Georges' position. The last two works cited are also of interest in that they begin exploration of the role of Wilson's mother in his development, a heretofore unexamined aspect of the whole controversy.

11. Gould (1979), in an interesting paper analyzing the legend of King Arthur and the Round Table, noted that at mid-life there was a change in the nature of Arthur's dream. In his thirties, Arthur's ambition is to be "the knightliest knight," but towards the end of his thirties the vision of the Round Table, which Gould characterizes as "a political vehicle fused with love and cooperation," begins to form.

References

Abraham, K. 1927. *Selected Papers*. London: Hogarth Press.

Alexander, F. 1948. *Fundamentals of Psychoanalysis*. New York: Norton.

Anderson, P. A. 1986. "The Act of Choice and the Choice of Acts: Foreign Policy

Decision Making as a Social Process." Paper presented at the annual meeting of the International Studies Association, Anaheim, Calif.

Ascher, W. 1986. "The Evolution of the Policy Sciences: Understanding the Rise and Avoiding the Fall." *Journal of Policy Analysis and Management* 5: 365–89.

Baldino, T. J. 1980. "Adult Development and Political Behavior." Paper presented at the Northeastern Political Science meeting. New Haven, Conn.

Barber, J. D. 1965. *The Lawmakers*. New Haven: Yale University Press.

———— 1985 [1972]. *The Presidential Character: Predicting Performance in the White House*. 3d editon.

Bem, D. 1970. *Beliefs, Attitudes and Human Affairs*. Belmont, Calif.: Brooks-Cole.

Beyle, T. L. 1978. "The Governor as Chief Legislator." *State Government* 51: 2–10.

Bright, J. G., J. S. Nye, Jr., and D. A. Welch. 1987. "The Cuban Missile Crisis Revisited." *Foreign Affairs* (Fall): 170–88.

Bongiorno, J. A. 1985. "Woodrow Wilson Revisited: the Prepolitical Years." In C. B. Strozier and D. Offer, eds., *The Leader*. New York: Plenum Press, pp. 133–79.

Boyd, D. 1973. *Elites and Their Education*. London: National Foundation for Education Research.

Brim, O. G., Jr. 1968. "Adult Socialization." In John A. Clausen, ed., *Socialization and Society*. Boston: Little Brown.

Brodie, F. 1981. *Richard Nixon: The Shaping of His Character*. New York: Norton.

Browning, R. P., and H. E. Jacob. 1964. "Power Motivation and the Political Personality." *Public Opinion Quarterly* 28: 75–90.

Buhler, C. 1935. "The Curve of Life as Studied in Biographies." *Journal of Applied Psychology* 19: 405–9.

Burns, J. McG. 1978. *Leadership*. New York: Harper and Row.

Calabresi, G. and P. Bobbitt. 1979. *Tragic Choice*. New York: Norton.

Clarke, J. W. and M. M. Donovan. 1980. "Personal Needs and Political Incentives: Some Observations on Self-Esteem." *American Journal of Political Science* 24: 536–52.

Dahl, R. 1961. *Who Governs?* New Haven: Yale University Press.

Dror, Y. 1978. "The Work Environment of Rulers." Paper presented to the Fifth Annual IRA Symposium. Tel-Aviv, Israel.

————. 1986. *Policymaking under Adversity*. New Brunswick, N.J.: Transaction Books.

Easton, D. 1965. *A Systems Analysis of Political Life*. New York: Wiley.

Edinger, L. J., and D. Searing. 1967. "Social Background in Elite Analysis: A Methodological Inquiry." *American Political Science Review* 61: 428–45.

Erikson, E. 1958. *Young Man Luther*. New York: Norton.

————. 1969. *Gandhi's Truth*. New York: Norton.

————. 1980 [1959]. *Identity and the Life Cycle*. New York: Norton.

Etheredge, L. S. 1985. *Can Governments Learn?* New York: Pergamon.

Fenichel, O. 1945. *The Psychoanalytic Theory of Neurosis*. New York: Norton.

Fenno, R. 1978. *Home Style: House Members in Their Districts*. Boston: Little-Brown.

Freud, S. 1908B. "Character and Anal Eroticism." In *Standard Edition*, pp. 167–77.

————. 1916D. "Some Character Types Met with in Psychoanalytic Work." In *Standard Edition*, pp. 311–40.

George, A. L., et al. 1975 *Towards a More Soundly Based Foreign Policy: Making Better Use of Information.* Commission on the Organization of the Government for the Conduct of Foreign Policy, vol. 2, pp. 3–136. Washington, D.C.: U.S. Government Printing Office.

George, A. L. 1969. "The 'Operational Code' Approach: A Neglected Approach to the Study of Political Leaders and Decision Making." *International Studies Quarterly* 13: 190–222.

——— 1974a. "Assessing Presidential Character." *World Politics* 26:234–82.

——— 1974b. "Adaptation to Stress in Political Decision Making." In G. V. Coelho, D. A. Hamburg, and J. E. Adams, eds., *Coping and Adaptation.* New York: Basic Books.

———. 1979. "The Causal Nexus between Cognitive Beliefs and Decision-making Behavior: The 'Operational Code' Belief System." In L. S. Falkowski, ed., *Psychological Models in International Politics.* Boulder, Colo.: Westview Press.

George, A. L., and J. L. George. 1964 [1956]. *Woodrow Wilson and Colonel House: A Personality Study.* New York: Dover.

Gilbert, R. E. 1988. "Psychological Pain and the Presidency: The Case of Calvin Coolidge." *Political Psychology.* In press.

Giovacchini, P. 1975. *Psychoanalysis of Character Disorders.* New York: Jason Aronson.

Glad, B. 1983. "Black and White Thinking: Ronald Reagan's Approach to Foreign Policy Thinking." *Political Psychology* 4: 33–76.

———. 1980. *Jimmy Carter: In Search of the Big White House.* New York: Norton.

———. 1987. "Reagan's Midlife Crises and the Turn to the Right." Paper presented to the International Society for Political Psychology, San Francisco, Calif.

Gould, L. J. 1979. "Political Vision and Political Action: A Developmental Perspective." Paper presented at the American Political Science Association, Washington, D.C.

Greenspan S. I., and G. Pollock, eds. 1980. *The Course of life: Psychoanalytic Contributions towards Personality Understanding.* Vol. 3. *Adulthood and the Aging Process.* Washington, D.C.: NIMH.

Greenstein, F. I. 1969 [1987]. *Personality and Politics.* Chicago: Markham.

———. 1987. "Adult Socialization in Pre-Presidential Roles and the Presidency." Paper presented to the American Political Science Association, Washington, D.C.

Hermann, M. G., 1979. "Indicators of Stress in Foreign Policy Makers during Foreign Policy Crises." *Political Psychology* 1: 27–46.

———. 1986. "Ingredients of Leadership." In Margaret G. Hermann, ed., *Political Psychology.* San Francisco: Jossey Bass.

Hersey, J. 1951. "Profiles: Mr. President, II—Ten O'Clock Meeting." *New Yorker,* April 14, 1951, pp. 38–55.

———. 1975. "A Day with the President." *New York Times Sunday Magazine.* April 20.

Hoagland, S. W., and S. G. Walker. 1979. "Operational Codes and Crises Outcomes." In L. Falkowski, ed., *Psychological Models in International Politics.* Boulder, Colo.: Westview Press.

Holsti, O. R. 1977. "The Operational Code as an Approach to the Study of Belief Systems." Report to the National Science Foundation, Grant no.Soc75–15368.

———. 1982. "The Operational Code Approach: Problems and Some Solutions." In C. Jonsson, ed. *Cognitive dynamics and international politics*. New York: St. Martin's Press.

Hook, S. 1962. *The Hero in History*. Boston: Beacon.

Janis, I. 1982. *Victims of Groupthink*. Boston: Houghton Mifflin.

Janis, I. and L. Mann. 1977. *Decision making*. New York: Free Press.

Jaques, E. 1965. "Death and the Mid-Life Crisis." *International Journal of Psychoanalysis* 46: 502–514.

Jervis, R. 1976. *Perception and Misperception in International Politics*. Princeton, N.J.: Princeton University Press.

Johnson, L. K. 1977. "Operational Codes and the Prediction of Leadership Behavior: Senator Frank Church at Mid-Career." In M. G. Hermann, Ed., *A Psychological Examination of Political Leaders*. New York: Free Press

Kearney, R. N. 1984. "The Mentor in the Commencement of a Political Career: The Case of Subhas Chandra Bose and C. R. Das." *Journal of Political and Military Sociology* 12: 37–48.

Kellerman, B. 1978. "Mentoring in Political Life: The Case of Willy Brandt." *American Political Science Review* 72: 422–33.

———.1979. "Is There Life after Adolescence and, If So, Should Political Scientists Care?" Paper presented to the American Political Science Association, Washington, D.C.

———. 1983. *All the President's Kin*. New York: The Free Press.

———. 1984. "Leadership as a Political Act." In Barbara Kellerman, ed., *Political Leadership: Multidisciplinary Perspectives*. Englewood Clifs, N.J.: Prentice-Hall.

Kellerman, B., ed. 1986. *Political Leadership: A Source Book*. Pittsburgh: University of Pittsburgh Press.

Kernberg, O. 1975. *Borderline Conditions and Pathological Narcissism*. New York: Jason Aronson.

Kohut, H. 1971. *The Analysis of the Self*. New York: International Universities Press.

———. 1985. "Creativeness, Charisma, Group Psychology: Reflections on the Self-analysis of Freud." In Charles B. Strozier, ed., *Heinz Kohut and the Humanities*. New York: Norton.

Kotter, J., and P. R. Lawrence. 1974. *Mayors in Action*. New York: Wiley.

Lasswell, H. D., 1930. *Psychopathology and Politics*. Chicago: University of Chicago Press.

———. 1936. *Politics: Who Gets What, When, How*. New York: McGraw-Hill.

———. 1948. *Power and Personality*. New York: Norton.

———. 1965. "Introduction: The Study of Political Elites." In H. D. Lasswell and D. Lerner, eds., *World Revolutionary Elites: Studies in Coercive Ideological Movements*. Cambridge: MIT Press.

———. 1971. *A Pre-view of the Policy Sciences*. New York: Elsevier.

Lasswell, H. D., and A. Kaplan. 1950. *Power and Society*. New Haven: Yale University Press.

Lasswell, H. D., and A. Rogow. 1963. *Power, Corruption and Rcctitude*. New York: Prentice-Hall.

Leites, N. 1951. *The Operational Code of the Politburo*. New York: McGraw-Hill.

Levinson, D. J. Forthcoming. *The Seasons of a Woman's Life*. New York: Knopf.

Levinson, D. J., with C. N. Darrow, E. B. Klein, M. H. Levinson, and B. McGee. 1978. *The Seasons of a Man's Life*. New York: Knopf.

Lifton, R. J. 1983. *The Broken Connection*. New York: Basic Books.

Matthews, D. R. 1960. *U.S. Senators and Their World*. New York: Vintage.

Mazlish, B. 1972. *In Search of Nixon*. New York: Basic Books.

Mazlish, B. and E. Diamond. 1979. *Jimmy Carter: An Interpretive Biography*. New York: Simon and Shuster.

McGlashan, T. H., and G. H. Miller. 1982. "The Goals of Psychoanalysis and Psychoanalytic Psychotherapy." *Archives of General Psychiatry* 39: 377–88.

McIntyre A. 1983. "The Aging Narcissistic Leader: The Case of Sir Oswald Mosley at Mid-life." *Political Psychology* 4: 483–99.

Michaelson, D. D. 1972. "An Analysis of the Chief Executive: How the Governor Uses His Time." *State Government* 3: 153–60.

Mills, C. W. 1956. *The Power Elite*. New York: Oxford University Press.

Moore, W. E. 1969. "Occupational Socialization." In D. A. Goslin, ed., *Handbook of Socialization Theory and Research*. Chicago: Rand McNally.

Muir, W. Ker. 1975. *Legislature: California's School for Politics*. Chicago: University of Chicago Press.

National Governors' Association. 1978. *Governing the American States: A Handbook for New Governors*. Washington, D.C.

Nelson, 1978. "The Matched Lives of the U.S. House Leaders: An Exploration." Paper presented at the annual meeting of the American Political Science Association, New York.

Neustadt, R. E. 1960. *Presidential Power: The Politics of Leadership*. New York: Wiley.

Neustadt, R. E., and E. R. May 1986. *Thinking in Time: The Uses of History for Decision Makers*. New York: The Free Press.

New York Times. 1974. *The White House Transcripts*. New York: Bantam.

Orbovich, C. B. 1986. "The Influence of Cognitive Style on the Social Process of Foreign Policy Decision Making." Paper presented at annual meeting of the American Political Science Association, Washington, D.C.

Paige, G. D. 1977. *The Scientific Study of Political Leadership*. New York: The Free Press.

Patrick, J. J. 1977. "Political Socialization and Political Education in Schools." In S. A. Renshon, ed., *Handbook of Political Socialization: Theory and Research*. New York: The Free Press.

Post, J. 1980. "The Seasons of a Leader's Life: Influences of the Life Cycle on Political Behavior." Political Psychology 2:35–49.

Putnam, R. 1973. *The Political Beliefs of Politicians*. New Haven: Yale University Press.

Ransone, C. B., Jr. 1982. *The American Governorship*. Westport: Greenwood Press.

Reich, W. 1949 [1933]. *Character Analysis*. New York: Farrar, Straus, and Giroux.

Renshon, S. 1977. "Assumptive Frameworks in Political Socialization Theory." In S. Renshon, ed., *Handbook of Political Socialization: Theory and Research*. New York: The Free Press.

————. 1980. "Life History and Character Development: Some Reflections on Political Leadership." In Mel Albin, ed., *New Directions in Psycho-history: The Adelphi Papers in Honor of Erik H. Erikson.* New York: Lexington.

————. 1989. "Educating Political Leaders in a Democracy." In Orit Ichilov, ed., *Political Socialization and Democracy.* New York: Teachers College Press.

Rhoads, J., and A. J. Stern. 1981. "Regulation of Self-esteem in Some Political Activists." *Annals of Psychoanalysis* 8: 271–89.

Rokeach, M. 1972. "A theory of Organization and Change within Value-attitude Systems." In G. D. Paige, ed. *Political Leadership: Readings for an Emerging Field.* New York: The Free Press.

————. 1960. *The Open and Closed Mind.* New York: Basic Books.

Rubinow, O. 1933. "The Course of a Man's Life—A Psychological Problem." *Journal of Abnormal and Social Psychology.* 28: 209–15.

Searing, D. D. 1969. "The Comparative Study of Elite Socialization." *Comparative Political Studies* 1: 471–500.

Searing, D. D., J. J. Schwartz, and A. E. Lind.1973. "The Structuring Principle: Political Socialization and Belief Systems." *American Political Science Review* 62: 415–32.

Sears, D. O. 1975. "Political Socialization." In F. I. Greenstein and N. Polsby, eds., *Handbook of Political Science.* Vol. 4. Reading, Mass.: Addison-Wesley.

Shapiro, D. 1965. *Neurotic styles.* New York: Basic Books.

Smith, M. B., J. Bruner and R. White. 1956. *Opinions and Personality.* New York: Wiley.

Sniderman, P. 1975. *Personality and Democratic Politics.* Berkeley: University of California Press.

Stern, A. J. 1987. "The Achieving Narcissist and His Father." Paper presented at the annual meeting of the International Society for Psychology, San Francisco, Calif.

Tetlock, P. E. 1983. "Cognitive Style and Political Ideology." *Journal of Personality and Social Psychology* 45: 118–26.

————. 1984. "Cognitive Style and Political Belief Systems in the British House of Commons." *Journal of Personality and Social Psychology* 46: 365–75.

Tucker, R. 1981. *Politics as Leadership.* Columbia,Mo.: University of Missouri Press.

Vaillant. G. E. 1977. *Adaptation to Life.* Boston: Little Brown.

Weinstein, E. A. 1981. *Woodrow Wilson: A Medical and Psychological Biography.* Princeton: Princeton University Press.

Weinstein, E. A., S. W. Anderson, and A. S. Link. 1978/1979. "Woodrow Wilson's Political Personality: A Reappraisal." *Political Science Quarterly* 93: 585–98.

Wilkens, L. 1986. "Leadership as Political Mentorship: The Example of Wayne Morse." *Political Psychology* 7: 53–65.

Winter, D. 1971. *The Power Motive.* New York: The Free Press.

Wolfenstein, E. V. 1967. *The Revolutionary Personality.* Princeton: Princeton University Press.

Wolfinger, R. E. 1974. *The Politics of Progress.* Englewood Cliffs, N.J.: Prentice-Hall.

Wrong, D. 1961. "The Oversocialized Conception of Man in Modern Sociology." *American Sociological Review* 26: 183–93.

Part III

Introduction:
Social Movement and Immigration

"The 1960's was one of those decades that occurs two or three times a century and has a profound transformative effect on society" (Freeman 1983, pp. xiii) The civil rights movement and the women's liberation movement clearly constitute such transformative movements. While the last few decades have seen the rise (and sometimes the fall) of other social movements, none have made as profound an impression on contemporary American life as these two. For that reason alone we have singled them out for this part of the volume. But they were also chosen because—as we shall discuss presently—these two protest movements, though frequently opting for similar tactics, had very different etiologies.

The third chapter in this part deals with immigration. Immigration differs from the two protest movements in that it rests on individual rather than collective initiative (with some exceptions) and frequently seeks individual rather than group benefits (although the latter are not precluded); unlike the other two movements it does not strive for a basic change in the social order of the host country or region. Yet all three phenomena make demands for resocialization on those who are caught up in them. It is for this reason that the topic of immigration was included here, although it could conceivably also have been included in the part after this because immigration, like the more dramatic episodes discussed later, frequently is a very wrenching and alienating experience calling for much desocialization and resocialization.

Definitions of social movements are numerous and not always compatible with each other. There is some agreement, however, that a social movement enters the public scene when a stratum or segment of the population feels excluded from the benefits the social system bestows on others, and when these "locked-out" individuals transform their private grievances into collective political demands on the system. "Social movements are one of the primary means of aggregating private grievances into political disputes and appealing to public authorities for redress" (Klein 1984, p. 12). However,

"Social strain does not create social movements; it only creates the potential for movements" (Freeman 1975, p. 44). For that potential to be realized, as Morris, Hatchett, and Brown point out, the larger environment and the resources the locked-out can bring to bear upon it have to be such as to make it probable that demands for social change will not fall on deaf ears. Another necessary precondition, of course, has to be that the locked-out are aware of being locked out, i.e., are conscious of their disadvantaged position and become aware of the fact that other members of their group are also conscious of it. It is precisely with respect to group consciousness that the civil rights movement and the women's movement form such startling contrasts.

There was never a time, as Morris, Hatchett, and Brown make clear, that the black population was not keenly aware of its locked-out status and judged it to be grossly unfair. Protest on the scale witnessed during the 1960s however, was not possible earlier (though sporadic attempts had been made, dating back to the days of slavery) for a variety of reasons, among them the blacks' structural location (in rural areas with inadequate communication networks), impoverishment, with the attendant lack of resources (material as well as psychological), not to mention the horrendous cost and danger involved in protest. It would, however, be highly misleading were we to attribute the relative quietude prior to the 1960s to a lack of consciousness in blacks of their deprived status. What was lacking was the second ingredient of group consciousness, the readiness to engage in collective political action. What facilitated the growth of the civil rights movement in the sixties were changes that took place in society at large: "major societal changes such as migration, urbanization . . . generate profound changes and new possibilities within a group even if that group's relative position in the social, economic and political order remains unchanged" (Morris et al. p. 277 below). As these larger social conditions changed, so did the political demands and activities of black Americans. In other words, the changing social climate gave rise to major changes among adult black Americans, showing that political learning is a continuous process.

By contrast—as Susan Carroll points out—women did not initially have such a sense of group consciousness, and some would say they still do not have it (Gurin, Miller, and Gurin 1980; but see Gurin 1985). Debates will probably continue for a long time as to what came first, the birth of the women's movement and its endeavor to raise women's consciousness or the changes in women's structural position which then in turn made women susceptible to the message of the women's movement. Most likely, as Carroll suggests, both affected each other. She credits the women's movement with providing women "with a framework for understanding the difficulties and discrimination they often face as they enter a more public existence." To that extent, the movement clearly acted as an important agent of political socialization. That such socialization was necessary can be deduced from the fact that women—unlike blacks—had not grown up with the sense of belonging to a disadvantaged and/or discriminated-against group (Hacker 1951). To be sure, they were aware that their treatment was not the same as the treatment accorded men and that the spheres in which the two genders operated (the private and the public) were vastly different. But—again unlike the black population—differential treatment was not perceived as discrimination; it was attributed to innate differences in temperaments, competencies, and life goals, which were said to set women and men apart from each other. Again it was life experiences (employment and higher levels of education first and foremost) that created tension between earlier socialization patterns (what it means to be female) and the transition into new roles (employee, divorced head of household, and so on). What the women's movement (as well as other catalysts, such as Betty Friedan's *Feminine Mystique*) did for such women was to legitimize the tension and, even more importantly, to alter women's consciousness, so that the tension then began to be seen as illegitimate and unjust. To gain that consciousness obviously represented a break with one's earlier socialization; thus the women's movement, where it succeeded, gave rise to adult political resocialization.

The difference between these two major social movements that followed each other closely in temporal terms was that blacks were highly aware long before the civil rights movement of the discrimination perpetrated against them, whereas women's sense of minority consciousness did not develop to any significant degree prior to the women's movement and probably even today does not yet characterize most women (Sigel and Whelchel 1986a, b). These differences notwithstanding, once private grievances had been aggregated into collective demands on the political system, both movements began to tread some of the same political-action paths.[1] What is important here from a political socialization perspective is that both movements made ample use of, in fact created, institutions designed for the specific purpose of resocializing susceptible individuals. Whether these institutions went by the name of consciousness-raising groups, freedom schools, or some other name, the purpose was always the same: to socialize or resocialize the worldview of the participants. Before a movement can hope to alter the public's view of what is unjust, it first has to alter that perspective among its own followers.[2] The movements were able to accomplish this, especially among their younger adherents. Both Carroll and Morris show that chronological age does play a role in this respect. The movements' resocialization efforts clearly had more impact on younger people. Openness to new perspectives and new life-patterns is not independent of the length to which one has been exposed to previously socialized patterns. The longer one has been used to these, the more difficult it is to change, even when change would be in one's own best interest. Both chapters, as did an earlier one by Delli Carpini, point to the crucial part played by generational replacements in effecting social change.

Any social movement to be successful, however, has to accomplish more than resocializing movement followers. It also has to raise the consciousness of a sufficient number of noninvolved people, i.e., it has to aim for large-scale popular resocialization. "[A]ny major social movement promotes and in fact depends upon some normative revision of the social order. Those movements having the greatest significance in terms of social change are those in which this normative revision of demand takes the form of a revision in the sense of what is just and unjust in society" (Ragan and Dowd 1971, p. 143). It seems that, up to a point, both movements succeeded in making the public aware of the injustice perpetrated against blacks and women.

Changing the public's cognitive awareness of injustice, nonetheless, is not the same as resocializing people to new feelings and behaviors. Thus a 1985 study of New Jersey men and women showed widespread agreement between the sexes that society discriminated against women. Among women, this realization gave rise to resentment and demand for major and swift change. Men, on the other hand, felt rather unperturbed by the discrimination they saw and tended to see less need for further change (Sigel and Whelchel 1986b). This would lead to yet another speculation, namely, that the receptivity to resocialization may be dependent not only on chronological age, as I suggested above, but also to the threats or rewards one anticipates from resocialization. Those who stand to benefit most from the status quo might be most hesitant, understandably, to exchange old patterns for new ones.

Coping with social change, of course, is a far more arduous task for the new immigrant than it is for either of the two groups just described. In the immigrant's case, changing is hardly an optional matter. Immigrants are *expected* to resocialize in order to get along well in the new environment, whether that is a city for a native rural migrant or a new land itself for someone from another country. A demand is made on the in-migrant to abandon some old ways and to adopt those of the host. Socialization, according to Hoskin, is a response to the demands for individual and group change. To meet demands for change may be particularly difficult for immigrants, not only because they often are no longer young adults but also because they may find themselves in a culture alien to the values and norms they had come to internalize long ago. Hence change is almost tantamount to changing one's identity, and immigrants, of course, are no more willing than people in general to contemplate identity change. Socialization to the new country, therefore, requires "[B]alancing of demands for change against strains for continuity," as Hoskin asserts. No wonder, then, that the history of immigration has at times been called the history of alienation.

A comparison of the socialization experiences of the newcomer with those of the modern feminist or the civil rights advocate offers some interesting insights into the process of adult political socialization. All three may seek the company and comfort of a group of like-minded individuals. For the immigrant it tends to be the comfort and security of his own ethnic group which permits him to maintain, perhaps even cling to, his old identity, the way of looking at the world as he had been taught. Because the ethnic group is more likely to fortify old ways than to make demands for dramatic and rapid resocialization, the group tends to function as an agent for continuity rather than for change.[3] By contrast, the feminist consciousness-raising groups had as their aim to help women to divest themselves of traditional gender attitudes to which they had been socialized and to learn to look at the world of gender relations with totally new eyes. Resocialization may not always have been easy, even in the feminist groups, but resocialization was what they were all about. Similar observations can be made about various civil rights activities and reeducation programs, notably those of the black churches in the South, as Morris, Hatchett, and Brown point out.

Many of the activities and groups organized by the two social movements have yet another purpose which sets them apart from immigrant groups. They—like the movements themselves—are frankly political. The goal is to bring about systemic political reform by making demands on government and other institutions for far-reaching changes; changes that are to benefit the movement's constituency, not any one individual. Immigrants, whether or not they are political refugees, do not come to the host country with any notion of wanting to change its political structure. Immigration, seen from this perspective, is essentially a nonpolitical and individual phenomenon. It is the host country which by its immigration policies tends to respond politically to immigrants. The few political immigrant-initiated overtures to which Hoskin refers usually came in response to such policies and mostly for the purpose of protecting the group's interests, but demands for major changes in the system were not on their agenda. The population at large and maybe even its government may consider immigration, as well as the feminist and the civil rights movements, as a disequilibrating challenge to the status quo, but in reality only the two social movements deliberately seek to make the challenge.

Although all three phenomena described in this section address themselves to human potential for political learning and change during the adult years, there is yet another difference which separates the social movements from the immigration phenomenon. For all their challenge to the status quo, the movements' challenge builds on a tradition to which both challenger and challenged have been socialized, namely, the tradition of political equality of opportunity. All share this common political tradition to which they were socialized from kindergarten days on. The same cannot be said for the immigrant. As Hoskin shows, a vast difference characterizes the socialization of children and that of immigrants, for unlike "most adults, the immigrant is not just extending the natural political orientations of his childhood. Rather, he faces the challenge of reconciling old expectations and loyalties with a new political environment." It is precisely for that reason that immigration is a topic excellently suited for the study of adult political socialization. As such, the study of immigration has the potential to help us formulate a theory of adult socialization. Immigration research with a political socialization perspective—which hardly exists as yet—would permit us to find answers to the more general question of how much change and what kind can one expect in adult life. It can ask: What kind of people having to cope with what kind of change are most able to resocialize, and who is least able to do so?

R.S.S.

Notes

1. Although both movements included protest activities in their behavioral repertoire, it played a more central and essential role in the civil rights movement than in the women's movement, since the latter possessed far more alternate resources than did the former. For a good discussion of these alternate resources and how they were used, see Freeman (1975).

2. Actual participation in protests, demonstrations, meetings, and the like further enhanced the political resocialization process, so much so that many women who originally participated only in the civil rights movement began to see parallels to the situation of women. Often they adopted both ideology and tactics acquired during the battle for civil rights as they joined the women's movement. Cf. S. Evans, 1980, *Personal Politics* (New York: Vintage Books, Random House).

3. Ethnic groups, however, frequently are very helpful in facilitating the process of acculturation by acquainting the newcomer with practical routines necessary to get along in the host country, such as how to seek employment, apply for welfare, request affidavits for relatives, and so on.

References

Freeman, J. 1975. *Politics of Women's Liberation*. New York: Longman.

———.1983. *Social Movements of the Sixties and Seventies*. New York: Longman.

Gurin, P. 1985. "Women's Gender Consciousness." *Public Opinion Quarterly* 49: 143–63.

Gurin, P., A. Miller, and G. Gurin. 1980. "Stratum Identification and Consciousness." *Social Psychological Quarerly* 43: 30–47.

Hacker, H. 1951. "Women as a Minority Group." *Social Forces* 30: 60–69.

Klein, E. 1984. *Gender Politics*. Cambridge: Harvard University Press.

Ragan, P. K., and J. J. Dowd. 1971. "The Emerging Political Consciousness of the Aged: A Generational Interpretation." *Journal of Social Issues* 27: 137–58.

Sigel, R. S., and N. L. Whelchel. 1986a. "Changing Gender Roles: Male and Female Reactions." Paper presented at the meeting of the International Society for Political Psychology, Amsterdam.

———. 1986b. "Assessing the Past and Looking Toward the Future: Perceptions of Change in the Status of Women." Paper prepared for the Annual Meeting of the American Political Science Association, Washington, D.C.

Seven

The Civil Rights Movement and Black Political Socialization

ALDON D. MORRIS, SHIRLEY J. HATCHETT, AND
RONALD E. BROWN

The civil rights movement caught America and the academic community by surprise. Prior to this movement, white America, including the social science community, had no idea of the extent to which black Americans abhorred racial inequality and domination. Part of the naiveté of the social science community stemmed from the lack of a discipline that systematically focused on black political socialization and black political behavior. Major studies of the black community (DuBois 1899; Johnson 1934; Myrdal 1944; Frazier 1949; Drake and Cayton 1954; Cox 1959) certainly existed prior to the 1960s, but they tended to be general studies on all aspects of black life. All in all, prior to the sixties, no identifiable political sociology of the black community existed.

The rise of a potent civil rights movement in the late fifties sent shock waves throughout America and the scientific community. Political authorities and social scientists began to search for the causes of the racial conflict that rocked the nation. They were also concerned with the short- and long-term consequences of such conflict. These concerns generated numerous studies of black political socialization and black politics. This chapter will discuss the conceptual thrust of this research, and suggest an alternative perspective for assessing the impact of the black political movements of the sixties on black political attitudes and behavior.

The chapter is divided into six sections. The first section briefly discusses major conceptual thrusts in research on black political socialization and, by way of critique and extension, suggests another approach to study of political socialization and behavior among blacks. The second section describes the political choices available to blacks in the era before the civil rights move-

The authors would like to acknowledge the assistance of Beverly Williams and Cathy Jenkins in the preparation of this chapter. We appreciate the enthusiasm and competence they brought to the task.

ment and sets the stage for the third section, which describes the emergence of the Southern civil rights movement and the mechanisms by which blacks were socialized to the reformist protest politics of that movement. In the fourth section, we describe the shift to more "revolutionary" protest politics, and the mechanisms by which some blacks were resocialized to black nationalist ideology. The fifth section examines changes in the racial and political attitudes of blacks during this period of widespread mobilization and protest. Our conclusions are presented in the last section.

Research Perspectives in Black Political Socialization

Although political socialization research has been seen as the study of the macro- and micro-level processes leading to constancy and change in political systems, researchers in this area have not fully attended to all dimensions of this charge. Rather they have tended to focus more on stability or constancy (Sears 1975; Renshon 1977; Cutler 1977). The centrality of this focus is underscored by the large number of studies that examine the influence of childhood socialization on the development of the political adult and the smaller number of studies that examine the influence of changing political environments on both early and adult socialization. This section briefly discusses the research that has been done on black political socialization within these two conceptual thrusts—one focusing on the persistence of childhood socialization, and the other on life-long openness to resocialization in changing environmental contexts.

Childhood Influences

Given the centrality of a childhood persistence-perspective in political socialization research on the civil rights movement, the vast majority of this research has been conducted on pre-adults (see Abramson 1977). A major question asked by political socialization researchers during the turbulent sixties was whether black parents and other agents of early socialization in the black community were socializing young blacks to views of the political system which predisposed them to rebellion, and whether such rebellion would lead to the instability of the system (see Greenberg 1970). The resultant research on black pre-adults was focused on substantive areas pertinent to this concern with possible upheaval—perceptions of system responsiveness and the extent and nature of discontent with political authorities and institutions.

The first, and to our knowledge, only book on black political socialization, was focused almost exclusively on political efficacy and trust among black children. In his review of this research, Abramson documented rather consistent findings of lower levels of political efficacy among blacks when compared to whites. While there were essentially no racial differences in political trust when this research began in the early sixties, by the end of the decade black children also had lower levels of trust. Although political efficacy and trust were generally seen as political resources important for political participation, Abramson's discussion and evaluation of these results suggested that rather than being an indication of political deficiency, the racial differences stemmed from realistic reactions to constraints deriving from the disadvantaged social, economic, and political position of blacks in America.

Indeed, the idea that the psychological resources of one group might be the bane of another group, given certain social structural relationships, was explored in the work of Gurin, Gurin et al. (1969). In this important study of group differences and perceptions of personal effectiveness and control, they suggested that for certain groups—blacks, the socioeconomically disadvantaged—external attributions for personal outcomes may derive from real factors such as discrimination rather than fate or chance. Moreover, they suggested that this variant of external control for such groups was relevant not only to personal functioning but also to collective political actions.

Other research had noted such a relationship between blacks' socio-political position and their political perceptions, attitudes, and behaviors. Sears's (1975) summary of the major studies on black political socialization indicated that black political discontent was directed more towards particular political officials and institutions than toward the general political system. For example, black children were more likely than white children to hold negative orientations toward those perceived to be against their racial group's interest, and more positive orientations toward their perceived political allies (see Sigel 1968 and 1970).

Sears noted that while blacks appeared to believe in the American creed more than whites, they grew up more disaffected with the political system. This observation cannot be easily explained by existing conceptual frameworks in the political socialization literature. The black political movements of the sixties, however, alerted social scientists to the importance of perceptions of one's racial group's position to evaluations of and participation in the political system. A number of studies found that racial awareness not only shaped political perceptions and attitudes but candidate choice and participation (see Campbell et al. 1966; Verba and Nie 1972; Murray and Vedlitz 1978). Group-based voting led some scholars to contend that the black community fosters a sense of racial awareness that emphasizes a common-fate orientation (see Lane 1959; Orum and Cohen 1973; Pitts 1975). Within a persistence-perspective, such findings suggest the importance of family and other agents of early socialization in the development of negative perceptions of system responsiveness and legitimacy as well as a collective political ideology among blacks. Indeed, race and ethnicity, along with party identification and religion, have been seen as important forces for continuity in the face of environmental or contextual changes (Sigel and Hoskin 1977).

Environmental Influences

Another focus of research on black political socialization has been on adult resocialization. Again, the impetus for this research came from the black protest era of the 1960s. Because the civil rights movement, in particular the black-power phase, was seen as a major departure from past political behavior of blacks, adult resocialization became a focus. Two related types of research came out of this emphasis—one assessing the impact of settings, events, or experiences on political socialization, and the other examining the process by which these different socialization environments, inasmuch as they coincide with the coming of age of various cohorts, effect generational change.

The studies of black student activism in the civil rights and black power movements, and of riot participants, fall in the first category of research. In perhaps the most important study of black student activism, Gurin and Epps (1975) examined the impact of activism on political ideology. They noted that ideological changes could also result from vicarious experience, e.g., being on an activist campus. Along with others (Matthews and Prothro 1966; Orbell 1967; Orum and Orum 1968; Searles and Williams 1962), they found that early on in the black-protest era student activists were more likely to be at black urban and academically prestigious colleges.

Sears and McConahay's (1970; 1973) studies of the Watts riot and Paige's (1968) study of the Newark riot are examples of a body of research that examined the relationship between such activism and political resocialization. Certain characteristics were found to predispose blacks to riot participation—urban residence, age, and racial-political disaffection. Also, this research suggests that the riots themselves appeared to have generated a type of "riot" ideology that further resocialized not only the direct participants but those who only vicariously experienced them (see *Report of the National Advisory Commission on Civil Disorders*, 1968; and Campbell and Schuman 1968).

The other type of research within this focus on adult socialization is intimately related to this study of environmental impact on political socialization. In the studies dealing with the impact of settings and events, age was found to be an important correlate of activism and ideology. The question which arises is, to what extent are differences found across age groups a result of young people being particularly receptive to new events and settings because of life cycle, or from birth cohorts coming of age in a particular period in history? Generational research has attempted to disentangle effects associated with life-cycle position, birth cohort, and period (Cutler 1977 and Delli Carpini, chap. 1 in this volume). The work of Jennings and Niemi (1974, 1981) is an example of this research focus. Their panel study of black and white pre-adults suggested a cohort effect on political socialization stemming from coming of age in the protest era of the sixties. These effects, however, were conditioned by several factors which we will discuss later in this chapter.

Both of the research perspectives discussed in this section—persistence of childhood socialization and openness to adult resocialization as a consequence of changing environments and experiences—are limited in their ability to fully capture political socialization among blacks. This limitation derives from both the conceptualization of political socialization and the political process, and the methodologies employed to document and understand these phenomena. A major flaw in political socialization research, as in socialization generally, stems from the fact that it is largely ahistorical (see Renshon 1977). Although generational or cohort research takes into account the fact that people are socialized in different historical eras, the research on blacks has been insensitive to the continuities of the black political process. Similarly, persistence-perspectives of black socialization are unable to explain sudden mass changes in political consciousness and mobilization. Given this, political socialization and the political process need to be examined within a broader conceptual framework and with multimethod approaches.

A great deal of political socialization research has relied on survey methodology. Whether cross-sectional or based on a particular type of individual, the survey interview format sometimes leads to a decontextualized assessment of the phenomena of interest. In addition, as noted by Cutler (1977), studies attempting to assess differences or similarities between the old and the young, or to look at changes over time in cross-sections of persons, often confuse what might be cohort effects with life-cycle or period effects. Multigenerational panel studies such as the one conducted by Jennings and Niemi (1974, 1981) allow the disentanglement of these influences and provide a temporal framework for understanding continuity and change. In addition, field methodologies, such as participant observation and ethnographic study, and historical analysis can provide the sociocultural context often lacking in research relying only on survey methods.

Indeed, we fully agree with C. Wright Mills that "Whatever else he may be, man is a social and a historical actor who must be understood, if at all, in close and intricate interplay with social and historical structures" (1959, p. 158). It is in this vein that we present a perspective on the political process which stresses the importance of history and of political resources associated with structural position—both organizational and psychological. This perspective also leads us to a multimethod approach to the assessment of the impact of the black political movements of the sixties on black political socialization.

A Structural-Interactive Approach

We suggest an approach that is both structural and interactive. It is structural because we begin from the premise that one's group membership and the location of that group in the social, economic, and political order will play an important role in shaping one's orientation to the political system (see Danigelis 1977, 1982; McAdam 1982; Piven and Cloward 1979). It is interactive in the sense that human actors are conceptualized as creative because they generate culture, ideas, and behaviors throughout their life cycles that challenge and at times change those conditions typically associated with their structural positions. Incorporated in this approach is the view that a group's structural position is dynamic, not fixed or immutable. Thus, major societal changes such as migration, urbanization, industrialization, proletarianization, and institution building may generate profound changes and new possibilities within a group even if that group's relative position in the social, economic, and political order remains unchanged. In essence, our structural-interactive approach incorporates the principles underlying the lifelong openness model of adult socialization described by Sears (1975) and Jennings and Niemi (1981). Just as the lifelong openness model assumes that political learning is a continuous process influenced by new knowledge and information, the political orientations and actions of black Americans are influenced by a changing racial-political climate.

In our perspective, we assume that racial group membership, to the extent that it is transformed into racial consciousness, will play an instrumental role in determining the nature of black political behavior (see Miller, Gurin, et al, 1981). A problem we see with most political socialization research is its conceptualization and measurement of the political process. By focusing on system-maintenance variables such as political efficacy, trust, political interest, and attachment to traditional political authorities, political scientists have, for the most part, failed to consider the "legitimacy" of the disorderly side of politics to which locked-out groups are usually constrained. The work of Miller, Gurin, et al. (1981), however, suggests that perceptions of system rather than individual blame for lack of social mobility and discontent with the power and influence associated with one's group position are political resources. When combined with a sense of common fate with one's group and a collective orientation, these resources foster a different brand of political participation.

Our structural approach is characterized by a broader view as to what constitutes the political process. Drawing from resource mobilization theory (Gamson 1975; Tilly 1978), we view the political process as a struggle between groups over the political and economic resources of the society. In this view, the political process has both an orderly side and a disorderly side. The political process is one of groups acting together in pursuit of their interests, whether they choose the orderly or disorderly side of the political process. Moreover, the structural position of a group largely determines whether that group pursues the orderly or disorderly route. In our view, social movements, political protest, riots, and the like are enduring components of the political

278   *Aldon D. Morris/Shirley J. Hatchett/Ronald E. Brown*

process. We agree with Gamson that "rebellion in this view, is simply politics by other means. It is not some kind of irrational behavior. It is as instrumental in its nature as a lobbyist trying to get special favors for his group or a major political party conducting a presidential campaign" (1975; p. 139).

Political protest is a form of power behavior initiated by groups excluded from the established political order. Thus, protest politics is a supranational phenomenon stemming from systemic forms of social stratification. From a study of political protest in five western democracies during the sixties, Barnes and Kaase (1979) concluded that protest was rooted in the very structure of those societies. Moreover, they concluded that the potential for protest is a "lasting characteristic of democratic mass publics and not just a sudden surge in political involvement bound to fade away as time goes by" (1979, p. 524). Given the systemic and supranational nature of protest, it is imperative that political socialization research comes to grips with the disorderly side of the political process.

The Politics of Protest and the Afro-American Community

In this chapter, the disorderly side of the political process is referred to as "the politics of protest." Focusing on the politics of protest, we will examine the changing structural conditions that made it possible for blacks to engage in widespread nontraditional politics in the late 1950s and throughout the 1960s. We will argue that certain structural changes made it possible for a population portrayed as politically passive and alienated to engage in political activism in unprecedented numbers. We also argue that such political activism suggests that political values and orientations, whether acquired in childhood or during later periods, are relatively malleable and potentially responsive to changes in political opportunities and options. We shall demonstrate, also, how human actors deliberately and, at times, successfully engage in socialization activities that change political orientations and make possible a range of political activities which previously seemed impossible. In short, we will stress how people, by acting back on the socialization process, can shape and influence it in important ways.

Political Choices in the Pre–Civil Rights Era

On the eve of the modern civil rights movement, southern blacks were negatively affected by a pervasive system of segregation and subordination. As a group, they had little political power because most were disenfranchised. Owing to the repressive and violent actions of whites, and discriminatory requirements such as poll taxes and literacy tests, only 20 percent of eligible black voters were registered in 1952 (Matthews and Prothro 1966, p. 18).

Additionally, blacks were at the very bottom of the socioeconomic order (see Farley 1984).

In the North, black oppression was more subtle and complex. Although northern blacks were not hampered by the deliberate impediments that prevented most of their southern counterparts from voting, they were, nevertheless, largely shut out of the decision-making process. Urban machine politics controlled, for the most part, by white ethnic groups constrained black political participation and influence (Katznelson 1976). Moreover, northern blacks, like their southern counterparts, found themselves at the very bottom of the socioeconomic structure. In essence, as Dr. Martin Luther King, Jr., suggested in his "I Have a Dream" speech (at the March on Washington, 1963), blacks in the South, prior to the civil rights movement, could not vote, and those in the North had little for which to vote.

Thus, the objective social position of black people created an antagonistic relationship between them and the established political order controlled by whites. Because of their oppressed and disadvantaged position, blacks had few political options available through which to realize their interests. Nevertheless, in the mid 1950s, blacks had the same political options available to their forebears during slavery and every subsequent decade thereafter—the politics of protest and social disruption.

Social protest has always been, and continues to be, an enduring component of the black experience. Gunnar Myrdal, in discussing the centrality of black protest historically and its manifestation in the 1940s, concluded that protest "has, in fact, become part of the ideology of the entire Negro people to an ever increasing extent" (1944, p. 744). For Myrdal, black protest stemmed from what he called race consciousness and racial solidarity. The detailed fieldwork used in *American Dilemma* enabled the researchers to ascertain the extraordinary extent to which the protest mentality was embedded in blacks in both the North and South. Speaking of blacks in the South during the 1940s who are often portrayed in the literature as passive victims of a docile socialization process, Myrdal wrote, "Deep down in the most dependent and destitute classes of Negroes in the rural south, the individual Negro of the masses ordinarily keeps a recess in his mind where he harbors the Negro protest" (p. 744). Given the sociopolitical position of blacks, it is not surprising that they developed a protest tradition. Indeed, protest was one of the limited political options available to blacks.

Yet, the political socialization research on blacks during the 1960s and 70s did not adequately take this tradition of black protest into account. Such an omission leads that literature to an imagery which suggests that an entirely new race consciousness emerged in the 1960s that produced unprecedented levels of black protest within a previously alienated and passive population. However, careful historical analyses of black politics suggest a strikingly different reality. Blacks have been engaged in social protest since their capture in Africa and enslavement in America. The legacy of this tradition of protest and political involvement was an independent political infrastructure composed of black institutions and organizations—churches, colleges, self-help and fraternal organizations, and the black press. This infrastructure has undergirded conventional and protest politics. Here, we present a sketch of this history highlighted by a brief discussion of important political movements in each century.

For blacks, the political process has comprised a wide range of behaviors. While in bondage, slaves formulated escape plans and executed them via the underground railroad. They also planned and carried out slave revolts (Aptheker 1943). Free blacks voted when they had the chance; participated in the underground railroad; founded black abolitionist organizations and at times formed coalitions with white abolitionists; established black newspapers to voice black sentiments regarding slavery, inequality, and the treatment of blacks; and initiated a series of all-Negro national conventions to organize grassroot protest (Walton 1972a, 1972b; Morris 1975; Moses 1978). During the Reconstruction period, blacks exercised their newly acquired right to vote and began to participate in large numbers in electoral politics. This participation was quickly curtailed by judicial decisions which narrowed the interpretation of the constitutional amendments and other legislation enacted after the Civil War, and by restrictive clauses and taxes which prevented most blacks from exercising their right to vote. During this period, blacks were rejected by the party which had once courted their votes. To ensure some participation in electoral politics, blacks formed satellite Republican parties known as the Black and Tans and challenged the regular party organizations at the local level (Walton 1972a, 1972b). Also, during this period, black women's clubs launched campaigns against lynching and racial discrimination (Davis 1983; Giddings 1984).

By the turn of the nineteenth century, black political behavior was largely confined to the politics of protest. Meier and Rudwick (1976) have documented how blacks boycotted Jim Crow streetcars throughout most of the South between 1900 and 1906. These boycotts were clearly forerunners of the bus boycotts of the 1950s and 60s. It was in 1905 that the Niagra movement emerged with the explicit purpose of black protest aimed at achieving full black equality. Five years later, the NAACP was organized and subsequently became a national protest organization committed to achieving black equality.

The 1920s and 30s witnessed the emergence of major mass movements. Garvey's nationalistic protest movement, anchored in the United Negro Improvement Association, drew millions of black people. Father Divine's Peace Mission was another mass-based protest movement. Most analysts have dismissed the Peace Mission as a black cult. However, recent research (e.g.,

Weisbrot 1983) clearly shows that Divine's movement was largely a protest movement against all forms of racial injustice. Moreover, during the 1920s, blacks in various states developed protest movements. Thus, Bank's careful and illuminating analysis of the black statewide movement in Texas between 1920 and 1950 shows that blacks "developed a well organized movement for equality which has served as a model for Negro freedom fighters in other states of the south" (1962, p. 111). It should also be pointed out that this was the same period in which a militant cultural movement known as the Harlem Renaissance emerged, producing literature, music, and art that embraced and promoted black protest.

Finally, the 1940s witnessed the development of the mass-based A. Philip Randolph March on Washington Committee. This was a major movement which organized a mass following able to act in a concerted fashion (Garfinkel 1959). It generated sufficient power to persuade President Roosevelt to issue an executive order desegregating the defense industry. The nonviolent tactics and mass character of this movement served as a direct forerunner of the modern civil rights movement.

Clearly, then, protest movements and protest activities have been an integral part of the black experience. In their fight to attain liberation, blacks have had to utilize the disorderly side of the political process. These movements and protest activities have been central to black political socialization and political behavior. Analysts of these various activities (Walton 1985; Myrdal 1944; Banks 1962; Weisbrot 1983; Garfinkel 1959) have consistently pointed to a number of socializing agents that produced the consciousness underneath black protest. These include mass meetings, the black press, and a number of institutions including the church, fraternal orders, and a host of protest organizations. Additionally, World Wars I and II were also critical because of the democratic rhetoric they spawned and the international perspective they imparted to black soldiers who often participated in protest activities upon their return to racist America.

In the next section, we examine the rise and remarkable spread of the modern civil rights movement. This movement is rooted in the protest tradition and socialization processes discussed above. The fact that different forms of black protest emerge in different eras and situational contexts implies that political socialization is indeed a dynamic process. But, as will be clear in our discussion of the modern civil rights movement, there has been historical continuity in terms of black political socialization. Political socialization is a process rooted in a group's history and shaped by available political options.

The Civil Rights Movement and the Political Process

In 1955, the black community of Montgomery, Alabama, ushered in the mass-action phase of the modern civil rights movement. In December of that year, Montgomery's black community organized a mass boycott of city buses in response to the arrest of Rosa Parks, who had refused to give her seat to a white man. Mrs. Parks's act of defiance proved significant in that it violated local segregation laws and reflected the extent to which black people were dissatisfied with racial segregation. Our purpose is not to present a detailed account of the Montgomery bus boycott, for that has been done elsewhere (King 1958; Yeakey 1979; Thornton 1979–80; and Morris 1984). The intent here is to distill the broad political significance of the Montgomery bus boycott.

The Montgomery bus boycott was a ground-breaking political development. First of all, it endured for an entire year (381 days) despite the intense opposition of the local white community. The long duration of the boycott maximized its local, regional, and national influence and visibility. Second, the boycott was clearly a mass movement because it involved the entire community, which meant that it successfully mobilized across class, age, educational, religious, and gender lines. This remarkable mobilization was accomplished through existing black organizations and especially the mass-based black church. Third, the boycott movement represented a tactical breakthrough for the black community by introducing the method of nonviolent civil disobedience. The boycott demonstrated that, given the fact that blacks were excluded from the formal political process, nontraditional and extrainstitutional politics were needed to overthrow racial segregation. Fourth, the movement itself functioned as a consciousness-raising tool for the black masses by giving rise to continuous mass meetings, nonviolent workshops, formal and informal political discussions and through the practice of distributing informational leaflets throughout the black community. Finally, the Montgomery movement served as a model of successful resistance for black communities throughout the South because it was victorious. After a year of protest, the Supreme Court declared bus segregation to be illegal in Montgomery.

From a political standpoint, the black community was never to be the same after the Montgomery bus boycott. Indeed, nonviolent movements against racial segregation began to emerge in other communities such as Tallahassee, Florida, and Birmingham, Alabama, even while the Montgomery movement was still in process (Morris 1984). For the next fifteen years, the "politics of protest" would become the dominant political expression of the black community within and outside the South. During this period economic boycotts, sit-ins, freedom rides, marches, demonstrations, mass arrests, and urban riots became commonplace. Clearly the Montgomery bus boycott provided a method and a blueprint of resistance that unleashed black political activism that spilled far beyond the boundaries of traditional political behavior.

There is little evidence that blacks underwent a fundamentally different socialization experience prior to the civil rights movement. We believe that structural and demographic changes that occurred prior to and concurrently with the modern civil rights movement, rather than fundamentally different socialization experiences, are primarily responsible for the heavy volume of black political activism of the late fifties and throughout the sixties. It is important to reemphasize the point that the protests which epitomized the civil rights movement were not new. Indeed, protest activities have occurred during every decade of black existence in America. Therefore, what has to be accounted for is the heavy volume of protest during the civil rights movement rather than the mere presence of protest.

Research by social-movement scholars (Gamson 1975; Zald and McCarthy 1979; McAdam 1982; Morris 1981 and 1984) has demonstrated that a variety of social and economic resources are required for an oppressed group to sustain and successfully use protest to accomplish political goals. At minimum, such a group needs communication networks, an organizational base, leadership, money, and group solidarity. Scholars of the civil rights movement (Piven and Cloward 1979; Morris 1984; McAdam 1982) have demonstrated that the urbanization of blacks during World Wars I and II and throughout the first half of the twentieth century facilitated the assemblage of resources needed to launch and sustain a successful protest movement. The urban environment promoted the growth of resourceful black churches that linked the masses through elaborate communication networks and provided an autonomous institutional, financial, and leadership base capable of generating group solidarity and sustaining collective action. Additional community organizations including the NAACP, black colleges, and a variety of political and civic organizations, as well as the black press, grew in the southern urban environment.

In short, the urbanization of blacks spawned the structural resources—communication networks, leadership, financial capabilities, and institutional solidarity—crucial to the rise and success of the modern civil rights movement. In our view, political consciousness as a product of political socialization is a necessary but not sufficient condition for the wide-scale use of social protest. Indeed, without the structural resources outlined above it is doubtful that the civil rights movement would have taken root when it did. Yet, the availability of structural resources within a subordinate group does not guarantee that such a group will engage in political activism.

Scholars of political movements have long recognized the close relationship between political consciousness and political action. This relationship has its most classical formulation in Marxist theory, which argues that, for a class to become revolutionary, a class in itself must become a class for itself. Thus, for Marx, revolution is a product of both objective and subjective conditions. Our structural/interactive approach similarly assumes a complementary relationship between consciousness and political action. In this chapter, we explore the nature of the political consciousness that undergirded the civil rights movement and seek to understand the mechanisms and processes through which this consciousness was disseminated to black masses.

One of the distinguishing features of the modern civil rights movement was its strategy of mass participation. The movement relied on "direct action," which included boycotts, sit-ins, marches, demonstrations, filling up the jails through arrests, and so on. For civil disobedience to work, mass participation is required. Thus, the movement through its utilization of nonviolent direct action installed a tactical innovation in the black community and directly pulled masses of blacks into the disorderly side of the political process, instantly shattering the illusion that politics had to be pursued within formal channels.

The movement itself was a tool of political socialization. Its mass tactics required people to learn and execute new forms of political behavior. On the whole, blacks were more able to identify with and grasp the politics of protest because they had been systematically excluded from participation in electoral politics. Also, the institutionalized political process normally had only incremental impact if any at all. Direct-action tactics gave more immediate feedback to efforts and, thus, affected efficacy and commitment. With protest politics, there was the real possibility they could bring about the desired political end: the overthrow of legal segregation and the implementation of racial equality. Reverend James Lawson (1978), a key practitioner of nonviolent direct action during the early years of the movement, recalls how it affected the masses: "The point of the whole problem is that when people are suffering, they don't want rhetoric and processes which seem to go slowly. . . . many people want direct participation." He went on to point out that the magnetic appeal of mass boycotts, demonstrations, and the like, is that they "put into the hands of all kinds of ordinary people a positive alternative to powerlessness and frustration. That's one of the great things about direct action." Thus, what emerged from these tactics was a heightened sense of group political efficacy. Within a short period of time, masses of people learned how to engage in civil disobedience, and how to nourish and sustain the appropriate consciousness which promotes group solidarity and rebellion.

How did the movement accomplish this political socialization? This consciousness resulted from a creative synthesis of preexisting attitudes and new attitudes generated within the situation. The black church provided both the organizational and attitudinal context for the movement. Organizationally, the church supplied the movement with a mass base, leadership, finances, communication networks, and an autonomous structure in which to meet and plan protest. Ideologically, the church housed a substantial portion of the institutionalized consciousness of black people. The concrete expressions of that consciousness—music, sermons, prayers, and the like—reveal that a protest philosophy undergirded black religion. Scholars of the black church have long noted the protest theme within black religion, even though, out of necessity, it has often been camouflaged. In fact, within black religion two warring themes—submission and protest—have clashed throughout the centuries.

The submission theme suggested that God would punish the oppressor, while the oppressed would experience equality and bliss in the afterlife. The other side of black religion spoke to the rebellious. DuBois (1903) captured this thrust when he wrote, "His [the rebellious] religion became darker and more intense, and into his ethics crept a note of revenge, into his songs a day of reckoning close at hand. The 'Coming of the Lord' swept this side of death, and came to be a thing hoped for in this day" (DuBois 1903, p. 200). Then, too, Christian doctrine stresses equality, justice, fairness, and liberation. It is no surprise that oppressed blacks found affinity with such a message. As Benjamin Mays (1978), an authority on black religion, put it, "the Negro was selective in his preaching. He usually selected biblical passages which emphasized that all men are children of God." In short, the protest theme within black religions was an enduring dimension of the black protest tradition.

The political consciousness that guided the Montgomery bus boycott and the numerous movements which followed were not entirely new. Rather, the leaders of the movements, usually ministers, deliberately anchored the protest within the framework of black religion. Speaking of the Montgomery bus boycott, Dr. King wrote (1958, p. 84) "From the very beginning a basic philosophy guided the movement. . . . it was Jesus of Nazareth that stirred the Negroes to protest with the creative weapon of love." In other words, the political consciousness that gripped the early civil rights protesters was familiar in that it came directly out of that reservoir of black religion that emphasized the necessity and appropriateness of social protest.

While the philosophical consciousness beneath the movement was not new to blacks, the actual practice of nonviolent direct action was. Suddenly, blacks were being asked to boycott, sit-in, march, go to jail, risk jobs and lives. A comprehensive consciousness entailing both an appropriate philosophical outlook and the tactical knowledge of how to engage in civil disobedience was needed. Blacks had to be taught these new techniques and socialized into a strategy of nonviolent resistance. Beginning with the Montgomery bus boycott, the Gandhian method of nonviolent resistance was chosen as the new thrust of black protest politics. The preexisting attitudes associated with militant black religion and the new attitudes and knowledge associated with nonviolent resistance combined to produce the comprehensive consciousness that gripped black Americans who participated in the civil rights movement. In Dr. King's words (1958, p. 85):

> I had come to see early that the Christian doctrine of love operating through the Gandhian method of non-violence was one of the most potent weapons available to the Negro in his struggle for freedom. . . . In other words, Christ furnished the spirit and motivation, while Gandhi furnished the method.

The civil rights movement developed specific mechanisms through which this comprehensive consciousness was disseminated to the black masses. We turn now to a brief description of those mechanisms.

Mass Meetings. The most important consciousness-raising device of the movement was the mass meeting. Throughout the civil rights movement, mass meetings were held on a weekly and sometimes daily basis. Those attending these meeting were a cross-section of the black community—representatives of all ages, socioeconomic classes, and religions. These meetings provided large numbers of people the opportunity to interact collectively. The overwhelming majority of these meetings were held in black churches (King 1963; Clarke 1962; and Morris 1984). It was in this comfortable and familiar atmosphere that the black masses were socialized into the techniques and philosophies of the movement. A pattern evolved at these mass meetings whereby traditional songs, prayers, and Scripture readings were intertwined with the nontraditional tactical and strategic matters (King 1958; Clarke 1962).

It was in these meetings that the masses were taught the philosophy and techniques of nonviolent resistance. For example, during the Birmingham confrontation of 1963 King (1963, p. 60), revealed that sixty-five mass meetings were held where he spoke "nightly on the philosophy of non-violence and its method." Because mass meetings rotated from church to church, they generated solidarity in the black community and provided the communication networks which facilitated the resocialization processes the masses underwent. Clarke's (1962, p. 65) empirical study of mass meetings during the period found that they "present the leaders with an opportunity to state publicly their major goals and ideologies, which, in turn, influences and helps to make individual goals consistent with the group goal." She concluded that mass meetings functioned as inspirational, educational, and instructional media.

Workshops. Workshops were designed to accomplish specific tasks of the movement. They taught movement participants how to demonstrate, how to react nonviolently when attacked, how to vote, and the like. Workshops were enormously important "how to" clinics because they trained people in the art of participating in the disorderly side of the political process. Indeed, most southern blacks lacked skills in traditional politics because throughout their lifetimes they had been deliberately excluded from the political process. Dr. Simpkins (1978), an activist in Louisiana in the late 1950s, recalls that the workshops taught people their rights and how to acquire them. He explained that people had to be taught how to use the voting machines, appear before the Board of Registration, and how to fill out complicated registration forms. We emphasize here that activities directed at acquiring the vote for blacks during this period cannot be classified as traditional politics. That is, extra-institutional measures including boycotts, marches, and demonstrations had to be carried out before southern blacks gained the franchise supposedly guaranteed them in the U.S. Constitution. The task of the workshop was to teach blacks how to engage in various forms of political activity. James Lawson (1978), another expert on the topic, explained that a variety of approaches including role-playing, game simulation, and the development of novel ways of strategizing and thinking were used during workshops. Although mostly conducted during mass meetings, workshops were sometimes held on an on-going basis; at other times, they were convened as the need arose.

Citizenship Schools. Literacy tasks were part of the arsenal of weapons used by white officials in the South to disenfranchise blacks. When blacks attempted to register to vote, they were often asked to interpret state constitutions and complete complicated forms (Zinn 1964, p. 66). This proved an effective method of disenfranchisement because most blacks were illiterate due to a discriminatory system of education. The citizenship schools were developed by the Highlander Folk School and King's Southern Christian Leadership Conference with the explicit goal of teaching blacks how to read and write so they could vote and become part of the political process. From the outset, the citizenship schools were political and their activities fell squarely within the domain of protest politics.

Instructors in the schools traveled throughout the South and found local blacks who could read and write; they then sent them to the central training center in McIntosh, Georgia, where they taught them methods they could use in teaching others on their return to their local communities (Clark and Blythe 1962). The curriculum of the citizenship schools informed blacks of the inner workings of the political system and showed how blacks were excluded from the political process. In these schools, blacks were taught how to raise questions about political power, and how to engage in activities aimed at acquiring power. The task of the schools was to stir up rebellion among the black masses by teaching them that they had no democracy in an allegedly democratic society (Adams 1975, p. 119). Dorothy Cotton (1978), one of the leaders in the schools, explained that they "unbrainwashed" black folk and started them thinking of themselves in new and different ways. That is, the citizenship schools were in the business of resocializing black people. Many of the people who attended these schools became involved in the civil rights movement and prepared others who eventually became involved (Morris 1984).

Within a short period of time, citizenship schools, because of mass demand, spread throughout the South. They were conducted in barbershops, beauty shops, churches, private homes,and open fields. Adams (1975) wrote that in 1963, Septima Clark, one of the founders of the citizenship schools, reported that "more than 26,000 blacks in twelve southern states had learned enough reading to register." At that time, she noted, volunteer teachers were running more than 400 schools attended by 6,500 adults. In 1970, she estimated that nearly 100,000 blacks had learned to read and write through citizenship schools (p. 118). In short, the citizenship schools were a carefully honed tool which contributed greatly to the development of political consciousness.

Freedom Schools. Freedom schools arrived in Mississippi in 1964. These schools were developed by a coalition of civil rights organizations, but it was the Student Nonviolent Coordinating Committee (SNCC) that played the central role in their development. In 1964, SNCC implemented its Mississippi Summer project, whose goal was to register thousands of disenfranchised blacks across the South so that they could unseat and, in fact, replace the racist white elected officials during the Democratic convention which was to be held in the fall of 1964 in Atlantic City.

The freedom schools were established to facilitate this grand strategy. To be successful, SNCC attempted to develop indigenous black leadership on a rapid basis throughout the state. They targeted the young. However, most blacks in Mississippi had been socialized by the public schools and white society not to question white domination. The freedom schools were designed with the explicit goal of teaching young blacks to question the overall white system of domination (Holt 1965, p. 105). Included with the curriculum were courses titled "The Movement," "Introducing the Power Structure," "Revolution" and "Negro History." The anthem of the Civil Rights Movement, "We Shall Overcome," was used as a teaching and inspirational device. Most of the teachers of the freedom schools were northern white college students from the most prestigious universities in the United States who agreed to work with SNCC that summer in Mississippi.

Over two thousand young black Mississippians flocked to these "schools of question" throughout Mississippi (Carson 1981; Holt 1965). These classes were held in churches, lodge halls, storefronts, sheds, and fields. By all accounts (Zinn 1964; Holt 1965; Carson 1981), these schools produced hundreds of indigenous young leaders who became a central part of the civil rights movement. As Carson put it, "many youngsters were deeply and permanently affected by the unique educational experience" (p. 120). Like mass meetings, workshops, and citizenship schools, freedom schools were devices deliberately designed by the movement to resocialize blacks into the nontraditional political activism of the sixties.

From the beginning, the southern civil rights movement had national impact. In particular, it served as a socialization tool for blacks across the nation. Electronic media, especially television, as well as print media, brought blacks outside the South into close contact with black resistance and white brutality. Also, civil rights leaders, organizers, and ministers conducted northern rallies, workshops, and lectures for the explicit purpose of informing blacks of the movement and mobilizing them in support of the struggle. Thus, by the early 1960s, thousands of blacks outside the South were actually initiating demonstrations against both southern and northern racism (*Report of the National Advisory Commission on Civil Disorders* 1968; Whalen and Whalen 1985). In fact, a significant amount of the financial support for the southern civil rights movement came from northern black communities (Morris 1984).

In short, the southern black movement quickly became a national black movement because oppression was nationwide. Additionally, many northern blacks had fresh memories of southern oppression and still had relatives and friends in the South. The black church, which was a national black institution, also linked southern and northern blacks. Therefore, both the mechanisms for socialization discussed above and the media coverage of the southern civil rights movement shaped black political consciousness from coast to coast.

Black Power—The Shift to Black Nationalist Ideology

The nonviolent southern civil rights movement achieved a number of important victories. Among these were the passage of the 1964 Civil Rights Act and the 1965 Voting Rights Act. Nevertheless, by the mid-sixties, the movement had failed to achieve racial integration nor had it accomplished Dr. King's dream of a "beloved community" where people would not be judged by the color of their skin.

To the contrary, in the mid-sixties blacks were still highly segregated and occupied inferior economic and political positions. Moreover, civil rights victories occurred in the context of white violence and major setbacks: black children were attacked, beaten, arrested, and at times killed when they challenged the established order; civil rights workers, including Medgar Evers,

James Chaney, Andrew Goodman, Michael Schwerner, Jimmy Lee Jackson, Viola Liuzzo, James Reeb, and others were murdered; SNCC's Mississippi Freedom Democratic party, which attempted to unseat the racist Democratic party of Mississippi, was defeated in Atlantic City in 1964 with the assistance of white liberals; the poverty and exploitation of northern ghettos remained largely untouched; and James Meredith was shotgunned down by racist whites as he attempted a one-man march against fear across the state of Mississippi.

This was the repressive and unrelenting atmosphere from which the "black power" movement emerged. Thus, the philosophy of black power emerged out of the struggles and outcomes of the civil rights movement itself. It is no accident, then, that the "black power" movement emerged in the South. More specifically, the cry for "black power" came to the attention of the black community and the nation in June of 1966 from Greenwood, Mississippi. This turning point occurred during the march begun by Meredith but completed by King of SCLC, McKissick of CORE, and Carmichael of SNCC after Meredith was shot and unable to continue. Shortly after the marchers entered Greenwood, Carmichael shouted out to the local audience:

> "What we gonna start saying now is 'black power.'" He shouted the slogan repeatedly, each time the audience shouted back "black power!" Willie Ricks [SNCC activist] leaped to the platform and asked, "What do you want?" Again and again the audience shouted in unison the slogan that had suddenly galvanized their emotions (Carson 1981, p. 210).

Thus, a militant and controversial phase of the civil rights movement crystallized in Mississippi. Before the march ended, both CORE and SNCC adopted the new philosophy of "black power," while King insisted that he and his organization would hold steadfast to the goal of nonviolent integration.

The black-power ideology signaled a more radical thrust in the movement. First, its proponents either relaxed or rejected the goal of racial integration. Obtaining economic, political, and cultural power for blacks became far more important than racial integration. Second, the strategy of nonviolence was rejected in favor of self-defense and the view that change should be achieved by "any means necessary." Finally, black-power advocates either relaxed or rejected the assumption that the civil rights movement should have an interracial character. The view emerged that only black people could pursue black power and that the motives and actions of white liberals were suspect at best.

The shift to black power and black nationalist ideology was merely a resurgence of similar political responses to American society followed by blacks in earlier periods. As for the civil rights movement, what distinguished this thrust from earlier movements was the extent to which it mobilized blacks, the impact it had on the wider society, and the manner in which it transformed blacks from "Negroes" to Afro-Americans. The roots of this movement can be traced to the decision of some slaves to return to Africa after emancipation and to Booker T. Washington's doctrine of separate development of the races. In the 1920s, the Garvey movement flourished and spawned a number of other organizations which survived the original Garvey organization. In the decade preceding the civil rights movement, more than twenty-five black nationalist organizations were said to have existed (Brisbane 1974). Most of these were located in Harlem, the hub of Garveyism. The Black Muslim organization also came out of this period but was distinct in its religious doctrine. So, out of a tradition that has been called "emigrationist" black nationalism there came the new black nationalist movement.

At the center of this movement was the Black Muslim leader Malcolm X. Initially, Malcolm X's nationalist ideology was similar to that of the emigrationist or back-to-Africa movements. However, it later evolved into a black nationalist ideology focused on a separate nation in America and aligned with worldwide struggles against colonial oppression. As the ideologies of Malcolm X (1964) and Frantz Fanon (1968), a former colonial subject, were incorporated into the new black nationalist philosophies of young blacks, new black nationalist organizations emerged and took on more aggressive militant stances. Among these were the Revolutionary Action Movement (RAM), the Black Panthers and the Republic of New Africa (RNA). Prior to this, SNCC, through its increasingly militant stance, had distanced itself from the main black civil rights organizations—NAACP, Urban League, and CORE.

The riots became the main mechanism for the resocialization of blacks and the crystallization of the new nationalist ideology. The riots of the sixties were different from those of earlier periods which stemmed from conflict and competition associated with black migration and urbanization. In particular, the riots prior to the 1960s were "pure" race riots in the sense that whites indiscriminately attacked blacks under the guise of a white supremacy ideology (Marx 1970, p. 33). In the riots of the 1960s, blacks attacked specific targets including ghetto merchants and their property, and the police force and their property. The majority of blacks viewed the 1960s riots as a form of political protest directed at social oppression (Feagin and Hahn 1973, pp. 1–55). The riots of the sixties emerged during the civil rights movement and expressed the disappointment of blacks with a racist system that denied them equal rights and confined them to a bleak existence in politically oppressed and economically depressed ghettos. Thus, riots—from Birmingham in 1963 to Watts in 1965, to those in Detroit and Newark in 1967, to the hundreds which exploded following the King assassination—expressed the growing political dissatisfaction with the slow pace and the meager accomplishments of the nonviolent movement. Early nationalist traditions, worldwide struggles for liberation, new separatist movements, black student nationalistic activism, and urban violent protest all combined into a new ideological thrust for black protest politics.

As noted above, this "new" ideology was forged out of past and contemporary struggles of blacks on the campuses and in the streets. Gurin and Epps (1975), in their study of students on predominantly black campuses, found four factors pertaining to what they called political nationalism and two factors of cultural nationalism. The dimensions of political nationalism were self-determination, separatism, community control (of schools and economic development), and violence as strategy. One of the cultural factors focused on the Afro-American heritage and the other on African roots. These factors, for the most part, captured the themes expressed in the various separatist organizations and in what some have called "riot ideology." By the end of the protest period, most black Americans ascribed to this ideology in one form or another: from simple affirmation of their heritage through hairstyles and dress or support for community control and black capitalism to the promotion of separatism or violent revolution. We now turn to the mechanisms which fostered this resocialization.

Mechanisms For Resocialization

The riots themselves were catalytic agents in the resocialization of both rioters and blacks as a whole. While a very small proportion of blacks, most of them young and male, took part in the riots, a much larger proportion sympathized with the rioters and saw the riots as protest. Campbell and Schuman (1968) report that only 2 percent of the more than 3,000 blacks interviewed in fifteen major cities where riots occurred in the late sixties said that they had taken part in a riot. However, more than half, 54 percent, said that they sympathized with the rioters, and nearly three-fifths said that the riots were protests. As noted earlier, Sears and McConahay (1970), Paige (1968), and others saw black youth as being particularly susceptible to resocialization in this setting. In addition to riots, other mechanisms for the resocialization of black youth included student-power movements on black campuses, black studies programs, and black student unions (Exum 1985). Almost all blacks were exposed to some mechanism for resocialization to black political and cultural nationalism during this period. Here we briefly describe two key mechanisms which had the most potential for resocializing a large proportion of the black masses.

The Media. The latter part of the 1960s evidenced a marked increase in the number of black people and black issues—political and cultural—in the print and electronic media. New black newspapers, journals, and magazines joined the ranks of those already in existence, some dating back to the abolitionist period (Brisbane 1974). In addition, the mainstream or majority media, urged on by the Kerner Commission Report, increased the presence of black issues and concerns in their programming as well as the number of black journalists and actors. This new presence of blacks in mainstream media aimed to counteract past stereotypic and negative images of black people and black life. Also, in this period, the black media, some of which had concentrated on other issues in the past, began to concentrate on black political issues and new images of black identity and culture.

Cultural Events and Projects. The visual, literary, and performing arts in black communities also began to focus on the new images of blacks and black life that stemmed from black-power ideology. Private foundations and state and municipal governments supported the development of black dance and theater groups in many communities. Poetry readings, African dance performances, and black theater in this period went beyond mere artistic expression to presentations that were labeled agitation-propaganda.

Although the proportion of blacks espousing black nationalism in its more extreme separatist and revolutionary form was never large, the mechanisms for resocialization we have discussed can be said to have touched the lives of most blacks and changed the way they viewed themselves and the world.

Thus far, we have discussed the structural conditions which gave rise to the modern civil rights movement in the South and described the mechanisms by which the movement socialized individuals for their participation in not only the protest politics of the period but in the political system as a whole. In addition, we described how the environmental responses (violence and the intransigence of racism) to the nonviolent movement, with its emphases on both litigation and direct action, issued a change in both direction and strategy in the movement. The aim of this chapter was to examine evidence addressing the political socialization impact of this period of protest politics. We have stressed throughout that the civil rights movement and the black-power movement were not drastic breaks in patterns of political thinking and behavior among blacks but rather that they flowed from a long tradition of protest politics. What distinguished this era from earlier periods was the extent of the mobilization of the masses, its ultimate impact on the broader society, and its lasting effects on those individuals who experienced that era. And it is to the latter that we now turn.

The Political Resocialization of Black Americans

On a group level, the impact of the black political movement of the 1960s was manifested in a great mobilization of black Americans into a political force with which the traditional political system had to reckon. The foundation of this collective political expression was made up of the political and racial attitudes of individuals which coalesced into what some called a new black consciousness. Within our structural/interactive approach, we have explored the process whereby a group's history, and the organizational and psychological resources associated with the group's structural position, lead to a nontraditional approach to the political process. Up to this point, we have examined indicators of this process largely at a micro-level. By describing changes in racial and political attitudes among blacks in the sixties and early seventies, we examine the process on a micro-level. We first discuss the methodological issues involved in an assessment of the impact on individuals, and then review the trends in racial and political attitudes over this period, and discuss how these attitudes differed within various sub-groups of the black population. Finally, we will discuss the implications of these findings for a generational or cohort impact of the protest era on black political socialization.

Methodological Issues

Age differences found in cross-sectional studies often confuse cohort and life-cyle effects (Cutler 1977). Glenn (1977) defines age, cohort, and period effects as those produced by influences associated with, respectively, aging or life-cycle, those produced by influences associated with birth-cohort membership, and those produced by influences associated with a given point in time. These effects are so interrelated that few believe their distinct contributions can be estimated. However, a growing body of research addresses these methodological issues and suggests techniques for unraveling these effects (Rodgers et al. 1980; Mason and Feinberg, 1985; Delli Carpini, chap. 1 in this volume). Here, with these issues in mind, we discuss the changes in racial and political attitudes during and after the protest period of the sixties.

Trends in Black Political and Racial Attitudes

In view of the special character of political life among blacks owing to a history of racism and participation in protest politics, most distinctions between racial and political attitudes are essentially arbitrary. Nevertheless, for purposes of discussion, we separate such attitudes into two groups. We designate as racial attitudes those dealing explicitly with racial issues and that can be said to be part of black group consciousness or racial political ideology. Political attitudes are those that do not explicitly address racial issues or domains but address general political concerns.

One of the problems in assessing the impact of the protest era on black attitudes is the virtual lack of baseline data. The black political movement of the 1960s affected not only black Americans but the social science community as well. Most of the studies of black racial and political attitudes come out of this period. Another problem is the lack of systematic study of attitude change in the black population. With the exception of Schuman and Hatchett (1974), Farley, Hatchett, and Schuman (1979), and Schuman, Steeh, and Bobo (1985), nothing comparable to the numerous systematic studies of racial attitudes among whites exists for blacks.

Racial Attitudes and Perceptions. We can discern three different periods characterized by the research findings on black racial attitudes—during the civil rights movement (1963–65), during the riots and the black-power movement (1965–75), and afterwards (1976–present). The first period was characterized by large-scale perceptions of discrimination, support for governmental intervention in dismantling segregation, support for the use of laws and persuasion and nonviolent protest, strong collective orientations, and interest in black issues (Brink and Harris 1963, 1967; Marx 1967; Schuman, Steeh, and Bobo 1985). While showing continuing high levels of perceptions of discrimination, support for governmental intervention and group solidarity, the next period evidenced an increasing association of antiwhite sentiment with militancy, and increases in discontent with white officials and institutions generally, not just those associated with the system of segregation. In addition, in this period, increased support was found for the use of violence if other strategies failed, and support for black power or black self-determination and black pride in African and Afro-American heritage (Campbell and Schuman, 1968; Schuman and Hatchett, 1974).

The changes found between these two periods can be described as a shift from conventional or "reformist" militancy (Marx 1967) to a more "revolutionary" militancy involving changes in the group's perception of itself and the wider society, an emphasis on self-determination and more aggressive strategies (i.e., violence) for redressing grievances (Carmichael and Hamilton 1967; Caplan 1970; Tomlinson 1970). Three aspects which particularly distinguished the second period from the first—antiwhite sentiment, support for violence as a principal strategy, and support for separatism—were never prevalent among the general black population.

While the protest era fostered many studies of black attitudes, its decrease in intensity was accompanied by a sharp decrease in such studies. There are few systematic studies which examine changes between what we are calling periods two and three. One study by Farley, Hatchett, and Schuman (1979) shows a reversal in what was felt to be a trend towards increasing disaffection with white society. Although their study focused only on blacks in Detroit, early findings on differences in racial attitudes among blacks in fifteen cities (Schuman and Hatchett 1974), indicated that black Detroiters were on the whole less disaffected than blacks in other cities. Hence, their results can be conservatively generalized to the country as a whole. In sum, they found that while there were increases in disaffection with white society and black consciousness between 1968 and 1970, in 1976 the level of discontent with white society had returned to 1968 levels while levels of black consciousness as indicated by support for emphasizing black cultural heritage increased significantly over the eight-year period.

Several observations conditioned this general impression of reversal in disaffection with white society. First, while the level of disaffection with white society and perceptions of no progress in eliminating discrimination returned to 1968 levels, these levels were still high. Also, one item which best summarizes changes in blacks' perceptions of white attitudes toward blacks evidenced a shift rather than a reversal. That item asked whether blacks thought whites wanted to "give them a better break, keep them down, or don't care." The modal response on this item changed from "better break" in 1968 to "keep down" in 1970 to "don't care" in 1976. Changes in another measure similarly captured the shift in the thrust of the movement. The modal response on an item asking what was the "best means" for redressing grievances of blacks went from "laws and persuasion" in 1967 (Detroit data from the study of fifteen American cities contracted by National Advisory Commission on Civil Disorders) to "non-violent protest" in 1968 (Detroit-area study conducted right after assassination of Martin Luther King, Jr.). In 1971, this item evidenced a rise in "violence" responses. Although only a minority still supported violence as a primary strategy at this time, a large increase occurred from 1968 to 1971 in those supporting violence "if all else fails." So by 1971 more than half of the blacks in these Detroit studies supported violence as either a primary or secondary means of gaining their rights. In 1976, the majority of blacks again supported either litigation or direct nonviolent action. Over this eight-year period, there was a gradual increase in support for traditional politics, indicated by the "laws and persuasion" response, such that in 1976 this was the modal response. Hence, blacks went from optimistic perceptions of responses from white society to their protest actions to perceptions of a repressive stance toward blacks. And finally, in the post-protest era, blacks came to feel whites were simply apathetic to their concerns. Also, over that period, the perceived need for disorderly politics rose and then declined in the aftermath of the protest period.

Political Attitudes and Perceptions. As one would expect, the 1960s witnessed changes in political perceptions and attitudes parallel to those found for more explicitly racial views. Studies conducted early in this period found lower levels of political efficacy among blacks when compared to whites, but similar levels of trust in government. By the end of the 1960s, both political efficacy and trust had eroded among blacks (Miller et al. 1980). Thus, a collective protest ideology characterized by disaffection with the majority society, and support for self-determination, black pride, and solidarity came together in the process of the struggle to gain equal rights.

Youth as Vanguard of the Ideological Shift. Young blacks, both those on campuses and in black communities, played an important role in both the civil rights movement and the black-power movement. They were particularly central in the shaping of the ideology and focus of the latter movement. In their study of black students, Gurin and Epps (1975) reported attitudinal changes among college students from 1964 to 1968 and from 1968 to 1970 which paralleled to a great extent those found for the general population. What most distinguished these students from the general population was the greatly higher levels of activism and support for black cultural and political nationalism. The urban riots beginning with Watts in 1965 were dramatic evidence of the shift from reformist to more militant ideology and tactics. Those active in these uprisings were primarily young, politically aware, and had high levels of disaffection, and, like the students, had higher levels of support for black cultural and political nationalism (*Report of the National Advisory Commission on Civil Disorders* 1968; Caplan 1970). In essence, the militant thrust of the black political movement of the sixties was shaped, in a large part, by an interaction of the protest dynamics of the campus with those of the streets.

Of the demographic factors which have distinguished levels of militancy and ideological stances—both reformist and "revolutionary"—among blacks, age has been the most important. Findings for education and income have been less clear and consistent. Some studies have found no education effect, while others have found positive or curvilinear relationships. The findings for income are similarly mixed, from no relationship to negative relationships (Schuman and Hatchett 1974). Therefore, a generational or cohort approach is central to any assessment of the impact of the black political movement of this period on black political socialization.

Age, Period, or Cohort

A number of studies have examined the political socialization impact of the protest era of the 1960s (e.g., Flacks 1970; Barnes and Kaase, 1979; Delli Carpini, chapter 1, in this volume). For the most part, these studies have focused on whites, and on the student and antiwar protest movements of this era. The evidence for generational effects along the line of cohort effects is mixed. While some studies have found little evidence of such effects, other more recent studies designed to tap these effects suggest that, while these effects exist, they may be conditioned by several factors. General cohort effects were found to be "overshadowed" by effects of having been actively involved in this protest era versus only having vicariously experienced it, and by predisposing outlooks rooted in family background (Jennings and Niemi 1981; Roberts and Lang 1985). Therefore, these findings reflect the Mannheimian conceptualization of cohorts as generation units: "those groups within the same actual generation which work up the materials of their common experiences in different specific ways" (Mannheim 1972, pp. 119–20). To what extent are these findings true for blacks?

Although blacks were in the Jennings and Niemi study, the numbers were too small for any examination of the separate impact of the civil-rights and black-power movements. Gurin and Epps's study of black students and other studies of black activists (Matthews and Prothro 1966; Orbell 1967; Orum and Orum 1968; Searles and Williams 1962), however, shed light on the generational or cohort impact of the black-protest movement on black students and the extent to which this impact was similar to that found for white students. Most of these studies suggest that, early in the movement, student activists were more likely to come from high socioeconomic backgrounds than nonactivists and were more likely to be on urban campuses. While finding little evidence of SES differences in family backgrounds, Gurin and Epps found that what distinguished activists and nonactivists most was whether students were from rural or urban areas. They suggest that rural and urban differences in recruitment to activism had more to do with opportunity to participate than greater conservatism among students with rural backgrounds.

Overall, the heterogeneity of students increased as the focus of activism shifted from the civil rights movement to the black-power and student-power movements. Gurin and Epps conclude from their analyses of background correlates of all three types of activism that family SES and urbanicity were important only for the civil rights movement. Also, as noted in Mankoff and Flacks (1972), Jennings and Niemi (1981), and Roberts and Lang (1985), heterogeneity in background increased among white students over the protest period. All in all, however, it seems reasonable to conclude that the generational effect of the black-protest movement on black political socialization was not conditioned by the same predisposing factors noted for whites. Rather, because of their common experience of racial oppression, most black youths, regardless of their background, were predisposed to protest ideology and activism. What remains to be assessed is the extent to which blacks as a whole were affected by this period of black political protest.

In exploratory analyses using data from Detroit-area studies conducted in 1968, 1970, and 1976, Hatchett (1982) examined the relative impact of age, period, and cohort on the racial attitudes of blacks in Detroit. Her findings suggest that period, operationalized as year of study, explained more of the variance in blacks' disaffection with white society than any other variable. The next important variable was age. In an attempt to distinguish cohort from life-cycle influences, age was recoded into four cohorts defined by period of racial and political socialization—cohorts for those who reached the age of sixteen before 1957; those who came of age during the major protest era (1957–68); those who came of age in the immediate post-protest period (1969–71); and those who came of age in the early seventies.

The results presented in cohort tables for each study year (with each successive year showing new cohorts), suggested strong period and cohort effects among blacks. Regardless of age, disaffection from white society increased from 1968 to 1971 and went back to 1968 levels in 1976. Following each cohort across the study years revealed that blacks who came of age before the major protest era were less disaffected than those who grew up in the heat of the sixties. And although they were more disaffected than the oldest cohort, the youngest cohort (entering in 1976), came of age in the post-protest era, was less disaffected than the children of the sixties.

While these analyses did not attempt to assess the impact of life-cycle position, age has been suggested in numerous studies as a factor predisposing people to the acceptance of new ideas and behaviors. As noted above, it was the single most important correlate of both reformist and "revolutionary" ideology. Urban residence has also been suggested as an important predisposing factor (Gurin and Epps 1975; Caplan 1970). More systematic research needs to be done in this area, in particular in regards to background and other differences that may have conditioned the impact of the protest era on black Americans.

From our macro-and micro-analyses, it is clear that the black protest period of the sixties had a profound effect on the political consciousness and behavior of black Americans. Although continuing in a long protest tradition, blacks experiencing the political movements of the sixties, because of changes in structural conditions and resources, were mobilized to such an extent that they were able to effect certain basic changes in American society that were only the substance of dreams for their forebears. During this period they also rediscovered their unique African and Afro-American heritage, thus beginning a phase of black ethnic group politics. What is different now is that the protest of the 1960s made it possible for blacks to engage in traditional politics on a scale unattainable during earlier periods. Given that protest politics also continue, contemporary black politics now embrace both the orderly and the disorderly sides of the political process.

Conclusions

The goal of this chapter was to investigate the role that political socialization played in the origins and outcomes of the modern civil rights movement. This investigation unfolded within the context of a dialogue with the existing literature on political socialization, especially as it relates to the black population. In our conclusions, we tease out some of the implications we feel our chapter has for political socialization research.

Our analysis suggests that it is very important to link the process of political socialization with a group's history and structural location. Political socialization is not a process with a beginning or end but one occurring within and shaped by a historical context. Thus, black political socialization has been shaped by the overarching relations that have existed historically between blacks and whites in the United States. A crucial feature of these relations has been a dominant/subordinate situation whereby blacks have found themselves at the bottom of the social order. This unenviable structural location has greatly shaped how blacks view the political order and how those views have been transmitted across generations. At the same time, the character and level of political consciousness and political behavior vary according to the organizational and psychological resources available to a given group. It is clear from our analyses that political socialization research needs to examine more closely the relationship between the organizational and psychological resources of groups and their structural position.

This particular history and structural location have led blacks to pursue the politics of protest in some form or another since they found themselves involuntarily on American shores. Taking this reality into account, we have argued that political socialization research must broaden its focus to include both the orderly and disorderly sides of the political process. Indeed, the failure to view the entire spectrum of the political process leads to the exclusion of a whole set of socializing agents—church, protest organizations, and the press—important in any analysis of black political life. Moreover, the political behavior that follows from such socialization will either fall outside the analytical net or be incorrectly viewed as sporadic or aberrant action fueled by a consciousness disconnected from history and social structure. Thus, future research on political socialization will be enriched if it encompasses both the orderly and disorderly sides of the political process.

Our analysis is consistent with other research which maintains that socialization is a fluid, open-ended process. To be sure, political consciousness is shaped by situational and contextual variables. Throughout, we have attempted to show how the civil rights movement itself generated mechanisms and situations which socialized blacks and affected their political behavior. We also know that this ground-breaking movement played an important role in resocializing other groups—white students, women, migrant farm-workers, Hispanic Americans, native Americans—to the politics of protest. We need to know more about how this cross-fertilization process operates. This is ripe territory for future work on political socialization.

Finally, political socialization research needs to examine the current political attitudes and behaviors of the black community. Crucial questions remain that need to be answered. For example, given the gains of the civil rights and black-power movements, is it likely that blacks will continue to pursue the politics of protest or will they embrace institutional politics? On the other hand, to what extent can contemporary black electoral behavior still be usefully conceptualized as protest politics? Then too, from a political standpoint, what are we to conclude about the political orientation of the huge underclass within most major cities? Wilson (1981) argues that these blacks have not benefited from the political movement of the sixties to the same extent as the black middle-class. Their situation is desperate, and rising conservatism in governmental circles portends measures that will only increase their misery. Will members of this class, like their counterparts in the sixties, choose riots as a viable strategy for social change or will they follow innovative electoral politics like those of Jesse Jackson and his Rainbow Coalition? We believe these kinds of issues can be illuminated by political socialization research if it broadens its conceptual focus while treating history and social structure as important variables.

References

Abramson, Paul R. 1977. *The Political Socialization of Black Americans: A Critical Evaluation of Research on Efficacy and Trust.* New York: The Free Press.

Adams, Frank, 1975. *Unearthing Seeds Of Fire: The Idea of Highlander.* Winston-Salem, N. C.: John Blair.

Aptheker, Herbert. 1943. *American Negro Slave Revolts.* New York: International Publishers.

Banks, Melvin J. 1962. "The Pursuit Of Equality: The Movement For First-Class Citizenship among Negroes in Texas, 1920–1950." Ph.D. dissertation, Syracuse University.

Barnes, Samuel H., and Max Kaase. 1979. *Political Action: Mass Participation in Five Western Democracies.* Beverly Hills: Sage Publications.

Brink, W., and L. Harris. 1963. *The Negro Revolution in America.* New York: Clarion.

———. 1967. *Black and White.* New York: Simon and Schuster.

Brisbane, Robert H. 1974. *Black Activism: Racial Revolution In The United States, 1954–1970.* Valley Forge, Pa: Judson Press.

Campbell, Angus, Philip Converse, Warren E. Miller, Donald Stokes. 1966. *Elections and the Political Order.* New York: Wiley.

Campbell, Angus, and Howard Schuman. 1968. *Racial Attitudes in Fifteen American Cities.* Ann Arbor: Institute for Social Research.

Caplan, Nathan. 1970. "The New Ghetto Man: A Review of Recent Empirical Studies." *Social Issues* 26 (1): 59–73.

Carmichael, Stokely, and Charles V. Hamilton. 1967. *Black Power.* New York: Random House.

Carson, Clayborne. 1981. *In Struggle: SNCC and the Black Awakening of the 1960's.* Cambridge: Harvard University Press.

Clark, Septima P., and LeGette Blythe. 1962. *Echo in My Soul.* New York: E. P. Dutton.

Clarke, Jacquelyne J. 1962. *These Rights They Seek: A Comparison of the Goals and Techniques of Local Civil Rights Organizations.* Washington, D.C.: Public Affairs Press.

Cotton, Dorothy. 1978. Interview. November 13. Atlanta, Ga.

Cox, Oliver Cromwell. 1959. *Caste, Class, and Race.* New York: Monthly Review Press.

Cutler, Neal E. 1977. "Political Socialization as Generational Analysis: The Cohort Approach Versus the Lineage Approach." In Stanley A. Renshon, ed., *Handbook of Political Socialization: Theory and Research.* New York: The Free Press.

Danigelis, Nicholas L. 1977. "A Theory of Black Political Participation in the United States." *Social Forces* 56: 31–47.

———. 1982. "Race, Class, and Political Involvement In The U.S." *Social Forces* 61: 532–50.

Davis, Angela Y. 1983. *Women, Race and Class.* New York: Random House.

Drake, St. Clair, and Horace Cayton. 1954. *Black Metropolis.* New York: Harcourt Brace.

DuBois, W. E. B. 1899. *The Philadelphia Negro: A Social Study.* Philadelphia: University of Pennsylvania Press.

———. 1903. *The Souls of Black Folk.* Chicago: McClurg.

Exum, William H. 1985. *Paradoxes of Protest: Black Student Activism in a White University.* Philadelphia: Temple University Press.

Fanon. Frantz. 1968. *The Wretched of the Earth.* New York: Grove Press.

Farley, Reynolds 1984. *Blacks and Whites: Narrowing the Gap?* Cambridge: Harvard University Press.

Farley, Reynolds, Shirley Hatchett, and Howard Schuman. 1979. "A Note on Changes In Black Racial Attitudes in Detroit: 1968-1976." *Social Indicators Research* 6: 439–43.

Feagin, Joe R., and Harlan Hahn. 1973. *Ghetto Revolts.* New York: Macmillan.

Flacks, Richard 1970. "The Revolt Of The Advantaged: Explorations of the Roots Of Student Protest." In Roberta S. Sigel, ed., *Learning about Politics: A Reader in Political Socialization.* New York: Random House.

Frazier, E. Franklin. 1949. *The Negro in the United States.* New York: Macmillan.

Gamson, William. 1975. *The Strategy of Social Protest.* Homewood, Ill.: Dorsey Press.

Garfinkel, Herbert. 1959. *When Negroes March.* Glencoe, Ill.: The Free Press.

Giddings, Paula. 1984. *When and Where I Enter. The Impact of Black Women on Race and Sex in America.* New York: William Morrow.

Glenn, N. 1977. "Cohort Analysis." In *Quantitative Applications in the Social Sciences,* Sage University Paper Series. Beverly Hills: Sage Publications.

Greenberg, Edward S. 1970. "Black Children and the Political System." *Political Opinion Quarterly* 34: 333–45.

Gurin, Patricia, and Edgar Epps. 1975. *Black Consciousness, Identity, and Achievement.* New York: Wiley.

Gurin, Patricia, Gerald Gurin, Rosina C. Lao, and Muriel Beattie. 1969. "Internal-External Control in the Motivational Dynamics of Negro Youth." *Journal of Social Issues* 25: 29–54.

Hatchett, Shirley J. 1982. "Black Racial Attitude Change in Detroit: 1968–1976." Ph.D. dissertation, University of Michigan.

Holt, Len. 1965. *The Summer That Didn't End.* New York: William Morrow.

Jackson, James S., and Shirley J. Hatchett. 1986. "Intergenerational Research: Methodological Considerations." In N. Datan, A. L. Greene and H. W. Reese, eds., *Intergenerational Relations.* Hillsdale, N. J.: Earlbaum Associates.

Jennings, M. Kent, and Richard E. Niemi. 1974. *The Political Character of Adolescence.* Princeton: Princeton University Press.

———. 1981. *Generations and Politics: A Panel Study of Young Adults and Their Parents.* 2d ed. Princeton: Princeton University Press.

Johnson, Charles S. 1934. *Shadow of the Plantation.* Chicago: The University of Chicago Press.

Katznelson, Ira. 1976. *Black Men, White Cities: Race Politics and Immigration in the United States, 1900–1930, and Britain, 1948–1968.* Chicago: University of Chicago Press.

King, Martin Luther, Jr. 1958. *Stride Toward Freedom.* New York: Harper and Row.

———. 1963. *Why We Can't Wait.* New York: New American Library.

Lane, Robert. 1959. *Political Life: Why People Get Involved in Politics.* New York: The Free Press.

Lansford, H. E. 1968. "Isolation, Powerlessness and Violence: A Study of Attitudes and Participation in the Watts Riot." *American Journal of Sociology* 73, 581–91.

Lawson, James. 1978. Interview. October 2 and 6. Los Angeles.

Malcolm X., and Alex Haley. 1964. *The Autobiography of Malcolm X.* New York: Grove Press.

Mankoff, Milton, and Richard Flacks. 1972. "The Changing Social Base of the American Student Movement." In Philip G. Altbach and Robert S. Laufer, eds., *The New Pilgrims: Youth Protest in Transition.* New York: David McKay.

Mannheim, Karl. 1972. "The Problem of Generations." In Philip G. Altbach and Robert S. Laufer, eds., *The New Pilgrims.* New York: David McKay.

Marx, Gary T. 1967. *Protest and Prejudice: A Study of Belief in the Black Community.* New York: Harper and Row.

———. 1970. "Civil Disorder and the Agents of Social Control." *Journal of Social Issues* 26: 19–57.

Mason, William, and Stephen Feinberg. 1985. *Cohort Analysis in Social Research: Beyond the Identification Problem.* New York: Springer-Verlag.

Matthews, Donald R., and James W. Prothro. 1966. *Negroes and the New Southern Politics.* New York: Harcourt Brace.

Mays, Benjamin. 1978. Interview. September 20. Atlanta.

McAdam, Doug. 1982. *Political Process and the Development of Black Insurgency, 1930–1970.* Chicago: University of Chicago Press.

Meier, August, and Elliot Rudwick. 1976. *Along the Color Line.* Urbana: University of Illinois Press.

Miller, Arthur H., Patricia Gurin, Gerald Gurin, and Oksana Malanchuk. 1981. "Group Consciousness and Political Participation." *American Journal of Political Science* 25: 494-511.

Miller, Warren E., Arthur H. Miller, and Edward J. Schneider. 1980. *American National Election Studies Data Source Book, 1952–1978.* Cambridge: Harvard University Press.

Mills, C. Wright. 1959. *The Sociological Imagination.* New York: Oxford University Press.

Morris, Aldon D. 1981. "Black Southern Student Sit-In Movement: An Analysis of Internal Organization." *American Sociological Review* 46: 746–67.

————. 1984. *The Origins of the Civil Rights Movement: Black Communities Organizing for Change.* New York: The Free Press.

Morris, Milton. 1975. *The Politics of Black America.* New York: Harper and Row.

Moses, Wilson J. 1978. *The Golden Age of Black Nationalism, 1850–1925.* Hamden, Conn.: Archon Books.

Murphy, R. J., and J. M. Watson. 1970. "The Structure of Discontent: The Relationship between Social Structure, Grievance and Support for the Los Angeles Riots." In N. E. Cohen, ed., *The Los Angeles Riots: A Socio-Psychological Study.* New York: Praeger.

Murray, Richard, and Arnold Vedlitz. 1978. "Racial Voting Patterns in the South: An Analysis of Mayoral Elections, 1960–1977, in Five Cities." In John Howard and Robert C. Smith, eds., *The Annals* 439: 29–40.

Myrdal, Gunnar. 1944. *An American Dilemma: the Negro Problem and Modern Democracy.* New York: Harper and Row.

Orbell, John W. 1967. "Protest Participation among Southern Negro College Students." *American Political Science Review* 61: 446–56.

Orum, Anthony W., and Amy W. Orum. 1968. "The Class and Status Bases of Negro Student Protest." *Social Science Quarterly* 49: 521–33.

Orum, Anthony, and Roberta S. Cohen. 1973. "The Development of Political Orientations among Black and White Children." *American Sociological Review* 38: 62–74.

Paige, Jeffery. 1968. "Collective Violence and the Culture of Subordination." Ph.D. dissertation, University of Michigan.

Pitts, James P. 1975. "The Study of Race Consciousness: Comments on New Directions." *American Journal of Sociology* 80: 660–68.

Piven, Frances, and Richard A. Cloward. 1979. *Poor People's Movement: How They Succeed, Why Some Fail.* New York: Vintage.

Renshon, Stanley A., ed. 1977. *Handbook of Political Socialization: Theory and Research.* New York: The Free Press.

Report of the National Advisory Commission on Civil Disorders. 1968. U.S. Riot Commission Report. New York: Bantam Books.

Roberts, Carl W., and Kurt Lang. 1985. "Generations and Ideological Change." *Public Opinion Quarterly* 49:460–73.

Rodgers, Willard, A. Regula Herzog, and John Woodworth. 1980. "Extensions of Procedures for the Analysis of Age, Period, and Cohort Effects." Ann Arbor: Institute for Social Research Working Paper Series.

Schuman, Howard, and Shirley J. Hatchett. 1974. *Black Racial Attitudes: Trends and Complexities*. Ann Arbor: Institute for Social Research.

Schuman, Howard, Charlotte Steeh, and Lawrence Bobo. 1985. *Racial Attitudes in America*. Cambridge: Harvard University Press.

Searles, Ruth, and J. Allen Williams, Jr. 1962. "Negro College Students' Participation in Sit-Ins." *Social Forces* 40: 215–20.

Sears, David O. 1975. "Political Socialization." In Fred I. Greenstein and Nelson W. Polsby, eds., *Handbook of Political Science, Micropolitical Theory*. Vol. 2. Reading, Mass: Addison-Wesley.

Sears, David O. and John B. McConahay. 1970. "Racial Socialization, Comparison, Levels, and The Watts Riot." *Journal of Social Issues* 26: 121–40.

———. 1973. *The Politics of Violence*. Boston: Houghton Mifflin.

Sigel, Roberta S. 1968. "Image of a President: Some Insights into the Political Views of School Children." *American Political Science Review*. 62: 216–26.

———. 1970. *Learning about Politics*. New York: Random House.

Sigel, Roberta S., and Marilyn B. Hoskin. 1977. "Perspectives on Adult Political Socialization—Areas of Research." In Stanley A. Renshon, Ed., *Handbook of Political Socialization: Theory and Research*. New York: The Free Press.

Simpkins, C. O. 1978. Interview. October 25. Merrick, N.Y.

Thornton, J. Mills III. 1979–80. "Challenges and Responses in the Montgomery Bus Boycott of 1955–1956." *Alabama Review: A Quarterly Journal of Alabama History* 32–33: 163–235.

Tilly, Charles. 1978. *From Mobilization to Revolution*. Reading, Mass.: Addison-Wesley.

Tomlinson, T. M. 1970. "Ideological Foundations for Negro Action: A Comparative Analysis of Militant and Non-militant Views of the Los Angeles Riot." *Journal of Social Issues* 26: 93–120.

Verba, Sidney, and Norman Nie. 1972, *Participation in America*. New York: Harper and Row.

Walton, Hanes, Jr. 1972a. *Black Political Parties*. New York: The Free Press.

———. 1972b. *Black Politics: A Theoretical and Structural Analysis*. New York: J. R. Lippincott.

———. 1985. *Invisible Politics: Black Political Behavior*. New York: Suny Press.

Weisbrot, Robert. 1983. *Father Divine: The Utopian Evangelist of the Depression Era Who Became an American Legend*. Boston: Beacon Press.

Whalen, Charles, and Barbara Whalen. 1985. *The Longest Debate*. Cabin John, Md.: Seven Locks Press.

Wilson, William J. 1981. *The Declining Significance of Race*. Chicago: University of Chicago Press.

Yeakey, Lamont H. 1979. "The Montgomery, Alabama, Bus Boycott." Ph.D. dissertation, Columbia University.

Zald, Mayer N., and John D. McCarthy. 1979. *The Dynamics of Social Movements*. Cambridge, Mass.: Winthrop Publishers.

Zinn, Howard. 1964. *SNCC: The New Abolitionists*. Boston: Beacon Press.

Eight

Gender Politics and the Socializing Impact of the Women's Movement

SUSAN J. CARROLL

The impact of the contemporary women's movement on political socialization in Western societies must be analyzed and understood within the broader context of the existing system of gender relations that characterizes those societies. Gayle Rubin has observed that every society has a "sex/gender system," defined as "a set of arrangements by which the biological raw material of human sex and procreation is shaped by human, social intervention and satisfied in a conventional manner" (1975, p. 165). Hypothetically, sex/gender systems could take different forms, but all Western societies are patriarchies in which men dominate women (Eisenstein 1981).

Although recent scholarship has emphasized that both the structure of gender relations and the analytic utility of the distinction between public and private depend on the historical and cultural context (Nicholson 1983; Rosaldo 1980), the division of life into private and public realms with the sexual assignment of women to the former and men to the latter is a pervasive characteristic of sex/gender systems in Western societies. According to Alison Jaggar, "the private realm has always included sexuality and procreation, has always been viewed as more 'natural' and therefore less 'human' than the public realm, and has always been viewed as the realm of women" (1983, pp. 127–28). Similarly, since the days of Aristotle, the public realm has included government and political activity and has been viewed primarily as the realm of men (Elshtain 1974).

The public/private division is reflected not only in the structure of the modern Western state, with its sharp demarcation between family and political life, but also in its ideology. Liberal theory, which developed concurrently with capitalism as the dominant political ideology of contemporary Western societies, posited a division between public and private as a logical and necessary distinction. Linda Nicholson has explained, "theorists associated with the liberal tradition assume that there are two different kinds of human needs best satisfied by two different kinds of institutions," state and family (1983,

p. 224). Most liberal theorists historically have also viewed the domination of the public sphere by men as natural and inevitable (Eisenstein 1981).

The process of socialization into gender roles has been critical to the continued domination of public life by men. John Stuart Mill, among others, emphasized the comprehensive nature of society's efforts to socialize women into subordinate public roles:

> The masters of women wanted more than simple obedience, and they turned the whole force of education to effect their purpose. All women are brought up from the very earliest years in the belief that their ideal of character is the very opposite to that of men; not self-will and government by self-control, but submission and yielding to the control of others. All the moralities tell them that it is the duty of women, and all the current sentimentalities that it is their nature, to live for others, to make complete abnegation of themselves, and to have no life but in their affections. (1980, p. 15).

This description of the socialization of women is quite inconsistent with the qualities that many liberal democratic theorists envisioned as desirable for effective citizenship. The ideal democratic citizen was to be rational, well-informed about public affairs, and self-interested in his or her behavior (Berelson, Lazarsfeld, and McPhee 1954, pp. 306–11). These are qualities far more consistent with the socialization of men than women.

The contemporary women's movement has posed a challenge to the well-entrenched system of patriarchal relations that characterizes Western societies and to the socialization processes that help to maintain this system. Like other social movements, the feminist movement has served as an agent of political socialization. It has done so both by contributing to material changes in women's lives and by providing them with an alternative framework for viewing the world. In part because of historical processes that preceded the contemporary women's movement and in part as a consequence of the movement, increasing numbers of women have in recent years pursued college educations, entered the paid labor force, lived apart from men, headed households, and/or become active in politics. As a result of these changes in women's lives, increasing numbers of women have experienced an incongruity between the demands and realities of their present lives and the expectations generated by their childhood socialization, which prepared them for an adulthood focused largely on private-sphere concerns and lived out in a state of economic dependence on men. The feminist movement has provided women engaging in nontraditional experiences with a framework for understanding the difficulties and discrimination they often face as they enter a more public existence. The changes in women's lives that have come about in part because of the women's movement, as well as the altered consciousness that many women have experienced because of the movement, have had important implications for women's political behavior.

This chapter examines the effect of the contemporary women's movement on political socialization in Western societies, focusing primarily on the United States. It begins with an overview of the political consequences of gender-based socialization as reflected in adult political behavior prior to the development of the contemporary feminist movement. Next, three major trends in women's political behavior evident since the emergence of the women's movement are reviewed. The chapter then explores the question of the extent to which, as well as the processes through which, resocialization brought about by the women's movement can be considered to be responsible for these trends. The chapter concludes with a review of issues needing further research and an assessment of the impact of the women's movement in resocializing political scientists.

Political Consequences of Socialization into a Patriarchal System of Gender Relations

The patriarchal nature of Western societies, the division between private and public life, and the association of women with the private realm have had important implications for women's political behavior. Empirical studies conducted prior to the advent of the contemporary women's movement showed the effects of women's marginal relationship to the public sphere and their socialization for, and frequent confinement to, a life focused largely on private-sphere concerns.

When judged against the behavior of men socialized for a life in which the concerns of public life were central, women were indeed found by political scientists to be inferior political beings. It is difficult to separate fact from fiction in much of the traditional political behavior literature because political scientists themselves judged women's behavior through a lens distorted by sex stereotyping. Their expectations about women's behavior affected the choice of questions they asked, the behaviors they examined, the interpretations they applied to data, and even the measures they used in their research (Bourque and Grossholtz 1974; Iglitzin 1974; Goot and Reid 1975). Nevertheless, several notable differences between women and men do seem to have existed prior to the development of the contemporary feminist movement.

Attitudes toward Women's Participation in Public Life

The political consequences of gender-based socialization have been most directly apparent in responses to survey questions examining attitudes toward women's involvement in politics. The views of both women and men have historically reflected the extent to which the public sphere was viewed as a domain reserved primarily for men. Hazel Erskine (1971) has comprehensively reviewed the results of questions about women's participation in public life drawn from public opinion polls conducted in the years between 1935 and 1970. While questions about women were asked irregularly and sporadically by pollsters, those that exist are sufficient to illustrate the prevalence of beliefs supporting a strong sexual division of labor.

Support for women in political roles remained low throughout the decades preceding the 1970s and was largely unaffected by war or other events. In 1936, only 36 percent of the American public believed that "we need more women in politics" and only 31 percent thought President Roosevelt should name another woman to his cabinet. By 1945, the proportion favoring the appointment of a woman to the cabinet had grown only to 38 percent (Erskine 1971, pp. 279–80). When the question was first asked in 1936, only 31 percent of the public said that they would vote for a qualified woman candidate for president. Although support grew gradually over the years, as late as 1969 only 54 percent of the public expressed support for the idea of a woman candidate for the nation's highest office (Erskine 1971, pp. 277–78).

Sex Differences in Mass Participation

Women have traditionally differed from men on fundamental political orientations that are regarded by political scientists as antecedents of political participation. First, women have expressed lower levels of political efficacy than men (Campbell et al. 1960, p. 490; Baxter and Lansing 1983, pp. 47–51). These differences have been most apparent on measures of internal efficacy (subjective competence) rather than on measures of external efficacy (government responsiveness) (Sapiro 1983, p. 99).

Differences between the sexes have also been evident historically on measures of political interest. Studies have repeatedly found women more likely than men to fail to give responses, or to give "don't know" responses, on various attitudinal items relating to politics (Smith 1984; Rapoport 1981, 1982). Women also have expressed less interest in politics generally and in following campaigns more specifically (Hansen, Franz, and Netemeyer-Mays 1976; Baxter and Lansing 1983; Sapiro 1983). In contrast to differences in political efficacy which seem to stem primarily from adult roles (Jennings and Niemi 1981), sex differences in political interest have clear childhood antecedents, and most researchers have attributed adult differences to anticipatory socialization that takes place in childhood (Sapiro 1983, pp. 88–91; Rapoport 1981; Orum et al. 1974).

As one might expect from the sex differences in these basic political orientations which are antecedents of participation, women traditionally have been less likely than men to participate in some forms of political activity examined by political scientists, although differences have been small and frequently overstated. Sex differences in voter turnout have perhaps been most significant. In the United States women voted at a much lower rate than men following passage and ratification of the Nineteenth Amendment. However, the gap between the sexes in voter turnout declined in the years after 1920, and by the early 1980s women were voting at a rate equal to that of men (U.S. Census 1983). In part, historic differences between American women and men can be explained by sex differences in education and age (Baxter and Lansing 1983; Wolfinger and Rosenstone 1980). Nevertheless, part of the explanation would also seem to lie with the fact that presuffrage generations of women were socialized to believe that voting was inappropriate for women (Wolfinger and Rosenstone 1980). Other Western societies seem to have followed the same pattern; postsuffrage differences in turnout have greatly diminished over time and are no longer significant (Lovenduski and Hills 1981, p. 323).

Sizeable sex differences have been apparent in at least one other self-reported form of behavior, persuading others how to vote. Ronald. B. Rapoport has argued that this difference has its origins in the greater reluctance of female than male children to express political attitudes (Rapoport 1981). Sex differences in several other forms of conventional political participation have been so small, at least since the advent of survey research, that they are almost negligible statistically. Although only small proportions (less than 15 percent) of either sex participate in these activities, women in the United States have been found to be as likely or only slightly less likely than men to work in campaigns, to write political letters, to attend political meetings, and to contribute money to a candidate or party (Baxter and Lansing 1983; Hansen, Franz, and Netemeyer-Mays 1976; Welch 1977). The fact that sex differences are small suggests that gender-based socialization is not a critical factor determining who engages in these forms of participation and who does not. Rather, social class seems a more important determinant.

Sex Differences in Candidacy and Officeholding

Candidacy for office and public officeholding are additional forms of political participation engaged in by proportionately few citizens—so few, in fact, that survey researchers do not even ask about them. In a general population survey, questions about these activities would yield too few cases for statistical analysis and almost certainly would show sex differences of only a tiny magnitude. Nevertheless, numerically many fewer women than men seek public office, and in the United States women constitute no more than 16 percent of the incumbents nationally at any level of government (Center for the American Woman and Politics 1987b). Campaigning for or holding public office allows far greater individual influence on politics and policy than do most other forms of participation. Consequently, questions about the relationship between gender-based socialization and the numbers of female candidates and officeholders are important, even if the proportions of women and men who seek or hold office are small.

There are many reasons for women's underrepresentation among public officeholders, including sex discrimination and structural impediments. Nevertheless, even those scholars who place the greatest emphasis on factors other than socialization generally acknowledge that gender-based socialization plays some role in explaining why few women seek or hold office (e.g., Carroll 1985; Welch 1978).

The demands of candidacy and officeholding are highly inconsistent with traditional female socialization. Lynne B. Iglitzin has noted, "as the socialization process proceeds girls are taught to accept *femininity*, a role equated with dependency, submissiveness, conformity, and passivity" (1974, p. 26). Seeking and holding public office requires quite a different set of characteristics. As Jeane J. Kirkpatrick observed in her landmark study of women legislators: "To campaign it is necessary to put oneself forward, to 'blow one's own horn,' to somehow demonstrate one's superiority and dominance. What can conventionally well-behaved ladies do in such an arena?" (1974, pp. 85–86). Characteristics such as nurturance, compassion, and sensitivity, which are often celebrated by feminists as female virtues, have not been especially valued in political leaders.

Studies of women who are politically active but have not sought public office have frequently pointed to women's own attitudes about appropriate roles for women, learned through socialization processes, as a factor that limits their political ambition (Lee 1977; Sapiro and Farah 1980). There is also considerable evidence that voters and party leaders have traditionally believed that women are unsuited for political leadership, although the proportions holding such beliefs have declined in recent years (Harris 1972, p. 15; Kirkpatrick 1976, pp. 462–70).

Finally, the effects of gender-role socialization in helping to account for the paucity of women candidates and officeholders is apparent in a set of findings focusing on family relationships. Research has found that women elective and appointive officeholders are less often married than their male counterparts and less likely to have young children. Among those officeholders who are married, women almost uniformly, and more often than men, report that their spouses are very supportive of their political activities (Carroll and Strimling 1983; Carroll and Geiger-Parker 1983, 1984; Stoper 1977). In part, these findings undoubtedly reflect the reality of the sexual division of labor; women's disproportionate responsibility for domestic work and childrearing may take it more difficult for women than men to take on the additional responsibilities of officeholding if there is a young child or an uncooperative spouse at home. However, these findings may also reflect the greater centrality that women, as a result of gender-based socialization, accord to private-sphere concerns. Virginia Sapiro, in a study of delegates to the 1972 national conventions, found that both women and men experience conflicts between domestic life and public commitments. However, she observed,

> women reduce conflict by avoiding taking on public commitments. Men, on the other hand, appear to increase conflict by committing themselves to officeseeking despite the demands and responsibilities of their family lives. . . . When conflict might arise, women appear to choose in favor of their families, men in favor of their political ambition. (1982, p. 274)

Just as the behavior of women activists reflects a strong sense of women's special responsibility for private-sphere concerns, so too do the attitudes of those who control women's access to positions of power. Women who seek positions of political leadership report that they are often questioned about, and criticized for, neglecting their domestic responsibilities (Mandel 1981; Lynn and Flora 1977).

Socialization into Gender Relations and the Nature of Women's Political Involvement

Socialization into gender relations has affected not only the extent of women's participation in politics but also the nature of their involvement. When women traditionally have participated in politics, their participation frequently has taken a form that would seem to be an extension of their domestic roles and/or has been rationalized in private-sphere terms. In the United States, the roots of this private-sphere justification for women's political involvement are found in what Linda K. Kerber has termed "Republican Motherhood," an ideology that developed during the early years of the American republic. Although women's participation in the postrevolutionary polis was extremely curtailed, women were allowed to serve a political role through educating their sons to be virtuous and public-spirited citizens. In this manner, some political knowledge and interest on the part of women was justified, but women's concerns remained clearly focused on private life. Kerber has observed, "From the time of the Revolution until our own day, the language of Republican Motherhood remains the most readily accepted . . . justification for women's political behavior" (1980, p. 12).

A number of findings from more contemporary studies examining women's political behavior also illustrate the relationship between the nature of women's political participation and traditional gender roles. Studies have found women to be more oriented than men toward local political issues, especially those pertaining to schools and education. Men, in contrast, show greater interest in national and international affairs (Jennings and Niemi 1981, pp. 276–77; Jennings 1979; Jaquette 1974, p. xxiii). This greater concern of women with politics closer to home has generally been explained as an extension of women's responsibilities within the family. Jennings's interpretation is illustrative: "the rearing of the young is still predominantly the prescriptive and descriptive province of mothers. Becoming involved in the politics of education serves as an extension of this primary role" (1979, p. 769).

In a similar vein, Kathleen McCourt, in a study of working-class women active in community organizations in Chicago in the early 1970s, found that women activists were most often motivated by issues such as changes in the racial composition of the neighborhoods and concern over the quality of neighborhood schools that were closely related to their domestic roles. McCourt observed: "the issues themselves do not far remove the women from traditional female concerns. Homes and children continue to be the objects of attention" (1977, p. 93). Moreover, despite their political involvement, these working-class women activists expressed very traditional views of gender roles and continually reaffirmed that their most important commitment was to home and family (McCourt 1977, pp. 133–58).

Even when women have ventured into forms of participation more removed from the concerns of home and family, the nature of, and reasons for, their involvement have often shown the effects of the sexual division of labor and the socialization into gender roles that helps to maintain this division. Women have a long history of activism in political parties, but they have generally been found in roles that support male leadership rather than in leadership roles themselves (Gruberg 1968; Costantini and Craik 1972). M. Kent Jennings and Norman Thomas, for example, found women delegates more active than their male counterparts in contacting voters and distributing literature and less active in making speeches and managing campaigns (1968, p. 481). Similarly, a common route into Congress and other high-level political offices for women historically has been to assume the seat of a deceased husband (Bullock and Heys 1972; Gertzog 1984). While almost half of the widows who took over their husbands' seats in Congress subsequently ran for election in their own right (Bullock and Heys 1972), their roles as wives serving in support of their husbands provided the initial justification for their political behavior.

In part, the gender-specific nature of women's involvement in conventional politics may reflect the effects of gender-based socialization on women's political aspirations and motivations for involvement. Edmond Costantini and Kenneth H. Craik, for example, argued that the reasons for becoming active in parties differed for women and men. While men saw their involvement as a "vehicle for personal enhancement and career advancement," women viewed their involvement as a "labor of love" through which they could serve others (1972, pp. 234–35). However, the frequency with which women have been confined to support roles in parties and to dependency on the widow's succession for gaining access to high-level office also suggests that gender-based socialization has affected the expectations of activist men. Men seem more readily to accept women's involvement in public life when women's participation is in service to men, just as much of women's work in the domestic realm traditionally has been in service to men.

Sex Differences in Perspectives

Historical sex differences in perspectives between women and men may also be a product of the sexual division of labor and the socialization into gender relations that helps to maintain it. Although on most issues women and men have traditionally expressed similar attitudes, differences have been apparent in a few issue-areas.

First, women have been more opposed than men to the use of force, and the largest sex differences in public opinion have occurred historically in this issue-area. The evidence for women's greater pacifism on issues of war and peace spans several wars and many years of survey research (Smith 1984; Baxter and Lansing 1983, 57–60; Pomper 1975; Gruberg 1968, pp. 13–15; Shapiro, Mahajan, and Veith 1984). However, women also have been more opposed than men to the use of force in domestic politics, as illustrated, for example, by their greater support for gun control and opposition to capital punishment (Smith 1984; Baxter and Lansing 1983, p. 59; Center for the American Woman and Politics 1987a; Shapiro, Mahajan, and Veith 1984).

Other notable differences between the sexes in political attitudes have been apparent historically. Women have exhibited what some have labeled greater "moralism" than men. They have, for example, shown greater support for prohibition, jail terms for drunk drivers, bans on cigarette advertisements, and school prayer. Women have been more likely than men to oppose legalized gambling, drug use, and prostitution (Shapiro, Mahajan, and Veith 1984; Jaquette 1974, p. xxiii; Center for the American Woman and Politics 1987a; Gruberg 1968, p. 13). Women's historical involvement in temperance movements both in the United States and in other countries is another manifestation of this traditional gender difference. Historically, many of the leading activists in reform causes have also been women, and there is evidence, although not always consistent, that women have traditionally been more supportive than men of social welfare measures (Baxter and Lansing 1983, p. 60; Shapiro, Mahajan, and Veith 1984).

In addition to these attitudinal differences between the sexes, women have historically been characterized as more conservative in their voting behavior and in their preferences among parties. In the United States, the evidence in support of this contention stems largely from the Eisenhower era, when women were found to have been slightly more likely than men to vote Republican and to identify with the Republican party (Campbell et al. 1960; Baxter and Lansing 1983, pp. 65–67). These differences probably occurred because women of higher social class and greater education entered the electorate more rapidly than did lower-class and less educated women (Baxter and Lansing 1983, pp. 66–67). Thus, in the United States, women's greater conservatism in the 1950s seems to have been largely an artifact of the expansion of suffrage. In other Western countries, women's greater conservatism cannot be so readily dismissed. While controls for occupation and education help to account for women's lesser support for parties on the left in some countries, for other countries evidence of women's greater conservatism persists despite the application of statistical controls. Joni Lovenduski and Jill Hills have argued that religion is a key factor in accounting for this difference among countries. Women's greater conservatism has been most evident in those countries (Italy, France, Spain, and West Germany) in which there is a strong, usually Roman Catholic, influence and a religious party that contests elections (1981, p. 324).

The various historical differences in perspectives between women and men do not reflect a consistent difference in political ideology between the sexes. In some respects, women can be considered historically to have been more "conservative" than men, but in other respects women's perspectives have been more "liberal." The logic that seems to underlie these traditional sex differences in perspective is not a logic based on liberal/conservative ideology, but rather one based on sex differences in objective life-circumstances and on the socialization of women and men to different roles. The objective circumstances of women's and men's lives have differed in ways that may well be related to the sex differences in perspectives discussed above. For example, women's more pacifist attitudes may stem in part from their marginal relationship to the military. Similarly, women's more marginal and vulnerable position in society may have led them to be more conservative than men in their voting choices and more opposed to social forces that might threaten the social fabric. Women's greater "moralism" also might well be due at least in part to the fact that women have often suffered from men's use and abuse of alcohol, drugs, gambling, and prostitution. Historical sex differences in perspectives would also seem in part to be a product of women's socialization into private roles. Through the process of socialization, women have learned a set of expectations that may help to shape their political attitudes and behavior. Sapiro has argued that both the pacifism and the greater moralism of women are a product of role expectations that women learn through socialization:

> As the traditional guardians of domestic tranquility and harmony
> . . . women are . . . supposed to be particularly concerned with
> peace issues. . . . In their capacity as traditional guardians of reli-
> gion and morality they are expected to bring these values to bear on
> their consideration of public issues. (1983, pp. 146–47)

Changes Since the Emergence of the
Contemporary Women's Movement

The origins of the contemporary women's movement in the United States are
usually traced to the founding of the National Organization for Women in
1966 and the independent formation of several small women's liberation
groups throughout the country in 1967 and 1968 (Freeman 1975). In the
period of time since the movement began, three major changes have been
apparent in the pattern of gender relations described thus far.

First, there has been a trend toward greater public acceptance of women's
involvement in political activities. The electorate, both female and male, has
come increasingly to view women as public, as well as private, persons.

The second trend is one of convergence between the sexes. In the basic
antecedents of participation and in rates of participation in conventional politics, women's political behavior has increasingly resembled the behavior of
men. Women have, in fact, become more active in the public sphere.

With greater integration of women into public life, a third trend has also
become evident. This trend is the increasing divergence of women and men
in their political perspectives. As women have become more politically active, their "private" values seem to be finding greater political expression.

Changes in Attitudes toward Women's Involvement in Public Life

Since the mid- to late-1960s, attitudes toward women's participation in public
life have changed dramatically. Change is apparent, for example, in attitudes
toward women working outside the home, in responses to the integration of
women into business and government, and in support for women who assume
political roles. Change in attitudes has been evident among adult cohorts as
well as among those who have reached adulthood in recent years. A few
examples will suffice to demonstrate the rapid change that has occurred.

The 1985 Virginia Slims American Women's Opinion Poll found a substantial increase from the mid-1970s to the mid-1980s in the proportion of
women who said they would prefer to have a job outside the home if they
were free to choose either to stay at home or to be employed for pay. In 1975
only 35 percent said they would choose to have a job outside the home while

51 percent chose this option in 1985. The proportion preferring to stay at home declined from 60 percent to 45 percent over the decade (Roper 1985).

Since 1972 the American National Election Studies conducted by the Institute for Social Research at the University of Michigan have included a question asking respondents to place themselves on a seven-point scale where one end was represented by the statement, "Women should have an equal role with men in running business, industry, and government." The other end of the scale was represented by the statement, "Women's place is in the home." In 1972, 48.9 percent of the public placed themselves at one of the three positions on the egalitarian end of the scale. By 1984 this proportion had grown to 59.6 percent.

A similar, but broader, question was included in the five Virginia Slims American Women's Opinion Polls conducted in the years between 1970 and 1975. In 1970 only 40 percent of women and 44 percent of men favored "most of the efforts to strengthen and change women's status in society today." By 1985 the proportions favoring such efforts had climbed to 73 percent of women and 69 percent of men (Roper 1985).

The item measuring willingness to vote for a woman candidate for president is another question that has been asked frequently by political pollsters since the advent of the contemporary women's movement. More than three-fourths of the American public now say that they would vote for a woman for their nation's highest political office, a significant increase from the late 1960s when just over one-half expressed support for a woman presidential candidate (Gallup 1985). Significant change began to occur in the very early 1970s. As Myra Marx Ferree has noted, there was a "lack of any significant decrease in prejudice (toward a woman presidential candidate) over time until 1972, when the drop was suddenly 13 percent (compared with 1969)" (1974, p. 392).

Voter prejudice against women candidates is even lower for other levels of office, and like the pattern for a woman presidential candidate, has declined in recent years. A 1984 Gallup Poll found 90 percent of Americans said they would vote for a woman candidate for mayor, 87 percent for a woman gubernatorial candidate, and 91 percent for a woman congressional candidate (Gallup 1985).

Finally, polls conducted during the decade of the 1970s found slight to substantial change on various attitudinal items relating directly to women's involvement in politics. Polls conducted several years apart showed declining proportions agreeing that men are emotionally better suited to politics, that women should leave running the country to men, and that there will not be a woman president for a long time and that is just as well. Similarly, increasing proportions of women and men agreed that the country would be better off if women had more to say about politics (de Boer 1977; Welch and Sigelman 1982).

Convergence of Women's and Men's Levels of Participation

Throughout the 1970s and into the 1980s, several of the sex differences in rates of participation and in the antecedents to participation apparent prior to the emergence of the women's movement declined, and in some cases, disappeared. Perhaps most significant is the fact that women no longer lag behind men in their rate of voter turnout in the United States. In the 1980, 1982, 1984, and 1986 elections, women voted at rates that were virtually identical to, or slightly higher than, the turnout rates for men (U.S. Bureau of the Census 1987).

The difference in proportions of women and men who reported that they tried to influence the votes of other people also declined over this time period, although it did not disappear. Data from the University of Michigan's American National Election Studies show that 26.6 percent of women, compared with 39.9 percent of men, reported in 1968 that they tried to persuade others how to vote; in 1984, 30.4 percent of women, compared with 35.0 percent of men, reported this behavior.

Sex differences in some antecedents of participation have also diminished since the contemporary women's movement first emerged in the United States. Differences between women and men in political efficacy have decreased, and according to Sandra Baxter and Marjorie Lansing, on measures of political efficacy "by 1976, women of all ages ranked very similarly to men of the same ages" (1983, pp. 49–50). Similarly, sex differences in propensity to give "don't know" responses to questions on political issues have declined notably since the women's movement developed (Shapiro, Mahajan, and Veith 1984, table 4).

Finally, while women and men are far from parity in political officeholding, women have made great strides in recent years. In 1969 only 4 percent of state legislators were women. By 1986 the number of women among state legislators had more than tripled, with women holding 15 percent of state legislative seats nationally. Similarly, the proportion of women serving as mayors and municipal council members increased from 4 percent in 1975 to 14 percent in 1986, the proportion of women among county governing board members grew from 3 percent in 1975 to 8 percent in 1984, and the proportion of statewide elective officials who were women increased from 10 percent in 1975 to 14 percent in 1986. Except for the presidency, Congress is the only level of elective office where little progress has been made since the beginning of the women's movement. In 1987, more women, twenty-five, served in Congress than ever before, but women still held only 4.7 percent of congressional seats (Center for the American Woman and Politics 1987b).

Women have also moved in the direction of parity with men in appointive office. More women held high-level positions in the Carter and Reagan administrations than in previous administrations. Both presidents appointed three women to cabinet-level posts, and Reagan appointed the first woman justice to the Supreme Court. During Reagan's first term in office, 9 percent of all Reagan's full-time, Senate-confirmed, nonjudicial appointments went to women, compared to 13.5 percent of Carter's appointments (U. S. House of Representatives Subcommittee on Civil Service 1984).

Divergence of Women's and Men's Political Perspectives

The trends toward increasing public acceptance of women's involvement in public life and increasing convergence of women's and men's rates of participation in conventional politics have been accompanied by an increase in the scope of politically relevant values and attitudes showing sex differences. The increasing divergence in perspectives between the sexes first came to public attention in the United States during the 1980 election, when a "gender gap" appeared in voting in the presidential election. Since 1980, a number of studies have documented a "gender gap" not only in voting choices but also in evaluations of Ronald Reagan's performance as president, in party identification, and in policy preferences.

The election-day voter polls conducted by the three major television networks in 1980 showed that women split their votes about evenly between Reagan and Carter while men voted overwhelmingly for Reagan. The gender gap in the vote for Reagan was 6 to 9 percentage points, depending on the particular poll. Women's lesser enthusiasm for Reagan was also apparent once he assumed office. Women consistently evaluated Reagan's performance as president less favorably than did men (Center for the American Woman and Politics 1987a; Frankovic 1982; Blydenburgh and Sigel 1983; Carroll 1988).

The gender gap in voting apparent in 1980 was again evident in 1982, when election-day voter polls showed that women more often than men voted Democratic in U.S. House races and that differences in the voting preferences of women and men were evident in several U.S. Senate and gubernatorial races. Women were credited with providing the margin of victory for Democratic gubernatorial candidates in New York, Michigan, and Texas (Center for the American Women and Politics 1987a; "Opinion Roundup" January 1983, pp. 34–35; Epstein and Carroll 1983; Blydenburg and Sigel 1983).

Although a majority of women voted for Reagan in the 1984 presidential election, the gender gap in that election was of approximately the same magnitude (6–9 percent) as for the 1980 presidential election. Again the votes of women provided the margin of victory for Democratic candidates in several statewide races, including senatorial races in Illinois, Iowa, Massachusetts, and Michigan and the gubernatorial race in Vermont (*New York Times,* November 8, 1984; *Eleanor Smeal Report,* November 12, 1984; Klein 1985).

Women's greater preference for the Democratic party since 1980 has been reflected not only in their voting choices but also in their party identification. A composite of three CBS News/*New York Times* polls conducted in 1985 showed that 41 percent of women compared with 33 percent of men identified with the Democratic party. A composite of Gallup polls conducted during 1985 showed almost identical results ("Opinion Roundup" 1985, p. 40). Although more women identify with the Democratic party, they are not significantly less likely than men to be Republicans. Rather, they less often are independents. Thus, unlike the 1950s when women were slightly more Republican and were considered to be more "conservative" than men, they appear in the 1980s to be more Democratic and "liberal" than men.

By the late 1970s and into the 1980s, sex differences on issues also became more pronounced and consistent across a larger number of issue areas. Historical sex differences on issues pertaining to the use of force in both domestic and foreign contexts continued into this period and did not increase significantly (Smith 1984; Shapiro, Mahajan, and Veith 1984; Center for the American Women and Politics 1987a). Differences between the sexes, evident in earlier eras, on "moral" issues such as the regulation of drugs, the use of alcohol, and school prayer also persisted into the contemporary period ("Opinion Roundup" 1982; Shapiro, Mahajan, and Veith 1984; Center for the American Woman and Politics 1987a). The most notable new developments were in the areas of social welfare and environmental protection. On policies aimed at helping the poor and other disadvantaged groups in society, sex differences became larger and more consistent in the mid- to late-1970s and early 1980s ("Opinion Roundup" 1982; Shapiro, Mahajan, and Veith 1984). Sizeable sex differences also emerged on issues relating to environmental protection and nuclear safety. Women appeared more sympathetic than men to government regulations to protect the environment and more opposed to the development of nuclear power (Center for the American Woman and Politics 1987a; "Opinion Roundup" 1982; Shapiro, Mahajan, and Veith 1984).

Finally, polls conducted in the late 1970s and the early 1980s showed women to be significantly more pessimistic than men about the future of the United States. Women expressed less confidence that the United States would be strong and prosperous in the future and were less certain that their country could solve the problems it faced ("Opinion Roundup" 1982; Center for the American Woman and Politics 1987a; Blydenburgh and Sigel 1983).

The Impact of the Women's Movement

To what extent are the trends toward greater liberalization of gender-role attitudes, increasing convergence in women's and men's rates of participation,

and increasing divergence in women's and men's perspectives due to resocialization brought about by the contemporary women's movement? This is a
difficult question to answer. The fact that the women's movement and these
trends have occurred simultaneously suggests that the phenomena are related
and that the women's movement has served as an important agent of socialization. However, specification of the causal relationships linking the women's
movement to the observed changes in behavior and attitudes is not an easy
task. As is true within the field of socialization generally (Sigel and Hoskin
1977, p. 291), research on gender differences has more often focused on
outcomes than on processes of socialization.

Nevertheless, it would appear that there are at least three distinct, although
interrelated, ways in which the women's movement has acted as a agent of
political socialization. The first is by accelerating changes in various areas of
women's lives. The second is by contributing to the autonomy of increasing
numbers of individual women from individual men, and the third is by increasing feminist consciousness.

In recent years important changes have occurred in women's lives—
changes which have helped to break down the separation between private and
public domains and have allowed women greater access to the public arena.
Four changes in women's lives stand out as most important. The changes are
in the areas of education, work, marriage, and motherhood. These changes
have been both cause and consequence of the women's movement. Changes
in women's lives made it possible for the women's movement to develop
(Freeman 1975; Klein 1984), and the women's movement, in turn, led to an
acceleration in the rate of change in women's lives.

The variables of education, work, marriage, and motherhood are familiar
to students of public opinion and adult political socialization, and they have
long been shown to be related to women's political behavior. Nevertheless,
to the extent that the women's movement through changing women's aspirations and altering society's conceptions about appropriate behavior for
women has led more women to pursue their educations, enter the paid labor
force, and change their family situations, any political socialization or resocialization that has occurred as a result of these changes can be attributed at
least in part to the movement.

To assess the impact of the women's movement in socializing women into
new patterns of political behavior, it is necessary to examine the relationship
of changes in each major area of women's lives to changes in their political
attitudes and involvement. Although the numbers of women who have experienced the socializing effects of changes in education, work-force participation, and family situations have increased in recent years, there is much continuity in the way that these variables have affected political behavior across
pre- and post-women's-movement eras.

However, change as well as continuity is evident, for changes in education, work-force participation, and family situations in the contemporary era have given rise to two further changes or developments in women's lives which are also related to changes in women's political attitudes and behavior. These new developments are greater autonomy of increasing numbers of individual women from individual men and increasing feminist consciousness, both of which reflect important ways in which the women's movement has contributed to the resocialization of women. Along with important material changes in women's lives, the increasing autonomy of women from men and the increase in feminist consciousness must be examined in order to assess the full impact of the women's movement on women's political attitudes and behavior.

The Resocializing Impact of Increased Education

The educational attainment of women has increased notably in recent years, reflecting a trend that has been evident since the early 1950s (Freeman 1975, p. 29). By the early 1980s, college enrollment rates for women were about equal to those for men, and women were receiving about one-half of all bachelors and masters degrees awarded by institutions of higher learning in the U.S. (Bianchi and Spain 1984, pp. 12–13).

Education has generally been viewed as an important variable in socialization research, in large part because it places a premium on critical thought and increases exposure to diverse experiences and points of views, leading to increased tolerance for nonconformity and increased receptivity to new ideas associated with social change. For women, college and postgraduate education also serves as an experience which broadens their horizons and builds their expectations by exposing them to, and preparing them for, involvement in public life.

Numerous studies have found that increased education is associated with more liberal gender-role attitudes as well as with greater support for women's involvement in politics (Thornton and Freedman 1979; Klein 1984; Welch and Sigelman 1982; Ferree 1974; Schreiber 1978; Sapiro 1983; Poole and Zeigler 1985; Fulenwider 1980). This relationship exists for both women and men, leading Klein to conclude, "The strong association between education and men's feminist views shows that education leads to feminism because it promotes tolerance rather than simply because it is a nontraditional experience for women" (Klein 1984, p. 111). However, as Poole and Zeigler have demonstrated, education seems to have a greater impact on attitudes toward egalitarianism among women than among men (1985, p. 18). This finding suggests that changes in women's attitudes occurring as a result of higher education probably cannot be attributed solely to consequent increases in tolerance and liberalism.

Education also has been found to be related to increased political participation for women as well as to higher levels of political interest and efficacy
(Sapiro 1983; Hansen, Franz, and Netemeyer-Mays 1976; Pomper 1975;
Welch 1977; Baxter and Lansing 1983; Poole and Zeigler 1985). These findings suggest that education plays an important role in increasing women's
sense of competence vis-à-vis the political world. However, there is little
evidence that education, in and of itself, is directly related to the "gender
gap" in political attitudes and voting behavior. Analyses of the gender gap
have generally found that sex differences are apparent across various levels of
education (Frankovic 1982; Miller and Malanchuk 1983).

The Resocializing Impact of Employment Outside the Home

Certainly one of the most significant, if not the most significant, of changes
in women's lives in the years since World War II has been the increased entry
of women into the paid labor force. While only one-fifth of women worked
outside the home at the turn of the century, more than one-half of the adult
female population was employed by 1980. Moreover, the rate of entry of
women into the paid labor force has clearly accelerated in recent years (Klein
1984, p. 34).

The potential impact of work as an agent of political socialization has long
been recognized (e.g., Sigel and Hoskin 1977). Work outside the home takes
women outside the private sphere and into the public arena. It exposes them
to new ideas and information. It gives them increased confidence in their own
abilities. It enhances the probability that women will directly experience sex
discrimination whether in the form of unequal pay or sexual harassment or
some other guise. For all these reasons, employment outside the home might
be expected to exert a powerful influence on women's political attitudes and
participation.

The increasing entry of women into the paid labor force has been found to
be associated with all three post-women's-movement trends in political attitudes and behavior. Several studies have found that women employed outside
the home differ from full-time homemakers in their gender-role attitudes
(Poole and Zeigler 1985; Klein 1984, p. 108; Andersen and Cook 1985; Ferree 1980; Sapiro 1983, pp. 73–75; Thornton and Freedman 1979). This relationship may be due in part to changes in women's attitudes that occur prior
to entry into the labor force. In one of the few studies examining longitudinal
data, Kristi Andersen and Elizabeth A. Cook found that homemakers who
entered the labor force differed significantly in their beliefs about the sources
of gender differences, even before going to work outside the home, from
those who remained full-time homemakers. However, there is evidence that
working outside the home does lead to attitude change on some gender-role

measures. For example, on two measures related to women's rights, one fo-cusing on whether women workers should be laid off first and the other on whether women should have equal roles with men in the public sphere, An-dersen and Cook found that entry into the work force did result in more feminist responses.

A number of studies have also found labor-force participation to be related to women's involvement in conventional forms of political participation. Em-ployed women participate at rates similar to those of men while women who are full-time homemakers participate at notably lower rates (Poole and Zeig-ler 1985, p. 123; Andersen 1975; Welch 1977, pp. 724–25). Moreover, stud-ies examining the relationship of employment to participation over time found that the apparent positive effect of labor-force participation on political participation had increased in more recent years (Andersen 1975; Welch 1977; Lafferty, chap. 3 this volume).

The findings of recent research suggest that the impact of labor-force par-ticipation in resocializing women to become more active in politics may be less straightforward and more limited than once thought. For example, Susan Welch (1977) found that the effect of employment seems to depend on level of education. Employment did seem to increase the participation rates of less-educated women, relative to the rates of their less-educated male counter-parts. However, employment did not have a significant impact on the partic-ipation rates of high-school and college-educated women when compared to men with the same level of education. Similarly, Eileen L. McDonagh has claimed, based on her analysis of data from five presidential election year surveys, that social status variables are more important than employment per se in determining women's levels of political participation. She has suggested that

> we discard the notion that the mere fact of being a housewife de-presses political participation, while being employed is a dramatic catalyzing force. The crucial factor with housewives, as with those employed outside the home, is their status level, which in the case of housewives is primarily derived through marriage and for those employed through their own jobs. (1982, p. 291)

Using data from a panel study spanning the years from 1972 to 1976, Andersen and Cook (1985) compared women who were full-time homemak-ers in 1972 but entered the labor force by 1976 with those who were home-makers and with those who were paid employees in both years. The political participation rates of new entrants into the labor force resembled those of full-time homemakers and were notably lower than those of paid employees in both years. Thus, in the short term, entry into the work force did not seem to have an effect on political participation. However, Andersen's and Cook's findings point to the possibility of a long-term impact, for those women who had been in the work force for some time (as evidenced by being employed in both 1972 and 1976) were notably more participatory than were home-makers.

Just as differences are apparent between full-time homemakers and women who work outside the home in their rates of political involvement, so too are differences apparent in their political preferences. Analyses of the gender gap have uncovered large differences in voting choices and attitudes between women who are and who are not employed outside the home (e.g., Schlicht-ing and Tuckel 1983; Carroll 1988; Poole and Zeigler 1985). When compared with either full-time homemakers or men, employed women have been found to be less supportive of President Reagan and his policies, more Democratic in their partisan identification, more liberal in their issue positions, and more likely to vote for Democratic candidates. In contrast to the pattern for em-ployed women, the voting behavior and preferences of full-time homemakers have been found to be very similar to those of men.

The Resocializing Impact of Changing Family Situations

Since 1950 women's family situations have changed dramatically. The aver-age age at which women marry and have children has increased, the fertility rate has declined, and women have spent more and more of their lifetimes living alone or heading households (Hartmann, forthcoming). From 1970 to 1982, the proportion of the female population that was single increased from 13.7 to 17.6 percent while the proportion that was divorced increased from 3.9 to 8.0 percent (U.S. Bureau of the Census 1983, p. 43). Over the same time period, the proportion of households headed by women increased from 21.1 to 29.4 percent (U.S. Bureau of the Census 1983, p. 48). Between 1960 and 1980, the birthrate fell from 3.1 children per woman to 1.8 (Bianchi and Spain 1984, p. 6).

The increase in the proportion of women who are divorced or never mar-ried and the decrease in the proportion of a woman's life span devoted to childrearing have had important consequences for women's political behav-ior. Marital status and motherhood have been found to be related to gender-role attitudes in expected ways. Thornton and Freedman (1979), for example, surveyed the same group of women in both 1962 and 1977 and found that divorce was associated with a slight shift toward more egalitarian attitudes while the birth of additional children was associated with the retention of traditional gender-role attitudes.

Marital status and motherhood have been found to be related to a variety of political orientations in addition to general gender-role attitudes (Sapiro 1983; Jennings and Niemi 1981; Githens 1984; Lynn and Flora 1977; Kirkpatrick 1974). Sapiro, for example, observed, "The women who were married were less favorable toward the women's movement, more trusting in political leaders, less likely to participate in protest activities, more conservative, and less favorable toward change in government than were women who were not married" (1983, p. 174). As for motherhood, Sapiro found that having children was associated with lower levels of political efficacy among all women, with lower levels of political knowledge among married mothers, and with restricted political participation among single mothers (1983, p. 177). Jennings and Niemi, in their longitudinal study of high-school seniors, found that marriage without children was not consistently related to political orientations. Rather, the critical variable was the presence or absence of children. They observed,"Basically, nonmothers had a closer political resemblance to men than did mothers" (1981, p. 297). When compared with mothers, nonmothers were more interested in politics, more knowledgeable politically, more attentive to public affairs, more likely to vote, more active in other forms of political participation, and more politically efficacious (1981, p. 296).

Although analyses of the gender gap generally have not investigated the relationship of motherhood to women's voting preferences and presidential evaluations, the role of marital status has been examined. Unmarried women have been found to be more Democratic in their voting choices in recent elections and more critical of President Reagan's performance (Plissner 1983; Miller and Malanchuk 1983; Carroll 1988).

The Effect of Women's Increasing Autonomy from Men

Increases in women's educational attainment, increases in their labor-force participation, and decreases in the proportion of women's lives spent living with men and raising children have occurred simultaneously and at an accelerated rate in the contemporary era. While each of these trends individually has had important implications for women's political attitudes and behavior, the combined effect of these changes also is important. In combination, these trends have meant that increasing numbers of women have become economically and politically independent of the control of individual men. Women are much more likely than they were even a decade ago to be living apart from men, either alone or as female heads of households. Although sex segregation in the labor force and great pay disparities between women and men mean that women who head households in the U.S. often do so under economic hardship, Heidi Hartmann (forthcoming) has argued that recent changes in women's lives are "largely positive for women, because they contribute to women's increased economic independence." In a similar vein, I have argued in another context that the changing circumstances of women's lives have made possible the increasing political autonomy of individual women from individual men (Carroll 1988). Women who are economically independent of men are more likely to make political decisions that reflect their own political interests. "When women and men make joint decisions or decisions based on joint interests in a patriarchal society, it is probably the interests of men that generally predominate. Women under patriarchy are socialized to view their interests as secondary, if not identical, to those of men" (Carroll 1988). While changes in women's lives may still leave them subject to the control of (and in many cases, more dependent on) a patriarchal state (Brown 1981; Hartmann forthcoming), they are less subject to patriarchal control by individual men and thus able to function politically more like the autonomous individuals envisioned by liberal democratic political theory.

Although the relationship between women's increased economic autonomy from men and their rates of participation in conventional politics has not been investigated, research has explored the links between women's increased economic independence and both the gender gap and gender-role attitudes. Women who were economically independent of men, either because they were well-educated managers or professionals who could provide for themselves or because they were unmarried and thus had no men upon whose income they could depend, voted for Ronald Reagan in notably smaller proportions in the 1980 election than did men. They also were much less likely than men to approve of his performance as president in 1982. In contrast, the voting choices and presidential evaluations of women who lacked economic independence from men did not differ significantly from those of men. Economic independence for women was also found to be related to women's gender-role attitudes. Women who were economically independent from men favored equal roles for women in business and government in notably larger proportions than did women who lacked economic independence (Carroll 1988).

The Impact of Feminist Consciousness

Accounts of the origins of the nineteenth- and twentieth-century women's movements in the U.S. suggest that nontraditional experiences for women— experiences that prepare women for, or bring them into, active involvement in public life—play an important role in the development of feminist consciousness. Many of the original activists in the nineteenth-century women's rights movement were well-educated women who were involved in the abolitionist movement (Flexner 1975). Similarly, one branch of the contemporary feminist movement had its origins among young, college-educated women involved in the New Left and civil rights movements of the 1960s (Freeman 1975; Evans 1980). The other branch was formed by somewhat older, largely professional women, many of whom had been involved with national or state commissions on the status of women established in the early 1960s (Freeman 1975).

Nontraditional experience is not the only, nor is it a sufficient, condition for the development of feminist consciousness—an internalized political ideology rooted in personal experience that reflects a recognition of discrimination against women and a preference for change in women's status. However, nontraditional experience does seem to be one of the factors most often associated with the emergence of feminist consciousness among women. Studies have identified at least three conditions that are necessary steps in the development of feminist consciousness. One is a sense of identification with women, a recognition of shared interests. The second is a recognition of disparities in the treatment of women, coupled with a sense that such treatment is unjust. The third is a realization that the problems women face demand collective, political solutions and cannot be solved through individual efforts (Klein 1984, p. 3; Gurin 1985, pp. 146–47). As long as American women's lives were confined to and focused largely on home and family, there were few opportunities for those women, often living with men and often isolated from each other, to develop a shared identification. There also was little chance they would come into contact with information suggesting that disparities in treatment of the sexes were unjust and demanded collective action. However, as American women became more educated, moved into the labor force in increasing numbers, and spent less of their life spans tending to husbands and children, opportunities for the development of feminist consciousness among significant numbers of women increased (Freeman 1975; Klein 1984).

Thus, it is not surprising that studies have found strong relationships between variables measuring important areas of change in women's lives and measures of feminism. Earlier sections of this chapter documented the fact that changes in education, labor-force participation, and family situations are associated with changes in gender-role attitudes. However, the impact of changes in women's lives seems to extend beyond gender-role attitudes. Studies have used as dependent variables a variety of measures of feminism, including but not limited to gender-role attitudes. Klein, for example, used a measure that combined gender-role attitudes with perceptions of discrimination (1984, pp. 103–4). Sigel and Whelchel developed a measure that included a cognitive component, awareness of discrimination, and an affective component, the salience of discrimination to the respondent (Sigel and Whelchel 1986a, 1986b). Similarly, Fulenwider employed a measure that combined a diverse range of items including gender-role attitudes, attitude toward abortion, a measure of group influence, perceptions of sex discrimination, and attitude toward the women's liberation movement (1980, pp. 42–45). Although more rigorous attempts to measure the incidence of feminist consciousness have not found it to be particularly widespread relative to other forms of consciousness (e.g., Gurin 1985), Klein and Fulenwider both found that even as early as 1972 sizeable proportions of women and men scored high on their measures of feminism. Moreover, the proportions supporting feminism grew from 1972 to 1976 (Fulenwider 1980, p. 59; Klein 1984, pp. 103–4). Gurin (1985), too, found a growth in feminist consciousness between 1972 and 1983. The studies of Gurin, Klein, and Fulenwider also all found strong relationships between measures of feminism and education, labor-force participation, and family situations (Gurin 1985, p. 161; Klein 1984, pp. 107–12; Fulenwider 1980, p. 110). Although the causal ordering of variables is not clear and in some cases feminist attitudes may have preceded increased education, entry into the labor force, or changes in family situations, these findings suggest the importance of recent changes in women's lives to the development of feminist consciousness.

The growth in feminism and feminist consciousness, which is related to changes in women's lives, is itself directly related to increased political participation and to the gender gap. Both Hansen et al. and Fulenwider have demonstrated that women with more feminist attitudes participate at higher rates in various forms of activity, ranging from voting to campaign activity to social protest (Hansen et al. 1976; Fulenwider 1980, 105–8). Moreover, this relationship holds even when variables such as education and employment are controlled and seems to be much stronger for black than for white women. Findings from studies of women who seek and hold elective office are consistent with these findings for women active in less demanding forms of participation. Women candidates and officeholders, like other women activists, appear to be more supportive of the concerns of the feminist movement than are women in the general population (Carroll 1985; Stanwick and Kleeman 1983; Johnson and Carroll 1978).

Nevertheless, as is true for many of the relationships discussed in this chapter, the direction of causality is not completely clear. While feminist attitudes may motivate political activism, they also may result from participation. Socially interactive participation may itself be an agent of socialization and perform a consciousness-raising function. As Hansen et al. have explained:

> Through work with others in campaigns and through informal politicking women may obtain information concerning women's problems and may meet other women actively working on these issues. They might also experience some subtle or not-so-subtle forms of sexism. In fact, one reason for the rebirth of the women's movement

in this country in the 1960's was that women already highly active
in the civil rights and anti-war movements resented being delegated
to serving coffee and stuffing envelopes. (1976, p. 586)

In addition to its relationship to participation, feminism also seems to be
related to sex differences in voting choices apparent in recent elections. Although women and men in the general population are about equally supportive of feminist positions on women's issues, Klein has argued convincingly
that the similarity in support between the sexes belies fundamental differences
in the nature of their support. She has suggested:

Men's feminist sympathy . . . is not the same as feminist consciousness. It is rather an abstract, ideological commitment to equality. In
contrast, consciousness refers to an internalized political perspective
derived from personal experience. Thus, feminism can be important
to both men and women, but the sexes support feminism for different
reasons, and consequently, their beliefs can have different political
implications. (1984, p. 7)

Indeed, Klein does show that women's and men's feminist attitudes have very
different political implications. Her analysis indicates that the voting calculus
of women and men in the 1980 election was very different, with women's
rights issues influencing women's votes far more than they influenced men's
(1984, pp. 161–62).

A Concluding Assessment of the Impact of the Women's Movement

Important changes in women's lives were underway prior to the development
of the contemporary feminist movement. These changes, even in the absence
of a social movement, had important effects on women's political attitudes
and involvement. However, the movement does appear to have accelerated
the rate of change in women's lives; consequently, changes in political behavior that came about as a result of increased education, entry into the labor
force, and changing family situations probably were experienced by more
women than would have been true in the absence of the movement.

Additionally, two new developments that have important effects on wom-
en's political behavior seem to be direct consequences of the women's movement. The first of these, the increased autonomy of women from men, stems
from the combined effects of changes in women's lives that have occurred at
an accelerated rate since the advent of the contemporary feminist movement.
Although a small minority of women have always been autonomous form
individual men, the incidence of autonomy has increased significantly in recent years. The women's movement has contributed to this increased auton-

omy through its attempts to create opportunities for women in the labor force, by its support for a wider variety of life-style options for women, through its advocacy of increased control of women over their reproductive and child-bearing capabilities, and by its struggles to increase educational opportunities for women.

The other new development affecting women's political attitudes and behavior that is even more clearly and directly linked to the women's movement is increased feminist consciousness. This increased consciousness, like increased autonomy, is in many ways a by-product of changes in women's lives which are themselves, in part, a product of the movement. In a more fundamental sense, feminist consciousness could not exist in the absence of a social movement aimed at changing the current status of women in society.

Overall, existing evidence suggests that the contemporary women's movement has had a significant impact on political attitudes and behavior in the two decades since it came into existence. The trends toward greater liberalization of gender-role attitudes, increasing convergence in women's and men's rates of participation and increasing divergence in women's and men's perspectives seem to be at least in part a product of changes in women's lives, increasing autonomy of women from men, and increasing feminist consciousness brought about by the feminist movement.

Although the women's movement seems clearly to have had a notable impact, the difficulty of untangling the causes and consequences of social change make a more precise assessment of the influence of the feminist movement in socializing people into new patterns of political behavior impossible at this time. Because we lack sufficient longitudinal research examining changes which have occurred during the past two decades, we may never know the extent to which recent changes in education, labor-force participation, and family situations are due to the women's movement and the extent to which these changes might have occurred even in the absence of the movement. Nevertheless, panel studies extending into the future would help to clarify some critical processes of social change and are very much needed. To what extent do changes in gender-role attitudes precede and motivate increased education for women and changes in women's family situations, and to what extent are changes in gender-role attitudes a consequence of such changes in women's lives? In the long term, does women's entry into the work force lead to changes in attitudes about feminism and/or increased involvement in conventional politics? Do women become more politically active as a result of their feminist beliefs, or do political activists support feminism because of their experiences as activists? Our knowledge of the impact of the women's movement on adult political socialization is hindered by our inability to answer these and similar questions about issues of causality. Only with more longitudinal research will we develop a clearer understanding of processes of social change as they relate to the women's movement and political behavior.

Issues for Future Research

Some research has examined generational differences in responses to the women's movement. Roberta S. Sigel and John Reynolds, for example, in a study of mothers and daughters who had attended the same college, found an overall pattern of similarity in support for the concerns of the feminist movement across the two generations (1979–80). Nevertheless, some signs of generational change were apparent. For example, as a group daughters were more likely than mothers to reject traditional views about the importance of marriage and motherhood and about male/female differences in emotions and sexual drives. These findings are, for the most part, consistent with those of other research. When generational differences have been found, the pattern is that older generations are generally more traditional in their views about women while younger generations show greater support for the positions advocated by the women's movement (Sapiro 1980; Klein 1984, pp. 117–19).

However, these studies are all based on an analysis of cohorts born prior to the development of the contemporary feminist movement. Women and men reaching adulthood in the mid- to late-1980s confront a society in which gender relations appear in some ways to be very different than they have been in the past. It has become far more acceptable for women to work outside the home, many of the most flagrant vestiges of sexism have disappeared, and female law-enforcement officers, bus drivers, and physicians are no longer rare sights. Some observers have suggested that changes such as these have led women who are coming of age in the mid- to late-1980s to view the women's movement as passé and without relevance for their lives (e.g., Bolotin 1982). Perhaps changing life experiences and patterns of socialization have altered the attitudes of cohorts born in the mid-1960s and after. If so, the women's movement may have a different meaning for these cohorts, with different implications for their political behavior. The question of generational change is one that clearly needs further research.

Also in need of further research is the question of how the impact of the women's movement on political socialization varies by race and class. A few studies have given serious attention to questions of difference among women of varying classes and races. These studies have examined the combined effects of gender and race or class on political attitudes and behavior, attitudes toward feminism, and the effects of the latter on the former (e.g., Fulenwider 1980; Baxter and Lansing 1983; Hershey 1980; McDonagh 1982). Nevertheless, we still know too little about how race and class affect the linkages between the women's movement and political behavior.

The Impact of the Women's Movement in Resocializing Political Scientists

Like the women and men they study, political scientists have been socialized into a patriarchal system of gender relations both inside and outside of academia. The women's movement has helped to make political scientists aware of the extent to which past work in the field has overlooked women's contributions to conventional politics and has judged women's behavior in terms of sex stereotypes. Consequently, more political scientists are now aware of the importance of explicitly examining women's political behavior, and they are more conscious of the values they bring to bear in assessing women's political attitudes and involvement.

The explicit focus on women and the attempt to correct the distortions and biases of the past are important steps. However, the implications of the women's movement for the discipline of political science are more far-reaching. This chapter has reviewed women's political behavior according to the categories and distinctions applied in conventional political analysis, in large part because almost all existing studies have analyzed women's political behavior in these terms. I have, however, attempted to place this presentation in a larger context by showing that the bifurcation into public and private and the association of women with the private have had great impact on both the political attitudes and involvement of women and the way that their behavior has been viewed and interpreted.

The women's movement has called into question the rigid separation of public and private in our thinking and our politics. In large part as a result of the movement, concerns that were once considered strictly private (sexuality, child care, domestic violence) have become public concerns. The boundaries between private and public are breaking down.

Within academia, feminist scholarship is also challenging the public/private dichotomy that has set women's activities apart as having lesser value than the activities of men. In political science the impact of feminist scholarship in challenging the public man/private woman dualism is just beginning to be felt. However, in disciplines such as history, where feminist scholars have a stronger foothold, significant inroads have been made. For example, a recent review of work in women's history noted the shift in emphasis that has taken place among those who study women's political history. Although scholars in the field of women's history initially accepted a "male definition of politics," one clearly linked to the public/private dichotomy, this definition proved too narrow to encompass women's political activities. As Mary Beth Norton, the author of the review, explained, "Drawing on the feminist movement's insight that 'the personal is political,' women's historians broadened the category to include women's attempts to gain control over their own lives—both inside and outside marriage—and to have an impact on the society in which they lived" (1986, p. 40). Consistent with this redefinition of the "political," feminist historians have focused on such subjects as the temperance movement, a variety of nineteenth-century women's organizations, and women's involvement in nineteenth-century foreign-mission activities in the Christian churches—all subjects not previously considered sufficiently "political" to merit much scholarly attention (Norton 1986).

Just as feminist scholarship is redefining the "political" in the discipline of history, so too is it likely to have an impact on conceptions of the "political" within the discipline of political science. In order to understand and appreciate fully women's political role, political scientists must begin to think about political behavior in ways that transcend the public/private dichotomy. As was true for women's history until recent years, our research has adopted the activities traditionally engaged in by men in the public sphere as the norm against which to judge women's "political" behavior. Given the strong sexual division of labor in Western societies and a tradition of socialization processes that have worked to maintain that division, it is not surprising that women have been judged by this norm to be inferior political beings. Indeed, what is perhaps most surprising is that women's "political" behavior has in some respects (voting and some other forms of conventional participation) come to resemble so closely the behavior of men.

If we were to change our approach and the questions we ask, we might well come to quite different conclusions about the extent, nature, and quality of women's (and men's) political behavior. Rather than accepting men's behavior as the norm and asking how women are similar to or different from men, we might instead begin to examine women's behavior on its own terms and through women's own eyes. This would lead to an interrelated set of research questions that might include the following: What are women's attitudes about their lives and the society in which they live? In what activities do they engage in an attempt to influence society and exercise control over their lives? To what extent and in what ways do women view their attitudes and activities as political? This need for new questions and different standards by which to judge women's political behavior—that is, the need for a more woman-centered approach to the study of politics—is perhaps both the most important issue confronting researchers in the area of gender and politics and the greatest challenge facing the women's movement as it attempts to resocialize political scientists.

References

Andersen, Kristi. 1975. "Working Women and Political Participation, 1952–1972." *American Journal of Political Science* 19: 439–53.

————, and Elizabeth A. Cook. 1985. "Women, Work, and Political Attitudes." *American Journal of Political Science* 29: 606–25.

Baxter, Sandra, and Marjorie Lansing. 1983. *Women and Politics: The Visible Majority.* Rev. ed. Ann Arbor: University of Michigan Press.

Berelson, Bernard R., Paul F. Lazarsfeld, and William N. McPhee. 1954. *Voting.* Chicago: University of Chicago Press.

Bianchi, Suzanne M., and Daphne Spain. 1984. *American Women: Three Decades of Change.* Washington, D.C.: U.S. Government Printing Office.

Blydenburgh, John C., and Roberta S. Sigel. 1983. "Key Factors in the 1982 Elections as Seen by Men and Women Voters: An Exploration into the Vulnerability Thesis." Paper presented at the Annual Meeting of the American Political Science Association, Chicago, Illinois, September 1–4.

Bolotin, Susan. 1982. "Voices from the Post-Feminist Generation." *New York Times Magazine.* October: pp. 28–31.

Bourque, Susan C., and Jean Grossholtz. 1974. "Politics an Unnatural Practice: Political Science Looks at Female Participation." *Politics and Society* 4: 225–66.

Brown, Carol. 1981. "Mothers, Fathers, and Children: From Private to Public Patriarchy." In *Women and Revolution,* ed. Lydia Sargent. Boston: South End Press.

Bullock, Charles S. III, and Patricia Findley Heys. 1972. "Recruitment of Women for Congress: A Research Note." *Western Political Quarterly* 25: 416–23.

Campbell, Angus, Philip Converse, Warren Miller, and Donald Stokes. 1960. *The American Voter.* New York: Wiley.

Carroll, Susan J. 1985. *Women as Candidates in American Politics.* Bloomington: Indiana University Press.

————. 1988. "Women's Autonomy and the Gender Gap." In *Politics of the Gender Gap,* ed. Carol Mueller. Beverly Hills: Sage Publications.

————, and Barbara Geiger-Parker. 1983. *Women Appointed to the Carter Administration: A Comparison with Men.* New Brunswick, N.J.: Center for the American Woman and Politics.

————, and Wendy S. Strimling. 1983. *Women's Routes to Elective Office: A Comparison with Men's.* New Brunswick, N.J.: Center for the American Woman and Politics.

————, and Barbara Geiger-Parker. 1984. *Women Appointed to State Government: A Comparison with All State Appointees.* New Brunswick, N.J.: Center for the American Woman and Politics.

Center for the American Woman and Politics. 1987a. *Gender Gap Fact Sheet.* New Brunswick, N.J.: Center for the American Woman and Politics.

————. 1987b. *Women in Elective Office Fact Sheet.* New Brunswick, N.J.: Center for the American Woman and Politics.

Costantinti, Edmond, and Kenneth H. Craik. 1972. "Women as Politicians: The Social Background, Personality and Political Careers of Female Party Leaders." *Journal of Social Issues* 28: 217–36.

de Boer, Connie. 1977. "The Polls: Women at Work." *Public Opinion Quarterly* 41: 268–77.

Easton David, and Jack Dennis. 1967. "The Child's Acquisition of Regime Norms: Political Efficacy." *American Political Science Review* 61: 25–38.

Eisenstein, Zillah. 1981. *The Radical Future of Liberal Feminism*. New York: Longman.

Eleanor Smeal Report. November 12, 1984.

Elshtain, Jean Bethke. 1974. "Moral Woman and Immoral Man: A Consideration of the Public-Private Split and Its Political Ramifications." *Politics and Society* 4: 453–72.

Epstein, Laurily K., and Susan J. Carroll. 1983. "Sex and the Vote: The 1982 Election Day Voter Polls." Paper presented at the Annual Meeting of the American Political Science Association, Chicago, Illinois, September 1–4.

Erskine, Hazel. 1971. "The Polls: Women's Role." *Public Opinion Quarterly* 35: 275–90.

Evans, Sara. 1980. *Personal Politics*. New York: Vintage Books, Random House.

Ferree, Myra Marx. 1974. "A Woman for President? Changing Responses: 1958–1972." *Public Opinion Quarterly* 38: 390–99.

———. 1980. "Working Class Feminism: A Consideration of the Consequences of Employment." *Sociological Quarterly* (Spring): 173–84.

Flexner, Eleanor. 1975. *Century of Struggle*. Rev. ed. Cambridge: Belknap Press, Harvard University Press.

Frankovic, Kathleen A. 1982. "Sex and Politics—New Alignments, Old Issues." *PS* (Summer): 439–49.

Freeman, Jo. 1975. *The Politics of Women's Liberation*. New York: Longman.

Fulenwider, Claire Knoche. 1980. *Feminism in American Politics*. New York: Praeger.

Gallup, George, Jr. 1985. *The Gallup Poll: Public Opinion 1984*. Princeton: Gallup.

Gertzog, Irwin. 1984. *Congressional Women*. New York: Praeger.

Githens, Marianne. 1984. "Women and State Politics: An Assessment." In *Political Women: Current Roles in State and Local Government*, ed. Janet A. Flammang. Beverly Hills: Sage Publications.

Goot, Murray, and Elizabeth Reid. 1975. *Women and Voting Studies: Mindless Matrons or Sexist Scientism?* London: Sage Publications.

Gruberg, Martin. 1968. *Women in American Politics: An Assessment and Sourcebook*. Oshkosh, Wis.: Academia Press.

Gurin, Patricia. 1985. "Women's Gender Consciousness." *Public Opinion Quarterly* 49: 143–63.

Hansen, Susan B., Linda M. Franz, and Margaret Netemeyer-Mays. 1976. "Women's Political Participation and Policy Preferences." *Social Science Quarterly* 56: 576–90.

Harris, Louis, and Associates. 1972. *The 1972 Virginia Slims American Women's Opinion Poll*. Louis Harris and Associates.

Hartmann, Heidi I. Forthcoming. "Changes in Women's Economic and Family Roles in Post World War II United States." In *Structural Transformations in the Work Place and Home*, ed. Lourdes Benería and Catharine R. Stimpson. New Brunswick, N.J.: Rutgers University Press.

Hershey, Marjorie Randon. 1980. "Support for Political Woman: The Effects of Race, Sex, and Sexual Roles." In *The Electorate Reconsidered*, ed. John C. Pierce and John L. Sullivan. Beverly Hills: Sage Publications.

Iglitzin, Lynne B. 1974. "The Making of the Apolitical Woman: Femininity and Sex-

Stereotyping in Girls." In *Women in Politics,* ed. Jane S. Jaquette. New York: Wiley.

Jaggar, Alison M. 1983. *Feminist Politics and Human Nature.* Totowa, N.J.: Rowan and Allanheld.

Jaquette, Jane S. 1974. Introduction. In *Women in Politics,* ed. Jane S. Jaquette. New York: Wiley.

Jennings, M. Kent. 1979. "Another Look at the Life Cycle and Political Participation." *American Journal of Political Science* 23: 755–71.

———, and Richard G. Niemi. 1981. *Generations and Politics.* Princeton: Princeton University Press.

———, and Norman Thomas. 1968. "Men and Women in Party Elites: Social Roles and Political Resources." *Midwest Journal of Political Science* 12: 469–92.

Johnson, Marilyn, and Susan Carroll. 1978. "Profile of Women Holding Office, 1977." In *Women in Public Office: A Biographical Directory and Statistical Analysis,* compiled by Center for the American Woman and Politics. Metuchen, N.J.: Scarecrow Press.

Kerber, Linda K. 1980. *Women of the Republic.* Chapel Hill: University of North Carolina Press.

Kirkpatrick, Jeane J. 1974. *Political Woman.* New York: Basic Books.

———. 1976. *The New Presidential Elite.* New York: Russell Sage Foundation and The Twentieth Century Fund.

Klein, Ethel. 1984. *Gender Politics.* Cambridge: Harvard University Press.

———. 1985. "The Gender Gap: Different Issues, Different Answers." *The Brookings Review* (Winter): 33–37.

Lee, Marcia M. 1977. "Toward Understanding Why Few Women Hold Public Office: Factors Affecting the Participation of Women in Local Politics." In *A Portrait of Marginality,* ed. Marianne Githens and Jewel L. Prestage. New York: McKay.

Lovenduski, Joni, and Jill Hills, eds. 1981. *The Politics of the Second Electorate.* London: Routledge and Kegan Paul.

Lynn, Naomi B. 1984. "Women and Politics: The Real Majority." In *Women: A Feminist Perspective,* 3d ed., ed. Jo Freeman. Palo Alto: Mayfield.

———, and Cornelia Flora. 1977. "Societal Punishment and Aspects of Female Political Participation: 1972 Convention Delegates." In *A Portrait of Marginality,* ed. Marianne Githens and Jewel L. Prestage. New York: McKay.

Mandel, Ruth B. 1981. *In the Running.* New York: Ticknor and Fields.

McDonagh, Eileen L. 1982. "To Work or Not to Work: The Differential Impact of Achieved and Derived Status upon the Political Participation of Women, 1956–1976." *American Journal of Political Science* 26: 280–97.

McCourt, Kathleen. 1977. *Working-Class Women and Grass-Roots Politics.* Bloomington: Indiana University Press.

Mill, John Stuart. 1980. *The Subjection of Women,* ed. Sue Mansfield. Arlington Heights, Ill.: AHM Publishing.

Miller, Arthur H., and Oksana Malanchuk. 1983. "The Gender Gap in the 1982 Elections." Paper presented at the 38th Annual Conference of the American Association for Public Opinion Research, Buck Hill Falls, Pennsylvania, May 19–22.

New York Times, November 8, 1984.

Nicholson, Linda. 1983. "Feminist Theory: The Private and the Public." In *Beyond Domination: New Perspectives on Women and Philosophy,* ed. Carol C. Gould. Totowa, N.J.: Rowman and Allanheld.

Norton, Mary Beth. 1986. "Is Clio a Feminist? The New History." *New York Times Book Review* (April 13).

"Opinion Roundup." 1982. *Public Opinion* (April/May): 21–32.

———. 1983. *Public Opinion* (January): 34–35.

———. 1985. *Public Opinion* (October/November): 40.

Orum, Anthony, Roberta Cohen, Sherri Grasmuck, and Amy W. Orum. 1974. "Sex, Socialization and Politics." *American Sociological Review* 39:197–209.

Plissner, Martin. 1983. "The Marriage Gap." *Public Opinion* (February/March):53.

Pomper, Gerald. 1975. *Voter's Choice.* New York: Dodd, Mead.

Poole, Keith T., and L. Harmon Zeigler. 1985. *Women, Public Opinion, and Politics.* New York: Longman.

Rapoport, Ronald B. 1982. "Sex Differences in Attitude Expression: A Generational Explanation." *Public Opinion Quarterly* 46: 86–96.

———. 1981. "The Sex Gap in Political Persuading: Where the Structuring Principle Works." *American Journal of Political Science* 25: 32–46.

Roper Organization. 1985. *The 1985 Virginia Slims American Women's Opinion Poll.* Storrs, Conn.: Roper Organization.

Rosaldo, Michelle Zimbalist. 1974. "Women, Culture and Society: A Theoretical Overview." In *Women, Culture and Society,* ed. Michelle Zimbalist Rosaldo and Louise Lamphere. Stanford: Stanford University Press.

———. 1980. "The Use and Abuse of Anthropology: Reflections on Feminism and Cross-Cultural Understanding." *Signs*: 389–417.

Rubin, Gayle. 1975. "The Traffic in Women: Notes on the 'Political Economy' of Sex." In *Toward an Anthropology of Women,* ed. Rayna R. Reiter. New York: Monthly Review Press.

Sapiro, Virginia. 1983. *The Political Integration of Women.* Urbana: University of Illinois Press.

———. 1982. "Private Costs of Public Commitments or Public Costs of Private Commitments? Family Roles versus Political Ambition." *American Journal of Political Science* 26: 265–79.

———. 1980. "News from the Front: Intersex and Intergenerational Conflict over the Status of Women." *Western Political Quarterly* 33: 260–77.

———, and Barbara G. Farah. 1980. "New Pride and Old Prejudice: Political Ambitions and Role Orientations Among Female Partisan Elites." *Women and Politics* 1: 13–36.

Schlichting, Kurt, and Peter Tuckel. 1983. "Beyond the Gender Gap: Working Women and the 1982 Election." Paper presented at the Annual Conference of the American Association for Public Opinion Research, Buck Hill Falls, Pennsylvania, May 19–22.

Schreiber, E. M. 1978. "Education and Change in American Opinions on a Woman for President." *Public Opinion Quarterly* 42: 171–82.

Shapiro, Robert, Harpreet Mahajan, and Kurt Veith. 1984. "Gender Differences in Policy Choices: Trends from the 1960s to the 1980s." Paper presented at the Annual

Meeting of the Midwest Association for Public Opinion Research, Chicago, November 16–17.

Sigel, Roberta, and Marilyn Brookes Hoskin. 1977. "Perspectives on Adult Political Socialization—Areas of Research." In *Handbook of Political Socialization*, ed. Stanley Allen Renshon. New York: The Free Press.

———, and John V. Reynolds. 1979–80. "Generational Differences and the Women's Movement." *Political Science Quarterly* 94: 635–48.

———, and Nancy L. Whelchel. 1986a. "Minority Consciousness and Sense of Group Power Among Women." Paper presented at the Annual Meeting of the Midwest Political Science Association, Chicago, Illinois, April 9–12.

———, and Nancy L. Whelchel. 1986b. "Changing Gender Roles: Male and Female Reactions." Paper presented at the Annual Meeting of the International Society for Political Psychology, Amsterdam, The Netherlands, June 29–July 3.

Smith, Tom W. 1984. The Polls: "Gender and Attitudes Toward Violence." *Public Opinion Quarterly* 48: 384–96.

Stanwick, Kathy, and Katherine E. Kleeman. 1983. *Women Make a Difference.* New Brunswick, N.J.: Center for the American Woman and Politics.

Stoper, Emily. 1977. "Wife and Politician: Role Strain Among Women in Public Office." In *A Portrait of Marginality*, ed. Marianne Githens and Jewel L. Prestage. New York: McKay.

Thornton, Arland, and Deborah Freedman. 1979. "Changes in the Sex Role Attitudes of Women, 1962–1977: Evidence From a Panel Study." *American Sociological Review* 44: 831–42.

Welch, Susan. 1977. "Women as Political Animals? A Test of Some Explanations for Male-Female Political Participation Differences." *American Journal of Political Science* 21: 711–30.

———. 1978. "Recruitment of Women to Public Office: A Discriminant Analysis." *Western Political Quarterly* 31: 372–80.

———, and Lee Sigelman. 1982. "Changes in Public Attitudes Toward Women in Politics." *Social Science Quarterly* 63: 312–21.

Wolfinger, Raymond E., and Steven J. Rosenstone. 1980. *Who Votes?* New Haven: Yale University Press.

U.S. Bureau of the Census. 1985. *Statistical Abstract of the United States: 1984.* Washington, D.C.: Government Printing Office.

———. 1987. *Voting and Registration in the Election of November 1986.* Current Population Reports, Series P-20, No. 414. Washington, D.C.: U.S. Government Printing Office.

U.S. House of Representatives Subcommittee on Civil Service. 1984. Statement of Representative Patricia Schroeder, Chairwoman, on Women Appointed by President Reagan and President Carter. October 10.

Nine

Socialization and Anti-Socialization:
The Case of Immigrants
MARILYN HOSKIN

Introduction

The movement and behavior of immigrants is by nature an expansive subject. At the most general level it is a phenomenon embracing the entire history of those migrating to seek the better life, thereby spanning centuries and continents. At a more pragmatic level it is a poignant indicator of the postwar divergence of rich and poor nations, reflecting the constant tensions associated with border and refugee politics. At an even more intimate sociopsychological level, it frames an ever-broadening academic field which studies how humans resolve to leave the familiar for the uncertain and how they succeed or fail in adapting to their new environments.

Not surprisingly, the range of perspectives found in the literature is also expansive. Economists have defined immigrant orientations as both motivator and by-product in labor and market theories, and demographers have used those orientations to model population trends. Historians have traced major phases of development to group movements and interactions, and sociologists expanded *that* notion to produce theories of integration and assimilation. Psychologists have explored the multiple personality dispositions of migrant minorities, leading public officials as well as political scientists to develop policies maximizing national interests while minimizing intergroup tension. In addition, a voluminous literature on the "immigrant experience" has furnished rich detail and sensitivity to the topic. In a real sense, the study of immigrants is as disrespectful of traditional boundaries as many of its subjects.

As a consequence of such varied attention, the study of immigration includes extensive treatments of continuity and change—both in theory and in concrete human relations. It is curious, therefore, that the important question of how immigrants are socialized *politically* has been addressed only infrequently and indirectly. In his recent analysis of Israeli immigrants, Zvi Gitelman notes that since Paul Wilson in 1973 rued the paucity of attention to political socialization of immigrants, only two books have been written on the subject (Gitelman 1982; Wilson 1973). Titles including "political" aspects of immigration appear, on the average, only once a year in the *International Migration Review*, and few of those are dedicated to socialization. Gitelman thus noted that only migration policies receive substantial academic treatment, while study of both the politics of migrants and the process of their political resocialization has been largely neglected.

Assessing the state of research on immigrant socialization is thus an indirect task, even in the face of a wealth of studies on the immigrant experience. Although there is no obvious consensus on how best to study the topic, students of migration tend to divide their subject into two distinct periods: all time before World War II (when, except for the abrupt and unique exoduses of refugees from 1918 Russia and Hitler's Germany, migrations occurred almost "naturally," reflecting mobility and absorptive capacity) and all time since (in which migration has become a clash of cultures, a threat to national integrity, and a strain on First World nations to accommodate new arrivals). A comprehensive review of works on migration, however, suggests that there is remarkable similarity in the two periods in both policy and immigrant response. In this chapter I concentrate on the evidence pertaining to immigration since 1945 and compare these patterns to those detailed in earlier studies where the comparison is instructive. Moreover, since socialization to a new environment is almost always smoother for that very small minority of immigrants who arrive with financial resources and connections, I concentrate further on the larger number with relatively fewer means. I begin by evaluating the contribution of the substantial number of theoretical perspectives on immigration for the study of political socialization and extrapolate elements which define a comprehensive socialization framework. I then proceed to evaluate the role of those elements in socializing migrants politically. Specifically, I address the relative contribution to the political socialization process of factors defined partly or mostly by immigrants (socioeconomic status and skills, group activity, political expectations and behavior) and those defined largely by the host society (official policy, informal organizational integration programs, public opinion).

Finally, I suggest lines along which this type of socialization encompasses elements of both continuity and change in defining the contours of adult socialization.

Sorting out Theory

The process by which immigrants are socialized is a long and varied one, extending from the decision to migrate to the establishment of a reasonably permanent (if still insecure) role in the new society. Since each step of the process involves multiple sources of influence (economic conditions, government policies, community norms, channels of opportunity), it is not surprising that the literature is extensive but disparate and largely unintegrated. Given this state of affairs, it makes sense to begin by sorting through the theoretical perspectives that have framed most of our current, if not final, wisdom on the topic. For my purposes three such perspectives are relevant: macro-theories of immigrant movement and its consequences; micro-theories of group adaptation or conflict in the host society; and individual-level theories of the resocialization process.

Macro-theories: The Primacy of Economic Forces

Immigration has most frequently been treated theoretically in terms of economic forces and global or systemic adjustment. As Daniel Kubat notes in his introduction to *The Politics of Immigration Policies.*

> Migration policies then, are short-term responses of nations faced with the consequences of steps, taken only recently before, to meet the needs for economic growth with their own supply of labor, to match their political aims with their population policies, and to accommodate the demographic pressures either from within or from outside the country. (Kubat 1979, p. xviii)

The major foci of this approach are international economic lures and crises. In their major academic volume on the American experience of Cuban and Mexican immigrants, for example, Portes and Bach (1985) classify three of four theoretical foci in economic terms: (1) *migration origins,* which are said to derive wholly from economic factors (push-pull forces associated with monetary incentives and lures; labor recruitment drives; and global economic trends); (2) *stabilization of economic imbalances* caused by government policies; and (3) *differential uses of migrant labor* (supplements to domestic labor supplies, colonized minorities, competition to domestic work forces). The economic theoretical umbrella thus defines immigrants largely by the forces of the market that direct labor flows (Piore 1975; Lebergott 1964; Chiswick 1976; Castles and Kosack 1973; Bonacich 1972).

The necessary corollary to economic dominance in migration is the adjustment of the larger society to population imbalances and shifts, and that concern defines the second type of macro-level theoretical focus. Zolberg, for example, considers the "world system" of population movement as a deviation from normal social organization; Hoffman-Nowotny sees migration as a "transfer of tension" in his general theory; and Boehning conceptualizes migration in terms of an "economic marketplace theory of surpluses and shortages in nation-states" (Zolberg 1981; Hoffman-Nowotny 1981; Boehning

1981). In this vein, Kritz and Keely, Kubat, and Bryce-LaPorte direct their major collections of essays to immigration as it presents societies with the universal dilemma of how to maximize both labor supplies and cultural integrity. As a consequence, systemically oriented frameworks see the immigrant as little more than a bit player in a larger game whose overall coherence is more important than any of its parts.

Finally, systemic responses to economic factors have been analyzed in terms of tangible national policy. Kritz and Keely (1981) note that, like other types of policy, immigration policy responds to perceived needs or obligations, indicating a systems-approach emphasis on adapation. In fact, most policies utilize the systems terminology in their specific laws. Canadian policy includes a formula which weights economic skills heavily; European programs have unabashedly invited migrants to fill temporary labor needs; and all states restrict immigration on the basis of economic capacity. More importantly, system capacity is also used to define acceptable limits for humanitarian, family reunion, and simple free-movement categories (Hawkins 1972; Rist 1978; Krane 1979; Keely 1982; Kubat 1979, among many examining immigration laws). Those policies then set the tone for related settlement and minority programs which will help the nation accommodate its new members. As with the economic and system frameworks, policy-oriented theoretical works assume a primacy of global or national factors in socializing immigrants but are distinguished by their focus on specific programmatic responses.

Micro-theories: Conflict, Integration, and Assimilation of New Groups

Where macro-theories view the immigrant primarily in terms of systemic factors, micro-level approaches shift the focus of study to variations in the experiences of definable groups. To be sure, economic variables and eventual system outcomes are not lost in the analysis, but the emphasis is clearly on *what happens* to Italians, Turkish guest-workers, or Haitian refugees as they confront a new environment. It is at this level that theory is best informed by literally hundreds of studies of particular groups.

A universal assumption of the early versions of this type of theory was that eventual assimilation of immigrants into the host culture was inevitable and desirable (Pedraza-Bailey 1985). Such an unvarying linear pattern was seen in groups whose migration was defined in those purposive terms, as described in a large number of sociologically oriented case studies (Warner and Srole 1945; Handlin 1941, 1951; Gordon 1964; Wittke 1952; Thomas and Znaniecki 1927; Child 1943, are excellent examples of this literature). Frequently this pattern was rationalized in moral or religious terms as well (as in Zangwill's reference to the U.S. melting pot as "God's Crucible" in his 1909 play).

Even after scholars determined that assimilation was almost always a long, multistage process, the path was nonetheless viewed as unidirectional. Gordon's well-known work, for example, eventually established six stages of integration for non-natives: (1) acculturation (adapting to the cultural norms of the new environment); (2) structural assimilation (acceptance of the economic and institutional structures of the new society); (3) amalgamation (merging into the mores and institutions of the host); (4) identificational assimilation (switching of affective ties to the new society); (5) attitudinal assimilation (adopting attitudes and beliefs consonant with those of long-term citizens); and (6) behavioral assimilation (the ultimate merge, in which behavior becomes indistinguishable from that of other residents). For our purposes, the important aspect of such work is its presumption of a linear process. It was assumed that "contact eventually leads to a merging of values and identities" benefiting both immigrants and the host society (Portes and Bach 1985, p. 23).

The fact that some immigrants never progressed through all stages forced a number of theoretical variations. Sowell (1981) documented permanent class and status variations according to national origin; Porter (1965) defined Canada in terms of a "vertical mosaic" in which immigrant ethnics occupied rather fixed strata in the society; Glazer and Moynihan introduced the "beyond the melting pot" concept of dignified differentiation according to ethnicity (1970); and the idea of multiculturalism emerged to accommodate the permanent but legitimate nonassimilation of groups within a benevolent host society. The recognition that ethnic identity persists, not only disrupted the notion of a nonvarying drive toward assimilation but also introduced to hosts the distinctly less appealing need for conscious policies of accommodation as well as integration.

The importance of this moment of nonlinear truth cannot be overemphasized, since it presaged the development of two contrasting models of nonintegrative immigration. One included research which began to document the consistent differentiation of an underclass perpetuated by successive waves of immigrants who seemed always to become classic victims of exploitation. Hoffman-Nowotny (1981) concluded that such differentiation forced immigrants to accept lower status as a judgment on themselves. Theoretically, some analysts interpreted such a pattern along Marxist lines (Castles and Kosack 1973; Piore 1979; Power 1979; Freeman 1979); others saw it as an unprecedented challenge to modern democracies to deal with "new" migrants who were quite different from earlier groups from more kindred nations (Miller 1981; Hoskin and Mishler 1983; Boehning 1981). Although they differ on how they define the underlying social dynamics of this phenomenon, most authors in this school argue that traditional immigration theories are insufficiently sensitive to the vulnerability of migrants who do not assimilate into the host societies.

The second nonintegrative model saw virtue in differentiation and lauded the sometimes trendy emphasis in multicultural policies. In this model, the ethnic identity of immigrants became a rallying point for theories of cultural pluralism, even in the face of evidence that ethnically identified migrants never seemed to achieve the sociopolitical access of other groups (Berry et al. 1984; Hoskin 1985).

The difficulty for group theorists, therefore, has been the persistence of evidence supporting contradictory models of immigrant orientation in the host society. Some immigrants strove to shed their earlier identities despite obstacles to assimilation; others experienced isolation and frustration and withdrew into the small comfort of poor ethnic enclaves; and still others sought ethnic parity with dominant national groups. Lacking a comprehensive group-level theory, some analysts turned to individual variation, which I review next.

Sub-Micro-Theories: Individual Political Response

Individually focused theories of the politics of immigration have been less prominent than others at least partially because immigrants do not fit into traditional conceptual frameworks easily. In the specific case of socialization theory, for example, immigrants tend to fall between the cracks of established lines of inquiry. As suggested throughout this volume, most research on socialization per se has concentrated on children (Brim and Wheeler 1966; Sigel and Hoskin 1977, are exceptions). Even when the focus is on adults, the immigrant presents a mixed case. Unlike most adults, he is not just extending the natural political orientations of his childhood. Rather, he faces the challenge of reconciling old expectations and loyalties with a new political environment. Since he is new, and often insecure within that environment, however, the process may be more similar to that experienced by children: authority looms large, information is scant, behavioral involvement seems remote. And, as I noted in the preceding section, his "proper" role in the new society—new lower-class, apprentice-citizen, proud ethnic—is anything but clear. Just as he experienced a major, even painful decision to leave home, he must decide which social and political path to pursue in the new society. In that process, *desocialization* and *resocialization* may need to occur simultaneously. As Gitelman notes in his study of American and Russian emigrés, these immigrants constitute "such a special case of adult resocialization, resembling childhood socialization in several crucial ways, that fundamental political orientations, and not just external behavior, may be transferred in the process of immigrant political socialization" (Gitelman 1982, p. 174).

Immigrants are thus caught between relatively firmly established theoretical guideposts. On the one hand, desocialization and resocialization are foreign concepts to the considerable body of theory on childhood socialization

(Greenstein 1965; Hess and Torney 1967; Hyman 1959; Sigel and Hoskin 1981; Searing et al. 1976), yet immigrants need to be analyzed in terms of many concepts keyed to initial political learning. At the same time, some of the more expansive theoretical constructs developed to accommodate socialization into adulthood (for example, the generational and life-cycle perspectives evaluated earlier in this volume) do not easily fit those who *enter* the system as adults. Thus where much socialization theory evolved from the debate over how significant the *primacy principle* of early learning is for adult orientations, attention has not been drawn to modifying this question in the study of immigrants (Searing et al. 1976).

In light of this fragmented theoretical picture, it is not surprising that attempts to study immigrants at the individual level have tended to dwell on factors which make the transition of the immigrant harder or easier, and by so doing they tend to overlap somewhat with those whose real focus is the group. Like a host of studies on adaptation in general, Portes and Bach (1985) analyze an extensive array of socioeconomic factors as predictors of Cuban and Mexican adaptation; Reitz has documented paths of immigrant families in Canada (1980); and others have analyzed the perceptions of migrants confronting the challenge of their new environments (Kudat 1974; Mehrlaender et al. 1981; Wilpert 1980, among many). Only a small number deal specifically with political orientations: Wilson's book on British and Italian immigrants in Brisbane, Australia (1973), Black's work on politicization of migrants in Canada (1982); the study by Ada and B. Finifter of American emigrants to Australia (1983), Gitelman's previously cited work on emigrés to Israel (1982); and Miller's less individualized analysis of political activities among foreign workers in Europe (1981). Only Gitelman and Finifter attempt to sketch out concepts basic to a theory of immigrant socialization, and even those attempts are made without an effort to integrate multiple aspects of politics into an explanatory theory. The most striking characteristic of analysis on this level, therefore, is sparse theoretical development despite a large target group whose experiences might well have inspired such development.

Sorting Out Theory: Guidelines for Studying Immigrant Socialization

Development of an integrated theory of immigrant socialization, it is clear, has been impeded by the disparate character of the phenomenon. What happens to immigrants is a question which appears at many levels of analysis (economic and refugee movements, policy debate, community politics) yet serves as a clear focus for none. In fact, in instances where immigrant adaptation has become a major issue, governments have shown a remarkable ability to defuse the question into ad hoc policy adjustments (Kubat 1979; Rist 1978). Even individually based perspectives suffer from the fact that immigrants are a diverse minority of adults in a field more at home with the study of relatively homogeneous children. To assess the state of immigrant socialization research, therefore, I need to bring together common themes which tend to reappear in the extant literature. Specifically, I extract three general but major theoretical propositions which can serve to structure a clearer picture of the socialization process of immigrants:

1. *Immigrant socialization analysis requires an individually defined focus.* However broadly the immigrant socialization phenomenon might be interpreted in policy or even global debate, it is ultimately one whose basic question asks how individuals and groups cope with the demands and opportunities of politics. That means that immigrants are never simply the dependent variable under study. Rather, they are subjects whose political characteristics may be more influenced by international forces and national policies than others, but who nonetheless play a key role in defining how they will confront such factors. The decision to emigrate is, after all, a choice made by individuals who, by that decision, defy any simple definition of them as mere pawns in a larger game. My assessment, therefore, will highlight direct evidence of political socialization in the language specific to that field of study—that is, in terms of developing and lingering loyalties, cognitive orientations, and behavioral involvement in the politics of the new home.

2. *Host policy and public opinion serve as variable correlates of socialization.* Defining the immigrant as the unit of analysis involves construing national policy and its correlates (economic trends, legal and social provisions for foreigners, public opinion) both as *external influences* on immigrant political orientations and behavior and *potential consequences* of those orientations and behavior. In some instances they may be formidable, perhaps even overwhelming forces, but utilizing them as sources and subjects of influence rather than as deterministic prime movers allows us to assess the varying degrees to which immigrant politics are shaped by external and internal factors. Evidence suggests that policy and opinion *are* malleable and subject to influence by how well immigrants either adapt to or challenge roles beneficial to the host. In short, policy, socioeconomic conditions, and opinion are parameters which define or limit immigrants in some cases but which are shaped by immigrant politics in others.

3. *Immigrant socialization is the balancing of demands for change against strains for continuity.* As several analysts have noted, socialization research has long been dominated by persistence theories emphasizing essential continuity in political learning (Gitelman 1982; Searing et al. 1976; Greenstein 1965; Hess and Torney 1967). For the immigrant, however, change is assumed to be instrumental to his very being: he chooses to change national residence; he chooses to risk the comforts of the familiar for the possible benefits and certain inconveniences of the unknown; he chooses a situation

which promises intergenerational family differences as his children grow up with little identification with (and perhaps hostility toward) his own culture. Since he is an adult, moreover, he must undertake desocialization and resocialization at the same time—changes which appear inherently destabilizing. Finally, whatever immediate gratifications there may be in maintaining the continuity of his earlier political existence through ethnic identity, the cold truth is that such gratification probably has a direct negative effect on his ability to benefit from identification with the host culture. The price of continuity for the immigrant is not a small one, yet ethnics pay it in large quantities. To better understand the tradeoffs involved in this process, I begin by examining my first major proposition, that immigrant socialization is best seen through the experience of the newcomer as he defines himself politically.

Immigrant-Defined Socialization Factors

Although socialization theory has tended to focus on *agents* involved in the process, the essence of the subject is still how people interpret the message of those agents and how they decide what to incorporate and what to reject. A substantial body of research documents some of the differential ways in which people make precisely these decisions. Here I examine if and how immigrants, as a specific category, establish distinctive attitudes and behavior within the context of a new environment.

The literature indicates that post-1945 immigrants may differ markedly from earlier groups, especially in the U.S. Perhaps because there was a sense that immigrants *could* be absorbed in the vast American expanse, political access prior to 1945 was easy: the right to vote was almost immediate, political parties wooed them, and second generations almost automatically moved up a notch or two in occupational and political circles (Riordan 1963). Although some groups certainly experienced initial difficulties, the promise of future improvement was always seen as genuine. Their more recent counterparts, however, have occupied a much more controversial position in national political debates. They are more likely to be seen as a threat to the labor force and perhaps to national integrity as well, and their long-term future is certainly not seen as automatically American.

How do immigrants define their socioeconomic and political outlook under these circumstances? They do so at least partly through their attitudes and behavior, and I identify five major areas in which the individual characteristics of immigrants come into play as they attempt to reorient themselves to the new political home: (1) individual motivations to emigrate; (2) the immigrant's initial position in the host society as defined by socioeconomic skills and cultural affinity; (3) group activity; (4) political information and attitudes; and (5) political behavior. Since only a very few studies address all five of these categories (Finifter and Finifter 1983; Gitelman 1982; Wilson 1973), I draw from a variety of analyses which contribute, indirectly or directly, to one or more of them.

Motivations to Emigrate: Defining Expectations of the New Life

It was noted earlier that theories of international migration most frequently employ a "push-pull" framework to classify original incentives. In fact, driving forces and allures have always worked together as the potential migrant makes this important decision, and my distinctions are used here primarily to establish categories of expectations which are likely to become part of the individual's socializing process. In fact, motivations are relatively simply categorized by most analysts as either political or economic.

Political factors are those emerging from dissatisfaction with political life in the home country. In the majority of cases such dissatisfaction has been rooted in persecution, leading to the flight or expulsion of refugees from nondemocratic nations (Hungarians in 1956; Asians in the 1970s, for example). In a much smaller number of cases, dissatisfaction has been with specific policy or with the general values of the home system, resulting in a search for a better political order elsewhere (Americans moving to Canada during the Vietnam War; many Europeans emigrating to New Zealand and Australia since 1960). In the strictest sense, those with only political motivations are relatively rare, but their political expectations are likely to be far more explicit than those with other reasons for migrating. In a study of potential emigrants in the U.S. and several other nations in 1983, Finifter documented greater cynicism about government, less nationalistic commitment, and sufficient education about the home system to criticize its capacity to perform. In her 1983 followup study of actual emigrants to Australia she documented dissatisfaction with political life as an important incentive to leave. Similarly, Gitelman's study of Americans and Russians in Israel found the more positive motivation of the attractiveness of the Israeli political form, as well as the desire to be a part of its struggle to survive in a hostile region (Gitelman 1982). Still, the numbers involved are very small compared to the total number of immigrants, and I note these purely political motivations primarily to document their specific incidence.

Much more frequent are combinations of political and *economic* motivations. Indeed, economic considerations have always ranked high among groups seeking to make major moves, and we note that irrespective of differences in the national origins of early and later twentieth-century migrations, this incentive has been remarkably constant. Portes and Bach's major study of Cuban and Mexican migrants (1985) documented the dominant role played by economic ties to the U.S. in defining the flight of 10 percent of the Cuban population between 1959 and 1980; and others have found an inextricable link between ideology and economics in the movement of migrants. More specifically, immigrants have defined their moves in terms of the inability of the home political/economic system to allow them to build decent lives. As I will note later, employers in host societies have periodically been very willing to encourage just such motivation (Freeman 1979; Rist 1978; Kudat 1974; Kubat 1979).

Whether the immigrant expects to stay permanently or to return triumphant to the home country, his views about politics are likely to be formed against the context of economic and political opportunity. For my purposes, therefore, the importance of the motivation is that it builds in expectations about how the migrant will fare in the new system. For those specifically intending a permanent move, expectations will cover the entire gamut of social and political life, *and will more likely extend to dissatisfaction with and claims upon the new system*—a pattern documented in the few studies that have examined initial motives and subsequent socialization (Gitelman 1982; Hawkins 1972; Finifter and Finifter 1983). Even though the migrant has made a decision to change his home, he brings major elements of continuity in his political inclinations with him, and he is consequently more likely to constantly compare expectations with achievement in the new environment. In short, he may be willing to change but he insists that changes work to his immediate and overall advantage. On the other hand, those who anticipate only a temporary stay will most likely limit their expectations to economic betterment (Portes and Bach 1985; Rist 1978; Castles and Kosack 1973), and they are unlikely to want to change their habits in more than minimal ways. That preference for continuity, however, may limit their ability to fulfill their economic expectations, and thus *may* eventually translate frustration into political expression in the new society (Mehrlaender et al. 1981; Miller 1981; Rist 1978; Portes and Bach 1985).

The Initial Socioeconomic Niche

The importance of socioeconomic factors in defining political orientations has never been questioned. Status factors indicate not only who will possess the skills needed to understand the complexities of politics, but also who will have the time and resources to translate them into involvement. There is no reason to expect that this relationship should not hold for immigrants as well, as long as we define background factors in terms relevant to their position as *new* entrants in the political game. Unlike some of the areas we have examined, the patterns in this one appear to be fairly clear in supporting the general hypothesis that cultural similarity and higher socioeconomic status are precursors of political integration. The initial niche the immigrant occupies is both defined by his relative advantage economically and culturally, and then used to facilitate a smoother transition to the new society. Since economic and cultural factors are prime in defining this important positional variable, I elaborate on each.

The obvious advantage of cultural similarity was noted by Oscar Handlin when he observed in 1959 that "From a historical perspective, immigration is always accompanied by social problems which are serious but resolvable *as long as the migrants and their host population did not differ too much from each other*" (p. 44). Immigration policies favored kindred regions and races for decades, and only expanded their vision under considerable pressure from Third World nations and human rights organizations after World War II. Even then, most in-migration countries modified the basis of admission less than radically by establishing desired categories of immigrants—usually skilled workers and professionals who "melted readily" into the new society (Portes and Bach 1985; Chiswick 1976; Richmond 1981; Kritz and Keely 1981). Although many immigrants with professional skills found themselves taking inferior positions at first, they were in many instances able to regain their status after a period of adaptation (Portes and Bach 1985).

The flip side of this coin is, of course, that those without similar backgrounds or skills would not fit in, and the literature documenting such a pattern is extensive (Castles and Kosack 1973; Power 1979; Freeman 1979; Rist 1978; Porter 1965). To take a specific example, in a relatively small host nation, the fairly smooth entry of Americans and Russians into the Israeli mainstream stands in stark contrast to the experience of Orientals, who found the gap between their economic position and that of other Israelis too great to bridge politically (Friendly 1972). Mexicans in the Southwest were concentrated in poor sections, yet produced few vocal representatives (Portes and Bach 1985); foreign workers throughout Europe settled into lower-class jobs but remained stoutly apolitical (Castles and Kosack 1973; Klasen and Drew 1973; Miller 1981); unemployment hit guest-workers in Germany especially hard, yet they made few claims on their hosts to extend benefits (Rist 1978). It is possible, of course, that many such immigrants simply do not expect much from government or society, perhaps as a result of their previous socialization in less democratic settings. Like many immigrants to the U.S. in earlier periods, these newcomers accept their economic niche as the way things are, at least partly because they cannot reasonably expect to know what to compare their situation to. Making economic demands, after all, involves questioning authority in at least one setting, and that experience is likely to be totally alien to many. The initial underclass position most experience acts as a quicksand from which they cannot emerge without the help of external factors—precisely those I will document in the next section as erratic or dependent on community goodwill. As a result, Kritz and Keely observe that "the characteristics which make groups suitable for a labor role [willingness to work in low-level jobs for low wages] make them unsuitable for membership in the society" (1981, p. 15). As they note, many societies resolve this dilemma by refusing citizenship to such groups, cutting them off from a whole host of political opportunities.

The cycle of economic disadvantage is a capricious one, often producing other characteristics which impede positive politicization. Zwingmann (1973) and others have documented extensive evidence of psychological disorders which appear more frequently among immigrants than citizens; Mehrlaender notes the reluctance to deal with outsiders (1981); Rist describes the dilemmas faced by parents whose children cannot do well in host schools (1978); Wilpert documents the destabilizing consequences of generational conflict (1980); Portes and Bach (1985) note the break in old-world tradition when women join the work force to supplement an inadequate income; Hoffman-Nowotny concludes that immigration acts as a "transfer of tension," in which immigrant groups accept lower status as judgments on themselves, and the retention of that status then becomes a self-fulfilling prophecy (1981).

Immigrants, it should be noted, most frequently do achieve an economic definition of integration. They find some kind of work and adopt the work habits and some of the living standards of others at their level. Cultural integration comes with much greater difficulty almost irrespective of how well they have fared economically (Handlin 1951; Portes and Bach 1985), and some immigrants (guest-workers, for example) simply avoid the effort entirely. What is important to observe in this cycle, then, is its starting point, since I suggest here that the initial niche is, for better or for worse, defined first by the immigrant but is likely to become a factor in its own right which will play a terribly critical role in further assimilation or nonassimilation into the host society.

In socioeconomic terms, therefore, the current realities of adult immigrants are not remarkably different from those in earlier periods. Those who entered with advantages found political integration easier, and those who lacked such resources had to hope their children would benefit from their labors. Lower-status immigrants *lack the ability to change;* they are forced by their very lack of resources to maintain a bleak continuity with their previous lives. Those entering with resources, on the other hand, can *change selectively,* adopting those aspects of host life necessary to complement their considerable store of advantages. Where there is a departure from earlier patterns is in the more recent efforts, particularly in Europe, to remove eventual integration from their policies. In those cases the immigrant has the choice of either accepting that bleak future for himself and his descendants, or choosing a decidedly more risky path of participation in which he fights for fuller opportunities. In either case, the possibility of immediate political integration is impeded by the need to work on the economic side first. Since recent migrants are if anything less likely than earlier groups to bring economic resources with them, this factor looms especially large in postponing political involvement.

Group Activity: Pluralist Approaches to Politics

In most societies, the only realistic defense minorities have against a more powerful system is collective. The isolated and poor immigrant, it has been shown, receives little encouragement to become politically involved, but a concerted group effort might provide an easier way for him to articulate the need for greater opportunities, both economic and political. Immigrants have not been blind to this fact, in many cases demonstrating remarkable imagination and resilience in the face of indifference or hostility from their hosts. Although the lines between general and political activity are not always clear, I focus in this section on the ways immigrants have utilized groups to either facilitate change or maintain some essential continuity in their lives.

Economic Groups. The most obvious examples of group activity derive from socioeconomic factors outlined in the preceding section. In the case of lower-class immigrants the grouping is the poor ghetto which, although it does provide a social network, is almost never a positive political force (Garcia 1981; Portes and Bach 1985). For middle-class immigrants, however, the unit is the economic enclave, often a source of prosperity and self-definition which exists almost totally independent of the host. Its best example is Cuban Miami, an expansive geographic collection of businesses and residences which are virtually self-sufficient and continue to bring new immigrants into the economy with a minimum of disruption (Cuban-owned enterprises in the enclave, for example, grew from 919 in 1967 to over 13,000 in 1985). Migrants adapt to the American economic system first, then proceed to adapt to the broader system with the benefit of financial security (Portes and Bach 1985). Similar enclaves have been developed by different ethnic groups elsewhere, promoting ethnic solidarity (continuity) at the same time that they open the door to profitable adaptation (change) for their residents (Bonacich 1972). Interestingly, economic enclaves exhibit almost universally conservative social and political values, tolerating little social deviance and no variation in loyalty from the virtues of the host system (Arguelles 1982). Not surprisingly, their residents also tend to become good citizens—with higher turnout and general participation rates than other ethnic groups. They thus promote eventual change and accommodation to the new system by fostering a measure of ethnic continuity which serves to promote economic security as well.

The importance of this form of social organization is underscored by the reiteration that immigrants have always tended to their economic roles before venturing into politics. When the residential setting is isolated and restricted to other economically dependent migrants (the more common case), the first crucial step to positive socialization is at best delayed, perhaps never really taken. When the resources of previous migrants and ethnic cohesion combine to create enclaves (the less common case), socialization is likely to be more rapid and predictably positive.

Ethnic Organizations. Almost by definition, ethnic organizations value continuity of identification over change to the norms of the host society. In some instances the groupings are created to preserve some ethnic heritage, but they have other functions as well. They are a natural lobby for ethnic programs, keeping the government aware of their presence and needs (Berry et al. 1984; Reitz 1980; Hawkins 1972). They also may reflect minority re-actions to bad conditions and encourage their members to unite against con-formity to any host norms (Schmitter 1980). Home organizations of foreign workers, Miller notes, do precisely this, maintaining the workers' cohesion at the expense of any efforts to become active in the European organizations that might welcome them (1981). This pattern is not unlike group solidarity historically. New York at the turn of the century included largely unintegrated East European Jews, Irish Catholics, Italian Catholics, and other religiously based groups, all dedicated to retaining ethnic solidarity despite at least the nominal availability of equivalent host organizations. Even union member-ship is sometimes separated by national grouping, protecting members without language fluency but encouraging isolation. By taking over such functions as instruction in home-country culture and language, ethnic orga-nizations present themselves as alternatives to (or even rejection of) adapta-tion. Such outlets are probably encouraged by the reluctance of governments to reconsider their policies on long-term citizenship and integration; nonethe-less they may ultimately serve to restrain immigrants from pushing for greater political opportunity (Hoffman-Nowotny and Killias 1979). As Hoskin (1985, p. 13) concluded: "Ironically, a major obstacle to full political partic-ipation appears to be ethnic cohesion."

Membership in Host-Society Groups. Immigrants are least likely to be in-volved in this type of group. Schmitter notes that, except in the United States, nonwork social groups are not terribly common, and participation by immi-grants even less so. In Europe, some church and welfare groups do make conscious efforts to recruit immigrants, but their activities tend to overlap with those of the home organizations, and some governments, such as the Swiss, simply leave this type of group activity to the consulate of the home country (Schmitter 1980; Miller 1981). The one organization in which im-migrant membership appears to be on the rise is that of the labor union, which foreigners now join in larger percentages than nationals in some countries

(Hoskin 1985; Mehrlaender et al. 1981). They actively participate in worker councils in a number of key industries in West Germany, and unions have begun to recruit them more actively, realizing that immigrants will continue to be a major labor presence in the host societies. In these instances, however, the problem of working-class hostility to the newcomers remains, and the overall effect of membership is still muted by the legal inability of the foreigners to extend their activity into the political activities reserved for citizens. Although there have been some instances where ethnic labor groups have engaged in strike activity, these have been relatively rare and not always supported by the parent organization.

It appears, then, that most forms of group activity are not necessarily conducive to positive resocialization. For ethnic groups the effect of membership is to emphasize continuity with the homeland, even at the expense of quicker adaptation to the host. For other social groups which attempt to link immigrant with host, the evidence provides little indication that the activity is widespread or especially effective. Only the economic enclave seems to combine features of continuity and change productively, thus hastening the melting-pot phenomenon for its residents. Interestingly, this conclusion is very similar to those drawn by analysts who studied earlier groups in the United States, especially those operating under the aegis of the party machines but retaining homeland ties. For those not attached to enclaves or who do not patronize political organizations, group activity is not a demonstrable impetus to integration. However important group activity has been as secondary socialization in general, therefore, it indicates few promising patterns among current immigrants.

Political Information and Attitudes

Although the previous sections revealed some general evidence of the push to conform to the new socioeconomic system and the strain to maintain some old-world identity, it is in the areas of concrete, explicitly political orientations and behavior that we should observe the most direct indication of how, and how much, socialization occurs. Unfortunately, this is also the area which has produced the least specific research. To lend some order to my review, I consider affective and cognitive dimensions of involvement first, then turn to the behavioral dimension in the next section.

Traditionally, immigrants have been portrayed as ideal precitizens. The literature on pre-1960 American immigrants is filled with illustrations. They were appropriately grateful to their new host for the opportunities provided and were supremely loyal; they eagerly attached themselves to parties and other political institutions; and they learned only enough to interpret political events in terms flattering to the system. Despite objective evidence that their lives were hard and that they were subjects of considerable discrimination, they apparently accepted their half loaves as better than none and displayed remarkably strong affective feelings (Riordan 1963; Handlin 1941, 1951; Child 1943; Carr 1975; Sowell 1981; Eisenstadt 1954, among many).

The patterns which have been found among post-1945 immigrants in the United States and elsewhere vary considerably from this earlier pattern, at least in part because the assumptions of permanent residence and assimilation have been qualified. Where earlier immigrants willingly undertook to de-socialize their former loyalties and behavior, many of the newer cohorts lack the promise of eventual citizenship to make them *want* to reorient themselves politically (Kubat 1979). It is wise, under these circumstances, to consider potential citizens and likely noncitizens separately. As I will note, the empirical evidence also justifies such a division.

For migrants whose purpose in the host country is predominantly economic, political information and attitudes are only relevant as they affect their ability to live in reasonable security and to make money. Mehrlaender's massive study of the situation and attitudes of guest-workers in Germany, for example, found little desire for contact with Germans as long as those workers perceived their stay as temporary. Those recognizing the likely permanence of their residence, in contrast, desired such contact, sought out information about Germany, and saw issues affecting them far more directly (1981). In the same vein, Wilpert found those with children more eager to find out about education policy and to have an opinion on which political factions would do better by them (1980); and Miller's extensive survey of foreign-worker politicization revealed evidence of high levels of information and concern with economic and social issues (1981). In Canada the pattern is similar, with newer ethnics exhibiting awareness of language and economic issues, in many cases at a higher level than nationals (Richmond and Kalbach 1977). Portes and Bach found Mexican and Cuban immigrants increasing their knowledge about the U.S. as their stay lengthened (1985).

When we turn to how they feel about the host political system, an interesting pattern appears. Almost without exception, migrants perceive discrimination. They know they perform jobs wanted by no one in the host society, they are keenly aware of the restrictions imposed upon them in work and residence, and they know they would have little support if the national economies were to turn sour (Mehrlaender et al. 1981; Kudat 1974; Miller 1981). In some instances, but not many, migrants have been inspired to voice protest, to strike, and to take their cases to union and government leaders (Miller 1981). Yet despite the perception of hostility and the absence of the promise of full citizenship, most economic migrants express positive affect for the host systems. Guzman (1976), Portes and Bach (1985), and Garcia (1981) are among those documenting very high loyalty to the U.S. among Mexicans;

Portes and Bach find even higher levels among Cubans. Among European migrants the feelings are less those of genuine affect than respect for the system which produces such economic success (Mehrlaender 1981; Power 1979), but they are nonetheless relatively positive.

There are three possible explanations for this pattern. One is that which applied to earlier immigrants. They have left conditions which are worse than any they find in the U.S. or Europe, conditions which offered no hope of betterment, and in which any critical response might well have meant political persecution. In this view, the new host—even an indifferent or restrictive one—deserves one's gratitude. A second is that discrimination can coexist with opportunity in the host, making it realistic for immigrants to come to terms with the society in a less idealistic way. As Portes and Bach (1985) conclude, "Refugees and immigrants who say that they are satisfied, intend to stay, and feel discriminated against are not expressing a contradiction. They are voicing instead a realistic assessment of their condition" (p. 297). The third and related explanation is that which has kept immigrants loyal for decades: the hope that from their sacrifices their children will benefit, if only through time and familiarity. In any case, the options of turning dissatisfaction into political opposition or moving on again are less attractive than reconciling one's position as at least tolerable. In short, considerable rationalization, but rationalization based on a definite realism, may well take place.

For those who have no real expectation of political integration themselves, the orientations I have described above are mostly those they *add* to their feelings associated with the homeland. Neither desocialization nor resocialization is involved to any significant degree. For those emigrating to politically receptive hosts, however, the process should be different. They enter with political expectations, they most frequently have very specific comparisons to make with their previous home, and they face few of the legal and social barriers so evident to the newer economic migrants. Since the time when nations happily opened their doors to foreigners is long past, the instances of this type of immigration are much fewer. Not surprisingly, the most explicit studies of adult resocialization (and the only ones based on substantial panel data) have been done in such a context. Although they differ in focus (Gitelman's book is an omnibus assessment of all orientations, Finifter deals primarily with participation), I rely heavily on them to review patterns of affective and cognitive socialization.

Both Gitelman's study of immigrants to Israel and the Finifters' work on Americans in Australia represent specific attempts to define desocialization and resocialization processes. Both studies found affective orientations to be influenced by previous experience and by expectations associated with the decision to migrate. Thus in Israel respondents' sense of political trust and efficacy remained mostly unchanged despite the change of system, and in

Australia levels of interest were directly related to political activity in the previous setting. Perhaps more relevant, immigrants in both cases developed their affective orientations toward the new host at least partially in the context of dissatisfaction with some aspect of life in the home country which had led them to consider emigration in the first place. Thus like economic migrants, they may well have tended to define their new loyalties as results of their previous orientations. Americans in both settings found it necessary to desocialize themselves from previous party identifications, even when the choices in the new system were not especially appealing to them. In both instances, the net effect was positive affective orientations, buttressed by substantial political information among those whose reason for emigrating was at least in part politically motivated.

One particularly interesting pattern documented by Gitelman was the extraordinary influence of war in producing commitment and loyalty. Since there was no equivalent in the Australian case it is impossible to compare the two, but we can note that in Israel this factor was stronger than any of the institutional or previous expectations factors in developing involvement in Israeli politics. Traditional agents, on the other hand, were simply not effective in resocializing immigrants. In Australia immigrants tended to reproduce patterns of previous involvement, including orientation to a new party and commitment to Australia as a political home, without conscious referents to political organizations, the church, or other groups. In neither case were the agents usually associated with socialization at all ages very noticeable.

It is clear that the research reviewed is unbalanced: the work on economically motivated migrants lacks a clear socialization focus, and that on the politically motivated emigrés in Australia and Israel may be special twentieth-century cases. Still, two patterns stand out from this review of findings on affective dimensions. For those inspired by economic need and received with little enthusiasm by the host nation, the tendency appears to be to try to fit in and be loyal first, reserving critical postures for later, if ever. For those inspired by political dissatisfaction and received with enthusiasm, on the other hand, the tendency appears to be just the reverse: to transfer their critical, not overwhelmingly loyal sentiments to the new host, reserving firm commitments to a later period. For both groups, the *motivation to migrate translates into a comparable affective orientation*. In both cases they manage, almost universally, to develop at least some positive orientations.

Second, immigrants acquire information relevant to their new existence. Like citizens, they are selective, but they also avail themselves of information that they may never have the opportunity to use on behalf of their interests. To be sure, most maintain an interest in the homeland, but that interest lessens with time. That suggests that some element of change/adaptation to the new system may be almost inevitable, even in the least congenial circumstances.

Behavioral Involvement in Politics

Characteristically, immigrants find other pursuits initially more pressing than participation in politics. Yet most of those who study the early experiences of immigrants note how important this period is for political learning which will then frame the activities they do undertake (Black 1982; Gitelman 1982). Not surprisingly, it is relatively easy to distinguish once again between the early images and subsequent behavior of those who see no expectation of citizenship, or no immediate integration, and those whose migrate with expectations of full political participation.

For the former group, the introduction to political learning is one which emphasizes barriers, dangerous acts, and generally restrictive norms. It is clear that they are certainly not *expected* to undertake political education, nor should they engage in any activity which is politically disruptive, since that is a possible cause for deportation (Rist 1978). Consequently, their orientation appears predominantly low-key, one of overall quiescence and passivity, perhaps even suggesting that their political involvement is hardly worth examination.

Miller argues against such an approach, preferring instead to view their participation as "politicization of the ordinarily nonpolitical" (p. 22). Viewed in those terms, there are a number of domains in which political behavior can be observed, including four of considerable note. First, they engage in expressive, extraparliamentary activities, primarily strikes and protest meetings. Such activities have sometimes been violent and linked to radical organizations, but they have always served the same function as demonstrative activities of nationals: drawing attention to a plight seen by demonstrators as in need of reform. Though not frequent, such activities have included wildcat strikes and protests by foreign workers in France and Germany and demonstrations by Caribbean immigrants in the U.S.

Second, there are less visible activities associated with consultative bodies. Most of these are local and most engage in more debate than decision-making, but they do provide at least a forum for issues affecting immigrants, and in recent years their members have used that forum to ask for voting rights for long-term residents (Decker 1982; Rath 1983). Although it is popular to scoff at their activity as nominal, it should be noted that it is in many instances more than that undertaken by citizens. Third, Miller points to industrial political activity which, in highly centralized economic systems such as Germany, carries enormous potential for political impact. Foreign workers are represented in industry councils and broader committees which offer benefits and programs to member families as well. Since the rate of unionization may be higher among foreigners, the possibility exists that labor policy may be influenced to cater to their needs. Finally, immigrants participate politically through allies—mostly political parties but also welfare, civil rights, and church groups. It is true that even where membership in parties is legal it is usually very low (less than .5 percent of foreigners belong to the Berlin SPD, for example), and some foreign workers prefer to work through ideological associations which oppose integration measures as patronizing (Decker 1982; Rath 1983). Still, those working with party and group allies keep the issue of immigrant treatment alive, much as nonparty groups of citizens force formal organizations to address issues of environment or child welfare.

The evidence accumulated here might lend itself to varying interpretations. On the one hand, it is clear that overt, traditional, political behavior by immigrants of this type (those not voluntarily moving from a generally prosperous nation) is not extensive. As many have noted, the new resident is more concerned with employment than elections, more worried about staying out of trouble himself than exposing government failures. In the most straightforward interpretation of such patterns the immigrant is timid, apathetic, unlikely to become highly active. On the other hand, even that level of watchful noninvolvement is similar to that exhibited by citizens, which in one sense would appear to make immigrants good prospects to fit in politically at some point in the future. Perhaps more important, however, is the observation that real political power often lies in the *potential* for its use rather than its superficial exercise, and in this respect immigrants have made impressive inroads. They dominate some industries, they make possible a domestic standard of living which most citizens would hate to lose, and they have won important support from groups that recognize their contribution to the society. In this sense, at least the *results* of their activities should be seen as potentially significant, given the legal limits to defining those activities in terms comparable to those of citizens. As Miller concludes, "West Europe's foreign workers possess considerable political resources as they increasingly utilize the avenues of political expression open to them." (p. 195).

When we turn to the behavior of those with political motivations and a receptive host society, the criteria for examining their involvement look even more like that employed in analyzing the activities of nationals. As Wilson (1973) pointed out in his study of immigrants in Australia, participation is highly dependent on socioeconomic mobility—not unlike participation among ordinary citizens—and that pattern has been redocumented in Israel and Australia some years later (Gitelman 1982; Finifter, 1983). The Finifters found American immigrants to reproduce participation orientations they had exhibited previously, just as others had documented a basic continuity of involvement or noninvolvement in other settings (Fagen, Brody, and O'Leary 1968). Commitment to remaining in Australia produced quicker commitment to desocialize from the previous party attachment and higher levels of activity—a pattern of special interest since it reveals an important predictor for permanent migrants which is simply not available for those whose stays *cannot* be defined in permanent terms under current national law. Finally, the Finifters were able to demonstrate that time was an important and consistent independent variable in the political resocialization process, producing greater (and perhaps reluctant) attachment to the new system almost by default.

Gitelman's book deals with behavior only in terms of partisan attachments, but it is interesting to note that a large number of Americans found the "instant socialization" offered by aggressive parties to be too strong a pitch. Those emigrating to Israel, it would appear, simply took time to revise their expectations and previous political inclinations to fit the Israeli context, such that "Three to six years after coming to Israel, the immigrants were in the political arena to the same extent as the general population" (Gitelman 1982, p. 299). Like Americans in Australia, this type of immigrant finds his own way in the new political system largely by translating his former political orientations into the new context. For this immigrant category, then, the inherent demands for change in migration are considerably less than those for the economic migrant. The former type possesses greater resources to begin with, his migration is more his choice, and his new home more likely to be one where his political inclinations will be welcome and reproducible. That he experiences far greater continuity in his political life is perfectly understandable in this context.

Parameters of Socialization: Host Needs, Policy, and Receptivity

To view immigrant socialization as an individualized process is not to downgrade the importance of environmental factors. Immigrants are especially likely to find their images and opportunities consciously shaped by official and unofficial policies of the host society; thus I assess here work relating such factors to migrants by examining (1) official policies and programs; (2) intermediary groups and organizations; and (3) public sentiment toward the status and socialization of newcomers.

Official Immigration Policies as Prime Movers in Socialization

I argued earlier that despite an apparently wide range of experiences with immigration, historical similarities among nations have been striking. Daniel Kubat contends that that parallel extends to specific policies as well: "host nations' responses to in-migration are essentially convergent" (1979, p. xviii). There has been one clear difference in national tradition, in which

American policy has expected immigrants to stay and European policy has assumed that most will not, but similarities still outweigh differences. Specifically, research documents three policy characteristics which can be observed across virtually all receiving states.

The first policy similarity is found in its intent. However altruistically immigration policies have been rationalized, nations have accepted migrants when they saw them as absorbable and/or necessary economically and have restricted their entry when they have been seen as a potential labor surplus. Global patterns have thus reflected cumulative national interests, usually defined in terms of economic deprivation and need (Portes and Bach 1985). Liberal policies accommodated labor shortages and a supply of foreign labor that was reliable, cheap, and largely docile; and in the process their advocates touted them as humanitarian as well (Hoskin and Mishler 1983; Klasen and Drew 1973). There is no evidence in the historical literature that this labor consideration was anything but primary in shaping policy across nations (Lanphier 1981 and Hawkins 1972 on Canada; Hoffman-Nowotny and Killias 1979 on Switzerland; Keely 1982 on the United States; Reimann and Reimann 1979 and Rist 1978 on Germany; Rees 1979 and Studlar 1979 on Britain; Miller 1981 on France; Power 1979 and Freeman 1979 on Europe more generally, to name prominent examples). Even more specifically, policies have been remarkably consistent in the way they incorporate economic conditions: Canada awards bonus admission points for desired economic skills in its "designated classes"; the U.S. emphasizes family reunion in order to maximize job-finding support for the immigrant; Germany requires a work permit (guaranteeing employability) before residence is authorized; Switzerland grants only short-period entry for seasonal employment. Even Britain, which traditionally felt obliged to offer free entry to applicants from former colonies, imposed economic restrictions in the early 1960s to curb the flow of poor Caribbeans.

A second major similarity among receiving nations has been a laissez-faire stance once immigrants arrive. Admission in many instances is the sum and substance of immigration policy, leaving questions of adaptation and integration unaddressed. Ashford's observation about Britain could easily be applied to most host nations: "British laws vacillate between stringent laws to keep minorities out and hoping more timid measures to encourage harmony will suffice" (1982, p. 236). With the exception of some relatively minor government educational and employment programs (Canada's financial support of multicultural festivals, limited German bilingual educational initiatives, for example), governments have confined their obligation to opening the door. In Britain, Parliament delegates all further questions of note to the civil service bureaucracy, the Germans assign immigrant issues to the Labor Ministry, and the U.S. limits official involvement to the already overextended Immigration and Naturalization Service. In Europe this sense of benign neglect may well be linked to the current expectation that most of the foreigners living there will not become naturalized citizens (Kubat 1979). In these instance, however, the fact of continued residence flies in the face of those expectations and should be viewed as a potential source of serious conflict. It is curious, therefore, that there as elsewhere the question is so easily pushed to the policy background.

A final common pattern is the somewhat ironic situation which arises out of the conviction by First World states that freedom to *leave* one's country is a basic right of individual expression. Those with such conviction on *exit*, however, view as entirely natural their right to deny *entry* (Kubat 1979). Apparently a place to go is not seen as a necessary corollary of the right to leave. Even more curious in this regard is the expectation among First World states that they may change their minds about those they admit. An increasing number of states have developed incentives for immigrants to return to their homeland, including programs of return bonuses, reintegration, and employment-creation (Rogers 1981; Miller and Martin 1982). To be sure, nations have always been most protective of their own citizens' rights. Where the difficulty arises is when those nations which take pride in their commitment to basic human rights make them an international policy statement as well, yet invoke specific reservations with respect to those on their doorstep and those only partially integrated into their societies. That host nations embrace contradictory theory and practice is thus a common if unfortunate pattern.

What emerges from this discussion of policy similarities is a series of logical anomalies. At base is the contradiction of principle just mentioned, in which states attractive to immigrants are vocally committed to lofty individualistic principles of democracy at the same time that they apply principles more appropriate to the marketplace to immigrants. Another is the tendency to respond to this chronic problem with policies which are reactive, ad hoc, and rarely more than incremental moves. Still another, more concrete discrepancy appears in the initial willingness of host states to accept those with markedly different cultural development, then assume that they will eventually blend into the national landscape or return home. A fourth, related anomaly is the vacillating character of national enthusiasm for the Old World variety which ethnic immigrants provide, as policies shift between support for ethnic activities and insistence on conformity to national values (Reitz 1980). As a group, these patterns can only be seen as a study in inconsistency, which for our purposes is best evidence of the context of challenge which migrants face as they attempt to cope with ambigous and shifting expectation from their new societies. Daniel Kubat aptly summarized the uncertainty of this aspect of the immigrant environment when he concluded that:

In a democracy, the politics of migration policies are either a response to pressure for more workers or a response to pressure to preserve the national identity by limiting in-migration. In any case, immigration policies will remain a matter of waiting to see what will happen next while issuing ad hoc regulations. (1979, p. xxx)

Intermediary Organizations and Programs: Secondary Movers

That temporizing policies are so pervasive is partly due to the absence of pressure for a coherent master policy from important groups in host societies. The argument could be made, in fact, that, policy has been at base a patchwork sum of separate group demands—none of which emphasizes the migrant's interest in smooth socialization. Since groups other than the family (secondary socializers) are usually categorized in the literature as major factors in the development of political orientations, I next take a brief inventory of how research has assessed the role on influential economic and political forces in defining immigrant socialization patterns.

By far the most consistent support for flexible immigration policy has been from business interests benefiting from the labor supply. They have favored relatively easy entry, but that generosity has not usually extended to favorable wage treatment, assistance in housing, or programs promoting integration into the host society (Miller 1981; Kudat 1974; Miller and Martin 1982). Where assistance has been provided, it has most often been at the insistence of the government, and even then has reflected an assumption that foreign workers are temporary residents rather than eventual citizens (Hoskin 1985). Consequently, businesses have emphasized programs which make the immigrant better able to handle employment but not necessarily better advised about handling permanent residence.

Not surprisingly, organized labor has reacted negatively to this view, arguing that migrants compete for scarce jobs and force wages down and should, therefore, be admitted in only limited numbers. At the same time, unions have been firm in their demand for fair wage and working conditions, both for members, who include growing numbers of immigrants, and nonmembers who might otherwise undercut domestic workers (Miller 1981; Castles and Kosack 1973; Freeman 1979). This strain has been complicated further by a pattern of working-class hostility to minorities (Gaugler et al. 1978; Studlar 1979), with the consequence that labor unions have not been consistently supportive of long-term plans that invite and integrate migrants. Even though migrants may well take jobs native workers shun in good times, the fear that they would prevent fallback employment in hard times keeps labor from enthusiastic support for their interests (Freeman 1979).

Groups without a definable economic base are more likely to be committed to smoothing the transition to life in the host society. Church associations, quasi-governmental agencies, and ethnic associations have historically been the most common source of actual sociopolitical aid for all types of immigrants (refugees, economic migrants, those reuniting with families). Canadian policy gives monetary encouragement to sponsor organizations (Lanphier 1981; Berry et al. 1984), and West Germany has enlisted the support of homeland associations in establishing bilingual education and other programs. One problem, however, is that such organizations are always less resourceful in influencing policy and, ultimately, what happens to immigrants. Their numbers are smaller and their constituency erratic as public support for their goals shifts. A second problem is that their activities sometimes run counter to official policy. The American sanctuary movements, for example, provide at least temporary aid to refugees but may increase the level of conflict between themselves and government and with some local groups which oppose further immigration not sanctioned by law. Similarly, welfare organizations may emphasize awareness of rights among immigrants and educational opportunities for their children, when official policy implies that foreign workers will not remain indefinitely. At least in theory these organizations could be the most effective socializers, but their influence is muted by both a relatively minor position and the possibility that their actions will be inconsistent with official positions that are more restrictive.

Given these group patterns, it is not surprising that political parties find themselves caught between conflicting internal constituencies on this issue. Liberal/Labor parties have an ideological commitment to the disadvantaged yet cannot ignore the fear and hostility expressed by their working-class members. More conservative organizations, on the other hand, want to support the needs of business without appearing to compromise national cultural integrity (Gehmacher 1978; Hoskin 1985). As noted above, British and other governments are fairly typical in their tendency to support only small and incremental programs (Ashford 1982; Keely 1982). Even the generally popular Canadian commitment to multiculturalism has been inconsistently supported as a ragtag collection of ideas with no clear overall goals, even within the context of a twenty-year period in which Liberals have been in almost constant control of government (Hoskin 1985; Palmer 1975). As a result, partisan conflict on the condition of immigrants has been remarkably muted, perhaps reflecting what one analyst calls a persistent if implausible hope by political leaders that that problem will somehow "resolve itself naturally" (Ashford 1982).

The absence of major political party roles in socializing immigrants is a real departure from the tradition that was central to the politicization of earlier waves of American immigrants. Documentation is abundant on the holistic approach taken by party machines to the Americanization of immigrants from the late 1870s through the slowdown in immigration between 1910 and 1920.

Such organizations took almost total responsibility for the welfare of immigrants in social and economic terms. They also took the role of prime socializer seriously in order to cultivate an army of political supporters, providing a thorough introduction to involvement in the political process (Riordan 1963). For better or for worse, however, the machine was totally dependent upon massive patronage and new immigrants, and its influence faded by the mid 1920s. Except for a brief period of Israeli politics when parties also hustled immigrants relentlessly (Gitelman 1982), this was a uniquely American creation, unmimicked in other democracies and thus not observable in other, tamer forms of party influence.

I noted above that the overriding characteristic of immigration policy has been its logical anomalies. For intermediary organizations the emergent theme is one of conflicting internal pressures. Groups with economic, social, and political rationales all suffer from serious divisions within their ranks, and all have tended to favor some mix of programs which would not totally offend any one base. Within such a context, the immigrant is almost necessarily subject to the possibility of frequent shifts in support, putting him in the unattractive position of dependence on both policy and group factors which have shown no consistent pattern of support for his long-term socialization. Secondary socializers, therefore, offer us only mixed evidence as to the direction as well as the intensity and manner of their influence on immigrant adaptation.

Public Opinion as the Climate for Adaptation or Nonadaptation

It should be evident from the discussion above that assessing the role of public opinion will not be simple. A wealth of research has shown that opinion on abstract issues often conflicts with specific applications, and even opinion on specific questions will vary according to how relevant the issue is to the respondent. Work on opinion toward immigrants verifies that these distinctions came into play here as well, in several ways.

I should note at the outset that the general concept of "cultural similarity" is one which appears throughout the literature on immigrant adaptation, often in language asserting its centrality to successful integration (Kunz 1981; Rose 1969). Similarity has historically been a consideration in defining policy options (Keely 1982). It is when we deal with the question of public acceptance of immigrants, however, that it is operationalized most clearly, and most research reveals that cultural nonsimilarity has a negative influence on public attitudes and, in turn, on the ability of nonsimilar immigrant groups to fit into the new society.

At the most general level, attitudes toward immigrants appear to range from relatively cautious to clearly hostile. As Hoskin (1985) reports in reviewing empirical studies, responses to most attitudinal batteries of questions reveal mixed patterns: respondents demonstrate some sympathy for the plight of migrants—their refugee background, the limited opportunities for their children—but more concern about their effect on the host society. Such negative opinion has been documented in numerous single-nation studies (Hoskin 1984 and 1985 on Germany; Hoskin and Mishler 1983 on the U.S. and Britain; Studlar 1978 and Freeman 1979 on Britain; Richmond 1981 and Palmer 1981 in his review of research, on Canada; Callan 1983 and Wilson 1973 on Australia).

That attitudes are generally negative does not explain the basis for that opinion or how intensely it is held, and much less evidence is available on these corollary questions. Some authors have simply cited the degree of societal tolerance as the reason for variation (Kritz and Keely 1979; Rose 1969). Numerous historical case studies have observed the fear of the strangeness of immigrants, resentment of their failure to assimilate quickly, and no small amount of concern that they would compete for status and power in the structure of home communities (Handlin 1951; Sowell 1981; and the vast literature on party machines are relevant examples). More systematic work is limited, but some have suggested that negative opinion may be based on the belief that immigrants pose a direct economic threat (Freeman 1979; Castles and Kosack 1973), and others have focused on the specific racial bases of hostility (Studlar 1978; Reitz 1980). The latter has been amply documented in studies detailing the hardships of specific racial minorities (Studlar's work on blacks in Britain; Portes and Bach on Mexicans and Cubans in the U.S.; Glazer and Moynihan 1970, to name a few). Examining other sources of negative attitudes, Hoskin and Mishler (1983) compared traditional party and class bases of hostility with that rooted in other values and found that obvious differences in background or political preference did not explain variations in attitudes toward immigrants. That finding suggests that opinion on this issue cannot be assessed in simple partisan or ideological terms. Finally, Hoskin (1985) tested four explicit theories of hostility to foreign workers (direct economic threat, disruption of system consensus, unpleasant personal contact, and personal insecurity) and found none to provide a clear basis for negative opinion. These studies indicate a range of explanations for hostility but no single or common source. What makes them similar, on the other hand, is the sense that, without some incentive to develop more congenial attitudes, opinion is likely to remain negative. "In the absence of either attention by existing political institutions or attempts by guestworkers to push their own interests, it would appear that public opinion will remain uncommitted to integration, or indeed to any long-term policy on this issue." (Hoskin 1985, p. 208).

What can be drawn from this overview of parameters of socialization? It is clear that host societies offer opportunity and hope for migrants on one level, one that inspires entry in the first place and likely encourages them to suffer inconvenience, isolation, even humiliation with some grace. On another level, however, these societies have never really deviated from their primary goal of serving their own national interests. That means that what they offer migrants will be tempered by both (1) host expectations that they owe immigrants less than they owe citizens, and (2) expectations that immigrants will fit into the dominant patterns of the society. If immigrants fail to meet these expectations, or even if they are *perceived* as not meeting them, the environment can be discouraging and hostile to their socialization.

This section, therefore, reinforces my organizing theme of socialization as *response to the demands for individual and group change*. Receiving nations are strikingly similar in their expectation that immigrants should present no major demands for host change. They have varied somewhat in the degree to which they demanded that newcomers adapt or assimilate to the host culture, but the instances where the host has actively encouraged immigrants to maintain ethnic characteristics have been essentially limited to some official rhetoric on the virtues (or the inevitability) of multiculturalism, and perhaps encouragement of some private sponsoring organizations. Host society parameters of socialization are thus almost always nonfacilitative at best, severely restrictive at worst. That immigrants have pressed demands successfully, improved their lot over time, and established the level of political presence described in the previous section, is testimony to their ability to combine continuity and change in both their personal adaptation patterns and those they apply to politics in the new home.

Conclusion: Continuity and Change in the Socialization of Immigrants

I began this essay by undertaking to integrate theory and research on the socialization of immigrants. In that process I had to confront two formidable obstacles all too familiar to the social scientist: (1) most extant theory on immigrants is indirect in its treatment of socialization and fragmentary in its coverage of this necessarily expansive phenomenon; and (2) research tends to be both geographically disparate and largely inattentive to the direct question of socialization as process. My task thus developed as one which would first pull together the strains relevant to immigrant socialization from existing theory on socialization and immigration, then assess the process through examination of the large but still incomplete literature. At this point I take stock of how useful the enterprise has been.

On Theroy

Social scientists are well acquainted with the proclivity of theorists to emphasize cause and effect variables, and the literature on immigration is replete with considerations of sources and consequences of this phenomenon, mostly at a macro-level. In the socialization field, a dominant concern with agents and outcomes is quite parallel, but mostly at a micro-level. Not surprisingly, therefore, studies of immigrant socialization as process, especially process which begins with fundamental life-changes in adulthood, have lacked theoretical guideposts. Perhaps because they sense the difficulty of integrating these levels of theory, most of those who have analyzed the process of immigrant socialization have done so through case studies of specific groups and subgroups. Although the fascinating store of ethnographic accounts of the experiences of immigrants have spoken quite eloquently to variations in that process, their disinterest in broader theory frustrated my search for a suitable framework.

A small number of analysts have worked to develop such a framework based on the twin concepts of desocialization and resocialization, and their studies have documented promising patterns. Those patterns were, however, mostly limited to relatively well-heeled, voluntary emigrants. My concern for the larger number of poorer immigrants, however, found this framework limited in the centrality of change within it—a pattern not always evident among culturally similar, resourceful immigrants and even less evident where immigrants are not especially welcome nor inclined to redefine themselves politically. In the absence of directive theory, I introduced a framework that (1) views the immigrant and his responses to political cues as central; (2) treats host policy and programs as possible sources of contextual influence; and (3) focuses on the extent of political continuity or change as the relevant dependent variable in immigrant socialization. Using this conception of socialization as degree of adaptation to demands for change, I proceeded to try to assess existing research. To the extent that the framework allowed me to interpret a wide range of empirical and more anecdotal studies in reasonably comparable terms, I can suggest that it is a promising approach to this question.

On the Dominance of Environment

I noted above that theoretical work in this area has been dominated by contextual factors, and empirical and quasi-empirical work has followed this lead. Viewing immigration from a socialization perspective, however, allows us to force an assessment of *how well* such environmental "agents" do in explaining the immigrant experience, and my review suggests that they do not do well at all. Three patterns evident from the literature support such a position. First, there is such wide variation in both policy and its interpretation and enforcement, even within host nations, that a claim that policy can or does simply control immigrants could not be reasonably tested and proved. Second, domestic interests within such nations are also of several minds, sometimes even diametrically opposed to each other, making their ability to define the lives of immigrants in more than superficial ways highly questionable. Finally, hard evidence on immigrants indicates that in practice they are not totally directed by environmental policy factors, even when that policy is unequivocal (as in universal legal prohibitions against illegal migrants). As we have seen, policy, parties, and even public opinion are all stimuli to which migrants respond in a variety of ways—including manipulation, accommodation, even noncompliance. My conclusion on the role of contextual factors is thus similar to that reached by Beck (1977) in his assessment of the role of agents in socialization more generally: such factors provide cues, even demanding cues, but immigrant response is conditioned rather than dominated by them.

On Immigrants as Socializers

In concluding his book on immigration to Israel, Gitelman half-seriously repeats the common wisdom that all immigrants go through stages of resentment, first against the host society, then against others in their situation. In a totally different context, the Finifters noted that the political activity of immigrants in Australia was "highly dependent on earlier experiences." In still other studies (Portes and Bach 1985 is the single best illustration), immigrants reacting to unfavorable conditions in host societies have marshalled their resources to force decent economic conditions as well as some measure of ethnic integrity. Although these are hardly exhaustive examples, they do point to the importance of immigrants as socializers, independent of context. This and other evidence I find supportive of my insistence on viewing socialization as individualized and group responses to continuous demands for change across nations.

The literature reveals vast differences in how immigrants take to political opportunity, ignore it, or create it where it is not offered. Early waves of immigrants arrived with few goals more explicit than bettering themselves and their families, yet many emerged as driving forces behind change in the host society itself: respect for their good citizenship, accommodation of some of their preferences, even new programs (bilingual education) which reflected their numerical strengths. Americans sought political change in Australia and Israel, yet most fell back on traditional ideological and involvement preferences or dropped out of politics entirely. Thousands of migrants to Europe sought mostly political anonymity and continued ethnic ties but have indicated their willingness to adapt and press for political solutions when their issues (the "ordinarily nonpolitical") were at stake. Immigrants in the U.S. and Canada have labored to keep ethnic traditions strong while adapting gradually to mainstream economic and political life.

What these patterns indicate is the importance of basic elements of continuity in the lives of all migrants confronted with challenge or opportunity to change. For those fortunate enough to select a host with some political considerations in mind, the pattern has been one in which change is sought, then gradually toned down. For those pursuing the economic opportunities of emigration the process is usually the reverse, with an initial preference for continuity modified to accommodate sufficient change to deal with the new environment. In either case, the immigrant or his group has been most productively studied as he considers the merits of both accommodation and tradition in getting the most out of life in the new society.

On Future Research

To a certain extent, the three sets of general observations made above are both a critique of the vast but disparate literature and a blueprint for new work. Rather than fitting itself into previous research, work needs to begin by extracting the essential focus on immigrants and how they react to elements of their new environment. I have repeatedly asserted that their need to change and adapt coexists with, conflicts with, and forces constant choices about, their need for continuity. The simple but basic organizing question is thus, what conditions promote greater or lesser change in the ways immigrants relate to politics?

Establishing a design for studying this question involves rather fundamental processes of conceptualization and operationalization of independent and dependent variables. With the basic concept of *change in relating to politics*—its absence or degree—accepted as the dependent variable, existing operational definitions may be utilized or modified as actual measures. Thus I might not entirely randomly suggest that my dependent variable of relating to politics be operationalized to embrace affective, cognitive, and behavioral orientations, orientations for which scores of concrete measures have been developed and applied in a number of different contexts (Sigel and Hoskin 1981, review and apply these three orientations). In a similar fashion, the independent variables that are thought to produce variation in involvement can be constructed creatively from interesting case examples (the influence of enclave norms, the strength of achievement ethics in the groups, for example) as well as gleaned from standard collections (socioeconomic status, strength of ethnicity, group membership). Intervening factors (such as the existence and quality of educational and remedial programs, the support of sponsors, unemployment rates, and the like) can be inserted into the growing empirical model for group and overall testing. Finally, the basic antecedent variables defined by host differences (policy, tradition, numbers of immigrants) can be used as important first-order controls to assess the importance of these factors in setting real limits on immigrant political involvement.

Ideally, all good socialization research requires panel data. For the analysis of immigrants, that requisite would permit the examination of the question in the form most interesting to me—namely, how changes in our independent variables affect changes in the dependent variable of political involvement. Since immigrants most commonly have to stay registered as resident aliens with their hosts, they are conceivably more traceable than other population groups. Even without panel studies, however, important base-line data may be gathered which may sort out initial questions (such as which forms of participation are worth asking about) and suggest central divisions among groups (enclave residents from others, those with language difficulties from those without) which can be derived even from cross-sectional analyses.

What I suggest is that analysts make an effort to address the simple question framing this volume by asking a simple question before adding the factors which make it realistically complex. To do so requires enormous restraint and a patience in adding the detail which gives the study of immigration its richness. I suspect, however, that such initial resolve will produce major achievements: theoretical simplicity, empirically validated patterns, and, consequently, a greater comprehension of how immigrants actually become more or less political in their new environments.

References

Allen, J. 1978. "The Economic Factor in Canadian Immigration Policy." In *The Canadian Ethnic Mosaic*, ed. L. Driedger. Toronto: McClelland and Stewart.

Arguelles, L. 1982. "Cuban Miami: the Roots, Development, and Everyday Life of an Emigré Enclave in the U.S. National Security State." In *The New Nomads*, ed. Marlene Dixon and Susanne Jonas. San Francisco: Synthesis Publications.

Ashford, D. E. 1982. *Policy and Politics in Britain*. Philadelphia: Temple University Press.

Beck, P. A. 1977. "The Role of Agents in Political Socialization." In *Handbook of Political Socialization*, ed. S. A. Renshon. New York: The Free Press.

Berry, J. B., et al. 1984. *Multiculturalism in Canada: Social and Educational Perspectives*. Toronto: Allyn and Bacon.

Black, J. 1982. "Immigrant Political Adaptation in Canada: Some Tentative Findings." *Canadian Journal of Political Science* 15: 3–28.

Boehning W. H. 1981. "Elements of a Theory of International Economic Migration to Industrial Nation States." In *Global Trends in Migration: Theory and Research in International Population Movements*, ed. M. M. Kritz, C. B. Keely, and Silvano M. Tomasi. New York: Center for Migration Studies.

Bonacich, E. 1972. "A Theory of Ethnic Antagonism: the Split Labor Market." *American Sociological Review* 37: 547–59.

Brim, O. G., and S. Wheeler. 1966. *Socialization after Childhood*. New York: John Wiley.

Brinley, T. 1973. *Migration and Economic Growth*. London: Macmillan.

Brown, L. G. 1969. *Immigration: Cultural Conflicts and Social Adjustments*. New York: Arno Press.

Bryce-Laporte, R. S., ed. 1980. *Sourcebook on the New Immigration.* New Brunswick: Transaction Books.

Callan, V. 1983. "Anglo-Australian Attitudes toward Immigration: A Review of Survey Evidence." *International Migration Review* 17: 120–37.

Carr, J. F. 1975. *Assimilation of the Italian Immigrant.* New York: Arno Press.

Castells, M. 1975. "Immigrant Workers and Class Struggles in Advanced Capitalism: The Western European Experience." *Politics and Society* 5: 33–66.

Castles, S., and G. Kosack. 1973. *Immigrant Workers and Class Structure in Western Europe.* New York: Oxford University Press.

Child, I. L. 1943. *Italian or American? The Second Generation in Conflict.* New Haven: Yale University Press.

Chiswick, B. 1976. *An Analysis of the Economic Progress and Impact of Immigrants.* Final report to the U.S. Department of Labor, Employment and Training Administration. Chicago: University of Illinois.

Decker, F. 1982. *Auslaender im politischen Abseits-Moeglichkeiten ihrer politischen Beteiligung.* Frankfurt: Campus Verlag.

Eisenstadt, S. N. 1954. *The Absorption of Immigrants.* London: Routledge and Kegan Paul.

Fagen, R., R. A. Brody, and T. J. O'Leary. 1968. *Cubans in Exile.* Palo Alto: Standford University Press.

Feagin, J. R. 1978. *Racial and Ethnic Relations.* Englewood Cliffs: Prentice-Hall.

Finifter, Ada. 1983. "Emigration from the United States: An Exploratory Analysis." Presented at the Conference on Political Support, Madison: University of Wisconsin.

———, and B. Finifter. 1983. "Political Socialization of International Migrants: American Immigrants in Australia." Presented at the Annual Meeting of the American Political Science Association, Washington, D.C.

Freeman, G. P. 1979. *Immigrant Labor and Racial Conflict in Industrial Societies.* Princeton: Princeton University Press.

Friendly, A. 1972. *Israel's Oriental Immigrants and Druzes.* London: Minority Rights Group.

Garcia, J. A. 1981. "Political Integration of Mexican Immigrants: Explorations into the Naturalization Process." *International Migration Review* 15: 608–25.

Gaugler, E., et al. 1978. *Auslaender in Deutschen Industriebetrieben.* Cologne: Happ Verlag.

Gehmacher, E. 1978. *Auslaenderpolitik in Konflikt.* Bonn. Neue Gesellschaft.

Gitelman, Z. 1982. *Becoming Israelis: Political Resocialization of Soviet and American Immigrants.* New York: Praeger.

Glazer, N., and D. P. Moynihan. 1970. *Beyond the Melting Pot: The Negroes, Puerto Ricans, Jews, Italians, and Irish of New York City.* Cambridge: MIT Press.

Gordon, M. 1964. *Assimilation in American Life: The Role of Race, Religion, and National Origins.* New York: Oxford University Press.

Grebler, L., J. W. Moore, and R. C. Guzman. 1970. *The Mexican-American People: the Nation's Second Largest Minority.* New York: The Free Press.

Green, A. G. 1976. *Immigration and the Postwar Canadian Economy.* Toronto: Macmillan.

Greenstein, F. I. 1965. *Children and Politics.* New Haven: Yale University Press.

Guzman, R. C. 1976. *The Political Socialization of the Mexican-American People.* New York: Arno Press.

Handlin, O. 1941. *Boston's Immigrants: a Study of Acculturation.* Cambridge: Harvard University Press.

—. 1959. *The Newcomers.* Cambridge: Harvard University Press.

—. 1951. *The Uprooted: The Epic Story of the Great Migrations That Made the American People.* Boston: Little, Brown.

Hansen, A., and A. Olivera-Smith, eds. 1982. *Involuntary Migration and Resettlement.* Boulder: Westview Press.

Hawkins, F. 1972. *Canada and Immigration: Public Policy and Public Concern.* Montreal: McGill-Queens University Press.

Herfurth, M., and H. Hogewog-Dehaart. 1982. *Social Integration of Migrant Workers and Other Ethnic Minorities: A Documentary of Current Research.* New York: Pergamon Press.

Hess, R., and J. Torney. 1967. *The Development of Political Attitudes in Children.* Chicago: Aldine.

Hoffman-Nowotny, H. J. 1981. "A Sociological Approach toward a General Theory of Migration." In *Global Trends in Migration: Theory and Research in International Population Research,* ed. M. M. Kritz, C. B. Keely, and S. M. Tomasi. New York: Center for Migration Studies.

—, and M. Killias. 1979. "Switzerland." In *International Labor Migration in Europe,* ed. R. Krane. New York: Praeger.

Holmes, C., ed. 1978. *Immigrants and Minorities in British Society.* London: Allen and Unwin.

Hoskin, M. 1987. "Immigration, Multiculturalism, and Pluralist Democracy in Canada." *Migraciones Internacionales en las Americas.*

—. 1984. "Integration or Nonintegration of Foreign Workers: Four Theories." *Political Psychology* 5: 661–86.

—. 1985. "Public Opinion and the Foreign Worker: Traditional and Nontraditional Bases of Opinion." *Comparative Politics* 18: 193–210.

—, and W. Mishler. 1983. "Public Opinion toward Foreign Workers: A Comparative Analysis." *International Migration* 21: 440–61.

Hyman, H. 1959. *Political Socialization: A Study in the Psychology of Political Behavior.* Glencoe: The Free Press.

Keely, C. B. 1982. "Immigration and the American Future." In *Ethnic Relations in America,* ed. Lance Liebman. Englewood Cliffs: Prentice-Hall.

Klasen, C. H., and P. Drew. 1973. *Migration Policy in Europe.* Lexington: Lexington Books.

Krane, R., ed. 1979. *International Labor Migration in Europe.* New York: Praeger.

Kritz, M. M. 1982. *U.S. Immigration and Refugee Policy.* Lexington: D. C. Heath.

—, and C. Keely, eds. 1981. *Global Trends in Migration.* New York: Center for Migration Studies.

Kubat, D., ed. 1979. *The Politics of Migration Policies.* New York: Center for Migration Studies.

Kudat, A. 1974. *Internationale Arbeitskraftwanderung.* Berlin: Wissenchaftszentrum.

Kunz, E. 1981. "Exile and Resettlement: Refugee Theory." *International Migration Review* 15: 42–51.

Lanphier, C. M. 1981. "Canada's Response to Refugees." *International Migration Review* 15: 113–30.

Lebergott, S., ed. 1964. *Men Without Work: The Economics of Unemployment*. Englewood Cliffs: Prentice-Hall.

Lee, E. S. 1966. "A Theory of Migration." *Demography* 3: 47–57.

Li, P. S., and B. S. Bolaria. 1979. "Canadian Immigration Policy and Assimilation Theories." In *Economy, Class, and Social Reality: Issues in Contemporary Canada*, ed. J. A. Fry. Toronto: Butterworths.

Lucas, R. E. B. 1981. "International Migration: Economic Causes, Consequences, and Evaluation." In *Global Trends in Migration: Theory and Research in International Population Movements*, ed. M. M. Kritz, C. B. Keeley, and S. M. Tomasi. New York: Center for Migration Studies.

Mangalam, J. 1978. "Toward a Migration Typology as a Prelude to Building Theories of Migration." Presented at the Ninth World Congress of Sociology, Uppsala.

Mehrlaender, U., et al. 1981. *Situation der Auslaendishcen Arbeitnehmer und ihre Familenangehoerigen in der Bundesrepublik Deutschland*. Bonn: Bundesminister fuer Arbeit und Sozialordnung.

Miller, M. J. 1981. *Foreign Workers in Western Europe*. New York: Praeger.

Miller, M. J., and P. L. Martin. 1982. *Administering Guest Worker Programs: Lessons from Europe*. Lexington: Lexington Books.

Palmer, H. 1981. "Canadian Immigration and Ethnic History in the 1970s and 1980s." International Migration Review 15: 471–501.

————. 1975. *Immigration and the Rise of Multiculturalism*. Vancouver: Copp Clark.

Pedraza-Bailey, S. 1985. *Political and Economic Migrants in America: Cubans and Mexicans*. Austin: University of Texas Press.

Piore, M. J. 1975. "Notes for a Theory of Labor Market Stratification." In *Labor Market Segmentation*, ed. R. C. Edwards et al., Lexington: D. C. Heath.

————. 1979. *Birds of Passage: Migrant Labor and Industrial Societies*. New York: Cambridge University Press.

Porter, J. 1965. *The Vertical Mosaic: An Analysis of Social Class and Power in Canada*. Toronto: University of Toronto Press.

Portes, A. 1969. "Dilemmas of a Golden Exile: Integration of Cuban Refugee Families in Milwaukee." *American Sociological Review* 34: 505–18.

————. 1978. "Immigrant Aspirations." *Sociology of Education* 51: 241–60.

————, and R. Bach. 1985. *Latin Journey: Cuban and Mexican Immigrants to the U.S.* Berkeley: University of California Press.

————, et al. 1980. "Assimilation or Consciousness: Perceptions of U.S. Society among Recent Latin American Immigrants to the United States." *Social Forces* 59: 200–224.

Power, J. 1979. *Migrant Workers in Western Europe and the United States*. New York: Praeger.

Pryor, R. J. 1981. "Integrating International and Internal Migration Theories." In *Global Trends in Migration: Theory and Research in International Population Movements,* ed. M. M. Kritz, C. B. Keely, and S. M. Tomasi. New York: Center for Migration Studies.

Rath, J. 1983. "Political Participation of Ethnic Minorities in the Netherlands." *International Migration Review* 17: 445–69.

Rees, T. 1979. "The United Kingdom." In *The Politics of Migration Policies,* ed. D. Kubat. New York: Center for Immigration Research.

Reimann, H., and H. Reimann. 1979. "Federal Republic of Germany." In *International Labor Migration in Europe,* ed. R. E. Krane. New York: Praeger.

Reitz, J. G. 1980. *The Survival of Ethnic Groups.* Toronto: McGraw-Hill.

Richmond, A. 1967. *Post-War Immigration in Canada.* Toronto: University of Toronto Press.

———. 1981. "Immigrant Adaptation in a Postindustrial Society." In *Global Trends in Migration: Theory and Research in International Population Movements,* ed. M. M. Kritz, C. B. Keely, and S. M. Tomasi. New York: Center for Migration Studies.

———, and W. Kalbach. 1977. *Factors in the Adjustment of Immigrants and Their Descendants.* Ottawa: Statistics Canada.

Riordan, W. 1963. *Plunkett of Tammany Hall.* New York: E. P. Dutton.

Rist, R. C. 1978. *Guestworkers in Germany.* New York: Praeger.

Rogers, R. 1981. "Incentives to Return: Patterns of Politics and Migrants' Responses." In *Global Trends in Migration: Theory and Research on International Population Movements,* ed. M. M. Kritz, C. B. Keely, and S. M. Tomasi. New York: Center for Migration Studies.

Rogg, E. M. 1974. *The Assimilation of Cuban Exiles: the Role of Community and Class.* New York: Aberdeen Press.

Rose, A. M. 1969. *Migrants in Europe: Problems of Acceptance and Adjustment.* Minneapolis: University of Minnesota Press.

Sassen-Koob, S. 1978. "Formal and Informal Associations: Dominicans and Colombians in New York." *International Migration Review* 13: 314–32.

Schmitter, B. E. 1980. "Immigrants and Associations: Their Role in the Socio-Political Process of Immigrant Worker Integration in West Germany and Switzerland." *International Migration Review* 14: 179–92.

Searing, D., et al. 1976. "The Primacy Principle: Attitude Change and Political Socialization." *British Journal of Political Science* 6: 83–114.

Sigel, R. S., and M. Hoskin. 1977. "Adult Socialization." In *Handbook of Political Socialization,* ed. Stanley Renshon. New York: The Free Press.

———. 1981. *The Political Involvement of Adolescents.* New Brunswick: Rutgers University Press.

Sowell, T. 1981. *Ethnic America: A History.* New York: Basic Books.

Studlar, D. T. 1978. "Policy Voting in Britain: the Coloured Immigration Issue in the 1964, 1966, and 1970 Elections." *American Political Science Review* 72: 46–64.

———. 1979. "Great Britain." In *Labor Migration in Europe,* ed. R. E. Krane. New York: Praeger.

Suttles, G. D. 1968. *The Social Order of the Slum: Ethnicity and Territory in the Inner City.* Chicago: University of Chicago Press.

Tabori, P. 1972. *The Anatomy of Exile.* London: George Harrop.

Thomas, W. I., and F. Znaniecki. 1927. *The Polish Peasant in Europe and America.* New York: Knopf.

Warner, W. L., and L. Srole. 1945. *The Social Systems of American Ethnic Groups.* New Haven: Yale University Press.

Wilpert, C. 1980. *Die Zukunft der Zweite Generation*. Koenigstein: Verlag Anton Hain.

Wilson, P. R. 1973. *Immigrants and Politics*. Canberra: Australian National University Press.

Wittke, Carl. 1952. *Refugees of the Revolution: the German Forty-Eighters in America*. Philadelphia: University of Pennsylvania Press.

Zolberg, A. R. 1981. "International Migrations in Political Perspective." In *Global Trends in Migration: Theory and Research in International Migration*, ed. M. M. Kritz, C. B. Keely, and S. M. Tomasi. New York: Center for Migration Studies.

Zwingmann, C., and M. Ammende. 1973. *Uprooting and After. . . .* New York: Springer Verlag.

Part IV

Introduction:
Coping with Traumatic Events

Natural disasters, war, or terror perpetrated on others in the name of a political ideal or cause all are events which tear men and women from their customary moorings and constitute a break with the past. Much of what they had come to expect of others and of themselves becomes inoperative. This holds particularly for those situations where the demands made on them are in direct conflict with moral and social demands made on them prior to the happening. The young man who had always been told not to inflict pain on others, let alone kill anyone, becomes a soldier and now must engage in systematic killings. The company executive trained to give orders quickly learns that to adopt a low profile and meekly follow the hijacker's orders may be the best strategy. The question here is not so much how capable people are of forsaking old behavior patterns—although that certainly is a most important question—but what happens once the ordeal is over? Can individuals resume earlier life-patterns and recapture their previous identities without too much stress and trauma, or will the terrorized self be incorporated into the former identity, thereby affecting social and political behaviors long after the ordeal is over?

In this section two such traumatic episodes will be examined. Laufer addresses the impact war has on the returning veteran and Horowitz the impact on victims of terror. Horowitz, in addition, will examine what drives people to terrorism, and what impact acts of terrorism have on society itself. Surely no stronger test case for the primacy of earlier socialization experiences could be devised than an observation of humans' behavior in crisis situations of great stress and of their behavior once the crisis has passed.

Before the reentry problem is discussed, it may be useful briefly to describe the customary immediate reactions observed in people who find themselves caught in such antagonistic situations. Whether a person is caught in a tornado, a kidnapping, or the first military battle, fear seems to be the first all-pervasive reaction, generally followed (at least in the first two situations) by a sense of disbelief or denial (this can't be true, this can't happen to me) and a sense of general disorientation or dislocation. "Whenever someone becomes victimized by a disaster, whatever its nature . . . their [sic] most basic assumptions about themselves and the world are undermined" (Janoff-Bulman as quoted in *The New York Times,* November 26, 1985, C1). Most significantly, people who previously considered themselves in control lose that sense as well as their faith that the world is predictable and fair as long as they play the game by the rules to which they had been socialized. Suddenly, who perishes and who survives becomes unpredictable and irrational.

A brief examination of behavior during natural disasters is instructive because it alerts us to both the similarities and differences in reactions when people are confronted with nature's versus man-made assaults on their security. Moreover, by focusing on a few different natural disasters, it is also possible to illustrate the role played by social structure and culture. Individuals' reactions to natural disasters—whether caused solely by nature, such as an earthquake, or by man's negligence, such as the breaking of a dam—seem to vary with the nature of the community and the culture prevailing in it. While the first reactions are, predictably, fear and disbelief or a feeling of being dazed and numb, victims in urban and organized communities fairly quickly begin to engage in mutual assistance as well as self-help in order to resume previous patterns. Reporting on one such disaster, Wallace (1956) in a study of the Worcester, Massachusetts, hurricane referred to victims' responses as a "disaster syndrome" and described them in the following way: During the first phase the victim felt dazed and withdrawn; after that he gratefully accepted whatever assistance was given and himself engaged in it; a "euphoric identity" with the community developed, outsiders (those living in areas not directly hit by the hurricane), driven by a sense of survivor guilt, also began to help. Energetic repair efforts began. After a while the euphoria wore off, residents began to feel ambivalent or critical of the official assistance offered, and life returned more or less to normal.

Contrast this behavior with the reactions of victims of the 1972 Buffalo Creek, West Virginia, flood, resulting from a break of the dam. Here the victims were rural, fairly impoverished inhabitants of the hollows of Appalachia. While their initial reactions were similar to those of the Worcester residents, no vigorous attempt at self-help or communal help was undertaken by them. Their sense of identity was coexistent with that of the community. This identity was damaged or lost when the flood destroyed these small, closely knit hamlets; with the destruction went the inhabitants' sense of belonging and their belief that they could on their own engage in a rebuilding. Why, one may well ask, did these residents sink into such despair and apathy when previously they had relied so much on each other? One might conjecture that the physical loss of home and loved ones in that rural culture may have been much more devastating because their individual identity was a communal one. Also, people had not acquired the habit of seeking help from agencies outside their narrow communities (in fact distrusted them), lacked the skills and resources to cope with such a disaster, and perhaps had been more accustomed than urban dwellers to accept fate. The urban dwellers, on the other hand, knew how to avail themselves of existing resources and actually had come to expect them; but they quickly returned to their own individualistic ways, their identity not being dependent on that of the community.[1] Studies of other disasters both here and abroad have shown that "disaster syndromes" characterize victims everywhere (at least as far as the first stages are concerned), but that the coping mechanism and with it the recovery process vary widely by cultures and are reflective of earlier socialization patterns (Clifford 1955; Wright et al. 1979).

What is less well known is whether living through disasters of this kind has permanent and destabilizing effects. Those who have studied natural disasters differ widely among themselves, in part because they have studied different types of communities and in part because there is a dearth of pre-post studies which would permit accurate measurements of effects (Frederick 1983; Friesema et al. 1979; Kasl et al. 1981; Logue et al. 1981; Rossi et al. 1978; Wright et al. 1979 and 1984). Researchers who approach the topic from a psychological perspective are among those inclined to conclude that events of this nature are bound to leave some permanent scars, especially among those people who had been socialized to assume that the world was relatively safe and predictable. The political withdrawal and apathy observed in some communities may well be attributable to such scars.

How much more destabilizing must the effect be when the pain or terror one experiences comes not from nature but from one's fellow man. Certainly men from time immemorial have inflicted pain and terror on each other, some of it on a gargantuan scale. Horowitz, rather than focusing on large scale episodes, such as the Holocaust, the Pol Pot massacres, and the like, puts the spotlight on the activities of the individuals or the small groups of terrorists who are operating with increasing frequency in the postwar world. He asks, who are these people, what in their socialization propels them to engage in violence, often against innocent people, and how do the victims of such violence react? Do the victims, provided they survive the violence, find it possible to resume, unscathed, their former life-patterns?

Horowitz distinguishes between terror initiated by individual groups and that initiated by the state. When the state chooses to pursue a policy of terror against specified groups in its midst—as in the current detention camps in South Africa or the concentration camps of Nazi Germany—the perpetrator of the terror no longer is seen as a violator of law and order but, quite the contrary, as the law enforcer. How do such perpetrators reconcile these deeds with the moral code to which they presumably had originally been socialized? This is a question we have difficulty answering because it is difficult to interview members of Central American death squads or concentration camp guards, to cite but two examples. A rare exception is the recent work by Robert Jay Lifton (1986), who studied the Nazi physicians who experimented on and otherwise abused inmates of the concentration camps. Lifton asked himself how could physicians, whose mission is to preserve life, become killers of innocent men, women, and children. He concludes—from interview with the few physicians still alive at the time—that they experienced no conflict between the two "missions" but rather saw themselves as fulfilling an important biological mission for the Nazi state. "As in a theocracy, the state itself is no more than a vehicle for the divine purpose, so in the Nazi biocracy was the state no more than a means . . . of assembling and preserving the most valuable stocks of basic racial elements." The absence of much firsthand information about officials at various levels of terror-inflicting official apparatuses does not permit us to reach firm conclusions about the socialization experiences of people who engaged in similar atrocities.[2]

Our knowledge is far greater about the impact these acts have on the victims of state-sponsored terror. Horowitz points to permanent psychological and political effects of the experience. The few who manage to be freed from the prisons and Gulags in Europe and South America, Asia, and Africa frequently have been so traumatized that they find it impossible or next to impossible to reenter their customary social world and to resume political attitudes and behaviors which once seemed natural. He notes that even victims of individual terrorist acts, whose suffering, generally, is not nearly as severe or as long-lasting (for example, individuals caught in a hijacking) emerge from the experience with a different legacy than the one with which they entered. Reactions can vary from sympathy for the cause of the terrorist to rage and demands for revenge. In addition Horowitz notes that the victim is not the only one who is affected by terrorist acts; he seems to see signs that states, in order to curb terrorism, are beginning to transform themselves in several ways—some of which he considers to be ominous.

Finally, Laufer turns to the most apocalyptic experience of our recent history, modern warfare. While concentrating on the experiences of veterans of the Vietnam War, he offers sufficient evidence from a rapidly growing field of study that all modern wars have a desocializing impact on young combatants. Even those who fought the "good war" (as Studs Terkel dubbed World War II) and felt that it was a just one have not escaped such reactions. This is so— as Laufer (1987, p. 1) argues in another paper—because

> the environments of war and civil society are radically different and
> psychologically at odds. This means that the process of going to war

and coming home requires sequential radical breaks between self systems as a consequence of participation in distinct social systems. The problem for the individual who experiences the process is adaptation of the fractured self after immersion in conflicting normative systems over the life course.

Warfare is constructed around striking terror, killing humans, causing pain and death. It directly conflicts with what the young soldier had been socialized to, prior to entering military service. If he wants to survive that experience—and help his country win the contest or at least defend itself—he has to divest himself of scruples which had taken a long time to become internalized and had become part of his identity. "Thus, the environment of warfare has a developmental component which requires that the individual attempt to construct a self system which is functional within the context of war" (Laufer 1987, p. 13). It is, however, not functional upon his return to civilian life. Although some studies (Jennings and Markus 1976) found that the political behaviors of returning veterans did not differ markedly from those of the rest of the population, others (among them Laufer) contend that for soldiers who had participated in active combat (and had witnessed deliberate atrocities or perhaps participated in them) reentry was not that smooth. Many remained politically isolated and apathetic. Jennings and Markus similarly observed that those veterans who entered the conflict earliest and served longest put less emphasis on active political citizenship. In fact, they valued it even less than they had a few years before, when they had been students in high school. As Laufer writes in this volume "[t]he war experience appears to become a filter through which subsequent events are given meaning."

In this context it must be remembered that most people who served in Vietnam,as well as in most recent wars, were very young. They were at a stage in their development where they were just beginning to form an adult self and to practice the lessons learned in childhood and adolescence. War told them to forget those lessons for the duration. War thus blocked for the time being the normal maturational process designed to fit the young person into civil society. It may have matured him in many other ways, but it interfered with his adaptation to civil society.[3] Laufer refers to this as "the truncated war self" and outlines the political consequences thereof.

One legacy shared by all survivors of traumatizing events is what is commonly known as "survivor's guilt." Whether the individual was caught in a hurricane, a bomb explosion in an airport, or at the battlefront, the death or injury of others always give rise to the question, why was I spared? Did I deserve it? Did I help as much as I could to save others? It is that feeling, as we have shown, which motivated individuals who were spared the consequences of the havoc caused by a flood or hurricane to come to the aid of the stricken community and help in rescue efforts, thereby presumably hoping to reduce feelings of guilt. Lifton (1973, p. 127) refers to this type of guilt as "animating guilt" in that it motivates and energizes man to come to the aid of his fellow men; whereas "static guilt" leads to numbness and inability to mobilize oneself. Here "the entire being is frozen or desensitized, in order to avoid feeling the 'wound' (or 'death') one has caused (or thinks one has caused), leaving one anesthetized from much of life itself." It seems plausible to assume that the anesthetized self is not likely to become an active participant in either community or polity. This, of course, is what observers have noted about survivors of the Holocaust and, more recently, about returning combat veterans from Vietnam.[4]

While the studies of victims of terrorism, especially terrorism initiated by groups rather than the state, are still sparse, studies of the impact of war and its consequences for those who fought in them have grown greatly both in volume and methodological as well as theoretical sophistication. Some of the parallels between the two chapters in this section are sufficiently striking that they should stimulate us to begin to develop some theory-informed notions about the consequences of such trauma for the political socialization of individuals.

R. S. S.

Notes

1. Of course, it should not be overlooked that the collapse of the dam at Buffalo Creek brought on far more devastating destruction in some communities than did the hurricane in Worcester.

2. One exception is Hannah Arendt's *Eichmann in Jerusalem: A Report on the Banality of Evil* (New York: Penguin Books, 1963). Arendt, however, did not interview Eichmann. Nor was Eichmann a small functionary. A few studies based on interviews or psychological examinations of top Nazi figures do exist, but the interviewees are no longer alive. Cf. G. M. Gilbert, *The Psychology of Dictatorship* New York: Ronald, 1950).

3. Oliver Stone, himself a combat veteran in Vietnam who encapsulated his combat experience in the movie *Platoon,* made the following observation in a recent interview as to the effect the war had had on soldiers. "Anyone in a combat troop comes back an older man, a more bitter man, an alienated man. [He is] "forever marked by his experiences in Vietnam. . . . the injuries prove not mortal but permanent." *The New York Times,* April 13, 1987, C13.

4. Public opposition to the war no doubt contributed to the returning veteran's sense of isolation and estrangement. Recently, Vietnam veterans have become more vocal and politically active, a development attributed to a change in the climate of public opinion and one that has found symbolic expression in the erection of the Vietnam War Memorial in Washington, D.C.

References

Clifford, R. A. 1955. *The Rio Grande Flood: A Comparative Study of Border Communities in Disasters*. NAS-NRC Publication 458, Washington D.C.

Frederick, C. J. 1983. "Violence and Disaster: Immediate and Long-Term Consequences." *Helping Victims of Violence*. Government Printing Office: The Hague.

Friesema, H. P., et al. 1979. *Aftermath: Communities after Natural Disasters*. Beverly Hills, Calif.: Sage Publications.

Jennings, K., and G. B. Markus. 1976. "Political Participation and Vietnam War Veterans: A Longitudinal Study." In N. L. Goldman and D. R. Segal, eds., *The Social Psychology of Military Service*. Beverly Hills, Calif.: Sage Publications.

Kasl, S. V., R. F. Chisholm, and B. Eskenazi. 1981. "The Impact of the Accident at Three-Mile Island on the Behavior and Well-Being of Nuclear Workers." *American Journal of Public Health* 71: 472–95.

Laufer, R. S. 1987. "The Serial Self: War Trauma, Identity and Adult Development." In Z. Harel, B. Kahana, and J. P. Wilson, eds., *Human Adaptation to Extreme Stress from the Holocaust to Vietnam*. New York: Putnam Books.

Lifton, R. J. 1973. *Home from the War*. New York: Simon and Schuster.

———. 1986. *The Nazi Doctors: Medical Killings and the Psychology of Genocide*. New York: Basic Books.

Logue, J. N., H. Hansen, and E. Struening. 1981. "Some Indication of Long-Term Effects of a Natural Disaster." *Public Health Reports* 96: 67–80.

Rossi, P. H., et al. 1978. "Are There Long-Term Effects of American Natural Disasters?" *Mass Emergencies* 3: 117–32.

Wallace, A. F. C. 1956. "Tornado in Worcester: An Explanatory Study of Individual and Community Behavior in an Extreme Situation." *NAS-NRC* Publication 392. Washington D.C.

Wright, J. D., et al. 1979. *After the Cleanup: Long-Range Effects of Natural Disasters*. Beverly Hills, Calif.: Sage Publications.

Wright, J. D., and P. H. Rossi, eds., 1984. *Social Science and Natural Hazards*. Boston: Abt.

Ten

The Texture of Terrorism: Socialization, Routinization, and Integration

IRVING LOUIS HOROWITZ

The extent to which the issue of terror has moved from the margins to the center of political discourse can be illustrated by the fact that many colleges and universities have introduced courses in terrorism "with student interest in the subject now higher than ever." (*New York Times*, February 18, 1986, C15). This increase in public attention is not hard to understand. While government-sponsored terrorizing of its own citizens is continuing in many parts of the world, group-sponsored, unofficial acts of political terrorism are accelerating at an alarming rate. In the last decade such acts of terrorism have become routine. The number of incidents of international terrorism, with or without the support of a foreign government or organization, almost doubled in the decade 1970–80. Deaths resulting from international terrorism in the same period increased from 131 to 642; casualties from terrorist attacks (especially bombings and assassinations) have risen dramatically. (National Foreign Assessment Center 1981.) Once extraordinary and unusual phenomena have become normal, everyday events.

Analyzing acts of terror has become a major activity for an enlarged intelligence industry. Nevertheless, we have not thought much about the social and political consequences of the routinization of terror. Social scientists and historians have made exhaustive analyses of everything from the causes of terrorism[1], to the "nature" of the terrorist, to the relationship of terrorism to ideology. But what are the lasting consequences of terrorism—unanticipated and otherwise?[2] Montandor (1983, p. 24) is correct when he asserts that "in general sociological and anthropological theories are still quite primitive" and that the act of violence has so far received more attention than its conse-

Let me acknowledge a special debt to Roberta S. Sigel, whose guidance went considerably beyond that of general editor. Her deep knowledge of the literature in political psychology had a salutary effect in correcting my own biases toward a political sociology. And in the study of terrorism, the balance and interplay between the political, sociological, and psychological is central.

quences. This relative inattention holds particularly with respect to the impact of such events. The social learning, value restructuring, and political reorientation they bring about have received very little systematic social science investigation, especially as they pertain to the victims of terror. Most of what we know of the temporary or permanent socializing effect comes from psychiatric case histories, journalistic accounts, personal memoirs, biographies, or works of fiction.[3] Nor do these works focus explicitly on *political* socialization. We are thus confronted with a serious gap in our knowledge of political socialization under conditions of political terror. It is perhaps no exaggeration to state that the study of the political socialization of terrorizers and terrorized is as yet in its infancy. This chapter seeks to fill some of the knowledge gaps by drawing inferences from available materials and above all by addressing crucial political questions which future research needs to study.

To that end I shall begin with an attempt to define and differentiate different types of political terrorism, both with respect to character and purpose. Next I shall discuss the political socialization experienced by political terrorists and then proceed to the same for victims of acts of terror. I shall conclude with observations and some speculation about the ways in which the prevalence and unpredictability of terrorism is beginning to affect and alter the conduct of daily affairs in many societies. The ultimate question then becomes: does political terror resocialize not only victims and victimizers but perhaps society as well?

The term "terror" is a quintessential psychological term widely employed to describe both unstructured political processes and unanticipated consequences. The term applies to both individual states of mind and to a collective social malaise. Terror is an interactive process, involving the perpetrators of acts of terror; the terror felt by those upon whom the acts are inflicted, their response; and on some occasions the response of the third parties. All of this makes the definition of terrorism a substantial task unto itself. Indeed, there are entire volumes dedicated to settling, alas without much success, taxonomic issues. (For an excellent summary, see Schmid 1988.) Thus rather than devote undue time to exploring the range of definitions, I have settled on a series of operational guidelines, which should be taken with caution, but yet permit discussion to move from etymological to operational levels, or more practically, from settling on the meaning of terms to an analysis and explanation of political problem-solving through violent means.

Political terror has in common with other, frequently random, forms of terror—such as homicide, infanticide, and killing for ransom—that it involves physical violence perpetrated against a victim. But unlike random forms of violence, political terror seeks a political, systemic outcome and not just personal gratification. When we speak of political terror, a distinction nonetheless has to be made between individual- or group-initiated acts of political terror, such as the hijacking of commercial aircraft in order to negotiate the release from prison of fellow terrorists on the one hand, and state-initiated terror such as the Gulags on the other.

The definition of group-sponsored, political terrorism I employ is this: the selective use of fear, subjugation, and intimidation to disrupt the normal operations of a society. The power to inflict such injury is a bargaining power which in its very nature bypasses due process of law. It seeks an outcome by means other than a democratic or consensual formula. The act of terror, whoever performs it, in some sense violates civil liberties. The cries and whispers about redressing generic injustices cannot disguise this fact of personal loss and suffering (Leites and Wolf 1970). Examples from current history would be the terrorist attacks of groups seeking ethnic or national autonomy, such as the Basque ETA movement in Spain or the IRA in Northern Ireland. State-initiated terror, by contrast, is the direct application (overtly or covertly) of the state's apparatus of coercion in order to obtain policy results. Its purpose may be to punish or destroy actual opponents or to intimidate potential opposition or to eliminate total populations (ethnic, religious, or social) or "undesirables." Both types of terrorism are based on a calculation of what its victim can or cannot tolerate. A threshold of pain replaces the articulation of shared values or the rationality produced by consensus politics. The act of terrorism, again without regard to who perfoms it, involves a substitution of pain for reason as the way to determine political and social issues.

Purposes and Policies of Terrorism

At its highest level of intellectual rationalization, recourse to group-sponsored terrorism that involves hijacking, kidnapping, and similar acts is a response and reaction to a perceived low rate of change. The recourse to terrorism is justified as a means for hastening the tempo and magnitude of the desired change. Group terrorists see their performance as an early or intermediate step to changing the general Zeitgeist or climate of public opinion. For example, by acts of terror as a series of cris de coeur, it is hoped by the Palestinian Arabs to weaken the bonds of American political support for Israel and to enlist the sympathies of nonterrorist spokespersons who share the goals of the terrorists while eschewing the instruments of direct violence. In short, it should not be thought that antistate group terrorists are naive in not recognizing the impact of social and political bonding on the community under direct attack. Rather, it is the larger, more amorphous "court of world opinion" to which supposedly random attacks are often addressed by these group terrorists. This, it would seem, is the motivation underlying PLO-engineered acts of terrorism. This type of terrorism as a policy is both antidemocratic and anti-civil-libertarian because the terrorists' ultimatums are addressed to leadership elites rather than to the people. It demands instantaneous decision-making. As a result, it places great strain on conventional legal mechanisms, which require due process and a strong evidentiary base to take action. Thus the appeal to swift action shifts power in the attacked society or community to its elites. (Bush et al. 1986, pp. 7–27.) Terror further violates the civil liberties of those who are nonparticipants or noncombatants. Indeed, terrorists usually have as their victims people who are innocent of any specific crime; and are not even guilty of being a part of the offending group. Whatever else the concept of civil liberties involves, it rejects holding people who have committed no specific criminal acts responsible for the alleged acts of others. In this sense, terrorist acts violate the civil liberties of individuals and collectivities alike.

Citizens who engage in terrorist acts against the political authority of their own state have a different goal in mind. The immediate aims of certain nationalist groups (such as the Basques' ETA and the Irish IRA) and of ultra-left-wing revolutionary ones (such as the Red Brigades) is to destabilize and eventually topple detested political regimes which are perceived as oppressive. Consequently, such groups frequently direct acts of terror not against innocent bystanders but against individuals who symbolize or represent the oppressive regime (British soldiers in the case of the IRA; government officials in the case of the Red Brigades). Notwithstanding the differences in targets chosen by the PLO or the Red Brigades, the motivation in either case is similar, namely the hope that the traumatization of some or many people will eventually lead to political changes desired by the terrorists and the people they claim to represent.

State-sponsored terror differs dramatically both in scope and intent from the aforementioned forms of terror. There is nothing random about it—victims or rather groups of victims—are carefully chosen and the full force of the state's coercive power is brought to bear on them, whether to terrorize them into acquiescence or, worse, to eliminate them altogether. Terror thus is a *direct* means to effect a specific policy desired by those in power. This is in distinction to group-sponsored terrorism which is conceived as an intermediate step to goal attainment.

Persecution, incarceration, torture, physical abuse, and murder are among the methods at the state's disposal. The history of mankind is replete with examples of governments that have resorted to wholesale terror in order to eradicate religious groups, political opposition, or whatever population elements are deemed to be "undesirable" or threatening to the state's political purpose. In more recent times we have again seen the state's coercive apparatus utilized in order to terrorize organized opposition (as for example in the case of the dictatorships of Idi Amin, Ferdinand Marcos, and Jean-Claude Duvalier). We also witnessed the use of terror in order physically to eliminate whole populations (as in the case of the genocide of the Armenian population by the Turkish government or that of the Jews in German-held territories).

If we compare group-initiated terrorism in terms of the number of people that have been killed by design or by accident, there is clearly no comparison between a hijacking or bombing and the genocidal behavior of Ataturk in Turkey, Stalin in Russia, and Hitler in Germany. The autocratic state has nearly unlimited power to terrorize entire communities, ethnic or racial groups, and, of course, religious networks. If terrorism is judged simply in terms of lives dispatched, the Nazi holocaust—the genocidal benchmark of our century—outstrips the desultory performances engaged in by contemporary terrorists.

Thus far I have emphasized ideological and tactical aspects of terrorism. However, behind the "ism" stands the person: the terrorist. And next to him or her "stands" the victim. In the section which follows I shall focus first on the terrorist and how his/her activities tend to socialize him/her, and next I shall seek to assess the impact acts of terror have on the victims, especially as they affect their subsequent political views and behaviors. I shall begin by drawing a composite profile of the terrorist.

Profiling the Terrorist

Although profiling the terrorist can be a dangerously unscientific venture, it nonetheless has the rare benefit of concretizing what can otherwise drift off into narcotizing abstractions. It is significant to start by conceptualizing terrorists as a subculture rather than to force the terrorist profile into broad class categories. One distinction which I find useful to make before proceeding with such a preliminary set of characterizations is between dramaturgical and political/ideological terrorists. Although both types are, of course, political actors, they differ nonetheless in goals, methods, and targets for their violence. Political/ideological terrorists (such as the Red Brigades in Italy and the Red Army faction in Germany) direct their violence against their own state, frequently targeting victims in high political office for the purpose of disrupting the political machinery of government, hoping thereby to destabilize it and eventually bring about the desired political change. (This does not preclude bombings and assaults on nonpolitical objects, such as the IRA's 1985 bombing of Harrod's department store in London.) Similar tactics are used by nationally or ethnically motivated political terrorists (such as the ETA in Spain and the IRA in Ireland) although their eventual goal tends to be autonomy or independence for their group rather than radical economic or political change.

Dramaturgical terrorists, in contrast, focus on the event itself—say hijacking, in which the planning and performance are related to an event rather than a person or persons. Thus, whoever happens to be aboard a plane or a boat or train is a victim in a much more randomized manner than in the form of terrorism described above and practiced in Europe or in some parts of Latin America. Nor is the target of dramaturgical terrorists' violence the government of their country of origin—far from it, these governments frequently encourage and finance the terrorists' activities.[4]

I shall have occasion shortly to comment in more detail on the difference between dramaturgical and political terrorists, but notwithstanding these differences there are some broad commonalities shared by both types. Let us proceed then with such a preliminary set of characterizations. (Horowitz 1973, pp. 147–157).

The terrorist is a person who is young (generally between twenty and thirty-five), usually male, and frequently economically marginal.

The terrorist defines himself differently from the casual homicide in several crucial respects: he murders systematically rather than at random; killing is a symbolic act rather than an impassioned one; that is, it is concerned with scoring political points rather than with responding to personal provocation; and his actions are usually planned (however clumsily) rather than spontaneous. Terrorism is thus primarily a sociological phenomenon, whereas homicide can more easily be interpreted in psychological terms.[5] Political terrorism essentially has a group nature rather than a personal nature or, for that matter, a strictly economic goal.

A terrorist is a person engaged in politics who makes little if any distinction between strategy and tactics on the one hand and principles on the other. For him, all politics is a matter of principle and, hence, nothing beyond the decision to commit a revolutionary deed of death and personal commitment requires examination, planning, and forethought.

Terrorists take care "to maximize the symbolic impact their violent actions have on the public at large. . . . the violent act is always a piece of showmanship played to the theater audience of the broader public" (Merkl 1986, p. 47).

The terrorist believes that the act of violence will encourage the uncommitted public to withdraw support from a regime or an institution, and hence make wider revolutionary acts possible by weakening the resolve of the opposition. Practically, however, such acts often work to lend greater support to the regime, by drying up fissures and contradictions in the name of opposing a common enemy: the terrorist.

Terrorists of all shades of the political spectrum share yet another common characteristic. As a rule, they are not likely to anticipate immediate systemic political change to follow from their actions. Left-wing radicals who assassinate a cabinet minister or kidnap a general do not imagine that the government will topple as a result. What they hope to accomplish is to erode the public's faith in the government's stability and/or the faith of people in the system's essential justice. Nor do PLO terrorists who attack a schoolhouse in Israel or hijack a plane anticipate that the world will immediately come to their aid and turn against Israel. But they too hope that by their acts they can lay the ground and dramatize the justice of their cause. By their acts terrorists aim to alter the consciousness of the public, to "convert" it to a cause they believe to be right. Consciously or unconsciously, they perceive themselves as political resocializers of the world's conscience.

Frequently a key event is the stimulus which pushes the alienated individual over the threshold from radicalism into terrorism. The strafing of a village with subsequent loss of property and lives—as occurs routinely in Lebanon—can be such an event. The death of a comrade (at the hands of the police or during incarceration) also can act as a catalyst. Speitel (1980, p. 41), commenting on the impact Holger Meins's death from a hunger strike had on radicals, noted: "Then came the day Holger Meins died. . . . For us this death was a key experience. . . . The death of Holger Meins and the decision to take up arms were one and the same. Reflection was not possible anymore."

No profile would be complete unless it made an effort to account for the subjective processes no less than the demographic features of the terrorist. For the terrorist, a key aspect of identity is the claim to be among the vanguard of an already marginal movement. Doris Lessing, in *The Good Terrorist* (1986) for example, captures this sense of the terrorist as a self-defined vanguard of the vanguard, so to speak. The arguments among the Communists are between essentially the extremists and the orthodox—thus replicating *within* the bowels of the revolutionary movement the normative division between extra-legal and legal modes of operation.

The terrorist claims of vanguardism imply the existence, among the adherents of a radical reactionary movement, of a scale for the measurement of merit: ideological purity, refusal to compromise with the established order, militant activism, readiness for self-sacrifice. But as one analyst has properly noted: "There is something tricky about vanguardism. It tends to be a self-liquidating form of distinction. To the degree that the vanguard is successful in persuading others to join them, they may destroy their own uniqueness. To maintain their position they may find it useful, or even necessary, to move the front lines—the benchmarks from which devotion to the cause is measured—forward. What was previously radical may now become reaction or collaboration with the enemy" (Cohen 1974, pp. 13–14).

What this entails is an escalation of violence by the terrorist, not in response to any particular objective political events, but as a consequence of the escalation of inner-directed or organizationally required demands for a bold action. What makes the study of terrorism so difficult is the absence of any correlation between specific worldly issues and terrorist actions. This is because the subjective side of terrorism has a momentum, a life of its own. Prediction of terrorist events is not like predictions in, say, electoral politics, because failure does not necessarily resolve participation; it only stimulates new levels of escalation.

The psychiatrist Martin Ostrow (1985), in reflecting on the attraction terrorist groups hold for the many different types of terrorists, observed that "terrorist groups offer a way of looking at the world that both explains the present feeling of hopelessness and offers a way out." Ideologically, they may be as far apart as the Marxist-inspired Red Brigades or the Khomeni-inspired Shiites, but they share an apocalyptic vision that divides the world into good and evil. Terrorists, Ostrow writes, believe that eventually the good will prevail but that it will come to pass only through forceful, dramatic action. Their own action will make the crucial difference. This, for example, is the view that impels Shiites in Lebanon to engage in suicide bombings (quoted in an article by Coleman, *New York Times,* September 9, 1986, sec. C).

Dramaturgical Terrorists

A dramaturgical terrorist is a person prepared to surrender his own life for a cause considered transcendent in value. A terrorist assumes not only that taking the lives of others will lead to desired political goals but that the loss of one's own life is a warranty that such a cause or political position is correct and obtainable.

A dramaturgical terrorist is a person who possesses both a self-fulfilling prophetic element and a self-destructive thanatotic element. The act of destruction of another person or group of persons itself becomes the basis upon which future politics can be determined and decided, and the absence of terror is hence held to signify the absence of meaningful events. The self-destructive element is coincidental with the previous point, namely, that one's own death is the highest form of the politics of the deed: the only perfect expression of political correctness.

A dramaturgical terrorist is a person for whom all events are volitional and none are determined. The terrorist, in contrast to the classic revolutionary, perceives the world pragmatically as a place to be shaped and reshaped in accord with the human will or the will of the immediate collective group. Beyond that, there is no historical or sociological force of a hidden or covert nature that can alter human relationships or geographic boundaries.

Dramaturgical terrorists may engage in violent attacks—such as a hijacking or a kidnapping—in order to secure the release of imprisoned fellow terrorists, or they may direct their activities against the symbols of establishments and agencies. Such forms of terror are less concerned with the individuals against whom terror is directed than with the organizations and agencies of which they are a part. For example, the Munich massacre of Israeli athletes was directed at the state of Israel; the specific people eliminated were not an issue. This kind of terrorist is usually under a strict political regimen and is responsible to counterorganizations and guerrilla groupings that define and determine the extent and types of terrorism (Russell and Miller 1978).

Such political terrorists are increasingly performing their own "profiles," i.e., taking on new forms of differentiation according to religion (Jew and Gentile), race (black or white), class (rich or poor), nationality (American, Israeli, Russian, South African), and sheer ethnicity of the victims. While some attacks remain undifferentiated, for the most part the new terrorism— as in the *Achille Lauro* and TWA hijackings—makes sharp differentiations along a social-ethnic stratification axis. This has had the impact of dividing the hostages and raising their "consciousness" of distinctions even after their release. The "enemy" no longer becomes the *terrorist,* but a carefully segmented portion of the *victim* population.

This newer trend of linkages between political psychology and political socialization is a modern-day reproduction of the fascist style: one in which the goal of ferreting out the rootless cosmopolitan, the enemy within, the alienated few, becomes crucial in the effort at terrorist purification and redemption. In this development of differentiation and stratification, terrorism has begun to achieve a long-sought goal, legitimation through the gun by the activities of the few. Again, the *Putschist* mentality of the Munich beer halls of the 1920s are recreated in the Beirut cafes of the 1980s. This parallelism and isomorphism is hardly complete or perfect, but there are enough commonalities to make inevitable a consideration of the nature of terror as an "ism."

Dramaturgical terrorists, such as key members of the PLO, often grew up in refugee camps and were socialized to feelings of deprivation, hatred, revenge, and the need to take up arms in order to gain statehood. While some terrorists have come from middle-class backgrounds and had attended universities (often quite sporadically), most are poor and relatively uneducated, driven more by fervor than intellectual sophistication. The witnessing of violence can be said to have been part of their early socialization experiences, and so may have been socialization to self-sacrifice for the attainment of the greater good. Engaging in acts of terror thus may not constitute a radical break with earlier socialization.[6]

Yet most of their fellow men and women, though equally victimized, do not embark on that path. What accounts for the fact that some will become terrorists while others, presumably equally unhappy, refrain from violence? Fields (1980), who has done extensive research on PLO members, suggests that the explanation often lies in the witnessing of a specifically upsetting event. Usually "it is a critical incident that propels a person to take the next step" (p. 1). She noted that the young male survivors of the Sabra and Shatila camp massacres had previously resented the forced military training imposed by the PLO and sought to evade it. "After the massacre, the boys felt both grief and intense guilt about their earlier feelings of resentment" (p. 1). Many subsequently joined terrorist groups. Fields, in fact, concludes that children's frequent witnessing of deprivation and violence predisposes them to affinity for terrorist groups. "For many of the children who later become terrorists, the only adults who seem to be able to control their destiny and who offer positive models are those who belong to terrorist groups" (p. 1). Habituation to violence has also been observed among children growing up in those districts of Northern Ireland where political violence is most intense. These children had become so accustomed to violence that they take it for granted and perhaps even sanction it (Bell 1978; Clark 1978; Cairns 1980).

Ideological Terrorists

Ideological terrorists differ in substantial ways from dramaturgical ones. Whereas dramaturgical ones tend to represent the sentiments and political ambitions of their fellow men and women (even though the nonterrorists may not condone the terrorists' tactics), the ideological one does not strike a responsive chord in the population; there is no sharing of a common political agenda. As Merkl (1986, p. 45) noted, the dramaturgical or ethnic liberationist (to use his terminology) has "a strong representational claim," but "none of the major terrorist groups can be said to represent or draw noticeable support from the proletariat they claim to fight for."

Moreover, ideological terrorists, especially those espousing leftist ideologies, frequently come from solid middle-class families (particularly in Western Europe), have attended universities, and are more or less ideologically sophisticated. Although here too we find considerable variation in background, especially among right-wing terrorists, none, probably, have grown up in the abject misery characteristic of the inhabitants of refugee camps. Moreover, few, if any, can be said to have come from political milieus that socialized for violence. Far from it; the most active of these terrorist groups originated in parliamentary-style democracies, such as France, Italy, and West Germany. Their resort to violence, therefore, has to be considered as evidence of unsuccessful political socialization. Why then did they reject the prevailing norms?

Explanations vary widely. Some attribute it to technological and societal changes, exacerbated by erosion of traditional familial and religious ties (see Gambino et al. 1979); others note the presence of generational conflicts

(Feuer 1969; Weinberg 1986); while yet others attribute it to the nature of the capitalist system itself or rather to youth's disillusionment with it (Ferrarotti 1978, 1979), as well as to a host of other possible "causes" (Pasquino and della Porta 1986). Personality no doubt plays a role. Merkl (1986, p. 42) traces terrorism's attraction to characterological deficits. "The recruits, with their insecure personalities and weak egos, were given a sense of political direction solely by these recruiters or protectors who took charge of their failed personal lives. . . . Commitment to a political cause . . . entered their lives through the back door and was not the prime mover in their terrorist careers." Explanations abound and vary widely but not one of them has yet been proven conclusively (Ferracuti and Bruno, 1981, 1984). Only one thing is certain: "nobody becomes a terrorist overnight. Even terrorist behavior has to be learned. This learning process is to be regarded as a complex procedure which is influenced by various factors. Thus mono-causative explanations cannot be considered an adequate means for explaining the motives for a terrorist career" (Wasmund, 1982).

Wasmund (1980, 1982, 1983), who studied the life histories of members of the Red Army faction, an underground left-radical West German terrorist group, noted that the learning process took place once the individual had joined a terrorist group and that the initial motivation for joining might not have had political sources. He observed that many originally were drawn to such groups because of a need for close human contacts, communal life, and from a search for self-definition. Merkl's study of young Nazi storm troopers (1980) as well as his more recent studies of postwar right-wing radicals (1986) similarly noted that ideological affinity tended to play a minor role in attraction to group life and violence.

For the German radical rightists and/or neo-Nazis a stress on weapons, explosives, "brawling," and soldierly camaraderie seem to take precedence over political ideology. Terrorist bombings perpetrated by Flemish, Austrian, English, and Italian youths (Drake 1986; Pasquino and Della Porta 1986; Merkl 1986) seem to have a similar etiology. Like the pre–World War II young storm-troopers Merkl described, these young men (there are few women among them) never entered the political mainstream but opted for violent confrontations, street- and soccer-game fights instead. Violent personal dislikes (especially of foreigners), gross prejudices, and anger over one's marginal position seem to serve them as a substitute for a political ideology (Weinberg 1986; Pasquino and Della Porta 1986). Such right-wing terrorists share with left-wing ones contempt and profound dislike of the capitalist, democratic postwar society. But whereas the latter look forward, hoping to bring about a new, frequently Marxist-inspired, society, the former look backward to the nondemocratic prewar society with its emphasis on weapons, manliness, battles, and super-patriotism. "The historical epoch to which they assign positive and legendary meaning is the post—World War I era when fascism, as they see it, used violence to defeat the menace of the Red revolution, and guile to replace a weak and inept liberal state" (Weinberg 1986, p. 149).

These documented similarities and differences between right- and left-wing terrorists notwithstanding, we lack as yet a sufficient number of empirically grounded investigations to permit us to draw any valid conclusions as to what elements during a terrorist's earlier socialization propelled him onto the path of terrorism. Some inferences can be drawn from studies of individuals and individual terrorist groups. For example, Wasmund's and other studies of terrorist groups (Clark 1986; Weinberg 1986; Ashkenasi 1986; Merkl 1980; Zimmerman 1986) all suggest that socialization to political terrorism takes place in a group but that an individual's act of joining such a group did not initially constitute readiness to become a terrorist, i.e., to engage in violence. Transition to violence occurs in the group—at times as a rite of passage. The group is effective as a socializer because of its isolation from outside contacts that might offer contrary clues, its persistent indoctrination until the new member becomes a victim of group thinking, and finally its ability to implicate the members personally through participation in acts of terrorism. Group experience thus becomes a vehicle of politicization to terror although, interestingly enough, the German terrorists described by Wasmund studiously avoid using terms such as "terror" or "terrorist acts" when describing their activities and instead refer to "the fight" (and to themselves as "fighters")—a choice of terms which suggests that some vestiges of earlier socialization (respect for human life, etc.) might still remain.

For some, socialization to the cause becomes permanent. Clark's (1986, p. 306) interviews with ETA members, then in exile in France, vividly illustrate this. By the time he talked to them, many had conceded that the fight might be futile, and they felt bitter that their sacrifices were not appreciated by the Basques on whose behalf they fought. What kept them fighting under these conditions? he asks. He attributes much to the solid support from the group as well as to the fact that it provided a "hermetically closed compartment where one simply did not raise depressing questions or challenge the ultimate victory of the organization" (p. 307).

Consequently, among ETA members as well as other West European terrorist groups, the number who voluntarily try to leave a group is exceedingly small, the number of those who succeed is smaller yet (Clark 1986; Ferracuti and Bruno 1984; della Porta 1985; Weinberg and Eubank 1985; Wasmund 1980). The recollections of the few who succeeded in making the break (voluntarily or after being apprehended by the authorities) are particularly revealing on this point (Homann 1971; Baumann 1977) and attest to the enormous socializing pressure the group exerts over its members. That fear of apprehension and persecution by the authorities adds extra weight to this pressure goes, of course, without saying.

These similarities, notwithstanding, it is in fact becoming increasingly difficult to make far-reaching generalizations about European terrorist groups. Between the years 1981 and 1984 a German commission of the Department of Interior issued a five-volume report on left- and right-wing terrorism. The second volume deals specifically with the background and life cycle of terrorists and corroborates Wasmund's point of the futility of searching for monocausative explanations. One commentator (Zimmerman 1986) correctly points out that while it is possible to point to certain features shared by most left-wing ideological terrorists—disillusionment over the failure of the student revolt of the 1960s, noncompleted school programs; "biographical burdens," such as broken family backgrounds—these features are shared with many youthful segments of society, segments that do not join terrorist groups. Similar comments apply to right-wing and ethnic terrorist groups in Europe, and possibly elsewhere. The search for politically meaningful explanations is an unfinished task and a challenge for the student of terrorism.

Resocialization of Terrorists

If the foregoing description is correct, then insufficient attention (both at the analytic and policy levels) has been given to issues of the resocialization of terrorists. Only a handful of terrorists are disposed of in the "line of duty." Hence, major questions arise as to how to reintegrate terrorists into the normative structure of a society, once social conditions or personal attitudes toward marginalized participation change. As one recent paper rhetorically asked: "After a terrorist group has surrendered, what is to be done with the surviving terrorists?" (Ferracuti and Bruno 1984).

The answers for a democracy are not readily forthcoming. The solutions of permanent incarceration or execution common in totalitarian systems are obviously not feasible. This problem is compounded by society's hostility toward or fear of terrorists who remain in the service of their causes. The issue of rehabilitation cuts two ways: the inability of the established order to induce normative behavior and the unwillingness of the revolutionary terrorists to admit erosion in their ranks, or to tolerate reentry into the established order by former comrades.

For the most part, in democratic societies at least, former radical activists (but not necessarily, indeed rarely, terrorists) reenter mainline society at the economic level while basically retaining their ideological beliefs at much lower levels of action (Nassi 1981). Clark's (1986) description of ETA activities fits that pattern. According to him, most ETA men spend relatively brief periods in the organization, usually only in their youth. He conjectured (p.

307) that in "the long run, ETA's major contribution to Basque and Spanish politics may turn out to be that it served as a crucial link that brought young Basques out of adolescence, radicalized and trained them, and then sent them back to attack the sources of their grievances through the institution of conventional politics."

For those who chose to remain with the group and to continue engaging in terrorist attacks, the picture is vastly different. Whether from fear of government reprisal in the event that they might decide to reenter civilian society[7] or from abiding group loyalty and ideological commitment or both, these men begin to rely more and more on the support of the group or cell and to distance themselves increasingly from former ties and the life of the village. Studies of other European radical terrorist groups also point to the difficulty as well as the reluctance of members of underground groups to reenter civilian society. Generally group socialization has been so thorough and so threatening that—at the very least—the individual's identity is merged indissolubly with the group's goals and strategies (Klein 1979; Rutschky 1978; Müller-Luckmann 1978; Wasmund 1980). Of course, fear of reprisal (by the state or by one's group) further adds to the terrorist's commitment to continue in the group and to participate in its violent activities. Wasmund (1980, p. 44), reflecting on the durability of German terrorist groups, asked: "How do terrorists react to the massive public rejection with which they are confronted? How do they work through their political lack of success and what conclusions do they draw from the failure of their fight?" He holds that, once the realization of failure dawns on them, it is the survival instinct that keeps them together. Incarceration being unacceptable, the fight for one's own survival (and possibly the freeing of one's jailed inmates) becomes the motivation to continue the terrorist group life. "What holds them together is the ethos of the lost battle position, the idea of proving one's worth as combatant, an idea now completely severed from its original ideological and political edifice" (p. 44). It may well be that for this type of unrepentant ideologue the answer to Ferracuti and Bruno's question, "What is to be done with the surviving terrorists?" will have to be: very little can be done. In all likelihood, resocialization is not going to occur.[8]

Resocialization isn't even an issue for those terrorists who believe their cause is divinely sanctioned and that it is ordained that their cause will eventually triumph (even though they personally might perish in the attempt). This, it is said, characterizes the Muslim perpetrators of the terrorist acts of this decade—the airplane hijackings, store and synagogue bombings, etc. Neither mission failure, apprehension by the authorities, nor incarceration or even the possibility of death act as deterrents here. Death in the attempt is converted into personal martyrdom and thereby eternal reward. For terrorists who manage to escape or are released after incarceration, the recycling into paramilitary structures replaces resocialization into civilian societies. Once the enemy is defined as a permanent source of evil, i.e., the state of Israel, the terrorist is likewise defined as a permanent source of creative energy. Dramaturgical and ideological terrorists may thus differ in their motivations for resisting conventional methods of rehabilitation or resocialization, but the results are the same: such attempts seem doomed to failure.

In short, just as I had earlier asserted that no one characterization fits all terrorists—their entrance into terrorist groups and their subsequent behavior—neither does one characteristic fit their exit. Only some generalizations apply to all or most: the "profile" of the terrorist begins with the entrance-level criteria, and the "typology" of the terrorist concludes with exit-level criteria. But in detailing a "life cycle," the researcher must be careful not to artificially create a social psychology of terrorism that exists in a vacuum apart from, or in isolation from, the social system as such. These macroelements make the tasks of analysis difficult and ready solutions virtually impossible, at least given the current line-up of states and powers in the world.

Victims and Targets of Terrorism

Let us now turn to the victims of terrorism. Here again we are handicapped by a dearth of systematic social science, especially political science research. Once again much of what we know comes from psychiatric case histories, individual memoirs, and historical accounts. I shall first examine victim reactions to group-initiated acts of terrorism, such as kidnapping, hostage-taking, and hijacking.

Group-Initiated Terrorism

For the victim, the sudden initiation of terrorism constitutes a drastic departure from expected modes of behavior. For someone first encountering terrorism—whether as a passenger on a hijacked plane or as the victim of a kidnapping—disbelief is the first reaction, followed—if the action persists over some time—by gradual perplexity and failure to know how to act. As a consequence, old political-socialization patterns may break down, and resocialization or desocialization may take their place. Terrorists become specialists in inflicting physical and mental pain on innocent victims, and victims find themselves in life-threatening situations where none of the old, long-established lessons of socialization seem to apply. For the victim, the formerly orderly (or at least comprehensible) world has lost its significance as a guidepost to action and feeling. The new world, however, has little meaning for the victim.

The range of victim responses to attacks by terrorists is just as wide as the range of human emotions themselves. At one pole is the resistance to terrorism in the form of immediate effort to retaliate, as in the case of the United States Navy diver who died resisting the 1985 airplane hijacking. At the other end is accommodation into the terrorist syndrome, e.g., the seeming absorption of Patti Hearst into the terrorist network after her abduction, the positive response of Napoleon Duarte's daughter, Isabel, to her abductors at least at the level of ideology. The full panoply of possible responses was exhibited during the Iranian hostage crisis, in which a few members of the U.S. embassy resisted and escaped, while a few others became spokesmen for the cause of the Ayatollah. In other words, the earlier mechanistic theories in which terrorist attacks would be met by civilized resistance do not uniformly hold. Indeed, a variety of behavior best described as passive and apathetic (with victims preferring to adopt a low profile) tends to prevail in specific terrorist situations and environments. High levels of confrontation tend to be marginal. In fact, Frederick (1980, p. 75) commented that the "behavioral phenomenon exhibited in the 'heroic' phase of major natural disasters exists rarely, if at all, among the victims of human-induced violence, whose experience offers less opportunity to unite as a community against an impersonal aggressor." What is far more likely to occur among victims of human-induced violence, especially terrorism, is the tendency to identify somewhat with the aggressor (the so-called Stockholm syndrome) and to sympathize with his plight and political goals. "This phenomenon has been observed on numerous occasions, such as during the airplane hijackings where hostages have been taken" (Frederick 1980, p. 74). The passengers victimized during the 1977 Moluccan train hijacking in the Netherlands, as well as some of the hostages of the 1977 Hanafi Muslim siege in Washington, D.C., displayed similar symptoms.

The fact that the victim may believe that the group-initiated acts of terror are likely to be of short duration would lead one to suspect that the experience is not likely to resocialize the victim permanently or in fundamental ways. This is not to say that such experiences cannot have long-lasting psychological consequences, such as reoccurring attacks of anxiety and depression, fear of strangers, and so on. German psychiatrists, for example, attested that hostages of the Mogadishu hijacking reported such reactions ten years after the incident (*Berliner Morgenpost,* May 18–19, 1986, p. 9). This being the case, one could equally well entertain a different hypothesis, namely, that even brief exposure to terrorism could lead to lasting political reorientations. Because the boundary line between psychological states and political dispositions is such an extremely fine one, as we have repeatedly seen in this volume, it would not be illogical to hypothesize that individuals whose faith in their fellow men had been shaken during such an experience and who continue to live with fear of its repetition, might now become advocates of sterner governmental antiterrorist policies or might (because they thought government help had been slow in coming forth during the incident) develop deep distrust of all political authority. In short, exposure to even short-lived terror could have the potential to restructure one's political orientation. As yet, not enough is known about victims' immediate and prolonged response patterns and the relation to socialization and resocialization. It is another area which calls for systematic political socialization research.

State-Initiated Terrorism

What, however, would we surmise concerning the stability of values and attitudes among people subjected to prolonged state-sponsored terror in concentration camps, Gulags, and the prisons or prison camps in other parts of the world? Although we have better documentation for these victims than for hostages, to a certain extent the same applies to them, namely, the range of responses is wide indeed, going from total self-alienation and dehumanization through collaboration; from acts of compassion and mutual help to resistance and annihilation (Boas 1986; Gilbert 1986; Cohen 1953; Hilberg 1962; Dobroszycki 1984; Nomberg-Przytyk 1986; Paul and Herberg 1963; Krystal 1968; Eitinger 1964, 1983; Kyle and Hoppe 1969). If anything, this literature has alerted us to the difficulty of making simple summary judgments on peoples' conduct in camps, prisons, and other arenas of state-sponsored terrorism. All that can be asserted so far is that the perpetrators' success in dehumanizing their victims, getting them to collaborate, and even to assist in their own self-destruction, varies not only with the length and severity of the incarceration but also with the psychological disposition, the cultural background, and the strength of the individual's value system, i.e., his or her earlier socialization (Segal et al. 1976; Fields 1976, 1980; Bettelheim 1943). Judging from the diaries and memoirs of victims of terror and torture, it would appear that prisoners who attributed their incarceration to their political convictions clung to their original belief system somewhat more easily than those who considered themselves to be punished merely for their social class, race, or ethnic-group membership. It must be remembered, however, that no body of scholarly knowledge exists as yet to explain systematically why and under what circumstances the horror of the experience desocializes some victims but causes other victims to reaffirm old value-patterns and to increase their determination not to abandon them. "The problem of genocide is not a new one, and the need for a literature to move beyond horror and into analysis becomes increasingly critical" (Horowitz 1983, p. 244).

Aftermath of Victimization

Because the choices available to the victim who is still at the mercy of the terrorist are severely restricted, if not actually nonexistent, it might be more heuristic to concentrate on the aftermath of the experience. Agreement exists in the psychological and medical literature that extreme victimization leaves a long-term mark on the victim once he or she returns to normal life-routines. As Laufer (in chap. 11 in this volume) points out, the deleterious effects have been so widely recognized as to receive a classificatory label, namely Post-traumatic Stress Syndrome (PTSS). A critical feature of many undesirable life events is that they often shatter the victim's perception of living in an orderly, meaningful world. (Wilkinson, 1974, pp. 81–88). The challenge posed to a person's previously internalized worldview, beliefs, and value system by the trauma of victimization is likely to leave its impact and even destabilize earlier socialization long after actual victimization has ceased. For example, comparisons of Latin Americans exposed to state-sponsored political terror who emigrated to Canada show wide variations between refugees (potential victims who left the country before becoming actual victims) and those who had become victims (being imprisoned and/or tortured). Not unexpectedly, refugees were better able to keep their earlier value system intact and encountered relatively fewer adjustment problems, whereas victims of incarceration and terror encountered the most problems.

However, even in the latter group the sense of social connectedness, co-operation, self-esteem, and trust in one's fellow men varied by previous socialization experiences, especially previous political integration and affiliation (Allodi and Rojas 1984b). Maintenance of original values and behaviors was most likely to be possible for those who continued participation after emigration and sought or maintained contact with human-rights organizations. Networking apparently served to reinforce earlier socialization patterns. The director of the International Rehabilitation Center for Torture Victims in Denmark, commenting on the difference between general psychiatric patients and those who arrived in Copenhagen as refugees from Chilean and other military prisons, told the New York Times (March 23, 1986) "The difference . . . is that torture victims usually prove to be strong and healthy personalities. The pathology was in the situation they encountered, not in themselves." The goal of psychotherapy, then, is to restore the victim's sense of self-worth and trust in himself and his fellow men and his capacity to resume social contact. What future research in political socialization needs to determine is whether previous political orientations and behaviors of former victims eventually reassert themselves, or become modified or extinguished, and what are the characteristics of a situation that make for extinction or reassertion.

The reactions of survivors of concentration camps bear resemblances to, as well as variations from, the pattern just described. While we must guard against overgeneralization, it does seem evident that several patterns have emerged. Due to the intense trauma of persecution and merciless declaration of their worthlessness, some Jewish victims suffered from conflicts based on simultaneous identification with both the persecuted and the persecutors "and transmitted these conflicts to their children" (Bergman and Incovy 1982, p. 224). For some survivors, fear of victimization, distrust of people, the inability to form friendships and to participate in society's organized life are the legacy of the trauma, compelling them to continue experiencing the past as present-day reality. Withdrawal from society and its rewards, as well as from its obligations, passivity, numbness, and fearfulness characterize these former victims. Politically this expressed itself in an unwillingness to participate, lest activity might bring about retribution—a fear survivors tried to transmit to their offspring. The children often felt called upon "to repair the fatal events in the histories of their parents. . . . Since they were burdened with a task stemming from a past reality that was incomprehensible to them, they could only act out what had been engraved, but not integrated, in their parent's memories" (Bergmann and Incovy 1982, p. 225).

Other survivors appear to have taken the opposite course, seeking to readjust and reintegrate themselves into the ongoing life of society as fast as humanly possible. Some of the observations Robert J. Lifton made concerning the war victims of the atomic blast at Hiroshima (1982, pp. 197–96) apply here as well: the desire to regain and rebuild as fast as possible a socially meaningful life and a rededication to a more moral, just intercourse among humans. While they share with all survivors what has come to be designated as survivors' guilt, these latter victims seek to alleviate it by dedicating themselves to the task of never letting "it" happen again.

Another consequence of the aftermath of organized official terror is the development of a heightened consciousness of anticipatory socialization, of political embodiments of resistance. The slogan of "never again" which arose not so much in the Holocaust generation but the offspring generation (many of them not even children of survivors) is an indication of this anticipatory socialization, or perhaps better said a post-hoc response to events of an earlier period.

The persistent links and occasional conflagration of national antagonism based on earlier genocides is another instance of such post-hoc response. For example, the slaughter of large numbers of Armenians under the Ottoman and later Kemalist regimes of Turkey, continues to this day to set in motion abiding desires for and reliance on retaliatory measures among Armenians (Horowitz 1982; Charney 1984.) Thus, the issue of terror is only seemingly mired in immediacy. In fact, it is a phenomenon with long-range, often structural consequences.

The diversity of the above reactions makes it difficult to reach firm conclusions concerning the socializing impact of terror on its victims. It would be futile to seek a single explanation or a single cause. Obviously duration and intensity of terror affect socialization. Personality probably also plays a role, especially the sense of self and self-esteem. Above all, previous socialization can be expected to play a role in present attitudes. People growing up in societies unaccustomed to state-sponsored violence might bring different reactions to the experience than those growing up in a culture of violence. Future research would do well to study such patterns. Without that knowledge it is next to impossible to reach any meaningful conclusions about the stability of early socialization during periods of terror and trauma.

Terror and The Nonvictimized Population

Finally, we must examine the response to terror of those who neither participate in it nor are victims. Sympathy for and assistance to victims or former victims are by no means inevitable responses.[9] It is not uncommon that victims returning home after having experienced traumatic events find themselves stigmatized or shunned by their community of origin as though they brought affliction and tragic memories to it. This has been observed in Japan (Lifton 1982), Northern Ireland, and elsewhere. Symonds (1975, p. 20) observed that "Society has strange attitudes towards victims. There seems to be a marked reluctance and resistance to accept the innocence . . . of victim behaviors. . . . The community has other attitudes to block sympathetic response. One is the primitive fear of contamination by the unlucky victim. The result. . . . is to isolate or exclude the victim."

Still different responses are elicited when terror is incorporated into the system or structure of society, as with the Nazi concentration camps or the Gulag archipelago during the Stalinist period in the Soviet Union. Then the response of the dominant population ranges from Erich Fromm's mechanisms of evasion (1971, 1978) to William Ryan's (1971) blaming the victims to acts of assistance and resistance. The adult German population's ignorance (feigned or genuine) of the existence and true nature of the concentration camps constitutes a classic example of evasion. Interestingly enough, evasion among those who were adults during that period continues even now. When in 1979 German television aired the American-made movie on the Holocaust, those then sixty years or older either disproportionately avoided watching it or doubted its veracity. Although younger generations (especially those under thirty years of age) wanted to learn more about that tragic episode, a majority of the oldest group objected (Ernst 1980; Magnus and Ernst 1980).[10] The scholarly literature on the process of evasion is slim, although journalistic accounts and memoirs suggest that it is a far from isolated phenomenon and does not apply exclusively to the German population (Boas 1986; Timerman 1981).

Very little is known as yet about the long-range effects of such evasion. Does the refusal to acknowledge one's past permit the "bystander" to keep an earlier-acquired value system intact—to cling to an earlier innocence so-to-speak—or does it prevent the person from looking into his or her self to examine individual and/or collective responsibility? The development and maintenance of responsibility, after all, is the goal of the socialization process.

Blaming the victim is another response to acts of victimization that bystanders might adopt if the observed acts of intimidation and terror inflicted on innocent victims conflict with long-established rules of socialization. When the evidence of injustice or even crimes committed against individuals becomes so pervasive as to make evasion no longer possible—as in the case of the human cargo carried by the German railroad system during the final stages of the Second World War—then the tendency to blame the victim increases. In such situations blaming the victim becomes the least painful reaction to be adopted by the unaffected, seemingly helpless bystander. William Ryan (1971) vividly describes the dynamics of the process and the self-protective function it serves for the practitioner. Although his analysis deals exclusively with American liberals' reactions to the condition of blacks in the United States, it is equally suitable for explaining public indifference to the victims of terror. For people who cannot condone such acts but do not wish (or are afraid) to challenge them, blaming the victim satisfies their conscience and patriotism, and "is an ideal, almost painless, evasion" (Ryan 1971, p. 9). Ryan makes a strong case that the myth of the victim's culpability "must not be a conscious, intentional process. . . . Finally, though they are not intentional, the ideas must serve a specific interest of a specific group. Blaming the victim fits the definition on all counts " (p. 11).

The aftermath of this process can be seen in the case of Germany. Illustrations abound of the reluctance with which the public that lived under Nazism has confronted its obligation to come to terms with its own culpability. Such reluctance, of course, raises problems not only for that generation itself but also for its capacity and willingness to socialize the next generation.[11] Failure to come to terms with one's own past may well constitute a legacy of the process of blaming the victim. Is it possible that blaming the victim desocializes, maybe even resocializes, people and their sense of social responsibility? This then would constitute another area begging to be researched systematically.

Neither evasion nor blaming the victim are inevitable responses to institutionalized terror. History also offers testimony of individuals and, on rare occasions, of whole communities that chose to come to the aid of victims—fully aware of the possibly mortal danger to which they exposed themselves (Klingemann 1985; Hallie 1979). But—just as with our insights into evasion and blaming-the-victim—much of our information here is derived from journalistic accounts, case histories, and individual memoirs rather than scholarly investigations. What little we know about these people would suggest that their choice constituted not a break with but rather an affirmation of beliefs and values to which they had been socialized long ago. Thus one of the inhabitants of Le Chambon-sur-Lignon—a small French, mostly Protestant, village which offered refuge to thousands of Jews during the last war—asserted that offering refuge, even at the risk of one's own life "was very much like what Protestants have done in France ever since the Reformation" (Hallie 1985). The almost unreflective choice to help the victim attests to the stability of socialization in certain cultures and subcultures, or—as Hallie commented—"[W]e fail to understand what happened in Chambon if we think *for them* their actions were complex and difficult." Klingemann (1985, p. 8), in a small study of Berlin residents who had chosen to rescue Jews made similar observations. All "rescuers, except one, made their decision at once." When interviewed many years later, some initially were at a loss to explain their choice but upon further reflection attributed it to the fact that they had, in Klingemann's words, "internalized the norms of social responsibility" (p. 13).

The very tentativeness of this discussion of terrorism's impact on victims and bystanders attests to the need for research in this area. At the moment the area constitutes terra incognita in the field of political socialization research. Systematic research on the topic needs to be given priority on the social science research agenda precisely because the acts of group-sponsored terrorism have increased so precipitously recently while state-sponsored terror shows few signs of abating.

Terrorism, Democracy, and Stable Systems

It is clear enough that terrorism as a tactic has had a dramatic effect on the course of many nations previously thought impregnable to such assaults. When a tactic reaches massive proportions, it can no longer be dismissed as something belonging to the backwaters of politics. For all of its distasteful aspects, terrorism has become a mode of doing politics—a tactic raised to a principle, as it were. In this concluding section, I wish to reflect on the impact terrorist activity exerts on current societies, especially on democratic ones.

As a tactic, terrorism for the most part has failed to reach its primary objective, changing the foundations of state power, and for that reason it has earned the scorn of revolutionaries no less than the wrath of conservatives. It has had mixed success in achieving its secondary objectives: being taken seriously by established authority, obtaining high media coverage, and insinuating itself as a factor in negotiations concerning critical economic or geopolitical areas. In its tertiary goals terrorism has been especially effective: it has reduced the operational range of democratic societies, has compelled democratic societies to curb essential freedoms in the name of survival, and, in so doing, has provided support to its prophecy that democracy is vulnerable and democratic societies are hypocritical with respect to their claims of political superiority. Frequently, the cycle begins with a terrorist kidnapping or killing, followed by enactment, enforcement, or strengthening of antiterrorist laws and a corresponding suspension of legal or constitutional safeguards. Policy proposals to that effect are not lacking: stronger weapons controls, computerized surveillance systems, censorship of the mass media to prevent undue publicity for terrorist activities, and so on. Such attempts to meet the challenge of terrorism by a heightened defense posture and increased security measures can convert democratic societies into garrison states or into a feudalism in which security firms usurp public policy power, often widening rather than limiting the scope of lawless operations (Nathan 1981).

Those who would support such surveillance systems have to contend with a surrender of the norms and values of democratic civilizations. These midway systems, where adopted, would in fact erode the democratic processes so widely taken for granted. The limits each society imposes on the civil liberties of its citizenry in order to secure its survival is essentially an issue in political culture. Seen in this way the consequences of terrorism have little to do with the rise and fall of societies and a great deal to do with political socialization. One would assume that a citizenry socialized to cherish its civil liberties would be loathe to see them diminished except under the most extreme of circumstances.

Considerations such as these should alert us that we cannot move directly to a policy designed to eliminate terrorism without a much clearer notion of the likely social consequences. For example, how much militarism is the American public likely to accept in efforts to curb domestic terrorism? (Farrell 1981). Just as benign tumors sometimes look like critical cancers, varieties of terrorism may also "look alike" but function differentially in a variety of social contexts. One must pay careful attention to such distinctions, not just to satisfy bad academic habits of nitpicking but to justify a continuing quest for democracy in a political universe of expanding social uncertainty.

What must be noted, as recent data indicate, is that terrorism can be stamped out, or at least drastically limited (U.S. Dept. of State 1985). However, in so doing society does not necessarily offer a demonstration of its health but perhaps a reflection of its weakness. If police-state methods are adopted in an effort to combat random terrorists, the social costs and political consequences alike become so grave that the foundations of the system become more menaced than could possibly be set by any random terrorist activities. Risk is part of the nature of the democratic system—to permit modes of behavior that are uncontrolled and experimental. What needs disaggregation, especially in terms of personal liberties, is society's willingness to respond to an immediate and dangerous threat with its capacity to build a social order that can absorb a certain level of risk while expanding its democratic potential. In short, to maintain an equilibrium between the passion for order and the compassion needed to instill change (Arendt 1963; Davies 1971; Eckstein 1966; Feierabend, Feierabend, and Gurr 1972; Gurr 1970; Walter 1969.) The ability to absorb some quanta of terrorism, like some protest violence, is a sign of a society's acceptance of the costs of liberty. It is also a measure of the citizenry's internalization of democratic norms, i.e., of its political socialization for democracy. And tough trade-offs are what characterize thriving open societies.

Notes

1. The literature on the specific causes of terrorism is rich. For example, Martha Crenshaw, "The Cause of Terrorism," *Comparative Politics* 13 (July 1981):379–99; Paul Wilkinson, *Terrorism and the Liberal State* (New York: Wiley, 1977); James W. Wilson, "The Terrorist's Goal Is Not to Solve the Problem," *Washington Star,* July 19, 1981, sec. F., p. 1.

2. Analysts of the terrorist phenomenon can be grouped into two general camps. In one are scholars such as Walter Laqueur (1980), who believes that in historical context terrorism has hardly ever had a lasting effect. Ted Robert Gurr (1979) shares Laqueur's conclusions, if not his intellectual disposition, and sees terrorism as an epiphenomenon of short-lived duration that has rarely been particularly effective. In the other camp are writers such as Albert Parry (1976), who sees terrorism as increasingly effective as it ceases to be a remote spectacle and becomes an immediate peril. Others, such as Brian Crozier (1974), emphasize contagion effect, likening terrorism to smallpox and global epidemics. Those who believe terrorism to be effective come from all ideological quarters; there is no apparent correlation between those who see terrorism as effective and any special political viewpoint.

3. This is not to say that the literature is not rich in historical accounts of specific episodes of terrorism, especially of the official type, such as the growing corpus of works on terrorism in Southeast Asia, the Soviet Union under Stalinism, and especially the holocaust literature. I am referring to systematic sociopolitical investigations of the consequences of these acts on those involved in them.

4. Peter Merkl (1986) distinguishes between extremist/radical ideologues of the left and right on the one hand and ethnic liberation ideologists on the other. He groups ETA and IRA terrorists together with those of the PLO, the Kurds, etc. All of them, he holds, are liberation ideologists.

5. Some scholars argue that violence holds an intrinsic attraction for the terrorist much as it does for criminals who resort to it (Merkl 1986, pp. 357–8).

6. Non-Muslim ethnic liberationist terrorists resist resocialization because of the ethnic identity consciousness-raising which they have experienced during their activities. It should be noted that "this seemingly ideological element of ethnocultural consciousness-raising comes not at the beginning of the involvement, but later" (Merkl 1986, p. 48).

7. Clark holds (1986, p. 307) that fear of reprisal works to discourage "*Etarras*

from leaving the organization, no matter how depressed they may become or how much they may yearn for a normal existence. There is, simply put, a fear of reprisals if they were to abandon the struggle and return to civilian life. The source of the reprisals is disputed. *Etarras* claim the Spanish secret police pursue former *Etarras* after they leave the protective cover of the organization."

8. Ferracuti (1984, pp. 33–40) comments that one of the real problems faced by the authorities is the ability of imprisoned terrorists to propagandize and socialize previously apolitical inmates to the cause of the terrorist.

9. I am referring to bystanders' sympathy for and assistance to *victims* of terrorism. Terrorists, by contrast, frequently can count on sympathetic bystanders who will assist them and their cause by supplying financial aid, weapons, or even shelter.

10. This question is very much at the base of the current debate in West Germany between Habermas, Jackel, and others on the one hand, and Hillgruber and Nolte on the other, with respect to accounts of the history of Nazi Germany. See for example, Gordon A. Craig, "The War of the German Historians," *The New York Review of Books,* 32 (January 15, 1987):16–19.

11. Of those nineteen years or younger who had watched the Holocaust broadcasts, 80 percent wanted to see it again; 49 percent of those forty years and older made a similar request, and the percentage dropped further for those sixty years and older.

References

Allodi, F., and Rojas, A. 1984a. "The Psychological Consequences of Political Violence and Torture in Latin America." Paper presented at the Annual Meeting of the International Society for Political Psychology, Toronto.

————. 1984b. "Authoritarianism—Dogmatism as Personality Trait and the Health and Adaptation of Latin American Victims of Persecution and Torture." Paper presented at the Annual Meeting of the International Society for Political Psychology, Toronto.

Arendt. H. 1963. *On Revolution.* New York: Viking Press.

Ashkenasi, A. 1986. "Social-Ethnic Conflict and Paramilitary Organization in the Near East." In P. H. Merkl, ed., *Political Violence and Terror: Motifs and Motivations.* Berkeley: University of California Press, pp. 311–34.

Baumann, B. 1977. *Wie alles Anfing.* Frankfurt/Main: Sozialistische Verlagsauslieferung.

Bell, J. B. 1978. "The Secret Army: The Finnish Republican Army, 1916–1974." In M. Livingston, ed., *International Terrorism in the Contemporary World.* Greenwich, Conn.: Greenwood Press, 1978, pp. 77–83.

Bergmann, M. S., and M. E. Incovy, eds. 1982. *Generations of the Holocaust.* New York: Basic Books.

Bettelheim, B. 1943. "Individual and Mass Behavior in Extreme Situations." *Journal of Abnormal and Social Psychology* 38: 417–52.

Boas J. 1986. *Boulevard des Misères: The Story of Transit Camp Westerbork.* Hamden, Conn.: Anchor Books, The Shoe String Press.

Bush, G., et al. 1986. *Public Report of the Vice President's Task Force on Combatting Terrorism.* Washington, D.C.: Government Printing Office.

Cairns, E., D. Hunter, and L. Herring 1980. "Young Children's Awareness of Violence in Northern Ireland: The Influence of Northern Irish Television in Scotland and Northern Ireland." *British Journal of Social and Clinical Psychology* 19: 36–46.

Charney, W., ed. 1984. *Toward the Understanding and Prevention of Genocide: Proceedings of the International Conference on the Holocaust and Genocide.* Boulder: Westview Press.

Clark, D. 1978. "Terrorism in Ireland: Renewal of a Tradition." In M. Livingston, ed., *International Terrorism in the Contemporary World.* Greenwich, Conn: Greenwood Press, pp. 77–83.

Clark, R. P. 1986. "Patterns in the Lives of ETA Member." In P. H. Merkl, ed., *Political Violence and Terror: Motifs and Motivations.* Berkeley: University of California Press, pp. 283–310.

Cohen, A. K. 1974. *The Elasticity of Evil: Changes in the Social Definition of Deviance.* Occasional paper no. 7 of the Oxford University Penal Research Unit. Oxford: Basil Blackwell.

Cohen, E. 1953. *Human Behavior in the Concentration Camp.* New York: Norton.

Coleman, D. 1986. "The Roots of Terrorism Are Found in Brutality of Shattered Childhood." *New York Times.* September 9, Section C, pp. 7–8.

Crozier, B. 1974. *A Theory of Conflict.* New York: Scribner and Sons.

Davies, J. C., ed. 1971. *When Men Revolt and Why.* New York: The Free Press.

Della Porta, D. 1985. "Left-Wing Political Violence in Italy During the Seventies: The Formation of Terrorist Organizations." Paper presented at the World Congress of the International Political Science Association, Paris.

Dobroszycki, L., ed. 1984. *The Chronicles of the Lodz Ghetto, 1941–1944.* New Haven: Yale University Press.

Drake, R. H. 1986. "Julius Evola and the Ideological Origins of the Radical Right in Contemporary Italy." In P. H. Merkl, ed., *Political Violence and Terror: Motifs and Motivations.* Berkeley: University of California Press, pp. 61–90.

Eckstein, H., ed. 1966. *International War: Problems and Approaches.* New York: The Free Press.

Eitinger, L. 1964. *Concentration Camp Survivors in Norway and Israel.* London: Allen & Unwin.

———. 1983. "Psychological Consequences of War Disturbances." In *Helping Victims of Violence. Proceedings of A Working Group on the Psychosocial Consequences of Violence.* The Hague: Government Publishing Office, pp. 47–56.

Ernst, T. 1980. "Holocaust—The TV-Event Seen From the Standpoint of Political Education." Bonn: Bundeszentrale für politische Bildung, October.

Farrell, W. R. 1981. "Military Involvement in Domestic Terror Incidents." *Naval War College Review* 34: 53–66.

Feierabend, I., R. L. Feierabend, and T. R. Gurr, eds. 1972. *Anger, Violence and Politics: Theories and Research.* Englewood Cliffs, N.J.: Prentice-Hall.

Ferracuti, F., 1984 "Consecuencias morales, sociales y politicas del terrorismo." *Terrorismo internacional.* Madrid, pp. 33–40.

Ferracuti, F., and F. Bruno. 1981. "Psychiatric Aspects of Terrorism in Italy." *The Mad, the Bad and the Different*. Lexington: D.C. Heath, pp. 179–213.

Ferracuti, F., and F. Bruno. 1984. "Exit From Terrorism." Paper presented at the Annual Meeting of the International Society of Political Psychology, Toronto 1984. Mimeographed.

Ferrarotti, F. 1978. "Riflessioni sul terrorismo italiano' vilenza comune e violenza politica." *I problemi di Ulisse* 32: 12–136.

———. 1979. *Alle radici della violenza*. Milan: Rizzoli.

Feuer, L. S. 1969. *The Conflict of Generations*. New York: Basic Books.

Fields, R. M. 1976. *Society under Siege*. Philadelphia: Temple University Press.

———. 1980. "Victims of Terrorism: The Effects of Prolonged Stress." *Evaluation and Change*, special issue, pp. 76–83.

Francis, S. T. 1981. *The Soviet Strategy of Terror*. Washington, D.C.: The Heritage Foundation.

Frederick, C. J. 1980. "Effects of Natural vs. Human-Induced Violence upon Victims." *Evaluation and Change*, special issue, pp. 71–75.

———. 1983. "Violence and Disaster: Immediate and Long-Term Consequences." In *Helping Victims of Violence. Proceedings of A Working Group on the Psychosocial Consequences of Violence*. The Hague: Government Publishing Office, pp. 32–46.

Fromm, E. 1978. *Anatomy of Human Destructiveness*. New York: Fawcett.

———. 1971. *Escape from Freedom*. New York: Avon Books.

Gambino, A. 1979. *Dal' 68 a oggi:come siamo e come eravamo*. Rome: Laterza.

Gilbert, M. 1986. *The Holocaust: A History of the Jews of Europe During the Second World War*. New York: Holt, Rinehart and Winston.

Gurr, T. R. 1979. "Some Characteristics of Political Terrorism in the 1960's." In M. Stohl, ed., *The Politics of Terrorism*. New York: Marcel Dekker, pp. 23–49.

———. 1970. *Why Men Rebel*. Princeton: Princeton University Press.

Hallie, P. P. 1979. *Lest Innocent Blood Be Shed: The Story of the Village of Le Chambon, and How Goodness Happened There*. New York: Harper and Row.

Hilberg, P. 1962. *The Destruction of the European Jews*. New York: Quadrangle Press.

Homann, P., 1971. "Andreas Baader? Er ist ein Feigling." *Der Spiegel* 48:47–62.

Horowitz, I. L. 1973. "Political Terrorism and State Power." *Journal of Political and Military Sociology* 1, no. 1: 147–157.

1977. "Can Democracy Cope with Terrorism?" *Civil Liberties Review* 4: 29–37.

———. 1981. "Leftwing Fascism: An Infantile Disorder." *Transaction Society* 18: 19–24.

———. 1982. *Taking Lives: Genocide and State Power*. New Brunswick and Oxford: Transaction Books.

———. 1983. Review of *Genocide: Its Political Use in the Twentieth Century*, in *Modern Judaism* 3: 243–47.

———. 1985. "Fascism with a Theological Face." *Freedom at Issue*, whole no. 87.

Klein, H. J. 1979. *Ruckkehr in die Menschlichkeit: Appell eines ausgestiegenen Terroristen*. Reinbeck: Rowohlt.

Klingemann, U. 1985. "The Study of Rescuers of Jews in Berlin: Progress Report." Paper read at the Annual Meeting of the International Society of Political Psychology, Washington, D.C.

Krystal, H., ed. 1968. *Massive Psychic Trauma*. New York: International Universities Press.

Kyle, N., and K. Hoppe. 1969. "Religiosity and Ethnocentric Idealism in Survivors of Severe Persecution." Paper presented at the International Psychological Congress, London.

Laqueur, W. 1980. "The Futility of Terrorism" and "Second Thoughts on Terrorism." In *The Political Psychology of Appeasement: Finlandization and Other Unpopular Essays*. New Brunswick and London: Transaction/Holt Saunder, pp. 101–25.

Leites, N., and C. Wolf 1970. *Rebellion and Authority: An Analytic Essay on Insurgent Conflicts*. Chicago: Markham.

Lessing, D. 1986. *The Good Terrorist*. New York: Vintage Books, Random House.

Lifton, R. J. 1973. *The Life of the Self: Toward A New Psychology*. New York: Basic Books.

———. 1982. *Survivors of Hiroshima*. New York: Basic Books.

Magnus, U., and T. Ernst 1980. "Die Fernsehserie HOLOCAUST: Empirische Ergebnisse." Bonn: Bundeszentrale für politische Bildung, October.

Merkl, P. H. 1980. *The Making of a Stormtrooper*. Princeton: Princeton University Press.

———., ed. 1986. *Political Violence and Terror: Motifs and Motivations*. Berkeley: University of California Press.

Montandor, C. 1983. "Psychosocial Mechanisms of Short-term and Long-term Reactions to Violence." In *Helping Victims of Violence. Proceedings of a Working Group on the Psychosocial Consequences of Violence*. The Hague: Government Publishing Office, pp. 20–31.

Müller-Luckmann. 1978. "Terrorism: Psychologische Deskription, Motivation, Prophylaxe aus Psychologischer Sicht." In H. D. Schwind, ed., *Ursachen des Terrorismus in der Bundesrepublik Deutschland*. Berlin, New York, pp. 60–68.

Nassi, A. J., 1981. "Survivors of the Sixties." *American Psychologist*. 36: 753–61.

Nathan, J. A. 1981. "The New Federalism." *Foreign Policy* whole no. 42: 156–66.

National Foreign Assessment Center. 1981. *Patterns of International Terrorism: 1980*. Washington: National Technical Information Service.

Navasky, V. 1981. "Society and Terrorism." *The Nation*. February 14, 1981, p. 168.

Nomberg-Przytyk. 1986. *True Tales from A Grotesque Land*. Trans. R. Hirsch. Chapel Hill: University of North Carolina Press.

Ostrow, M. 1985. "The Apocalyptic View, Seed of Terrorism." *Jewish Week*, August 16.

Parry, A. 1976. *Terrorism: From Robespierre to Arafat*. New York: Vanguard Press.

Pasquino, G., and D. Della Porta. 1986. "Interpretations of Italian Left-wing Terrorism." In P. H. Merkl, *Political Violence and Terror: Motifs and Motivations*. Berkeley: University of California Press, pp. 169–90.

Paul, H., and H. Herberg, eds. 1963. *Psychische Spatschaden nach politischer Verfolgung*. Basel, New York: Karger.

Russell, C. A. and B. H. Miller 1978. "Profile of a Terrorist." *Terrorism: An International Journal*. 1: 17–34.

Rutschky, M. 1978. "Über Schriften zum Terrorism." Cited in Wasmund, "Zur politischen . . . ," p. 37.

Ryan, W. 1971. *Blaming the Victim*. New York: Pantheon.

Schmid, A. P. 1988. *Political Terrorism: A Research Guide to Concepts, Theories, Data Bases and Literature*. Second edition. New Brunswick and Oxford: Transaction Books/ABC-CLIO.

Segal, J., E. J. Hunter, and Z. Segal 1976. "Universal Consequences of Captivity: Stress Reactions Among Divergent Populations of Prisoners of War and Their Families." *International Social Science Journal* 28: 3.

Speitel, V. 1980. "Wir wollten alles und gleichzeitig nichts. Ex-terrorist Volker Speitel über seine Erfahrungen in der Westdeutschen Stadtguerilla." *Der Spiegel* 31: 36–49; 32: 30–39; 33: 30–36.

Sterling, C. 1981. *The Terror Network: The Secret War of International Terrorism*. New York: Reader's Digest Press/Holt, Rinehart, and Winston.

Symonds, M. 1975. "Victims of Violence: Psychological Effects and Aftereffects." *American Journal of Psychoanalysis* 35: 19–26.

Timerman, J. 1981. *Prisoner without a Name, Cell without a Number*. New York: Knopf.

United States Department of State. *Patterns of Global Terrorism*. Washington, D.C.: United States Government Printing Office, 1985.

Walter, E. V. 1969. *Terror and Persistence: A Study of Political Violence*. New York: Oxford University Press.

Wasmund, K. 1980. "Zur politischen Sozialisation in terroristischen Gruppen." *Aus Politik und Zeitgeschichte*, 33–34, 39–46.

———. 1982. "Political Socialization in Terrorist Groups." Paper delivered at the Twelfth World Congress of the International Political Science Association in Rio de Janeiro.

———. 1983. "The Political Socialization of Terrorist Groups in West Germany." *Journal of Political and Military Sociology* 11: 223–40.

Weinberg, L. 1986. "The Violent Life: Left- and Right-Wing Terrorism in Italy." In P. H. Merkl, ed., *Political Violence and Terror: Motifs and Motivations*. Berkeley: University of California Press, pp. 145–68.

Weinberg, L., and W. L. Eubank 1985. "Change and Continuity in the Recruitment of Italian Political Terrorists: 1970–1984." Revised mimeo.

Wilkinson, P. 1974. *Political Terrorism*. London: Macmillan.

Wolin, S. 1981. "Separating Terrorism from Radicalism." *New York Times*, November 3.

Zimmerman, E. 1986. "Terrorist Violence in West Germany: Some Reflections on Recent Literature." Forthcoming in the *Journal of Political and Military Sociology*.

Eleven

The Aftermath of War: Adult Socialization and Political Development
ROBERT S. LAUFER

The impact of war on adult socialization is a relatively recent concern which asks in a more specific way the age-old question of how war changes the history of nations and the fate of humanity. This poses a serious problem for writing a coherent and limited chapter on the aftermath of war. To focus the chapter I have concentrated on how direct personal experience with war influences adult psychosocial and political development. My objective is to explore the relationship between adult psychosocial and political development in the aftermath of war.

Conceptually the chapter will rely on three general literatures. First, I shall draw from the work of researchers concerned with life-span development. Second, I shall utilize the literature on the effects of war. Empirically, for reasons which will be discussed below, I rely most heavily on the literature on veterans' postwar psychosocial and political adaptations. Finally, I shall draw on the political generation literature for insights into the processes which differentiate individuals located in common place and time.

We are currently at a stage of rapid development of the literature on the aftermath of war. A number of studies are in the field, the data analysis stage or planning stage, so that we can feel confident that our ability to understand the aftermath of war will grow considerably in the coming years. This essay, then, represents an effort to summarize findings in a field which is in rapid development and can serve best as a prod to both research design and data analysis.

The organization of the chapter will move from a discussion of relevant conceptual issues to a review of the studies which have examined the impact of exposure to war on postwar adaptation and conclude with a discussion of the research agenda and some key questions which require systematic investigation if we are to develop an understanding of the effects of war on adult development.

Adult Development: Key Concepts

Psychosocial and Political Development

The linking of psychosocial and political development derives from my interpretation of the impact of warfare on identity and identity formation. My approach to adult political development in the aftermath of war is based on a reading of the evidence that suggests the direct experience of the violence of war is a "life-organizing experience" that fundamentally alters life trajectories, by traumatizing the self system and forging a crystallized identity which is dysfunctional in civil society. In the aftermath of war, the need to integrate the "serial self", i.e., prewar, war, and postwar selves, generally contributes to a period of identity diffusion before an initial integrated identity functional in civil society emerges (Laufer, 1985). Political identity also evolves out of the interplay of the serial self during the postwar years.

Differentiation of the Life Course

Over the last twenty years Ryder (1965), Riley, Johnson, and Foner (1968), Neugarten and Datan (1973), Elder (1975, 1979, 1985), in sociology, and Keniston (1972), Schaie and Gribbin (1975), and Levinson et al. (1978) in psychology have emphasized the importance of viewing the life cycle in general and adulthood in particular as composed of an interrelated series of discrete phases. This literature also makes clear that the social meaning of age and expected behavior at chronological points in the developmental process vary over time and by society (Levinson et al. 1978; Elder 1979).

First, the conceptualization of the adult life course as composed of discrete phases or stages requires me to specify the stage(s) of adulthood on which I propose to focus in my analysis as well as the cultural/historical framework of my investigation.

Second, several concepts in life-span development theory are useful in developing a systematic approach to psychosocial and political adaptation in the aftermath of war (Elder 1985). This literature operationally defines the life line as a trajectory and specifies that events alter trajectories through individual adaptations and thereby initiate transitions, and that the duration of events and transitions are variable and are critical to the character of adjustments in life trajectories. Social adjustment to events can take different forms, such as altering the timing of scheduled life events (marriage, schooling, work, or beginning a family) (Hogan 1981; Elder 1985). Furthermore, the trajectories of an individual are interlocked in two ways. First, occupational, familial, and health trajectories evolve interdependently; and, second, early and later events are linked in personal histories. The trajectories of individuals are also interlocked with those of their kinship system.

Finally, Elder (1985) points out that the more drastic the life experiences, the more one's life organization must be recast, and the more the transition marks a probable turning point in trajectory. Drawing from Thomas's work, which portrayed the trajectory of life as one marked by the recurring loss and recovery of control potential, Elder concludes that "Novel adaptations to crisis situations are ways of dealing with resources and options in order to achieve control over the environment" (1985). In this chapter I shall be dealing with the problem of exerting control over the trauma of war in the postwar years. In my analysis I shall utilize this framework of concepts—trajectory, event, duration, transition, control, and interlocking trajectories—as a way of interpreting the findings on the impact of war on the life course.

Generations: Key Concepts

A second literature on political generations evolved during the same period as the life-span development studies and, like the former, was informed by Mannheim's (1928) seminal essay "On Generations." The political generation literature, in Keniston (1968), Laufer (1970), Lambert (1972), Laufer and Bengtson (1974), Bengtson, Furlong, and Laufer (1974), Katz (1974), and Esler (1979, 1982), emphasized the role of historical events in intra- and inter-generational differentiation. The critical insights from this literature for my analysis are that specific experiences with generic historical events produce intragenerational differentiation among individuals of a common age (i.e., each generation shares a general common history) but the interpretation of the experience varies as a function of how the event is experienced; and, that intergenerational political differentiation reflects identification with distinct historical experiences in early adulthood. Thus, it is critical to specify as clearly as possible the specific empirical pathways through a historical event (see Delli Carpini, chap. 1 in this volume). My approach to the problem of adult socialization and political development in the aftermath of war is informed by the concepts discussed above.

Warfare: Key Concepts

The third problem which confronts us is the nature of warfare itself. Modern warfare during this century has constantly expanded its arc of destruction and multiplied the destructive forces brought into play. The twentieth century can truly be described as a charnel house. While nearly ever continent and nation has suffered on its own soil, there have been a few nations, including the United States, Sweden, Switzerland, Canada, Australia, and New Zealand, which have not known civil war or colonial war in this century, nor experienced directly the devastation of World War II, Korea, or Vietnam-like wars.

Only two Western nations, Sweden and Switzerland, however, have escaped having large numbers of their young men go off to war in this century.

The impact of war has often preoccupied social historians, economists, political scientists. Yet, in no social science theory of society is the role of warfare central. In a world at war for nearly an entire century the question of what warfare means to the social and political fabric of a nation through the lives of its citizens has been largely ignored in the study of society during those years. Only in the wake of World War I and World War II was some attention given to that question (Freud 1921, 1939; Grinker and Spiegel 1945; Kardiner and Spiegel 1947; Futterman and Pumpian-Midlin 1951; Havighurst et al. 1951; Brill and Beebe 1955; Archibald et al. 1962, Archibald and Tuddenham 1965; Lifton 1967; Krystal 1968; Matussek 1971) and not until the Vietnam War has that question become central to scholars in the behavioral sciences (Lifton 1973; Robins 1974; Helzer et al. 1979; Horowitz and Solomon, 1975; Wilson 1978, Figley 1977, 1985; Laufer et al. 1981; Laufer, Gallops, and Frey-Wouters 1984; Laufer, Brett, and Gallops, 1985a, b; Laufer and Gallops, 1985; Laufer, Frey-Wouters, and Gallops, 1985; Laufer 1985; Laufer, Sloan, Joyce, and Surrey 1981; Yager, Laufer, and Gallops 1984; Frey-Wouters and Laufer 1986; Committee on Damage Caused by Atomic Bombs 1982; Stretch 1984a, b, c; Card 1983; Lindy, Grace, and Green 1984; Green, Lindy, and Wilson 1984; Sonnenberg, Blank, and Talbot 1985, Brende and Parson 1985; Smith, Parson, and Haley 1983; Parson 1985a,b; McCubbin et al. 1976; Elder and Maguro 1985; Elder and Clipp 1986; Elder 1986; Van Dyke, Zilberg, and McKinnon 1985; van der Kolk 1984). Today there is growing interest in the issue.

The literature on survivors of war indicates that exposure to the trauma of war leaves lasting scars on individuals and potentially serves as a turning point in life trajectories. What we know about the experience of war indicates that the resources, beliefs, and experiences individuals bring to it are wholly inadequate to cope with the actual experience. Warfare in the imagination cannot compare with warfare in situ; and the latter, especially modern warfare, is without romance, glamour or melodrama; it is terrifying beyond imagination, horrifying beyond what is known in civil society and, for those trapped in its grip, inescapable. The experience of warfare is so overwhelming that individuals rapidly find it necessary to develop a new repertoire of adaptive coping mechanisms for functioning in the warfare environment, i.e., the situation imposes a new subjective reality on the neophyte (Laufer 1985).

Thus, while it is true that what one brings to an event in the life course influences how one responds even to war, it is important to understand that hardly anyone who has not previously experienced warfare brings resources adequate to cope with the experience of war. Warfare is an event which overwhelms the most resourceful; and the breaking point beyond which the individual cannot endure is in comparison with the ability to handle the stress of everyday life or the stress of relatively short economic crises. Sustained exposure to combat situations for more than thirty to fifty days, the military estimates, is beyond the limits of most soldiers (Marlowe 1983). Under these circumstances the resources, beliefs, and experiences that individuals bring to a situation are likely to be of greatest import, not in response to the immediate trauma of war, but in how individuals adapt in the aftermath of war.

In order to understand the aftermath of war we need to utilize the literature on warfare to specify the key concepts in understanding warfare and adaptation to war. At the core of my analysis of the role of warfare in adult development is my definition of its implications for individuals. War is an event of extreme severity. The severity of war stress had led to its incorporation in the *Diagnostic and Statistical Manual*, third edition (DSM-III), of the American Psychiatric Association (1980), Axis IV, as a catastrophic life event, which is by definition out of the range of normal human experience and is associated with potential psychopathology e.g., post-traumatic stress disorder. War is one of the more extreme experiences, outside the normal range of human experiences, and is potentially traumatizing regardless of its duration, because of its severity.

There are three interrelated elements to the traumatizing potential of exposure to warfare relevant to this discussion. Exposure to war stress is by definition a formative life-transition experience. Stress experienced during war involves a loss of control; and the aftermath of war demands adaptations to reexert control over the life process and outcomes. Finally, the experience constitutes a potentially traumatizing situation in the sense that it acquires a fixed disruptive role in life trajectories, and marks a turning point which requires a recasting of the past.

Warfare, however, is not a single experience, but a differentiated group of experiences which have distinctive consequences for individuals. Thus, to say that an individual has gone through war is not, in itself very informative. In each of the literatures we find that, as research develops, efforts are made to differentiate the war experience.

The literature on World War II and Vietnam provides the most useful guides to specifying and differentiating the key independent variables in predicting adaptations to war. As the literature on soldiers/veterans indicates, the key factor(s) which differentiate men at war is whether there is exposure to war stress. Several indicators of war stress have been identified in the literature:

1. Combat
2. Loss of buddies
3. Proportion of unit which suffers casualties
4. Witnessing of abusive violence/atrocities

5. Direct participation in abusive violence/atrocities
6. Age of exposure to war stress
7. Particularly dangerous assignments such as graves registration, tunnel rats, demolition, etc.
8. Knowledge of personally killing enemy soldiers
9. Number of tours in Vietnam and length of tour in World War II

These measures distinguish among soldiers/veterans and allow us to make more precise comparisons between adaptations to war among men who served in the same war and across different wars. As the literature indicates, patterns of adaptation vary substantially by the extent and type of war stress to which soldiers are exposed.

The holocaust literature (Matussek 1971) begins to differentiate concentration camp inmates by the type of camp in which they were incarcerated. The POW literature (Ursano 1985) attempts to differentiate the length of time of incarceration among Vietnam veteran POWs. In the literature on Japanese survivors of the atomic bomb there are several criteria which differentiate survivors, including proximity to epicenter of the explosion, degree of scarring, scope of loss of family and kin. Among members of the Dutch resistance there is evidence that (a) the length of participation in the resistance; (b) the degree of danger resisters were exposed to; and (c) internment in camps, including exposure to torture, are among the factors which differentiate subsequent adaptations (Op den Velde 1985; Instituut Psychiatrie 1986; Dane 1984; Jacob-Stams 1981; Hugenholtz 1984; Ministerial Report on War Victims and Their Needs 1978). While such concerns may, at first, appear ghoulish, differentiating the nature of exposure to catastrophic stress is important if we are to understand differential patterns of adaptation to war over the life line.

A methodological point which deserves some attention is that what is understood by these concepts varies considerably in the literature. For example, combat has been measured in a variety of ways over several wars and the issue of atrocities, abusive violence, and other horrific aspects of war also has been treated differently by researchers in the field. While I will pay some attention to this problem, the reader of this chapter is advised to examine the cited literature for a more detailed discussion of the methodological complexities of the measurement issue (Laufer, Gallops, and Frey-Wouters, 1984; Laufer, Brett, and Gallops, 1985; Frey-Wouters and Laufer 1986; Green and Lindy 1985; Wilson and Krauss 1986). However, regardless of how the concepts are measured, the pattern of findings is remarkably consistent within populations and across wars.

The above discussion provides us with a framework and key concepts we will use to understand the war experience in the aftermath of war: differential exposure to war stress, war as a catastrophic stress event, a formative life-transition, and a critical experience in loss of control.

Adult Development in the Aftermath of War

My analysis takes as its point of departure the traumatization that within the trajectory of adult life occurs at a particular point, constitutes a key life-transition which involves the integration of antecedent life history and re-definition of self, social roles, values and attitudes, and is centered around the impact of the experience on the specific tasks which were interrupted and must be addressed in the immediate aftermath of war. This argues that study-ing the aftermath of war requires specification of the relationship between age at traumatization, social age, and key life tasks at the time of traumatization and immediately afterward; and subsequently, following the population over time, to specify how the experience of war interacts with aging trajectories and developmental transitions.

It follows that social or political developments will have different meanings for distinct adult age-strata in a population, i.e., in the aftermath of war dif-ferent political interpretations of the war experience will emerge, depending on the level of adult political development (crystallized vs. formative political identity).

There is growing evidence from a range of studies that the trauma of war is a potent long-term factor in postwar adjustment in a large sector of the affected population. However, the findings suggest that the problems which do emerge are not necessarily highly intercorrelated. This particular finding raises the problem of differentiating between severe psychosocial disorder and life-course disruption or temporary disorganization as a consequence of war.

Finally, the existing literature suggests that the political fallouts from World War I (Wohl 1979; Fussell 1979), World War II (Waller 1944; Havighurst et al. 1951), and Vietnam in the U.S. were distinct. Similar evidence has sug-gested that World War I and II had very different implications for various European societies.

Early Adulthood among Veterans of War

The first issue I need to address is the problem of specifying the discrete portion of the adult years on which I shall focus. Adulthood, as Levinson et al. (1978) have demonstrated, is hardly a single undifferentiated stage of life. Indeed, it is the tendency to treat adulthood as if it were a single concept which poses very serious problems for any analysis of the impact of warfare on adult development. If we look at the literature on adult socialization, we can see very clearly that the social and occupational tasks are distinctly dif-ferent at different stages of adulthood. For example, in early adulthood the key developmental tasks involve the establishment of careers and families; in the mid to late thirties there is a need for consolidation of career and family, while in the late forties and early fifties there is a contraction of family, career stability, and health issues are likely to emerge.

First, there is the problem of specifying when adulthood begins and ends. Operationally I shall define entry into adulthood as commencing at the age of eligibility for military service and political participation in the body politic (between eighteen and twenty in Western societies) and ending with the onset of old age, defined as the point where careers and generative activity generally end, around the age of seventy. If we take what appears to be the emerging entry and exit points for adulthood in western societies, then we have a long period of at least fifty years, from about twenty to seventy, which may legitimately constitute adulthood. As this indicates, where the war experience occurs in the trajectory of adulthood has potentially different implications for the subsequent years of adulthood and patterns of adaptation.

We know most about the impact of war on psychosocial development of people who, at the time of their encounter with war, were in the early adult stage of life—in their twenties. In World Wars I and II, Korea, and Vietnam the average age of the population of veterans never rose above twenty-six, and in Vietnam the average age of the soldier was about twenty. Among Holocaust survivors the age range was from fifteen to forty. Members of European resistance movements during the war also tended generally to be in their twenties or thirties. The age of civilian populations who are victimized by war covers a normal distribution of age strata in societies.

We are also confronted with one of those unfortunate but empirically limiting realities—our best data on psychosocial effects of war generally relate to the years immediately following the war experience. While there are some data on long-term implications of war across the life line, there are serious gaps in the literature once we move beyond approximately twenty years after the war. There are some exceptions to this rule in the Holocaust literature, but generally that literature is predominantly clinical or the data need to be extrapolated from fictional or autobiographical materials. The preponderance of data on the aftermath of war in the early adult years dictates that I will focus on the implications of experiencing warfare in the early years of adulthood for subsequent stages of the life course.

Second, the literature on the aftermath of war in early adulthood and subsequent pyschosocial and political development deals predominantly with soldiers/veterans. Therefore, the chapter will focus on what we know about this population to develop a more general approach to adult adaptations to war.

Our knowledge of the impact of war on political socialization is significantly less developed than the psychosocial literature. Studies which specifically attempt to understand the relationship between the war experience and political attitudes, values, or behavior of men or women in their fifties or sixties are even rarer. Thus I shall concentrate on the twenty-year span after exposure to war and cite relevant work which provides insight into political development in the later years.

Psychosocial Adaptation and War

The study of the effects of war on postwar adult political and psychosocial development should be concerned with how war recasts life trajectories; its implications for immediate and later life tasks; how the trauma of war affects political attitudes and orientations, the timing and sequencing of life events; and its relationship to interlocking trajectories, i.e., marriage, career, and mental health.

The literature on psychosocial development and war comes primarily from World War II, the Vietnam War, and to a lesser extent from Korea and some early observations from World War I. Currently there is considerable interest and research on Israeli soldiers (Dohrenwend and Levov, personal communication). The World War II literature covers three separate issues: war as it affects soldiers/veterans, Holocaust survivors, and survivors of the atomic blasts in Hiroshima and Nagasaki. The literature on Vietnam, while scientifically the most extensive, is primarily concerned with the fate of veterans. The Israeli research deals with veterans and soldiers. The Korean literature is generally very sparse and thus of limited value for this inquiry. The World War I literature is most interesting from a conceptual point of view as the point of departure for serious scientific concern with the psychological consequences of warfare for soldiers/veterans. In my discussion I shall examine the literature on the aftermath of war largely, though not exclusively, from data on the United States where I can compare research findings across several wars.

World War I

Psychological Adaptation

Psychological reactions to war among American soldiers have been noted at least as far back as the Civil War (Allerton 1969). Military observers of that period described a syndrome marked by restlessness and depression that was common in their troops. This condition was termed "nostalgia," a reference to the soldiers' yearning to return home. For the most part, however, extreme psychological reactions to combat were viewed as manifestations of cowardice.

During and immediately following World War I two additional explanations were put forth in response to the effects of war stress. One was physio-

logical (Kardiner and Spiegel 1947). "Shell shock," the physiological explanation, was thought to be an organic disease caused by the concussive effect
of exploding artillery shells. "War neurosis" was viewed as a purely psychological reaction to combat.

These traditions continued to influence military psychiatrists in World War
II. "Combat exhaustion" or "fatigue," like shell shock, was seen to have a
physiological etiology, whereas war neurosis continued to be considered a
functional psychological reaction to war experiences. Clinical interest in war
neurosis expanded extensively during World War II (Kardiner and Spiegel
1947; Grinker and Spiegel 1945). The work of Kardiner, especially, attempted to differentiate traumatic neurosis associated with war experience
from ordinary psychoneurosis.

These studies focused primarily on men who developed reactions during or
immediately after their war-zone experience. Consideration of the onset, incidence, and lifetime prevalence of psychiatric difficulties was extremely limited. In addition, factors other than war experience that contributed to these
problems were not examined.

Political Adaptation

Several studies which utilize material from World War I (Wohl 1979; Fussell
1979; Waller 1944) all suggest, in quite different ways, that the generation of
1914, the young men who fought World War I, returned home seriously disillusioned with war, bitter, and feeling that they had been badly used. The
pacifism and antimilitarism, especially in England and the U.S., of the post—
World War I era are generally attributed to the perception of warfare and its
meaningless destruction of a generation of young men. The portrayal of
World War I by intellectuals who suffered its wounds is bitterly accusatory.
In Sassoon's poetry and writings the war "is being deliberately prolonged by
those who have the power to end it . . . this war which I entered as a war of
defense and liberation, has now become a war of aggression and conquest"
(Fussell 1979, pp. 100–101), while in Aldington's *Death of a Hero* we find
"an angry indictment of the generation of late Victorians who had light-
heartedly sent their sons to die on the battlefields of France and Flanders"
(Wohl 1979, p. 107). There are two interconnected themes raised by this
critique of World War I. The carnage of war experienced by the writers leads
them to the conclusion that the death, mutilation, and destruction they witnessed constitute a bond which ties together the men of a generation that went
to war and fundamentally alters the trajectories of their lives. The bond which
the survivors share also enduringly differentiates them from those who have
not seen the face of war. The second issue which is raised is the moral basis
for exposing a generation to life-shattering violence. The predominant theme

in the literature of the post–World War I period is that there was no over-whelming justification for the mass destruction of human life wrought by the war. The issue of the moral justification for waging war and its implications for political elites and publics in Western societies is, as the destructive capacities of war grow, a vital theme throughout the rest of the century. The failure to sustain the legitimacy of wars, often reckoned in terms of human costs versus political gains, haunts political elites. This issue has profoundly affected the political dialogue in the West since World War I and may be one its enduring legacies.

The political implications of the experience vary by country. In Germany soldiers/veterans confronted by the horror of war moved in two opposite directions, repudiation of war on the left and glorification of militarism on the right. However, there is a common thread, the human cost of war at the front demands justification (Waller 1944; Wohl 1979). The political implication of the experience for later political development thus generates an effort to give meaning to the suffering and loss endured. This can occur in two ways. On the one hand pacifist or antiwar efforts attempt to characterize war as a craven waste of young human life by an older generation insensate to the tragedy of literally wasting a generation. This suggests that the meaning of the war experience is in the knowledge of horror that cannot be repeated. An alternative response to the war was the glorification of the warrior—the warrior myth—to sanctify war and validate the sacrifice. These alternative interpretations share a sense of social and political alienation born out of the reality of warfare; in each, the war is the core experience from which to shape political perspectives. Regardless of the political direction the adaption to the war experience takes, it places visceral imagery of war at the center of political and cultural consciousness. As Fussell points out, Sassoon spent his postwar life from 1920 to 1967 attempting to cope with the meaning of war.

The point I should emphasize is raised by Fussell's (1979, p. 112) citation from Carl Jung's reflections on a war dream in 1926 in which he was driving back from the front in a cart with shells exploding around him: "The shells falling from the sky were interpreted psychologically, missiles coming from the 'other side'. They were, therefore, effects emanating from the unconscious, from the shadow of the mind"; and Fussell goes on to say that "The happening in the dream suggested that the war, which in the outer world had taken place some years before, was not yet over, but was continuing to be fought within the psyche." As Fussell (1979) points out, this was characteristic of the writings of the twenties and the thirties. The psychological trauma of war was indeed fought out within the psyche long after the war ended. As is evident from the literature, the psychic trauma of war has political implications. As young men who went off to war between 1914 and 1918 returned to pick up their lives, it is evident, in the work of cultural and intellectual elites, that the trauma they endured became the centerpiece for their adult political development. If we examine the years between World War I and World War II, it appears that the elite were articulating the feelings, fears, and rages of their less articulate brethren about the war years. This suggests a point of departure for examining adult political development in subsequent wars. No single coherent political lesson was drawn by soldiers in the aftermath of World War I. Rather, the important impact of the experience of war for soldiers/veterans is that the war becomes a bedrock experience.

The question which remains is whether the war experience shapes views of political issues in general or only those issues which raise the spectre of the war. This is a complicated issue because in some societies, such as Germany, domestic issues were always in some way connected to the war years, i.e., the Weimar regime itself evoked the war. In other countries, such as England or the United States, only some aspects of the political debate related to World War I. On those issues it does appear that for men who fought the war the experience was important. However, precise data on this issue for World War I are accessible only through interpretative reading rather than compelling studies of the role World War I played in the attitudes of former soldiers on these issues.

World War II Veterans

In the aftermath of World War II a number of studies attempted to determine the aftereffects of the war experience among veterans (Waller 1944; Lewis and Engel 1954; Havighurst et al. 1951; Brill and Beebe 1955; Futterman and Pumpian-Midlin 1951; Archibald et al. 1962; Archibald and Tuddenham 1965). Subsequently, there were several additional efforts to explore the impact of World War II (Elder and Maguro 1985; Van Dyke et al. 1985; Vanden Heuvel 1985; Cook 1983; Meguro 1984; Terkel 1984; Dane 1984). These studies generally have a common concern with social and psychological adaptation to the war years. Most differentiate between social and psychological adjustment, and a few ask questions about the political impact of the war years.

War Stress

In the literature on World War II (Stouffer et al. 1949; Grinker and Spiegel 1945; Kardiner and Spiegel 1947), and in Freud's earlier work (1939) from the time of World War I it is clear that the role of combat and exposure to the traumatic character of war significantly contribute to traumatization and psychiatric disability in battle. Brill and Beebe (1955) found that for 42 percent of the men in their clinical sample combat was the precipitating stress in breakdowns. In the work of Futterman and Pumpian-Midlin (1951), Archibald et al. (1962) and Archibald and Tuddenham (1965) we find evidence that exposure to combat is a decisive factor in differentiating long-term reactions to war experience. Further, in Futterman and Pumpian-Midlin (1951) and Archibald and his colleagues (1962, 1965) we also find evidence that exposure to or participation in atrocities and/or behaviors which evoke shame play an important role in postwar reactions.

In more recent work on World War II we find similar evidence that combat experience plays a critical long-term role in postwar adult development (Van Dyke et al. 1985; Terkel 1984) and that we need a multidimensional model of war experiences to help us understand the enduring impact of war. A recent study by Elder and Clipp (1986) also indicates that a multidimensional model of war stress is important to understanding adaptations to war. In this study a continuing relationship between mental health outcomes and duration of service, exposure to fire, and killing or observing killing has been found among men who served in World War II and are currently in their sixties.

I should not, however, overstate the preoccupation of the World War II literature with differentiating the nature of warfare. For the most part it is primarily concerned with identifying those men who did and did not see combat. And, there are various measures of combat in these studies. Nonetheless, the literature from World War II and Korea, developed in the 1940s, 1950s, 1960s and 1980s indicates that in understanding the aftermath of war it is essential to differentiate between soldiers who have and have not been directly exposed to the violence of warfare, and that among those men it is of some consequence to specify the nature of their encounter with death and dying.

Psychological Adjustment

Evidence of psychopathology associated with the trauma of war comes through in the early studies. The Brill and Beebe (1955) study estimates that approximately 38 percent of the sample at the time of follow-up, generally five to six years after first admission to a medical facility for pyschoneurosis, showed evidence of serious psychiatric disturbances; 20 percent were classifed as moderately disabled and 8 percent as severely disabled short of hospitalization. Futterman and Pumpian-Midlin (1951) found, as did Archibald and his colleagues (1962,1965) evidence of delayed stress reactions, i.e., men who showed no prior evidence of psychological distress developing symptoms several years after release from the military. The findings of Archibald's studies (Archibald et al. 1962; Archibald and Tuddenham 1965, p. 475) are especially important because they come from both World War II and Korean veterans. They found that "There is now reason to believe that the symptoms following from sufficiently severe traumatic stress may persist over very long intervals, if indeed they ever disappear." Indeed they found evi-

428   *Robert S. Laufer*

dence for a chronic combat-related stress syndrome in which nineteen of twenty-two symptoms appeared with greater frequency at the time of the twenty-year follow-up compared to the time in combat. Furthermore, their findings indicate that war-related trauma involves more than simply combat. Other aspects of the experience that contributed to the combat syndrome included witnessing of atrocities and shame over specific acts committed.

The Havighurst et al. (1951) study examines the role of military experience on the lives of men in a small town near Chicago. While Havighurst et al. do not explore the implications of combat exposure for the sample, nonetheless, a number of their respondents show evidence of what was later to be called post-traumatic stress disorder (PTSD) as a consequence of their combat experience. The mother of one veteran in the study who had seen combat described her son as follows:

> When he came back, I like to went nuts, tryin' to keep up with him and all . . . he was just like a caged cat. He couldn't sit down for a minute without goin' to pieces. He couldn't read or stay in one place for any time at all. At night he couldn't sleep a wink—used to pace the floors all night long because he couldn't stand to lie abed without sleepin'. and he had them fainting spells—everythin' would just go black on him. He was out at the mill then and he'd conk out and have to come home and rest up. He couldn't work only two or three days a week. And he was so fidgety and nervous. . . . (Havighurst et al. 1951, p. 159)

Another veteran explained that he was "irritable":

> I suppose you'd say . . . when I first got back I used to snap at people a lot more than I ever did before. (Havighurst et al. 1951, p. 162)

Finally a veteran said,

> "It was just about the roughest period I've ever been through," and then went on to explain: Hell, yes. What do you think? Look at me now. Jesus Christ, you can't go through that without being influenced, stepping over dead bodies every day of the week, fellows just like me that got it. . . . I can't forget it; I dream about it and see it at night. (Havighurst et al. 1951, p. 172)

Thus, while Havighurst's work is of generally greater interest in understanding social and political adaptation, like other researchers he turns up evidence that men exposed to the trauma of war show psychological disturbance long after they leave the military.

The research on World War II and Korean veterans who experienced the trauma of war shows delayed expressions of symptomatology and persistence of symptoms many years after the war; and we find evidence that sympto-matic responses to war stress are in some portion of the population chronic and indeed may increase in severity over time. These findings indicate that the trauma of war plays an important disruptive role in the lives of veterans. Terkel (1984), and Van Dyke et al. (1985) in a more recent work, uncover similar evidence of enduring psychological traumatization forty years after the original events. The findings on the psychological sequelae of war expo-sure suggest that veterans' social careers (interpersonal and economic) would exhibit a similar pattern of disruption.

Social Functioning

The studies cited above generally present evidence that among veterans who have experienced combat or other aspects of warfare there is also a negative impact on marital careers. The research suggests that the pathogenic effects of combat on intrapersonal well-being is accompanied by significant detri-mental effects on marital relationships. Thus, in a period when divorce was less acceptable than today, there is evidence of relatively higher divorce rates and significantly higher rates of troubled marriages (Brill and Beebe 1955) and difficult relationships with spouses and children over time (Archibald and Tuddenham 1965).

However, if we look at military service generally in World War II rather than just combat, we do not find evidence that there is a significantly higher rate among veterans than among nonveterans (Havighurst et al. 1951). Furthermore, in Elder's work (1979) there is evidence that for younger men who looked as if they had relatively poor prospects there is no evidence of less satisifying lives or marital histories by the time they reach their forties. The data on marriage and family patterns in the aftermath of war indicates that it is the direct involvement with the trauma of war which is decisive in later life.

Careers

The data on the career implications of military service and exposure to war stress for adult development are not as clear as those just described for famil-ial and psychological adjustment. In Archibald and Tuddenham (1965) we find evidence of long-term occupational deficits associated with postwar ad-justment to war trauma in their clinical population. However, Brill and Beebe (1955, p. 184) argue that "Neither the particular stress associated with the first breakdown nor its severity bears any relation to ability to work or to occupational adjustment at follow-up." Thus, the implication of war stress on careers in the World War II literature is not entirely clear. It may be that time is an important factor in the development of occupational problems, related to war stress, i.e., the Archibald and Tuddenham data collected twenty years later may provide a more accurate picture of the impact of war on career development; or the clinical character of the Archibald and Tuddenham population at the time of the study is responsible for the association between career problems and war experience, and therefore the Brill and Beebe (1955) follow-up study is a better guide to postwar career patterns among war-stressed veterans. I shall come back to this issue later when I discuss Vietnam.

The relationship between military and service and career attainment is more clear-cut. In several studies—Havighurst et al. (1951), Elder and Maguro (1985), we find evidence that, among World War II veterans, American and Japanese men who entered the service at earlier ages, cohorts born between 1926 and 1930, "war mobilization was most likely to delay the transition of males to adulthood when it occured relatively early in their life course" (Elder and Maguro 1985, p. 15). In Havighurst's study there is evidence that the men who went into the service from older cohorts, born between 1916 and 1918, were likely to show, relative to their nonveteran peers, marginal, not statistically significant but persistent, career deficits. However, Elder's work suggests that veterans "who entered the service at a young age still rank above the nonveterans on educational achievement and life accomplishment in general." In addition, in earlier work Elder concludes that military service is especially helpful to younger men who came from disadvantaged families and had adolescent psychosocial profiles which were indicative of poor adjustment.

In addition, Havighurst and Elder find that men who were between the ages of seventeen and twenty at the time of entry were most likely to show significant career gains and changes in direction under the auspices of the G.I. Bill. Thus it appears that one critical factor in adapting to war and military experience after World War II is the age at entry. The impact of war on careers was considerably greater on those who entered younger than on those who entered in their twenties. Thus, career trajectories seem to be especially susceptible to alteration through participation in military institutions and war if that occurs at the first stages of the transition to adulthood. The World War II data remain ambiguous as to the long-term implications of exposure to war on career trajectories, and on the relationship between career trajectories and marital and mental health trajectories. In the latter cases we see stronger evidence that traumatization in early adulthood has significant largely negative implications for life trajectories.

The World War II literature provides a reasonable basis for arguing that exposure to war in the early adult life stage constitutes a catastrophic stress experience, contributes to a significant alteration of life trajectories, functions as a major transition event for men who went to war, and plays an apparently disruptive role in the lives of veterans over time. And as we can see in the work of Terkel (1984), Van Dyke et al. (1985), and Elder and Clipp (1986), life trajectories, especially mental health trajectories, in later life continue to show a relationship to the trauma experienced in war forty years ago.

Political Adaptation and World War II

The literature on World War II provides a complex picture of the meaning of that war. As Terkel's title indicates, it is perceived as "The Good War." Behind that metaphor is the "justification" soldiers found for sacrifices in World War II, or at least a sense of the enemy that in general political discourse has retrospectively as well as prospectively made World War II credible and usually laudatory. Yet, in the literature we see some evidence that, as in World War I, the carnage and loss experienced by veterans will not easily fit the mold that ideology and retrospection assigned to the war. We see in the literature, academic and more general, that men who fought that war came away with something less than unbridled enthusiasm for warfare and some skepticism that the vast military role the United States carved out for itself necessarily encouraged them to endorse subsequent American military adventures. There is again, though more muted than after World War I, a recognition that the trauma of war persists in the psyche long after the fields of fire are still. This type of feeling is evident in some of the war literature. The issue which emerges is again the meaning of death and dying, which can be glorified rhetorically for a general public, while at the same time those who experienced brutality feel a loss of dignity and a sense of betrayal because the rhetoric obscures the brutality. There is certainly disillusionment with war among veterans in the U.S.; and in a study of Dutch resistance members we often find political withdrawal after the end of the war and disillusionment because the sacrifices made during the war did not contribute to fundamental political changes in the postwar world. In this instance the alienation derives from a sense of failure of the postwar world to respond meaningfully to the survivors' trauma in shaping the political order of that world.

However, Havighurst's data suggests a different response among soldiers in his study. Havighurst shows that the notion that soldiers have a clear idea of what they were fighting for misses the mark dramatically. Most veterans, while they thought the war had to be fought, had only the vaguest idea about why they were fighting; generally they thought the reason there had been a war was that the political people had worked their way into one, or the money boys were responsible and will be for the next war.

Veterans also came back thinking that the "American way of life" was superior. Only 3 percent were found willing to let Jews into the country. They often came back with quite hostile views of former allies. There was resentment at aid for our allies and a feeling that the veterans were getting the short end of the stick.

Havighurst et al. (1951, pp. 220–21) also show that, among the veterans they studied, World War II contributed to the development of a perspective which defined the United States as "an integral and inseparable part of the world. The problems of Europe and Asia were also problems of America; we had become involved in them, and we must play our part in solving them. The days of smug isolationism were gone, and we must either help to keep the peace in our world or prepare to take our place in World War III." What we lack here is data on whether men who saw death and dying were in any way different from other veterans. Further, veterans were found not to be especially tolerant of diplomacy, as evidenced by their skepticism about the United Nations. As a group they were far more satisfied with the United States than their peers were; and they expected there to be another war either relatively soon or within twenty years.

The insights we can draw from Havighurst's data, collected shortly after the end of the war, is similar to the conclusion from the World War I accounts. The war experience does form a bedrock against which political development takes shape.

More recent research by Elder (1986) and Elder and Clipp (1986) shows that among younger veterans (twenty-two or younger at the time of entry into the military) military service and combat generally altered the life trajectories of these men significantly. Younger veterans took advantage of the G.I. Bill, which led to substantial upward mobility. However, combat exposure among World War II veterans, currently in their sixties, was found to be associated with psychological deficits.

The implications for proximal and distal adult political development among World War II veterans are less clear. Neither Terkel nor Havighurst et al. provides data from which we can generalize. Terkel's work, while rich textually, does not provide a reliable statistical basis for estimating the impact of the war experience on political attitudes; and Havighurst et al., while providing a solid study of a local community, does not allow us to extrapolate to the larger population. A more systematic exploration of the impact of the war on political attitudes and behavior will become available in the next few years. A recently initiated reanalysis of a longitudinal study started in the early 1920s, the Terman Gifted Men Sample, "Military Service in Adult Development" (Elder, Laufer, and Clipp 1986), will provide a better estimate of the general impact of World War II on adult political development. In addition, Elder's recent extension of the Oakland/Berkeley study will also provide clearer data on the enduring political impact of the war, though this sample is somewhat smaller than the Terman one. The available evidence suggests that the psychosocial problems which men bring back with them from the war persist well into late adulthood, and may also shape political orientations. This indicates that in order to understand adult political development in the aftermath of war, it is essential to explore psychosocial disruption associated with the war in veterans' lives. The best available data on this issue come from the Vietnam War, to which I now turn.

The Vietnam War

Research on Vietnam veterans[1] show a distinctly different development than did previous concern with war veterans. In prior wars it was during and immediately after the war that scholarly interest peaked; in succeeding years that interest waned. Studies of Vietnam veterans grew slowly in the later years of the war, from 1968 through the early 1970s, and then grew gradually to a crescendo in the late 1970s through the 1980s. A prior paper traced the development of that literature (Laufer 1985). Here I note that not only has research on Vietnam veterans continued to grow, this literature has also contributed to a general growth in awareness of the importance of the relationship between war experience and adult political and psychosocial development. The growing awareness of the importance of war experiences has led to renewed interest in World War II veterans as they move toward retirement.

War Stress

In the literature of the Vietnam War we find for the first time a serious concern with the conceptualization and measurement of war stress. The development of the measurement of war stress moved slowly in the first half of the 1970s, but has since become a concern for a number of scholars (Wilson and Krauss 1980; Laufer 1985; Laufer, Gallops, and Frey-Wouters, 1984; Frey-Wouters and Laufer, 1986; Foy et al. 1984; Green and Lindy 1985; Elder and Clipp, 1986; Brett and Mungine 1985). We can summarize the research as focused on differentiating the nature of war trauma, and specifying the relationship between particular war stressors and mental health, career and political attitude outcomes. The critical finding of this research is that differentiating types of war stress is important in specifying how life-course trajectories are altered, as well as the duration of war-related effects on the life course.

At this point several measures of war stress have been identified as critical to understanding the aftermath of war. All studies have some measure of combat. Virtually all of the major studies conducted in the last few years have developed scalar measures of combat (Harris 1980; Laufer et al. 1981; Green and Lindy 1985; Brett 1983; Polk et al. 1982; Begans 1985; Laufer, Gallops, and Frey-Wouters 1984).

A second concept which has received considerable attention is the general issue of atrocities. Several studies have approached this issue in different ways, but there has been consistent evidence that this aspect of the war experience has a powerful impact on life trajectories, and that it is an enduring effect (Wilson and Krauss 1980; Laufer, Gallops, and Frey-Wouters 1984; Foy et al. 1984; Green and Lindy 1985). In each study, whether the measure is labeled abusive violence (Laufer, Gallops, and Frey-Wouters 1984; Brett and Mungine 1985; Frey-Wouters and Laufer 1986) or atrocities (Foy et al. 1984; Green and Lindy 1985), there has been consistent evidence that this aspect of the war experience has a powerful impact on life trajectories.

A third category of events which have been differentiated include personal loss, i.e. loss of buddies (Green,Lindy, and Wilson 1984). There is also some indication that particularly dangerous assignments such as long-range reconnaisance patrol (LRPP), field demolition, entering tunnels (tunnel rats), and graves registration are distinguishable experiences.

A final type of stress relates to taking care of the victims of violence rather than necessarily being a participant in warfare. In some cases the individual may in addition have experienced combat or other aspects of war stress, but is also stressed by these caretaking activities. Treating victims of violence appears to be an important stressor among nurses, doctors, and medics (Van Deventer 1983; Schnaier 1986). While there is still a considerable amount of work to be done in this area, the research has established that a multidimensional model of war stress is essential to understanding postwar development.

Psychosocial Development

The research findings establish that war trauma during the late teens and early twenties appears to have a detrimental impact on mental health over the life course. If we consider the cross-sectional studies conducted between 1977 and 1984, a period of transition from early to middle adulthood for the majority of Vietnam veterans, we find that there is little diminution of the strength of the relationship between war-stress exposure and mental health outcomes. For a minority of veterans who were exposed to various forms of war stress, it is apparent that post-traumatic stress disorder, depression-type symptomatology, explosiveness, guilt, anger, perceived hostility, as well as alcohol abuse, persist and undermine their psychological well-being. While we have no longitudinal data to determine what proportion of this population exhibits chronic versus episodic disorder or symptomatic patterns, it is evident that both types of responses are associated with war experiences. Although the vast majority of Vietnam veterans continue to function without institutionalization, the evidence indicates that war stress irreparably alters their intrapsychic life trajectories by creating a series of identity crises whose resolution requires the integration of serial crystallized selves that often can only be partially integrated (Laufer 1985). The early adult development crisis around integration of the serial self creates confusion in social relations, career development, and parenting which, because they often come close together, negatively affect interlocking life trajectories.

The studies described above also indicate that participation in abusive violence, or what Green and Lindy (1985) call involvement in the "grotesque," has a somewhat different relationship to postwar development than combat, loss of a buddy, or the witnessing of abusive violence. The evidence indicates that participation in abusive violence is related to depressed affect, contributing to numbing, depression, and the use of psychoactive substances such as heroin.

Studies of Vietnam veterans also provide support for the thesis that postwar adaptation is an ongoing process in which the pressure of life-event stress triggers war-related symptomatology/disorder. The most important finding is that, although there is evidence that veterans who come back with PTSD experience diminution of symptoms and/or no longer have the disorder, the relationship between PTSD and war stress is remarkably stable in both longitudinal and cross-sectional studies conducted between 1977 and 1984. Thus, it appears that we are not only dealing with a small population of chronically disordered veterans but also with a much larger group of veterans who throughout their lives episodically undergo disruptive effects of their war experience.

Social Functioning

Evidence of the lasting disruptive effect of war traumatization is most evident in the studies which focus on familial issues as well as mental health. In the major studies of Vietnam veterans, studies which have substantial and/or randomly drawn samples, we find continuing evidence that the stress of war is related to marital problems and/or dissolution (McCubbin et al. 1976; Wilson 1978; Martin 1981: Laufer and Gallops 1985; Laufer, Joyce and Gallops 1985 Harris 1980; Begans 1985). The most important findings in this literature are that the relationship between war stress and marital dissolution and dissatisfaction is found over a range of studies over time. There is also some evidence that parenting is a source of stress in the Vietnam population (Haley 1977, 1986). The two issues are, of course, interrelated. Over time there has been a disproportionate growth of divorce among war-stressed veterans. Children in these families are subjected to prolonged familial stress, suggesting that developmental trajectories of children as well may be seriously affected by parental exposure to war stress. In addition, Haley's work indicates that normal developmental patterns during early childhood, when children act out, can create fears among veterans of having passed on to their children their capacity of violence.

Post-service arrest and conviction rates are also related to exposure to war stress. The findings from *Legacies of Vietnam*[2], a household probability sample of ten sites in the United States (Laufer et al. 1981; Yager, Laufer, and Gallops, 1984), indicate that post-service arrest and conviction rates are related to combat exposure and unrelated to preservice arrest histories. Similar findings were obtained in two other studies, Polk et al. (1982) and Laufer, Gallop and Joyce (1985). However, in both studies there is evidence that, as veterans age, the likelihood of getting arrested diminishes.

Veterans do not easily discuss their experiences with their peers unless the peers are also veterans; and they are generally reluctant to discuss their war years with family (Wilson 1978; Laufer et al. 1981; Polk et al. 1982; Brende and Parson 1985; Frey-Wouters and Laufer 1986). The persistent tendency of veterans to keep their experiences from their friends and family suggests that the Vietnam years remain hidden, implicitly menacing both to the veterans and their nonveteran social network.

Careers

The evidence on career patterns is far less clear. There is evidence of deficits in occupational attainment associated with service in Vietnam, especially among black veterans (Rothbart, Sloan and Joyce 1981; Polk et al. 1982; Card 1983). However, researchers have not generally found a relationship between war-stress measures and careers until recently (Laufer, Gallops, and Joyce 1985; Begans 1985). In *Opportunities for Intervention* (Laufer, Gallops and Joyce 1985) a strong relationship was found between combat and un-employment, downward career trajectories, and income measures. The *ABC/ Washington Post Poll* (Begans 1985) also found some evidence of underrepresentation of heavy-combat veterans in the higher-income categories. Only 40 percent of the heavy-combat veterans had incomes of $30,000, compared to other Vietnam veterans (47 percent) Vietnam-era veterans (49 percent) and nonveterans (53 percent). The delayed entry of veterans into the labor market as a consequence of the military service may be a factor in the more recent studies that found career deficits associated with war stress.

Only recently have researchers begun to investigate patterns of entry into early adulthood among Vietnam veterans (Laufer and Joyce 1986). As the literature developed by Hogan (1981) and Elder (1985) indicates, the timing and sequencing of early adult life-events play a potentially important role in career trajectories. Findings to date indicate that one aspect of the early adult transition, entry into marriage, occurs relatively earlier among veterans when compared to nonveterans if we take into account the fact that they spent three years in the military, i.e., we do not find a difference between age of marriage among Vietnam veterans, Vietnam-era veterans, and nonveterans (Laufer and

Gallops 1985). However there is an important finding in terms of entry into marriage. Vietnam veterans (84 percent) and Vietnam-era veterans (81 percent) are significantly more likely to have entered marriage by age thirty than are their nonveteran peers (70 percent).

In summary I can say that the evidence compiled over the last ten years does indicate that the stress of war plays a continuing role in life trajectories of Vietnam veterans. Indeed the evidence is rather clear that even in their late thirties and early forties the war experience remains a source of disruption in psychological health, social relations, and occupational attainment for a significant portion of the Vietnam veteran population. Furthermore, as my review demonstrates, the disruptive effects are often delayed, cyclical, or episodic in some segment of the population, and chronic for a quite small proportion of Vietnam veterans. What I should emphasize is that Vietnam veterans provide considerable evidence for the thesis that the war experience remains a potentially disruptive factor through early and middle adulthood.

Political Development

During the Vietnam War years researchers have pursued the relationship between military experience and political orientations and attitudes. Research in this area has focused on either the military as an institution of socialization, i.e., the impact of military service per se on political development (Barber 1972; Stenger 1974; Bachman and Jennings 1975; Segal and Segal, 1976; Jennings and Markus 1976; Kirkpatrick and Regens 1978); or on the role of the war experience in postwar political orientations (Polner 1971; Yankelovich 1972; Brady and Rappaport 1973; Harris 1980; Laufer et al. 1981; Laufer, Sloan, Joyce, and Surrey, 1981; Frey-Wouters and Laufer 1984; Begans 1985; Frey-Wouters and Laufer, 1986).

Studies which concentrate on military experience generally do not find significant differences between the political attitudes of veterans and their peers. Jennings and Markus (1976), in their panel study of men who graduated from high school in 1965, found no changes in political participation, general interest in political affairs, or the sense of political efficacy between veterans and nonveterans. Bachman and Jennings (1975) found that veterans and nonveterans did not significantly differ in their levels of trust in government, their ratings of the military, or their dissatisfaction with American involvement in Vietnam.

Jennings and Markus (1976) did find some modest differences between veterans and nonveterans. Vietnam veterans were more likely to report a higher level of support for involvement in Vietnam while in the military; they also tended to have a broader political attention frame. Veterans also showed slightly lower levels of political cynicism and slightly more faith in the national government. The magnitude of these differences was small, leading the authors to conclude that differences in the institutional experiences were more important in distinguishing attitude sets in groups of individuals than was the fact of military service itself.

In a study of the adult Detroit population Segal and Segal (1976) reported that there were no significant differences between groups distinguished by veteran status in levels of trust in government or support for military intervention in Vietnam. This study was different from the panel studies noted above in that its sample was a cross-sectional one and the key variable, military service, referred to service in any period and not just during the Vietnam War. Significant differences were also absent in comparisons they made between veterans of different wars, leading the authors to conclude that Vietnam veterans were not different from veterans from previous periods or other wars. Similar findings are reported by Kirkpatrick and Regens (1978). In this cross-sectional study of military-experience effects on foreign-policy attitudes the authors conclude that generally the data suggest an "absence of differences between veterans and nonveterans."

The findings discussed above are quite consistent with the pattern of findings on psychosocial adjustment, where, in general, military service per se is not significantly associated with distinctive outcomes.

However, research which differentiates between *military service, Vietnam experience,* and *exposure to war trauma* shows that the war experiences are important factors in influencing postwar adult political attitudes (Fendrich and Axelson 1971; Yankelovich 1972; Brady and Rappaport 1973; Wilson 1978; Harris 1980; Laufer, Sloan, Joyce and Surrey 1981; Surrey 1982; Laufer et al. 1981; Begans 1985; Frey-Wouters and Laufer, 1986). The impact of the Vietnam experience on subsequent political development in these studies provides evidence that the Vietnam experience is a factor in shaping current attitudes on some issues. Research which includes measures of Vietnam and war-stress effects indicates that specific experiences with war trauma further differentiates the Vietnam veteran population.

In this literature we can differentiate several distinct dimensions of political attitudes where we do and do not find differences as a result of the war experiences:

1. Alienation from society and distrust of government
2. War-related foreign and domestic policy issues
3. Political identification
4. Political participation
5. Attitudes toward violence
6. Domestic social issues

Alienation from Society and Distrust of Government

The most pervasive theme in the literature is one of social and political alien-ation among Vietnam veterans, especially among men who were exposed to the trauma of war. Fendrich and Axelson (1971) characterized their sample of Vietnam veterans as highly alienated. In addition, they found disillusion-ment and disenfranchisement. This sample included only black veterans liv-ing in northwest Florida. Their study lacked comparison groups in the sample and included a nonrepresentative all-black veteran sample.

Yankelovich (1972), in a national study of changing values among youth, found that, among noncollege youth, Vietnam veterans were more alienated and felt their values were not shared by other Americans. Pollack, White, and Gold (1975) in a study of 163 Vietnam veterans at a large university found that these veterans held themselves apart from the political process. Having killed someone in Vietnam was strongly correlated with general social alienation. Though the authors characterize Vietnam veterans as ex-tremely alienated, the lack of an effective comparison group of nonveterans and the lack of representatives of the general population to which the veterans belonged limits the generalizability of the findings. Wilson's (1978) study suffers from similar limitations though the population is not drawn from the academic world. Nonetheless, he too found that Vietnam veterans were alien-ated and had lost faith in government. In addition combat experience among whites sharply increased alienation.

Harris (1980), in a national study of Vietnam veterans and their age peers, *Myths and Realities,* found substantial differences between Vietnam veterans and their nonveteran peers on levels of political alienation. Veterans classified as heavy-combat, reported somewhat higher levels of political and social alienation more frequently than their Vietnam veteran counterparts; and the study shows that combat veterans also felt more rejected than other veterans when they returned home; and felt more strongly than light-combat veterans that the United States took unfair advantage of them (30 percent v. 18 percent). Laufer et al. (1981), Frey-Wouters and Laufer (1984) and Frey-Wouters and Laufer (1986) using the *Legacies of Vietnam* data set have re-ported similar findings using multivariate analysis. Vietnam veterans gener-ally reported they were more alienated from government than nonveterans; heavy-combat veterans express a higher level of alienation than low-combat veterans and are significantly more likely to say they are apolitical; Vietnam veterans who witnessed abusive violence report being significantly more alienated from government than other Vietnam veterans. Finally, the aliena-tion from government found in the Vietnam veteran population today, fits well with the finding that combat veterans, especially those who returned after 1967, report being alienated from society at the time they returned home.

The *ABC/Washington Post Poll* on Vietnam veterans (Begans 1985), shows that heavy-combat veterans (64 percent) are somewhat more likely to say that U.S. leaders' handling of the war made them personally distrustful "of our leaders in Washington" than the general population (57 percent). The distrust of leaders by combat veterans persists. Today 24 percent of the heavy-combat veterans are less sure that they can trust government officials to do what is right, compared to only 11 percent of their nonveteran age peers and 13 percent of the general population.

In a series of studies from 1971 through 1985 there is a consistent finding of increased social and political alienation related to both service in Vietnam and exposure to war stress. In light of the discussion which follows this may be the most important set of findings in the research literature on adult political development in the aftermath of war. Social and political alienation provides a direct link between psychosocial and political adjustment.

War-Related Foreign and Domestic Political Issues

The studies discussed above also explore in many instances the association between military service and attitudes toward the war, the conduct of the war, future military intervention, and feelings about those who protested the war and/or refused to serve and left the country. I shall now examine the evidence on these issues separately.

These studies all examine attitudes of the veteran population to the Vietnam War. Wilson's (1978) study shows that Vietnam veterans support for the war gradually diminished. The combat experience further eroded support for the war; combat veterans were distinguished from noncombat veterans by lower levels of support for the war, willingness to fight another war like Vietnam, or send their son to such a war. Harris (1980) found substantial differences between Vietnam veterans and their nonveteran peers on levels of support for American involvement in the Vietnam War. While a plurality of Vietnam veterans (49 percent) felt the U.S. should have stayed out of Vietnam, fully 60 percent of the age group 25–34 (defined as the Vietnam generation by Harris) felt that way; and among antiwar activists 90 percent felt the U.S. should have stayed out of Vietnam. Combat veterans were not found to differ from Vietnam veterans on level of support for American involvement in Vietnam. Frey-Wouters and Laufer (1984, 1986) found that a majority of Vietnam veterans either opposed the war (45 percent) or were confused by it (10 percent). Black veterans (13 percent) reported an extraordinarily low level of support for the war; and Vietnam veterans who served after 1967 were significantly more opposed to the war (54 percent) than those who served in the earlier years of the war (36 percent), before 1968. Nonetheless, Vietnam veterans were significantly more likely to support the Vietnam War than their nonveteran peers, especially those who were actively engaged in the antiwar movement. The *ABC News/Washington Post Poll* on Vietnam veterans (Begans 1985) shows that nonveteran males of the Vietnam generation (61 percent) are substantially more likely to say that the U.S. should not have become involved in the Vietnam War than Vietnam veterans (45 percent). Vietnam veterans are more likely to say American troops fought in a worthwhile cause (57 percent v. 39 percent).

Another major issue pursued in several of the studies is views of the Vietnamese. Harris (1980) asked whether they felt "It is shameful what my country did to the Vietnamese people." This item does significantly differentiate younger from older Vietnam veterans. Among the 25–34-year-old veterans, 33 percent agreed with the statement, compared to 25 percent of the 35–44 age group and only 16 percent of those between the ages of 45 and 54. However, combat does not differentiate Vietnam veterans' response to this item. Frey-Wouters and Laufer (1986) found differences among these groups on attitudes toward the Vietnamese, and the effects of the war on the Vietnamese. Vietnam veterans report a more complex view of the Vietnamese. Vietnam veterans reported hostile (31 percent) ambivalent (31 percent), and positive feelings (37 percent) while nonveterans generally expressed sympathy (71 percent); and among black veterans only a small proportion of them (10 percent) held negative views of the Vietnamese people. They also found that witnesses of abusive violence are somewhat less likely to report hostile views of the Vietnamese (21 percent) than either combat veterans (29 percent) or participants in abusive violence (41 percent).

A companion concern, perceptions of the conduct of the war, has been explored by Begans (1985) and Frey-Wouters and Laufer (1986). Frey-Wouters and Laufer found that Vietnam veterans were less likely than nonveterans to report that U.S. forces engaged in abuse of civilians, or used terror bombing tactics against civilian targets. However, a majority of Vietnam veterans who served after 1967 admitted that these actions took place. The effects of the three variables—combat, witnessing abusive violence, and participation in that violence—tend to differentiate the Vietnam veteran population. For example, combat generally has the effect of lowering estimates of abuse of Vietnamese civilians by U.S. forces, the extent of terror bombing of civilian targets to terrorize the population, and estimates of the frequency with which the U.S. employed environmental warfare. The witnessing of and participation in abusive violence generally increases estimates of such actions among Vietnam veterans. Combat and participation in abusive violence tend to increase legitimation of a broader range of weapons in more unrestricted ways, while those who witnessed abusive violence are more likely to restrict the use of such weapons and the conditions of their use. Begans (1985) also found that Vietnam veterans are more likely to say that the bombing of North Vietnam, the use of napalm and chemical weapons, and the destruction of villages harboring hostile forces were justified than their nonveteran peers.

A major focus of research on the Vietnam era has been the attitudes of veterans toward those who participated in the antiwar movement and/or resisted military service through resistance. Laufer, Sloan, Joyce, and Surrey (1981) found that Vietnam veterans were considerably more hostile to amnesty for draft resisters than either Vietnam-era veterans or nonveterans. Begans (1985) also finds that 68 percent of the Vietnam veterans report they are critics of protesters while 50 percent of the nonveteran males report they are supporters of protesters. Harris (1980) and Frey-Wouters and Laufer (1986) found no significant differences between Vietnam veterans and Vietnam-era veterans on attitudes toward resisters, but the latter study found that combat veterans were significantly more hostile to resisters and antiwar activists than other veterans.

However, support for resistance to military service in wars like Vietnam has become an option for a significant number of veterans. Frey-Wouters and Laufer (1986) asked whether or not the respondent would want to send his son to participate in future wars like Vietnam, and/or whether the respondent would be willing to send his son to Canada instead of military service. A substantial majority of all groups would prefer that their sons not serve in the military under these circumstances. Vietnam veterans are least likely to reject military service for their sons: 64 percent compared to 74 percent of Vietnam era veterans and 80 percent of the nonveterans. On the more divisive issue of resistance to military service during a future Vietnam-style war we find only a bare majority of the age group opposes resistance by emigration to Canada for their children. Veterans (37 percent) are significantly more reluctant to encourage their sons to resist military service by leaving the country during a war like Vietnam than nonveterans (54 percent). Heavy-combat veterans (38 percent) are as likely as their Vietnam-era peers to support resistance to military service by their children.

Finally, we find in Begans (1985) that Vietnam veterans are the most pessimistic about the prospects of preventing another war like Vietnam. Only 51 percent of Vietnam veterans feel the United States is less likely to become involved in subsequent wars because of Vietnam, compared to 64 percent of their nonveteran male peers. Frey-Wouters and Laufer (1986) and Begans (1985) found that Vietnam veterans are overwhelmingly opposed to future military intervention, though somewhat less so than either Vietnam-era veterans or nonveterans. Finally, Begans (1985) found the fear of another Vietnam-like intervention in Central America coming to fruition was more prevalent among heavy-combat veterans (39 percent) than among the nonveteran members of the Vietnam generation (21 percent).

Attitudes toward Violence

Brady and Rappaport (1973) in a study of orientation to the use of violence in domestic and foreign-policy-related issues found that heavy-combat veterans agreed more than others with items which stated that it is sometimes necessary to torture prisoners, take the law into your own hands, kill looting rioters, more force should have been used in Vietnam, and men prove their courage in physical combat. In addition the overall violence score for heavy-combat veterans was significantly higher than for either moderate- or low-combat veterans; the analysis suggests that socioeconomic factors are inadequate to account for the findings in light of the commonality of attitudes between officers and enlisted men. These authors conclude that "exposure to combat makes for a more positive general and specific orientation toward violence, and seems superior to any interpretation based on socioeconomic status."

General Political Orientation: Political Identification, Participation, Domestic Social Issues

The findings of the various studies are not in complete harmony concerning the relationship between military experience and general political orientation. In one of the early studies (Yankelovich 1972) there is evidence that Vietnam veterans were different from their noncollege-age peers. Yankelovich found that Vietnam veterans were more liberal and less traditional on social issues than their peers, more likely to be at the political extremes (radical-conservative), and for stricter gun-control laws. The Yankelovich study did not report on differences associated with exposure to combat or other war stressors. There is some supporting evidence for the Yankelovich study in Wilson's research. Wilson reported that Vietnam veterans' views generally moved from right to left after returning from the military.

In subsequent studies by Harris (1980), Frey-Wouters and Laufer (1986) and Begans (1985),[3] we do not find evidence to support the above findings. Harris found that there were no differences on political activism, social participation, or political identification. Frey-Wouters and Laufer examined political identification and attitudes to nonwar-related political issues. They found that on a range of indicators including social issues (such as support for social spending and defense spending), political orientation, and political involvement, there were no differences between veterans and nonveterans or among Vietnam veterans. Finally, in the *ABC News Washington Post Poll* there is also little evidence that there are substantial differences in general political orientation between veterans and nonveterans, or that such differences exist within the veteran population based on wartime experience. For example, views of the Reagan administration or propensity to vote for the Reagan ticket do not seem to be associated with military experience.

The persistent differences on general political orientation appear to be related to participation in the antiwar movement during the Vietnam years. In studies where an effort was made to differentiate the nonveteran population (Harris 1980; Frey-Wouters and Laufer 1986) antiwar activists during the Vietnam War were found to constitute a distinct subgroup which remained more hostile to the war, its conduct, and subsequent interventions, and more liberal on general political issues and identification, than their peers. Frey-Wouters and Laufer (1986) also found that witnesses to abusive violence among veterans are the group most likely to share the views of the antiwar activists. Thus, it appears that self-selected experiences which systematically shape consciousness, such as participation in the antiwar movement, and dramatic experiences which challenge and/or destroy the individual's taken-for-granted world are most likely to have enduring effects on political identification. Such experiences, however, touch only a small fraction of any cohort.

Interpreting The Findings

There are several basic insights we can draw from the studies of veterans of World War I, World War II, Korea, and Vietnam whose encounter with war occurred during the early stages of adulthood. I conclude that there is an important relationship between psychosocial and political adaptation. The experience of warfare also shapes the veterans' political frame of reference, because when war intrudes on early adulthood it is a decisive formative transition experience. The decisiveness of warfare in early adult development derives in large part from the intensity of the trauma, its duration, and the precipitous loss of control over the self and the environment into which the young soldier is plunged. However, the experience of warfare is a differentiated experience for the mass of soldiers; therefore, the trauma of war does not lead to a uniform political interpretation in the postwar years. The differential experience with and immediate response to the trauma provide the common ground from which the war's survivors draw their "lessons of war." Subsequently survivors use these "lessons," primarily on foreign-policy-related issues, to interpret and "define" postwar sociopolitical events. Finally, while we have little direct evidence in the area of political adaptation, it is evident from the psychosocial data that mental health, familial, and career trajectories interact with the war experience over the life course as the relationship of the trauma to the self evolves under the pressure of life-event stress and developmental transitions; and potentially this process reshapes the meaning of war in sociopolitical terms because the relationship of the self to society changes.

The evidence generally supports the conclusion that the experience of war contributes to social and political alienation. Even among World War II veterans we find evidence of disaffection/alienation in the short-and long-term. However, among World War II veterans we also find a sense of the war's necessity and some significant support for an active role by the United States in the world's affairs. In World War I and Vietnam, of course, the alienation from society and politics yields a more limiting vision of the American role in the world.

The implication of this finding is that in attempting to understand political adaptation we must pay attention to war-related psychosocial wounds which plague veterans in the years after, by contributing to and/or being exacerbated by life-event stress over the life course. The trauma remains a potential source of stress, and the disaffection and distancing between the self and others also contributes to political isolation. The process of intersection between political and psychosocial development appears to emerge out of the process of identity integration and establishment of a relationship between self and society.

In the light of the literature, a dynamic interpretation of this process can be elaborated through the work of Vaillant (1977), Levinson et al. (1978), Laufer (1985). This literature develops a conceptualization of the adaptation process in adulthood, emphasizing aspects of the early adult transition, elaborates the developmental stages of the adult years, and explores the role of war experience in early adult life. The initial adaptations to the trauma of war revolve around the difficulty of relating to the "serial self" and the process of reexerting control over life processes. The self which emerges from war is traumatized but plays the central role in defining the parameters of identity available to the individual. Serialization is the process of constructing a self-system congruent with civil society in the post-war period which integrates the warrior self into an "integrated" postwar identity. The discontinuities between identities poses a constant challenge to the survivor of war. This process evolves over the individual's life course and, I would argue, constantly creates a special vulnerability to identity diffusion or disintegration through the demands of developmental transitions of adulthood and subsequent stressful life events which either recall the original trauma and/or challenge the "partial" resolution of the serial self.

The centrality and evolving nature of the relationship between the war experience and psychosocial adaptation over the life line potentially influences political development. The war experience appears to becomes a filter through which subsequent events are given meaning. Political orientations and attitudes are thus substantially influenced by the particular relationship of the individual to the particular meaning of the war experience at a given time. There are, of course, stable elements to the self-system and the political-belief system. However, I hypothesize that as the war experience as a life-organizing (traumatic) event represents a constant potential for psychosocial disruption, it also potentially alters the perceived meaning of the event and hence the development of political attitudes and orientations.

Another important issue in the literature is that traumatization in war is variable; and the management of trauma is also variable. This variability of war experiences in soldiers is reflected in patterns of association between war experiences and political attitudes of veterans. We do not find a uniform political impact of war on adult development. Rather, we find that particular types of experiences and responses to the trauma contribute to distinct postwar political orientations. This supports an interpretation that war experiences form the basis of political development and opposing political perspectives for the survivors.

An insight we can draw from the research is that war trauma as experienced by individuals is the type of social historical event which contributes to the formation of political-generation units who struggle, during their lifetime, to apply the "lessons of the war" (Mannheim 1928; Laufer and Bengtson 1974). The differential war experiences then become an important factor in shaping the political imagery which dominates political debate among elites and which finds a resonance in the general population. While in public debate a dominant image of a war may emerge, the competing interpretations of the war, and of war itself, remain an active part of the postwar political debate, especially on issues of war and peace.

For example, while World War II has generally been regarded as a "Good War" (Terkel 1984), it is clear that "good", as Terkel demonstrates, is a simplistic idea in trying to understand the aftermath of the war. It is therefore an error to impose a single vision of World War II on its veterans. For example, World War II veterans' responses to subsequent foreign policy considerations varied in some measure by whether or not they felt badly used by the military during World War II, their experiences with death and dying in the war, and the lasting impact of the war on their lives. As Terkel demonstrates, there appears to be some relationship between the sense of war's destructiveness as personally experienced and sympathy for those who were less than enthusiastic about dying in Vietnam. It is unclear whether there is any systematic relationship between types of war experiences in World War II and responses to opposition to Vietnam. It would be of some interest to know whether men who experienced different aspects of warfare during World War II were more receptive to opposition to the Vietnam War as its costs became clearer and the objectives more obscure.

There seems little doubt from the Vietnam data that the military experience forms the root of political orientations and attitudes which are related to foreign policy considerations vis-à-vis America's role in the world, but not to general domestic social issues or political identification. If we look at the three wars, we see that in World War I and Vietnam there was substantially reduced enthusiasm among men who experienced war stress for subsequent uses of force by the United States. In Havighurst and Terkel we find a more expansionist view coming from World War II veterans. Nonetheless, even among World War II veterans we find considerable concern over, and reluctance to be involved in, future wars. It is important to keep in mind that in the Vietnam studies we find systematic evidence that Vietnam veterans and/ or combat veterans are more likely to believe that the U.S. will become involved in future interventions. While American veterans exposed to warfare appear more prone to support intervention, the proportion who are disaffected in the aftermath of the Vietnam War is very large. Further, the data on Vietnam veterans suggest that we are not dealing with soft attitudes. While we cannot tell whether individuals have changed their attitudes on particular issues, there appear to be some rather persistent findings from this war in the studies conducted over a fourteen-year period.

First, there is evidence that a significant portion of the Vietnam veterans and war-stressed veteran population has become politically alienated, although they are less disaffected than the antiwar activists. Nonetheless, the proportion of these veterans disaffected from the traditional political dogmas of the Cold War is impressive. The idea that a significant minority would at least entertain their children resisting Vietnam-type wars is a strong indication that alienation from the political system is accompanied by disaffection from specific policies. Though resistance to future intervention is generally lower among Vietnam veterans or combat veterans than among nonveterans, except for those who report supporting the Vietnam War, there still appears to be a majority of Vietnam and combat veterans who oppose such interventions. While Vietnam veterans oppose future military interventions like Vietnam, they also believe that such interventions are likely to occur. For these veterans the spectre of future U.S. military intervention remains vivid and, I suspect, a source of potential turmoil. It would be of considerable interest to know how Vietnam veterans are responding to the escalation in Nicaragua. To what extent does the gradual escalation of U.S. involvement fuel their fears and confirm their sense of future American military interventions? The question is whether or not the sense of alienation these veterans reported persists into the present and/or is revived by the spectre of American policy once again creating a situation which, to many of these veterans, may appear reminiscent of Vietnam.

The preceding discussion does not deal with a range of war environments relevant to the central concerns of the chapter. I have said little about the psychosocial and political implications of the Holocaust, Hiroshima and Nagasaki, Israeli wars, Northern Ireland, torture victims, survivors of the European resistance over the last generation as well as many other recent conflicts; and I have not explored the novels on war which have proliferated over the century. In part this is because the best systematic evidence on the aftermath of war is available on United States veterans of wars in this century, especially World War II and Vietnam. I felt that it was more useful to focus on a part of the problem which had definable parameters. Indeed, the limits of the data from which I could draw for insights into both political and psychosocial development in the aftermath of war helps set the agenda I will discuss for the future.

Research Agenda

This chapter implicitly and explicitly argues that postwar psychosocial development and political development during the early adult years are interlocked, i.e., life-course trajectories and political development around a life-organizing trauma such as war are intertwined. That interpretation is based on two types of findings. First, the same antecedent factors (independent variables) which predict or are correlated with psychosocial adaptation are also related to postwar political attitudes and orientations. Furthermore, I attach considerable significance to the finding of social and political alienation among war-stressed veterans as an important link between the psychological and political developmental tasks of the adult years. Studies designed to test the hypothesis that this link is significant are now required. Moreover, such studies need to focus on the precise relationship between war-related alienation and political development.

In my review of the developmental transitions in the life course my interpretation argues that stressful life events are reflective of and/or contribute delayed or episodic reopening of war trauma intrapsychically; and that the process of intrapsychic stress is a factor in altering politically derived meanings of the war. Studies which focus on the middle and later years of the adult life cycle need to be designed to take into account the traumatic histories of war survivors and determine the extent to which political shifts in perspective are associated with crises in life trajectories.

I have focused on the early and middle adult years in the aftermath of trauma among soldiers which occurs at the early stages of adult development. Wars do not happen only to men in the early adult years, nor are the effects felt only through the middle period. Subsequent studies must begin to examine systematically and cross-culturally adaptations to the trauma of war. This means we need life-history studies which use representative population samples of military and civilian populations who experienced the trauma of war in their adult years.

It is also important when studying the effects of war that the design of the research differentiates the population in terms of life stages. Adulthood is not a single undifferentiated time. As scholars studying the life course have shown, there are distinct stages of adulthood. While we do not as yet have adequately agreed upon chronological definitions of these stages, researchers must be cognizant of the fact that the impact on the life course and political development of the trauma is likely to vary significantly for individuals depending on whether it occurs in early, middle, or late adulthood. Studies must examine the impact of the war years in terms of the portion of the adult life-cycle which antedates the war trauma, and then attempt to explore the impact of the war through the remaining years of the life course. The problem, as I have tried to show, is that we can only understand the aftermath of war if we locate the experience within particular stages of the life course. Furthermore, it is essential to try and study populations where there is some degree of commonality in the war experiences.

One of the key points I have highlighted in the population of young adults is that the encounter with trauma creates what I have called the serial self (Laufer 1986); and the integration of the serial self into a stable identity remains a lifetime problem. However, identity formation is a critical task of the early stages of adulthood. Subsequent studies need to be concerned with the impact of war experiences on the self-system and its implications for postwar adaptation in older populations. The questions which needs exploration is the extent of the assault on the self-systems of adults in the middle and later years of life. Is there a comparable process, is it a function of the severity of the assault, i.e., are holocaust survivors, especially those who were in the death camps, likely to experience a similar phenomenon irrespective of age? Evidence from that literature suggests this may have been the case (Matussek 1971; Krystal 1968; Bergmann and Jucovy 1982; Danieli 1981, 1985). However, European civilians exposed to various aspects of devastation may not have been exposed to such severe traumatization that those in their middle years had their self-systems undermined. Thus, we need more comparative studies which elaborate on the psychosocial imprint of war at particular stages of the life course and how political development is affected by the experience and interacts with the psychological adaptation.

There are also some methodological implications which deserve attention in future research on war survivors. In order to clarify these issues it will be necessary to differentiate the nature of the war experience into categories which have been identified as predicting differential outcomes in studies where such data are available for that particular aspect of war. In other studies, developing conceptual categories and empirical measures for differentiating the war experience is a first-order priority. Indeed a great deal remains to be done in the conceptualization and measurement of war stress. Studies solely concerned with this methodological issue would be of considerable help.

The most important kind of research which is generally missing are longitudinal studies. Many of the interpretations of the findings in this review are based on multiple cross-sectional studies conducted over number of years. As Elder (1985) has shown, longitudinal data sets often provide insights into individual behavior which undermine generalizations derived from cross-sectional research. One interesting point is that Elder's work on veterans of wars is based on longitudinal studies and his most recent data do appear to support the finding that war trauma plays a disruptive role in the life course in the later years for at least a minority of the veteran population. The Polk et al. (1982) study of Vietnam veterans was likewise part of a longitudinal study.

Research now under way (Elder, Laufer, and Clipp 1986) with the Terman Gifted Men Study, will in the next several years provide data on both psychosocial and political development among World War 11 veterans well into their seventies. The Terman Gifted Men Study, which will have the benefit of the most recent waves of data collection in 1982 and 1986, suggests that it may be possible to explore many of the issues raised in this chapter through reanalysis of existing studies, longitudinal and cross-sectional. Researchers often tend to be enamored with the collection of new data, and existing data sets are rarely exhaustively analyzed. It would, of course, help if we identified the available data sets which have relevant indicators for research on the effects of war, whether or not they were intended for this purpose.

A question which has not been addressed to date is the impact of the war experience of parents on children. Though there has been some research on concentration camp survivors and resistance fighters of World War II in the psychiatric literature, there are few studies which examine the pattern of relationships between parental war-survivors and child and adolescent social, psychological, and political development. Such research is vital, because it may be that the societies that have had large parts of their populations exposed to the trauma of war, experience the social and political consequences of war beyond the original generation.

Finally, the design of research in this area must take into account the problem of age stratification. We need to develop research which uses large enough populations to differentiate the effects of war stressors over time depending on the point in the life course when traumatization occurs.

I conclude by reiterating what I said at the beginning of this chapter. Research on the effects of war is in a period of rapid development in a number of countries, but especially in the United States, Japan, Israel, the Netherlands, and Germany; and there is increasing interest in these issues elsewhere. This chapter is only an initial effort to raise a number of issues of consequence in the literature. Subsequent research will help clarify the answers to many questions about which we can only speculate at the moment.

Notes

I would like to thank my colleagues Dr. Glen Elder, Jr., and Dr. Ellen Frey-Wouters for their comments and suggestions on early drafts of the chapter. And I would like to express my appreciation to Dr. Roberta Sigel for her careful reading and helpful suggestions as the chapter evolved.

1.Throughout the discussion of the Vietnam experience I shall use the terms *Vietnam veterans* to refer to those veterans who served in Vietnam or the Southeast Asia theater of hostilities (Vietnam, Cambodia, Laos, the waters and/or airspace of those countries) during the war years; *Vietnam-era veterans* to refer to those men who served in the military during the war years but who did not serve in the war zones; and *nonveterans* to refer to those men eligible for military service during the years of the Vietnam War who did not enter the military.

2. *Legacies of Vietnam* was a national study of the Vietnam veteran population conducted for the Congress and the Veterans Administration which was completed in 1981. The study included 1,342 men stratified by veteran status, i.e., Vietnam, Vietnam-era, and nonveterans. The study was the most extensive study of this population and its findings remain the most authoritative on this population.

3.The combat scales in both Harris (1980) and Begans (1985) used the *Legacies of Vietnam* measure of combat exposure.

References

Allerton, W. S. 1969. "Army Psychiatry in Vietnam." In P. G. Bourne *The Psychology and Physiology of Stress*. New York: Academic Press.

American Psychiatric Association. 1980. *Diagnostic and Statistical Manual*. 3d ed. Washington, D.C.: American Psychiatric Press.

Archibald, H. C., D. M. Long, C. Miller, and R. D. Tuddenham. 1962. "Gross Stress Reaction in Combat: A 15 Year Follow-up." *American Journal of Psychology* 119: 317–22.

Archibald, H. C., and R. D. Tuddenham. 1965. "Persistent Stress Reaction after Combat: A 20-Year Follow-up." *Archives of General Psychiatry* 12: 475–81.

Bachman, J. G., and K. Jennings. 1975. "The Impact of Vietnam on Trust in Government." *Journal of Social Issues* 31: 141–55.

Barber, J. A. 1972. "The Social Effects of Military Service." In *The Military and American Society*, ed. S. E. Ambrose and J. A. Barber, New York: The Free Press.

Begans, P. 1985. *ABC News/Washington Post Poll: Survey 0186 and 0187*. New York: ABC News Polling Unit.

Bengtson, V., M. Furlong, and R. S. Laufer. 1974. "Time, Aging, and the Continuity of Social Structure." *Journal of Social Issues* 30: 1–30.

Bergmann, M. S., and M. E. Jucovy, eds. 1982. *Generations of the Holocaust*. New York: Basic Books.

Brady, D., and L. Rappaport. 1973. "Violence and Vietnam: A Comparison between Attitudes of Civilians and Veterans." *Human Relations* 26: 735–52.

452   Robert S. Laufer

Brende, J. O., and E. A. Parson. 1985. *Vietnam Veterans: The Road to Recovery*. New York: Plenum.

Brett, E. A. 1983. "Imagery and Posttraumatic Stress Disorder." *Veterans Administration Medical Center, Merit Review Study*. West Haven: Conn.

Brett, E. A., and W. Mungine. 1985. "Imagery and Combat Stress in Vietnam Veterans." *Journal of Nervous and Mental Disease* 173: 309–11.

Brill, N. Q., and G. W. Beebe. 1955. *A Follow-Up Study of War Neuroses*. Washington, D.C.: Veterans Administration Monograph.

Card, J. J. 1983. *Lives after Vietnam: The Personal Impact of Military Service*. Lexington: Lexington Press.

Committee for the Compilation of Materials on Damage Caused by the Atomic Bombs in Hiroshima and Nagasaki. 1981. *Hiroshima and Nagasaki: The Physical, Medical and Social Effects of the Atomic Bombings*. New York: Basic Books.

Cook, T. F. 1983. "Cataclysm and Career Rebirth: The Imperial Military Elite." In *Work and Life-course in Japan*, ed. David Plath. Albany: State University of New York Press.

Dane, J. 1984. *Keerzijde van de Bevrijding*. Deventer: van Loghum Slaterus.

Danieli, Y. 1981. "On the Achievement of Integration of Aging Survivors of the Nazi Holocaust." *Journal of Geriatric Psychiatry* 14: 191–210.

————. 1985. "The Treatment and Prevention of Long-Term Effects of Integenerational Transmission of Victimization: A lesson from Holocaust Survivors and Their Children." In *Trauma and Its Wake*, ed. C. B. Figley. New York: Bruner/Mazel.

Elder, G. 1975. "Age Differentiation and the Life Course." In *Annual Review of Sociology*, ed. A. Inkeles and N. Smelser. Palo Alto: Annual Reviews Inc.

————. 1979. "Historical Change in Life Patterns and Personality." In *Life Span Development and Behavior*, vol. 2, ed. P. B. Baltes and O. G. Brim. New York: Academic Press.

————. 1985. *Life Course Dynamics*. Ithaca: Cornell University Press.

————. 1986. "Military Times and Turning Points in Men's Lives." *Developmental Psychology* 22(2): 1–13.

Elder, G., and Y. Maguro. 1985. "Wartime in Men's Lives: A Comparative Study of American and Japanese Cohorts." Paper presented at meetings of the American Sociological Society, Washington, D.C.

Elder, G., and E. Clipp. 1986. "Combat Experience, Comradship, and Psychological Health." In *Human Adaptation to Extreme Stress: From the Holocaust to Vietnam*, ed. B. Kahana, B. Harel, J. P. Wilson. New York: Plenum Forthcoming.

Elder, G, R. S. Laufer, and E. Clipp. 1986. "Military Service in Adult Development." *NIMH Merit Grant, 1986–89*.

Esler, A. 1979. *Generational Studies: A Basic Bibliography*. Williamsburg: Esler.

————. 1982. *Generations in History: An Introduction to the Concept*. Williamsburg: Esler.

Fendrich, J. M., and L. J. Axelson. 1971. "Marital Status and Political Alienation Among Black Veterans." *American Journal of Sociology* 77: 245–61.

Figley, C. H., ed. 1977. *Stress Disorders Among Vietnam Veterans: Theory, Research and Treatment*. New York: Bruner/Mazel.

————. 1985. *Trauma and Its Wake*. New York: Bruner/Mazel.

Foy, D. W., R. C. Sipprelle, D. B. Rueger, and E. M. Carroll. 1984. "Etiology of Posttraumatic Stress Disorder in Vietnam Veterans: Analysis of Military and Combat Exposure Influences." *Journal of Consulting and Clinical Psychology* 52: 79–87.

Freud, S. 1921. *Beyond the Pleasure Principle*. In *Complete Psychological Works*. Standard Edition, volume 23. London: Hogarth Press, 1953.

———. 1939. *Moses and Monotheism*. In *Complete Psychological Works*. Standard Edition, volume 23. London: Hogarth Press, 1953.

Frey-Wouters, E. and R. S. Laufer. 1984. "The Political Legacy of the Vietnam War." Paper presented at the International Political Psychology meetings, Oxford, England.

———. 1986. *Legacy of a War: The American Soldier in Vietnam*. Armonk: M. E. Sharpe.

Fussell, P. 1979. *The Great War and Modern Memory*. New York: Oxford University Press.

Futterman, S., and E. Pumpian-Midlin. 1951. "Traumatic War Neurosis Five Years Later." *American Journal of Psychiatry* 108: 401–5.

Green, B. L., and J. D. Lindy. 1985. "Prediction of Delayed Stress after Vietnam: A Summary of Preliminary Study Findings." *NIMH Final Report*. Cincinnati: University of Cincinnati.

Green, B. L., J. D. Lindy, and J. P. Wilson. 1984. "Conceptualizing Post-Traumatic Stress Disorder: A Psychosocial Framework." In *Trauma and Its Wake*, C. H. Figley, ed. New York: Bruner/Mazel.

Grinker, R. R., and J. P. Spiegel. 1945. *Men under Stress*. Philadelphia: Blakiston.

Haley, S. A. 1977. "When the Patient Reports Atrocities: Specific Treatment Considerations of the Vietnam Veteran." *Archives of General Psychiatry* 30: 191–96.

———. 1986. "The Vietnam Veteran and His Pre-School Child: Child Rearing and Delayed Stress in Combat Veterans." In *Post-Traumatic Stress Disorder and the Veteran Patient*, P. Kelly, ed. New York: Bruner/Mazel.

Harris, L. 1980. *Myths and Realities: A Study of Attitudes toward Vietnam Veterans*. Washington, D.C.: U.S. Government Printing Office.

Havighurst, R. J., J. W. Baughman, W. H. Eaton, and E. W. Burgess. 1951. *The American Veteran Back Home*. New York: Longmans, Green.

Helzer, J. E., L. N. Robins, E. W. Wish, and M. Hesselbrock. 1979. "Depression in Viet Nam Veterans and Civilian Controls." *American Journal of Psychiatry* 136: 526–29.

Hogan, D. 1981. *Transitions and Social Change*. New York: Academic Press.

Horowitz, M., and G. F. Solomon. 1975. "A Prediction of Delayed Stress Response Syndromes in Vietnam Veterans." *Journal of Social Issues* 31: 67–80.

Hugenholtz, P. Th. 1984. "De Factoren bij de Instandhouding van de psychosociale Problematiek van Oorlogsgetroffenen." In *Keerzijde van de Bevrijding*, J. Dane, ed.

Instituut Psychiatrie. 1986. "Literatuuronderzoek: medische causaliteit bij oorlogsgetroffenen, 1940–1945." Manuscript. Rotterdam: Erasmus Universiteit.

Jacob-Stams, C. M. 1981. *Oorlog, een Breuk in het Bestaan: actergrond en prolemen van door de oorlog getroffenen*. Deventer: Van Loghum Slaterus.

Jennings, K., and G. B. Markus. 1976. "Political Participation and Vietnam War

Veterans: A Longitudinal Study." In *The Social Psychology of Military Service*, ed. N. L. Goldman and D. R. Segal. Beverly Hills: Sage Publications.

Kardiner, A., and H. Spiegel. 1947. *War Stress and Neurotic Illness*. New York: Harper and Brothers.

Katz, D. 1974. "Factors Affecting Social Change: A Social-Psychological Interpretation." *Journal of Social Issues* 30: 159–80.

Kirkpatrick, S. A., and J. L. Regens. 1978. "Military Experience and Foreign Policy Belief Systems." *Journal of Political and Military Sociology* 6: 29–47.

Keniston, K. 1968. *The Young Radicals*. New York: Harcourt, Brace, Jovanovich.

———. 1972. *Youth and Dissent*. New York: Harcourt, Brace, Jovanovich.

Krystal, H. 1968. *Massive Psychic Trauma*. New York: International Universities Press.

Lambert, T. A. 1972. "Generations and Change: Toward a Theory of Generations as a Force in Historical Process." *Youth and Society* 4: 21–46.

Laufer, R. S. 1970. "Sources of Generational Consciousness and Conflict." *ANNALS*, 395: 80–94.

Laufer, R. S., and V. Bengtson. 1974. "Generations, Aging and Social Stratification: On the Development of Generation Units." *Journal of Social Issues* 30: 181–205.

Laufer, R. S., T. Yager, E. Frey-Wouters, and J. Donnellan. 1981. *Post-War Trauma: Social and Psychological Problems of Vietnam Veterans in the Aftermath of the Vietnam War*. Vol. 3 in *Legacies of Vietnam*, ed. A. Egendorf, C. Kadushin, R. S Laufer, G. Rothbart, and L. Sloan. Washington, D.C.: U.S. Government Printing Office.

Laufer, R. S., M. S. Gallops, E. Frey-Wouters, 1984. "War Stress and Trauma: The Vietnam Veteran Experience." *Journal of Health and Social Behavior* 25: 65–85.

Laufer, R. S., E. Frey-Wouters, and M. S. Gallops. 1985. "Traumatic Stressors in the Vietnam War and Post-Traumatic Stress Disorder." In *Trauma and Its Wake*, ed. C. Figley, New York: Bruner/Mazel.

Laufer, R. S., E. A. Brett, M. S. Gallops. 1985a. "Dimensions of PTSD Among Vietnam Veterans." *Journal of Nervous and Mental Diseases* 173: 538–45.

Laufer, R. S., E. A. Brett, M. S. Gallops. 1985b. "Patterns of Symptomatology Associated with Post-Traumatic Stress Disorder Among Vietnam Veterans Exposed to War Trauma." *American Journal of Psychiatry* 141: 1304–11.

Laufer, R. S., and M. S. Gallops. 1985. "Life-Course Effects of Vietnam Combat and Abusive Violence." *Journal of Marriage and the Family* 47: 839–53.

———. 1985. "War Trauma and Human Development." In *The Trauma of War: Stress and Recovery in Vietnam Veterans*, ed. Sonnenberg, A. Blank, and J. Talbot. Washington, D.C.: American Psychiatric Press.

Laufer, R. S. and K. Joyce. 1986. "War Trauma, Career Patterns and Mental Health Over the Life-Span." Paper presented at the International Political Psychology Meetings, Amsterdam, The Netherlands.

Laufer, R. S., L. Sloan, K. Joyce, and D. Surrey. 1981. "Attitudes Towards Amnesty within the Vietnam Generation." *Journal of American Culture* 4: 176–94.

Laufer, R. S., M. S. Gallops, and K. Joyce. 1985. *Opportunities for Intervention: Employment Needs of Vietnam Veterans in New York City*. New York: New York City Vietnam Veterans Memorial Commission.

Levinson, D., C. Darow, E. B. Klein, M. H. Levinson, and B. McKee. 1978. *The Seasons of a Man's Life*. New York: Knopf.

Lewis, N. D. C., and B. Engel, eds. 1954. *Wartime Psychiatry: A Compendium of the International Literature*. New York: Oxford University Press.

Lifton, R. J. 1967. *Death in Life: Survivors of Hiroshima*. New York: Random House.

———. 1973. *Home from the War*. New York: Simon and Schuster.

Lindy, J. D., M. Grace, and B. L. Green. 1984. "Building a Conceptual Bridge between Civilian Trauma and War Trauma: Preliminary Psychological Findings from a Clinical Sample of Vietnam Veterans." In *New Perspectives on Post-Traumatic Stress*, ed. B. v. d. Kolk. Washington D.C.: American Psychiatric Press.

McCubbin, H. I., B. D. Dahl, G. R. Lester, D. Benson, and M. L. Robertson, 1976. "Coping Repertoires of Families Adapting to Prolonged War-Induced Separations." *Journal of Marriage and the Family*, pp. 461–76.

Marlowe, D. A. 1983. "Cohesion, Anticipated Breakdown, Endurance in Battle: Considerations for Severity and High Intensity Combat." Paper. Washington, D. C.: Walter Reed Army Institute of Research.

Mannheim, K. 1928. "The Problem of Generations." In *Essays in the Sociology of Knowledge*, ed. P. Keckscemeti, London: Routledge and Kegan Paul.

Martin, J. M. 1981. "Marital Status, Spouse Support and Mental Health." In vol. 4, *Legacies of Vietnam*, ed. A. Egendorf, C. Kadushin, R. S. Laufer, G. Rothbart, L. Sloan. Washington. D.C.: U.S. Government Printing Office.

Matussek, P. 1971. *Internment in Concentration Camps and Its Consequences*. New York: Springer-Verlag.

Maguro, Y. 1984. "Effects of World War II Experiences on Japanese Men's Lives." Honolulu: U.S.-Japanese Conference at the East-West Center, University of Hawaii.

Ministerial Report on War Victims and Their Needs, 1978. *Immateriele Hulpverlening aan Oorlogsgeroffenen*, Hague: Ministerie van Volksgezondheid en Milieuhygiene.

Neugarten, B., and N. Datan. 1973. "Sociological Perspectives on the Life Cycle." In *Life-Span Developmental Psychology*, ed. P. B. Baltes and K. W. Schaie, New York: Academic Press.

Op den Velde, W. 1985. "Postraumatische Stress-Stoornis al Laat Gevolgvan Verzetsdeelname." *Ned. T. Geneesk* 129: 834–38.

Parson, E. R. 1985a. "The Intercultural Setting Encountering Black Viet-Nam Veterans." In *The Trauma of War: Stress and Recovery in Vietnam Veterans*, ed. S. Sonnenberg, A. Blank, and J. Talbot. Washington. D.C.: American Psychiatric Press.

———. 1985. "Life After Death: Vietnam Veterans Struggle for Meaning and Recovery." *Death Studies* 10: 11–26.

Polk, K., S. Cordray, et al. 1982. "Cohort Careers and the Vietnam Experience." Manuscript. Eugene, Oregon: University of Oregon.

Pollack, J. C., and White, Gold. 1975. "When Soldiers Return: Combat and Political Alienation Among White Vietnam Veterans." In *New Directions in Political Socialization*, ed. D.C. Schwartz and S. K. Schwartz, New York: The Free Press.

Polner, M. 1971. *No Victory Parades: The Return of the Vietnam Veteran*. New York: Holt, Rinehart and Winston.

Riley, M. W., M. Johnson, and A. Foner, eds. 1968. *Aging and Society: A Sociology of Age Stratification.* Vol. 3. New York: Russell Sage Foundation.

Robins, L. 1974. *The Vietnam Drug User Returns.* Washington, D.C.: U.S. Government Printing Office.

Rothbart, G., L. Sloan, and K. Joyce. 1981. *Educational and Work Careers: Men in the Vietnam Generation.* Vol. 2, *Legacies of Vietnam.* Washington, D.C.: U.S. Government Printing Office.

Ryder, N. 1965. "The Cohort as a Concept in the Study of Social Change." *American Sociological Review* 30: 843–61.

Schaie, K. W., and K. Gribbin, 1975. "Adult Development and Aging." *Annual Review of Psychology* 26: 65–96.

Schnaier, J. A. 1986. "A Study of Women Vietnam Veterans and Their Mental Health." In *Post-Traumatic Stress Disorder and the Veteran Patient,* P. Kelly, ed. New York: Bruner/Mazel.

Segal, D. R., and M. W. Segal, 1976. "The Impact of Military Service on Trust in Government: International Attitudes and Social Status." In *The Social Psychology of Military Service,* ed. W. L. Goldman and D. L. Segal, Beverly Hills: Sage Publications.

Smith, J., E. R. Parson, and S. A. Haley, 1983. "On Health and Disorder in Viet Nam Veterans: An Invited Commentary." *American Journal of Orthopsychiatry* 53: 27–33.

Sonnenberg, S., A. Blank, and J. Talbot, eds. 1985. *The Trauma of War: Stress and Recovery in Vietnam Veterans.* Washington. D.C.: American Psychiatric Press.

Stenger, C. A. 1974. "Perspectives on the Post-Vietnam Syndrome." *Newsletter for Research in Mental Health* 16: 1–4.

Stouffer, S. A., M. H. Lumsdine, R. M. Williams, B. Smith, I. D. Janis, S. A. Starr, and L. S. Cottrell. 1949. *The American Soldier: Combat and Its Aftermath.* Vol. 2. Princeton: Princeton University Press.

Stretch, R. A. 1984a. "Assessment of Psychosocial and Physical Health Among Army Reserve Veterans." Manuscript. Washington D.C.: Walter Reed Army Medical Center.

————. 1984b. "Post-Traumatic Stress Disorder Among U.S. Army Reserve Vietnam and Vietnam-Era Veterans." Manuscript, Washington D.C.: Walter Reed Army Medical Center.

————. 1984c. "Post-Traumatic Stress Disorder Among Civilian Vietnam and Vietnam-Era Veterans." Manuscript, Washington D.C.: Walter Reed Army Medical Center.

Surrey, D. S. 1982. *Choice of Conscience: Vietnam Era Military and Draft Resisters in Canada.* New York: Praeger.

Terkel, S. 1984. *The Good War.* New York: Pantheon.

Ursano, R. J. 1985. "Viet Nam Era Prisoners of War: Studies of U.S. Air Force Prisoners of War." In *The Trauma of War: Stress and Recovery in Vietnam Veterans,* ed. S. Sonnenberg, A. Blank, and J. Talbot, Washington. D.C.: American Psychiatric Press.

Vaillant, G. E. 1977. *Adaptation to Life.* Boston: Little, Brown.

Vanden Heuvel, A. 1985. "Mortality and Morbidity Trends Among U.S. Veterans: Exploratory Perspectives." Paper. Chapel Hill: University of North Carolina.

van der Kolk, B. 1986. "The Psychological Consequences of Overwhelming Life Experiences." In *Psychological Trauma,* ed. B. v. d. Kolk. Washington, D.C.: American Psychiatric Press (in press).

van der Kolk, B., ed. 1984. *Post-Traumatic Stress Disorder,* Washington, D.C.: American Psychiatric Press.

Van Deventer, L. 1983. *Home before Morning.* New York: Beaufort.

Van Dyke, C., N. J. Zilberg, and J. A. McKinnon. 1985. "Post-Traumatic Stress Disorder: A Thirty-Year Delay in a World War II Veteran." *American Journal of Pyschiatry* 142: 1070–73.

Waller, W. 1944. *Veteran Comes Back.* New York: Dryden Press.

Wilson, J. P. 1978. "Identity, Ideology, and Crisis: The Vietnam Veteran in Transition." Monograph. Cleveland: Cleveland State University.

Wilson, J. P., and G. E. Krauss. 1980. *Vietnam Era Stress Inventory.* Cleveland: Cleveland State University.

Wilson, J. P., G. E. Krauss. 1986. "Predicting Post-Traumatic Stress Syndromes Among Vietnam Veterans." In *Post-Traumatic Stress Disorder and the Veteran Patient,* P. Kelly, ed. New York: Bruner/Mazel.

Wohl, R. 1979. *The Generation of 1914.* Cambridge: Harvard University Press.

Yager, T., R. S. Laufer, and M. S. Gallops, 1984. "Some Problems Associated with War Experience in Men of the Vietnam Generation." *Archives of General Psychiatry* 41: 327–33.

Yankelovich, D. 1972. *Changing Values on Campus.* New York: Washington Square Press.

Conclusion:

Adult Political Learning—
A Lifelong Process
ROBERTA S. SIGEL

For this concluding chapter I have set myself two tasks: to offer a synthesis (rather than a detailed review) of the eleven preceding chapters and to set an agenda for what still needs to be accomplished in adult political socialization research—theoretically as well as methodologically—if we want to attain a systematic understanding of the adult political learning process.

Synthesis

Two themes run through the eleven chapters: (1) adult political socialization essentially is an interactive phenomenon and (2) it is characterized by change as well as continuity. To discuss the latter first, all chapters point to much continuity in political-response patterns over the course of an individual's life, notwithstanding the fact that people have to cope with a variety of new tasks and assume a variety of new roles for which neither childhood nor adolescence prepares them adequately. The chapters, however, also point to considerable change in sociopolitical attitudes and behaviors as individuals are confronted with new conditions and contingencies. Some of the changes are attributable to factors intrinsic to the individual, such as those related to the physiological processes connected with aging or the cognitive and emotional transformations experienced by the person as he or she matures. Other changes have to be attributed to social phenomena external to the person but with which she or he has to attempt to come to terms, major technological changes being one example, transition from rural to urban life being another. Some changes people make constitute drastic departures from earlier patterns (the behavior of terrorists described by Horowitz), while others may constitute more superficial adaptations to novel conditions (the political behavior of workers in reorganized plants, described by Lafferty). Regardless of the degree of persistence or change observed by each author, they agree that individuals' political dispositions do not become frozen at the end of the adolescent period (as once believed) but that change of varying degrees continues throughout the entire life course.

The second theme which connects the chapters is an interactive one. Whether we speak of persistence or of change, we cannot approach the study of adult political socialization either from a purely individual, personal perspective or from an exclusively social, structural one. The adult is not only an individual; he or she is also a social being, and—more precisely—a social being functioning at a specific historical period, located in a social structure and a specific place therein. One's personal and unique mode of activity is constrained by these external or contextual realities, but how one interprets or constructs the "realities" depends in turn on the uniqueness of one's personality. In addition to reacting to their environment, humans also have the capacity to generate changes in the environment itself. Humans "generate culture, ideas, and behaviors throughout their life cycles that challenge and at times change those conditions typically associated with their structural position" (Morris, Hatchett, and Brown in this volume). Consequently, as Mahoney (1987, p. 13) writes, "we have become . . . the changers and the changed." We are changed by the social circumstances around us, and we in turn may attempt to affect or change these circumstances. *We* change as we make these attempts, but so does *society.* Minimally then, adult political socialization is a two-way street, representing an interactive process. To put it another way, adult political socialization is a social-learning process affected both by the individual's own development and the societal demands he or she has to cope with. It is impossible, therefore, to study either in isolation.

Since that is the nature of the adult political socialization process, it is essential that any study of it incorporate at least three aspects: the crystallization of an individual's own, unique identity; the assumption of new roles and responsibilities, including that of political citizen, which generally are associated with adult status; and the coping with less routine and more unanticipated novel demands brought on by major changes in the individual's sociopolitical status or conditions. None of them, of course, are completely independent of each other, and all interact and are shaped by the social environment or structure in which they occur.

The process of identity formation is a prolonged process which was begun already in childhood but will have been more or less completed by onset of adulthood or soon thereafter.[1] There exists in "humans a powerful drive to maintain the sense of one's identity, a sense of continuity that allays fears of changing too fast or being changed against one's own will by outside forces" (Brim and Kagan 1980, p. 17). The chapters by Hoskin, Horowitz, and Laufer document the stress, at times even pain, experienced by individuals caught in circumstances which challenge the value and/or authenticity of their identities. Thus Laufer shows how the "infantilization" of the young soldier who has barely had time to develop an adult self has far-reaching and dysfunctional consequences for assuming the role of adult citizen upon his return to civilian life.

Our sense of identity, i.e., how we perceive ourselves, of course is dependent not only on our cognitive and affective structures but on our social identities. A person's cognitive and affective perceptions of self arise "from innate dispositions and social interactions across a lifetime, characterized by thought, feeling, and action relative to social structure of roles, rules, norms and values" (Harre and Lamb 1983, p. 558). In other words, personal identity, and with it the sense of self-worth, although clearly a part of our "innate disposition," is very much dependent on our social position and the respect it is accorded in the world of significant others (frequently the dominant culture). Moreover, one's social position shapes one's notion of what constitutes behavior appropriate for one's position; affects the internal representations one makes to oneself of external events, and has an impact on one's affective as well as behavioral responses to society. In the end, it very much helps define personal identity.

This is most clearly seen when we observe the political behavior of so-called disadvantaged groups. Members of ethnic, religious, or social groups judged by society to be inferior or less worthy often run the risk of incorporating this negative judgment into their self-image. Feeling left out (or actually being left out), they respond by refraining from active political involvement or become involved only sporadically, at times with devastating results to themselves. For example, the second-class citizenship status accorded women in many societies is said to be the source of diminished self-esteem and the sense of "learned helplessness." Learned helplessness, of course, also affects the notion that one is impotent to change one's political situation. Carroll shows how one of the functions of the women's movement is to disabuse women of this notion and to legitimize for them new behaviors as well as new life-styles independent from men, thereby facilitating the development of new female identities. Similar observations have been made concerning the sense of self-definition in many other disadvantaged minority groups, as in the black population in the United States. The "Black is Beautiful" campaign therefore must be viewed as an attempt to overcome any diminished group-based sense of self-worth. The recent growth in black political participation has been attributed not only to the removal of structural barriers but also to a more positive sense of personal efficacy. Needless to say, it would be a gross overgeneralization—regardless of the group examined—to equate identity establishment and political participation, but the weight of the literature clearly suggests that sense of identity and political involvement are not unrelated.

Assuming a variety of adult roles and performing adequately in them constitutes the second developmental task. "In adulthood the main *issue* is the degree to which the individual accepts, and the quality of his performance in, the whole panoply of roles which accompany the statuses of adulthood, such as husband, father, earner of a living, member of a religious community, warrior, citizen of a polity, and so on "(Inkeles 1969, p. 628). Some of these roles can be adopted simultaneously while others may occur serially. Regardless of the timing, the adoption of each new role—as Steckenrider and Cutler indicate—represents a transition for the individual. Above, I discussed the transitions which characterize the process of identity crystallization and the changes to which they give rise. Here I want to focus on role transitions and their effect on continuity and change.

The Inkeles quotation makes a sharp distinction between seemingly private roles (such as husband) and the public or political role of citizen. On the surface only that last role may seem to be a truly political one. In reality, however, many of the seemingly nonpolitical roles cited by Inkeles involve or have the potential to involve political engagements, as the chapters in this volume suggest. Many of the opinions, dispositions, and behaviors which we tend to characterize as private—such as the definition of marital rape—are actually reflections of sociopolitical realities and norms.

As for the overtly political role of the citizen, most of the chapters have dealt with citizen behaviors at the mass level and have sought to demonstrate how these stabilize or change during various phases in the life cycle or in response to external contingencies. Renshon, on the other hand, focused on political leaders and showed how accession to political office has the potential to lead to considerable changes in political dispositions. Greenstein (1987), in this same vein, illustrates how the perspective from the Oval Office caused Gerald Ford to alter many previous tactics and preferences whereas Dwight Eisenhower could draw on his experiences as military leader when fashioning his presidential leadership style. Surely, in this case as well as in other instances, both individual predispositions and the magnitude of the transition affect continuity and change in adult political behavior.

While most of the examples offered so far did involve varying degrees of change—and without getting into a debate whether adaptations or minor changes constitute genuine change, let alone development—it is probably safe to assert that many changes may simply be minor modifications of earlier acquired dispositions or surface adaptations to new demands. Many transitions probably proceed fairly smoothly without much need for resocialization. The young man who had been led to believe that hard work and thrift will be rewarded in our system and who subsequently becomes a successful CEO need not be socialized by his company to devalue the social-welfare state. Many role transitions are in fact so smooth that persons undergoing them are hardly aware of changes they are making, and the chances are that these changes are not fundamental. The role transition from dependent adolescent to university student may make the student highly conscious of a new emotional and social status, but she or he may be much less open to new ideas which might conflict with earlier acquired beliefs; for some, on the other hand, exposure to new ideas may give rise to a modified or even a new political worldview.

Other transitions are less incremental and symbolize a more drastic departure from earlier socialization. It is here, of course, that it is easier, relatively speaking, to observe how adult identities are maintained. The bourgeois terrorist, described by Horowitz, who joins a radical cell does more than merely adapt to new conditions; he becomes resocialized to a whole set of new behaviors and dispositions which drastically break with past ones. Eventually he may even come to form a new identity. Up to now this third type of transition, which calls for coping with novel and often unsettling demands which conflict with or at least challenge earlier socialization lessons, has received relatively less systematic attention in the political science literature.

The underlying assumption in much of the socialization literature had been that new circumstances, events, or contingencies would in all likelihood not give rise to response patterns drastically different from those the individual had learned to internalize earlier. For example, for a long time it had been accepted folk wisdom that the natural transition to old age would pose few problems for the elderly (beyond those associated with declining health). It was assumed that they would willingly and relatively smoothly disengage from active participation because they had been socialized from childhood on to associate old age with disengagement. Steckenrider and Cutler, however, point to the trauma or near-trauma caused by the status and identity-diminution the elderly experience upon retirement. Similarly Hoskin shows that even those who voluntarily migrate seldom find the transition to their new status easy and smooth. Other studies have shown that the transition from the status of employed or temporarily unemployed worker to that of permanently unemployed causes profound alterations in a person's sense of identity and political self.

Of particular interest in this context are those transitions over an individual's life course which, though perhaps less dramatic than that of the terrorist, create much strain in the individual, frequently because of multiple-role conflicts. Upper-level black executives in white firms report experiencing such role-related strains. Playing their executive roles according to the norms of the corporate world, with its emphasis on competition and profits, frequently estranges them from the milieu from which they have come and from those whose friendship they do not want to lose. Many middle-aged women constitute another example of the strains ensuing from conflicts between early socialization and later life experiences. As Carroll has shown in this volume, the women's movement has raised the consciousness not only of the young but of many middle-aged, traditional women as well, causing them to reject the notion of second-class citizen. Simultaneously, however, they have misgivings about the social acceptability of the feminist movement. In the case of the female legislator this can lead to a particular kind of role strain. She would like to champion causes beneficial to women but refrains for fear of being typed as either a feminist or a one-issue representative (Kirkpatrick 1974; Carroll 1985).

All through this volume we have stressed the interactive nature of the adult learning process, especially the individual's interaction with the social environment and its institutions. So far in this summary I have focused on individual-level change, i.e. changes experienced by the individual. I now must turn to problems of stability and change at the system level. Most authors comment on the rapidity with which change has taken place in recent history and the profound effect it has had on some institutions. Had we been able to include a wider array of such institutions, we might have been able to determine which American institutions have most readily responded to sociopolitical change and have in turn socialized those connected with them. In general, institutions tend to be quite change-resistant. Nonetheless those featured in this volume all showed change—but to varying degrees—in response to demands made by those connected with them and/or to changes in the world around them. We singled out one institution notorious for its traditionalism, the military, in order to indicate that even it is not change-resistant. Lovell and Stiehm show that the military, without abandoning its main mission, nonetheless had to abandon some time-honored regulations and practices if it wanted to function as an effective socializer of young men. Lafferty in a different setting also highlights the ways in which changing institutions succeed or fail in socializing members for new attitudes and behaviors.

Much less attention has been paid in socialization research to the impact of historical processes and events. In fact, it would probably be no exaggeration were we to characterize socialization research as being essentially a-historic. Here the early research on childhood socialization offers an outstanding example. That work—done mostly during the relatively prosperous, peaceful, and contention-free years of the Eisenhower presidency—yielded an image of a politically naive but very trusting, idealistic, and even super-patriotic youth. From this the researchers concluded that youth—at least in the U.S.—respects, trusts, and perhaps even idealizes our government and its authorities. Research done a decade or two later—during the Vietnam and Watergate periods—yielded a very different picture, that of a much more critical and disillusioned young population, showing that even young people are sensitive to historical events transpiring around them. For that reason Sapiro (1987, p. 6) warns against "reaching conclusions about political -change on the basis of single-time relationships" and illustrates it by showing how shifts in the political orientations of the two genders simply cannot be understood unless we are cognizant of the historical and structural changes which preceded them. A similar point is made by Morris, Hatchett, and

Brown, who clearly illustrate how unprepared social scientists were for the black-protest movement of the 1960s and 1970s, precisely because they lacked sufficient knowledge of black history and hence "had no idea of the extent to which black Americans abhorred racial inequality and domination." The recent growth of worker-client coalitions in the field of social work described by Dressel and Lipsky and the absence of similar efforts during other periods "suggests that service workers and recipients take their political cues from social forces . . . apart from localized agency concerns," i.e., individuals not only are imbedded in social structures but have the capacity to shape those structures in consonance with sociohistorical changes in the environment.

To conclude, the eleven chapters have given evidence that adult political socialization is essentially an interactive process shaped by people's continuous interaction with a variety of social structures. Moreover both people and their social structures are affected by the nature of the historical period. It is thus a dynamic process and not mired in the socialization patterns acquired during youth, but modified by individual-level development (due to maturation and other factors) as well as societal demands and changes. But neither is it a process of constant change and unpredictable movement back and forth; much of it is characterized by continuity, building on patterns and preferences acquired earlier in life. All of which propels me to suggest we cease thinking in terms of continuity versus change. To me, posing the problem that way constitutes a false dichotomy. Continuity and change should be perceived as complementary phenomena. There are conditions (individual or social) which require men and women to change, or, minimally, to modify their feelings and behavior somewhat in order to cope; there are other situations which call for consolidation and continuity. To search exclusively for patterns of continuity (as did much of the early socialization literature) leaves us unprepared for the occurrence of sudden or dramatic social change (for example the protests of the 1960s generation). Conversely, to operate from the assumption that there is no predictable pattern to human political responses, that only random change prevails, is equally unproductive in that it ignores human resilience and adaptability to changed conditions when change is desirable and resistance when it is not desirable.

The Agenda for Future Research

Theoretical Considerations

The preceding comments on continuity and change have failed to answer a crucial question, namely, what are individual change and political change and, more importantly, under what conditions are they likely to occur? As early as 1971 Schonfeld (p. 556) faulted the socialization literature for failing to specify "the conditions under which attitudes will persist, will be subject to transformation, or will actually change." That criticism is as timely today as it was then. Nor is the current literature seeking to answer the question "What is fundamental change in political dispositions and how do we distinguish it from surface adaptation and/or simple conformity?" Authors of psychobiographies (George and George 1956; Glad 1966, 1980; Rogow 1963; Mazlish 1972; Kearns 1976; Brodie 1974, 1981) have attempted to answer the question but the general socialization literature has tended to ignore it.

Clearly one of the tasks ahead is to develop a scheme by which we can distinguish conditions likely to lead to dispositional and behavioral change from those likely to encourage stability and/or overt resistance to change. A second task which needs to be addressed concerns adults' cognitive and affective development as it relates to politics; a third calls for correcting our inattention to the historical context. Refering to the first task, one way of approaching it would be by starting with the socialization demands made upon the individual and distinguishing these on the basis of the following criteria: (1) the congruence or incongruence of new demands with entrenched or traditional socialization patterns, especially those internalized during youth; (2) the consonance or dissonance of simultaneous demands made of the individual—for example, the demands for cooperative citizenship behavior and competitive business behavior; (3) the degrees of freedom available to the individual to meet or reject demands. Presumably, the combat soldier lacks such freedom but the employee in the civilian workplace enjoys varying degrees of freedom. Yet even in many work situations company regulations or peer pressure can act as a constraint. Several chapters in this volume document how workplace organization and routines restrict individuals' freedom to resist or modify work-related demands. More insight into this topic will be gained if in the future—as Dressel and Lipsky suggest—we examine the specific organizational features and socialization practices of a given milieu.

A fourth area not well investigated concerns research in the ways people relate to change (both personal and social), i.e., how they calculate the cost and benefits of meeting socialization demands. In all likelihood the desire to meet or resist socialization demands will be affected by the individual's perception of the benefits to be derived from them. Knox (1977, p. 513) distinguishes between gain- and loss-events. Presumably—unless forced to do otherwise—people would refrain from adaptations to novel developments from which they might incur losses. The recent growth in social conservatism and female political mobilization on its behalf (as witnessed by the growth in right-to-life and stop-ERA movements) can be viewed in this way. The change in social mores advocated by feminists threatens many people who are comfortable with traditional gender relations. The change in women's status, far from being welcomed by traditional women, was viewed by them as a denigration of the status of housewife and hence a threat to their own status, i.e., a loss event (Mansbridge 1986). In contrast, highly educated and professionally trained women, because they perceived it as a gain event, welcomed it. Each side consequently mobilized itself politically in order either to ward off change or to promote it.

These observations raise a fifth point: it is crucial that the conditions be considered which make it likely that individuals will make counterdemands on the system, i.e., to become change agents. Several chapters, notably those by Carroll, Delli Carpini, and Morris et al., have shown some of the conditions under which individuals resist time-honored practices or demands and are likely to make counterdemands on the system. This work points to the need to develop a systematic and theoretically grounded category system by which we can reach generalizable axioms which will permit us to distinguish those conditions likely to lead to major or minor change from those representing accommodation to the status quo. I shall have occasion to return to this point in somewhat more detail presently.

The second topic begging for much more attention in the political science literature concerns the cognitive and emotional development of adult political dispositions. Cross-sectional (and a very few longitudinal) studies of children and adolescents have offered information about the changes in thought processes and affect characteristic of young people, but no comparable information is available for adults. To be sure the gerontological and life-span literature (Neugarten 1977; Glenn 1980; Baltes and Schaie 1973; Binstock and Shanas 1976;) has highlighted psychological and a few political developments characteristic of the aged, but no systematic study exists as yet which tries to trace and explain developmental changes in political outlook as they occur over the total life-span. We lack discrete, in-depth studies of the development of "politically relevant dispositions at various stages in the life cycle" (Schonfeld 1971 p. 569). In this respect it is particularly noteworthy how few studies (including those described in this volume) seek to trace the adult phenomena they describe to childhood or adolescent antecedents, notwithstanding the fact that the original justification for studies of childhood political socialization was that childhood learning provides the foundation for later adult behavior.

It would therefore seem crucial for future research in political socialization that it combine this developmental perspective with its more commonly accepted sociocultural one. As Dawson and Prewitt (1969, p. 13) so cogently commented, political socialization must be examined from two perspectives: it is essentially the interaction between "cultural transmission . . . and individual learning." Both represent "the developmental process through which the citizen matures politically. The citizen acquires a complex of beliefs, feelings and information which help him comprehend, evaluate, and relate to the political around him . . . . [It] produces a political self." The absence of a developmental perspective is partially accountable for the fact that as yet we lack a theory of political socialization. We would do well to ask ourselves, as did Daniel Levinson (1986, p. 12) with respect to adult personality development, "How can we bring together the developmental perspective and the socialization perspective?"

The third task in current research refers, as I indicated earlier, to the need to correct our relative inattention to the historical events and conditions which help shape individual political learning and/or dispositions. Several chapters in this book pay explicit attention to this phenomenon but it is not accorded sufficient attention in the general political socialization literature. Not only do we need to pay attention to major historical happenings (such as wars and revolutions) but increased attention will also have to be paid to the context in which our observations of people are made. Gustafssen (1974), for example, showed that political reactions of young people living in communities experiencing high unemployment varied considerably from the reactions of those living in more prosperous ones. David Sears (1984, p. 5) correctly commented that it is essential for us to include recognition of important contextual variables and events into adult socialization research, and that we cannot content ourselves with only studying predispositions as though they were unaffected by past experience. Precisely because socialization research pays inadequate attention to contextual constraints or to local and subgroup variations, we frequently are at a loss to interpret seemingly inexplicable behaviors and attitudes and/or misinterpret them. For example, recently fishermen in the Gulf Coast area of the U.S., who felt threatened in their livelihood by the competition from alien fishermen, advocated restrictive immigration policies and expressed xenophobic attitudes. Wealthy suburbanites of the same locality who were not equally threatened seemed to express more liberal attitudes. To what are we to attribute these differences—to previous socialization patterns or to differences in economic and social location? Too often we are tempted to rely on readily available demographic factors, such as social class, when the real explanation may lie in contextual factors.

Finally, all the above considerations, of course, are not independent of our conceptualization of political learning. It is our contention that much inquiry into adult political socialization's impact on politics focuses on a very narrow definition of politics. It excludes for one thing—as Morris et al. point out— many unconventional political acts, such as protest behavior. Equally serious, in my opinion, are the tendencies to focus on variables whose significance may be debatable, at least for large segments of the population (such as attending political meetings, party identity, etc.). As Lovell and Stiehm say, "the challenge is to go beyond statistically significant findings to politically significant ones." Currently too much research continues to exclude or ignore a whole range of endeavors in which individuals engage and which may well have indirect or even direct political implications. The politicizing effect of active membership in some churches, in unions, in gun clubs, etc. tends to be ignored. To cite but one example, volunteer fire companies prevalent in some sectors of the country seem, on the surface, to be far removed from politics. In actuality, in their exclusionary membership policies, in their attitudes toward governmental regulations, and in other ways they are highly political and succeed in politicizing their fellow volunteers.

Methodological Problems

Many of the authors of the preceding eleven chapters have pointed to the great methodological difficulties that confront the social scientists who wish to study the process. The study of political persistence and change in adult life is made especially difficult because of the absence of baseline data. How can we speak confidently of change when so often we don't know what people thought or felt before being confronted with a new situation? Not surprisingly, therefore, almost all authors spoke to the necessity of collecting longitudinal and/or panel data. The most desirable strategy, of course, would be to collect data going back to childhood in order to ascertain what political dispositions have been maintained over the life course. So far the studies conducted by Jennings and Niemi (begun when the subjects were adolescents in high school) are the only major ones of this genre, and it is highly unlikely that many new ones will follow, because of the enormous costs involved as well as other problems (such as sample mortality). Moreover, most childhood political experiences tend to be so removed from the world of politics with which the adult has to cope, that it is problematic how much insight we would gain from conducting studies of this kind. An alternative would be to inquire into children's social and moral values and the indoctrination they received into them, and then observe the extent to which such values get translated into adult political values. For example, does child training for empathy and cooperation versus child training for toughness and competition lead to different political preferences? In order to conduct that type of a study, the researcher, of course, first has to establish theoretically tenable links between certain general values acquired in childhood and their specific application in adulthood.

   In view of these technical difficulties in conducting extensive longitudinal research, researchers might have to content themselves with longitudinal research conducted exclusively over the adult life-span. In an earlier section, I referred to the debate relating to old age and conservatism. The debate really cannot be decided definitively until we conduct research beginning with young adults and observe whether or not their conservatism increases as they age. Morris, Hatchett, and Brown, for example, alerted us to the fact that civil rights protests might have been anticipated had we had better information on the feelings shared by many blacks adolescents and young adults.

Second, inasmuch as we always maintain that political socialization is a *process,* it is imperative to collect process data. For example, much current research on the socializing effect of workers' participation in company decision-making is not based on actual observation in the workplace—of how much and in what ways employees actually do participate. "Most often researchers rely upon the respondent as an informant about workplace conditions—a method that certainly raises problems of measurement reliability" (Abramson 1985, p. 2). An ongoing process cannot be studied by such methods and even less by the administration of mass survey instruments. It must be studied by observing it as it progresses, i.e., in the field. Consequently, political scientists would do well if they would include ethnographic studies in their repertoire. To be sure, such studies would not permit us to generalize about all adult Americans but they would have three advantages over the customary mammoth studies: (1) they offer us in-depth information; (2) they free us from having to rely on verbal or written responses to questionnaire-type schedules whose reliability we cannot always assess and whose meaning we frequently misunderstand; and (3) by conducting a number of small but intensive studies of different settings (different branches of the military, different communities during natural disasters) we may learn a great deal of the role that different structures and settings play in socializing adults.

Third, to explore more fully the topics raised by the authors in this volume we are in need of cross-national studies. While this is a suggestion that has been made almost from the outset of socialization studies, we still do not have enough cross-national studies, especially those conducted in the non-Western world. The importance of obtaining such information is so self-evident as not to require further elaboration here.

To conclude, even though the eleven chapters of this volume cover widely disparate areas of adult political socialization, and even though the authors differ in their theoretical frameworks, agreement far outweighs disagreement. Methodologically the authors agree that firm conclusions about the socialization process are vitally dependent on longitudinal data. Questions also are raised as to the suitability of studying process by such static methodologies as mass surveys. Almost all authors call for better and more reliable measures of individual change due to socialization experiences. Theoretically, the authors agree that the topic of adult socialization can only be studied from an interactive perspective. Finally, many authors also think it important to comment on the tentativeness with which they have reached some of their conclusions and to point to the immense terra incognita which still confronts us as we reflect on the subject. Such caveats notwithstanding, their explorations give us the outlines and contours of a map on the topic. With its help, it should not be too difficult in the future to fill in the blank spaces.

Notes

1. Erik H. Erikson, Daniel Levinson, and other psychoanalytically oriented authors, on the other hand, hold to a much more plastic and developmental view of identity formation, specifying definite states related more or less to chronological age.

2. Psychobiographers tend to seek explanations for leaders' adult political behavior by studying their childhood—as Renshon's chapter makes clear. It must be remembered, however, that here we deal with an atypical population and with retrospective, not longitudinal, data.

References

Abramson, P. R. 1985. "Research Directions on the Workplace as a Political Social-izer." Paper presented at the World Congress of the International Political Science Association, Paris, France.

Baltes, P. B., and K. W. Schaie, eds. 1973. *Lifespan Psychology: Personality and Socialization.* New York: Academic Press.

Binstock, R. and E. Shanas, eds. 1976. *Handbook of Aging and the Social Sciences.* New York: Van Nostrand Reinhold.

Brim, O. G., Jr., and J. Kagan, eds. 1980. *Constancy and Change in Human Development.* Cambridge, Mass.: Harvard University Press.

Brodie, F. 1974. *Thomas Jefferson: An Intimate History.* New York: Norton.

——— 1981. *Richard Nixon: The Shaping of His Character.* New York: Norton.

Carroll, S. J. 1985. *Women as Candidates in American Politics.* Bloomington: Indiana University Press.

Dawson, R. E., and K. Prewitt. 1969. *Political Socialization.* Boston: Little, Brown.

George, A., and J. George. 1956. *Woodrow Wilson and Colonel House: A Personality Study.* Ontario: Longman.

Glad, B. 1966. *Charles Evans Hughes and the Illusions of Innocence.* Urbana: University of Illinois Press.

——— 1980. *Jimmy Carter—In Search of the Great White House.* New York: Norton.

Glenn, N. D. 1980. "Values, Attitudes, and Beliefs." In O. G. Brim, Jr., and J. Kagan, eds., *Constancy and Change in Human Development.* Cambridge: Harvard University Press, pp. 596–640.

Greenstein, F. I. 1987. "The Impact of Presidential Experience on Presidential Leadership." Paper presented at the Annual Meeting of the American Political Science Association.

Gustafsson, G. 1974. "Environmental Influence on Political Learning." In R. G. Niemi, ed., *The Politics of Future Citizens.* San Francisco: Jossey-Bass, pp. 149–66.

Harre, R. H., and R. Lamb, R., eds. 1983. *The Encyclopedic Dictionary of Psychology*. Cambridge, Mass.: MIT Press.

Inkeles, A. 1969. "Social Structure and Socialization." In D. A. Goslin, ed., *Handbook of Socialization Theory and Research*. Chicago: Rand McNally, 615–32.

Kearns, D. 1976. *Lyndon Johnson and the American Dream*. New York: Harper and Row.

Kirkpatrick, J. J. 1974. *Political Woman*. New York. Basic Books.

Knox, A. B. 1971. *Adult Development and Learning*. San Francisco: Jossey-Bass.

LeVine, R. A. 1969. "Culture, Personality, and Socialization: An Evolutionary View." In D. A. Goslin, *Handbook of Socialization Theory and Research*. Chicago: Rand-McNally, 503–42.

Levinson, D. J. 1986. "A Conception of Adult Development." *American Psychologist* 41, no. 1–3: 3–13.

Mahoney, M. J. 1987. "Plasticity and Power: Emerging Emphasis in Theories of Human Change." Mimeo.

Mansbridge, J. 1986. *Why We Lost the ERA*. Chicago: University of Chicago Press.

Mazlish, B. 1972. *In Search of Nixon: A Psychohistorical Portrait*. New York: Basic Books.

Neugarten, B. L. 1977. "Personality and Aging." In J. E. Birren and K. W. Schaie, eds., *Handbook of the Psychology of Aging*. New York: Van Nostrand Reinhold.

Rogow, A. 1963. *James Forrestal: A Study of Personality, Politics, and Policy*. New York: Macmillan.

Sapiro, S. 1987. "Changing Gender Roles and Changing Political Socialization." Paper presented at the Conference on Socialization for Democracy, Tel Aviv University, March 1–8.

Schonfeld, W. 1971. "The Focus of Political Socialization Research: An Evaluation." *World Politics* 22: 554–78.

Sears, D. O. 1984. "Attitude Objects and Political Socialization through the Life Cycle." Paper presented at the Annual Meeting of the American Political Science Association, Washington D. C.

Contributors

RONALD E. BROWN is an assistant professor of political science at Eastern Michigan University. He is also adjunct research scientist at the Institute for Social Research, in the Program for Research on Black Americans, at the University of Michigan. Currently he is engaged in research and writing on the role of the black church as a political resource for black women and the aged.

SUSAN J. CARROLL is an associate professor of political science at Rutgers University and senior research associate at the Center for the American Woman and Politics of the Eagleton Institute of Politics. She is author of *Women as Candidates in American Politics* and several articles on women's political participation.

NEAL E. CUTLER is professor of political science and gerontology, and co-director of the Andrus Gerontology Center's Institute for Advanced Study in Gerontology and Geriatrics, at the University of Southern California. He is the author of numerous articles on gerontology and served as issue editor of *"Aging and Public Policy: The Politics of Agenda-Setting,"* an issue of the Policy Studies Journal.

MICHAEL X. DELLI CARPINI is a member of the Political Science Department of Barnard College, Columbia University. He is author of *Stability and Change in American Politics*: The Coming of Age of the Generation of the 1960s. His articles on generational politics, public opinion, and the mass media have appeared in journals such as *Public Opinion Quarterly, The Journal of Politics, American Politics Quarterly,* and *Western Political Quarterly.*

PAULA DRESSEL is an associate professor of sociology at Georgia State University in Atlanta. She is the author of *The Service Trap: From Altruism to Dirty Work* and articles on social welfare in journals such as *Social Problems, Social Service Review,* and *The Gerontologist.*

SHIRLEY J. HATCHETT is a sociologist and assistant research scientist at the Institute for Social Research at the University of Michigan. She is the co-author of the forthcoming *Hope and Independence: Blacks' Struggle in the Two-Party System* as well as the co-author of books and articles about racial attitude change, black political attitudes and behaviors, and selected issues in survey research methodology.

IRVING LOUIS HOROWITZ is Hannah Arendt professor of sociology and political science at Rutgers University, and editor in chief of Transaction/SOCIETY. Among his writings are *Winners and Losers: Social and Political Polarities in America; Radicalism and the Revolt against Reason; Ideology and Utopia in the United States; Foundations of Political Sociology;* and of a biography of C. Wright Mills, *An American Utopian.*

MARILYN HOSKIN is associate dean of social sciences and associate professor of political science at the State University of New York at Buffalo. She is the co-author of *The Political Involvement of Adolescents* and the author of numerous articles on immigrant socialization appearing in *Comparative Politics, International Migration, Political Psychology,* and other journals.

WILLIAM M. LAFFERTY is professor of political science at the University of Oslo. His publications include *Economic Development and the Response of Labor in Scandinavia; Industrialization, Community Structure and Socialism;* and *Participation and Democracy in Norway.* He is at present working on a cross-national study of citizenship in Norway and the United States.

ROBERT S. LAUFER is professor of sociology at Brooklyn College and the Graduate School, CUNY, and vice-president of the Society for the Study of Traumatic Stress. He was director, a principal investigator, and author of *Legacies of Vietnam* and *Opportunities for Intervention: Employment Needs of New York City Vietnam Veterans,* and co-author with Ellen Frey-Wouters of *Legacy of a War: The American Soldier in Vietnam,* as well as numerous articles in leading journals and books on the effects of war.

MICHAEL LIPSKY is professor of political science at the Massachusetts Institute of Technology. He is the author of *Protest in City Politics; Commission Politics: The Processing of Racial Crisis in America;* and *Street-Level Bureaucracy.* His current research includes U.S. policy toward hunger in America and the politics of nonprofit organizations.

JOHN P. LOVELL, professor of political science at Indiana University. He is the author of *The Challenge of American Foreign Policy: Purpose and Adaptation.* Lovell also is the author of *Neither Athens Nor Sparta? The American Service Academies in Transition* and co-editor of and contributor to *New Civil-Military Relations: The Agonies of Adjustment to Post-Vietnam Realities* as well as of numerous articles on the U.S. military establishment and its relation to American society.

ALDON MORRIS is associate professor and associate chair of sociology at the University of Michigan. He is currently national president of the Association of Black Sociologists. His research interests include social movements, political sociology, social change, and sociological theory. In 1986, his book *The Origins of The Civil Rights Movement: Black Communities Organizing for Change* received the Distinguished Contribution to Scholarship Award from the American Sociological Association.

STANLEY RENSHON is an associate professor of political science at the City University of New York (Herbert Lehman College and the Graduate School and University Center). He is the author of *Psychological Needs and Political Behavior,* editor of the *Handbook of Political Socialization: Theory and Research,* and has published a number of articles in the fields of political psychology and behavior.

JANIE S. STECKENRIDER is a doctoral candidate in Political Science at the University of Southern California. She has twice been named as National Institute on Aging predoctoral research fellow in aging, politics, and public policy at the Andrus Gerontology Center. She is the co-author of "How Golden is the Future?" (*Generations*), and "Electronic Participation by Citizens in U.S. Local Government" (*Information Age*).

JUDITH HICKS STIEHM is the provost at Florida International University. Among the books she has written or edited are *Bring Me Men and Women: Mandated Change at the U.S. Air Force Academy; Women and Men's Wars* (edited); *Men, Women, and State Violence; Government and the Military; Women's View of the Political World of Men* (edited).

Index